AMERICAN FAMILIES

AMERICAN FAMILIES

A MULTICULTURAL READER

EDITED BY
STEPHANIE COONTZ
WITH MAYA PARSON
AND GABRIELLE RALEY

WITH THE ASSISTANCE OF
BETH VAIL, TAMARA ANDERSON,
AND BEN ANDERSON

ROUTLEDGE
NEW YORK   LONDON

Published in 1999 by
Routledge
29 West 35th Street
New York, NY 10001

Published in Great Britain by
Routledge
11 New Fetter Lane
London EC4P 4EE

10   9   8   7   6   5   4   3   2   1

Library of Congress Cataloging-in-Publication Data

American Families : a multicultural reader / edited by Stephanie Coontz ... [et al.]
   p.   cm.
  includes bibliographical references.
   ISBN 0-415-91573-2 (HB : alk. paper). — ISBN 0-415-91574-0 (PB : alk. paper)
    1. Family—United States.   2. Multiculturalism—United States.
3. Ethnicity—United States.   4. Work and family—United States.
I. Coontz, Stephanie.
HQ535.A583   1999
306.85'0973—dc21   98-6092
                                        CIP

CONTENTS

ACKNOWLEDGMENTS

The articles included in or considered for this book served as the basis of a two-quarter seminar on race, class, and gender in family scholarship. Stephanie Coontz and five of her then-current students reviewed the multicultural family literature and discussed what mix of articles or chapter excerpts would best meet the needs both of other students and of the general reader. Although only two of the original seminar members were able to remain involved in the next stage of article review and editing decisions during the following year, the participation of Ben Anderson, Tamara Anderson, and Beth Vail in the first half of this project was absolutely vital to the finished product. Their skilled library research and thoughtful comments on the articles we read were invaluable. In addition, Beth Vail was able to rejoin us for the meetings where we did the final reorganization of the book, and her contributions to this were extraordinarily helpful.

We want to thank the many researchers who sent us copies of articles and books to review for this collection or took time out from their busy schedules to suggest other sources. We especially thank the members of the Council on Contemporary Families, who were unfailingly generous with ideas and citations. Among the many individuals to whom we owe debts of gratitude are Lee Lyttle, Peta Henderson, Donna Franklin, Robert-Jay Green, Peggy Papp, Rich Simon, Minda Concha, Constance Ahrons, Judith Stacey, Delia Aguilar, Louise Lamphere, Peggy Penn, Sandra Wagner-Wright, and Craig Severance, as well as most of the authors represented in this volume.

We would also like to acknowledge the support of the administration and staff at The Evergreen State College Library. As a group, we placed a significant burden on the reference and circulation staff. Their skills and dedication enabled us to locate hard-to-find citations and receive articles under tight deadlines.

Stephanie Coontz
Maya Parson
Gabrielle Raley

INTRODUCTION

Stephanie Coontz

What is a family? What makes one work? Everyone has personal experience, both positive and negative, with the tremendous variety, complexity, and contradictory effects of family arrangements. At the same time, most of us tend to sift those experiences through the sieve of a social recipe for what "the Family" ought to be. The result is that the different ingredients of family life lose their distinctive character, and large clumps of people's experience never even get through.

For the past two decades, Americans have engaged in a protracted, emotional debate about whether our measuring and sifting utensils should be retooled to accommodate "nontraditional" family structures and to permit the development of new recipes for healthy family life. Part of the controversy revolves around whether our prevailing family measures take adequate account of long-term changes in the nature of marriage, the prevalence of divorce and unwed motherhood, and the (re)emergence of stepfamilies and working mothers. Another part has to do with increasing cultural and racial diversity in the United States. Our old directions for "doing" family have also been called into question by the realization that class divisions have not disappeared, as so many postwar social scientists predicted, but rather have deepened and in some ways become more intractable.

The intersection of old and new types of diversity has made it impossible to pretend any longer that all families can be forced through the same analytical or moral grid. It has also produced much confusion about how to analyze the origins and consequences of contemporary family variance. On the one hand, some leaders of the recent "family values" crusade argue that family "breakdown," especially the absence of a biological father in the home, has replaced race and class as the major cause of socioeconomic inequality and psychological disadvantage in America.[1] A slightly different tack is taken by more traditional conservatives such as George Will, who claims that "what is called the race crisis is a class problem arising from dysfunctional families and destructive behaviors."[2]

Other observers suggest that many "deviant" family forms are not dysfunctional at all. Rather, they are highly adaptive, flexible arrangements for coping with distinctive challenges posed by inequities of class, race, and gender. When family rearrangements *are* problematic, many scholars argue that this is the result rather than the cause of race and class inequities.

This reader sheds light on such debates and differences of emphasis by bringing together articles by leading researchers in the field of family diversity, past and present. What their work reveals is that in every historical period, including today, the United States has had several distinct but interconnected family systems, all of which form part of a larger constellation of power relations, unequal access to resources, and struggles over ideological representations of family life. Each group must adapt its family strategies and roles to the climate set up by its distance from the dominant sources of social and economic control. At the same time, the family trajectories of each group are shaped by the particular economic, political, and racial circumstances through which its productive and reproductive labor is organized, as well as by the orbits and gravitational pull of other groups in the system. Such variations on the basis of mutual dependency constitute the theme of the articles in this reader.

The authors in this volume examine the impact of class, race, and ethnicity on family forms, values, and definitions, as well as on the relations between men and women, parents and children. While many "new" family structures or arrangements are found in all class, race, and ethnic groups, the articles in this reader suggest that the origins, dynamics, and consequences of such family forms must be understood in the context of long-standing differences in the power, resources, status, and culture of various class and racial-ethnic groups. Because our authors situate diversity of family form in the context of group differences in social power, status, and resources, we have chosen to call this book a multicultural reader on families rather than a reader on family diversity per se.

Obviously, there are trade-offs in this choice. We have not been able to include any of the rich research comparing male-breadwinner–female-homemaker, dual-earner, and remarried families, divorced or never-married parents, and cohabitating couples, whether same-sex or heterosexual. Instead, we have chosen to focus on differences that complicate or cut across such family categories, giving them differing meanings and outcomes. In particular, we are interested in patterns of family difference created by the dynamics of resistance or accommodation among groups of unequal power and socioeconomic status.

The issue of how to conceptualize diversity in a manner that takes into account the relationships among different groups is an underlying theme in all the articles in this reader. It was even a matter for debate in our choice of the word *multicultural* in the title. Two of the authors whose work we include in this volume have argued elsewhere that *multiracial* is a better term for describing the "primary and pervasive" role of race in organizing difference in family life and gender roles within the United States.[3]

We agree that an emphasis on culture rather than on race can understate the powerful gravitational force of the color line in determining the orbits of families within the U.S. constellation of power and prestige. Latino immigrants, for example, come from countries where racial organizing principles have been more subtly intertwined with social class and less dichotomized by skin color than in the United States. Once they enter the United States, however, prevailing racial ideologies tend to rearrange immigrant hierarchies and opportunities by color, with darker-skinned Hispanics experiencing higher residential segregation and less-desirable job opportunities. Similarly, immigrants of European origin have an advantage that transcends skill differences, with Germans and Poles receiving higher incomes than more-educated Iranians or Indians, and poorly skilled Portuguese doing better than Mexicans or Dominicans, even though the educational attainments of these groups are comparable.[4]

We were concerned, however, that for some readers the term *multiracial* might reinforce the myth that race is a biological fact. As Evelyn Brooks Higginbotham warns, race language tends to cloak other organizing principles such as gender and class, while it also "blurs and disguises, suppresses and negates its own complex interplay" with these other social relations.[5] To avoid these problems, we have chosen to call this book a multicultural reader, defining culture as the set of behaviors and "ideological frame of reference through which people attempt to deal with the circumstances in which they find themselves"—circumstances in which racial hierarchies often play a pivotal role.[6]

Not that the term *multicultural* is without difficulty. Too often, multicultural studies serve up a buffet of different family arrangements and values without specifying the relationships and struggles among different groups. A "celebration of diversity" obscures the power and resource differentials among various groups, overlooking their symbiotic (or parasitical) relationships. John Garvey suggests that multicultural education can become a kind of managed care, offering the palliative medicine of tolerance rather than aggressively treating the disease of oppression.[7]

Recognizing that much cultural and racial difference is the product of enforced inequalities in access to power and resources is not the same thing as a victim model of family diversity. The rich historical traditions and creative contemporary adaptations described in this volume demonstrate the tremendous ingenuity and resourcefulness of "minority" families and individuals. But without a theoretical analysis of how social relations of race, gender, class, and ethnicity interact with personal decision making, we can mistake such creative, even heroic, adaptations for unconstrained choice.

As Maxine Baca Zinn and Bonnie Thornton Dill write, "intersecting forms of domination produce both oppression and opportunity."[8] They place some families at the top of a social hierarchy and others at the bottom, shaping the choices that all families can make. But the hierarchy itself is not static, and even at the bottom some types of oppression open up other opportunities for personal action or collective organization. At the same time, many of the gains achieved by families or individuals remain limited by larger power and productive relations. When a woman charms her way out of a speeding ticket, she is not demonstrating that men and women have "separated but equal" sources of power, merely that the stereotypes perpetuating male dominance can sometimes be manipulated to individual advantage. When an African-American or Puerto Rican woman strikes out on her own, acting independently of men in a way that a white middle-class woman sometimes envies, it is hard to separate out how much of this is gender equality and how much dire necessity.

The key to acknowledging power differences without denying the agency of less privileged groups is to understand that power is never a one-way street. A slave family, for example, was not a simple imitation of its owner's family nor a helpless victim of the traffic in human beings. Neither, however, was it a self-made creation free from the constraints of white owners. Yet slave owners' families themselves were *also* forged by slavery. Their internal relations were profoundly affected by external racial hierarchies and by anxieties about social control.[9] Today, similarly, white working-class and middle-class families forge their strategies in the context of growing income inequality interacting with the social disorientation engendered by polarization within racial categories, where a few people of color have been admitted to formerly all-white professions and income levels, while the ranks of the extremely poor are more visibly filled by African Americans and Latinos than ever.

Part One: The American Tradition of Family Diversity

Many discussions of family diversity start from the assumption that the white middle-class family ideal popularized by the sitcoms of the 1950s was the historical norm for most families and that diversity is a recent development in family life. The articles in this section demonstrate that there has never been a single family model in the United States and that change has been a constant feature of every kind of family.

When political pundits hold up the "Ozzie and Harriet" ideal as the traditional American family, they ignore not only the existence of other family forms and values in different economic, racial, or ethnic groups, but the fact that this was a new norm even for the white middle class. Not until the 1920s did a majority of white children come to live in a family where the wife was a full-time homemaker—instead of working beside her husband on the farm or in a small shop—and where the children went on to high school instead of out to work in fields or factories. This reorganization of family life was disrupted by the Great Depression and World War II, only to emerge more strongly after the war.

Following World War II, the age of marriage and the percentage of women remaining unmarried or childless fell to a 100-year low. The fertility rate soared and the divorce rate dropped, reversing the previous eighty-year pattern. These demographic trends were accompanied by a novel idealization of nuclear family togetherness. Such 1950s family values differed not only from the extended-family models of working-class immigrants and ethnic groups but also from a nineteenth-century middle-class tradition in which female networks of kin and friends were the emotional center of family life. That nineteenth-century family pattern, often referred to by historians as the "separate spheres" model, in turn represented a departure from the colonial and Revolutionary patterns, where white middle-class women worked alongside men in household production, with child rearing occupying only a minor portion of their time.[10]

Bonnie Thornton Dill begins this section by reminding us that each of these distinct phases in the history of Anglo-American middle-class families coexisted with and was in fact dependent upon different family arrangements and definitions in other classes and racial-ethnic groups. The native-born white middle class, for instance, could not have reorganized family life in the nineteenth century to keep children at home longer and to redirect maternal time from clothes or food production to childcare without the foreclosure of any extended childhood for the slaves who provided cotton to the new textile mills and the immigrant children who provided cheap factory clothes or household help for middle-class families.[11]

The family constellation of early America was forged out of the interactions and clashes between three groups. These were the politically, economically, and militarily dominant Euro-American colonizers; the original Native American inhabitants; and the Africans brought by Europeans as indentured servants and then as lifetime slaves. Native American family arrangements ranged from simple monogamy (usually with divorce rights) to various forms of multiple marriage. Some groups had complex descent systems traced either through the maternal or the paternal lines; others were comparatively unconcerned with lineal descent rules. But all of them organized production, distribution, and even justice through kin networks, rather than adherence to the authority of a territorial state, while the private ownership of land by individuals or independent nuclear families was unknown among North American indigenous peoples. Most Native American societies had a division of labor by gender, but it differed greatly from that brought by European settlers. Indeed, several early Native American societies allowed for a third gender, whose sexual orientation is not adequately described by modern dichotomous notions of heterosexuality and homosexuality.[12]

Despite some mingling of customs and knowledge, European colonization resulted in the physical decimation of many Native American societies through disease and war, while magnifying the role of young men at the expense of the traditional roles of elders and women. The selection from David Adams, however, shows that even after the physical conquest and relocation of Native American groups had been accomplished, Anglo-American political leaders felt compelled to destroy Native American communal values and kinship norms.

The Africans brought to America in the forced service of white settlers also came from kinship-based societies, although some of these had greater internal status differentiation and more complex political institutions than those of the North American Indians. In the New World, they had to adapt to a very different political and economic structure, the loss of their languages, and the imposition of a wholly new way of organizing their labor. Family conditions varied depending on whether African Americans lived in free black settlements, Anglo villages where there were only a few personal slaves or servants, great cotton plantations utilizing gang labor, or small backwoods farms where one or two slaves worked under a master's close supervision. All African-American families, however, had to deal with their involuntary relocation to America, the existence of slavery, and the gradual hardening of racial attitudes over the first two centuries of colonization.

While many writers have emphasized the ways that slavery shaped the experience of black family life, Niara Sudarkasa's article suggests that many African-American family forms and practices were actually a continuation of a West African heritage. This is complicated, Leith Mullings has pointed out, by the fact that some working-class Euro-American groups have developed similar family strategies, such as child-exchange networks and reliance on matri-focal extended-kinship ties, in reaction to economic necessity rather than cultural tradition. Similarly, Gabrielle Raley (this volume) argues that economic factors ultimately outweigh cultural ones in explaining teenage childbearing. Still, the case for a continuing African-American cultural legacy of extended-kin networks and flexible definitions of family is supported by considerable research. At the same time, some studies suggest that these social support systems have been severely strained in recent years.[13]

Evelyn Nakano Glenn's selection points out that cultural values can never be easily disentangled from structural conditions such as racism or political and economic constraints, or from the attempts of groups to change their position in the racial-economic hierarchy. She describes how Chinese Americans altered their family strategies over time, using their cultural resources selectively to adapt to shifting institutional pressures and opportunities.

My own article explores how seemingly analogous cultural values can be deployed for different goals, with very different outcomes. I suggest that although many working-class families attempted to replicate some white middle-class family strategies, such as withdrawing wives from the paid labor force whenever possible, the content of their family life cannot be understood as an imitation of middle-class domesticity even where the form seems superficially similar.

For many groups, migration to America set up work and residence patterns, as well as interactions with larger mainstream institutions, that forged a new cultural identity. The selection from George Sánchez stresses the diversity among Mexican families before migration and the varying types of adaptation afterward. Sánchez traces the emergence of a distinctive barrio culture in portions of Los Angeles, along with a Chicano identity quite different from earlier Mexican ones.

Jacqueline Jones examines how economic and social pressures on African-American families have created or interacted with cultural traditions. Comparing the situations faced by impoverished black and white Southern families since the Civil War, and their experiences in migrating to Northern cities, Jones finds differences that cannot be explained by economic and educational background alone. On the other hand, she argues that while blacks brought with them a stronger pre-existing cultural identity than did white Appalachians, based on their experiences during and after slavery, they were also less able to renounce older patterns even if they wanted to, due to racist hiring and housing practices.

Taken together, the articles in this section remind us that while change in family life has been a constant in American history, it has not been random. Each author stresses a slightly different mix of historical forces and sociological processes that produced the patterns he or she describes.

Part Two: Integrating Race, Class, and Gender Into Family Theory

Whatever its distinctive characteristics, every family system channels people into the prevailing structure of obligations, rights, and labor division, then attaches the tasks and rewards associated with that structure to a definition of self. The family is the physical and the mental location where we link our personal relationships to our socioeconomic relationships, our reproductive relations to our productive ones.

One's family of origin is the first building block of social placement; it defines and limits the obligations individuals owe each other and the way they relate to the dominant political apparatus. But the family is also a place where people can cooperate or struggle with other family members to change their position in the social structure.

Often what is adaptive for a family in one socioeconomic or political setting is dysfunctional in another. By the same token, what is adaptive for one family member may not be so, or at least not equally so, for another. Researchers must pay attention not only to the interaction, conflicts, and mutual dependencies *among* families but also to the struggles or accommodations *within* families over roles, resources, power, and autonomy. But the study of adaptations, struggles, and compromises frequently raises the question of how to understand the relative weight of race, class, ethnicity, sexuality, and gender in determining family dynamics. In part two, we present a few views on this question.

Disentangling the various influences of race relations, class, ethnicity, gender, and sexuality, as well as distinguishing between family adaptations that reflect defeats for a particular group and those that reflect victories, is a major analytical challenge. Even defining the terms separately poses difficulties.

Ethnicity describes people by their supposedly common ancestry, language, and cultural heritage. Unlike ethnicity, race is based on no distinctive cultural or linguistic heritage. Unlike gender, it is based on no irreducible physical difference. Racialization draws on real or imagined physical differences to define and separate people, but race is a socially constructed and constantly changing phenomenon that has no coherent biological base and has never been shown to explain differences in human behavior. Nevertheless, ideologies of race have real consequences, such that acting in a "race-blind" way on an individual level allows and even encourages the racial structuring of society to continue.[14]

As Eric Wolf points out, the cultural construction of ethnicity has served historically to stratify, while racial constructions have served to exclude. But the difference between race and ethnicity is not always clear-cut. Race can divide people of the same ethnicity or unite people of very different ethnic traditions on the basis of the way their color is perceived and labeled by others. Latinos, for example, unlike African Americans, are *divided* rather than united by race, even though all are subject to discrimination from white society.[15]

Some former racial categories have become ethnic ones over time. Numerous researchers, for example, have shown that the Irish, original-ly considered a nonwhite race, won their whiteness in large part through participation in the fabrication of color as a category that was thought to outweigh class. More recently, other groups whose original ethnic patterns were tied to a subordinate place in the socioeconomic and cultural hierarchy of America, and who therefore struggled to shed their ethnicity in favor of a "white" identity, have now rediscovered eth-nicity, as Lillian Rubin demonstrates in this volume.[16]

Ethnicity, moreover, despite its seeming connection to a shared her-itage, is a product not just of the traditions brought by immigrants but of the particular immigrant group's class origins and occupational skills interacting with the historically or regionally specific jobs, housing stock, and political conditions they meet. Immigrants have experienced what Alejandro Portes and Cynthia Truelove call distinctive "modes of incor-poration" into the United States. These have encouraged groups to selec-tively rework and occasionally actively invent aspects of their cultural "traditions." Thus immigrants frequently celebrate holidays, rituals, sto-ries, and even dialects that were unimportant or actually considered undesirable in their home territory. Alternatively, groups that had little in common in "the old country" may be lumped together on the basis of shared traits that assume importance only in contrast to features of the new social environment. Despite a common language, for instance, Hispanic ethnicity was originally a creation for the convenience of cen-sus takers; many writers prefer the term *Latino*. Portes and Truelove refer to Hispanics/Latinos as "a group in formation whose boundaries and self-definition are still in a state of flux."[17]

Similarly, Asian Americans do not come from the same culture or speak the same language. The term includes more than two dozen sub-groups who differ in class and cultural origins, immigration experiences, religion, physical features, language, gender roles, and intergenerational relations. Since the 1960s, though, many of these groups have forged a pan-ethnic identity, in large part as a reaction to their experience with mainstream American institutions and ideologies. At the same time, a very different political current has tended to blur these groups together to create the myth of the Asian "model minority," against which Latinos and African Americans are often unfavorably compared.[18]

Class refers to people's socioeconomic roles and resources. It can thus be measured in several quantitative ways or it can be conceptualized as a historical *relationship* among groups. Readers should be alert to differences between authors in this volume who define class in terms of an individual's income or educational level and those who see class as the outcome of people's relative positions in the larger economic system of production, distribution, and exchange. According to the latter definition, class cannot be defined in terms of what one earns or even what one does, but only by a person's experience as a member of one group that engages in a historically specific pattern of interaction with other socioeconomic and political groups.[19]

The second definition, unlike the first, sometimes puts people of similar income in different class categories, usually because of their different experiences and customary ways of relating to others. It may offer more insight than simple quantitative measures of income or education into the reasons that people choose different family strategies or bring different assumptions and goals to their child rearing. But both definitions raise the problem of how to conceptualize a *family's* class status. Is it determined by that of the major income earner, by the combination of the parent's occupations and earnings, or by some characteristic relationship between income earners and their dependents? And how do definitions of class coincide or interact with racial categories?

Barbara Fields argues that class and race are qualitatively different concepts that "do not occupy the same analytical space." Class is determined by the structural relationship among groups with different points of access to or leverage within the prevailing system of economic production and social reproduction. It is a material condition, mediated by ideology but able to "assert itself independently of people's consciousness," as when workers who define themselves as middle class find that they have no more control over their work conditions than the blue-collar employees from whom they formerly differentiated themselves. Race, by contrast, is purely ideological. Belief in race has real consequences, Fields suggests, but there is no underlying mechanism of race that can assert itself independently of what people believe about it.[20]

On the other hand, racial ideologies can create or cement class differences, while changes in class relations can also transform racial beliefs. Few societies have constructed material class inequalities without the aid of subjective racial or ethnic categories. Class thus involves multifaceted relationships both with economic and political institutions and with prevailing ideologies of difference, including race, ethnicity, religion, gender, and sexuality. Multivariate analyses often show that socioeconomic status accounts for more variables in family patterns than race, but it seldom explains all, and multivariate analysis has trouble explaining factors that are analytically but not practically separable. As Jodie Kliman and

William Madsen point out, a black executive may be able to hire and fire white employees, but he "has less *effective* class standing than subordinates when trying to hail a cab, join a country club, buy an elegant home"—or even protect his children from police brutality.[21]

Similarly, Douglas Massey argues that despite the huge impact of industrial restructuring on job prospects and dependency in the cities, described by Thomas Sugrue in this volume, the emergence of a socially isolated "underclass" would not have happened without the prior existence of historically enforced racial segregation.[22] The fact that so-called "underclass" behaviors occur in areas of white rural poverty, however, also raises the possibility that racism accounts for the labeling rather than the existence of marginalized groups.

While much work remains to be done in conceptualizing the ways that ethnicity, race, class, gender, and sexuality interact in family life, many contributors to this volume draw on the notion of "social location" developed by Louise Lamphere, Patricia Zavella, and Felipe Gonzales. These authors suggest that the strategies and meanings fashioned by families and their individual members must be understood through specific examination of "the way in which regional and local political economy interact with class, ethnicity, culture, and sexual preference."[23]

Patricia Hill Collins argues that gender is constructed through a matrix of intersecting inequalities, as well as by the attempts of individuals and groups to thread their way through the cracks or occasional openings in the perimeters that circumscribe their lives. The same can be said of the way that families are constructed and in turn organize or rearrange themselves (including by what is often called "family dissolution"). Evelyn Nakano Glenn points out that family analysis is especially useful as a corrective to theories of racial hierarchy that do not include analysis of reproductive labor as well as to theories of gender hierarchy that assume all women do the same *kinds* of reproductive labor.[24]

As these citations indicate, there has been an explosion of theory about diversity in family life. Due to space limitations, we can provide only a few examples of the ways that authors have grappled with the thorny question of how to understand the interactions of race, ethnicity, class, and gender in shaping family life and values. Rayna Rapp's comparatively early article helped pave the way for much subsequent research by distinguishing between family and household, not only because some families are not bounded by households, but because households are where daily reproduction takes place and families are the way we recruit people into household labor. Families, she argues, also are more ideologically loaded than households.

The other side of the coin, as Andrew Billingsley points out, is something that contemporary family-values rhetoric often ignores: Single-person households are often made up of members of functioning families. In some communities, the family involvement of many fathers has been rendered invisible by the confusion of family and household. Tamara Hareven argues that we have not yet discovered a clear way of conceptualizing the different functions and meanings of household membership and family membership.[25]

If many varieties of fatherhood have been ignored or slandered by writers who assume that only one kind of parenting can work, motherhood, Patricia Hill Collins explains, has been falsely homogenized. Her article illuminates the racial and ethnic differences Rapp found in the ways women evaluate the family's impact on their lives. Women in most race, class, and ethnic groups are subordinate to men of the same group, and family relations often enforce that subordination. But as Nancy Cott has noted, the critique of male dominance within the family "was historically initiated by, and remains prejudiced toward, those who perceive themselves first and foremost as 'woman,' who can gloss over their class, racial, and other status identifications because those are culturally dominant and therefore relatively invisible." As bell hooks has written, women who belong to groups where men do not have social or economic power seldom place the demand for male-female equality at the top of their agenda, though they will often act both collectively and individually to resist abuse or maltreatment.[26]

Multicultural family scholarship, then, challenges universal generalizations about femininity, masculinity, motherhood, fatherhood, and family dynamics. It also undermines the traditional additive model of diversity, where white maleness is taken as the base, gender is added to that, race or ethnicity makes a woman "doubly oppressed," and working-class status substracts points from white-male privilege. The brief excerpt from Karen Brodkin Sacks argues that we need to redefine class in ways that integrate both race and gender. Thus she suggests that the working class is defined by "membership in a community that is dependent upon waged labor, but that is unable to subsist or reproduce by such labor alone." Race and ethnicity help define that community, both through the discrimination that members face in finding waged labor and the constraints imposed on them in seeking other forms of subsistence and reproduction, as well as by the cultural resources they can mobilize. Family and gender are integral to and are also shaped by that class-race-ethnicity dynamic. So are parent-child relations, since class is connected not just to immediate income and social status but also to the resources parents can pass on to the next generation.[27]

Maxine Baca Zinn discusses five key components of family analysis that have been overlooked or downplayed in traditional social-science frameworks such as modernization theory, assimilation models, and functionalism. She then argues that these must be integrated into a theory of family interaction and change that no longer marginalizes racial-ethnic families. Zinn further warns against the tendency of some writers on race to assume a bipolar model, where the experience of African Americans is taken as representative of all racial and ethnic minorities. She points out that the dynamics of race and cultural identity among Latinos cannot be explained by such a paradigm.

The bipolar racial model also ignores variation *within* the African-American experience. Studies of African Americans, for example, are heavily skewed toward the inner-city poor, with a handful of books on black professionals. Very little is written about working-class African Americans. Similarly, describing some immigrant groups solely as "black" obscures tremendous class and cultural diversity. In the early 1960s, many Haitian refugees were from the upper middle class; "by 1972, the number of Haitian physicians in the United States represented an incredible 95 percent of Haiti's stock." In the 1980s and 1990s, however, well-to-do Haitian immigrants have been overshadowed by the desperately poor boat people. As these and other disruptions of established race and class alignments continue to mount, theorizing difference and interaction of race, class, gender, and ethnicity must continue to be a high priority for researchers as well as policy makers.[28]

Parts Three through Seven: Contemporary Issues in Family Diversity

Most Americans recognize that global economic, demographic, and technological trends have recently created new possibilities and new challenges in family life for all social groups. Some writers have argued, indeed, that the family experiences of many subordinated racial groups are now becoming more common throughout the population.[29] The remaining sections of the book show how our understanding of contemporary issues in families, gender roles, and child rearing must be informed by multicultural and class analysis.

Part Three: Working-Class and Inner-City Families Under Economic Stress

The articles here deal with the impact of changing job opportunities both on white working-class families and on their predominantly black counterparts in the impoverished inner cities, as well as on public understandings of the origins of poverty. On the one hand, as the selections by Thomas Sugrue and Gabrielle Raley demonstrate, racism not only "colors" the discussion of industrial restructuring but also its outcome, helping to ensure that the worst effects will be felt by people of color. Additionally, racism has deformed our understanding of welfare policy, Raley argues, with the result that recent changes in the welfare laws may have devastating effects on impoverished children.

Many political ideologues blame inner-city poverty on a self-perpetuating "underclass" culture that destabilizes families, producing individual pathologies that block social and economic mobility. Sudarkasa and, later in this volume, Margaret Crosbie-Burnett and Edith A. Lewis point out that many "nontraditional" family values of racial-ethnic groups are adaptive rather than pathological. Yet few would deny that the support systems, community cohesion, and informal methods of social control of many isolated and poverty-stricken neighborhoods have been gravely eroded in recent years and that the instability of many inner-city families is indeed a serious problem. Sugrue argues that such family instability is the effect rather than the cause of long-term economic deprivation, class marginalization, and racism.

Raley makes a similar argument about unwed teen motherhood. Rates of unwed motherhood have risen dramatically in the United States, and the incidence of unwed motherhood is more widespread among African Americans than among whites. This masks an important difference in trends: Rates of unwed motherhood among white women have been rising steadily for the past twenty-five years. The likelihood that an unmarried black woman will bear a child out of wedlock, however, is lower today than it was in 1970. But rates of unmarried childbearing among blacks remain higher than those among whites. In addition, the sharp decline in births to married African-American women and the rise in the numbers of unmarried black women mean that a larger proportion of children who are born to African-American women are born out of wedlock.[30]

Contrary to conventional wisdom, most unmarried births are not to teens but to women in their 20s and 30s. A quarter are to unmarried but cohabitating parents. In many cases, the increase of births to unmarried older women results from the growth in women's economic independence and social options. The causes and outcomes of births to unwed teens are quite different, however, and Raley tries to answer misconceptions about teen childbearing that she argues have led to ill-advised changes in welfare law.

Unfavorable economic forces also impact working-class families that have been more stably employed since the end of World War II. Much family conflict and divorce, for instance, is caused when a husband loses his job or a wife enters the workforce as a result of unanticipated necessity rather than conscious choice. Indeed, Judith Stacey's ethnography of working-class families in Silicon Valley suggests that they, rather than "cultural elites" or members of the so-called "underclass," are the true pioneers of modern forms of family diversity.[31]

But Lillian Rubin argues that many white working-class Americans accept racially charged, value-laden explanations of family distress that ultimately undermine their ability to analyze where their own setbacks originate. Revisiting the working-class families that she first studied in the 1970s, Rubin found that many women had gained a heightened sense of competence and self-worth when they entered the labor force or improved their position there, but that these personal benefits were counteracted by new time stresses and family instabilities connected to the decline in union-wage jobs and benefits available to their husbands.[32] She found in her interviews with white working-class families that lack of a class analysis often led them to translate their economic insecurity and family frustrations into racial or anti-immigrant hostility. Even minority groups, she points out, are sometimes sucked into this search for scapegoats.

At one level, the families Rubin interviewed can be described as trying to hang on to their white-skin privilege. But many white working people find it hard to see themselves as privileged when they compare themselves to consumerist visions of what a white, middle-class "lifestyle" should entail. A better way to describe their racial and gender prejudices might be as a search for "leverage" or "purchase"—something to brace against as they feel themselves slipping downward on the American social ladder, or even just unable to climb further up.

One such source of leverage has been the rediscovery of ethnicity among whites. After years of trying to escape ethnic stereotypes by claiming the homogenized label of "white" or "American," some working-class whites have begun to rework or recreate ethnic identities as a way of differentiating their needs and concerns from those of more affluent whites and also from those of other working-class groups whom they view as competitors for resources. These "optional ethnicities," as Mary Waters terms them, can make the celebration of diversity a new excuse to avoid confronting racism. Asserting that everyone has an ethnic identity worth recognizing, many whites deny that there is anything especially distinctive in the histories of groups whose racial or ethnic identity was societally imposed in order to facilitate discrimination against them.[33]

This argument has been a linchpin of the campaign against affirmative action, and it reinforces the danger of allowing discussion of diversity to be separated from analysis of power relations and socioeconomic inequalities. Rubin argues further that the pan-ethnic "European-American" identity claimed by some whites is especially dangerous in its potential to serve as a code word for reassertion of white interests.

Yet it would be wrong to conclude that working-class whites are more likely than upper-class ones to oppose efforts to rectify racial inequalities. If competition for jobs can produce prejudice, collaboration on the job can produce respect. In Houston, Texas, a 1997 referendum to abolish affirmative action was defeated, mainly because of the many Hispanic and African-American voters in the city. But while 71 percent of upper-income whites voted to abolish affirmative action, with only 29 percent in favor of retaining it, low-income whites were split nearly evenly on the issue.[34]

Part Four: Globalization and Today's Immigrant Families

Globalization is another concept that camouflages power differentials when it is used to suggest impersonal forces operating beyond anyone's control. In part five of this volume, Sarah Ryan describes how employers have both responded to and initiated growing global competition by trying to drive down workers' living standards and control over working conditions. She argues that despite appeals to the "remorseless logic" of global competition, resistance is possible. Part four, meanwhile, focuses on how the internationalization of economic and political power struggles has rearranged ethnic and racial migration patterns.

As of the late 1990s, nearly one in ten Americans was born in a foreign country, the highest rate in more than fifty years. A larger proportion of these immigrants are people of color than at any time since the involuntary importation of Africans. Nearly two-thirds come from a handful of countries in Latin America, the Caribbean, and Asia, most of which have a history of economic dependency on and external intervention by the United States: Mexico, Cuba, El Salvador, Guatemala, Nicaragua, the Dominican Republic, Haiti, the Philippines, Vietnam, South Korea, China, and India. Part four turns to the family adaptations and strategies of recent immigrants.[35]

Some of the economic fears described by Rubin have combined with racial prejudices and national chauvinism to produce anti-immigrant campaigns such as those outlined by Pierrette Hondagneu-Sotelo. Despite the stereotypes mobilized in these campaigns, immigrant family patterns vary widely. Grace Chang and Nazli Kibria describe two very different strategies (or necessities) used by different groups of immigrant women.

Chang discusses how women from indebted nations such as the Philippines are in a sense exported by their own governments to fill the demand for caregiving and household work created by the labor-market entry of women in the "host" countries. A similar pattern has been identified by Christine Ho, who asserts that Caribbean migrants have created international family networks that are now more central than spatially bound households to people's identity, exchange networks, and even child-rearing practices.[36]

Kibria argues that Vietnamese immigrant women, while taking advantage of the erosion of patriarchal power that accompanied their migration to the United States, have adopted a strategy of maneuvering within the comparatively traditional restraints of their culture. Susan Ostrander has described a similar pattern within the top reaches of the upper class. Here, however, women's acceptance of traditional roles has little to do with personal vulnerability, since many upper-class women possess major inheritances. Rather, Ostrander argues, they see significant class advantages to a gendered division of labor that keeps them subordinate to husbands but puts them in charge of regulating access to high-status social institutions. Forsaking their gendered sphere of activity might jeopardize the monopoly of status and power enjoyed by the class to which they belong.[37]

Most immigrants, however, are part of the working class or a precariously situated middle class where the maintenance of separate spheres is neither possible nor, for the most part, advantageous. More and more women of every racial and ethnic group are joining the labor force, and not leaving it after childbirth. In 1995, for the first time, a solid majority of new mothers returned to work within a year of giving birth. Reversing older historical trends, college-educated women from economically advantaged backgrounds were more likely to return to work within a year than women from lower socioeconomic strata, but there has been a growing convergence in the relative likelihood that women, except among the very elite, will combine paid work with motherhood for most of their lives.[38]

Despite the increase in employment among upper middle-class and professional women, only a minority of working women in the United States face the problem of bumping into a glass ceiling. Most are more concerned with getting off the ground floor. And while equal pay is a major concern for working women of all income and ethnic groups, those married to men in the bottom seventy percent of the income ladder are painfully aware that the narrowing of the gender gap in pay has partly been a result of losses for men rather than absolute gains for women.

Part Five: Work-Family Issues

Sarah Ryan describes the stress of recent trends in income inequality, loss of benefits and security, rise of part-time work, and new management techniques, as well as reliance on overtime and contingent workers. These trends multiply the pressures on both male and female workers, making it harder but also more necessary for both men and women to combine work and family life. However, Ryan points to the 1997 UPS strike as evidence that working people not only need to fight battles over working conditions but also have the chance to win them.

The entry of women into the workforce and the eclipse of sequencing, an earlier pattern where most women quit work for at least a short period while their children were young, has created some new commonalities in women's experience. Women who work must renegotiate the household division of labor with their husbands, a process that has been difficult and painful in all economic and racial-ethnic groups. Women at all income levels also tend to bear the responsibility for arranging child care. The next two articles deal with these issues.

A stereotype widespread in the popular press is that middle-class white men have been most enlightened in their adjustment to the entry of wives into the workforce. In fact, however, employed African-American men do more housework and child care than employed white men. Contrary to stereotypes about Latino "machismo" and African-American "hypermasculinity," gender relations in racial-ethnic groups are extremely variable and complex. Pierrette Hondagneu-Sotelo and Michael Messner argue that the white middle-class image of the "New Man" confuses style with substance, ignoring deeper and more important gender changes taking place in other segments of the population.[39]

Where many discussions of the household division of labor exaggerate the problems in racial and ethnic families while downplaying those faced by white middle-class women in getting cooperation from their partners, Tamara Anderson and Beth Vail find that much discussion of child care errs in the opposite direction. There is a tendency to focus only on the concerns of white middle-class women, overlooking the dilemmas faced by racial-ethnic women who need child care and who often are also the ones expected to provide it for others. Anderson and Vail suggest that the way class and race inequalities play themselves out in child-care arrangements raises problems for all women, even those who derive short-term advantages from being able to exploit the labor of low-paid workers with less economic and social privilege than themselves.

Part Six: New Forms of Family Diversity

The growing workforce participation and economic independence of women has combined with new cultural freedoms and reproductive technologies to create novel kinds of diversity in family forms and arrangements, ranging from the increasing visibility of same-sex relationships to the high numbers of single-parent families. Surrogate mothering and in vitro fertilization challenge traditional ideas about the biological composition of a family. Growing numbers of "mixed race" marriages challenge older racial categories as well. Part six discusses how these new forms of family diversity cut across and interact with old forms of diversity in complex ways.

Gays and lesbians are in one sense a form of "minority" family. However, there are tremendous variations by class, race, and ethnicity in the experience and meaning of sexuality. Even the markers by which gay men and lesbians have proclaimed or disguised their interests or activities have differed by class, ethnicity, and culture.[40]

Judith Stacey's article outlines how gay and lesbian families can create new ways of understanding gender roles and parenting possibilities that might benefit all families. Yet Ruthann Robson has suggested elsewhere that demands for legalizing gay marriage have a conservatizing effect, since she believes that such unions will win acceptance "only to the extent that they represent the traditional [Anglo-American] couple, a tradition based on property relations."[41] At the same time, Beverly Greene and Nancy Boyd-Franklin remind us that gays and lesbians face considerable opposition and prejudice within minority cultures.

If gay and lesbian families call into question traditional middle-class conceptions of marital and parental roles, interracial marriages call into question traditional racial classifications. The incidence of such marriages has increased by 114 percent since 1980.

Some individuals are proud of their mixed heritage and reluctant to identify as one race or another. Yet racial solidarity has been a strong basis of mutual aid for people of color, and an important source of identity for children facing adversity. Maria Root explores the dilemmas faced by individuals whose parents come from differently defined or ranked racial or ethnic groups. What happens, she asks, when individuals don't have the coherent and cohesive alternative group identities that many researchers have found to be so important for minority children?[42]

Reproductive technology has challenged traditional biological definitions of families. The authors who comment on the Baby M case, which pitted the claims of the biological mother against those of the biological father and adoptive mother, remind us that while advances in reproductive technologies offer new freedoms, they also open new ways of reproducing class and ethnic inequalities. Many surrogate and adoptive parent disputes have opened people's eyes to the fact that a biological parent is not necessarily "better" than a social parent. However, the definition of what constitutes an acceptable social parent can be subject to many class and racial biases.

Margaret Crosbie-Burnett and Edith A. Lewis close this section on a note of hope. They argue that traditional African-American and Native American family norms can help *all* families deal with the dilemmas posed by rising rates of divorce and single parenthood. In the Anglo-European tradition, obligations to children have often been conceived as part of a package deal, contingent upon marriage and blood relatedness. Many minority cultures, by contrast, have long-standing traditions of shared child rearing beyond the nuclear family.

In Ghana, the Caribbean, and the Polynesian islands, children are often "loaned" to other households in ritual and reciprocal exchanges that extend ties of affection and mutual aid beyond the nuclear family household. These children seem perfectly capable of sustaining strong emotional ties with several psychological parents. Another basis of sharing child raising beyond the nuclear family lies in the African-American tradition of female self-identity and participation in social networks based on "sisterhood" instead of "wifehood." Valorizing rather than stigmatizing such child-centered family systems may be a better way to give children a claim on adult time and resources than trying to channel fathering and mothering exclusively through a marriage-centered family system.[43]

Part Seven: Recognizing Diversity, Encouraging Solidarity

The final section of the book asks how we can recognize and accommodate diversity in American family life while building the kind of solidarity that can gain all families an expansion of their support systems. Many of the social programs that modern families need cross the boundaries of race and class. But a recurring issue is the extent to which we can and should take account of racial and class differences in the programs we seek, especially when it comes to economic support systems.

Roger Lawson and William Julius Wilson suggest that working for a universal family-support program is necessary to avoid stigmatization of poor families, especially those of color, and to counter the backlash against social welfare. Stephen Steinberg argues that a universalist program (and by implication, even an affirmative-action program based on diversity per se) ignores the unique, historical oppression of African Americans and Native Americans in our society. He believes that these groups must be targeted for special attention if we are to avoid the cycle described by Sugrue, in which blacks and Indians get continually pushed off the job ladder while other ethnic groups are allowed on at the bottom rungs. Steinberg reminds us that diversity is not just about adding color and dialect to the sights and sounds of America; it is also about power relations and questions of economic justice.

One problem in implementing Steinberg's proposal is the question of how to rank Puerto Rican and Mexican-American families in the hierarchy of oppression. And what about the increasing impoverishment of newer immigrant groups such as the Hmong? Yet it is certainly true that the historical weight of slavery and Jim Crow has exerted a long-term intergenerational impact on the ability of African Americans to achieve economic stability, especially when it comes to accumulation of assets. Many of the losses sustained by blacks historically were translated into gains for whites, with the result that even where African Americans have won equal pay, the median worth of household assets among whites is twelve times higher than among blacks. Without some sort of racial redistribution or affirmative action, this economic gap may for the most part perpetuate itself.[44]

During the past twenty years the educational achievement gap between white and minority workers has narrowed dramatically, both in years of schooling completed and in test scores. At the same time, wages for white blue-collar workers have stagnated. It might be thought that this would lead to increasing convergence between African Americans and whites of the same general class origins. Yet over the same time period, the wage gap has widened for high school–educated black and white men, for black and white females with some college education, and for Latinas at all levels of schooling. In California, the state that has been at the leading edge of attempts to roll back affirmative action, even the wage gap between black and white college graduates widened from 1980 to 1995.[45]

What is the correct balance between reversing the historical momentum of past injustices and uniting around issues that apply to the concerns of all workers, such as stagnating wages, increasing job insecurity, and the erosion of medical benefits and pension plans? These questions will continue to be debated in social policy. Our hope is that the articles in this text will help readers get past the racial stereotypes and misinformation that so often drive debates over family support programs.

In the meantime, there are certainly some family issues that cut across such divisions. First among these is the need to reject the "family values fable" that Judith Stacey discusses in the final piece: the myth that all of America's problems could be solved if we would only renew our commitment to the strong family values America used to have in the 1950s and that supposedly broke down in the 1960s.

The family-values fable described by Stacey sounds plausible to some Americans because many families *did* succeed in establishing a secure and stable existence during the postwar era. The successes they achieved, however, rested on exceptionally favorable economic and political trends. The

United States emerged from World War II with the strongest economy in the world, and the profits gained from its international head start over our war-damaged economic rivals did trickle down to many American workers. In addition, the government gave much more assistance and many more subsidies to young families than it does today. Forty percent of young men starting families after World War II were eligible for veterans' benefits, allowing an unprecedented number of working-class Americans to gain an education that provided entry into the middle class. The government paid for ninety percent of the highway program that created secure, well-paying jobs for blue-collar workers and opened up suburbia to middle-class and union-wage Americans. It also reorganized home financing, underwriting low down payments and long-term mortgages that had been rejected as bad business by private industry.[46]

In consequence, real wages rose more in each year of the 1950s than in the entire decade of the 1980s. It is no wonder that many modern families look back nostalgically to a time when the average thirty-year-old man could buy a median-priced home on fifteen to eighteen percent of his salary. But these gains resulted from the economic and political climate of the postwar era, not its family arrangements. It is hypocritical for politicians to tell families to return to the family values and forms of the 1950s when they are unwilling to restore the jobs programs and family subsidies of that era, not to mention the limits on corporate relocation and financial wheeling and dealing, the much higher share of taxes paid by corporations, the availability of union jobs for non-college youth, and the subsidies for higher education, such as the National Defense Education Act loans.

Furthermore, the greater economic security of young workers in the 1950s did not apply to all families or individuals, and did not necessarily produce idyllic family relationships. Fifty percent of African-American married-couple families were poor in the fifties, and poverty was also widespread among rural Americans, including whites. Segregation was enforced by daily acts of coercion and violence. Political dissidents, gays, and lesbians were subject to widespread persecution. Women were discriminated against in almost every sphere of life, while battering, incest, and spousal rape were routinely ignored.

Even the seeming successes of the period had a downside. The subsidies that helped many families escape to suburbia, for instance, also helped create today's urban crisis. Government policy diverted funds from urban housing and public transport to building parking lots and offices for commuters without rehousing the thousands of families that were displaced or crowded into slums as a result.

Despite the underside of 1950s family arrangements, it's not surprising that many people believe family life has gotten harder over the past two decades. Partly this is because the postwar promise of rising wages, steady employment, government investment in education, and corporate commitment to local communities has eroded steadily since the early 1970s; by 1996 the United States had reached greater economic inequality than at any time since the 1920s. Partly it's because there have been massive and irreversible changes in gender roles and demographic trends without any comparable adjustment of our work policies, school arrangements, medical programs, and child-care institutions, resulting in new stresses and worries both for parents and for children of aging parents.[47]

Stacey points out, however, that we won't relieve these stresses by telling people fables about a past that is largely romanticized and wholly unrecoverable. If we're going to have a wish list, she argues, let's fill it with items that today's families could really use. We need to adjust our school schedules, work hours, parental leave policies, and definitions of family to recognize that household diversity and working mothers are here to stay. Unemployed or underemployed parents need jobs with adequate medical benefits. Working parents need flextime, quality child care, and an end to forced overtime. Young people need more options for apprentice-type work programs. We should institute paid parental leave, as every other industrial nation has done without going broke; offer parents or other caregivers the option of cutting hours and pay with no loss of benefits or seniority; reorganize school hours to recognize the reality that many mothers work; invest as much in child-care, preschool, and parks programs as we do in failed savings and loan banks. Only with such support systems can families be expected to rise to the challenges of the twenty-first century and can our society hope to avoid further racial and class polarization.

A Note on How to Use This Book

Not everyone, of course, will want to read or use this book in the same order outlined here, or be equally interested in all articles. People concerned with gender issues might want to read Dill, Coontz, Collins, Rapp, Raley, Hondagneu-Sotelo, Chang, Kibria, Hondagneu-Sotelo and Messner, Anderson and Vail, and Greene and Boyd-Franklin. A class on race in contemporary America might use Dill, Sacks, Collins, Zinn, Rubin, Sugrue, Raley, Hondagneu-Sotelo and Messner, Root, Lawson and Wilson, and Steinberg. Those interested in the interaction between people's cultural heritage and the economic or political pressures they face could focus on Sudarkasa, Glenn, Jones, Sanchez, Sugrue, Raley, and Crosbie-Burnett and Lewis. Family dynamics and the psychological impact of race, class, gender, sexuality, and ethnicity are addressed by Adams, Kibria, Hondagneu-Sotelo and Messner, Collins, Stacey, Greene and Boyd-Franklin, Root, and Crosbie-Burnett and Lewis. Our bibliography directs readers to other sources in all of these fields.

NOTES

1. David Blankenorn, *Fatherless America* (New York: Basic Books, 1995).
2. George Will, "The 'Race' Problem," *The Olympian*, 16 April 1995, A9.
3. Maxine Baca Zinn and Bonnie Thornton Dill, "Theorizing Difference From Multiracial Feminism," *Feminist Studies* 22 (1996): 324.
4. E. Douglas Massey, Ruth Zambrana, and Sally Alonzo Bell, "Contemporary Issues in Latino Families," in *Understanding Latino Families: Scholarship, Policy, and Practice*, ed. Ruth Zambrana (Thousand Oaks, Calif.: Sage, 1995), 194; Roger Waldinger and Greta Gilbertson, "Immigrants' Progress: Ethnic and Gender Differences Among U.S. Immigrants in the 1980s," *Sociological Perspectives* 37 (1994): 441
5. Evelyn Brooks Higginbotham, "African-American Women's History and the Metalanguage of Race," *Signs* 17 (1992): 255.
6. Leith Mullings, *On Our Own Terms: Race, Class, and Gender in the Lives of African-American Women* (New York: Routledge, 1997), 80.
7. John Garvey, "My Problem With Multicultural Education," in *Race Traitor*, ed. Noel Ignatiev and John Garvey (New York: Routledge, 1996), 25–30.
8. Baca Zinn and Dill, "Theorizing Difference," 327.
9. See, for example, Stephanie McCurry, *Masters of Small Worlds: Yeoman Households, Gender Relations, and the Political Culture of the Antebellum South Carolina Low Country* (New York: Oxford University Press, 1995).
10. Karen Calvert, *Children in the House* (Boston: Northeastern Press, 1992); Mary Ryan, *Cradle of the Middle Class: The Family in Oneida County, New York, 1790–1865* (New York: Cambridge University Press, 1981); Elaine Tyler May, *Homeward Bound: Families in the Cold War Era* (New York: Basic Books, 1988); Anthony Rotundo, *American Manhood* (New York: Basic Books, 1993); Carroll Smith Rosenberg, *Disorderly Conduct: Visions of Gender in Victorian America* (New York: Oxford University Press, 1985).
11. Mary Ryan, *Cradle of the Middle Class*; Leith Mullings, *On Our Own Terms: Race, Class, and Gender in the Lives of African-American Women* (New York: Routledge, 1997).
12. For more references on Native American diversity, see Stephanie Coontz, *The Social Origins of Private Life: A History of American Families, 1600–1900* (London: Verso, 1988); Brian Schnarch, "Neither Man Nor Woman: Berdache— A Case for Non-Dichotomous Gender Construction," *Anthropologica* XXXIV (1992): 106–21.
13. Mullings, *On Our Own*, 82; Andrew T. Miller, "Social Science, Social Policy, and the Heritage of African-American Families," in *The Underclass Debate*, ed. Michael Katz (Princeton: Princeton University Press, 1993); Mary Benin and Verna Keith, "The Social Support of Employed African-American and Anglo Mothers," *Journal of Family Issues* 16 (1995): 275–97; Anne Roschelle, *No More Kin: Exploring Race, Class, and Gender in Family Networks* (Thousand Oaks, Calif.: Sage, 1997).
14. Michael Omi and Howard Winant, *Racial Formation in the United States* (New York: Routledge, 1994).
15. Eric Wolf, *Europe and the People Without History* (Berkeley: University of California Press, 1982); Douglas Massey, Ruth Zambrana, and Sally Alonzo Hall, "Contemporary Issues in Latino Families: Future Directions for Research, Policy, and Practice," in *Latino Families: Laying a Foundation for Research, Policy, and Practice*, ed. Ruth Zambrana (Thousand Oaks, Calif.: Sage, 1995).

16. David Roediger, *The Wages of Whiteness: Race and the Making of the American Working Class* (London: Verso, 1988); Noel Ignatiev, *How the Irish Became White* (New York: Routledge, 1995).

17. Alejandro Portes and Cynthia Truelove, "Making Sense of Diversity: Recent Research on Hispanic Minorities in the United States," *Annual Review of Sociology* 13 (1987): 359–85.

18. Omi and Winant, "Contesting the Meaning of Race in the Post–Civil Rights Movement Era," in *Origins and Destinies*, ed. Silvia Pedraza and Ruben Rumbaut, (Belmont, Calif.: Wadsworth, 1996), 472; Sucheng Chan, *Asian Americans: An Interpretive History* (Boston: Twayne, 1991); Masako Ishii-Kuntz, "Chinese American Families," in *Families in Cultural Perspective* ed. Mary Kay DeGenova (San Francisco: Mayfield, 1997); Iishi-Kuntz, "Japanese American Families," in *Families*, DeGenova; Iishi-Kuntz, "Intergenerational Relationships Among Chinese, Japanese, and Korean Americans," *Family Relations* 46 (1997): 23–32; Harry Kitano and Roger Daniels, *Asian Americans: Emerging Minorities* (Englewood Cliffs, N.J.: Prentice-Hall, 1988); Laura Uba, *Asian Americans: Personality Patterns, Identity, and Mental Health* (New York: Guilford, 1994).

19. For further discussion of the relational aspect of class, see E.P. Thompson, *The Making of the English Working Class* (New York: Vintage, 1963), 9.

20. Barbara J. Fields, "Ideology and Race in American History," in *Region, Race, and Reconstruction: Essays in Honor of C. Vann Woodward*, ed. J. Morgan Kousser and James M. McPherson (New York: Oxford University Press, 1982), 150–51.

21. Jodie Kliman and William Madsen, "Social Class and the Family Life Cycle," in *The Changing Family Life Cycle*, ed. Betty Carter and Monica McGoldrick (Boston: Allyn and Bacon, in press).

22. Douglas Massey, "American Apartheid: Segregation and the Making of the Underclass," *American Journal of Sociology* 96 (1990): 329–57.

23. Louise Lamphere, Patricia Zavella, and Felipe Gonzales with Peter B. Evans, *Sunbelt Working Mothers: Reconciling Family and Factory* (New York: Cornell University Press, 1993), 4.

24. Patricia Hill Collins, *Black Feminist Thought: Knowledge, Consciousness, and the Politics of Empowerment* (Boston: Unwin Hyman, 1990); Evelyn Nakano Glenn, "From Servitude to Service Work: Historical Continuities in the Racial Division of Paid Reproductive Labor," *Signs* 18 (1992).

25. Andrew Billingsley, *Climbing Jacob's Ladder: The Enduring Legacy of African-American Families* (New York: Touchstone, 1992); Sandra Danziger and Norma Radin, "Absent Does Not Equal Uninvolved: Predictors of Fathering in Teen Mother Families," *Journal of Marriage and the Family* 52 (1990); Tamara Hareven, "Historical Analysis of the Family," in *Handbook of Marriage and the Family*, ed. Marvin Sussman and Suzanne Steinmetz (New York: Plenum Press, 1987).

26. Nancy Cott, *The Grounding of Modern Feminism* (New Haven: Yale University Press, 1987); bell hooks, *Feminist Theory From Margin to Center* (Boston: South End Press, 1984), 1–2, 18.

27. Joan Acker, "Class, Gender, and the Relations of Distribution," *Signs* 13 (1988).

28. Robert B. Hill, *Research on the African-American Family: A Holistic Perspective* (Westport, Conn.: Auburn House, 1993); Ruben Rumbaut, "Origins and Destinies: Immigration, Race, and Ethnicity in Contemporary America," in *Origins and Destinies*, Pedraza and Rumbaut, 39.

29. Mullings, *On Our Own*.
30. For documentation of this and the following two paragraphs, see Coontz, *The Way We Really Are: Coming to Terms With America's Changing Families* (New York: Basic Books, 1997).
31. Judith Stacey, *Brave New Families: Stories of Domestic Upheaval in Late Twentieth Century America* (New York: Basic Books, 1990).
32. The original study appeared as *Worlds of Pain: Life in the Working-Class Family* (New York: Basic Books, 1992, first published 1976).
33. Mary C. Waters, "Optional Identities: For Whites Only?" in *Origins and Destinies*, Pedraza and Rumbaut, 449.
34. Carl Rowan, "Houston Voters Send America a Message," *Houston Chronicle*, November 6, 1997.
35. Suzann Evinger, "How Shall We Measure Our Nation's Diversity?" *Change* 8 (1995): 9; Rumbaut, "Origins and Destinies," in *Origins and Destinies*, Pedraza and Rumbaut, 28.
36. Christine Ho, "The Internationalization of Kinship and the Feminization of Caribbean Migration: The Case of Afro-Trinidadian Immigrants in Los Angeles," *Human Organization* 52 (1993): 32–40.
37. Susan Ostrander, *Women of the Upper Class* (Philadelphia: Temple University Press, 1984), 152.
38. Faye Fiore, "Full-Time Moms a Minority Now, Census Bureau Finds," *Los Angeles Times*, November 26, 1997; Daphne Spain and Suzanne M. Bianchi, *Balancing Act: Motherhood, Marriage, and Employment Among American Women* (New York: Russel Sage, 1996).
39. Beth Anne Shelton and Daphne John, "Ethnicity, Race, and Difference: A Comparison of White, Black, and Hispanic Men's Household Labor Time," in *Men, Work, and Family*, ed. Jane Hood (Thousand Oaks, Calif.: Sage, 1993); Stephanie Coontz and Maya Parson, "Complicating the Contested Terrain of Work/Family Intersections," *Signs* 22 (1997): 440–52.
40. George Chauncey, *Gay New York: Gender, Urban Culture, and the Making of the Gay Urban World*, 1890–1940 (New York: Basic Books, 1994); E.S. Morales, "Ethnic Minority Families and Minority Gays and Lesbians," in *Homosexuality and Family Relations,* ed. F.W. Bozett and M.B. Sussmen (New York: Harrington Park Press, 1990), 217–39.
41. Ruthann Robson, "Resisting the Family: Repositioning Lesbians in Legal Theory," *Signs* 19 (1994): 987.
42. See, for instance, Algea Harrison et al., "Family Ecologies of Ethnic Minority Children," *Child Development* 61 (1990): 347–62.
43. Carol Stack, "Cultural Perspectives on Child Welfare," in *Family Matters: Readings on Family Lives and the Law*, ed. Martha Minow (New York: The New Press, 1993), 344–49; E. Alan Howard, Robert Heighton, Cathie Jordan, and Ronald Gallimore, "Traditional and Modern Adoption Patterns in Hawaii," in *Adoption in Eastern Oceania*, ed. Carroll. (Honolulu: University of Hawaii Press, 1970), 21–51; Jean Peterson, "Generalized Extended Family Exchange: A Case From the Philippines," *Journal of Marriage and the Family* 55 (1993); Kate Porter Young, "Notes on Sisterhood, Kinship, and Marriage in an African-American South Carolina Island Community," *Center for Research on Women, Working Paper 6*, August 1992, 12.
44. Richard America, ed., *The Wealth of Race: The Present Value of Benefits From Past Injustices* (Westport, Conn.: Greenwood, 1990); Melvin Oliver and Thomas Shapiro, *Black Wealth/White Wealth: A New Perspective on Racial Inequality* (New York: Routledge, 1995).

45. Martin Carnoy and Richard Rothstein, "Are Black Diplomas Worth Less?" *The American Prospect* 10 (1997): 45.

46. The points in this and the following paragraphs are documented in my books, *The Way We Never Were: American Families and the Nostalgia Trap* (New York: Basic Books, 1992) and *The Way We Really Are: Coming to Terms With America's Changing Families* (New York: Basic Books, 1997).

47. Sheila Kamerman, "Gender Role and Family Structure Changes in the Advanced Industrial West," in *Poverty, Inequality, and the Future of Social Policy*, ed. Katherine McFate, Roger Lawson, and William Julius Wilson (New York: Russell Sage, 1995); Barbara Bergmann, *Saving Our Children From Poverty: What the United States Can Learn From France* (New York: Russell Sage, 1996).

Part I

THE AMERICAN TRADITION OF FAMILY DIVERSITY

1

FICTIVE KIN, PAPER SONS, AND *COMPADRAZGO*: WOMEN OF COLOR AND THE STRUGGLE FOR FAMILY SURVIVAL

Bonnie Thornton Dill

Race has been fundamental to the construction of families in the United States since the country was settled. People of color were incorporated into the country and used to meet the need for cheap and exploitable labor. Little attention was given to their family and community life except as it related to their economic productivity. Upon their founding, the various colonies that ultimately formed the United States initiated legal, economic, political, and social practices designed to promote the growth of family life among European colonists. As the primary laborers in the reproduction and maintenance of families, White[1] women settlers were accorded the privileges and protection considered socially appropriate to their family roles. The structure of family life during this era was strongly patriarchal: denying women many rights, constraining their personal autonomy, and making them subject to the almost unfettered will of the male head of the household. Nevertheless, women were rewarded and protected within patriarchal families because their labor was recognized as essential to the maintenance and sustenance of family life.[2] In addition, families were seen as the cornerstone of an incipient nation, and thus their existence was a matter of national interest.

In contrast, women of color experienced the oppression of a patriarchal society but were denied the protection and buffering of a patriarchal family. Although the presence of women of color was equally important to the growth of the nation, their value was based on their potential as workers, breeders, and entertainers of workers, not as family members. In the eighteenth and nineteenth centuries, labor, and not the existence or maintenance of families, was the critical aspect of their role in building the nation. Thus they were denied the societal supports necessary to make their families a vital element in the social order. For women of color, family membership was not a key means of access to participation in the wider society. In some instances, racial-ethnic families were seen as a threat to the efficiency and exploitability of the work force and were actively prohibited. In other cases, they were tolerated when it was felt they might help solidify or expand the work force. The lack of social, legal, and economic support for the family life of people of color intensified and extended women's work, created tensions and strains in family relationships, and set the stage for a variety of creative and adaptive forms of resistance.

AFRICAN AMERICAN SLAVES

Among students of slavery, there has been considerable debate over the relative "harshness" of American slavery, and the degree to which slaves were permitted or encouraged to form families. It is generally acknowledged that many slave owners found it economically advantageous to encourage family formation as a way of reproducing and perpetuating the slave labor force. This became increasingly true after 1807, when the importation of African slaves was explicitly prohibited. The existence of these families and many aspects of their functioning, however, were directly controlled by the master. Slaves married and formed families, but these groupings were completely subject to the master's decision to let them remain intact. One study has estimated that about 32 percent of all recorded slave marriages were disrupted by sale, about 45 percent by death of a spouse, about 10 percent by choice, and only 13 percent were not disrupted (Blassingame 1972). African slaves thus quickly learned that they had a limited degree of control over the formation and maintenance of their marriages and could not be assured of keeping their children with them. The threat of disruption was one of the most direct and pervasive assaults on families that slaves encountered. Yet there were a number of other aspects of the slave system that reinforced the precariousness of slave family life.

In contrast to some African traditions and the Euro-American patterns of the period, slave men were not the main providers or authority figures in the family. The mother-child tie was basic and of greatest interest to the slave owner because it was essential to the reproduction of the labor force.

In addition to the lack of authority and economic autonomy experienced by the husband-father in the slave family, use of rape of women slaves as a weapon of terror and control further undermined the integrity of the slave family.

> It would be a mistake to regard the institutionalized pattern of rape during slavery as an expression of white men's sexual urges, otherwise stifled by the specter of the white womanhood's chastity.... Rape was a weapon of domination, a weapon of repression, whose covert goal was to extinguish slave women's will to resist, and in the process, to demoralize their men. (Davis 1981:23–24)

The slave family, therefore, was at the heart of a peculiar tension in the master-slave relationship. On the one hand, slave owners sought to encourage familiarities among slaves because, as Julie Matthaei (1982:81) states, "These provided the basis of the development of the slave into a self-conscious socialized human being." They also hoped and believed that this socialization process would help children learn to accept their place in society as slaves. Yet the master's need to control and intervene in the family life of the slaves is indicative of the other side of this tension. Family ties had the potential to become a competing and more potent source of allegiance than the master. Also, kin were as likely to socialize children in forms of resistance as in acts of compliance.

It was within this context of surveillance, assault, and ambivalence that slave women's reproductive labor[3] took place. They and their menfolk had the task of preserving the human and family ties that could ultimately give them a reason for living. They had to socialize their children to believe in the possibility of a life in which they were not enslaved. The slave woman's labor on behalf of the family was, as Angela Davis (1971) has pointed out, the only labor in which the slave engaged that could not be directly used by the slave owner for his own profit. Yet, it was crucial to the reproduction of the slave owner's labor force, and thus a source of strong ambivalence for many slave women. Whereas some mothers murdered their babies to keep them from being slaves, many sought within the family the autonomy and creativity that were denied them in other realms of the society. The maintenance of a distinct African American culture is testimony to the ways in which slaves maintained a degree of cultural autonomy and resisted the creation of a slave family that only served the needs of the master.

Herbert Gutman (1976) gives evidence of the ways in which slaves expressed a unique African American culture through their family practices. He provides data on naming patterns and kinship ties among slaves that fly in the face of the dominant ideology of the period, which argued that slaves were immoral and had little concern for or appreciation of family life. Yet Gutman demonstrates that, within a system that denied the father authority over his family, slave boys were frequently named after their fathers, and many children were named after blood relatives as a way of maintaining family ties. Gutman also suggests that after emancipation a number of slaves took the names of former owners in order to reestablish family ties that had been disrupted earlier. On plantation after plantation, Gutman found considerable evidence of the building and maintenance of extensive kinship ties among slaves. In instances where slave families had been disrupted, slaves in new communities reconstituted the kinds of family and kin ties that came to characterize Black family life throughout the South. The patterns included, but were not limited to, a belief in the importance of marriage as a long-term commitment, rules of exogamy that excluded marriage between first cousins, and acceptance of women who had children outside of marriage. Kinship networks were an important source of resistance to the organization of labor that treated the individual slave, and not the family, as the unit of labor (Caulfield 1974).

Another interesting indicator of the slaves' maintenance of some degree of cultural autonomy has been pointed out by Gwendolyn

Wright (1981) in her discussion of slave housing. Until the early 1800s, slaves were often permitted to build their housing according to their own design and taste. During that period, housing built in an African style was quite common in the slave quarters. By 1830, however, slave owners had begun to control the design and arrangement of slave housing and had introduced a degree of conformity and regularity to it that left little room for the slaves' personalization of the home. Nevertheless, slaves did use some of their own techniques in construction, often hiding them from their masters.

> Even the floors, which usually consisted of only tamped earth, were evidence of a hidden African tradition: slaves cooked clay over a fire, mixing in ox blood or cow dung, and then poured it in place to make hard dirt floors almost like asphalt.... In slave houses, in contrast to other crafts, these signs of skill and tradition would then be covered over. (Wright 1981:48)

Housing is important in discussions of family because its design reflects sociocultural attitudes about family life. The housing that slave owners provided for their slaves reflected a view of Black family life consistent with the stereotypes of the period. While the existence of slave families was acknowledged, they certainly were not nurtured. Thus, cabins were crowded, often containing more than one family, and there were no provisions for privacy. Slaves had to create their own.

> Slave couples hung up old clothes or quilts to establish boundaries; others built more substantial partitions from scrap wood. Parents sought to establish sexual privacy from children. A few ex-slaves described modified trundle beds designed to hide parental love-making.... Even in one room cabins, sexual segregation was carefully organized. (Wright 1981:50)

Perhaps most critical in developing an understanding of slave women's reproductive labor is the gender-based division of labor in the domestic sphere. The organization of slave labor enforced considerable equality among men and women. The ways in which equality in the labor force was translated into the family sphere is somewhat speculative. Davis (1981:18), for example, suggests that egalitarianism between males and females was a direct result of slavery: "Within the confines of their family and community life, therefore, Black people managed to accomplish a magnificent feat. They transformed that negative equality which emanated from the equal oppression they suffered as slaves into a positive quality; the egalitarianism characterizing their social relations."

It is likely, however, that this transformation was far less direct than Davis implies. We know, for example, that slave women experienced what has recently been called the "double day" before most other women in this society. Slave narratives (Jones 1985; White 1985; Blassingame 1977) reveal that women had primary responsibility for their family's domestic chores. They cooked (although on some planta-tions meals were prepared for all the slaves), sewed, cared for their chil-dren, and cleaned house after completing a full day of labor for the mas-ter. John Blassingame (1972) and others have pointed out that slave men engaged in hunting, trapping, perhaps some gardening, and furniture making as ways of contributing to the maintenance of their families. Clearly, a gender-based division of labor did exist within the family, and it appears that women bore the larger share of the burden for house-keeping and child care.

In contrast to White families of the period, however, the division of labor in the domestic sphere was reinforced neither in the relationship of slave women to work nor in the social institutions of the slave com-munity. The gender-based division of labor among the slaves existed within a social system that treated men and women as almost equal, independent units of labor.[4] Thus Matthaei (1982:94) is probably correct in concluding that

> whereas the white homemaker interacted with the public sphere through her husband, and had her work life determined by him, the enslaved Afro-American homemaker was directly subordinated to and determined by her owner.... The equal enslavement of husband and wife gave the slave marriage a curious kind of equality, an equality of oppression.

Black men were denied the male resources of a patriarchal society and therefore were unable to turn gender distinctions into female sub-ordination, even if that had been their desire. Black women, on the other hand, were denied support and protection for their roles as moth-ers and wives, and thus had to modify and structure those roles around the demands of their labor. Reproductive labor for slave women was intensified in several ways: by the demands of slave labor that forced them into the double day of work; by the desire and need to maintain family ties in the face of a system that gave them only limited recogni-tion; by the stresses of building a family with men who were denied the standard social privileges of manhood; and by the struggle to raise chil-dren who could survive in a hostile environment.

This intensification of reproductive labor made networks of kin and fictive kin important instruments in carrying out the reproductive tasks of the slave community. Given an African cultural heritage where kin-ship ties formed the basis of social relations, it is not at all surprising that African American slaves developed an extensive system of kinship ties and obligations (Gutman 1976; Sudarkasa 1981). Research on Black families in slavery provides considerable documentation of participa-tion of extended kin in child rearing, childbirth, and other domestic, social, and economic activities (Gutman 1976; Blassingame 1972; Genovese and Miller 1974).

After slavery, these ties continued to be an important factor linking individual household units in a variety of domestic activities. While kinship ties were also important among native-born Whites and European immigrants, Gutman (1976:213) has suggested that these ties

> were comparatively more important to Afro-Americans than to lower-class native white and immigrant Americans, the result of their distinctive low economic status, a condition that denied them the advantages of an extensive associational life beyond the kin group and the advantages and disadvantages resulting from mobility opportunities.

His argument is reaffirmed by research on African American families after slavery (Shimkin et al. 1978; Aschenbrenner 1975; Davis 1981; Stack 1974). Niara Sudarkasa (1981:49) takes this argument one step further, linking this pattern to the African cultural heritage.

> Historical realities require that the derivation of this aspect of Black family organization be traced to its African antecedents. Such a view does not deny the adaptive significance of consanguineal networks. In fact, it helps to clarify why these networks had the flexibility they had and why they, rather than conjugal relationships, came to be the stabilizing factor in Black families.

In individual households, the gender-based division of labor experienced some important shifts during emancipation. In their first real opportunity to establish family life beyond the controls and constraints imposed by a slave master, Black sharecroppers' family life changed radically. Most women, at least those who were wives and daughters of able-bodied men, withdrew from field labor and concentrated on their domestic duties in the home. Husbands took primary responsibility for the fieldwork and for relations with the owners, such as signing contracts on behalf of the family. Black women were severely criticized by Whites for removing themselves from field labor because they were seen to be aspiring to a model of womanhood that was considered inappropriate for them. The reorganization of female labor, however, represented an attempt on the part of Blacks to protect women from some of the abuses of the slave system and to thus secure their family life. It was more likely a response to the particular set of circumstances that the newly freed slaves faced than a reaction to the lives of their former masters. Jacqueline Jones (1985) argues that these patterns were "particularly significant" because at a time when industrial development was introducing a labor system that divided male and female labor, the freed Black family was establishing a pattern of joint work and complementarity of tasks between males and females that was reminiscent of preindustrial American families. Unfortunately, these former slaves had to do this without the institutional supports given White farm families and within a sharecropping system that deprived them of economic independence.

CHINESE SOJOURNERS

An increase in the African slave population was a desired goal. Therefore, Africans were permitted and even encouraged at times to form families, as long as they were under the direct control of the slave master. By sharp contrast, Chinese people were explicitly denied the right to form families in the United States through both law and social practice. Although male laborers began coming to the United States in sizable numbers in the middle of the nineteenth century, it was more than a century before an appreciable number of children of Chinese parents were born in America. Tom, a respondent in Victor Nee and Brett de Bary Nee's book, *Longtime Californ'*, says: "One thing about Chinese men in America was you had to be either a merchant or a big gambler, have lot of side money to have a family here. A working man, an ordinary man, just can't!" (1973:80).

Working in the United States was a means of gaining support for one's family with an end of obtaining sufficient capital to return to China and purchase land. This practice of sojourning was reinforced by laws preventing Chinese laborers from becoming citizens, and by restrictions on their entry into this country. Chinese laborers who arrived before 1882 could not bring their wives and were prevented by law from marrying Whites. Thus, it is likely that the number of Chinese American families might have been negligible had it not been for two things: the San Francisco earthquake and fire in 1906, which destroyed all municipal records, and the ingenuity and persistence of the Chinese people, who used the opportunity created by the earthquake to increase their numbers in the United States. Since relatives of citizens were permitted entry, American-born Chinese (real and claimed) would visit China, report the birth of a son, and thus create an entry slot. Years later, since the records were destroyed, the slot could be used by a relative or purchased by someone outside the family. The purchasers were called "paper sons." Paper sons became a major mechanism for increasing the Chinese population, but it was a slow process and the sojourner community remained predominantly male for decades.

The high concentration of males in the Chinese community before 1920 resulted in a split household form of family. As Evelyn Nakano Glenn observes:

> In the split household family, production is separated from other functions and is carried out by a member living far from the rest of the household. The rest—consumption, reproduction and socialization—are carried out by the wife and other relatives from the home village.... The split household form makes possible maximum exploitation of the workers.... The labor of prime-age male workers can be bought relatively cheaply, since the cost of reproduction and family maintenance is borne partially by unpaid subsistence work of women and old people in the home village. (1983:38–39)

The Chinese women who were in the United States during this period consisted of a small number who were wives and daughters of merchants and a larger percentage who were prostitutes. Lucia Cheng Hirata (1979) has suggested that Chinese prostitution was an important element in helping to maintain the split household family. In conjunction with laws prohibiting intermarriage, it helped men avoid long-term relationships with women in the United States and ensured that the bulk of their meager earnings would continue to support the family at home.

The reproductive labor of Chinese women, therefore, took on two dimensions primarily because of the split household family. Wives who remained in China were forced to raise children and care for in-laws on the meager remittances of their sojourning husbands. Although we know few details about their lives, it is clear that the everyday work of bearing and maintaining children and running a household fell entirely on their shoulders. Those women who immigrated and worked as prostitutes performed the more nurturant aspects of reproductive labor, that is, providing emotional and sexual companionship for men who were far from home. Yet their role as prostitutes was more likely a means of supporting their families at home in China than a chosen vocation.

The Chinese family system during the nineteenth century was a patriarchal one and girls had little value. In fact, they were considered temporary members of their father's family because when they married, they became members of their husband's family. They also had little social value; girls were sold by some poor parents to work as prostitutes, concubines, or servants. This saved the family the expense of raising them, and their earnings became a source of family income. For most girls, however, marriages were arranged and families sought useful connections through this process. With the development of a sojourning pattern in the United States, some Chinese women in those regions of China where this pattern was more prevalent would be sold to become prostitutes in the United States. Most, however, were married to men whom they saw only once or twice in the twenty- or thirty-year periods during which these men sojourned in the United States. A woman's status as wife ensured that a portion of the meager wages her husband earned would be returned to his family in China. This arrangement required considerable sacrifice and adjustment by wives who remained in China and those who joined their husbands after a long separation.

Maxine Hong Kingston tells the story of the unhappy meeting of her aunt, Moon Orchid, with her husband, from whom she had been separated for thirty years: "For thirty years she had been receiving money from him from America. But she had never told him that she wanted to come to the United States. She waited for him to suggest it, but he never did" (1977:144). His response to her when she arrived unexpectedly was to say: " 'Look at her. She'd never fit into an American household. I have important American guests who come inside my house to eat.' He turned to Moon Orchid, 'You can't talk to them. You can barely talk to me.' Moon

Orchid was so ashamed, she held her hands over her face" (1977:178).

Despite these handicaps, Chinese people collaborated to establish the opportunity to form families and settle in the United States. In some cases it took as long as three generations for a child to be born on U.S. soil.

> In one typical history, related by a 21 year old college student, great-grandfather arrived in the States in the 1890s as a "paper son" and worked for about 20 years as a laborer. He then sent for the grandfather, who worked alongside great-grandfather in a small business for several years. Great-grandfather subsequently returned to China, leaving grandfather to run the business and send remittance. In the 1940s, grandfather sent for father; up to this point, none of the wives had left China. Finally, in the late 1950s father returned to China and brought his wife back with him. Thus, after nearly 70 years, the first child was born in the United States. (Glenn 1981:14)

CHICANOS

Africans were uprooted from their native lands and encouraged to have families in order to increase the slave labor force. Chinese people were immigrant laborers whose "permanent" presence in the country was denied. By contrast, Mexican Americans were colonized and their traditional family life was disrupted by war and the imposition of a new set of laws and conditions of labor. The hardships faced by Chicano families, therefore, were the results of the U.S. colonization of the indigenous Mexican population, accompanied by the beginnings of industrial development. The treaty of Guadalupe Hidalgo, signed in 1848, granted American citizenship to Mexicans living in what is now called the Southwest. The American takeover, however, resulted in the gradual displacement of Mexicans from the land and their incorporation into a colonial labor force (Barrera 1979). Mexicans who immigrated into the United States after 1848 were also absorbed into that labor force.

Whether natives of northern Mexico (which became part of the United States after 1848) or immigrants from southern Mexico, Chicanos were a largely peasant population whose lives were defined by a feudal economy and a daily struggle on the land for economic survival. Patriarchal families were important instruments of community life, and nuclear family units were linked through an elaborate system of kinship and godparenting. Traditional life was characterized by hard work and a fairly distinct pattern of sex-role segregation.

> Most Mexican women were valued for their household qualities, men by their ability to work and to provide for a family. Children were taught to get up early, to contribute to their family's labor to prepare themselves for adult life.... Such a life demanded discipline, authority, deference—values that cemented the working of a

family surrounded and shaped by the requirements of Mexico's distinctive historical pattern of agricultural development, especially
its pervasive debt peonage. (Saragoza 1983:8)

As the primary caretakers of hearth and home in a rural environment,
Chicana's labor made a vital and important contribution to family survival.
A description of women's reproductive labor in the early twentieth century may be used to gain insight into the work of the nineteenth-century
rural women.

> For country women, work was seldom a salaried job. More often it
> was the work of growing and preparing food, of making adobes and
> plastering houses with mud, or making their children's clothes for
> school and teaching them the hymns and prayers of the church, or
> delivering babies and treating sickness with herbs and patience. In
> almost every town there were one or two women who, in addition
> to working in their own homes, served other families in the com-
> munity as *curanderas* (healers), *parteras* (midwives), and school-
> teachers. (Elasser et al. 1980:10)

Although some scholars have argued that family rituals and community life showed little change before World War I (Saragoza 1983), the
American conquest of Mexican lands, the introduction of a new system
of labor, the loss of Mexican-owned land through the inability to document ownership, and the transient nature of most of the jobs in which
Chicanos were employed resulted in the gradual erosion of this pastoral
way of life. Families were uprooted as the economic basis for family life
changed. Some people immigrated from Mexico in search of a better
standard of living and worked in the mines and railroads. Others, who
were native to the Southwest, faced a job market that no longer required
their skills. They moved into mining, railroad, and agricultural labor in
search of a means of earning a living. According to Albert Camarillo
(1979), the influx of Anglo[5] capital into the pastoral economy of Santa
Barbara rendered obsolete the skills of many Chicano males who had
worked as ranch hands and farmers prior to the urbanization of that
economy. While some women and children accompanied their husbands to the railroad and mining camps, many of these camps discour-
aged or prohibited family settlement.

The American period (after 1848) was characterized by considerable
transiency for the Chicano population. Its impact on families is seen in
the growth of female-headed households, reflected in the data as early
as 1860. Richard Griswold del Castillo (1979) found a sharp increase in
female-headed households in Los Angeles, from a low of 13 percent in
1844 to 31 percent in 1880. Camarillo (1979:120) documents a similar
increase in Santa Barbara, from 15 percent in 1844 to 30 percent by
1880. These increases appear to be due not so much to divorce, which
was infrequent in this Catholic population, as to widowhood and tem-

porary abandonment in search of work. Given the hazardous nature of work in the mines and railroad camps, the death of a husband, father, or son who was laboring in these sites was not uncommon. Griswold del Castillo (1979) reports a higher death rate among men than women in Los Angeles. The rise in female-headed households, therefore, reflects the instabilities and insecurities introduced into women's lives as a result of the changing social organization of work.

One outcome, the increasing participation of women and children in the labor force, was primarily a response to economic factors that required the modification of traditional values. According to Louisa Vigil, who was born in 1890, "The women didn't work at that time. The man was supposed to marry that girl and take care of her.... Your grandpa never did let me work for nobody. He always had to work, and we never did have really bad times" (Elasser et al. 1980:14).

Vigil's comments are reinforced in Mario Garcia's (1980) study of El Paso. In the 393 households he examined in the 1900 census, he found 17.1 percent of the women to be employed. The majority of this group were daughters, mothers with no husbands, and single women. In Los Angeles and Santa Barbara, where there were greater work opportunities for women than in El Paso, wives who were heads of household worked in seasonal and part-time jobs, and lived from the earnings of children and relatives in an effort to maintain traditional female roles.

Slowly, entire families were encouraged to go to railroad work camps and were eventually incorporated into the agricultural labor market. This was a response both to the extremely low wages paid to Chicano laborers and to the preferences of employers, who saw family labor as a way of stabilizing the work force. For Chicanos, engaging all family members in agricultural work was a means of increasing their earnings to a level close to subsistence for the entire group and of keeping the family unit together. Camarillo provides a picture of the interplay of work, family, and migration in the Santa Barbara area in the following observation:

> The time of year when women and children were employed in the fruit cannery and participated in the almond and olive harvest coincided with the seasons when the men were most likely to be engaged in seasonal migratory work. There were seasons, however, especially in the early summer when the entire family migrated from the city to pick fruit. This type of family seasonal harvest was evident in Santa Barbara by the 1890s. As walnuts replaced almonds and as the fruit industry expanded, Chicano family labor became essential. (1979:93)

This arrangement, while bringing families together, did not decrease the hardships that Chicanas had to confront in raising their families. We may infer something about the rigors of that life from Jesse Lopez de la Cruz's description of the workday of migrant farm laborers in the 1940s. Work conditions in the 1890s were as difficult, if not worse.

> We always went to where the women and men were going to work, because if it were just the men working it wasn't worth going out there because we wouldn't earn enough to support a family.... We would start around 6:30 a.m. and work for four or five hours, then walk home and eat and rest until about three-thirty in the afternoon when it cooled off. We would go back and work until we couldn't see. Then I'd clean up the kitchen. I was doing the housework and working out in the fields and taking care of two children. (Quoted in Goldman 1981:119–120)

In the towns, women's reproductive labor was intensified by the congested and unsanitary conditions of the barrios in which they lived. Garcia described the following conditions in El Paso:

> Mexican women had to haul water for washing and cooking from the river or public water pipes. To feed their families, they had to spend time marketing, often in Ciudad Juarez across the border, as well as long, hot hours cooking meals and coping with the burden of desert sand both inside and outside their homes. Besides the problem of raising children, unsanitary living conditions forced Mexican mothers to deal with disease and illness in their families. Diphtheria, tuberculosis, typhus and influenza were never too far away. Some diseases could be directly traced to inferior city services.... As a result, Mexican mothers had to devote much energy to caring for sick children, many of whom died. (1980:320–321)

While the extended family has remained an important element of Chicano life, it was eroded in the American period in several ways. Griswold del Castillo (1979), for example, points out that in 1845 about 71 percent of Angelenos lived in extended families, whereas by 1880, fewer than half did. This decrease in extended families appears to be a response to the changed economic conditions and the instabilities generated by the new sociopolitical structure. Additionally, the imposition of American law and custom ignored, and ultimately undermined, some aspects of the extended family. The extended family in traditional Mexican life consisted of an important set of family, religious, and community obligations. Women, while valued primarily for their domesticity, had certain legal and property rights that acknowledged the importance of their work, their families of origin, and their children. In California, for example,

> equal ownership of property between husband and wife had been one of the mainstays of the Spanish and Mexican family systems. Community-property laws were written into the civil codes with the intention of strengthening the economic controls of the wife and her relatives. The American government incorporated these Mexican laws into the state constitution, but later court decisions interpreted these statutes so as to undermine the wife's economic rights. In 1861, the legislature passed a law that allowed the deceased wife's property to revert to her husband. Previously it had

been inherited by her children and relatives if she died without a will. (Griswold del Castillo 1979:69)

The impact of this and similar court rulings was to "strengthen the property rights of the husband at the expense of his wife and children" (Griswold del Castillo 1979:69).

In the face of the legal, social, and economic changes that occurred during the American period, Chicanas were forced to cope with a series of dislocations in traditional life. They were caught between conflicting pressures to maintain traditional women's roles and family customs, and the need to participate in the economic support of their families by working outside the home. During this period the preservation of traditional customs—such as languages, celebrations, and healing practices—became an important element in maintaining and supporting familial ties.

According to Alex Saragoza (1983), transiency, the effects of racism and segregation, and proximity to Mexico aided in the maintenance of traditional family practices. Garcia has suggested that women were the guardians of Mexican cultural traditions within the family. He cites the work of anthropologist Manuel Gamio, who identified the retention of many Mexican customs among Chicanos in settlements around the United States in the early 1900s.

> These included folklore, songs, and ballads, birthday celebrations, saints' days, baptisms, weddings, and funerals in the traditional style. Because of poverty, a lack of physicians in the barrios, and adherence to traditional customs, Mexicans continued to use medicinal herbs. Gamio also identified the maintenance of a number of oral traditions, and Mexican style cooking. (Garcia 1980:322)

Of vital importance to the integrity of traditional culture was the perpetuation of the Spanish language. Factors that aided in the maintenance of other aspects of Mexican culture also helped in sustaining the language. However, entry into English-language public schools introduced the children and their families to systematic efforts to erase their native tongue. Griswold del Castillo reports that in the early 1880s there was considerable pressure against speakers of Spanish in the public schools. He also found that some Chicano parents responded to this kind of discrimination by helping support independent bilingual schools. These efforts, however, were short-lived.

Another key factor in conserving Chicano culture was the extended family network, particularly the system of *compadrazgo* (godparenting). Although the full extent of the impact of the American period on the Chicano extended family is not known, it is generally acknowledged that this family system, though lacking many legal and social sanctions, played an important role in the preservation of the Mexican community (Camarillo 1979). In Mexican society, godparents were an important way of linking family and community through respected friends or authorities. Participants in the important rites of passage in the child's life, such as baptism, first Communion, confirmation, and marriage, godparents had a moral obligation to act as guardians, to provide financial assistance in times of need, and to substitute in case of the death of a parent. Camarillo (1979) points out that in traditional society these bonds cut across class and racial lines.

The rite of baptism established kinship networks between rich and poor, between Spanish, mestizo and American Indian, and often carried with it political loyalty and economic-occupational ties. The leading California patriarchs in the pueblo played important roles in the *compadrazgo* network. They sponsored dozens of children for their workers or poorer relatives. The kindness of the *padrino* and *madrina* was repaid with respect and support from the *pobladores* (Camarillo 1979: 12–13).

The extended family network, which included godparents, expanded the support groups for women who were widowed or temporarily abandoned and for those who were in seasonal, part- or full-time work. It suggests, therefore, the potential for an exchange of services among poor people whose income did not provide the basis for family subsistence. Griswold del Castillo (1979) argues that family organization influenced literacy rates and socioeconomic mobility among Chicanos in Los Angeles between 1850 and 1880. His data suggest that children in extended families (defined as those with at least one other relative living in a nuclear family household) had higher literacy rates than those in nuclear families. He also argues that those in larger families fared better economically and experienced less downward mobility. The data here are too limited to generalize to the Chicano experience as a whole, but they do reinforce the actual and potential importance of this family form to the continued cultural autonomy of the Chicano community.

CONCLUSION

Reproductive labor for African American, Chinese American, and Mexican American women in the nineteenth century centered on the struggle to maintain family units in the face of a variety of assaults. Treated primarily as workers rather than as members of family groups, these women labored to maintain, sustain, stabilize, and reproduce their families while working in both the public (productive) and private (reproductive) spheres. Thus, the concept of reproductive labor, when applied to women of color, must be modified to account for the fact that labor in the productive sphere was required to achieve even minimal levels of family subsistence. Long after industrialization had begun to reshape family roles among middle-class White families, driving White women into a cult of domesticity, women of color were coping with an extended day. This day included subsistence labor outside the family and domestic labor within the family. For slaves, domestics, migrant farm laborers, seasonal factory workers, and prostitutes, the distinctions between labor that reproduced family life and labor that economically sustained it were minimized. The expanded workday was one of the primary ways in which reproductive labor increased.

Racial-ethnic families were sustained and maintained in the face of various forms of disruption. Yet the women and their families paid a high price in the process. High rates of infant mortality, a shortened life span, and the early onset of crippling and debilitating disease give some insight into the costs of survival.

The poor quality of housing and the neglect of communities further increased reproductive labor. Not only did racial-ethnic women work hard outside the home for mere subsistence, they worked very hard inside the home to achieve even minimal standards of privacy and cleanliness. They were continually faced with disease and illness that resulted directly from the absence of basic sanitation. The fact that some African women murdered their children to prevent them from becoming slaves is an indication of the emotional strain associated with bearing and raising children while participating in the colonial labor system.

We have uncovered little information about the use of birth control, the prevalence of infanticide, or the motivations that may have generated these or other behaviors. We can surmise, however, that no matter how much children were accepted, loved, or valued among any of these groups of people, their futures were precarious. Keeping children alive, helping them to understand and participate in a system that exploited them, and working to ensure a measure—no matter how small—of cultural integrity intensified women's reproductive labor.

Being a woman of color in nineteenth-century American society meant having extra work both inside and outside the home. It meant being defined as outside of or deviant from the norms and values about women that were being generated in the dominant White culture. The notion of separate spheres of male and female labor that developed in the nineteenth century had contradictory outcomes for Whites. It was the basis for the confinement of upper-middle-class White women to the household and for much of the protective legislation that subsequently developed in the workplace. At the same time, it sustained White families by providing social acknowledgment and support to women in the performance of their family roles. For racial-ethnic women, however, the notion of separate spheres served to reinforce their subordinate status and became, in effect, another assault. As they increased their work outside the home, they were forced into a productive labor sphere that was organized for men and "desperate" women who were so unfortunate or immoral that they could not confine their work to the domestic sphere. In the productive sphere, racial-ethnic women faced exploitative jobs and depressed wages. In the reproductive sphere, they were denied the opportunity to embrace the dominant ideological definition of "good" wife or mother. In essence, they were faced with a double-bind situation, one that required their participation in the labor force to sustain family life but damned them as women, wives, and mothers because they did not confine their labor to the home.

Finally, the struggle of women of color to build and maintain families provides vivid testimony to the role of race in structuring family life in the United States. As Maxine Baca Zinn points out:

> Social categories and groups subordinate in the racial hierarchy are often deprived of access to social institutions that offer supports for family life. Social categories and groups elevated in the racial hierarchy have different and better connections to institutions that can sustain families. Social location and its varied connection with social resources thus have profound consequences for family life. (1990:74)

From the founding of the United States, and throughout its history, race has been a fundamental criterion determining the kind of work people do, the wages they receive, and the kind of legal, economic, political, and social support provided for their families. Women of color have faced limited economic resources, inferior living conditions, alien cultures and languages, and overt hostility in their struggle to create a "place" for families of color in the United States. That place, however, has been a precarious one because the society has not provided supports for these families. Today we see the outcomes of that legacy in statistics showing that people of color, compared with whites, have higher rates of female-headed households, out-of-wedlock births, divorce, and other factors associated with family disruption. Yet the causes of these variations do not lie merely in the higher concentrations of poverty among people of color; they are also due to the ways race has been used as a basis for denying and providing support to families. Women of color have struggled to maintain their families against all of these odds.

Notes

Acknowledgments: The research in this study was an outgrowth of my participation in a larger collaborative project examining family, community, and work lives of racial-ethnic women in the United States. I am deeply indebted to the scholarship and creativity of members of the group in the development of this study. Appreciation is extended to Elizabeth Higginbotham, Cheryl Townsend Gilkes, Evelyn Nakano Glenn, and Ruth Zambrana (members of the original working group), and to the Ford Foundation for a grant that supported in part the work of this study.

1. The term "White" is a global construct used to characterize peoples of European descent who migrated to and helped colonize America. In the seventeenth century, most of these immigrants were from the British Isles. However, during the time period covered by this article, European immigrants became increasingly diverse. It is a limitation of this chapter that time

and space do not permit a fuller discussion of the variations in the White European immigrant experience. For the purposes of the argument being made herein and of the contrast it seeks to draw between the experiences of mainstream (European) cultural groups and those of racial-ethnic minorities, the differences among European settlers are joined and the broad similarities emphasized.

2. For a more detailed discussion of this argument and the kinds of social supports provided these families, see an earlier version of this paper: "Our Mothers' Grief: Racial-Ethnic Women and the Maintenance of Families," *Journal of Family History* 13 (4) (1988): 415–431.

3. The term "reproductive labor" is used to refer to all of the work of women in the home. This includes, but is not limited to, the buying and preparation of food and clothing, provision of emotional support and nurturance for all family members, bearing children, and planning, organizing, and carrying out a wide variety of tasks associated with socialization. All of these activities are necessary for the growth of patriarchal capitalism because they maintain, sustain, stabilize, and reproduce (both biologically and socially) the labor force.

4. Recent research suggests that there were some tasks assigned primarily to males and some others to females. Whereas some gender-role distinctions with regard to work may have existed on some plantations, it clear that slave women were not exempt from strenuous physical labor.

5. This term is used to refer to White Americans of European ancestry.

REFERENCES

Aschenbrenner, Joyce. 1975. *Lifelines: Black Families in Change.* New York: Holt, Rinehart, and Winston.

Baca Zinn, Maxine. 1990. "Family, Feminism and Race in America." *Gender and Society* 4 (1) (March): 68–82.

Barrera, Mario. 1979. *Race and Class in the Southwest.* Notre Dame, Ind.: Notre Dame University Press.

Blassingame, John. 1972. *The Slave Community: Plantation Life in the Antebellum South.* New York: Oxford University Press.

———. 1977. *Slave Testimony: Two Centuries of Letters, Speeches, Interviews, and Autobiographies.* Baton Rouge: Louisiana State University Press.

Camarillo, Albert. 1979. *Chicanos in a Changing Society.* Cambridge, Mass.: Harvard University Press.

Caulfield, Mina Davis. 1974. "Imperialism, the Family, and Cultures of Resistance." *Socialist Review* 4 (2) (October): 67–85.

Davis, Angela. 1971. "Reflections on the Black Woman's Role in the Community of Slaves." *Black Scholar* 3 (4) (December): 2–15.

———. 1981. *Women, Race, and Class.* New York: Random House.

Degler, Carl. 1980. *At Odds.* New York: Oxford University Press.

Elasser, Nan, Kyle MacKenzie, and Yvonne Tixier Y. Vigil. 1980. *Las Mujeres.* New York: The Feminist Press.

Garcia, Mario T. 1980. "The Chicano in American History: The Mexican Women of El Paso, 1880–1920—A Case Study." *Pacific Historical Review* 49 (2) (May): 315–358.

Genovese, Eugene D., and Elinor Miller, eds. 1974. *Plantation, Town, and County: Essays on the Local History of American Slave Society.* Urbana:

University of Illinois Press.

Glenn, Evelyn Nakano. 1983. "Split Household, Small Producer, and Dual Earner: An Analysis of Chinese-American Family Strategies." *Journal of Marriage and the Family* 45 (1) (February): 35–46.

Goldman, Marion S. 1981. *Gold Diggers and Silver Miners*. Ann Arbor: University of Michigan Press.

Griswold del Castillo, Richard. 1979. *The Los Angeles Barrio: 1850–1890*. Los Angeles: University of California Press.

Gutman, Herbert. 1976. *The Black Family in Slavery and Freedom, 1750–1925*. New York: Pantheon.

Hirata, Lucia Cheng. 1979. "Free, Indentured, Enslaved: Chinese Prostitutes in Nineteenth Century America." *Signs* 5 (Autumn): 3–29.

Jones, Jacqueline. 1985. *Labor of Love, Labor of Sorrow*. New York: Basic Books.

Kennedy, Susan Estabrook. 1979. *If All We Did Was to Weep at Home: A History of White Working-Class Women in America*. Bloomington: Indiana University Press.

Kessler-Harris, Alice. 1981. *Women Have Always Worked*. Old Westbury, N.Y.: The Feminist Press.

———. 1982. *Out to Work*. New York: Oxford University Press.

Kingston, Maxine Hong. 1977. *The Woman Warrior*. New York: Vintage Books.

Matthaei, Julie. 1982. *An Economic History of Women in America*. New York: Schocken Books.

Nee, Victor G., and Brett de Bary Nee. 1973. *Longtime Californ'*. New York: Pantheon Books.

Saragoza, Alex M. 1983. "The Conceptualization of the History of the Chicano Family: Work, Family, and Migration in Chicanos." In *Research Proceedings of the Symposium on Chicano Research and Public Policy*. Stanford, Calif.: Stanford University, Center for Chicano Research.

Shimkin, Demetri, E. M. Shimkin, and D. A. Frate, eds. 1978. *The Extended Family in Black Societies*. The Hague: Mouton.

Spruill, Julia Cherry. 1972. *Women's Life and Work in the Southern Colonies*. New York: W. W. Norton. (First published Chapel Hill: University of North Carolina Press, 1938).

Stack, Carol S. 1974. *All Our Kin: Strategies for Survival in a Black Community*. New York: Harper & Row.

Sudarkasa, Niara. 1981. "Interpreting the African Heritage in Afro-American Family Organization." In *Black Families*, Harriette Pipes McAdoo, ed. Beverly Hills, Calif.: Sage.

White, Deborah Gray. 1985. *Ar'n't I a Woman? Female Slaves in the Plantation South*. New York: W. W. Norton.

Wright, Gwendolyn. 1981. *Building the Dream: A Social History of Housing in America*. New York: Pantheon.

Zaretsky, Eli. 1978. "The Effects of the Economic Crisis on the Family." In *U.S. Capitalism in Crisis*, edited by Crisis Reader Editorial Collective. New York: Union of Radical Political Economists.

2

Excerpts from *Education for Extinction:*

American Indians and the Boarding School Experience, 1875–1928

David Wallace Adams

In retrospect it is not surprising that reformers should look to schools as central to the solution of the Indian problem. As an instrument for fostering social cohesion and republicanism, no institution had been more important in the spread of the American system. In the case of Indians, the challenge facing educators was particularly difficult: the eradication of all traces of tribal identity and culture, replacing them with the common-place knowledge and values of white civilization. Reformers believed that the school's capacity to accomplish this transformation would determine the long-term fate of the Indian race, for if the doctrine of historical progress and the story of westward expansion taught anything, it was the incompatibility of white civilization and Indian savagism. The former must inevitably supplant the latter. Fortunately, Indians need not perish as a race. Once they shed their attachment to tribal ways—that is to say, their Indianness—and joined the march of American progress, their continued existence in the nation's future was assured. Schools would show them the way.

Boarding schools, especially the off-reservation variety, seemed ideally suited for this purpose. As the theory went, Indian children, once removed from the savage surroundings of the Indian camp and placed in the purified environment of an all-encompassing institution, would slowly learn to look, act, and eventually think like their white counterparts. From the daily regimentation and routine, Indian children would learn the need for order and self-discipline. In the half-day schedule devoted to academics they would master the fundamentals of English, take to heart the moral maxims of McGuffey, and from their history textbook appreciate the meaning of 1492. Balancing the academic side would be classes in industrial training and domestic science, a rotating system of institutional chores, and outing assignments, all designed to prepare them for the path ahead. Sunday sermons, midweek prayer meetings, holiday ceremonies, patriotic drills, and football contests, all in their own way, would contribute to the students' cultural metamorphosis. When it was all over, the onetime youthful specimens of savagism would be thoroughly Christianized, individualized, and republicanized, fit candidates for American citizenship and ideal agents for uplifting an older generation still stranded in the backwaters of barbarism—"a little child shall lead them."

Judged by the ambitious scope of their assimilationist vision, reformers clearly failed to achieve their objective. Beyond the fact that congressional parsimony never allowed the educational assault to be waged with the intensity that reformers envisioned, the reasons for their failure go much deeper. Underlying the reform program was the presupposition that the acculturation process was a relatively simple matter of exchanging one cultural skin for another. The possibility that Indians, either as students or returnees, once having been exposed to the white man's cultural system would react in any manner other than complete embracement, that the acculturation process itself could involve various forms of selective incorporation, syncretization, and compartmentalization, was beyond their comprehension. [But] Indian students were anything but passive recipients of the curriculum of civilization. When choosing the path of resistance, they bolted the institution, torched buildings, and engaged in a multitude of schemes to undermine the school program. Even the response of accommodation was frequently little more than a conscious and strategic adaptation to the hard rock of historical circumstance, a pragmatic recognition that one's Indianness would increasingly have to be defended and negotiated in the face of relentless hegemonic forces.

If the boarding school failed to fulfill reformers' expectations, it still had a profound impact on an Indian child's psychological and cultural being. Returning students, whatever their disposition toward their late experience, could not help but be affected by their sustained exposure to white ways of knowing and living during which time they inevitably acquired new attitudes, values, skills, prejudices, desires, and habits of behavior. Like it or not, most returned students were agents of cultural change, and over time white education would constitute one of the major acculturative forces shaping Indian society. On the other hand, one of the chief consequences for students attending an off-reservation facility was an enlarged sense of identity as "Indians." At schools like Carlisle and Haskell, Sioux children were regularly thrown into intimate association with Comanche and Navajo. At Sherman Institute, Hopi slept, ate, drilled, and played alongside Cahuilla and Serrano. At such institutions students learned that the "Great Father" made no allowances for tribal distinctions; Indians were simply Indians. Ironically, the very institution designed to extinguish Indian identity altogether may have in fact contributed to its very persistence in the form of twentieth-century pan-Indian consciousness.

In the final analysis, the boarding school story constitutes yet another deplorable episode in the long and tragic history of Indian-white relations. For tribal elders who had witnessed the catastrophic developments of the nineteenth century—the bloody warfare, the near-extinction of the bison, the scourge of disease and starvation, the shrinking of the tribal land base, the indignities of reservation life, the invasion of missionaries and white settlers—there seemed to be no end to the cruelties perpetrated by whites. And after all this, the schools. After all this, the white man had concluded that the only way to save Indians was to destroy them, that the last great Indian war should be waged against children. They were coming for the children.

INSTITUTION

The boarding school, whether on or off the reservation, was the institutional manifestation of the government's determination to completely restructure the Indians' minds and personalities. To understand how it functioned in this regard one must attempt to understand how Indian students actually came to know and experience it. And this effort must necessarily begin at that point in time when Indian youths left behind the familiar world of tribal ways for the unfamiliar world of the white man's school. For philanthropists, of course, the journey of Indian children to boarding school was that first step out of the darkness of savagery into the light of civilization. For most Indian youths it meant something entirely different. In any event, the day they left for boarding school could never be forgotten.

For a young Lakota Sioux named Ota Kte, or Plenty Kill—later named Luther Standing Bear—the idea of attending the white man's school first presented itself in the fall of 1879, when he and a friend noticed a crowd gathering around one of the agency buildings at Rosebud. Curious, the two boys approached the building and peered through a window. The room was mostly filled with Sioux, but there were also a few whites among them.

> When they saw us peeping in at the window, they motioned for us to come inside. But we hesitated. Then they held out some sticks of candy. At this, we ran away some little distance, where we stopped to talk over this strange proceeding. We wondered whether we had better go back again to see what the white people really wanted. They had offered us candy—and that was a big temptation. So we went back and peeped in at the window again. This time the interpreter came to the door and coaxed us inside. He was a half-breed named Charles Tackett. We called him Ikubansuka, or Long Chin. We came inside very slowly, a step at a time, all the time wondering what it meant.[1]

From Long Chin, Plenty Kill learned that the whites had come to collect children for a school in the East (the man in charge of the white party was Captain Pratt, recruiting his first volunteers for Carlisle). If Plenty Kill wanted to go to the white man's school, Long Chin explained, he must bring his father, Standing Bear, to the agency to enter his son's name in the ledger. Plenty Kill was both suspicious and intrigued with the proposal. After giving the matter some thought, however, he decided he wanted to go with the captain. As for his reasons, he later recalled:

> When I had reached young manhood the warpath for the Lakota was a thing of the past. The hunter had disappeared with the buffalo, the war scout had lost his calling, and the warrior had taken his shield to the mountain-top and given it back to the elements. The victory songs were sung only in the memory of the braves. So I could not prove that I was a brave and would fight to protect my home and land. I could only meet the challenge as life's events came to me. When I went East to Carlisle School, I thought I was going there to die; ... I could think of white people wanting little Lakota children for no other reason than to kill them, but I thought here is my chance to prove that I can die bravely. So I went East to show my father and my people that I was brave and willing to die for them.[2]

The next day, Plenty Kill, the other recruits, and a number of parents left for the Missouri, where the final parting would take place as the children boarded a steamer to take them south. The final farewell was emotional. The children had no sooner boarded the steamer than both parents and children began to sob. "It was a sad scene," Plenty Kill recalls. "I did not see my father or stepmother cry, so I did not shed any tears. I just stood over in a corner of the room we were in and watched the others all crying as if their hearts would break."[3]

The next day, the steamer pulled into shore whereupon the recruits were directed to a "long row of little houses standing on long pieces of iron which stretched away as far as we could see." Each house had a little stairway. Instructed to climb up into the "little houses," the Indians found them to be lined with cushioned seats.

> I took one of these seats, but presently changed to another. I must have changed my seat four or five times before I quieted down. We admired the beautiful room and the soft seats very much. While we were discussing the situation, suddenly the whole house started to move away with us. We boys were in one house and the girls in another. We expected something terrible would happen. We held our blankets between our teeth, because our hands were both busy hanging to the seats, so frightened were we.

As the locomotive picked up speed, Plenty Kill noticed the line of telegraph poles passing by. "It seemed to me that the poles almost hit the windows, so I changed my seat to the other side."[4]

When the train pulled into Sioux City, Iowa, the Indians were informed that they would be taken from the train to one of the city's restaurants. Not knowing what to expect, some of the older boys placed feathers in their hair and painted their faces. Just three years after the Custer debacle, this act further excited a crowd of spectators who were on hand to see firsthand the sons and daughters of Sitting Bull's Sioux. Indeed, as Pratt ushered the Indians through the mob of onlookers, they heard frightening imitations of the Sioux war whoop. "We did not like this," recalls Plenty Kill, "and some of the children were naturally very much frightened. I remember how I tried to crowd into the protecting midst of the jostling boys and girls." Once in the restaurant, the Indians noticed a crowd of whites pressing their faces against the window. Too upset to eat, the Indians scooped up the food in their blankets and took it back to the train.[5]

By the next day, the "iron road" had taken them as far as "Smoky City," or Chicago. "Here we saw so many people and such big houses that we began to open our eyes in astonishment. The big boys said, 'The white people are like ants; they are all over—everywhere.'" Since the layover in Chicago was a long one, the Indians were placed in a large waiting room where they entertained themselves by dancing. Back on the train, "the big boys began to tell us little fellows that the white people were taking us to the place where the sun rises, where they would dump us over the edge of the earth, as we had been taught that the earth was flat, with four corners, and when we came to the edge, we would fall over." On the second night out of Chicago the anxiety was at fever pitch.

> Now the full moon was rising, and we were traveling toward it. The big boys were singing brave songs, expecting to be killed any minute. We all looked at the moon, and it was in front of us, but we felt that we were getting too close to it for comfort. We were very tired, and the little fellows dozed off. Presently the big boys woke everybody. They said they had made a discovery. We were told to look out the window and see what had happened while we were dozing. We did so, and the moon was now behind us! Apparently we had passed the place where the moon rose![6]

After a journey of several days, the train finally arrived at Carlisle, Pennsylvania. A two-mile walk brought the travel-weary recruits to the great gate that served as the entrance to the Carlisle barracks. Plenty Kill would later lay claim to a very special distinction: "I was the first Indian boy to step inside the Carlisle Indian school grounds."[7]

Such is Plenty Kill's remembrance. It is, of course, just one story. How others experienced the journey depended on several factors. Younger children, for instance, must have felt the pain of being separated from family and community more severely than older ones. Those coerced into attending school were surely more bitter than those who went voluntarily and with their parents' blessing. Children who had attended a day school, which constituted a sort of intermediate introduction to white schooling, must have found it easier than those taken directly from the camp. Moreover, it must have been much more difficult for the first generation of children, who had no idea of what lay ahead, than it was for later recruits, who had the benefit of learning from returned students what to expect. Finally, because different tribes had been exposed to white ways with varying intensity, it stands to reason that those children coming from cultures where there had been sustained contact with whites would find both the idea and necessity of schooling more comprehensible than those to whom the school was the first taste of white civilization.

But regardless of these differing circumstances, leaving for boarding school was almost always a painful affair, as evidence by an account left by Hoke Denetsosie, a Navajo, who, at the age of six, was carted off to a reservation boarding school in 1926. In this instance the departure occurred after an all-night ceremony of ritualistic praying and singing, an apparent effort by parents to protect their children against any evil that might lie ahead.

> Early in the morning, after we had eaten, the police assembled us near ... two old black Model "T" Fords. They started to warm up the cars, and the machines just shook all over. Altogether there were 14 boys and girls, all taller than I was. Some of the parents gathered around talking to their kids. Some were weeping. There was a wave of sadness all around. All of us wore our hair long, tied into bundles behind our necks. Just before we climbed into the cars some of the girls' parents got shears, and cut off the hair bundles and kept them. As we moved out everyone wept again, and we all waved good-bye; then we were on our way.[8]

The Assault on Cultural Identity

From the policymakers' point of view, the civilization process required a twofold assault on Indian children's identity. On the one hand, the school needed to strip away all outward signs of the children's identification with tribal life, that is to say, their savage ways. On the other, the children needed to be instructed in the ideas, values, and behaviors of white civilization. These processes—the tearing down of the old selves and the building of new ones—could, of course, be carried out simultaneously. As the savage selves gave way, so the civilized selves would emerge. As a "total institution," the boarding school was designed to systematically carry out this mission.[9]

For boys the stripping away process began when the school sheared off their long hair. Shortly after arriving at Carlisle, Luther Standing Bear noticed "some white men come inside the school grounds carrying big chairs." The interpreter informed the boys that the men had come to cut their hair. While sitting in class Standing Bear noticed that one by one the boys were being quietly removed: first, Ya Slo; then, Whistler. Each returned looking strange in his short hair. When it came to Standing Bear's turn, he comments that "it hurt my feelings to such an extent that the tears came into my eyes." All the short-cropped Sioux boys felt strange. "We still had our Indian clothes, but were all 'bald-headed.' None of us slept well that night; we felt so queer. I wanted to feel my head all the time."[10]

The short-hair policy was rooted in two considerations. First, it made it easier to control the problem of head lice. Head lice were by no means universal among recruits, but a general policy of short hair made dealing with the problem much simpler. Frank Mitchell, a Navajo, recalls that after bathing and having his hair cut, a "blue ointment" was immediately applied "to kill the bugs." After this, "they checked our heads every now and then and would give us treatments. They kept us clean by bathing us every so often. And of course, finally, they got rid of all of those scabs and sores."[11]

But the reason for short haircuts went deeper than cleanliness. At the heart of the policy was the belief that the children's long hair was symbolic of savagism; removing it was central to the new identification with civilization. It is interesting that Standing Bear rejects the idea that cleanliness was the primary reason for the short-hair policy: "The fact is that we were to be transformed, and short hair being the mark of gentility with the white man, he put upon us the mark." This motivation can clearly be seen in an incident recalled in a letter from S. M. McCowan to a former student at Fort Mohave Boarding School. McCowan, who had been superintendent of the institution, recalled:

> I can remember when I first took you into the Ft. Mojave school and what a time I had in cutting your hair for the first time. I can see now all the old Mojave women standing around crying, while you covered your long hair with your arms and told me that I wouldn't dare to cut that hair off, but the hair was cut in spite of all your efforts and the direful predictions of the Mojave women. I compelled you to have your hair cut off, not because of any objections to the long hair in itself, but merely because the long hair was a symbol of savagery.[12]

The haircutting exercise, in addition to being a traumatic experience, could also spark deep resentment and occasionally even resistance. Commissioner Morgan made note of this fact after witnessing a haircutting session involving Hopi boys. "The boys had beautiful, glossy, black, long straight hair," reports Morgan, "but unfortunately it did not bear close examination, and when they had submitted their hair to the scissors and their locks were thrown into the fire there was, ... a great destruction of the innocents." Morgan went on to confess that a number of school superintendents were having difficulty keeping older boys in school, in part because of their aversion to losing their hair.[13]

Perhaps the most serious rebellion occurred at the opening of Pine Ridge Boarding School. Anticipating that the Sioux would not take kindly to having their braids cut off, the plan of operation was for each child to be called individually into a room where a teacher and a matron, supplied with a pair of scissors, would carry out the hair removal beyond the view of the anxious onlookers who were outside pressing against shade-drawn windows. But just as the first child was seated, a breeze swept aside the window shades, revealing the horrible sight of the matron about to slice off a long braid. According to one account:

> Like a war whoop rang out the cry: "*Pahin Kaksa, Pahin Kaksa!*" The enclosure rang with alarm, it invaded every room in the building and floated out on the prairie. No warning of fire or flood or tornado or hurricane, not even the approach of an enemy could have more effectively emptied the building as well as the grounds of the new school as did the ominous cry. "They are cutting the hair!" Through doors and windows the children flew, down the steps, through the gates and over fences in a mad flight toward the Indian villages, followed by the mob of bucks and squaws as though all were pursued by a bad spirit. They had been suspicious of the school from the beginning; now they knew it was intended to bring disgrace upon them.[14]

According to Luther Standing Bear, a revolt against Pratt's haircutting order by Carlisle's first recruits nearly occurred as well. On the evening after the boys were informed that their hair must be cut, they held a secret "council." Standing Bear remembers Robert American Horse proclaiming, "If I am to learn the ways of the white people, I can do it just as well with my hair on." Almost to a person, the assembled boys shouted "Hau," signifying their agreement. But this resolve weakened the next day as, one by one, they were summoned to the barber's chair. The question remained whether any of the boys would actually make a stand.[15]

Pratt knew nothing about any of this. Instead, thinking that all was going smoothly with the barbers, he left for a scheduled trip to Indian Territory, leaving the school under Mrs. Pratt's charge. It was after his departure that one of the older boys steadfastly refused to have his braids removed. Wishing to avoid an incident, Mrs. Pratt sent the barbers away, declaring that the fate of the one holdout would be resolved upon her husband's return. Late that night, however, Mrs. Pratt and the white staff were awakened suddenly by a general commotion. The long-haired recalcitrant had undergone a change of heart. Securing a knife, he had walked out on the parade ground to publicly cut off his braids. Since by Sioux tradition the cutting off of hair was always associated with mourning, the boy's dramatic act spontaneously evoked a characteristic response from those in the barracks. Boys and girls alike now filled the night air with a shrill wailing that was both eerie and not a little unsettling to the staff. Mrs. Pratt feared that the nearby residents of Carlisle might be aroused, provoking even a worse situation. Finally, however, order was restored.[16]

The second step in the civilization process called for changing the students' dress. It made little difference whether students arrived wearing elegant buckskin or threadbare trade blankets; shortly after their arrival, their traditional clothing was exchanged for the standard school uniform. Indian service regulations held that each boy should be provided with two plain suits, with an extra pair of trousers, and each girl with three dresses. In some instances, boys also received a Sunday suit of better quality. The annual clothing ration also included the necessary underwear, nightclothes, and finally, boots.[17]

In spite of such standards, considerable variability in the quality of clothing existed among schools. Generally speaking, students at off-reservation schools were better provided for, in part because such schools were showcases for the government's Indian policy. Another factor was that these schools possessed large sewing and tailoring classes, where capable students were expected to turn out sufficient uniforms and dresses to meet the school's needs. A number of schools—Carlisle, Haskell, Genoa, Phoenix, and others—were well-known for their handsome and smart-looking dress. At Carlisle, for instance, the shoulders of the boys' dark blue uniforms were decorated with red braid, with student officers sporting red stripes as well. Carlisle girls, meanwhile, had their dark blue cloaks lined in bright red. In 1893, the superintendent of the boarding school at Albuquerque reported that since the Indian girls had recently taken to comparing their own dress with the pervading style of white girls, they had been allowed to adorn their school dresses with a few ruffles and a bit of lace. This change, it was noted, had "made a vast difference in the general feeling among the girls, who are much more willing and cheerful."[18]

The situation was decidedly different at remote reservation schools. Students often had to make do with tattered clothes, oversized boots, and beaten hats, while an overworked seamstress patched, mended, and prayed daily for a new clothing allotment. "Wearing mended clothes may implant habits of economy and be of some practical value," one agent complained in 1897, "but the wearing of crownless, brimless, and otherwise illshapen hats, and the continued wear of boots and shoes long after they have served their purpose, lessens the wearer's self-respect, lowers the school in his estimation, and in short, creates a formidable barrier to the attainment of the end and aim of education." Sometimes, students gave up a finer quality of clothing than what they received in return. One Hopi boy, for instance, recalls being separated from a "beautiful new blanket with colored stripes" that his grandfather had specially woven for him in exchange for the standard school issue—in this case, a blue shirt, mustard-colored pants, and heavy shoes. As for the fate of the blanket, "I saw it later, in the possession of the wife of the superintendent."[19]

Students reacted differently to this aspect of their transformation. According to one school official: "A school uniform is a great cross to Indian pupils. One Indian never likes to appear like any other." Besides going against the grain of Indian youngsters' individuality, some articles of white clothing were resented simply because they were uncomfortable. Stiff boots and woolen underwear were clearly in this class. And of course many students must have seen the emphasis on uniform dress for what it was: yet another aspect of the school's design to turn Indians into carbon copies of their white overseers. Still, it appears that this aspect of the transformation process was less traumatic than the haircutting policy. Indeed, some appear to have experienced a certain excitement in dressing up like whites, even though, as we see below, the occasion was sometimes marked by a good deal of confusion.

> How proud we were with clothes that had pockets and boots that squeaked! We walked the floor nearly all that night. Many of the boys even went to bed with their clothes all on. But in the morning, the boys who had taken off their pants had a most terrible time. They did not know whether they were to button up in front or behind. Some of the boys said the open part went in front; others said, 'No, it goes at the back.' There is where the boys who had kept all their clothes on came in handy to look at. They showed the others that the pants buttoned up in front and not at the back. So here we learned something again.[20]

Yet another assault on tribal identity came in the form of new names. The policy of renaming students was motivated by several concerns. First, many students arrived at school with names the teachers could neither pronounce nor memorize. Most teachers had little patience with such names as Ain-dus-gwon, John Sang-way-way, Wah-sah-yah, Min-o-ke-shig, and Mah-je-ke-shig. As one Indian Office official observed at a national educational conference, "a teacher would be at a disadvantage in trying to be either affectionate or disciplinary with an eight-syllabled girl like Sah-gah-ge-way-gah-bow-e-quay." Second, some students had names that, once translated, were perceived to be ridiculous and occasionally humiliating—such as Mary Swollen Face, Nancy Kills-a-Hundred, Sam Slow-Fly, John Bad-Gum, Ada Parts-His-Hair, and Lizzie-Looks-Twice.[21]

Finally, renaming students was part of a conscious government policy to give Indians surnames. As Indians became property owners and thoroughly imbued with the values of possessive individualism, it would be virtually impossible to fix lines of inheritance if, for example, the son of Red Hawk went by the name Spotted Horse. "When Indians become citizens of the United States under the allotment act," Commissioner Morgan informed agents and school superintendents, "the inheritance of property will be governed by the laws of the respective states, and it will cause needless confusion and, doubtless, considerable ultimate loss to the Indians if no attempt is made to have the different members of a family known by the same family name on the records and by general reputation." For this reason, Indian Office employees in the field were instructed to move forward with the renaming process. The work proceeded slowly, and although most of the responsibility fell to the Indian agent, school officials also played a vital role, particularly in the early years.[22]

The renaming process followed several patterns. One pattern was to use the original untranslated Indian name, although sometimes in shortened form, as a surname. When practical, this was the preferred policy of the Indian Office. In a circular issued in 1890, Commissioner Morgan admitted that in many instances "the Indian name is difficult to pronounce and to remember," but then went on to say that "in many other cases the Indian word is as short and as euphonious as the English word that is substituted." Fourteen years later, an Indian Office official reiterated the point by saying: "Let the Indian keep both his personal and race identity ... for the sake of his property it is necessary that he adopt our system of family names, but that is no reason why we should ruthlessly thrust upon him our English names when his own will answer just as well, even better. We want to educate the Indian—lead him on, not stamp him out."[23] By this liberal policy, if it may be termed as such, a Kiowa man with the name of Richard Sitahpetale or a Navajo woman called Ruth Chesehesbega could make their way in civilized society as easily as a Richard Smith or a Ruth Miller.

Another pattern was to use the translated Indian name as a surname. Under this system a Robert Redhawk or a William Swiftriver would do nicely. But such translations were not always workable. As noted earlier, some Indian names, once translated, appeared to be ridiculous and even uncouth, others were too long, and many simply could not be translated without losing their original meaning. As Alice Fletcher pointed out, the translated Dakota name Young-Man-Afraid-of-His-Horses conveyed little of the meaning behind the original, which actually meant "the young man whose valor is such that even the sight of his horses brings fear to his enemies." In such instances, if the Dakota original was short and pronounceable, it would be retained. Otherwise, it would be abandoned.[24]

A third pattern was to give children completely new names. At this point, agents and superintendents were presented with several options. One approach, recommended by John Wesley Powell, was to select from the tribal vocabulary names for geographical forms and animal life with which Indians could readily identify. For instance, the Sioux word for "roan horse" might be received with greater enthusiasm than Miller or Erickson. Another option was simply to randomly bestow common American names such as Smith, Brown, and Clark. Still another method, and one practiced for many years with conscious intent, was to rename students after famous historical figures. Harriet Patrick Gilstrap tells us that when her father, the agent at Sac and Fox Agency, gave the Indians new names, "first came the names of the presidents, then the vice-presidents, then prominent people of the day."[25]

But the Indian Office increasingly frowned on such ridiculous changes, and some schools made a conscious effort to retain at least a modicum of the Indian name. Thus, Hampton Institute was critical of the fact that two of its new transfer students had arrived with the names Julius Caesar and Henry Ward Beecher. Such names were nonsensical, declared the *Southern Workman*. A more humane approach was the

Hampton method. When a boy arrived at the school with the name Hehakaavita (Yellow Elk), an inquiry about the boy's father's name evoked the response "Good Wood." Hence, the boy's new name became Thomas Goodwood. On another occasion, the son of an old chief, Medicine Bull, was given the new name of Samuel M. Bull. Such alterations, Hampton held, met the necessity of assigning a new name yet recognized the individuality, if not the heritage, of the student. Besides, renaming alone would not civilize savages: "Old Sitting Bull would be nonetheless a savage were he to take to himself the most honorable name we know ... George S. Bull Washington."[26]

Whatever process superintendents used in bestowing new names, the fact remains that it constituted a grave assault on Indian identity. This is true for two reasons. First, as George A. Pettit has made clear in his landmark study *Primitive Education in North America*, traditional Indian names and the naming process itself were fundamentally connected to the process of cultural transmission and served a variety of educational purposes: as a stimulus to self-improvement, as a reward for a special achievement, and finally, as a means of transferring the traits of a revered relative or tribal figure to a member of a new generation. Because some Indian youth were sometimes given a series of names in the course of their development, and since the giving of names was frequently ritualized in elaborate ceremony, tribal naming practices were clearly central to the perpetuation of cultural outlook.[27] Second, as already discussed, a major justification for changing names was the argument that assigning surnames was an essential step in transforming Indians into self-reliant property owners. Thus, the renaming process was pregnant with cultural significance.

It is difficult to judge how students actually experienced the renaming process or what meanings they ascribed to it, but three instances from Carlisle are suggestive. Luther Standing Bear recalls that after a few days at Carlisle the interpreter announced: "Do you see all these marks on the blackboard? Well, each word is a white man's name. They are going to give each one of you one of these names by which you will hereafter be known." The first boy stepped forward and with a long pointer touched one of the names, which was written on a piece of tape and attached to the back of his shirt.

> When my turn came, I took the pointer and acted as if I were about to touch an enemy. Soon we all had the names of white men sewed on our backs. When we went to school, we knew enough to take our proper places in the class, but that was all. When the teacher called the roll, no one answered his name. Then she would walk around and look at the back of the boys' shirts. When she had the right name located, she made the boy stand up and say "Present." She kept this up for about a week before we knew what the sound of our new names was.[28]

Another boy at Carlisle was given the name "Conrad."

> Dear Captain Pratt:
>
> I am going to tell you something about my name. Captain Pratt, I would like to have a new name because some of the girls call me Cornbread and some call me Cornrat, so I do not like that name, so I want you to give me a new name. Now this is all I want to say.
>
> Conrad[29]

Jason Betzinez, an Apache youth from Geronimo's band, was more fortunate. Shortly after arriving at Carlisle,

> Miss Low selected for me the name of Jason. She said that Jason was some man who hunted the golden fleece but never found it. I thought that was too bad but it didn't mean anything to me at that time so I accepted the name. In the intervening years I believe that the story of Jason and his search for the golden fleece has set a pattern for my life.[30]

In this instance the name "Jason" served the same instructional function that many tribal names had served in traditional Indian life; it gave meaning and guidance to his life. The object of Betzinez's search and that of the famous mythological figure were, of course, altogether different. The Jason of Greek lore sought the golden fleece; Jason, an Apache thrown into the strange world of the white man, would seek something far more precious, his very identity. Still, the Carlisle Apache's new name could serve as a metaphor for his life, and for that matter, for countless other Indians as well.

Adjustments to New Surroundings

Meanwhile, students were adjusting to their new physical surroundings. Since the overriding purpose of the boarding school was to bring about the student's civilization, it logically followed that the physical environment should approximate a civilized atmosphere as closely as possible. At the very least, physical facilities should be of firm structure, should be large enough to house the students enrolled, and should reflect a mindful consideration for sanitation and hygiene. This was the ideal. Unfortunately, it was not always achieved. In 1882, Indian Commissioner Price lectured Congress: "Children who shiver in rooms ceiled with canvas, who dodge the muddy drops trickling throughout worn-out dirt roofs, who are crowded in ill-ventilated dormitories, who recite in a single school-room, three classes at a time, and who have no suitable sitting-rooms nor bathrooms, are not likely to be attracted to or make rapid advancement in education and civilization." According to Price, the Indian Bureau was currently forced to use facilities "which long ago should have been condemned as unserveable and even unsafe."[31]

In the next decade living conditions improved markedly, especially at off-reservation schools. Touring several schools in 1892, Special Indian Agent Merial A. Dorchester found that the best ones provided each girl with a single bed, washstand, towel, bowl and pitcher, and brush and comb. Some dormitories had sliding curtains between the beds, "making a retired place for each girl, which helps her on the line of modesty." Others were divided into small rooms where the girls "are taught how to arrange and beautify them in a pretty and hygienic manner." Superintendent of Indian Schools William Hailmann also stressed the progress being made when he addressed the Lake Mohonk Conference in 1897. In school after school, he explained, the kerosene lamp was giving way to the electric light, the wood stove to steam heat, the bathtub to the "needle bath." At remote reservation schools, however, such renovations were slow in coming. Just a year after Hailmann's optimistic assessment, Commissioner William Jones admitted that too many schools suffered from a "deplorable deficiency" in providing Indian youth with acceptable living facilities.[32]

Adjusting to a new physical environment also meant adjusting to new conceptions of space and architecture.[33] The boarding school, the new recruits quickly learned, was a world of lines, corners, and squares. Rectangular dormitories and dining rooms and square classrooms were filled with beds, tables, and desks—all carefully arranged in straight rows. Whites, Indians surmised, largely conceived of space in linear terms. This was no mean observation, especially for students who came from cultures where definitions of space and the meanings assigned to it were radically different. For Lakota students, for instance, the essential touchstones of cultural reality—the sky, the sun, the moon, the tepee, the sundance lodge, and the "sacred hoop"—were all circular phenomena. Thus, an old Lakota, Black Elk, would tell John Neihardt in 1931: "You will notice that everything the Indian does is in a circle. Everything that they do is the power from the sacred hoop." But now, Black Elk would lament, his people were living in houses. "It is a square. It is not the way we should live.... Everything is now too square. The sacred hoop is vanishing among the people.... We are vanishing in this box."[34] Although the circle held less symbolic significance in other cultures than it did for the Sioux, the larger point should not be missed: conceptions of space are not neutral.

The same could be said for the layout of school grounds. "Our sense of place—of space—is largely determined by the manner in which we see ourselves in relation to nature," writes Jamake Highwater. In the landscaping of school grounds, Indian students received another lesson on white civilization's attitude toward space and nature. In his annual report in 1898, Commissioner William Jones informed superintendents that in order to impress upon the minds of Indian youths a new conception of "order," "system," and "the beautiful," they should attempt to reconstruct "unsightly banks and rugged hillsides so as to make them more pleasing to the eye." Elsewhere, superintendents were instructed, "The grounds around the buildings must receive proper attention, insofar that agreeable designs in landscaping be improvised, diversified with flowers, shrubs, and trees and swarded areas, producing pleasing and attractive surroundings." In other words, weeds, cactus, and earth must give way to manicured lawns, pruned trees, and contoured gardens. The lesson in all this was clear: nature existed to serve man's ends. In the interest of symmetry and order, the wild must be tamed, just as the Indian must be civilized.[35]

Adjusting to the white man's food—and the lack of it—was another challenge. According to official policy as stated in 1890, "Good and healthful provisions must be supplied in abundance; and they must be well cooked and properly placed on the table." Moreover, schools were urged to offer a varied menu and to use the school farm and dairy to furnish the necessary amount of fruits, vegetables, and dairy products. Although coffee and tea could be served on occasion, milk was deemed preferable. In those instances where school farms produced great amounts of fresh produce and where dairy, stock raising, and poultry departments were going concerns, the stipulated standards were met. One Navajo boy who attended the school at Fort Defiance recalls: "When I entered school there was plenty to eat there, more food than I used to get at home.... So I was happy about that; I was willing to go to school if they were going to feed me like that."[36]

But most would remember this aspect of boarding school life with considerable bitterness. Sometimes this displeasure stemmed from being forced to abandon traditional foods for those of the white man. Others complained about the way the food was cooked. Perhaps the most serious complaint was that they left the table half-starved. A Klamath Indian, who was detailed as a meat cutter at his boarding school, recalls that the best cuts went to the employees, while the children got only the necks and ribs. He remembers, "I learned to steal at school to keep from going hungry." Don Talayesva, a Hopi, vividly recalls his first meal at Keams Canyon Boarding School. It was a hearty breakfast consisting of coffee, oatmeal, fried bacon and potatoes, and syrup. Not a bad breakfast by white standards perhaps, but Talayesva found the bacon to be too salty and the oatmeal too "sloppy." Lunch was worse.

> We went to the dining room and ate bread and a thing called hash, which I did not like. It contained different kinds of food mixed together; some were good and some were bad, but the bad outdid the good. We also had prunes, rice, and tea. I had never tasted tea. The smell of it made me feel so sick that I thought I would vomit. We ate our supper but it did not satisfy me. I thought I would never like hash.

Helen Sekaquaptewa, who attended the same school, recalls: "I was always hungry and wanted to cry because I didn't get enough food.

They didn't give second helpings, and I thought I would just starve. You can't go to sleep when you are hungry."[37]

Were Indian children underfed? The evidence seems to suggest that conditions varied greatly from school to school. But there is little doubt that great numbers suffered from undernourishment. From the very beginning, Pratt found the school service per capita food allowance inadequate and managed to have Carlisle put on army rations, a unique distinction that the school enjoyed during its entire existence. Estelle Brown says that she was at her first post only a week when she realized that the children were undernourished. "I did not know that for sixteen years I was to see other children systematically underfed." Describing her experience at another school she comments, "I knew these girls were consistently overworked, knew that they were always hungry. Simply, they did not get enough to eat. We all knew it; most of us resented it, were powerless—or too cowardly—to try to do anything about it."[38]

So students endured it as best they could. Some resorted to stealing, a risky enterprise. Others were occasionally the beneficiary of a small gift of Indian food brought by a relative on a visit to the agency. One Sioux girl who attended boarding school in the early 1920s recalls: "There was a place called the trunk room. That's where we kept our steamer trunks. They were filled with dried foods like *papa* and *wasna* because our parents thought that the white people wouldn't feed us right." After school, she relates "we would get the keys to our trunks from the matrons. And we'd go down and open our trunks and eat the Indian food." But in the main, students were dependent upon the often inadequate school ration, causing the girls at one school to compose the jingle: "Too much government gravy / Make me lazy."[39]

As students soon learned, they were not only expected to eat new foods but to eat them in a special manner. In short, they must acquire the food rites of civilized society. Enter the world of knives, forks, spoons, tablecloths, and napkins. In the finer schools, tin plates and cups would eventually give way to glassware and white china. Thus equipped, the school dining room became a classroom for instructing Indians in the rudiments of middle-class table manners. Frank Mitchell recalls:

> One of the problems we faced ... was that we did not know how to eat at a table. We had to be told how to use the knife, fork and spoons. And when we started eating, we were so used to eating with our fingers that we wanted to do it that way at school, and we had to be taught. Although we had things there to eat with, like a fork, we had never used them at home, so we did not know what they were or how to use them; so we always wanted to stick our fingers in our food. Of course, it took some time before we got used to how we were to conduct ourselves with these different things.[40]

Food not only had to be eaten in a certain manner but it had to be eaten at precise intervals in the day, which typified another distinctive feature of boarding school life—the relentless regimentation. As every new recruit soon discovered, nearly every aspect of his day-to-day existence—eating, sleeping, working, learning, praying—would be rigidly scheduled, the hours of the day intermittently punctuated by a seemingly endless number of bugles and bells demanding this or that response. As one school official observed, the Indian "knew he was coming to a land of laws, but his imagination could never conceive of such a multiplicity of rules as he now finds thrown about them; bells seem to be ringing all the time, and the best he can do is to follow his friendly leader." Follow his "friendly leader" is exactly what Jim Whitewolf did on his first day of boarding school.

> Logan was still with me. He told me that when the first bell rang, we would go to eat. He said that when we got down there he would tell me what to do. The second bell had rung and we were going to dinner. We all lined up according to height. Logan told me to watch the others who had been there some time already. Some fellow there gave a command that I didn't understand, and I saw all the others were standing there at attention with their arms at their sides. Then this fellow said something else and we all turned. This fellow would hit a bell he was carrying and we were supposed to march in time to it. I didn't know at the time what it was for. My legs just wouldn't do it so I started walking. When we got to the eating place, there were long tables there in rows.... When we got to a certain table he told me to just stand there. There was a lady there in charge who had a little bell and, when she hit it, everybody sat down.... I watched the others and did what they did. After we sat down they rang the bell again and everybody had his head bowed.... The bell rang again and we started eating.[41]

As Whitewolf's narrative suggests, the boarding school environment was patently militaristic. This was especially the case at off-reservation schools, where students organized into army units and drilled in elaborate marching routines. On special celebrations, when marching students shouldered rifles, brass bugles gleamed in the sunlight, drums pounded out marching rhythms, and school banners flapped in the breeze, the military atmosphere was only enhanced. No aspect of school life left a more profound impression on students. One Hopi who attended an off-reservation school at the turn of the century remembers that it was like "a school for Army or soldiering." "Every morning," he recalls, "we were rolled out of bed and the biggest part of the time we would have to line up and put guns in our hands." In broken English, a former student at Albuquerque recalls:

> We would be in the school, but part of the time we can practice something else. That was being soldiers with the gun. Line up with it different ways, learn how to handle gun, like we being soldiers. This was sure hard thing for me to do. The most hard thing was to

do this early in the morning early while it was cold; hands cold on the guns. We got more than one captain to take care of these soldiers. Then we boys made a lot of mistakes when we doing that. Sometimes we don't take the right step like they wanted us to. The ones that don't know how to do, the captain would go up to this boy and take him by the shoulders and shake him and tell him to do like the way he was told to do. The ones that are making a lot of mistakes, they can be punished for it.

While learning to march, one student at Chilocco acquired a lifelong nickname—Dizzy. Years later he would recall: "I remember, many times [the] company commander saying 'You dizzy bastard, get in step!' And it kind of stuck with me."[42]

Although spared the burden of bearing rifles, girls were subjected to the same drill routines. In fact, for Anna Moore Shaw, who attended Phoenix Indian School, the cadence of military marching was so internalized that it was hard to walk in a normal manner.

> At first the marching seemed so hard to learn, but once we had mastered the knack, we couldn't break the habit. Sometimes on our once-a-month visit to town, a talking machine would be blasting band music outside a store to attract customers. Then we girls would go into our act; try as hard as we could, we just couldn't get out of step. It was impossible! We'd try to take long strides to break the rhythm, but soon we would fall back into step again. How embarrassing it was![43]

Why were schools organized like military training camps? Part of the answer lies in the sheer organizational problems created by having to house, feed, teach, and, most significantly, control several hundred "uncivilized" youths. Good health, neatness, politeness, the ability to concentrate, self-confidence, and patriotism were also attributed to military regimen. The superintendent of Haskell even reported in 1886 that by organizing the school into a battalion of five companies, he had managed to break up persisting tribal associations; forcing students to sleep in dormitories and to sit in the mess hall by their assigned companies required them to converse in English.[44]

But there were deeper reasons for the military atmosphere, reasons related to policymakers' perceptions of the "wildness" of Indian children. Indian children, it was argued, were products of cultures almost entirely devoid of order, discipline, and self-constraint, all prized values in white civilization. It was a well-known fact, according to Commissioner Morgan, that Indian parents "generally exercise very little control over their children and allow them the utmost freedom." Part of the problem, policymakers surmised, stemmed from Indians' unfamiliarity with the white man's clock and, once exposed to it, their general disdain for it. From a less ethnocentric perspective, anthropologist Bernard Fontana has made a similar observation, namely, that Indian and white societies have historically subscribed to different conceptions of time. Whereas white society has increasingly become governed by "clock time," Indians have traditionally been oriented to "natural time." "In devising a mechanical means of arbitrarily segmenting the day into regularly spaced units," writes Fontana, white society has "made an artifact of time.... Our notion of time and our methods of time-keeping are the very underpinnings of our entire industrial system." Indians, on the other hand, have traditionally lived out their lives in accordance with natural phenomena. Fontana makes an important point. The cultural and psychological distance separating the two orientations was immense, as this Arapaho remembrance makes clear:

> It was a long time before we knew what the figures on the face of a clock meant, or why people looked at them before they ate their meals or started off to church. We had to learn that clocks had something to do with the hours and minutes that the white people mentioned so often. Hours, minutes, and seconds were such small divisions of time that we had never thought of them. When the sun rose, when it was high in the sky, and when it set were all the divisions of the day that we had ever found necessary when we followed the old Arapaho road. When we went on the hunting trip or to a sun dance, we counted time by sleeps.[45]

Until the students' concept of natural time was supplanted by that of clock time, school authorities reasoned, it would be next to impossible to develop in them an appreciation for the importance of promptness and punctuality, key values in civilized life. "Make the most of time," one school newspaper exhorted. "You have no right to waste your own time; still less, then, the time of others. Be punctual in the performance of all your duties." By constantly marching and drilling, the clocklike, mechanical movements on the drill field would hopefully carry over to other areas of student behavior. As students internalized the measured units of the clock, so too would they come to discipline and regulate their bodies and lives. "Be punctual to the minute. Even a little beforehand is preferable to being behind time. Such a habit ... no doubt will mean a great deal to you in the after life"—that is, life after boarding school.[46]

Part of being civilized, the logic went, was being able to follow orders in a hierarchical organization, and what better training than that gained on the drill field? Thus, when Secretary of the Interior Richard Ballinger spoke to Phoenix Indian students in 1909, he referred to the school's military organization to make his major point: "We have got to become men and women and we have got to take our place in line in life, just as you take your places in the ranks of your companies. You have got to march through this world; the world expects you to do something, not simply to play and not simply to have pleasure." Or as students at one school were reminded:

Obedience is the great foundation law of all life. It is the common fundamental law of all organization, in nature, in military, naval, commercial, political, and domestic circles. Obedience is the great essential to securing the purpose of life. Disobedience means disaster. The first disastrous act of disobedience brought ruin to humanity and that ruin is still going on. "The first duty of a soldier is obedience" is a truth forced upon all soldiers the moment they enter upon the military life. The same applies to school life. The moment a student is instructed to do a certain thing, no matter how small or how great, immediate action on his part is a duty and should be a pleasure.... What your teachers tell you to do you should do without question. Obedience means marching right on whether you feel like it or not.[47]

Students entered boarding school with vastly different religious backgrounds. Some came already converted to Christianity. In this regard, schools were reaping the harvest of missionary efforts across Indian country. Thus, shortly after a group of Dakota children arrived at Hampton in 1879, they sang for the student body "Nearer My God to Thee," although in a language unrecognizable to all but a few.

> Mita Wakantanka,
> Nikiyedan,
> Kakix mayanpi xta,
> He taku ani;
> Nici waun wacin,
> Mita Wakantanka,
> Nikiyedan.

"My thoughts went to and fro," reported one observer of the scene, "and when I looked at their beaming faces and knew that they understood the words they were singing, for they sang in their own language, I felt that they were nearer to Him at that hour."[48]

Most, however, came from cultures still permeated by a traditional religious outlook. What were the common denominators of this worldview?[49] First, traditional Indian cultures were so thoroughly infused with the spiritual that native languages generally had no single word to denote the concept of religion. It would have been incomprehensible to isolate religion as a separate sphere of cultural existence. For the Kiowa, Hopi, or Lakota, religion explained the cosmological order, defined reality, and penetrated all areas of tribal life—kinship relations, subsistence activities, child raising, even artistic and architectural expression. The theistic structures of native religions differed greatly. Some religious systems were polytheistic, but others, as Joseph Epes Brown observes, represented "a form of theism wherein concepts of monotheism and polytheism intermingle and fuse without being confused." Thus, the Lakota universe, to cite just one example, was populated by a pantheon of gods, spirits, and personalities, but pervading all was *Wakan-Tanka*, or the "Great Mysterious." Hence, Brown quotes Black Elk, "Wakan-Tanka, you are everything, and yet above everything." The spirit world pervaded all.[50]

A second theme was man's fundamental interrelatedness with nature. Unlike Christianity where God and man stood apart—really above—nature, Indians lived in ecological harmony with their environment, approached it with reverential humility, and ultimately, ascribed to it a spiritual significance unknown to European-Americans. According to the Indian worldview, all creatures—the buffalo, the eagle, the spider—and the inanimate world as well, possessed their own unique soul or spiritual essence. In such a world nature was filled with spiritual lessons, to be read and interpreted just as the white man read his Jesus book. Nature, moreover, was not something to be objectified and conquered, nor to be seen as merely a source of sustenance and shelter; it was, rather, a profound source of spiritual awareness from whence man could reaffirm his elemental relationship with all living things.[51]

A third characteristic was the richness and variety of religious expression. On one level this manifested itself in elaborate tribal ceremonies—the sun dance of the Plains peoples, the kachina dances of the Pueblo, the Midewiwin of the Objibwa, the chantways of the Navajo, to name just a few. Added to these are the culturally prescribed provisions for individual religious expression. Particularly noteworthy in this regard are the role of dreams and the almost ubiquitous vision quest. In the latter instance the supplicant sought direct communication with the supernatural, which might appear in the form of a hawk, a fox, an ant, or perhaps a "thundering being." The knowledge and power gained from such an experience often shaped the entire life course and personality of the vision seeker. Also, most cultures singled out those significant transitions in the life cycle—birth, puberty, marriage, and death—for public ceremonial recognition although, again, the manner of expression differed greatly from one culture to another. Finally, each religious system possessed its own songs, dances, myths, and ritual dramas.[52]

Fourth, and by way of comparison to Christianity, Native American religions tended not to conceive of personal morality or ethics as the special domain of religion. Although it is true that all cultures certainly knew of "evil" and possessed their own definition of proper social behavior, the social regulation of interpersonal behavior had its source in the larger social fabric of tribal existence. This, of course, was in direct contradiction to Christianity, which, from the Indians' perspective, seemed preoccupied with "sin" and provided a biblical prescription for nearly all aspects of social relations. It was for this reason that Indians who had converted to Christianity soon discovered they had embraced not only a new God but an entirely new way of life. An extension of the morality issue was the whites' conception of heaven as the exclusive destiny of the righteous, as compared with the Indians' view of the afterlife, which was rarely as restrictive. What Henry Warner Bowden says of northeastern cultures applies to Indians generally:

"They thought the gods would punish sacrilegious acts almost immediately, just as socially destructive behavior met with swift communal justice. But they assumed that everyone would eventually reside in the same place after death."[53]

If Christianity and traditionalism were the polar extremes of Indian religious belief, by the turn of the century other forms of religious expression had come upon the scene. By the 1880s, for instance, some tribes in the Northwest were converting to Shakerism, which took its name from the fact that its followers frequently achieved a trembling, trancelike state in the course of praying, singing, and dancing—in all, a ritualized synthesis of white and native religious expression. An even more powerful movement was the rapid spread of the so-called peyote religion, later designated the Native American Church. The most sensational aspect of this new faith involved chewing peyote buttons, which produced powerful and transcendent visions wherein the worshiper achieved an enhanced sense of self, power, and spiritual consciousness. Beyond this, the new religion proved to be a highly flexible configuration of native and Christian traditions: core elements included the worship of a supreme being (the "Great Spirit" or God); the belief in both white and Indian spirits (angels, the devil, the thunderbird), the fusion of Christian ethics with native values, and the blending of native and Christian ritualistic practices. Finally, discussion must include the brief but ill-fated ghost dance religion that swept across the Central and High Plains in the late 1880s, culminating in the tragic episode at Wounded Knee in December 1890. Given the brevity of the movement, its long-term influence on Indian youth is questionable. Still, some students home for the summer surely observed relatives swept up in the fervor of the moment, observed the dancing and ritualized trances, and heard firsthand accounts from dancers who told of seeing the utopian world to come, a world without whites, where Indians would be reunited with fallen warriors and the prairies once again would be teeming with bison.[54]

What else can be said about the religious background of students? For one thing, many students came from communities characterized by religious factionalism and thus may have arrived deeply divided themselves. On the other hand, many students came from cultures that either had managed to integrate various aspects of Christianity into their own religious system without destroying the latter's essence or had simply accepted and compartmentalized it in the spirit of what one scholar has termed "nonexclusive cumulative adhesion."[55] Finally, and this point cannot be overstated, except for the early years when schools recruited older students fully enculturated into tribal ways, nearly all students entered boarding school with only a partial understanding of their tribal belief system and ceremonial cycle. Reservation boarding schools cut students off from religious experiences that by tradition could only be had in the fall, winter, and spring. For nonreservation students the deprivation was even more complete.

It was in this context that boarding school superintendents waged an aggressive campaign of Christianization. By the 1890s Indian Office rules stipulated, "Pupils of Government schools shall be encouraged to attend the churches and Sunday-schools of their respective denominations." Even though local churches were encouraged to open their doors to Indian students, schools also were expected to develop a systematic program of religious instruction. A typical week's activities included Sunday morning, afternoon, and evening services, daily morning and evening prayers, and a special Wednesday evening prayer meeting. As for the content of religious instruction, teachers were encouraged to emphasize the Ten Commandments, the beatitudes, and prominent psalms. Superintendent William Hailmann urged in 1894, "Prayer, song, and Bible reading should be wholly free from mystifying allusions and sentiments, but rich and forceful in the simple earnestness with which they lead the heart to God, to virtue, to benevolence, to reverence, to self-abnegation, and to devotion."[56]

For younger children, Sunday school was probably the most effective format for instruction. In Sunday school, Hampton Institute reported, "the teacher endeavors to put into these almost empty minds the simplest, and at the same time the most strengthening, truths of God's Word." Bible stories, especially when given a creative rendering by an enthusiastic teacher, were a favorite of students. According to one account: "As soon as an Indian understands enough English to follow the simple stories, he can never get enough of them. Some of the friskiest boys will sit like graven images through a whole evening, listening to them." Stories of David and Goliath, the separation of the waters, the slaying of the Philistines, and the resurrection of Christ were easily the equals of the wonders told by tribal medicine men. "When I found the place in the Bible," one teacher related, "and read about the holy city which we all hope to enter, their merry eyes opened wide and their little faces grew thoughtful, and they wondered if the little boy who died last autumn went there, and asked 'Did the angels come to take him?'"[57]

An inordinate amount of time was spent on moral training. In the eyes of educators, Indian children were products of cultures that placed little emphasis on "virtue," at least as it was understood in the context of Christian ethics. In the words of one Indian agent, "The Indians are simple children of nature, and many things condemned as immoral among whites are with them without offense."[58] In particular, Indian children needed to be taught the moral ideals of charity, chastity, monogamy, respect for the Sabbath, temperance, honesty, self-sacrifice, the importance of pure thoughts and speech—indeed, an almost endless array of personal characteristics important to the formation of "character."

Fundamental to this aim was implanting the idea of sin and a corresponding sense of guilt. And sometimes it worked. One Carlisle boy caught writing "vile thoughts" to a friend was moved to write to Pratt:

> I want to tell you that I cry inside of my heart when I was in church for the bad and sin I have done. Oh I am very *sorry*, but Captain I only believe that God has power to take way our sins. So please

Captain help me and pray for me to come out of this wrong where I am in. I will promise you that I will *never* write nor say such words to any body here after this.

I will do what you told me, that is if I get a letter from someone is bad, I will throw it in stove or I will not answered it.

Captain Pratt now from today I will commence my way to follow the Christians. If I do fall into sin I will get up again. Ever since I get into trouble I feel as though I am by my self. But I have parents and I must try to do what is right to see that I am in right side here after this.

Captain I hope to help me and pray for me that I may become Christian and I will give my self to Christ. I have long sin and gives me but a sorrow life. Now Captain Pratt I will not mind any one that will try to pull me down and lead me into wrong direction.[59]

Efforts to build Christian character were not limited to Sunday sermons and prayer meetings. McGuffey Readers were hardly deficient in moral content, nor were most teachers shy about offering advice on moral questions; indeed, they were expected to. Student essays were yet another medium for reinforcing the character theme, and one example was the Indian Office's efforts on behalf of temperance. Because alcoholism was both a health and moral issue, in 1915 it became the subject of a system wide essay contest. Student response to the issue, at least measured by several seventh grade essays printed in Haskell's newspaper, was deeply felt.

Alcohol wrecked my life, but two years ago I reformed and am trying to lead a good life. Alcohol has wrecked the lives of many people and is still at it. I have seen men killing each other, cutting up each other, frozen to death, killed by railroad trains because they were going home along the track and were to drunk to get out of the way. Whose fault is it? Who is to blame? Alcohol!

According to a second:

We once had a nice home but after alcohol entered it kept on going down and down until we had no home. Papa drank up everything. He caused mother to sell her land and now mother has no home at all. She works. If I had the power, I would crush every saloon to pieces. Fight well, hard and forever until this great enemy is banished from our Nation. I pray God to give us strength to fight this enemy.[60]

Undoubtedly, many students could identify with admonitions against alcohol because they had seen the havoc it could wreak on an Indian community.

More difficult to assess is their overall response to the constant proselytizing. Some students were apparently confused by it all. In some schools pupils were forced to repeat the words of Bible verses and hymns with no explanation of the meaning behind the phrases. For younger students, language presented a problem. A former student at Tuba City Boarding School bitterly remembers two-hour Sunday sermons, even though "some of us who did not understand the full meaning of the sermons would get bored and fall asleep." Similarly, Frank Mitchell, who attended Fort Defiance, recalls that when the priests and missionaries came to school: "We did not know much English, and we did not understand what they were talking about half of the time. They talked about God, and most of us did not understand it. So I guess they were just talking to themselves."[61]

The pressure to convert was sometimes immense. Jason Betzinez, an Apache student at Carlisle, recalls that "the most powerful influence on my life at this ... time was my introduction to the teachings of Christianity.... This influence became stronger and stronger as I came to understand English better. It changed my whole life." Similarly, Thomas Wildcat Alford, who, before leaving for school, was warned by Shawnee chiefs against converting to the white man's religion, eventually fell under the spell of the evangelical promise. In time, he came to know "deep in my soul that Jesus Christ was my Savior." Even Don Talayesva, who was torn between his ancestral Hopi beliefs and Christianity while at Sherman Institute, and who would promptly reject Christianity upon his return to Oraibi, managed to conjure up this sermon for a school YMCA meeting.

> Well, my partners, I am asked to speak a few words for Jesus. I am glad that I came to Sherman and learned to read and cipher. Now I discover that Jesus was a good writer. So I am thankful that Uncle Sam taught me to read in order that I may understand the Scriptures and take my steps along God's road. When I get a clear understanding of the Gospel I shall return home and preach it to my people in darkness. I will teach them all I know about Jesus Christ, the Heavenly Father, and the Holy Ghost. So I advise you boys to do your best and pray to God to give us a good understanding. Then we will be ready for Jesus to come and take us up to heaven. I don't want any of my friends to be thrown into the lake of hellfire where there is suffering and sorrow forever. Amen.[62]

The evidence about student's reaction to conversion efforts is sketchy at best. But most students, like Helen Sekaquaptewa, probably went through the motions, kept their counsel, and endured the hours of preaching and praying as best they could.

> I remember one preacher especially, although they were all about the same. I couldn't understand a thing he was talking about but had to sit and listen to a long sermon. I hated them and felt like crying. If I nodded my head going to sleep, a teacher would poke me and tell me to be good. It seemed as if this preacher would talk all night. He put a great deal of emotion into his sermons. He would work himself up to a climax talking loud and strong, and then calm

down to a whisper, and I would think, "Now he is going to stop." But no, he would start all over again and go on and on.[63]

How many students simply rejected the school's conversion efforts outright? Again, the evidence is sketchy. Helen Sekaquaptewa relates that the various missionaries "were always urging and bribing us with little presents to join their church," and then goes on to say: "It didn't appeal to me and I didn't join any of them." Even more suggestive is a missionary newspaper's account of Pratt's effort at a school assembly to extract from students a public declaration of their religious inclinations. When asked how many were already Christian, thirty-four students stood. When asked how many were "trying" to become Christians, another seventy-two rose from their seats. Interestingly, this account was presented as evidence that the school's missionary program was rapidly winning converts. But it also provides an indication of the number who remained skeptical of the Christian message; the vast majority had remained seated.[64]

A particularly intriguing question—for which there is no answer—is, how many students surreptitiously carried out native rituals in defiance of the official religious program? Also, how many students were involuntarily visited by visions or dreams, traditionally powerful mediums of religious experience? Consider the truly extraordinary account left by Don Talayesva of his spirit journey back to Hopiland while laying unconscious and hospitalized at Sherman Institute.[65] Several examples of religious counter-culture are presented in Morris E. Opler's *Apache Odyssey: A Journey Between Two Worlds.* Discussing his boarding school experiences, Opler's Mescalero informant relates how one boy sought to acquire power from the towhee bird. "He used to tie the feathers to his bed. At night he used to say he wished to see the bird so that it might show him something." The ritualistic approach to the bird apparently had its effect.

> So one night the towhee came in and slept under his pillow. He spoke to the bird that night, and the bird stayed right there. Early in the morning the boy got up, and the towhee flew out. Others tried to catch it, but it came to this boy, and he held it in his hand. Others asked for it, but the towhee told the boy to turn it loose, and he did. It came for the next three nights too. But no one but the boy saw it these other times. He learned supernatural power from it.

Indeed, the bird became a powerful spirit guide and protector. When the boy was selected for transfer to an off-reservation school, the bird's power was invoked to reverse the superintendent's decision. "He got the help of the towhee, and he didn't go. He stayed right where he was."[66]

Another instance occurred when a school employee purchased a large quantity of bear meat. A Mescalero schoolboy crippled with a bad leg managed to get a piece of the roasted meat and ate it in the belief that the power of the bear might correct his deformity. According to Mescalero tradition, bear meat, ritualistically eaten under the direction of a shaman, possessed special healing power. In this case, however, the ritual prescriptions had been forgotten, which constituted a reckless and stupid act. Indeed, the bear's spirit was angered.

> About midnight we heard this boy crying. The bear was after him; he saw it go out the door. The boys tried to keep him quiet but they couldn't. And so he kept crying 'til morning and also vomited. He said the bear was coming in and putting its paws down his throat, trying to catch something. He was very sick all that day. They didn't know what to do. The doctor gave him some medicine, but it didn't help him. The relatives of the boy were told, and they went to Swinging-Lance, who was a chief.... Swinging-Lance talked to the agent, who was his friend, and got the boy out of school, for that boy saw the bear every night, and every night it put its paws in and out of his mouth, and he cried.[67]

After the boy was taken from the school, his relatives found a shaman who carried out a public curing ceremony, which included, among other things, a ritualistic feeding of bear meat. Somehow, the boy recovered. The Mescalero present were understandably impressed. "The white doctor said that the boy just had an upset stomach, that there was nothing wrong with him. But the Mescalero said he had Bear sickness and would have died if it weren't for them."[68] Presumably, once word spread back to the school, many students adopted the same opinion. What the episode illustrates beyond all doubt is the complex configuration of the forces shaping Indian students' religious attitudes.

RESISTANCE

The Indian agent Eugene White would never forget the day one seven-year-old Ute boy was enrolled at Uintah Boarding School. The induction should have gone smoothly. Even though the lad was brought in "wild as a jack rabbit," he was delivered to the school by his father, normally a strong indicator that the boy would be cooperative. As a matter of procedure, White turned the youngster over to Fannie Weeks, the school superintendent, and Clara Granger, the matron, and invited the boy's father into the office for a bit of friendly conversation. It was all a matter of routine. The father would seek assurances he had done the right thing in bringing the boy in; the agent would praise him for his intelligence and foresight in doing so and would promise to watch over the boy like his, the agent's, very own son.[69]

All was proceeding according to script until, as White later recounted: "I heard a tremendous disturbance break out up at the schoolhouse. Tables and chairs were being hurled about, women were screaming, children were running in every direction." When White reached the schoolhouse he could scarcely believe the scene before him. In one part of the room Superintendent Weeks was almost in a "swoon." "Her dress was torn, her face badly scratched, and two-thirds of her hair missing." In another stood Mrs. Granger, "her face and neck showed several ugly fingernail scratches, one ear was bitten almost off, and her nose was swollen to ridiculous size, and bleeding profusely." Meanwhile, crouched upon a corner woodbox was the silent but defiant culprit, "the worst scared little animal I ever saw."[70]

Calm restored, White reconstructed events. After the boy had been turned over to the two women, they had "petted" and fed him, all the while coaxing him, in a tongue he had never heard before, to speak to them. Then Miss Weeks turned to other duties, and Mrs. Granger was to lead him to the storeroom for a new set of clothing. When Mrs. Granger

> stooped to take his hand, the little fellow sprang up on her shoulders and went to snatching, biting, and pulling hair like a real wildcat. Of course, when Miss Weeks heard the screaming she rushed heroically to the rescue of Mrs. Granger. In trying to pull the boy loose she bent Mrs. Granger over on the table. The little Indian jumped off on the table, kicked Mrs. Granger on the nose, leaped upon Miss Weeks' shoulders and commenced to pluck her head. She struggled and screamed tremendously at first, but in a little while she dropped on her hands and knees and commenced to pray. When she sank entirely to the floor the little fellow jumped off, ran to the far corner of the room and climbed up on the woodbox. The ladies said he did not utter a word—did not even whimper—during the melee, and did not look at all mad, but just seemed to be scared almost to death.[71]

What is one to make of this episode, especially considering the fact that the defiant youth eventually became "one of the brightest and most amiable children in school"?[72] Is it possible that once acclimated, the boy found boarding school life completely agreeable? Perhaps, but not necessarily. As will be shown shortly, the fact of resistance need not take such dramatic form. What was the reason for the boy's rebellion? Was it simply a matter of fear or the pain of being separated from his father? Was it possibly a reaction to the cultural assault about to be performed? Perhaps both of these. One wonders also if the boy's eventual cooperation was elicited by virtue of the fact that his father had voluntarily brought him to school. How different would the young Ute's adjustment have been if the agent had been compelled to take him by force?

Although the evidence for this particular episode is incomplete, the historical record on student response in general makes one thing abundantly clear: students, often in collaboration with their parents, frequently went to great lengths to resist. In this chapter, I explore the manner, extent, and motivation for such a response.[73]

Parents' Opposition to Boarding Schools

The opposition of Indian parents to white schooling was both deeply felt and widespread. "The Indians have a prejudice against schools," the agent at Sac and Fox Agency reported in 1882, and another agent complained, "The Crows are bitterly opposed to sending their children to school and invent all kinds of excuses to get the children out or keep from sending them." Similarly, the Lemhi in Idaho were said to be "constantly at rebellion against civilizing elements," the school being a prime irritant. The problem, the agent lamented, was that the Indians in his charge had "not yet reached that state of civilization to know the advantages of education, and consequently look upon school work with abhorrence." Frustrated over recruitment problems, the superintendent of one school could only conclude that the average Indian had as much regard for education "as a horse does for the Constitution."[74]

When parents refused to enroll their children in school, agents normally resorted to either withholding rations or using the agency police. When one agent at Fort Peck met with resistance, he sent the police to round up the children, denied rations to the parents, and then, to drive the point home, locked several of the most intractable fathers in the agency guardhouse. In any event, the forced procurement of children was usually unpleasant business.[75] In 1886, the agent to the Mescalero Apache reported:

> Everything in the way of persuasion and argument having failed, it became necessary to visit the camps unexpectedly with a detachment of police, and seize such children as were proper and take them away to school, willing or unwilling. Some hurried their children off to the mountains or hid them away in camp, and the police had to chase and capture them like so many wild rabbits. This unusual proceeding created quite an outcry. The men were sullen and muttering, the women loud in their lamentations, and the children almost out of their wits with fright.[76]

Resistance to the annual fall roundup took a number of forms. Most dramatic were those instances when an entire village or tribal faction refused to turn over their children. Sometimes parents simply slipped away from the main camp for several weeks until the pressure for students had let up. Another response was to offer up orphans or children living on the fringe of extended kinship circles. Occasionally, resistance took the form of bargaining. This occurred on those reservations where the school-age population was in excess of dormitory space, thus allowing tribal leaders and agents to negotiate a family quota until the school was filled. In other instances, the whole matter was simply dropped in the lap of tribal policemen, who in turn might put the agonizing question to a mother—which child to give up, which to hold back? In his memoirs, Frank Mitchell readily admits that he was the first child to be given over because he was the "black sheep" of the family. Indeed, he argues that when Navajo police-men were looking for children, they consciously avoided taking the "prime." Rather, "they took those who were not so intelligent, those the People thought could be spared because of their physical conditions, and those who were not well taken care of."[77]

Even after children were enrolled, parents still found ways to oppose the school. In the face of a particularly obnoxious school policy, or in time of crisis, parents were known to withdraw their children en masse or to encourage runaways. Sending delegations to the agency, drawing up petitions to Washington, and catching the ear of an inspector were other methods of protest. From the Indian Office's point of view, the most insidious form of resistance was the conscious efforts of tribal elders to undermine the school's teachings during vacation periods by enculturating youth in the curriculum of traditional culture, a phenom-enon that, it may be remembered, was one of the major reasons for pol-icymakers' preference for off-reservation schools. And finally, after 1893 some parents took full advantage of their legal right to deny the transfer of older students to off-reservation institutions.

What prompted such resistance? In part, the answer lies in the dis-tinction Edward Dozier makes between "forced" and "permissive" accul-turation. "The forceful imposition of religion, ideologies and behavior patterns by the dominant society on a subordinate one appears to be met in every case with resistance and rejection," writes Dozier. On the other hand, when cultural interchange takes place free of compulsion in a "per-missive contact situation," then "the resultant product is a new cultural whole where the cultural traits of both groups are fused harmoniously in both meaning and form."[78] To be sure, Dozier's distinction overstates the case; forced acculturation need not always result in resistance. Still, the argument is sound in the main. Conquered and colonized, Native Americans were hardly of a mind to view government policies, including that of compulsory education, as benign.

If nothing else, the policy of forced acculturation exacerbated an age-old characteristic of native life, tribal factionalism.[79] "Upon close study," Hamlin Garland observed in 1902,

> each tribe, whether Sioux, or Navajo, or Hopi will be found to be divided,.... into two parties, the radicals and the conservatives—those who are willing to change, to walk the white man's way; and those who are deeply, sullenly skeptical of all civilizing measures, clinging tenaciously to the traditions and lore of their race. These men are often the strongest and bravest of their tribe, the most dig-nified and the most intellectual. They represent the spirit that will break but will not bow. And, broadly speaking, they are in the majority. Though in rags, their spirits are unbroken; from the point of view of their sympathizers, they are patriots.[80]

Although Garland's analysis fails to do justice to the complexity of tribal opinion, it does offer a major motivation for resistance, namely, that a significant body of tribal opinion saw white education for what it was: an invitation to cultural suicide. If white teachings were taken to heart, almost every vestige of traditional life would be cast aside. At the very least, whites expected Indians—and here, of course, the extent of the list differed with cultures—to abandon their ancestral gods and ceremonies; redefine the division of labor for the sexes; abolish polygyny; extinguish tribal political structures; squelch traditions of gift giving and communalism; abandon hunting and gathering; and restructure traditional familial and kinship arrangements. Across campfires, tribal elders weighed the issues. And many, like this Papago parent, asked:

> Now, are we a better people than we were years ago when we sang our own songs, when we spoke to the Great Spirit in our own language? We asked then for rain, good health and long life. Now what more do we want? What is that thought so great and so sacred that cannot be expressed in our own language, that we should seek to use the white man's words?[81]

When such attitudes translated into a complete indictment of white ways, the agent's call for students was almost certain to meet with staunch resistance.

But opposition to schools did not always spring from a comprehensive rejection of white ways. It might just as well represent opposition to some selective aspect of the school program: punishing children for speaking their native tongue, pressuring them to convert to Christianity, forcing them to perform manual labor. Especially obnoxious to some was the school's manner of disciplining Indian children, and even more, the practice of dressing and drilling them like soldiers.[82] One of the reasons given by Spotted Tail for withdrawing his children from Carlisle in 1880 was his discovery that Pratt had turned the school into "a soldier's place."[83]

Parents also were certain to dig in their heels if they suspected that a superintendent was unusually mean-spirited. In early 1890, for instance, it appears that one of the major reasons for the Navajo's refusal to fill the agency school at Fort Defiance was the widespread belief that Superintendent G. H. Wadleigh, nicknamed "Billy Goat" by the local Navajos, was mistreating their children. In a special investigation, one Navajo mother testified how her eight-year-old son, Henry, was confined in the school belfry for two days, only to be released in leg irons. In this condition the boy ran away, and his mother found him

> crawling on his hands and knees. His legs were tied up with iron shackles. I picked up and carried him in my arms. When I got my boy home—the Billy Goat came after the boy, and said he wanted to take him to the school again.... I told him to take the iron strings off of my son Henry, and I would let him go—he took the iron strings off and left my house returning to the school leaving my son

with me, telling me not to tell the agent. Next day I sent the boy back to school—he is there now.[84]

One of the headmen in the area, Sour Water, frankly told the inspector that Billy Goat Wadleigh was a major cause for parents holding back children. "I told Mr. Wadleigh," the old man related, "that we put our children into school to learn to read and write. That we did not want our children whipped. That the school was no jail for them."[85] At the recommendation of the inspector, Wadleigh was eventually removed; meanwhile, the school had received a setback.

Many parents also had suspicions that boarding schools posed a threat to their children's health. When the agent at Uintah went looking for students in 1900, one of the major reasons for opposition was the school's high death rate. Still, by November the school had managed to boost its enrollment to sixty-five. And then, in the words of the agent, "came the catastrophe"—an epidemic of measles. After word reached the villages, parents swooped down upon the school and carried their children off to camp, turning them over to medicine men. Upon hearing that the Indians planned to burn down the school, the agent called in a troop of cavalry. Meanwhile, the school staff listened to the "tom-tom and the barbarous howl of the medicine man at night, and the death wail from the same wickiup in the morning." A few students were coaxed back again and things began to improve until it was announced that the children were to be vaccinated. Not waiting for their parents this time, the frightened students bolted for home, and there they stayed until the year's end.[86]

Parents especially associated off-reservation schools with death. In 1889, Washington received word from Navajo Agency that since two boys of a leading chief had died at Carlisle, "no Navajo will listen to a proposition to send a child of his to an eastern school."[87] By 1891, the Spokane, who had lost sixteen of twenty-one children sent to eastern schools, also were fed up with the idea of off-reservation schools. "I made up mind that my people were right in being afraid to send the children away," one chief declared. "My people do not want to send their children so far away. If I had white people's children I would have put their bodies in a coffin and sent them home so that they could see them. I do not know who did it, but they treated my people as if they were dogs." But then, in reference to an old government promise to build the Spokane their own school, the old man continued: "They should give me that school house. When they buried sixteen of our children they should pay by building a school."[88]

For some parents the distinction between reservation and off-reservation schools was a fundamental one. "Why is it," one Ute parent asked, "that Washington does not build a school-house here, as he agreed to when we sold him our lands in Colorado?" Similarly, at Rosebud the agent was informed: "We have been promised for a long time by the Great Father that we should have a boarding school at this agency. Why do we not have it? Have such a one built here or at other agencies and we will send our children. We do not want to send our children from home."[89]

The bottom line was that parents resented boarding schools, both reservation and off-reservation, because they severed the most fundamental of human ties: the parent-child bond. The reservation school, by taking the child for months at a time, was bad enough; the off-reservation term of three to five years was an altogether hellish prospect, especially if the child had been shipped off without the parent's consent. "It has been with us like a tree dropping its leaves," one distressed Navajo parent protested in council.

> They fall one by one to the ground until finally the wind sweeps them all away and they are gone forever.... The parents of those children who were taken away are crying for them. I had a boy who was taken from this school [Fort Defiance] to Grand Junction. The tears come to our eyes whenever we think of them. I do not know whether my boy is alive or not.[90]

NOTES

1. Luther Standing Bear, *My People, the Sioux* (1928; reprint, Lincoln: University of Nebraska Press, 1975), 123.
2. Standing Bear, *Land of the Spotted Eagle* (Boston: Houghton Mifflin Company, 1933), 68–69, 230–31. Also, Standing Bear, *My People, the Sioux*, 124, 128.
3. Standing Bear, *My People, the Sioux*, 187.
4. Ibid., 128–29.
5. Standing Bear, *Land of the Spotted Eagle*, 231–32; and Standing Bear, *My People, the Sioux*, 129–30.
6. Standing Bear, *My People, the Sioux*, 130–32.
7. Ibid., 133.
8. "Hoke Denetsosie" in *Stories of Traditional Navaho Life and Culture*, ed. Broderick H. Johnson (Tsaile, Ariz.: Navajo Community College Press, 1977), 81. For other accounts see "Max Hanley," in ibid., 36–37; Frank Mitchell, *Navajo Blessingway Singer: The Autobiography of Frank Mitchell, 1881–1967*, ed. Charlotte J. Frisbie and David A. McAllester (Tucson: University of Arizona Press, 1978), 57–61; Albert Yava, *Big Falling Snow: A Tewa-Hopi Indian's Life and Times and the History and Traditions of His People*, ed. Harold Courlander (Albuquerque: University of New Mexico Press, 1978), 14–18; Richard Henry Pratt, *Battlefield and Classroom: Four Decades with the American Indian, 1867–1904*, ed. Robert M. Utley (New Haven: Yale University Press, 1964), 203–4; Clark Wissler, *Indian Cavalcade or Life on the Old-time Indian Reservations* (New York: Sheridan, 1938), 183–84; and *Southern Workman*, August 1881, 85. For an excellent analysis of autobiographical accounts of leaving for school see Michael C. Coleman, *American Indian Children at School, 1850–1930* (Jackson: University Press of Mississippi, 1993), chap. 4.

9. According to Erving Goffman total institutions include the following characteristics. "First, all aspects of life (eating, sleeping, playing, working, learning) are conducted in the same place and under the same single authority. Second, each phase of a member's daily activity is carried out in the immediate company of a large batch of others, all of whom are treated alike and required to do the same thing together. Third, all phases of the day's activities are tightly scheduled, with one activity leading at a prearranged time into the next, the whole circle of activities being composed from above through a system of explicit, formal rules and a body of officials. Finally, the contents of the various enforced activities are brought together as parts of a single, overall, rational plan purportedly designed to fulfill the official aims of the institution." By Goffman's definition, examples of total institutions include concentration camps, mental hospitals, army barracks, prisons, and work camps. See Erving Goffman, "The Characteristics of Total Institutions," in *Complex Organizations: A Sociological Reader*, ed. Amitai Etzioni (New York: Holt, Rinehart, and Winston, 1961), 313–14; also see Goffman, *Asylums: Essays on the Social Situation of Mental Patients and Other Inmates* (Chicago: Aldine Publishing, 1961), 3–124, and C. A. McEwen, "Continuities in the Study of Total and Nontotal Institutions," *Annual Review of Sociology* 6 (1980): 143–85. Historians have applied the concept with varying degrees of accuracy and insight. One of the most important results of this discussion has been the recognition that there are great differences between total institutions—for instance, concentration camps and prisons—in their capacity to shape and control behavior. Slavery historians, for instance, have argued that the concept is of limited use in understanding the "peculiar institution." See, for instance, John W. Blassingame, *The Slave Community: Plantation Life in the Antebellum South* (New York: Oxford University Press, 1972), appendix. Other applications include David Rothman, *The Discovery of the Asylum* (Boston: Little, Brown, 1971); George Harwood Phillips, "Indians and the Breakdown of the Spanish Mission System in California," *Ethnohistory* 21 (Fall 1974): 291–302; and Thomas James, *Exile Within: The Schooling of Japanese Americans, 1942–1945* (Cambridge: Harvard University Press, 1987), 92. Were Indian boarding schools total institutions? They clearly fulfill the requirements of Hoffman's definition and even appear to go beyond it when he states that "total institutions do not substitute their own unique culture for something already formed. We do not deal with acculturation as assimilation but with something more restricted than these. In a sense, total institutions do not look for cultural victory" (Goffman, "The Characteristics of Total Institutions," 317). Boarding schools, of course, existed for the express purpose of achieving "cultural victory." It is also suggestive that in 1891 Commissioner Morgan compared boarding schools to juvenile asylums and houses of correction. ARCIA, 1891, 62–63. Still, as this book later shows, the boarding school's control over Indian students was not absolute.

10. Standing Bear, *My People, the Sioux*, 140–41.

11. Mitchell, *Navajo Blessingway Singer*, 62.

12. Standing Bear, *Land of the Spotted Eagle*, 189. McCowan is quoted in Lorraine M. Scherer, "Great Chieftains of the Mohave Indians," *Southern California Quarterly* 48 (March 1966): 18.

13. ARCIA, 1892, 615.

14. Julia B. McGillycuddy, *McGillycuddy, Agent: A Biography of Dr. Valentine T. McGillycuddy* (Standford: Stanford University Press, 1941), 205–6.

15. Standing Bear, *My People, the Sioux*, 140.
16. Pratt, *Battlefield and Classroom*, 232.
17. ARCIA, 1890, cli; and U.S. Office of Indian Affairs, *Rules for the Indian School Service* (Washington, D.C.: Government Printing Office, 1898), 31.
18. Carnelita S. Ryan, "The Carlisle Indian Industrial School" (Ph.D. dissertation, Georgetown University, 1962), 42; and ARCIA, 1893, 429.
19. ARCIA, 1897, 161; and Helen Sekaquaptewa (as told to Louise Udall), *Me and Mine: The Life Story of Helen Sekaquaptewa* (Tucson: University of Arizona Press, 1969), 32.
20. Frederick Riggs, "Peculiarities of Indian Education," *Southern Workman*, February 1901, 69; and Standing Bear, *My People, the Sioux*, 142.
21. ARCIA, 1904, 424; ARCIA, 1890, clx; and U.S. Office of Indian Affairs, *Rules for the Indian School Service*, 1898, 26.
22. ARCIA, 1890, clx. See Daniel F. Littlefield, Jr., and Lonnie E. Underhill, "Renaming the American Indian: 1890–1913," *American Studies* 12 (Fall 1971): 33–45.
23. ARCIA, 1890, clx-xlxi; and ARCIA, 1904, 424.
24. ARCIA, 1904, 426.
25. ARCIA, 1890, clxi; and Harriet Patrick Gilstrap, "Memories of a Pioneer Teacher," *Chronicles of Oklahoma* 38 (Spring 1960): 23.
26. *Southern Workman*, May 1889, 55.
27. George A. Pettit, *Primitive Education in North America* (Berkeley: University of California Press, 1946), 59–74.
28. Standing Bear, *My People, the Sioux*, 137.
29. Quoted in Pratt, *Battlefield and Classroom*, 293.
30. Jason Betzinez, *I Fought with Geronimo*, ed. Wilber S. Nye (Harrisburg, Pa.: Stackpole Company, 1959), 154.
31. ARCIA, 1882, p. 30. Agents continually complained of conditions. See ARCIA, 1886, 222, 230; ARCIA, 1887, 148; ARCIA, 1888, 77; ARCIA, 1889, 343–44; and ARCIA, 1900, 266.
32. ARCIA, 1892, 605; LMC, 1897, 36; and ARCIA, 1898, 18.
33. For contrasting definitions of Indian and white concepts of space see Bernard L. Fontana, "The Melting Pot that Wouldn't: Ethnic Groups in the American Southwest Since 1846," *American Indian Culture and Research Journal* 1 (1974): 21; Jamake Highwater, *The Primal Mind: Vision and Reality in Indian America* (1981; reprint, New York: New American Library, 1982), chap. 5; Peter Nabokov and Robert Easton, *Native American Architecture* (New York: Oxford University Press, 1989); and Joseph Epes Brown, *The Spiritual Legacy of the American Indian* (New York: Crosswood Publishing, 1982), 50–52.
34. Raymond J. DeMallie, ed., *The Sixth Grandfather: Black Elk's Teachings Given to John G. Neihardt* (Lincoln: University of Nebraska Press, 1984), 290–91. Also see George W. Linden, "Dakota Philosophy," *American Studies* 18 (Fall 1977): 33; and John (Fire) Lame Deer and Richard Erdoes, *Lame Deer: Seeker of Visions* (1972; reprint, New York: Washington Square Press, 1976), 96–97, 100–101.
35. Highwater, *The Primal Mind*, 119; ARCIA, 1898, 20; and U.S. Office of Indian Affairs, *Rules for the Indian School Service*, 1898, 25.
36. ARCIA, 1890, cli; and Mitchell, *Navajo Blessingway Singer*, 62.
37. Quoted in Theodore Stern, *The Klamath Tribe: A People and Their Reservation* (Seattle: University of Washington Press, 1965), 107; Don Talayesva, *Sun Chief: The Autobiography of a Hopi Indian*, ed. Leo

Simmons (New Haven: Yale University Press, 1942), 95–96; and Sekaquaptewa, *Me and Mine*, 94–95. Also see Edmund Nequatewa, *Born a Chief: The Nineteenth Century Hopi Boyhood of Edmund Nequatewa, as told to Alfred F. Whiting*, ed. P. David Seaman (Tucson: University of Arizona Press, 1993), 87–89.

38. Pratt, *Battlefield and Classroom*, 233, and Estelle Aubrey Brown, *Stubborn Fool: A Narrative* (Caldwell, Idaho: Caxton Printers, 1952), 60, 185.

39. K. Tsianina Lomawaima, *They Called It Prairie Light: The Story of Chilocco Indian School* (Lincoln: University of Nebraska Press, 1994), 59, 133, 135–38; Sally Hyer, *One House, One Voice, One Heart: Native American Education at the Santa Fe Indian School* (Santa Fe: Museum of New Mexico Press, 1990), 25; Jim Whitewolf, *The Life of a Kiowa Apache Indian*, ed. Charles S. Brant (New York: Dover Publications, 1969), 96; Fred Kabotie (as told to Bill Belknap), *Fred Kabotie: Hopi Indian Artist* (Flagstaff: Museum of Northern Arizona and Northland Press, 1977), 18; Nequatewa, *Born a Chief*, 93; and Marla N. Powers, *Ogalala Women: Myth, Ritual, and Reality* (Chicago: University of Chicago Press, 1986), 109–10.

40. ARCIA, 1890, cli; ARCIA, 1892, 604–5; and Mitchell, *Navajo Blessingway Singer*, 63.

41. ARCIA, 1887, 348; and Whitewolf, *The Life of a Kiowa Apache Indian*, 84.

42. Hopi hearings, July 15–30, 1955, BIA, Phoenix Area Office, Hopi Agency, Keams Canyon, Arizona, 33; Alexander H. Leighton and Dorothea C. Leighton, *The Navajo Door: An Introduction to Navajo Life* (Cambridge: Harvard University Press, 1945), 125–26; and K. Tsianina Lomawaima, "Oral Histories From Chilocco Indian Agricultural School, 1920–1940," *American Indian Quarterly* 11 (Summer 1987): 250. Also Peter Blaine, Sr. (as told to Michael S. Adams), *Papagos and Politics* (Tucson: Arizona Historical Society, 1981), 23–25; Kabotie, *Fred Kabotie*, 17–18; Jerry Suazo, Interview no. 868, Doris Duke Collection, University of New Mexico; Lomawaima, *They Called It Prairie Light*, 101–5; Hyer, *One House, One Voice, One Heart*, 11; Robert A. Trennert, *The Phoenix Indian School: Forced Assimilation in Arizona, 1891–1935* (Norman: University of Oklahoma Press, 1988), 115–18; and Coleman, *American Indian Children at School*, 86–88.

43. Anna Moore Shaw, *A Pima Past* (Tucson: University of Arizona Press, 1974), 133.

44. ARCIA, 1898, 357; E. P. Grinstead, "Value of Military Drills," *Native American*, 21 March 1914, 151–52; and ARCIA, 1886, 224.

45. ARCIA, 1892, 616; Fontana, "The Melting Pot that Wouldn't," 20; and Althea Bass, *The Arapaho Way: A Memoir of an Indian Boyhood* (New York: Clarkson N. Potter, 1966), 6.

46. *Sherman Bulletin*, 21 December 1910, 1; and Grinstead, "Value of Military Drills," 153.

47. *Native American*, 23 October 1909, 342; and *Sherman Bulletin*, 21 December 1910, 1.

48. *Southern Workman*, January 1897, 7.

49. For an introduction to this aspect of Indian societies, see Brown, *The Spiritual Legacy of the American Indian*; Ake Hultkrantz, *Belief and Worship in Native North America* (Syracuse, N.Y.: Syracuse University Press, 1981); Hultkrantz, *The Religions of the American Indians* (Berkeley: University of California Press, 1979); Hartley Burr Alexander, *The World's Rim: Great Mysteries of the North American Indians* (Lincoln: University of

Nebraska Press, 1953); and Sam D. Gill, ed., *Native American Religions: An Introduction* (Belmont, Calif.: Wadsworth Publishing, 1982).

50. See Brown, *Spiritual Legacy of the American Indian*, x, 69.
51. Ibid., 38–40, 53–54, 71–72, 124; Christopher Vecsey, "American Indian Environmental Religions," in *American Indian Environments: Ecological Issues in Native American History*, ed. Christopher Vecsey and Robert W. Venables (Syracuse, N.Y.: Syracuse University Press, 1980), 1–37; Hultkrantz, *Belief and Worship in Native North America*, chap. 7; and N. Scott Momaday, "Native American Attitudes to the Environment," in *Seeing with a Native Eye: Essays on Native American Religion*, ed. Walter Holden Capps (New York: Harper and Row, 1976), chap. 6.
52. See works cited in note 49.
53. Henry Warner Bowden, *American Indians and Christian Missions: Studies in Cultural Conflict* (Chicago: University of Chicago Press, 1981), 121.
54. Homer G. Barnett, *Indian Shakers: A Messianic Cult of the Pacific Northwest* (Carbondale: Southern Illinois University Press, 1957); James S. Slotkin, *The Peyote Religion: A Study in Indian-White Relations* (Glencoe, Ill.: Free Press, 1956); Weston LaBarre, *The Peyote Cult* (New York: Schocken Books, 1969); Omer C. Stewart, *Peyote Religion: A History* (Norman: University of Oklahoma Press, 1987); James Mooney, *The Ghost-Dance Religion and the Sioux Outbreak of 1890*, Fourteenth Annual Report of the Bureau of American Ethnology, 1892–1893, pt. 2 (Washington, D.C.: Government Printing Office, 1896); and Robert M. Utley, *The Last Days of the Sioux Nation* (New Haven: Yale University Press, 1963), chap. 5.
55. Brown, *Spiritual Legacy of the American Indian*, 27.
56. U.S. Office of Indian Affairs, *Rules for the Indian School Service,* 1898, 25; ARCIA, 1880, 302–3; ARCIA 1881, 132–33; ARCIA, 1882, 120; ARCIA, 1886, 225; ARCIA, 1887, 350; ARCIA, 1891, 542; and LMC, 1903, 86–87. Hailmann quoted in Indian Rights Association, *Answers to Charges Made Against William N. Hailmann, Superintendent of Indian Schools, Submitting Quotations from His Writings, etc.* (Philadelphia: Indian Rights Association, 1898), 5.
57. ARCIA, 1887, 350; and ARCIA, 1883, 231.
58. ARCIA, 1884, 68.
59. Harry Raven to Richard H. Pratt, 7 November 1887, Pratt Papers, BRBML.
60. *Indian Leader*, March 1915, 4. Also *Indian Leader*, 8 May 1915, 2–3, and *Indian Leader*, October 1915, 14.
61. "Hoke Denetsosie," in *Stories of Traditional Navajo Life and Culture*, ed. Broderick H. Johnson (Tsaile, Ariz.: Navajo Community College Press, 1977), 93; and Mitchell, *Navajo Blessingway Singer,* 65–66.
62. Betzinez, *I Fought with Geronimo*, 257; Thomas Wildcat Alford (as told to Florence Drake), *Civilization, and the Story of the Absentee Shawness* (Norman: University of Oklahoma Press, 1936), 105–6; and Talayesva, *Sun Chief*, 116–17. Also Charley Joseph Atsye, Interview no. 522, Doris Duke Collection, University of New Mexico; and Nequatewa, *Born a Chief*, 111–12, 121–22.
63. Sekaquaptewa, *Me and Mine*, 129.
64. Ibid. and *Iapi Oaye: The Word Carrier*, February 1882, 15.
65. Talayesva, *Sun Chief*, 119–28.
66. Morris E. Opler, *Apache Odyssey: A Journey Between Two Worlds* (New York: Holt, Rinehart and Winston, 1969), 126–27.
67. Ibid., 123.

68. Ibid., 123–24.
69. Eugene E. White, *Experiences of a Special Indian Agent* (Norman: University of Oklahoma Press, 1965), 168–69.
70. Ibid., 169–70.
71. Ibid., 170–72.
72. Ibid., 172.
73. For discussions of student response, including resistance, see David Wallace Adams, "From Bullets to Boarding Schools: The Educational Assault on the American Indian Identity," in *The American Indian Experience: A Profile*, ed. Philip Weeks (Arlington Heights, Ill.: Forum Press, 1988), 230–37; Coleman, *American Indian Children at School*, esp. chaps. 4 and 8–9; Coleman, "Motivations of Indian Children at Missionary and U.S. Government Schools," *Montana: The Magazine of Western History* 40 (Winter 1990): 30–45; Coleman, "The Responses of American Indian Children to Presbyterian Schooling in the Nineteenth Century: An Analysis Through Missionary Sources," *History of Education Quarterly* 27 (Winter 1987): 473–97; Coleman, "The Mission Education of Francis La Flesche: An Indian Response to the Presbyterian Boarding School in the 1860's," *American Studies in Scandinavia* 18 (1986): 67–82; Lomawaima, *They Called It Prairie Light*, 94–99, 115–26, chap. 6; Sally J. McBeth, *Ethnic Identity and the Boarding School Experience of West-Central Oklahoma American Indians* (Washington, D.C.: University Press of America, 1983), esp. 127–34; and Alice Littlefield, "The B.I.A. Boarding School: Theories of Resistance and Social Reproduction," *Humanity and Society* 13 (1989): 428–41.
74. ARCIA, 1882, 152; ARCIA, 1890, 307; ARCIA, 1897, 164; and ARCIA, 1900, 220. Also see ARCIA, 1881, 188; ARCIA, 1884, 100; ARCIA, 1895, 278; ARCIA, 1899, 168, 202; and ARCIA, 1906, 237.
75. ARCIA, 1886, 318; and ARCIA, 1887, 226–27.
76. ARCIA, 1886, 417.
77. Mitchell, *Navajo Blessingway Singer*, 57.
78. Edward Dozier, "Forced and Permissive Acculturation," *The American Indian* 7 (Spring 1955): 38.
79. On the role of factionalism see Richard P. Metcalf, "Who Should Rule at Home? Native American Politics and Indian-White Relations," *Journal of American History* 61 (December 1974): 651–65; and Robert B. Berkhofer, Jr., *Salvation and the Savage: An Analysis of Protestant Missions and American Indian Response 1787–1862* (New York: Atheneum, 1972), chap. 7.
80. Hamlin Garland, "The Red Man's Present Needs," *North American Review* 174 (April 1902): 479.
81. Quoted, LMC, 1901, 76.
82. See for example ARCIA, 1882, 223–24; Alford, *Civilization*, 90; ARCIA, 1879, 124; ARCIA, 1887, 321; ARCIA, 1888, 253; and LMC, 1893, 1025.
83. For an account of Spotted Tail's visit to Carlisle see George E. Hyde, *A Sioux Chronicle* (Norman: University of Oklahoma Press, 1956), 51–57; and Pratt, *Battlefield and Classroom*, 236–40.
84. Inspection Report no. 9020 (Navajo), 23 December 1892, OSI.
85. Ibid. For a fuller firsthand account of Navajo opposition to the school at Fort Defiance see Council of the Chief Men of the Navajo Tribe, 25 November 1892, encl., David L. Shipley to Commissioner of Indian Affairs, 13 December 1892, LR, no. 45001, OIA; and Open Council of the Chiefs and Head Men of the Navajo Tribe, 25 November 1892, encl., Commissioner of

Indian Affairs to Secretary of the Interior, 6 December 1892, LR, no. 43345, OSI.

86. ARCIA, 1901, 382.

87. ARCIA, 1890, 35; ARCIA, 1884, 89; ARCIA, 1891, 214–15; ARCIA, 1883, 195–96; and ARCIA, 1889, 259.

88. Quoted in Robert H. Ruby and John A. Brown, *The Spokane Indians: Children of the Sun* (Norman: University of Oklahoma Press, 1970), 216–18.

89. ARCIA, 1883, 195–96; and ARCIA, 1884, 89.

90. Proceedings of Council Held at Navajo School, 20 April 1891, LR, no. 15559, OIA.

3

Interpreting the African Heritage in Afro-American Family Organization

Niara Sudarkasa

Introduction

Whereas it is generally agreed that the history of the family in Europe is pertinent to an understanding of European-derived family organization in America (and throughout the world), many—if not most—scholars working on Black American families have argued or assumed that the African family heritage was all but obliterated by the institution of slavery. This view has retained credence, despite the accumulation of evidence to the contrary, in large measure because E. Franklin Frazier (1939 [1966]), the most prestigious and prolific student of the Black American family, all but discounted the relevance of Africa in his analyses.

This chapter takes its departure from W.E.B. DuBois (1908[1969]), Carter G. Woodson (1936), and M.J. Herskovits (1941 [1958]), all of whom looked to Africa as well as to the legacy of slavery for explanations of Afro-American social institutions. Herskovits is the best-known advocate of the concept of African survivals in Afro-American family life, but DuBois was the first scholar to stress the need to study the Black American family against the background of its African origins. In his 1908 study of the Black family, DuBois prefaced his discussions of marriage, household structure, and economic organization with observations concerning the African antecedents of the patterns developed in America.

> In each case an attempt has been made to connect present conditions with the African past. This is not because Negro-Americans are Africans, or can trace an unbroken social history from Africa, but because there is a distinct nexus between Africa and America which, though broken and perverted, is nevertheless not to be neglected by the careful student. [DuBois, 1969: 9]

Having documented the persistence of African family patterns in the Caribbean, and of African-derived wedding ceremonies in Alabama, DuBois noted:

> Careful research would doubtless reveal many other traces of the African family in America. They would, however, be traces only, for

the effectiveness of the slave system meant the practically complete crushing out of the African clan and family life. [p. 21]

With the evidence that has accumulated since DuBois wrote, it is possible to argue that even though the constraints of slavery did prohibit the replication of African lineage ("clan") and family life in America, the principles on which these kin groups were based, and the values underlying them, led to the emergence of variants of African family life in the form of the extended families which developed among the enslaved Blacks in America. Evidence of the Africanity to which DuBois alluded is to be found not only in the relatively few "traces" of direct *institutional transfer* from Africa to America, but also in the numerous examples of *institutional transformation* from Africa to America.

No discussion of the relevance of Africa for understanding Afro-American family organization can proceed without confronting the issue of the "diversity" of the backgrounds of "African slaves" (read "enslaved Africans") brought to America. Obviously, for certain purposes, each African community or each ethnic group can be described in terms of the linguistic, cultural, and/or social structural features which distinguish it from others. At the same time, however, these communities or ethnic groups can be analyzed from the point of view of their similarity to other groups.

It has long been established that the Africans enslaved in the United States and the rest of the Americas came from the Western part of the continent where there had been a long history of culture contact and widespread similarities in certain institutions (Herskovits, 1958: chs. 2 and 3). For example, some features of kinship organization were almost universal. Lineages, large co-resident domestic groups, and polygynous marriages are among the recurrent features found in groups speaking different languages, organized into states as well as "segmentary" societies, and living along the coast as well as in the interior (Radcliffe-Brown, 1950; Fortes, 1953; Onwuejeogwu, 1975).

When the concept of "African family structure" is used here, it refers to those organizational principles and patterns which are common to the different ethnic groups whose members were enslaved in America. These features of family organization are known to have existed for centuries on the African continent and are, therefore, legitimately termed a part of the African heritage.

African Family Structure: Understanding The Dynamics of Consanguinity and Conjugality

African families, like those in other parts of the world, embody two contrasting bases for membership: *consanguinity*, which refers to kinship that is commonly assumed or presumed to be biologically based and rooted in "blood ties," and *affinity*, which refers to kinship created by law and rooted "in-law." *Conjugality* refers specifically to the affinal kinship created between spouses (Marshall, 1968). Generally, all kinship entails a dynamic tension between the operation of the contrasting principles of consanguinity and affinity. The comparative study of family organization led Ralph Linton (1936: 159–163) to observe that in different societies families tend to be built either around a conjugal core or around a consanguineal core. In either case, the other principle is subordinate.

According to current historical research on the family in Europe, the principle of conjugality appears to have dominated family organization in the Western part of that continent (including Britain) at least since the Middle Ages, when a number of economic and political factors led to the predominance of nuclear and/or stem families built around married couples. Certainly for the past three or four hundred years, the conjugally based family has been the ideal and the norm in Western Europe (Shorter, 1975; Stone, 1975; Tilly and Scott, 1978). Whether or not the European conjugal family was a structural isolate is not the issue here. The point is that European families, whether nuclear or extended (as in the case of stem families), tended to emphasize the conjugal relationship in matters of household formation, decision making, property transmission, and socialization of the young (Goody, 1976).

African families, on the other hand, have traditionally been organized around consanguineal cores formed by adult siblings of the same sex or by larger same-sex segments of patri- or matrilineages. The groups which formed around these consanguineally related core members included their spouses and children, and perhaps some of their divorced siblings of the opposite sex. This co-resident *extended family* occupied a group of adjoining or contiguous dwellings known as a compound. Upon marriage, Africans did not normally form new isolated households, but joined a compound in which the extended family of the groom, or that of the bride, was already domiciled (Sudarkasa, 1980: 38–49).

African extended families could be subdivided in two ways. From one perspective, there was the division between the nucleus formed by the consanguineal core group and their children and the "outer group" formed by the in-marrying spouses. In many African languages, in-marrying spouses are collectively referred to as "wives" or "husbands" by both females and males of the core group. Thus, for example, in any compound in a patrilineal society, the in-marrying women may be known as the "wives of the house." They are, of course, also the mothers of the children of the compound. Their collective designation as "wives of the house" stresses the fact that their membership in the compound is rooted in law and can be terminated by law, whereas that of the core group is rooted in descent and is presumed to exist in perpetuity.

African extended families may also be divided into their constituent conjugally based family units comprised of parents and children. In the traditional African family, these conjugal units did not have the characteristics of the typical "nuclear family" of the West. In the first place, African conjugal families normally involved polygynous marriages at some stage in their developmental cycle. A number of Western scholars have chosen to characterize the polygynous conjugal family as several distinct nuclear families with one husband/father in common (Rivers, 1924: 12; Murdock, 1949: 2; Colson, 1962). In the African conception, however, whether a man had one wife and children or many wives and children, his was *one* family. In the case of polygynous families, both the husband and the senior co-wife played important roles in integrating the entire group (Fortes, 1949: chs. III and IV; Sudarkasa, 1973: ch. V; Ware, 1979). The very existence of the extended family as an "umbrella" group for the conjugal family meant that the latter group differed from the Western nuclear family. Since, for many purposes and on many occasions, *all* the children of the same generation within the compound regarded themselves as brothers and sisters (rather than dividing into siblings versus "cousins"), and since the adults assumed certain responsibilities toward their "nephews" and "nieces" (whom they term sons and daughters) as well as toward their own offspring, African conjugal families did not have the rigid boundaries characteristic of nuclear families of the West.

The most far-reaching difference between African and European families stems from their differential emphasis on consanguinity and conjugality. This difference becomes clear when one considers extended family organization in the two contexts. The most common type of European extended family consisted of two or more nuclear families joined through the parent-child or sibling tie. It was this model of the stem family and the joint family that was put forth by George P. Murdock (1949: 23, 33, 39–40) as the generic form of the extended family. However, the African data show that on that continent, extended families were built around consanguineal cores and the conjugal components of these larger families differed significantly from the nuclear families of the West.

In Africa, unlike Europe, in many critical areas of family life the consanguineal core group rather than the conjugal pair was paramount. With respect to household formation, I have already indicated that married couples joined existing compounds. It was the lineage core that owned (or had the right of usufruct over) the land and the compound where families lived, farmed, and/or practiced their crafts. The most important properties in African societies—land, titles, and entitlements—were transmitted through the lineages, and spouses did not inherit from each other (Goody, 1976).

Within the extended family residing in a single compound, decision making centered in the consanguineal core group. The oldest male in the compound was usually its head, and all the men in his generation constituted the elders of the group. Together they were ultimately responsible for settling internal disputes, including those that could not be settled within the separate conjugal families or, in some cases, by the female elders among the wives (Sudarkasa, 1973, 1976). They also made decisions, such as those involving the allocation of land and other resources, which affected the functioning of the constituent conjugal families.

Given the presence of multiple spouses within the conjugal families, it is not surprising that decision making within them also differed from the model associated with nuclear family organization. Separate rather than joint decision making was common. In fact, husbands and wives normally had distinct purviews and responsibilities within the *conjugal* family (Sudarkasa, 1973; Oppong, 1974). Excepting those areas where Islamic traditions overshadowed indigenous African traditions, women had a good deal of control over the fruits of their own labor. Even though husbands typically had ultimate authority over wives, this authority did not extend to control over their wives' properties (Oppong, 1974; Robertson, 1976; Sudarkasa, 1976). Moreover, even though women were subordinate in their roles as wives, as mothers and sisters they wielded considerable authority, power, and influence. This distinction in the power attached to women's roles is symbolized by the fact that in the same society where wives knelt before their husbands, sons prostrated before their mothers and seniority as determined by age, rather than gender, governed relationships among siblings (Sudarkasa, 1973, 1976).

Socialization of the young involved the entire extended family, not just the separate conjugal families, even though each conjugal family had special responsibility for the children (theirs or their relatives') living with them. It is important to note that the concept of "living with" a conjugal family took on a different meaning in the context of the African compound. In the first place, husbands, wives, and children did not live in a bounded space, apart from other such units. Wives had their own rooms or small dwellings, and husbands had theirs. These were not necessarily adjacent to one another. (In some matrilineal societies, husbands and wives resided in separate compounds). Children ordinarily slept in their mothers' rooms until they were of a certain age, after which they customarily slept in communal rooms allocated to boys or girls. Children usually ate their meals with their mothers but they might also eat some of these meals with their fathers' co-wives (assuming that no hostility existed between the women concerned) or with their grandmothers. Children of the same compound played together and shared many learning experiences. They were socialized by all the adults to identify themselves collectively as sons and daughters of a particular lineage and compound, which entailed a kinship, based on descent, with all the lineage ancestors and with generations unborn (Radcliffe-Brown and Forde, 1950; Uchendu, 1965; Sudarkasa, 1980).

The stability of the African extended family did not depend on the stability of the marriage(s) of the individual core group members. Although traditional African marriages (particularly those in patrilineal societies) were more stable than those of most contemporary societies, marital dissolution did not have the ramifications it has in nuclear family systems. When divorces did occur, they were usually followed by remarriage. Normally, all adults other than those who held certain ceremonial offices or who were severely mentally or physically handicapped lived in a marital union (though not necessarily the same one) throughout their lives (for example, Lloyd, 1968). The children of a divorced couple were usually brought up in their natal compound (or by members of their lineage residing elsewhere), even though the in-marrying parent had left that compound.

Several scholars have remarked on the relative ease of divorce in some traditional African societies, particularly those in which matrilin-eal descent was the rule (for example, Fortes, 1950: 283). Jack Goody (1976: 64) has even suggested that the rate of divorce in precolonial Africa was higher than in parts of Europe and Asia in comparable peri-ods as a corollary of contrasting patterns of property transmission, con-trasting attitudes toward the remarriage of women (especially widows), and contrasting implications of polygyny and monogamy. If indeed there was a higher incidence of divorce in precolonial Africa, this would not be inconsistent with the wide-ranging emphasis on consan-guinity in Africa as opposed to conjugality in Europe.

Marriage in Africa was a contractual union which often involved long-lasting companionate relationships, but it was not expected to be the all-encompassing, exclusive relationship of the Euro-American ideal type. Both men and women relied on their extended families and friends, as well as on their spouses, for emotionally gratifying relation-ships. Often, too, in the context of polygyny women as well as men had sexual liaisons with more than one partner. A woman's clandestine affairs did not necessarily lead to divorce because, in the absence of publicized information to the contrary, her husband was considered the father of all her children (Radcliffe-Brown, 1950). And in the context of the lineage (especially the patrilineage), all men aspired to have as many children as possible.

Interpersonal relationships within African families were governed by principles and values which I have elsewhere summarized under the concepts of respect, restraint, responsibility, and reciprocity. Common to all these principles was a notion of commitment to the collectivity. The family offered a network of security, but it also imposed a burden of obligations (Sudarkasa, 1980: 49–50). From the foregoing discussion, it should be understandable that, in their material form, these obliga-tions extended first and foremost to consanguineal kin. Excepting the gifts that were exchanged at the time of marriage, the material obliga-tions entailed in the conjugal relationship and the wider affinal rela-tionships created by marriage were of a lesser magnitude than those associated with "blood" ties.

Afro-American Family Structure: Interpreting the African Connection

Rather than start with the question of what was *African* about the fam-ilies established by those Africans who were enslaved in America, it would be more appropriate to ask what was *not* African about them. Most of the Africans who were captured and brought to America arrived without any members of their families, but they brought with them the societal codes they had learned regarding family life. To argue that the trans-Atlantic voyage and the trauma of enslavement made them forget, or rendered useless their memories of how they had been brought up or how they had lived before their capture, is to argue from premises laden with myths about the Black experience (Elkins, 1963: 101–102; see also Frazier, 1966: ch. 1).

Given the African tradition of multilingualism and the widespread use of lingua francas (Maquet, 1972: 18–25)—which in West Africa would include Hausa, Yoruba, Djoula, and Twi—it is probable that many more of the enslaved Africans could communicate among themselves than is implied by those who remark on the multiplicity of "tribes" represented among the slaves. As Landman (1978: 80) has pointed out:

> In many areas of the world, individuals are expected to learn only one language in the ordinary course of their lives. But many Africans have been enculturated in social systems where multiple language of dialect acquisition have been regarded as normal.

The fact that Africans typically spoke three to five languages also makes it understandable why they quickly adopted "pidginized" forms of European languages as lingua francas for communicating among themselves and with their captors.

The relationships which the Blacks in America established among themselves would have reflected their own backgrounds *and* the conditions in which they found themselves. It is as erroneous to try to attribute what developed among them solely to slavery as it is to attribute it solely to the African background. Writers such as Herbert Gutman (1976), who emphasize the "adaptive" nature of "slave culture" must ask what it was that was being adapted as well as in what context this adaptation took place. Moreover, they must realize that adaptation does not necessarily imply extensive modification of an institution, especially when its structure is already suited (or "preadapted") to survival in the new context. Such an institution was the African extended family, which had served on that continent, in various environments and different political contexts, as a unit of production and distribution; of socialization, education, and social control; and of emotional and material support for the aged and the infirm as well as the hale and hearty (Kerri, 1979; Okediji, 1975; Shimkin and Uchendu, 1978; Sudarkasa, 1975b).

The extended family networks that were formed during slavery by Africans *and their descendants* were based on the institutional heritage which the Africans had brought with them to this continent, and the specific forms they took reflected the influence of European-derived institutions as well as the political and economic circumstances in which the enslaved population found itself.

The picture of Black families during slavery has become clearer over the past decade, particularly as a result of the wealth of data in Gutman's justly heralded study. Individual households were normally comprised of a conjugal pair, their children, and sometimes their grandchildren, other relatives, or nonkin. Marriage was usually monogamous, but polygynous unions where the wives lived in separate households have also been reported (Gutman, 1976: 59, 158; Blassingame, 1979: 171; Perdue et al., 1980: 209).

Probably only in a few localities did female-headed households constitute as much as one-quarter of all households (Gutman, 1976: esp. chs. 1–3). The rarity of this household type was in keeping with the African tradition whereby women normally bore children within the context of marriage and lived in monogamous or polygynous conjugal families that were part of larger extended families. I have tried to show elsewhere why it is inappropriate to apply the term "nuclear family" to the mother-child dyads within African polygynous families (Sudarkasa, 1980: 43–46). In some African societies—especially in matrilineal ones—a small percentage of previously married women, or married women living apart from their husbands, might head households that were usually attached to larger compounds. However, in my view, on the question of the origin of female-headed households among Blacks in America, Herskovits was wrong, and Frazier was right in attributing this development to conditions that arose during slavery and in the context of urbanization in later periods (Frazier, 1966; Herskovits, 1958; Furstenberg et al., 1975).

Gutman's data suggest that enslaved women who had their first children out of wedlock did not normally set up independent households, but rather continued to live with their parents. Most of them subsequently married and set up neolocal residence with their husbands. The data also suggest that female-headed households developed mainly in two situations: (1) A woman whose husband died or was sold off the plantation might head a household comprised of her children and perhaps her grandchildren born to an unmarried daughter; (2) a woman who did not marry after having one or two children out of wedlock but continued to have children (no doubt often for the "master") might have her own cabin built for her (Gutman, 1976: chs. 1–3).

It is very important to distinguish these two types of female-headed households, the first being only a phase in the developmental cycle of a conjugally headed household, and the second being a case of neolocal residence by an unmarried female. The pattern of households headed by widows was definitely not typical of family structure in Africa, where normally a widow married another member of her deceased husband's lineage. The pattern of neolocal residence by an unmarried woman with children would have been virtually unheard of in Africa. Indeed, it was also relatively rare among enslaved Blacks and in Black communities in later periods. Before the twentieth-century policy of public assistance for unwed mothers, virtually all young unmarried mothers in Black communities continued to live in households headed by other adults. If in later years they did establish their own households, these tended to be tied into transresidential family networks.

The existence during slavery of long-lasting conjugal unions among Blacks was not a departure from African family tradition. Even with the relative ease of divorce in matrilineal societies, most Africans lived in marital unions that ended only with the death of one of the spouses. In the patrilineal societies from which most American Blacks were taken, a number of factors, including the custom of returning bridewealth payments upon the dissolution of marriage, served to encourage marital stability (Radcliffe-Brown, 1950: 43–54). Given that the conditions of slavery did not permit the *replication* of African families, it might be expected that the husband and wife as elders in the household would assume even greater importance than they had in Africa, where the elders within the consanguineal core of the extended family and those among the wives would have had major leadership roles within the compound.

When the distinction is made between family and household—and, following Bender (1967), between the composition of the co-resident group and the domestic functions associated with both households and families—it becomes apparent that the question of who lived with whom during slavery (or later) must be subordinate to the questions of who was doing what for whom and what kin relationships were maintained over space and time. In any case, decisions concerning residence per se were not always in the hands of the enslaved Blacks themselves, and space alone served as a constraint on the size, and consequently to some extent on the composition, of the "slave" cabins.

That each conjugally based household formed a primary unit for food consumption and production among the enslaved Blacks is consistent with domestic organization within the African compound. However, Gutman's data, and those reported by enslaved Blacks themselves, on the strong bonds of obligation among kinsmen suggest that even within the constraints imposed by the slave regime, transresidential cooperation—including that between households in different localities—was the rule rather than the exception (Gutman, 1976: esp. 131–138; Perdue et al., 1980: esp. 26, 256, 323). One might hypothesize that on the larger plantations with a number of Black families related through consanguineal and affinal ties, the households of these families might have formed groupings similar to African compounds. Certainly we know that in later times such groupings were found in the South Carolina Sea Islands and other parts of the South (Agbasegbe, 1976, 1981; Gutman, 1976; Johnson, 1934: ch. 2; Powdermaker, 1939: ch. 8).

By focusing on extended families (rather than simply on households) among the enslaved Blacks, it becomes apparent that these kin networks had many of the features of continental African extended families. These Afro-American groupings were built around consanguineal kin whose spouses were related to or incorporated into the networks in different degrees. The significance of the consanguineal principle in these networks is indicated by Gutman's statement that "the pull between ties to an immediate family and to an enlarged kin network sometimes strained husbands and wives" (1976: 202; see also Frazier, 1966: pt. 2).

The literature on Black families during slavery provides a wealth of data on the way in which consanguineal kin assisted each other with child rearing, in life crisis events such as birth and death, in work groups, in efforts to obtain freedom, and so on. They maintained their networks against formidable odds and, after slavery, sought out those parents, siblings, aunts, and uncles from whom they had been torn (Blassingame, 1979; Genovese, 1974; Gutman, 1976; Owens, 1976). Relationships within these groups were governed by principles and values stemming from the African background. Respect for elders and reciprocity among kinsmen are noted in all discussions of Black families during slavery. The willingness to assume responsibility for relatives beyond the conjugal family and selflessness (a form of restraint) in the face of these responsibilities are also characteristics attributed to the enslaved population.

As would be expected, early Afro-American extended families differed from their African prototypes in ways that reflected the influence of slavery and of Euro-American values, especially their proscriptions and prescriptions regarding mating, marriage, and the family. No doubt, too, the Euro-American emphasis on the primacy of marriage within the family reinforced conjugality among the Afro-Americans even though the "legal" marriage of enslaved Blacks was prohibited. As DuBois noted at the turn of the century, African corporate lineages could not survive intact during slavery. Hence, the consanguineal core groups of Afro-American extended families differed in some ways from those of their African antecedents. It appears that in some of these Afro-American families membership in the core group was traced bilaterally, whereas in others there was a unilineal emphasis without full-fledged lineages.

Interestingly, after slavery, some of the corporate functions of African lineages reemerged in some extended families which became property-owning collectivities. I have suggested elsewhere that "the disappearance of the lineage principle or its absorption into the concept of extended family" is one of the aspects of the transformation of African family organization in America that requires research (Sudarkasa, 1980: 57). Among the various other issues that remain to be studied concerning these extended families are these: (1) Did members belong by virtue of bilateral or unilineal descent from a common ancestor or because of shared kinship with a living person? (2) How were group boundaries established and maintained? (3) What was the nature and extent of the authority of the elder(s)? (4) How long did the group last and what factors determined its span in time and space?

CONCLUSION

Obviously, Black families have changed over time, and today one would expect that the evidence for African "retentions" (Herskovits, 1958: xxii–xxiii) in them would be more controvertible than in the past. Nevertheless, the persistence of some features of African family organization among contemporary Black American families has been documented for both rural and urban areas. Although this study cannot attempt a full-scale analysis of these features and the changes they have undergone, it is important to make reference to one of them, precisely because it impacts upon so many other aspects of Black family organization, and because its connection to Africa has not been acknowledged by most contemporary scholars. I refer to the emphasis on consanguinity noted especially among lower-income Black families and those in the rural South in discussions of "matrifocality" and "female-headed households." Too often, the origin of this consanguineal emphasis in Black families, which can be manifest even in households with both husband and wife present, is left unexplained or is "explained" by labelling it an "adaptive" characteristic.

In my view, historical realities require that the derivation of this aspect of Black family organization be traced to its African antecedents. Such a view does not deny the adaptive significance of consanguineal networks. In fact, it helps to clarify why these networks had the flexibility they had and why they, rather than conjugal relationships, came to be the stabilizing factor in Black families.

Some writers have viewed the consanguineally based extended family as a factor of *instability* in the Black family because it sometimes undermines the conjugal relationships in which its members are involved. I would suggest that among Black Americans the concept of "family" historically meant first and foremost relationships created by "blood" rather than by marriage. (R. T. Smith [1973] has made substantially the same point with respect to West Indian family organization.) Children were socialized to think in terms of obligations to parents (especially mothers), siblings, and others defined as "close kin." Obligations to "outsiders," who would include prospective spouses and in-laws, were definitely less compelling. Once a marriage took place, if the demands of the conjugal relationship came into irreconcilable conflict with consanguineal commitments, the former would often be sacrificed. Instead of interpreting instances of *marital* instability as prima facie evidence of family instability, it should be realized that the fragility of the conjugal relationship could be a consequence or corollary of the *stability* of the consanguineal family network. Historically, such groups survived by nurturing a strong sense of responsibility among members and by fostering a code of reciprocity which could strain relations with persons not bound by it.

Not all Black families exhibit the same emphasis on consanguineal relationships. Various factors, including education, occupational demands, aspirations toward upward mobility, and acceptance of American ideals concerning marriage and the family, have moved some (mainly middle- and upper-class) Black families toward conjugally focused households and conjugally centered extended family groupings. Even when such households include relatives other than the nuclear family, those relatives tend to be subordinated to the conjugal pair who form the core of the group. This contrasts with some older types of Black families where a senior relative (especially the wife's or the husband's mother) could have a position of authority in the household equal to or greater than that of one or both of the spouses. Children in many contemporary Black homes are not socialized to think in terms of the parent-sibling group as the primary kin group, but rather in terms of their future spouses and families of procreation as the main source of their future emotional and material satisfaction and support. Among these Blacks, the nuclear household tends to be more isolated in terms of instrumental functions, and such extended family networks as exist tend to be clusters of nuclear families conforming to the model put forth by Murdock (1949: chs. 1 and 2).

For scholars interested in the heritage of Europe as well as the heritage of Africa in Afro-American family organization, a study of the operation of the principles of conjugality and consanguinity in these families would provide considerable insight into the ways in which these two institutional traditions have been interwoven. By looking at the differential impact of these principles in matters of household formation, delegation of authority, maintenance of solidarity and support, acquisition and transmission of property, financial management, and so on (Sudarkasa, 1981), and by examining the political and economic variables which favor the predominance of one or the other principle, we will emerge with questions and formulations that can move us beyond debates over "pathology" and "normalcy" in Black family life.

References

Agbasegbe, B. (1976) "The role of wife in the Black extended family: perspectives from a rural community in Southern United States," pp. 124–138 in D. McGuigan (ed.) *New Research on Women and Sex Roles*. Ann Arbor: Center for Continuing Education of Women, University of Michigan.

———(1981) "Some aspects of contemporary rural Afroamerican family life in the Sea Islands of Southeastern United States." Presented at the Annual Meeting of the Association of Social and Behavioral Scientists, Atlanta, Georgia, March 1981.

Allen, W. R. (1978) "The search for applicable theories of Black family life." *Journal of Marriage and the Family* 40 (February): 117–129.

———(1979) "Class, culture, and family organization: the effects of class and race on family structure in urban America." *Journal of Comparative Family Studies* 10 (Autumn): 301–313.

Aschenbrenner, J. (1973) "Extended families among Black Americans." *Journal of Comparative Family Studies* 4: 257–268.

————(1975) *Lifelines: Black Families in Chicago.* New York: Holt, Rinehart & Winston.

————(1978) "Continuities and variations in Black family structure," pp. 181–200 in D. B. Shimkin, E. M. Shimkin, and D. A. Frate (eds.) *The Extended Family in Black Societies.* The Hague: Mouton.

————and C. H. CARR (1980) "Conjugal relationships in the context of the Black extended family." *Alternative Lifestyles* 3 (November): 463–484.

Bender, D. R. (1967) "A refinement of the concept of household: families, co-residence, and domestic functions." *American Anthropologist* 69 (October): 493–504.

Billingsley, A. (1968) *Black Families in White America.* Englewood Cliffs, NJ: Prentice-Hall.

Blassingame, J. W. (1979) *The Slave Community.* New York: Oxford University Press.

Colson, E. (1962) "Family change in contemporary Africa." *Annals of the New York Academy of Sciences* 96 (January): 641–652.

DuBois, W. E. B. (1969) *The Negro American Family.* New York: New American Library. (Originally published, 1908).

Elkins, S. (1963) *Slavery: A Problem in American Intellectual Life.* New York: Grosset and Dunlap. (Originally published, 1959).

English, R. (1974) "Beyond pathology: research and theoretical perspectives on Black families," pp. 39–52 in L. E. Gary (ed.) *Social Research and the Black Community: Selected Issues and Priorities.* Washington, D.C.: Institute for Urban Affairs and Research, Howard University.

Fortes, M. (1949) *The Web of Kinship among the Tallensi.* London: Oxford University Press.

————(1950) "Kinship and marriage among the Ashanti," pp. 252–284 in A. R. Radcliffe-Brown and D. Forde (eds.) *African Systems of Kinship and Marriage.* London: Oxford University Press.

————(1953) "The structure of unilineal descent groups." *American Anthropologist* 55 (January-March): 17–41.

Frazier, E. (1966) *The Negro Family in the United States.* Chicago: University of Chicago Press. (Originally published, 1939).

Furstenberg, F., T. Hershberg, and J. Modell (1975) "The origins of the female-headed Black family: the impact of the urban experience." *Journal of Interdisciplinary History* 6 (Autumn): 211–233.

Genovese, E. D. (1974) *Roll Jordan Roll: The World the Slaves Made.* New York: Random House.

Goody, J. (1976) *Production and Reproduction: A Comparative Study of the Domestic Domain.* Cambridge: Cambridge University Press.

Gutman, H. (1976) *The Black Family in Slavery and Freedom: 1750–1925.* New York: Random House.

Herskovitz, M. J. (1958) *The Myth of the Negro Past.* Boston: Beacon. (Originally published 1941).

Johnson, C. S. (1934) *Shadow of the Plantation.* Chicago: University of Chicago Press.

Kerri, J. N. (1979) "Understanding the African family: persistence, continuity, and change." *Western Journal of Black Studies* 3 (Spring): 14–17.

Landman, R. H. (1978) "Language policies and their implications for ethnic relations in the newly sovereign states of Sub-Saharan Africa," pp. 69–90 in B. M. duToit (ed.) *Ethnicity in Modern Africa.* Boulder, Colo.: Westview Press.

Linton, R. (1936) *The Study of Man.* New York: Appleton-Century-Crofts.

Llyod, P. C. (1968) "Divorce among the Yoruba." *American Anthropologist* 70 (February): 67–81.

Maquet, J. (1972) *Civilizations of Black Africa.* London: Oxford University Press.

Marshall, G. A. [Niara Sudarkasa] (1968) "Marriage: comparative analysis," in *International Encyclopedia of the Social Sciences*, Vol. 10. New York: Macmillan/Free Press.

Murdock, G. P. (1949) *Social Structure.* New York: Macmillan.

Okediji, P. A. (1975) "A psychosocial analysis of the extended family: the African case." *African Urban Notes*, Series B, 1(3): 93–99. (African Studies Center, Michigan State University).

Onwuejeogwu, M. A. (1975) *The Social Anthropology of Africa: An Introduction.* London: Heinemann.

Oppong, C. (1974) *Marriage among a Matrilineal Elite: A Family Study of Ghanaian Senior Civil Servants.* Cambridge: Cambridge University Press.

Owens, L. H. (1976) *This Species of Property: Slave Life and Culture in the Old South.* New York: Oxford University Press.

Perdue, C. L., Jr., T. E. Barden, and R. K. Phillips [eds.] (1980) *Weevils in the Wheat: Interviews with Virginia Ex-Slaves.* Bloomington: Indiana University Press.

Powdermaker, H. (1939) *After Freedom: A Cultural Study in the Deep South.* New York: Viking.

Radcliffe-Brown, A. R. (1950) "Introduction," pp. 1–85 in A. R. Radcliffe-Brown and D. Forde (eds.) *African Systems of Kinship and Marriage.* London: Oxford University Press.

——and D. Forde [eds.] (1950) *African Systems of Kinship and Marriage.* London: Oxford University Press.

Rivers, W. H. R. (1924) *Social Organization.* New York: Alfred Knopf.

Robertson, C. (1976) "Ga women and socioeconomic change in Acera. Ghana." pp. 111–133 in N. J. Hafkin and E. G. Bay (eds.) *Women in Africa: Studies in Social and Economic Change.* Stanford: Stanford University Press.

Shimkin, D. and V. Uchendu (1978) "Persistence, borrowing, and adaptive changes in Black kinship systems: some issues and their significance," pp. 391–406 in D. Shimkin, E. M. Shimkin, and D. A. Frate (eds.) *The Extended Family in Black Societies.* The Hague: Mounton.

Shimkin, D., E. M. Shimkin, and D. A. Frate [eds.] (1978) *The Extended Family in Black Societies.* The Hague: Mouton.

Shorter, F. (1975) *The Making of the Modern Family.* New York: Basic Books.

Smith, R. T. (1973) "The matrifocal family," pp. 121–144 in J. Goody (ed.) *The Character of Kinship.* Cambridge: Cambridge University Press.

Stack, C. (1974) *All Our Kin.* New York: Harper & Row.

Stone, L. (1975) "The rise of the nuclear family in early modern England: the patriarchal stage," pp. 13–57 in C. E. Rosenberg (ed.) *The Family in History.* Philadelphia: University of Pennsylvania Press.

Sudarkasa, N. (1973) *Where Women Work: A Study of Yoruba Women in the Marketplace and in the Home.* Anthropological Papers No. 53. Ann Arbor: Museum of Anthropology, University of Michigan.

——(1975a) "An exposition on the value premises underlying Black family studies." *Journal of the National Medical Association* 19 (May): 235–239.

——(1975b) "National development planning for the promotion and protection of the family." *Proceedings of the Conference on Social Research and National Development*, E. Akeredolu-Ale, ed. The Nigerian Institute of Social and Economic Research, Ibadan, Nigeria.

———(1976) "Female employment and family organization in West Africa," pp. 48–63 in D. G. McGuigan (ed.) *New Research on Women and Sex Roles.* Ann Arbor: Center for Continuing Education of Women, University of Michigan.

———(1980) "African and Afro-American family structure: a comparison." *The Black Scholar* II (November-December): 37–60.

———(1981) "Understanding the dynamics of consanguinity and conjugality in contemporary Black family organization." Presented at the Seventh Annual Third World Conference, Chicago, March 1981.

Tilly, L. A. and J. W. Scott (1978) *Women, Work, and Family.* New York: Holt, Rinehart & Winston.

Uchendu, V. (1965) *The Igbo of South-Eastern Nigeria.* New York: Holt, Rinehart & Winston.

Ware, H. (1979) "Polygyny: women's views in a transitional society, Nigeria 1975." *Journal of Marriage and the Family* 41 (February): 185–195.

Woodson, C. G. (1936) *The African Background Outlined.* Washington, D.C.: Association for the Study of Negro Life and History.

4

Split Household, Small Producer, and Dual Wage Earner: An Analysis of Chinese-American Family Strategies

Evelyn Nakano Glenn

Most research on family patterns of black and other urban poor minorities points to the decisive impact of larger institutional structures. Particular attention has been paid to structures that lock certain classes of people into marginal employment and/or chronic unemployment (Drake and Cayton, 1962; C. Valentine, 1968). It has been argued that many characteristics of family organization—for example, reliance on female-based kinship networks—represent strategies for coping with the chronic poverty brought about by institutional racism (Stack, 1974; Valentine, 1978). Structural factors are considered sufficiently powerful to outweigh the influence of cultural tradition, especially in the case of blacks.[1]

Chinese Americans, despite their historical status as an economically exploited minority, have been treated in almost exactly opposite terms. Studies of the Chinese-American family have largely ignored social and economic conditions. They focus on purely cultural determinants, tracing characteristics of family life to Chinese values and traditions. The resulting portrayal of the Chinese-American family has been highly favorable; the family is depicted as stable and problem-free—low in rate of divorce (Huang, 1976), delinquency (Sollenberger, 1969), and welfare dependency (Light, 1972). These virtues are attributed to the family-centered values of Chinese society.

Given this positive assessment, the absence of challenge to the cultural approach is understandable. Still, the case of the Chinese cannot be disengaged from controversies involving other minority groups. The apparent fortitude of the Chinese has been cited as evidence supporting the view of black and Hispanic families as disorganized. Along with other "model" minorities, notably the Japanese and Cubans, the Chinese seem to have offered proof that some groups possess cultural resources that enable them to resist the demoralizing effects of poverty and discrimination. By implication, the difficulties experienced by blacks and Hispanics are due in some measure to the cultural weaknesses of these groups.

On the basis of an historical review and informant interviews,[2] this study argues that a purely cultural analysis does not adequately encompass the historical realities of Chinese-American family life. It argues, furthermore, that a fuller understanding of the Chinese-American family must begin with an examination of the changing constellation of economic, legal, and political constraints that have shaped the Chinese experience in America. When followed by an analysis of the strategies adopted to cope with these constraints, such an examination reveals the many institutionally created problems the Chinese have confronted in forming and maintaining family life, and the variety of strategies they have used to overcome limitations. By positing a more or less passive cultural determinism and a continuity of Chinese culture, the cultural approach used up to now by many writers tends to obscure not only the problems and struggles of Chinese-American families but also their heterogeneity over time.

CULTURAL VS. INSTITUTIONAL APPROACHES TO THE CHINESE-AMERICAN FAMILY

The cultural approach grows out of the dominant assimilative perspective in the race- and ethnic-relations field (Gordon, 1964; Park, 1950). This perspective focuses on the initial cultural and social differences among groups and attempts to trace the process of assimilation over time; much literature on Chinese Americans is framed in these terms (Hirata, 1976). The rather extreme emphasis on traditional *Chinese* culture, however, seems to require further explanation. The emphasis may be due in part to the prevailing conception of the Chinese as perpetual foreigners or "strangers" (Wolfe, 1950). The image of the Chinese as strange, exotic and different seems to have preceded their actual arrival in the United States (Miller, 1969). Since arriving, their marginal position in the larger society, combined with racist ideology, has served to perpetuate and popularize the image. First, laws excluding the Chinese from citizenship and preventing them from bringing over spouses and children ensured that for over 130 years a large proportion of the Chinese-American population consisted of non–English-speaking alien residents. Second, discriminatory laws and practices forced the Chinese to congregate in ethnic ghettos and to concentrate in a narrow range of enterprises such as laundries, restaurants, and tourist-oriented businesses (Light and Wong, 1975) that simultaneously reinforced and exploited their foreignness. Moreover, because of distinctive racial features, Americans of Chinese ancestry have been lumped together in the public mind with Chinese foreign nationals and recent immigrants, so that third-, fourth- or even fifth-generation Americans are assumed to be culturally as well as racially Asian. It is not surprising, therefore, to find that until recently studies of Chinese Americans interpreted social and community organizational patterns as products of Chinese culture rather than as responses to economic and social conditions in the United States (Lyman, 1974, is an exception; see also Hirata, 1976; and

Kwong, 1979 for related critiques).

Studies of family life follow in this same mold. Authors typically begin by examining traditional Chinese family patterns, then attempt to show how these patterns are expressed in a new setting and undergo gradual change through acculturation (e.g., Hsu, 1971; Haynor and Reynolds, 1937; Kung, 1962; Sung, 1971; Weiss, 1974). The features identified as typical of Chinese-American families and as evidence of cultural continuity are (a) stable family units as indicated by low rates of divorce and illegitimacy; (b) close ties between generations, as shown by the absence of adolescent rebellion and juvenile delinquency; (c) economic self-sufficiency, demonstrated by avoidance of welfare dependency; and (d) conservatism, expressed by retention of Chinese language and customs in the home.

Each of these characteristics is interpreted in terms of specific aspects of Chinese culture. For example, the primacy of the family unit over the individual in Chinese society is credited for the rarity of divorce. Similarly, the principles of Confucianism (filial piety, respect for elders, and reverence for tradition) are cited as the philosophical bases for close control over children by parents and retention of Chinese language and customs in the home; and the family-based production system in the Chinese agricultural village is seen as the precedent for immigrants' involvement in family enterprise and economic self-sufficiency.

An institutional approach starts at a different point, looking not at Chinese society but at conditions in the United States. More specifically, it focuses on the legal and political restrictions imposed on the Chinese, particularly with respect to immigration, citizenship, residential mobility, and economic activity. The Chinese were the first group excluded on racial grounds from legally immigrating, starting in 1882 and continuing until the mid-1950s. When they were allowed entry, it was under severe restrictions which made it difficult for them to form and maintain families in the United States. They also were denied the right to become naturalized citizens, a right withheld until 1943. This meant that for most of their 130-year history in the United States, the Chinese were categorically excluded from political participation and entrance into occupations and professions requiring citizenship for licensing (see Konvitz, 1946). In addition, during the latter part of the nineteenth century and through the early twentieth, California and other western states in which the Chinese were concentrated imposed head taxes and prohibited Chinese from carrying on certain types of businesses. The Chinese were routinely denied most civil rights, including the right to testify in court, so they had no legal recourse against injury or exploitation (Wu, 1972; Jacobs and Landau, 1971). Having initially worked in railroad building, agriculture, and mining, the Chinese were driven out of smaller towns, rural areas, and mining camps during the late nineteenth century and were forced to congregate in urban ghettos (Lyman, 1977). The effect of these various restrictions was to keep the Chinese in the status of alien guests or commuters going back and forth between China and America. In addition, the restrictions led to a population made up disproportionately of male adults, concentrated in Chinatowns, and limited to a few occupations and industries.

These circumstances provide an alternative explanation for some of the features previously described as originating in Chinese culture: (a) low divorce rates result when spouses are forced to stay together by the lack of economic options outside of family enterprises; (b) low delinquency rates may reflect the demographic composition of the population which, up to the mid-1950s, contained few adolescents who, therefore, could be more effectively controlled by community sanctions; (c) avoidance of welfare is necessitated by the illegal status of many immigrants and the lack of access to sources outside the community; (d) retention of Chinese language and custom is a logical outcome of ghetto life and denial of permanent membership in American society.

Being able to generate plausible explanations does not itself constitute support for one approach over the other. However, in addition to offering alternative interpretations, the two approaches lead to quite different expectations regarding the degree of types of changes which the Chinese-American family has undergone over time. By tracing family patterns to a specific cultural system, the *cultural approach* implies a continuity in family organization over time, with change occurring gradually and linearly via acculturation. By connecting family patterns to contemporaneous institutional structures, the *institutional approach* implies that family organization could and probably would undergo dramatic change with alteration in external constraints. A related point is that the cultural approach suggests that Chinese-American family patterns are unique to this group, while the institutional approach suggests that other groups with differing cultural traditions might display similar patterns under parallel conditions.

The analysis that follows tests these expectations against the historical evidence by documenting the existence of qualitatively different family forms among Chinese Americans in different historical periods, with occasional reference to similar family forms among other groups in comparable circumstances. Three distinct family types are identified, corresponding to three periods demarcated by shifts in institutional constraints.

THE SPLIT-HOUSEHOLD FAMILY

For the first seventy years of Chinese presence in the United States, from 1850 to 1920, one can hardly speak of family life, since there were so few women or children (Lyman, 1968; Nee and Nee, 1974). As Table 1 shows, from the late nineteenth to the early twentieth century, the ratio of males to females ranged from 13:1 to 20:1. In 1900 less than 4% of the Chinese population consisted of children fourteen years and under, compared to 37.4% of the population of whites of native parentage (U.S. Census, 1902).

The first thirty-two years, from 1850 to 1882, was a period of open immigration, when over 300,000 Chinese left Guangdong Province to work in California and the West (Lyman, 1974). Most were able-bodied young men, recruited for labor on the railroads and in agriculture, mining and manufacturing. Although some men of the merchant class came and brought wives or concubines, the vast majority of immigrants were laborers who came alone, not intending to stay; over half left wives behind in China (Coolidge, 1909). Many were too impoverished to pay for passage and came on the credit ticket system, which obligated them to work for a fixed term, usually seven years, to pay for transport (Ling, 1912). These "birds of passage" labored to send remittances to relatives and to accumulate capital to enable them to acquire land in China. Two-thirds apparently succeeded in returning, as there were never more than 110,000 Chinese in the United States at any one time.

It is possible that, like other Asian immigrants, Chinese laborers eventually would have sent for wives, had open immigration continued. The passage of the Chinese Exclusion Act of 1882 precluded this possibility. The Act barred laborers and their relatives but exempted officials, students, tourists, merchants, and relatives of merchants and citizens. Renewals of the Act in 1892 and 1902 placed further restrictions on entry and return. Finally, the Immigration Act of 1924 cut off all immigration from Asia (Wu, 1972). These acts achieved their aim, which was to prevent the Chinese from settling in the United States. With almost no new immigration and the return of many sojourners to China, the Chinese population dwindled from a high of 107,000 in 1890 to 61,000 in 1920. Chinese men of the laboring class—faced with an unfavorable sex ratio, forbidden as non-citizens from bringing over wives, and prevented by laws in most western states from marrying whites—had three choices: (a) return permanently to China; (b) if single, stay in the United States as bachelors; or (c) if married, remain separated from families except for occasional visits.

Faced with these alternatives, the Chinese nevertheless managed to take advantage of openings in the law; if they had not, the Chinese population in the United States would have disappeared. One category for which entry was still allowed was relatives of citizens. Men born in the United States could return to China, marry, and father children, who were then eligible for entry. The 1906 earthquake and fire in San Francisco that destroyed most municipal records proved a boon for the large Chinese population of that area. Henceforth, residents could claim American birth without officials being able to disprove the contention (Sung, 1971). It became common practice for American-born Chinese (actual or claimed) to visit China, report the birth of a son, and thereby create an entry slot. Years later the slot could be used by a relative, or the papers could be sold to someone wanting to immigrate. The purchaser, called a "paper son," simply assumed the name and identity of the alleged son.

Table 1.
Chinese Population in the United States, by Sex, Sex Ratio, Percentage
Foreign Born, and Percentage Under Age 15, 1860–1970

Year	Total	Male	Female	Male/Female Ratio	% Foreign Born	% Aged 14 or Under
1860	34,933	33,149	1,784	18.58		
1870	63,199	58,633	4,566	12.84	99.8	
1880	105,465	100,686	4,779	21.06	99.0	
1890	107,475	103,607	3,868	26.79	99.3	
1900	89,863	85,341	4,522	18.87	90.7	3.4
1910	71,531	66,856	4,675	14.30	79.3	a
1920	61,639	53,891	7,748	6.96	69.9	12.0
1930	74,954	59,802	15,152	3.95	58.8	20.4
1940	77,504	57,389	20,115	2.85	48.1	21.2
1950	117,140	76,725	40,415	1.90	47.0	23.3
1960	236,084	135,430	100,654	1.35	39.5	33.0
1970	431,583	226,733	204,850	1.11	46.9	26.6

Source: U.S. Censuses for the years 1872, 1883, 1895, 1902, 1913, 1922, 1933, 1943, 1953, 1963, and 1973. List of specific tables available upon request.

a Figures for California, Oregon, and Washington—which together had a somewhat lower male-female ratio (11.33) than the United States as a whole—show 7.0% of the Chinese population to be under age 15 in those states.

Using these openings, many families adopted a strategy of long-term sojourning. Successive generations of men emigrated as paper sons. To ensure loyalty to kin, young men were married off before leaving. Once in America they were expected to send money to support not only wives and children but also parents, brothers, and other relatives. In some villages overseas remittances constituted the main source of income. It has been estimated that between 1937 and 1940 overseas Chinese remitted more than $2 billion, and that an average of $7 million per annum was sent from the United States in the years between 1938 and 1947 (Lyman, 1968; Sung, 1971). In one typical family history, recounted by a 21-year-old college student, great-grandfather arrived in the United States in the 1890s as a paper son and worked for about twenty years as a laborer. He then sent for the grandfather, who helped great-grandfather run a small business. Great-grandfather subsequently returned to China, leaving grandfather to carry on the business and forward remittances. In the 1940s grandfather sent for father. Up to this point, none of the wives had left China; finally, in the late 1950s, father returned to China and brought back his wife, so that after nearly seventy years, a child was finally born in the United States.

The sojourning strategy led to a distinctive family form, the *split-household family*. A common sociological definition of a family is: a group of people related by blood or marriage, cooperating to perform essential domestic tasks such as production, consumption, reproduction, and socialization. In the split-household family, production would be separated from other functions and carried out by a member living far away (who, of course, would be responsible for his own consumption needs). The other functions—reproduction, socialization, and the rest of consumption—would be carried out by the wife and other relatives in the home village. The family would remain an interdependent, cooperative unit, thereby fulfilling the definition of a family, despite geographical separation. The split-household form made possible the maximum exploitation of the worker. The labor of prime-age male workers could be bought relatively cheaply, since the cost of reproduction and family maintenance was borne partially by unpaid subsistence work of women and old people in the village. The sojourner's remittances, though small by U. S. standards, afforded a comfortable standard of living for family members in China.

The split household is not unique to the Chinese and, therefore, cannot be explained as a culturally preferred pattern. Sojourning occurs where there are (a) large differences in the level of economic development of receiving vs. sending regions, and (b) legal/administrative barriers to integration of the sending group. Three examples of the phenomenon are guest workers in Western Europe (Castles and Kosack, 1973); gold-mine workers in South Africa (Boserup, 1970); and Mexican braceros in the American Southwest (Power, 1979). In all three cases, prime-age workers from disadvantaged regions are issued limited-duration permits to reside in regions needing low-wage labor but are prevented from bringing relatives or settling permanently. Thus, the host country benefits from the labor of sojourners without having to incorporate them into the society. Although the persistence of sojourning for several generations makes the Chinese somewhat unusual, there is evidence that legal restrictions were critical to maintaining the pattern. Other societies to which the Chinese immigrated did not prohibit intermarriage or limit economic competition—for example, Peru and the Philippines. In these societies a high proportion of the Chinese intermarried with the native population (Wong, 1978; Hunt and Walker, 1974).

The life of the Chinese sojourner in the United States has been described in sociological and historical studies (see Nee and Nee, 1974; Lyman, 1977). Employed as laborers or engaged in small enterprises, the men lived in rented rooms alone or with other "bachelors." In place of kin ties, they relied on immigrant associations based on fictive clan relationships. As is common in predominantly male societies, many sojourners found outlets in gambling, prostitution, and drugs. Those successful enough or frugal enough to pay for passage returned periodically to China to visit and to father more children. Others, as a result of bad luck or personal disorganization, could never save enough to return. Even with movement back and forth, many sojourners gradually came to feel remote from village ties, and attached to life in the Chinese-

American colony. Thus, they ended up staying in the United States more or less by choice (Siu, 1952).

The situation of wives and relatives in China has not been documented in the literature. According to informants, wives generally resided with in-laws; and remittances were sent to the husband's kin, usually a brother or son, to insure that wives remained chaste and subject to the ultimate control of their husbands. Despite the lack of formal authority, most wives had informal influence and were consulted on major decisions. An American-born informant, the daughter of an herbalist and his concubine, was sent as a young girl to be raised by her father's first wife in China. This first wife never wanted to join her husband, as she lived quite comfortably in the village; with remittances from her husband, she maintained a large house with two servants and oversaw substantial landholdings and investments. The father's concubine led an arduous life in the United States, raising several children, running the household, and working long hours in the shop.

Parent-child relations were inevitably affected by separation. The mother-child tie was strengthened by the absence of the father. The mother's tie with her eldest son, normally an important source of leverage within an extended-kin household, became particularly close. In contrast, prolonged absence made the father's relationship with his children more formal and distant. The long periods between visits meant that the children were spaced far apart, and the father was often middle-aged or elderly by the time the youngest child was born. The age gap between fathers and later children added to the formality of the relationship.

THE SMALL-PRODUCER FAMILY

Despite obstacles to family formation, the presence of families was evident in the major U.S. Chinatowns by the 1920s. As Table 1 shows, the male-female ratio fell, and the proportion of children nearly doubled between 1920 and 1930. These early families were started primarily by small entrepreneurs, former laborers who had accumulated enough capital to start a small business alone or in partnership. Due to occupational restrictions and limited capital, the enterprises were confined to laundries, restaurants, groceries, and other small shops. Once in business they could register as merchants, return to China, and bring over wives and children. There was an economic incentive to bring over families; besides providing companionship and affection, women and children were a source of free labor for the business.

The number of families grew steadily, then jumped dramatically during the 1950s due to changes in immigration regulations. The first small opening was created in 1943 with the repeal of the Chinese Exclusion Act. In recognition of China's position as an ally in World War II, a token quota of 105 entrants per year was granted, and permanent residents were declared eligible for citizenship. A larger opening was created by the "Brides Act" of 1946, which permitted entry to wives and children of citizens' and permanent residents, and by the Immigration Act of 1953, which gave preference to relatives of citizens (Lee, 1956; Li, 1977b). For the first time in over sixty years, sizable legal immigration flowed from China; and for the first time in history, the majority of entrants were women. The women fell into two general categories: wives separated from their husbands for periods ranging up to thirty years or more, and brides of servicemen and other citizens who took advantage of the 1946 and 1953 laws to visit China and get married (Lee, 1956). The marriages were usually arranged hastily; Chinese families were eager to have eligible daughters married to Americans, so the men had no problem finding prospects on short notice. At the same time, parents of American-born men often preferred Chinese-born brides (Lee, 1956). An American-born woman explained why; she once had an engagement broken off because her fiancé's parents objected to the marriage:

> They thought American girls will be bossy; she'll steal the son and go out freely. They said, "She will ruin your life. She'll be free spending with money." Also, she won't support the parents the rest of their life. They want a typical Chinese girl who will do what the father wants. [Interview with subject]

At his parent's urging, the fiancé later visited China and brought back a wife.

During the period from about 1920 to the mid-1960s, the typical immigrant and first-generation family functioned as a productive unit in which all members, including children, worked without wages in a family business. The business was profitable only because it was labor-intensive and members put in extremely long hours. Often, for reasons of thrift, convenience, or lack of options, the family's living quarters were located above or behind the shop; thus, the workplace and home were physically joined.

Some flavor of the close integration of work and family life is seen in this description of the daily routine in a family laundry, provided by a woman who grew up in Boston's Chinatown during the 1930s and 1940s. The household consisted of the parents and four children. The work day started at 7:00 in the morning and did not end until midnight, six days a week. Except for school and a short nap in the afternoon, the children worked the same hours as the parents, doing their homework between midnight and 2:00 A.M. Each day's routine was the same. All items were marked or tagged as they were brought in by customers. A commercial cleaner picked up the laundry, washed it, and brought it back wet. The wet laundry was hung to dry in a back room heated by a coal burner. Next, items were taken down, sprinkled, starched, and rolled for ironing. Tasks were allocated by age and sex. Young children of six or seven performed simple tasks such as folding socks and wrapping parcels. At about age ten they started ironing handkerchiefs and underwear. Mother operated the collar and cuff press, while father hand-ironed shirts and uniforms. Only on Sunday did the family relax its hectic regimen to attend church in the morning and relax in the afternoon.

This family may have been unusually hard working, but this sort of work-centered family life was common among the generation that grew up between 1920 and 1960. In fact, the close-knit small-business family was portrayed in several popular autobiographies covering this period (Lowe, 1943; Wong, 1950; Kingston, 1976). These accounts describe a life of strict discipline, constant toil, and frugality. Family members constantly interacted, but communication tended to revolve around concrete details of work. Parents directed and admonished the children in Chinese as they worked, so that the American-born Chinese became fluent in Chinese as well as in English, which they learned in school. Education was stressed, so that children's time was fully occupied by studying, working, and caring for younger siblings. Not so apparent in these accounts was the high incidence of disease, including tuberculosis, due to overcrowding and overwork (Lee et al., 1969).

The small-producer family had several distinct characteristics. First was the lack of any clear demarcation between work and family life. Child care, domestic maintenance, and income-producing activities occurred simultaneously in time and in the same location. Second was the self-contained nature of the family as a production and consumption unit. All members contributed to family income and domestic maintenance, including the children. Third was the division of labor by age and gender, with gradations of responsibility according to capacity and experience. Elder siblings were responsible for disciplining and taking care of younger siblings, who in turn were expected to defer to their older brothers and sisters. Finally, there was an emphasis on the collectivity over the individual. With so many individuals working in close quarters for extended periods of time, a high premium was placed on cooperation. Self-expression, which might engender conflict, had to be curbed.

While these features are in some way similar to those found in Chinese peasant families, they do not necessarily represent carryovers of Chinese patterns; they can be attributed equally to the particular material and social conditions arising from the family's involvement in small enterprise, an involvement dictated by limited economic options. There is evidence that these features are common to small-producer families in various societies and times (see, for example, Demos's 1970 account of the early Puritan families of the Massachusetts Bay Colony). Moreover, the Chinese-American small-producer family had some features that differed from those of rural Chinese families due to circumstances of life in America. Of great significance was the family's location in a society whose dominant language and customs differed greatly. Children had the advantage in this regard. Once they started school, children quickly learned to speak and write English, while parents were rarely able to acquire more than rudimentary English. The parents came to depend on their children to act as mediators in relation to the outside society. As a result children gained a great deal of status at an early age, in contrast to the subordinate position of children in China. American-born Chinese report that, starting at age eight or nine, they helped their parents in business and domestic matters by reading documents and contracts, accompanying them to the bank to fill out slips, negotiating with customers, and translating notices in stores.

A second circumstance was the age composition of immigrant communities, which were made up primarily of childbearing-aged men, and later, women. In the initial period of family formation, therefore, there were no grandparents; and households tended to be nuclear in form. In China the preferred pattern was for sons to live with parents, and wives were required to defer to mothers-in-law. The young immigrant mother, however, did not have to contend with in-laws. As a result of this, and the fact that she was an equal producer in the family economy, the wife had more autonomy. Many informants recall their mothers as the disciplinarians and central figures in the household.

THE DUAL WAGE EARNER FAMILY

Following World War II, particularly after the Civil Rights Movement of the 1960s, discrimination against Asian Americans eased. College-educated Chinese Americans were able to enter white-collar occupations and industries formerly barred to them and to move into previously restricted neighborhoods. Among these socially mobile families, the parents still shop and visit friends in Chinatown; but their children tend not to have ties there. The lowering of barriers also speeded the integration of the so-called scholar-professional immigrants. Educated in Hong Kong, mainland China or Taiwan, many are Mandarin-speaking, in contrast to the Cantonese-speaking resident population. The older segment of this group arrived as students in the 1940s and 1950s and stayed, while the younger segment entered under the 1965 immigration act, which did away with national quotas and gave preference to relatives of citizens and permanent residents and to those in needed occupations. Employed as professionals, this group tends to live in white neighborhoods and to have little connection with Chinatown. Thus, for the socially mobile American-born and the scholar/professional immigrants, the trend has been toward assimilation into the mainstream of American society.

At the same time, however, there has been a countertrend that has re-Sinicized the Chinese-American population. The same immigration law that brought in professionals and scholars has brought in an even larger influx of working-class Chinese. Under the liberalized law, over

20,000 Chinese have entered the United States each year since 1965, primarily via Hong Kong (U.S. Department of Justice, 1977).[3] About half the immigrants can be classified as working class, having been employed as service workers, operatives, craftsmen, or laborers in Hong Kong (Nee and Nee, 1974). After arrival, moreover, a significant proportion of professional, managerial and white-collar immigrants experience a drop in occupational status into blue-collar and service jobs because of language and licensing difficulties (U.S. Department of Health, Education and Welfare, 1974).

Unlike the earlier immigrants who came over as individuals, most new immigrants come over in family groups—typically a husband, wife and unmarried children (Li, 1977a). The families have pulled up stakes in order to gain greater political security, economic opportunity, and educational advantages for their children. Since the law gives preference to relatives, most families use kinship ties with previous immigrants to gain entry. Frequently, the ties are used in a chainlike fashion (Li, 1977b). For example, a couple might sponsor the wife's sister, her husband and children; the sister's husband in turn sponsors his parents, who later bring over one of their children, and so forth. In this way an extended-kin network is reunited in the United States.

Initially, the new immigrants usually settle in or near Chinatown so that they can trade in Chinese-speaking stores, use bilingual services, and find employment. They are repopulating and stimulating growth in Chinatowns at a time when these communities are experiencing declines due to the mobility of American-born Chinese (Hong, 1976). The new immigrants have less dramatic adjustments to make than did earlier immigrants, having lived for some years in an urban society that exposed them to Western goods and lifestyles. In addition, although bilingual social services are frequently inadequate, municipal and country agencies now provide medical care, advice on immigration problems, family counseling, and the like. The immigrants rely on these public services rather than on the clan associations which, thus, have lost their old influence.

Despite the easier adjustment and greater opportunities for mobility, problems of language, and discrimination in small trade, construction and craft unions still affect immigrants who are not professionally trained. Having given up property, businesses or jobs, and having exhausted their resources to pay for transportation and settlement, they must quickly find a way to make a living and establish their families in a highly industrialized economy. The strategy most families have adopted is for husband and wife to find employment in the secondary labor market, the labor-intensive, low-capital service and small manufacturing sectors. The wage each earns is low, but by pooling income a husband and wife can earn enough to support a family. The typical constellation is a husband, who works as a waiter, cook, janitor, or store helper, and a wife who is employed in a small garment shop (Nee and Nee, 1974; Ikels and Shiang, 1979; "Tufts' lease...," 1981; cf. Lamphere, Silva and Sousa,

1980 for parallels with Azorean immigrants).

Although many women have been employed in Hong Kong, for most it is a new experience to juggle fulltime work outside the home with child care and housework. In Hong Kong mothers could do piecework at home, stitching or assembling plastic flowers during spare hours (Ikels and Shiang, 1979). In the United States employment means a long complicated day involving dropping off children at school, going to work in a shop for a few hours, picking up children from school, preparing food, and returning for a few more hours of work in the shop. Another change in many families is that the women's earnings comprise a greater share of family income in the United States. The pay differential between men and women, which is large in Hong Kong, becomes less or even reversed because of the downward shift in the husband's occupation (Hong, 1980). Wives and husbands become more or less coequal breadwinners.

Perhaps the most striking feature of the dual-worker family is the complete segregation of work and family life. As a result, in contrast to the round-the-clock togetherness of the small-producer family, parents and children in the dual-worker family are separated for most of the day. While apart they inhabit totally different worlds. The parents' lives are regulated by the discipline of the job, while children lead relatively unstructured and unsupervised lives, often in the company of peers whose parents also work (Nee and Nee, 1974). Furthermore, although mothers are usually at home by early evening, the father's hours may prevent him from seeing the children at all. The most common shift for restaurant workers runs from 2:00 in the afternoon until 11:00 at night. The sons and daughters of restaurant workers reported that they saw their fathers only on their days off.

The parents' fatigue, the long hours of separation, and the lack of common experiences combine to undermine communication. Children complain that their parents are not around much and, when they are, are too tired to talk. One young student notes, "We can discuss things, but we don't talk that much. We don't have that much to say." In addition, many parents suffered serious trauma during World War II and the Chinese Revolution, which they refuse to discuss. This refusal causes blocks to intimacy between parents and children since certain topics become taboo. For their part parents complain that they have lost control over their children. They attribute the loss of influence to the fact that children adjust to American ways and learn English much more quickly than parents. Over a period of years, a language barrier frequently develops. Since parents are not around to direct and speak to children in Chinese, the children of wage-earning parents lose the ability (or willingness) to speak Chinese. When they reach adolescence, moreover, children can find parttime employment, which gives them financial independence as well as money to spend on outside recreation.

The absence of a close-knit family life among dual-worker families has been blamed for the eruption of youth rebellion, delinquency, and gang violence in Chinatowns during the 1960s and 1970s (Lyman, 1974; Nee and Nee, 1974). While the change in family patterns undoubtedly has been a factor, other demographic and social changes have contributed to the surfacing of youth problems (Light and Wong, 1975). Adolescents make up a higher proportion of the new immigrants than they did in previous cohorts, and many immigrants arriving as adolescents encounter difficulties in school because of the language barrier. When they leave school they face unemployment or the prospect of low-wage service jobs. Similar obstacles were faced by the early immigrants, but they take on a new meaning in the present era when expectations are higher and when there is more awareness of institutional racism.

In a similar vein, dual-worker families are beset by the chronic difficulties that plagued Chinese-American families in the past—rundown crowded housing, low incomes, immigration problems, and language difficulties; but their impact is different now that the family faces them in a less unified fashion. Social workers employed in Chinatown report that the immigrant family is torn by a multiplicity of problems.[4] Ironically, the resilience of the Chinese-American family until recently has retarded efforts at relief. It has taken the visible outbreak of the youth unrest mentioned above to dramatize the fact that the Chinese-American family cannot endure any and all hardships without support. For the first time, social services, housing programs, and other forms of support are being offered to Chinese-American families.

SUMMARY AND CONCLUSIONS

This sociohistorical examination of the Chinese-American immigrant family has emphasized three main points: first, throughout their history in the United States, Chinese Americans have faced a variety of economic, social and political constraints that have had direct effects on family life. Second, Chinese-American families have displayed considerable resourcefulness in devising strategies to overcome structural obstacles and to take advantage of the options open to them. Third, the strategies adopted have varied according to the conditions prevailing during given historical periods, resulting in three distinct family types.

The characteristics and differences among the family types, discussed in the previous sections, are summarized in Table 2. Each type can be characterized in terms of six major dimensions: the economic strategy, the make-up of the household(s), the nature of the relation between production or work and family life, the division of labor in the household, conjugal roles, and relations between generations.

The split-household type, prevalent until 1920, adopted the strategy of sending married men abroad to specialize in income-producing activities. This created two separate households, one in the United States consisting of a primary individual—or, in some cases, a pair of related males such as a father and son—and another in China, consisting of the relatives of the sojourner—wife, children, parents, and brothers and their wives. Production was separated from the rest of family life, with the husband/father engaging in paid work abroad while the other relatives engaged in subsistence activities (e.g., small-scale farming) and carried out other domestic functions. Husband and wife, therefore, led completely separate existences, with the husband's relation to parents taking precedence over his relation to his wife, and the wife forming her primary attachment with children.

The small-producer type succeeded the split-household type around 1920 and became more common after the late 1940s when women were allowed to join their spouses in the United States. The economic strategy was to engage in small-scale enterprises that relied on the unpaid labor of husband, wife, and children. The nuclear household was the basic unit, with no separation between production and family life, and was focused around work. Close parent-child relations resulted from the enforced togetherness and the constant interaction required to carry on the business. The economic roles of husband and wife were basically parallel, and most daily activities were shared in common.

Finally, the dual-wage type, which has predominated among immigrants arriving after 1965, is based on a strategy of individual wage work, with husband and wife engaged in low-wage employment. The pooling of two wages provides sufficient income to support the family. The household is primarily nuclear, with production and family life separate, as is common in industrial society. The clearest division of labor is between parents and children, with parents specializing in income-producing activities while children are economically inactive. The roles of husband and wife are symmetrical; that is, they engage in similar proportions of paid and unpaid work but in separate settings (cf. Young and Wilmott, 1973). Because parent's employment schedules often keep them away from home, there is little shared activity. The parent-child tie becomes attenuated, with children involved in a separate world of peers.

The existence of three distinctly different family types corresponding to different historical periods calls into question the adequacy of purely cultural explanations of Chinese-American family patterns. If cultural patterns were the sole or primary determinants, we would expect to find greater continuity in family patterns over time; instead, we find discontinuities associated with shifts in institutional conditions. These discontinuities underline the importance of the larger political economic structures in which the family is embedded.

At the same time, the family is shown as actively striving to survive and maintain ties within the constraints imposed by these structures. The persistence of ties and the variety of strategies adopted by Chinese-American families testify to their resilience and resourcefulness in overcoming obstacles. Further insights into the relationships among and between culture, larger institutional structures, and family strategies might be gained through comparative historical analysis of different racial and ethnic groups.

Table 2.
Characteristics of Three Types of Chinese Immigrant Families

CHARACTERISTICS	SPLIT HOUSEHOLD	SMALL PRODUCER	DUAL WAGE
Historical period [a]	c. 1882–1920	c. 1920–1965	c. 1965–present
Economic strategy	male sojourning	family business	individual wage work
Household composition	two households: (a) in United States—primary individual; (b) in China— extended	nuclear	nuclear
Work and family life	separated	fused	separated
Division of labor	husband/father— paid work; wife/other relatives—unpaid domestic and subsistence work	husband, wife and children— unpaid production work	husband and wife—paid and unpaid work; children— unpaid domestic work
Conjugal roles	segregated	joint or shared	symmetrical
Intergenerational relations	strong mother- child tie; weak father-child tie	strong parent- child tie	attenuated parent- child tie

[a] The occurrence of each type is not exclusive to one period but is more prominent during the designated period.

NOTES

The author is grateful to Gloria Chun, Judy Ng and Yee Mei-Wong for discussions that provided valuable insights; and to Ailee Chin, Gary Glenn, Larry Hong, Charlotte Ikels, Peter Langer, S. M. Miller, T. Scott Miyakawa, and Barbara Vinick for comments on earlier drafts. A previous version of this paper was presented at the meetings for the Study of Social Problems, Toronto, August, 1981.

1. Although some scholars (e.g., Herskovitz, 1958; Levine, 1977) have argued for the continuity of African cultural patterns among American blacks, family sociologists have not systematically explored the possible influence of an autonomous black culture with African roots. This is true even for those who depict the black family as strong and resilient (e.g., Billingsley, 1968; Hill,

1971). Those who characterize it as weak and disorganized (e.g., Frazier, 1939; Moynihan, 1965) have relied on a particular type of cultural formulation, one that views the culture as degraded, a legacy of past economic and social deprivation.

2. The analysis is based on review of the English-language literature on Chinese Americans and informant interviews of twenty-nine individuals of varying ages, nativity, and family status, mainly residing in the Boston area. Informants were interviewed about family immigration histories, economic activities, household composition, residence, and relations among family members. Social and community workers provided broader information on typical tensions and problems for which help was sought.

3. Although the immigrants enter via Hong Kong, they mostly originate from the same region of southern China as the earlier immigrants. They or their parents fled Guangdong during the Sino-Japanese War or during the land reform following the Communist victory. Hence, they tend to have kinship ties with earlier immigrants.

4. According to community workers and government agencies, the most common problems are low, though not poverty-level, family income; substandard and dilapidated housing; language difficulties; legal problems with immigration; and unresolved past traumas, including separation between family members.

REFERENCES

Billingsley, A. 1968. *Black Families in White America*. Englewood Cliffs, NJ: Prentice-Hall.

Bonerup, E. 1970. *Women's Role in Economic Development*. New York: St. Martin's Press.

Castles, S. and Kosack, G. 1973. *Immigrant Workers and Class Structure in Western Europe*. London: Oxford University Press.

Coolidge, Mary. 1909. *Chinese Immigration*. New York: Henry Holt.

Demos, John. 1970. *A Little Commonwealth*. London: Oxford University Press.

Drake, S. C. and Cayton, H. R. 1962. *Black Metropolis* (rev. ed.). New York: Harper and Row.

Frazier, E. F. 1939. *The Negro Family in the United States* (rev. ed.). New York: Macmillan.

Gordon, M. M. 1964. *Assimilation in American Life: The Role of Race, Religion, and National Origin*. New York: Oxford University Press.

Haynor, N. S. and Reynolds, C. N. 1937. "Chinese family life in America." *American Sociological Review* 2:630–637.

Herskovitz, M. 1958. *The Myth of the Negro Past*. Boston: Beacon Press.

Hill, R. A. 1971. *The Strengths of Black Families*. New York: Emerson Hall.

Hirata, L. C. 1976. "The Chinese American in sociology." Pp. 20–26 in E. Gee (Ed.), *Counterpoint: Perspectives on Asian Americans*. Los Angeles: Asian American Studies Center, University of California, Los Angeles.

Hong, L. K. 1976. "Recent immigrants in the Chinese American community: issues of adaptations and impacts." *International Migration Review* 10 (Winter):509–514.

———. 1980 Personal communication.

Hsu, F. L. K. 1971. *The Challenge of the American Dream: The Chinese in the United States*. Belmont, CA: Wadsworth.

Huang, L. J. 1976. "The Chinese American family." Pp. 124–147 in C. H. Mindel and R. W. Habenstein (Eds.), *Ethnic Families in America*. New York: Elsevier.

Hunt, C. I. and Walker, L. 1974. "Marginal trading peoples: Chinese in the Philippines and Indians in Kenya." Ch. 4 in *Ethnic Dynamics: Patterns of Intergroup Relations in Various Societies*. Homewood, IL: Dorsey Press.

Ikels, C. and Shiang, J. 1979. "The Chinese in Greater Boston." Interim Report to the National Institute of Aging.

Jacobs, P. and Landau, S. 1971. *To Serve the Devil, Volume II: Colonials and Sojourners*. New York: Vintage Books.

Kingston, M. H. 1976. *The Woman Warrier*. New York: Knopf.

Konvitz, M. G. 1946. *The Alien and Asiatic in American Law*. Ithaca, NY: Cornell University Press.

Kung, S. W. 1962. *Chinese in American Life: Some Aspects of Their History, Status, Problems, and Contributions*. Seattle, WA: University of Washington Press.

Kwong, P. 1979. *Chinatown, New York: Labor and Politics, 1930–1950*. New York: Monthly Review Press.

Lamphere, L., Silva, F. M. and Sousa, J. P. 1980. "Kin networks and family strategies; working class Portuguese families in New England." Pp. 219–245 in L. S. Cordell and S. Beckerman (Eds.), *The Versatility of Kinships*. New York: Academic Press.

Lee, L. P., Lim, A. and Wong, H. K. 1969. Report of the San Francisco Chinese Community Citizen's Survey and Fact Finding Committee (abridged ed.). San Francisco: Chinese Community Citizen's Survey and Fact Finding Committee.

Lee, R. H. 1956. "The recent immigrant Chinese families of the San Francisco-Oakland area." *Marriage and Family Living* 18 (February):14–24.

Levine, L. W. 1977. *Black Culture and Black Consciousness*. New York: Oxford University Press.

Li, P. S. 1977a. "Occupational achievement and kinship assistance among Chinese immigrants in Chicago." *Sociological Quarterly* 18(4):478–489.

———. 1977b. "Fictive kinship, conjugal tie and kinship claim among Chinese immigrants in the United States." *Journal of Comparative Family Studies* 8(1):47–64.

Light, I. 1972. *Ethnic Enterprise in America*. Berkeley and Los Angeles: University of California Press.

Light, I. and Wong, C. C. 1975. "Protest or work: dilemmas of the tourist industry in American Chinatowns." *American Journal of Sociology* 80:1342–1368.

Ling, P. 1912. "The causes of Chinese immigration." *Annals of the American Academy of Political and Social Sciences* 39 (January):74–82.

Lowe, P. 1943. *Father and Glorious Descendant*. Boston: Little, Brown.

Lyman, S. M. 1968. "Marriage and the family among Chinese immigrants to America, 1850–1960." *Phylon* 29(4):321–330.

———. 1974. *Chinese Americans*. New York: Random House.

———. 1977. "Strangers in the city: the Chinese in the urban frontier." In *The Asians in North America*. Santa Barbara, CA: ABC Clio Press.

Miller, S. C. 1969. *The Unwelcome Immigrant: The American Image of the Chinese, 1785–1882*. Berkeley: University of California Press.

Moynihan, D. P. 1965. *The Negro Family: The Case for National Action*. Washington, DC: U.S. Department of Labor, Office of Planning and Research (reprinted in Lee Rainwater and William Yancey, The Moynihan Report and the Politics of Controversy. Cambridge, MA: MIT Press, 1967).

Nee, V. G. and Nee, B. 1974. *Longtime Californ'*. Boston: Houghton Mifflin.

Park, R. E. 1950. *Race and Culture*. Glencoe, IL: The Free Press.

Power, J. 1979. *Migrant Workers in Western Europe and the United States*. Oxford: Pergamon Press.

Siu, P. C. T. 1952. "The sojourners." *American Journal of Sociology* 8 (July):32–44.

Sollenberger, R. T. 1968. "Chinese American childbearing practices and juvenile delinquency." *Journal of Social Psychology* 74 (February):13–23.

Stack, C. B. 1974. *All Our Kin: Strategies for Survival in a Black Community*. New York: Harper and Row.

Sung, B. L. 1971. *The Story of the Chinese in America*. New York: Collier Books.

"Tufts' lease on two Kneeland Street buildings threatens over 600 jobs in Chinatown." *Sampan* (May 1981).

U.S. Bureau of the Census 1872. Ninth Census. Vol. I: The Statistics of the Population of the United States. Washington, DC: Government Printing Office.

———. 1883. Tenth Census. Statistics of the Population of the United States. Washington, DC: Government Printing Office.

———. 1895. Eleventh Census. Report on Population of the United States, Part I. Washington, DC: Government Printing Office.

———. 1902. Twelfth Census of the United States Taken in the Year 1900. Census Reports, Vol. II: Population, Part II. Washington, DC: United States Census Office.

———. 1913. Thirteenth Census of the United States Taken in the Year 1910, Vol. I: Population, General Report and Analysis. Washington, DC: Government Printing Office.

———. 1922. Fourteenth Census Taken in the Year 1920, Volume II: Population, General Report and Analytic Tables. Washington, DC: Government Printing Office.

———. 1933. Fifteenth Census of the United States: 1930. Population, Vol. II: General Report, Statistics by Subject. Washington, DC: Government Printing Office.

———. 1943. Sixteenth Census of the Population: 1940. Population Characteristics of the Non-White Population by Race. Washington, DC: Government Printing Office.

———. 1953. U.S. Census of the Population: 1950. Vol. IV: Special Reports, Part 3, Chapter B, Non-White Population by Race. Washington, DC: Government Printing Office.

———. 1963. U.S. Census of the Population: 1960. Subject Reports. Nonwhite Population by Race. Final Report PC(2)-1C. Washington, DC: Government Printing Office.

———. 1973. Census of Population: 1970. Subject Reports. Final Report PC(2)-1G, Japanese, Chinese and Filipinos in the United States. Washington, DC: Government Printing Office.

U.S. Department of Health, Education and Welfare. 1974. A Study of Selected Socioeconomic Characteristics of Ethnic Minorities Based on the 1970 Census, Vol. II: Asian Americans. HEW Publication No. (OS) 75–121. Washington, DC: U.S. Department of Health, Education and Welfare.

U.S. Department of Justice. 1977. Immigration and Naturalization Service Annual Report. Washington, DC: U.S. Department of Justice.

Valentine, B. L. 1978. *Hustling and Other Hard Work*. New York: The Free Press.

Valentine, C. 1968. *Culture and Poverty: Critique and Counter-proposals*.

Chicago: University of Chicago Press.

Weiss, M. S. 1974. *Valley City: A Chinese Community in America.* Cambridge, MA: Schenkman.

Wolff, K. 1950. *The Sociology of Georg Simmel.* Glencoe, IL: The Free Press.

Wong, B. 1978. "A comparative study of the assimilation of the Chinese in New York City, and Lima, Peru." *Comparative Studies in Society and History* 20 (July):335–358.

Wong, J. S. 1950. *Fifth Chinese Daughter.* New York: Harper and Brothers.

Wu, C. 1972. *"Chink": A Documentary History of Anti-Chinese Prejudice in America.* New York: Meridian.

Young, M. and Wilmott, P. 1973. *The Symmetrical Family.* London: Routledge and Kegan Paul.

5

WORKING-CLASS FAMILIES, 1870–1890

Stephanie Coontz

One of the most striking features of working-class history from the 1870s to the 1890s is the presence of a vibrant, cohesive, even 'universal' working-class culture, paradoxically distributed in separate, localized, occasionally competing forms of social organizations and customs. The gulf between working-class and middle-class values, behaviors, and everyday life was perhaps greater than at any time before or since; and it occasionally surfaced in dramatic confrontations with the industrial order. Yet due to the uneven development patterns around the country, the recruitment of different immigrant groups to different industries at various points in the evolution of work relations and housing stock, divisions between skilled and unskilled workers, and other cleavages, the working-class ethic assumed divergent cultural and political forms. The middle class confronted—and workers operated within—a multiplicity of working-class cultures. These comprised a clear-cut alternative to bourgeois individualism and work patterns without coalescing into a unified national movement that could sustain a political and economic challenge to the emerging industrial order. 'This moral universality amid the particularities of the workers' daily sectoral struggles' was the peculiar characteristic of late-nineteenth-century labor.[1]

The absence of a unified ideological or structural challenge to American capitalism should not be confused with lack of militancy. As Steven Ross points out: 'In the two decades after the Centennial Exhibition of 1876, with its grand celebration of American industry and progress, there were more strikes and more people killed or wounded in labor demonstrations in the United States than in any other country in the world.' Over the course of the period, as we shall see, a greater sense of class solidarity was forged, culminating in the Great Upheaval of 1886. But while this upsurge changed the terms of debate and struggle within American industry, labor was unable to maintain its organizational and ideological gains after 1886. (Ironically, by the end of the 1890s more effective national organizations and campaigns were being built, but many of the values and institutions that had challenged bourgeois cultural hegemony steadily eroded, and the 'moral universality' was 'ruptured.')[2]

To understand the role of the family in the working class during the Gilded Age, it is necessary to grasp both the specificity—even fragmentation—of working-class experience and organization *and* the universality of working-class values. There was tremendous variety in the work experiences of the wage-earning population. In industrial cities such as Philadelphia and Detroit, marked variation was the norm in the scale of firms, rates of pay, application of mechanical power, the proportions and relationships of skilled and unskilled labor in any industry, and the organization of production and authority within various work settings. American industries tended to have far greater pay differentials between skilled and unskilled workers than what was prevalent in Europe, while other aspects of industrial employment also varied. Textile mills in Massachusetts, for instance, regulated the work pace and even the personal lives of their employees in strict detail, but they also put up with high employee turnover and rehired workers who had left without proper notice. European observers were amazed by the extent to which speed-ups and sobriety had been imposed on American textile workers: cotton workers in the 1870s operated four looms instead of the two worked by their English contemporaries. Yet, as late as 1904, managers gave in to workers' tendency to vote with their feet by closing down the mill on the day the circus came to town. The Winchester Repeating Arms factory in New Haven, Connecticut, began to require on-time attendance only in the 1890s, while skilled iron- and steel-workers set their own hours and hired their own help.[3]

These differences hampered the emergence of movements that could raise demands or coordinate actions extending beyond a craft or local community. Although local communities, especially in smaller, one-industry towns, often provided some support for workers' demands against absentee capitalists, this usually occurred on the basis of older, ambiguous republican slogans or on a new consciousness of ethnic homogeneity. It thereby imposed limits on the growth of workers' organization and class consciousness. While the petit bourgeoisie sometimes aided workers by blocking elite projects, 'the ideological and programmatic influence of such a political force on the workers was certainly at least as pervasive as the obstacles it raised to the wishes of the industrialists.'[4]

David Roediger has shown that the St. Louis General Strike of 1877 failed in part because its unrepresentative leadership—disproportionately composed of skilled workers, small proprietors, professionals, and white-collar workers—refused to mobilize unskilled workers or to sanction the widespread cooperation of Blacks and whites that occurred at the rank-and-file level. Identification with local institutions, he argues, encouraged some labor reform but also 'limited the tactical flexibility of labor organizations by committing them to a local boosterism shared with the upper and middle classes.' This divided skilled workers from the 'underclasses' and accentuated racism 'as a means of expressing those workers' inclusion in the community by dwelling on the otherness of Black workers....'[5]

The tremendous divisions between big cities and small towns also impeded solidarity. In places such as Rochester, even the Knights of Labor 'desired social harmony and wished to preserve the sense of individual moral accountability possible in a small town.' Despite the radicalism of full-time organizers, local groups were likely to join Knights of Labor head Terence Powderly in condemning militant actions in the big cities.[6]

Even the strongest protest movements in small towns rarely mounted a supra-local challenge to business interests or to the two-party system; working-class political alignments were often cross-cut by conflicts over cultural or local issues, especially as immigration mounted. In the big cities, politics were based on the ward system and its patronage apparatus. Political machines filled the gaps left between the private sector and government, and the machine bosses parleyed local constituencies and favors into particularistic power bases. Labor often found itself unable to compete with these machines. In addition, the waves of immigrants that poured into the larger cities entered the workforce at different places and with different sets of experiences: factors that initially prevented their collective identification and set them apart from small-town workers. These conditions are reflected in the way contemporaries, both pro- and anti-labor, usually talked about the working or producing *classes*.

IMMIGRATION AND ETHNICITY

Over the course of the nineteenth century, America recruited the bulk of its working class through immigration. While the majority of manual workers in America were native-born, many came from recently immigrated families, and first-generation immigrants—one-seventh of the population—comprised more than two-fifths of the workers in manufacturing and extractive industries. Immigrants made up a majority of the workforce in some of the larger cities, and their ethnic characteristics often seemed more significant than their occupational experience in shaping their lives and values. This has led some historians to elevate ethnicity above class in discussing American family history.

Certainly each group of immigrants drew on its own heritage to develop distinctive work and family patterns, and ethnic divisions frequently cut across class solidarities. But ethnicity cannot be readily or rationally disentangled from class in American history. Ethnicity was fundamental to the making of the American working class, not a historically separate feature laid on top of or opposed to class formation. Most ethnic sub-cultures evolved out of the working-class experience of immigrants, 'and people did not divide ethnic and class feelings into separate components in their minds.'[7]

True, there were important variations in family and gender patterns by ethnic group. While many differences between immigrants and native-born Americans—and between different immigrant groups—are explicable by economic and demographic factors, important cultural differences are equally evident, especially for females. One study, for example, found that non-ethnic variables accounted for all the so-called ethnic differences in labor-force participation for boys, yet not for girls. Girls from immigrant families started work and left home earlier than girls from native-born families, but there were also variations between immigrant groups. After marriage, Irish women tended to withdraw more completely from paid employment than did German women. German immigrants tended to socialize in family groups, while Southern Italians maintained stricter sex segregation. Polish families tolerated children's peer groups far less than did Irish, Italian, or black families. Italian mothers who had to work outside the home chose cannery and field work over factory work because it permitted them to work alongside their children. Polish women preferred domestic work to factory work after marriage, while Jewish women avoided domestic work and sought industrial employment, whether at home or in the factory. Immigrant groups had different propensities to purchase their own homes, in part because of different experiences of proprietorship in Europe. Immigrant families consistently had higher fertility rates, higher rates of child labor, and lower percentages of non-kin living with them than did natives. Multivariant analyses of such patterns generally find that ethnic differences 'remain significant even after allowing for the varying occupational distribution.'[8]

But the same study that judged ethnic differences more significant than occupational ones also found in its sample that only 8 percent of the Irish and 6 percent of the Canadian household heads, as opposed to 34 percent of the native-born, were non-manual workers. Immigrants were so overwhelmingly working-class that their tiny 'middle class' was not in any way comparable to the native-born middle class. Most immigrants who rose to middle-class status did so through manipulating their working-class environments, becoming petty landlords, shopkeepers, or ethnic power brokers. This led them, regardless of occupation, to share the class and cultural characteristics of their neighborhoods, giving an impression of independence to 'ethnic' factors that actually reflected a particular group's location in the larger industrial system. Another study purporting to show the impact of ethnicity after 'controlling' for occupation found that *literal* location in the city greatly modified even supposedly ethnic patterns in fertility. Micaela di Leonardo points out that 'the households that immigrants formed, while labeled by themselves and others as "ethnic," varied greatly depending on region, era, and economic circumstance' rather than flowing from some constant cultural 'tradition.'[9]

Differing ethnic patterns, moreover, should be related not just to pre-migration values but to separate times of arrival, conditions of leaving the old country, and points of entry into American industry, all of which fit groups into the labor market and housing system in distinctive ways. Different nationalities arrived with dissimilar skill levels and age or gender distributions, as well as disparate values, and these attributes interacted with the particular state of the housing stock, the configuration of the labor market, and the reaction of previous arrivals to forge ethnicity and class together. Immigrants drew on older cultural patterns in adapting to their new conditions, but they drew selectively, often recasting their old values considerably or highlighting characteristics that had not been predominant in the Old World.[10]

If ethnicity and class cannot be disentangled in their origins, they also served overlapping functions as sources of mutual aid, joint action, and collective identification against bourgeois individualism. Nevertheless, unions and cultural/ethnic institutions were often *alternative* ways in which American workers responded to pressure and organized to meet their needs. Sometimes ethnic ties could facilitate labor solidarity. German bakers in Chicago, for example, were able to organize successfully because they could count on local support from fellow Germans in their neighborhoods for boycott and label campaigns. Such successful organization in turn led the bakers to recognize that the growth of larger bread manufactories required supra-local and intra-ethnic institutions. Jewish solidarity provided a powerful radical base for organizing in the New York garment industry. Sometimes, however, even groups that built a common cultural community outside of work competed with each other on the job market, while in other areas workers called united job actions but failed to build solidarity outside the workplace.[11]

Up until 1880, many ethnic areas were merely small enclaves—perhaps a block or two—that maintained their links to the larger working-class communities of which they were a part. In Philadelphia, industrial affiliation rather than ethnicity remained the 'primary organizing factor' in white residential patterns. In Pittsburgh and in Lynn, Massachusetts, centralized working-class districts helped overcome differences among the waves of ethnic groups that poured into various levels of the factory, allowing ethnicity to complement rather than compete with class organization. On the other hand, in the Massachusetts industrial towns of Fall River and Worcester, scattered mills and housing concentrations reinforced the divisions introduced by segregated hiring practices and led to deep divisions within the working class. In many areas ethnic divisions deepened in the late nineteenth century as 'increasing class segregation of housing was overlaid by simultaneously expanding ethnic differentiation.'[12]

Immigrant families, then, faced special circumstances and created varied strategies for coping with them, while the working class often divided along ethnic lines. But in analyzing the changing patterns of family life in the nineteenth century, it is possible—perhaps even necessary—to discuss immigrant families as part of a general working-class configuration, remembering that they tended to be employed in the lower occupational strata. As Richard Ostreicher comments: 'Each of the ethnic working-class cultures included components of mutualism, solidarity, and egalitarian politics which provided the basis for a common ground on which they might come together....'[13] Each also had family structures and strategies that are best explained by their articulation with the industrial system.

The black family, however, despite its almost completely working-class character, requires distinctive treatment, for the position of black workers in the industrial system was qualitatively different from that of other ethnic groups. Their residential patterns, unlike those of the Irish, Germans, and native whites, cannot be explained by their industrial position; they seldom had access to factory jobs except when temporarily imported as strikebreakers; and new immigrant labor, far from pushing native-born Blacks up in the occupational scale, generally pushed Blacks entirely out of certain industries and job categories. Not surprisingly, Blacks developed some special family patterns which deserve separate consideration. We will return to the black family after examining white working-class families.

PATTERNS OF WORK AND FAMILY LIFE IN THE WORKING CLASS

For all the differences outlined above, working-class people shared many common experiences and values which imparted a distinctive cast to their family patterns, despite important variations by occupation and ethnicity. The majority of the working class lived very close to minimum levels of subsistence. Forty percent of industrial workers fell below the poverty level of $500 per year; another 45 percent barely stayed above it. Another 15 percent comprised highly skilled workers, usually Protestant and native-born, who might earn two to three times this amount. But the exceptionally high pay that could be earned by skilled workers did not always compensate for other aspects of the American industrial system— seasonal layoffs, no public social security measures such as pensions or unemployment compensation, no national labor party, unsafe working conditions, and possibly a harsher attitude than elsewhere in the industrializing world toward welfare for men (though not for women and children, who were 'allowed' to be dependent in proportion as men were required to be independent). The cumulative impact of all this, claims Peter Shergold, was that by the early twentieth century even skilled workers' higher pay and greater social mobility still left American workers as a group behind their British counterparts. The British worker

> generally had longer leisure time ... ; he was far less likely to be killed or maimed while at the workplace; he labored under less pressure; and he was provided with superior social services and facilities—hospital accommodations, city-based unemployment benefits, garbage collection, park space, and so on.[14]

Earnings of male workers, moreover, especially for manual workers but also in the skilled trades, peaked very early, leaving families vulnerable as fathers aged and children left home. A 'man of 23 earned as much as or more than a man two score years his senior.' In Michigan, only 5.2 percent of the workers surveyed in 1885 had savings accounts to help them through layoffs, illnesses, or old age. In addition to these shared insecurities, most workers also encountered authoritarian or arbitrary treatment on the job, increasing pressure to conform to industrial discipline, and numerous attempts at paternalistic control over their leisure lives. They simultaneously gained common experiences in organizing to resist such control, both at work and in their communities.[15]

Another common experience for American workers was geographic mobility. Population turnover in the cities, small as well as large, seems to have ranged from 40 to 60 percent in every decade of the nineteenth century. Such high transiency rates may have hampered the consolidation of working-class political and union institutions in some ways, but they also helped to establish a universal working-class culture, marked by an openness to newcomers and a recognition of the need to give and receive aid through associational networks and personal hospitality. Much migration was organized through kinship or ethnic networks, while some was a result of occupational and labor solidarities. Migration was also not simply a one-way, one-time process. Communication and assistance flowed in both directions and set up far-reaching linkages among working-class people.[16]

The effect of these common experiences on working-class family life was twofold. On the one hand, reliance on distinctive family strategies was greatly reinforced; on the other, there was a constant need to look beyond the family for other sources of aid and solidarity. Like the middle-class family, the working-class family in the nineteenth century was the primary source of class reproduction. Working-class status translated directly into specific family strategies and family position greatly influenced an individual's place within the working class. The family, moreover, was the main institution available to cushion the shocks of a deflationary period in which falling profit rates led to cutthroat competition, frequent layoffs, and attempts to impose more control over labor.

Low rates of pay, chronic economic and personal insecurity, and the lack of developed state or trade union institutions to provide social welfare measures ensured that the working-class family had to organize itself as an economic unit, closely coordinating its reproductive and domestic strategies with its position in industrial production. In some factories, especially the mills, families contracted to work together. The male might be paid the wages for the entire family and be held responsible for supervising their behavior on the job. Many industrial enterprises recruited labor through the extended family networks of immigrant males, while in the sweated trades whole families worked together on various parts of products made on piecework terms. Even in occupations in which families did not work together, most working-class families required one or more secondary earners in order to make ends meet. Child-rearing strategies and husband-wife interactions had to reproduce 'a collective family economic unit.'[17]

For unskilled and semi-skilled workers, high fertility rates were a rational response to the problem of declining income for an aging father.

Among French-Canadian textile workers, 'one child wage earner could boost the family income, on average, by more than half, and two child wage earners could double it.' Among these workers, large families were the *most* likely to escape poverty.[18] In other industries too, the employment of children could allow the family to buy a house, which would then serve as security when the father's income fell off and the children had left the family. It is no wonder that birth rates rose among unskilled and semi-skilled workers in this period, independently of religion and national origin.

In many industrializing cities, 'ethnicity became an increasingly important factor in fertility. The reason, however, rested not in culture but in the dominant class position of different ethnic groups':

> The great rise in Irish Catholic fertility was at least in part of a function of its working class character, and the decline among the Scottish Presbyterians, English Methodists, and Canadian Protestants related to the prominence of business-class occupations among them. Ethnicity, in short, served as a mediator between class and fertility.[19]

While most working-class families put their children to work early, they were unlikely to have the wife working outside the home unless the husband was incapacitated in some way. First-generation immigrant wives often worked, but second-generation immigrant families tended to withdraw wives from the paid labor force. Although this is sometimes interpreted as assimilation, it can be more plausibly explained by the exigencies of life in working-class America, where the sharp split between domestic and productive work and the lack of national social security systems or large-scale workers' aid organizations required a full-time worker in the home if wage-earners' returns were to be translated into a minimum level of comfort and long-term security. As Michael Haines observes: 'Child-rearing was apparently an adequate substitute for a wife's labor-force participation outside the home and ... a good investment for later stages in the life cycle.'[20]

We have already noted Jeanne Boydston's calculation that a woman's work inside the home, prior to the Civil War, had more value than her potential earnings outside. This conclusion would apply equally to the postwar period, given the continuity of wage differentials by gender and the failure of new technology to ease household chores and food preparation. The wife who stayed home, coordinated the schedules of the working members of the family, made their clothes and food, and possibly took in boarders or did piecework as the children aged might contribute more to the family economy than one who worked for wages that were often less than a third of a man's. As late as 1905, a national survey found that women's wages averaged $5.25 a week. Assuming year-round full employment, seldom possible for women, their average yearly wage would have been $273. When one considers that the work week necessary to earn this sum was often sixty hours, it seems likely that the income earned by a working wife would not equal the extra expenditures on clothes, transportation, food, and cleaning that would have been necessary to maintain a barely comfortable living. Unless the family was living substantially below subsistence (as were many Blacks), the family was better off having the wife free to prepare food, keep house, and perhaps earn a little extra money by taking in boarders or doing some piecework on the side.[21]

Homemaking in the nineteenth-century working class was still a full-time job. Many working-class families, even in the cities, had to grow at least part of their own food, because of the prohibitive cost of fresh vegetables. As late as 1890, half the families in the main centers of coal, iron, and steel employment kept livestock or poultry, grew vegetables, or both. Almost 30 percent grew enough food so that they purchased no vegetables other than potatoes. Of 7,000 working-class families interviewed between 1889 and 1892, fewer than half purchased even prepared bread. Other prepared foods were beyond the means of most working-class families. The housewife, consequently, was involved with food preparation on an almost full-time basis. Workers could seldom afford ice boxes—ice alone cost 42 cents a week in Pittsburgh—nor could they afford to buy larger, theoretically more economical quantities of food, so that marketing and cooking had to be done almost daily. Margaret Byington's 1910 study of the steel town of Homestead, Pennsylvania, found that twenty-one of the ninety families examined spent less than the 22 cents per person a day estimated as the rock bottom figure for adequate nutrition. The average expenditure was 24 cents, leaving most families a 'surplus' of only 2 cents. Survival on such budgets required careful, constant work, and a housewife might increase the real income of her family more by staying home and devoting herself to such work full-time than by going out to look for a job.[22]

Susan Strasser has pointed out the limited diffusion of nineteenth-century technology into most American households. Few homes had the mechanical cooking or cleaning devices that were illustrated in popular journals. Laundering was an arduous and time-consuming task, requiring hours of work even for the few who owned machines. The job must have been particularly demanding when the family included workers in heavy industry. In Pittsburgh, working-class homes in the 1880s had no indoor water. Women had to haul water by hand for every task, from cooking to cleaning, and then dispose of it afterwards. Wood and coal stoves required hours of tending and cleaning, while the soot they produced made general housecleaning a formidable undertaking. In 1893 the Commission of Labor revealed that only 47 percent of New York City's families, 30 percent of Philadelphia's, 27 percent of Chicago's, and 12 percent of Baltimore's had inside toilets. In the New York City primary tenement tract of the 1890s, only 306 of 255,000 residents had access to bathtubs.[23]

In these circumstances, working-class families who wished to maintain a modicum of cleanliness or to eat nutritious and adequate meals would, if they could afford to, assign a full-time worker to household tasks. Given the higher wages of the husband and the earnings advantage of youth, this was most likely to be the wife.

The day-to-day economic dependence of family members upon one another created strong pressures against individualism and toward family solidarity. Such solidarity extended beyond the nuclear family. Contrary to older myths, immigrant extended-family networks were not broken up by the process of migration or the transition to industrial work. Such networks were often the impetus to and the means of migration; family connections determined where immigrants would live and helped newcomers adjust to city life, while links with the community of origin were maintained to the extent that many migrants sent remarkably high proportions of their wages back to relatives they had left behind. Evidence suggests that immigrant families were *more* cohesive in America than in the Old World, as they settled together, sought work together, extended the length of parent/child co-residence, and often incorporated other kin into their households. Immigrants, of course, were especially likely to work at piecework or home industry, thus reinforcing extended kinship networks, but extended family networks were important among the entire working class, for males as well as females. Most visiting and vacationing, for example, was done in the homes of relatives.[24]

The same factors that strengthened general reliance on family strategies prevented the nuclear family from operating as an entirely independent unit, even where kin were not present: 'The prevailing native middle-class culture stressed the value of independence and self-reliance, but even workers who fully believed in these virtues could never know when they, too, would need the help of neighbors, friends, or fellow workers.'[25] In consequence, the working-class ethos extended beyond job-related acts of solidarity—supporting strikes, boycotts, and associations—to less formal means of sharing resources, even with newcomers seeking work. As we shall see, working-class families made fewer divisions between family and street life or public and private roles than did middle-class families, though they drew sharper distinctions between work and personal behavior. Working-class families did accept a clear division of labor on the basis of gender, however, and often formulated it in terms of domesticity.

WORKING-CLASS DOMESTICITY

The working-class family partook of several elements associated with middle-class domesticity: the wife seldom worked for wages outside the home; a gender-based division of labor prevailed in the family and the workforce, defining men as producers and women as potential wives and mothers; and home-ownership was an important value often linked to ideas about the sanctity of the home. 'Next to being married to the right woman,' editorialized the *Ontario Workman* in 1872, 'there is nothing so important in one's life as to live under one's own roof.' The author then waxed eloquent in his dramatization of what home-ownership meant to a working-class wife:

> We have our cosy house; it is thrice dear to us because it is our own. We have bought it with the savings of our earnings. Many were the soda fountains, the confectionery saloons, and the necessities of the market we had to pass; many a time my noble husband denied himself the comfort of tobacco, the refreshing draught of beer, wore his old clothes, and even patched-up boots; and I, O me! I made my old bonnet do, wore the plainest clothes, did the plainest cooking; saving was the order of the hour, and to have 'a home of our own' had been our united aim. Now we have it; there is no landlord troubling us with raising the rent, and expecting this and that. There is no fear in our bosom that in sickness or old age we will be thrown out of house and home, and the money saved to pay rent is sufficient to keep us in comfort in the winter days of life.[26]

In the absence of social security, home ownership could mean the difference between a comfortable old age and a miserably impoverished one. Since male earnings dropped sharply with age and few pension plans existed, such sacrifices to buy a home were rational and even imperative, despite the fact that they frequently meant pulling children out of school to maximize purchasing power for the home.

This is not to deny a partial acceptance of middle-class values here. Religious and political organizations stressed economic individualism and the possibilities of upward mobility. Upper- and middle-class women influenced working-class women and children in their role as Sunday school teachers, charity workers, or even employers of maidservants.[27] Perhaps even more important was the exceptionally strong and pervasive presence of a lower middle class in America and the real, if limited, possibilities for advancement into white-collar work. The earnings advantage of skilled over unskilled labor created a small group of workers who could afford some of the comforts of middle-class domesticity and who undoubtedly spread such values and aspirations to other sections of the class. It is also worth remembering that middle-class domesticity, in its original form, was critical of excessive accumulation, ambition and individualism—values that would have resonated positively for working-class people.

But it will not do to see working-class family values and organization as a mere reflection or even creative adaptation of middle-class values. First, many working-class family values and practices, such as early employment of children, insistence on the role of active leisure in personal life, and toleration of youthful peer groups outside the family remained remarkably distinct (even though they were later adopted—and reworked—by the middle class). Second, even practices and values that were similar in form possessed a very different content.

The demand for a family wage, for instance, did not necessarily originate in acceptance of middle-class values about woman's sphere. One possibility is that withdrawal of the wife's labor may have been a more or less conscious attempt to resist the exploitation of the family. Hans Medick has commented that the early phases of capitalist expansion rested 'on an increasing exploitation ... of the *total* family labour force.' As competition reduced returns to labor, the preindustrial family typically increased its expenditure of labor, falling back on 'self-exploitation' to ensure the subsistence of the family. Although Medick is here talking about handicraft production, so that his remarks apply particularly to home industries in nineteenth-century America, the same principle operated in many early factories, where men could not earn enough to support their family without mobilizing the labor of other family members.[28] Withdrawal of wives from the workplace and the use of domestic ideology to demand a family wage may have represented one attempt to break this pattern, especially as changing technology and increased employer control over work led to a deterioration in wages and working conditions in industries that had initially offered relatively good opportunities for women workers.

Skilled workers had another reason to oppose the employment of women. It was not simply male prejudice which led to the charge that women were often hired to undercut male wage rates. Women were certainly not hired because employers wished to affirm any commitment to sexual equality or female capacity. They were hired only where and when they could be paid less than men. The employment of women often led to a decline in wage rates for the entire industry involved, as happened with the transition to a female labor force in the clerical field. Given the craft-union mentality of the time, the logical response of organized workers was to attempt to exclude the cheap competition, and many wives probably acquiesced in this primitive attempt to maintain their husbands' wage rates. The probability that this consideration weighed more heavily than simple male prejudice is supported by the fact that male unionists often worked amicably and showed strong solidarity with women workers who were not directly competitive with them, as in the shoe industry.

Of course, the exclusion of women from many jobs was not a long-term solution to employers' attacks on workers' living standards, given the unequal power of craft unions and industrial employers. A craft organization that successfully limited entrance to the trade and maintained high wages was soon likely to find its entire craft obsolete, as employers substituted new jobs or mechanized the task completely. The only long-run solution, as some women and men began to recognize in the 1880s, was to eliminate sources of cheap labor and strikebreakers by achieving equal pay. Nevertheless, in the context of the nineteenth-century labor movement, poorly organized and divided along craft and ethnic lines, most working men responded to the problem of competition from cheap labor by attempting to exclude women (and Blacks or Chinese) from the labor force. The reluctance of men to have their wives work was thus a logical—if ultimately ineffective—response to a real problem, not merely an irrational patriarchal prejudice.

Martha May argues that the demand for a family wage originated among male and female workers, against middle-class, employer, and state opposition. It 'represented a dual claim to subsistence and industrial justice to its early advocates,' as well as a desire to remove the power of economic and social superiors over the working-class household. Clearly the demand did not benefit working women, especially single or widowed ones, in the way it benefited working men: it adopted the limiting theory of the fundamentally different natures of men and women, elevated the male public role, and obscured the productive activity of women in the household. 'But gender divisions remained subordinate to class claims; the working-class family ideology continued to be qualified by its emphasis on subsistence, justice and the demand for better hours and wages,' unlike the middle-class family ideology, which explicitly made domesticity a *substitute* for labor reform or modification of the market system. 'The arguments for the family wage invoked the interests of the entire family, thus going beyond a simple assertion of gender privilege.'[29]

Unlike middle-class domesticity, which reduced morality to gender roles, the working class used gender roles to raise larger issues of industrial justice and social democracy. In the radical union town of Cripple Creek, Colorado, for example, 'Miners opposed capitalism partly because it forced women to work and destroyed the home'; they justified unionism on the basis that it made a dignified life possible for families. Only in the twentieth century was the family wage demand transformed by Progressive reformers and conservative unionists into a cross-class issue that divided workers on the basis of gender more than it furthered the aims of class autonomy.[30]

Similarly, working-class rhetoric about the sanctity of the home had an entirely different content than did apparently similar sentiments held by the middle class. The home, argues Linda Schneider, was 'a symbol of autonomy' for working-class people, a place where workers could assert their own standards of comportment, escape factory regulation, and resist middle-class interference into their leisure life. It was also a counterweight to the opportunities and pressures in industrial society that might lead individuals to abandon class and family obligations.[31]

The sexual division of labor within the working class, and the ideologies of male and female spheres, could actually elevate labor solidarity outside the home. Where men and women were not in competition for jobs, for example, their sense of mutual dependence and complementary roles could heighten labor militancy. In Louisville, Kentucky, male spinners and female weavers cooperated in labor organization and militant strike activity; women's labor efforts garnered strong support from the male labor movement during the 1887 woolen strike. In Troy, New York, ideas about proper work for men and women helped to create an economy based on male labor in the iron foundries and female work in laundering, but the fact that most female industrial workers were single or widowed allowed an ideology of the domestic family to coexist with support for women's economic rights. Many of the Irish women among the Troy collar laundresses were the sisters, daughters, or in-laws of male ironworkers, and the powerful male union movement in Troy showed them what organization could do. The Troy Collar Laundry Union, organized in 1864 by Kate Mullaney, was strong enough by 1866 to donate $1,000 to the Iron Molders' Association when ironworkers were locked out by their employers. The laundrywomen organized a strike in 1869 and received in their turn substantial financial and organizational support from the Troy Molders and several New York City Unions. (The invention of a new paper collar, however, which threatened the very existence of the collar laundresses, gave employers enough leverage to break the strike.) Carole Turbin suggests that the strong labor community in Troy was supported by the sexual division of labor in both the city and the home:

> Since the city was dominated by two industries, one employing women and the other employing men, when men went out on strike they could rely on the earnings of female family members in the other industry and vice versa.... [T]he relationship between industrial structure and family patterns is an important part of the explanation for Troy's strong labor community.[32]

During the latter part of the nineteenth century, women proved again and again that acceptance of prevailing gender distinctions did not necessarily moderate militancy. In 1875, the male textile workers at Fall River voted to accept a pay cut announced by the employers. The women held their own meeting afterwards and voted to strike, on their own if necessary. The men then reversed their decision, joined the women, and together the men and women of Fall River won their strike. In the 1880s, women members of the Knights of Labor led militant strike actions that earned them the praise of Terence Powderly, head of the Knights, as 'the best men in the Order,' a phrase that evidently did not rankle as it would today. Women also used the ideology of gender to shame men into taking part in strikes or to get away with actions for which men might have more readily been shot, such as harassing militia members, crossing military lines to run messages for strikers or bring supplies, and tossing strike-breakers into ditches or subjecting them to the 'water cure'—dowsings in buckets of cold water. Moreover, as we have already seen, where men and women did not manage to cooperate, a shared sense of gender could occasionally reinforce and harden the class solidarity of women workers. 'We are a band of sisters,' wrote a mill operative in the *Voice of Industry*, 'we must have sympathy for each other's woes.'[33]

Still, it would be wrong to romanticize working-class domesticity any more than middle-class domesticity, or to deny the ultimately conservatizing effects of the Victorian sexual division of labor in the working class. Steven Dubnoff has found that among Lowell mill workers, parents had a much greater tendency to work consistently, whatever the wage rate (though women were absent more often then men), than non-parents; single boarders tended to trade extra income for leisure, taking more absences when they received more pay. Parents, in other words, were forced to develop a 'moral orientation' toward work, while boarders, both male and female, were 'strongly calculative' in absenting themselves from work once immediate economic ends were met. Daniel Walkowitz also points to the conservative role of the working-class family in the Gilded Age: it was 'a relatively small private-interest group ... [that] filled the normative role of accommodator, while ... the neighborhood usually remained the arena for collective organization.'[34] The self-sacrifice of the wife at home—some accounts even indicate that women denied themselves food to feed male workers—gave her little of the middle-class woman's 'expanded sphere,' while the 'privileges' of the male worker also forced him into steady employment, limited his mobility, and hampered his ability to stay out on strike.

Parents were not the only ones constrained by family responsibilities. Many young people sacrificed their personal dreams of education or independence to work for the family unit. The role of secondary wage-earners in the family, especially when they were young women, also inhibited labor organization. The majority of the female industrial workforce prior to 1920 was composed of young single women living with their parents. On the one hand, since they were not primary bread-winners, they were not forced to organize in order to survive; on the other, inasmuch as their small wages made the difference between family subsistence and absolute poverty, these women faced many pressures to keep on working whatever the conditions and pay. A study of Italian women in industry, undertaken between 1911 and 1913, found that two-thirds of the workers were under twenty-one and more than 80 percent lived with a parent or parents. Almost all simply turned their pay checks over, unopened, to the head of the family. Such women were unlikely to be able to resist family pressures against striking or other activities that might jeopardize the family's weekly subsistence. Many females shared the situation of thirteen-year-old Fannie Harris, who testified before a New York legislative committee on female labor that she had been earning $2 a week, for sixty hours' work, at a necktie factory:

> Q. What did you do with that two dollars? A. Gave it to my mamma.
> Q. Did your mamma give you anything to spend? A. Yes, sir ... two cents every week ...
> Q. Have you got any older brothers and sisters? A. I have an older sister.
> Q. Does she work? A. Yes, sir.
> Q. Does your mamma work? A. Now she ain't working because I am working, but before, when I didn't work, she worked ...

Q. Does your papa do anything; does he work? A. Yes, sir; he works, but just now he is not at work—he is sick.[35]

Adopting domesticity was in some ways, then, a defensive maneuver with long-run disadvantages. It was a response partly to the deterioration of working conditions for women, partly to the threat of industrialization to skilled craftsmen, and partly to the failure of middle-class women to address the special needs of women workers. As May points out, 'the family-wage ultimately ... worked against the interests of working-class men, women and families, by accepting and deepening a sexual double standard in the labor market.' The double standard allowed the state to forestall union demands by granting charity to women without 'providers' and employers in order to hold down women's wages on the grounds that they worked for 'pin money.' It also gave some women an incentive to act as strikebreakers or non-union workers. Finally, the double standard closed off opportunities to explore alternative family and gender roles within the industrial working-class that might have strengthened working-class solidarity. Indeed, by the early twentieth century,

> Middle-class social reformers and activists came to embrace the family wage as a means of restoring social stability, while some employers recognized its possibilities as a means to control and divide labor. At the same time, within the ranks of organized labor, the family wage increasingly became a defense of gender privilege. Defense of gender privilege, in turn, was closely connected to a craft exclusiveness that hampered male organizing as well as female.[36]

WORKING-CLASS GENDER ROLES AND THE LIMITS OF DOMESTICITY

The most important thing to grasp about working-class domesticity and family life, whatever their pros and cons for labor organizing, is that they had a different social content than did middle-class domesticity and family life. Working-class gender roles were not always as clearly divided, nor were they defined along the same lines, as middle-class ones. Although the separation of paid work and home life appeared earlier in the working class than elsewhere, this was not necessarily equated with the separation of male and female spheres. Home remained a center of important productive activity and of mixed-gender leisure activity for both men and women. The earliest working-class taverns, for example, were often located in private homes, and up through the 1870s much drinking 'remained rooted in the ... kitchen grog shop. The saloon, as a spatially distinct public and commercialized leisure-time institution, had not yet entirely triumphed.'[37]

City officials increasingly legislated against kitchen taverns and women liquor-sellers, thereby creating the very split between home life and male sociability that they later denounced, and encouraging the male saloon to develop as 'the mirror image of the male factory.' Yet like the factory, the public image of the saloon as a male preserve hid significant participation by women. Perry Duis denies that the saloon was

> a uniquely male preserve. In small 'ma and pa' operations the wife was at home behind the bar as well as behind the stove preparing the free lunch.... The crusades against the dance hall and the white slave menace after 1900 also indicate that drinking became less sexually divided as the years passed, while Boston license officials fought a losing cause ... to enforce temporary segregation-of-sex rules.[38]

Although some working-class wives complained of husbands who ran off to the saloon, in Boston and Chicago, at least, 'Court statistics ranked drinking low on the list of causes of divorce.'[39] Most working-class women seem to have had no objection to their husbands bringing home a bucket of beer from the local tavern. Home-based beer parties were quite common, with both sexes participating.

Under normal circumstances, the saloon was perhaps less a competition to the working-class family than a necessary supplement to it. The majority of its regular clients were the bachelors who made up such a high proportion of the working-class city population. It provided these men with food, companionship, a mailing address, often even a place to sleep. Additionally, the saloon served certain functions for married men that were in the interests of the entire family—they provided free lunches or cheap breakfasts, information or even contracts for work, and political patronage. Finally, women also utilized the saloon, which was often rented out for social functions or meetings. Women as well as men bought beer or wine, usually in little pails to take home with them, though German beer gardens were gathering places for the entire family.[40]

Despite an ideology of male production and female domesticity, necessity often blurred the distinctions. Although married working women tried not to work outside the home, they did much income-generating work within it, taking in boarders or lodgers, doing laundry, preparing food goods for sale; the cash raised in these ways was often an important component of the family's budget. Working-class families were also far more vulnerable than those in the middle class to economic and personal catastrophes that might force a wife into wage-work. Working-class men and women blamed the capitalist, not the woman, when married women had to work. Few derogatory comments about the lack of femininity of women workers, no matter how dirty and arduous their work, are to be found in working class writings.

Although distinct male and female networks existed in the late-nineteenth-century working class, comments Kathy Peiss, 'there was no simple or rigid gender-based dichotomy between public and private realms of leisure.'[41] Part of the reason for this was the increase in young women working outside the home. By 1890, nearly four million women, almost one in seven, were so employed, one million of them in factories. The proportion of working women in domestic service shrank from 50 percent in 1870 to 38 percent in 1890. These women had a period before marriage when they worked and socialized, and might even live, away from their families and in contact with young men of their class.

Ironically, the lack of physical amenities in working-class homes and the greater amount of housework to be done there may also have diminished the distance between male and female responsibilities:

> In the 1880s, when the first modern investigations of working-class family life were undertaken by the Massachusetts Bureau of Labor Statistics, one of the findings that most shocked and dismayed the middle-class male investigators was that working-class men would cook, clean, and care for the children while their wives were at work and they were not.[42]

When housewives got sick in urban tenements, someone had to haul water, dump excrement, and tend the fire; the working class did not have servants to protect men from these realities.

NEIGHBORS, COMMUNITY, AND FELLOW WORKERS IN THE WORKING-CLASS FAMILY

Despite ideology, there were important limits on the privacy of the middle-class family. Male business and female kin networks cut across the couple relationship, while the family often felt it had to live its life on display, proving to neighbors, peers, and social superiors its 'respectability' and conformity to middle-class standards. Yet the middle-class family clearly emphasized economic privatism, put itself forward as a self-sufficient unit, and sanctioned a degree of ambition for individual mobility, at least for males. The working-class family, by contrast, put forward neither privacy nor escape from community obligations as an ideal. The boundaries of the working-class nuclear family, both conceptually and physically, were far more fluid than was true in the middle class.

Conditions of life in the industrial working class strongly militated against a withdrawal into the nuclear unit. I have already noted the increase in extended families and subfamilies between 1850 and 1880 in urban, industrial areas. Boarding and lodging seem to have increased for the working class as well. Once characteristic of the middle class, these situations became in late-nineteenth-century cities more of a working-class phenomenon, though particularly associated until the end of the century with native-born Americans. (Newly settled cities in the West, however, tended to follow older patterns, where boarding and extended families were more common among affluent sectors of the population.) The incidence of boarding or lodging at any given census was 15 to 20 percent (more in the cities), but a substantial majority of native-born workers probably lived in such settings at some time in their life, for boarding was associated with what some authorities call the life cycle but might be more usefully termed the job cycle. Working-class youths tended to lodge when they were selecting among occupations or establishing themselves in their jobs. After gaining a family, a steady job record, and a home, they were more likely to take in boarders.[43]

The choice of boarding over residence with relatives is sometimes interpreted as preference for an economic transaction over an affective relationship, but this seems dubious, since lower-class families who lived together also had to operate on economic principles in order to survive. (Family sweatshops in which children as young as four or five had to work all day, fetching materials or pasting roses onto hats, can scarcely be offered as examples of affective relationships.) More likely, the prevalence of boarding among the native-born working class testifies to occupational and ethnic solidarities (the match between boarders and household head was close in both categories) and to the greater income security of these workers: boarding seems to have offered an institutionalized way of progressing from mobile worker to settled household head while receiving the financial benefits of co-residence. Immigrants, on the other hand, until the turn of the century were less likely to take in boarders than to share housing with relatives. The difference is probably related to the divergent job experiences of these members of the working class. Immigrants tended at first to fill low-skilled jobs involving entire families, or to work in preindustrial jobs as family units. Such families would naturally tend to live together. It was also more difficult for low-paid immigrant workers to establish the independence needed to become or to take in boarders.[44]

Although increasing numbers of white-collar workers lived a significant distance from their workplaces, most blue-collar workers continued to live within a mile of their jobs, often within a block or two. With fellow workers nearby, crowded and uncomfortable tenement apartments, and little money to spend on travel even for day trips, working-class men, women, and children did much of their socializing out of doors:

> Streets served as the center of social life in the working-class districts, where laboring people clustered on street corners, on stoops, and in doorways of tenements, relaxing and socializing after their day's work.... [O]rgan grinders and buskers played favorite airs, itinerant acrobats performed tricks, and baked-potato vendors, hot-corn stands, and soda dispensers vied for customers. In the Italian community ... street musicians and organ grinders made their melodies

heard above the clatter of elevated trains and shouting pushcart vendors, collecting nickels from appreciative passers-by. Maureen Connelly, an Irish immigrant, remembered listening to the German bands that played in Yorkville.... 'Something was always happening,' recalled Samuel Chotzinoff of his boyhood among lower East Side Jews, 'and our attention was continually being shifted from one excitement to another.'[45]

The lack of separation between family and neighborhood life in the working class helps to explain the fact that the sexual division of spheres was different, and often less rigid, than in the middle class. Some areas of recreation were gender-specific (more of these for men than for women). A male leisure culture grew up around cigar stores, barber shops, workingmen's or ethnic societies, and saloons. Women often combined domestic chores with social time by doing laundry in tenement yards or congregating at the pumps and fire hydrants where they got their water; they also simply hung out on stoops or fire escapes while their children played nearby. But the separation of working-class men and women should not be exaggerated. Many men brought beer home for socials with kin and neighbors, and 'workers who were too tired, poor, or temperate [to go to taverns] "congregated in groups on the leeside of some house"....' Interestingly, George Bevans's 1913 study of New York workmen found that the higher-paid native-born workers, not the immigrants and unskilled laborers, spent the least amount of leisure time with their families. This contradicts the usual portrayal of immigrant and manual laborers as particularly 'macho' and patriarchal in comparison with more 'enlightened' natives.[46]

For the many working-class couples who spent a majority of their leisure time in each other's company, family recreation was seldom confined to the nuclear unit. When families were not socializing outdoors they might set up evenings at another family's apartment. These often involved shared housekeeping or cooking by the women alongside male card-playing. In an article derived from her detailed investigation of early-twentieth-century life in Homestead, Margaret Byington offers us a glimpse of life in the courtyards of working-class housing, where women exchanged pleasantries as they did their wash and waited to use the pump, men gathered to play cards on summer evenings, and on pay Saturdays households pooled funds to buy beer and socialize.[47]

Boarding and lodging ensured a turnover of unrelated people within the household and seem to have contributed to labor solidarity in working-class communities. In many nineteenth-century labor disputes, for example, the fact that many workers boarded in other workers' homes ensured strong community sympathy for strikes and facilitated mutual aid during hard times. Even in expanding rural towns where families were experiencing a contraction in the yards where neighbors had formerly gathered, porches became places of neighborhood sociability. In Middletown, the Lynds found that it was only the owners of 'business class homes' who began after 1900 'to divert the money formerly put into front porches to ... other more private and more often used parts of the house.'[48] These 'business class' families were to become increasingly worried by the continuing sociability of lower-class households: the turn of the century saw a concerted effort to impose middle-class ideals of privacy on lower-class families.

Meanwhile, however, most working-class families provided little space for privacy and next to no support for personal ambition and individual mobility. Wages were pooled within the household, and the educational prospects or future earnings of children were often sacrificed to the security of the family unit. And not only that of the co-residential family: between 1851 and 1880, Irish immigrants sent $30 million back to the Old Country through the Emigrant Industrial Savings Bank of New York alone. Immigrants also financed local churches with donations that represented an extremely high proportion of their income.[49]

Gender divisions within the working class, moreover, were less connected to the aim of family self-sufficiency than in the middle class, and more rooted in a mutualistic tradition of reciprocity that put group solidarity above family ambition. Where the middle-class cult of domesticity supported rather than challenged the world of business and the free play of the market, the working-class cult of domesticity sometimes complemented and extended union organization and worker resistance to the industrial order. In the 1880s, for example, the Knights of Labor set up cooperative laundries and stores to socialize women's work. The Knights also organized picnics, sociables, and railroad excursions that 'brought the family together within the context of the wider working-class movement. For all their talk of "hearth and home," the Knights of Labor conceived of the family, not as an isolated haven from the world, but rather as the cornerstone of the working-class community.' Leon Fink argues that the Knights

> beckoned both to wage-earning women and workingmen's wives to join in construction of a 'cooperative commonwealth,' which, without disavowing the Victorian ideal of a separate female sphere of morality and domestic virtue, sought to make that sphere the center of an active community life.[50]

If working-class manliness meant, as in the middle class, the ability to work hard to support a family, it also meant meeting one's responsibility to the labor movement and standing up for workers' rights. If working-class womanliness meant—as in the middle class—being a good wife and mother, it could also mean being a dedicated 'union girl.' The female members of the New York Knights of Labor, in a nice blend of gender and class solidarity, passed this resolution:

> whenever the Knights of Labor girls went to a picnic or ball they were to tell all the brother Knights that none of the latter were to

walk with a non-union girl in the opening promenade so long as a union girl was without a partner. Should any male Knight violate this rule, all the girl Knights are to step out of the promenade and boycott the entire crowd.[51]

THE BLACK FAMILY IN THE LATE NINETEENTH CENTURY

Many of these comments about working-class families apply equally to Blacks, who also had a rich community life, a strong youth culture, an orientation toward extended family networks, and values and behaviors clearly opposed to bourgeois individualism. But mention should be made here of the special characteristics of black families in industrializing America, particularly in view of persistent myths that black family and community life was destroyed by slavery and that the resultant 'matriarchal' structure of black communities resulted in a 'tangle of pathology' which prevented Blacks from achieving upward mobility. This alleged 'disorganization' of black culture and family life has been variously attributed to the 'legacy of slavery,' the disruptive effects of migration North, and a 'culture of poverty' caused by severe material deprivation and then reinforcing that deprivation by creating 'weak ego structure, confusion of sexual identity, a lack of impulse control, and ... little ability to defer gratification and plan for the future.'[52]

Attacks on these stereotypes have come from many different angles. First, numerous researchers have demonstrated that Blacks developed their own culture and community both before and after slavery, maintaining group traditions while flexibly adapting and innovating where necessary. The rich community life constructed by Blacks in the period under consideration here is revealed in the list of groups that participated in the 1883 parade in the District of Columbia celebrating the twentieth anniversay of emancipation:

> Hod-carriers Union (500 men), Sons and Daughters of Liberty (50), Fourth Ward Ethiopian Minstrels (26), West Washington Union Labor Association (40), Young Men's Social Club, Washington Star Pioneers (20), Washington Brick Machine Union Association (16), Gay Heart Social Club, Cosmetic Social Club, the Invincible Social Club, Knights of Labor, East Washington Social Club, Knights of Jerusalem, Chaldeans, Knights of Moses, Galilean Fishermen, Sons and Daughters of Samaria, Osceolas, Solid Yantics, Monitor, Celestial Golden Links, Lively Eights, Imperials, Independent Fern Leaf Social Club, The Six Good Brothers, Twilight Social Club, and the Paper Hangers' Union.

A newspaper reporter commented in the same year that there were approximately 100 black societies in Washington, D.C., 'supported almost entirely by the laboring colored people.'[53]

Second, many researchers have argued that the incidence of broken and female-headed families among nineteenth-century Blacks has been exaggerated: two-parent nuclear families were in actuality the normal residential unit. Herbert Gutman reports that between 1855 and 1880, 70 to 90 percent of black households were male-headed, and at least 70 per cent were nuclear. In Ohio, as well, most black households were nuclear and headed by males.[54]

However, it is important not to overstate the resemblance of black families to what has become the white, middle-class ideal. In Boston, Elizabeth Pleck initially reported that only 18 percent of black families were headed by just one parent in the late nineteenth century, but more extensive research convinced her that this statistic seriously underestimated the extent of household dissolution. Pleck now estimates that about 25 percent of black households in northern cities and 34 percent of those in southern cities were female-headed during this period.[55]

What is at issue is the source of this phenomenon, and this brings us to a third critique of arguments about the legacy of slavery and migration: the important structural differences that did exist between black and white families cannot be attributed to either slavery or migration. In Boston and Philadelphia, the highest proportion of one-parent households was found among long-term residents rather than among ex-slaves or migrants from the rural South. In both North and South, female-headed families were associated with urban poverty, unemployment, and underemployment rather than with the heritage of slavery or the direct effects of migration.[56]

Between 1880 and 1900, the number of two-parent nuclear families among urban Blacks seems to have declined in at least some areas. Although this change is partly attributable to a rise in the proportion of female-headed households, the greatest single cause was increasing numbers of augmented households or subfamilies—a marked rise in the co-residence of black families and individuals. By 1905, in New York City, one out of 7.9 black households included a subfamily, compared to one in 22.9 for Jews and one in 11.2 for Italians, while female-headed households represented 17 percent of the black total and 7 percent for both Jews and Italians. In New York, the proportion of nuclear families among Blacks had declined to 49 percent by 1905; in Richmond, Virginia, it had fallen to 40 percent by 1900. The decline in the proportion of nuclear families began earlier in Philadelphia, and centered in the poorest section of the black population. By midcentury, almost one-third of the families in the poorest half of the black community were headed by women.[57]

Differences in black family structures, then, were direct consequences of urban poverty. Clearly, the viability of a household dependent upon a central male breadwinner declined for many Blacks during the second half of the nineteenth century. The most probable reason for this development is the increase in unemployment, underemployment, and job discrimination against black males. Job opportunities 'narrowed both relatively and absolutely' for northern and southern Blacks in the latter part of the century. In Buffalo, New York, Blacks were driven out of skilled occupations between 1855 and 1905 and were hit harder than other groups by the depressions of the 1870s and 1890s. In Birmingham, Alabama, Blacks 'were constantly pushed out of various occupations toward the bottom of the occupational hierarchy.' Throughout the South, 'traditional black artisanal skills, which had reached a high point in the late eighteenth century and were maintained throughout the antebellum period by free Negroes, were liquidated in the last decades of the nineteenth century.'[58]

The exclusion of Blacks from skilled trades and even factory work led to poverty and unemployment that undoubtedly made it necessary for many families to pool their resources and for others to split up, as members went different directions in search of work or security. It also produced high mortality rates for black males and led to diseases such as tuberculosis, which caused sterility among black men and women. Childless marriages were more likely than others to be dissolved. The increase in female-headed families also reflected a different consequence of racism: while black men suffered from constant unemployment, black women were able to find jobs in domestic service as white women domestics moved on to more desirable office and manufacturing jobs.

Elizabeth Pleck argues that, at least in northern cities, it was the virulence of racist discrimination rather than the failure of Blacks to adopt middle-class values that best explains the high rates of marital dissolution in the late nineteenth century. Indeed, she suggests that the adoption of mainstream values was part of the problem rather than the solution, for the realities of racial discrimination made such values unrealistic guides to family life and caused strain in many marriages.[59]

The distinctive history of Blacks in America, compared to other ethnic groups, illustrates a point made by Eric Wolf about the different functions of racial and ethnic categories in the modern world:

> The function of racial categories is exclusionary. They stigmatize groups in order to exclude them from more highly paid jobs and from access to the information needed for their execution.... While the categories of race serve primarily to exclude people from all but the lower echelons of the industrial army, ethnic categories express the ways that particular populations come to relate themselves to given segments of the labor market.

Thus, despite discrimination, ethnic groups in America have over time achieved at least limited job and residential mobility. Segregation and concentrations of poverty, however, have *increased* among Blacks over time, and this has required them to adopt qualitatively different coping strategies than those used by white immigrant workers.[60]

We should regard those different coping strategies, however, less as a sign of *disorganization* than *reorganization* of family life. For the final critique to be leveled against the theorists of black family 'pathology' is that their assumptions about what is 'normal' and 'functional' are seriously flawed. Carol Stack and Demetri Shimkin have shown that the extended family networks of both northern and southern Blacks in the twentieth century provide flexible, effective ways of building community while coping with poverty and discrimination. That such networks functioned similarly in the nineteenth century is illustrated by James Borchert's study of alley residents in Washington, D.C. Other studies reveal that black families maintained far tighter and more supportive kin ties than other urban families, more frequently taking care of elders, paupers, and orphans within the family rather than institutionalizing them.[61]

As in other sections of the working class, family life among Blacks, whether one- or two-parent, nuclear or extended, did not develop in isolation from the community; nor did it mirror the fragmentation of life characteristic of industrial capitalist society. Borchert writes that black Washingtonians 'turned the alley into a commons where children could play safely, adults could lounge and talk, and people could even sleep on hot summer nights.' Although 'outsiders were made to feel uncomfortable,' residents developed a strong community life, based on 'clear lines of social order' and expressed in extensive social rituals such as those surrounding death and hospitality:

> Extended kinship networks and the incorporation of friends and neighbor into the family made it difficult to determine where the family ended and neighborhood or community began. The distinction between work and recreation was also unclear in the alleys, if only because there was little time for activities that did not add to the family's limited resources. Children's world was also play, 'Some women regard housework as a form of recreation,' and men fished for both sustenance and pleasure.

Alley dwellers also 'drew no sharp lines between the sacred and the secular. Like everything else in alley life, religion and folklife were intertwined almost completely.'[62]

The ways in which necessary adaptations to poverty interacted with creative innovations in family life and sex roles are well illustrated in the history of black women and children. As Eugene Genovese has pointed out apropos the slave community, far from there being a debilitating black matriarchy, male and female relations may have been healthier than in much of white society. Jacqueline Jones argues that after Reconstruction black women continued to play a leading role in work and community-building, helping black families to develop work patterns that gave them at least some independence from white interference. Nineteenth-century black children's commitment to both work and education suggests that if anyone had a problem with weak ego structure it was the overprotected, passive children of white middle-class families in Chicago described by Sennett.[63]

In the late nineteenth century, many more black wives worked than white: Approximately 20 percent of married black women worked for wages, in contrast to only 4 percent of married white women. Elizabeth Pleck has examined possible explanations for this and suggests 'that black women's wage earning was a means of coping with [black men's] long-term income inadequacy.' Although other working men faced low wages and chronic unemployment, they had some possibility of wage raises over time. Jobs available to black men, by contrast, 'were more often dead ends.' Claudia Goldin reports that her research might support either 'the hypothesis that black women worked to enable sons to remain in school or the hypothesis that they worked because their children were discriminated against in the labor market.' The difficulty black children had in finding jobs certainly reinforced an emphasis on education: history bears out modern assertions by Blacks that they have to be twice as qualified as whites to earn almost as much. Even today, for example, Blacks with four years' college education earn an average of $800 less per year than white high school graduates.[64]

Although poverty, discrimination, and commitment to children's education explain much of the tendency for black wives to work, they do not account for all of it. Black wives were more likely to work than white wives from the same income level. This may have been due partly to realistic fear of discrimination and partly to a greater need to protect the family against the strong probability of downward mobility. But it may also have reflected a self-confidence and independence among black women connected to their central role in work and community, as well as an acceptance of and respect for that role by black men.[65]

A final characteristic of black families in the late nineteenth century runs counter to many impressionistic accounts: between 1860 and 1910 the fertility of Blacks was lower than that of their white neighbors in any given region except the South. And 'by 1910 even southern blacks had lower levels of childbearing than did their white neighbors.' Thus the high overall fertility of Blacks in the nineteenth century was a function of the fact that most Blacks lived in the South, a region whose economic and social characteristics tended to foster high fertility among most of its residents. In urban areas, black households were consistently smaller than white ones.[66]

THE GREAT UPHEAVAL AND ITS DEFEAT

There were times, of course, when divergent family strategies, ethnic and racial divisions, and local or regional variations were transcended or fused into a larger expression of class solidarity and united action. In 1878, the Knights of Labor, initially organized as an underground union to avoid repression, came out into the open by holding a national convention. The Knights quickly moved to the forefront of attempts to organize workers across religious, ethnic, and even gender divisions. They tried seriously to build not only a unified working-class culture and movement, but alternative working-class institutions. In addition to the cooperative stores and laundries discussed above, they even set up assemblies that allowed workers to settle domestic and community disputes without depending on the bourgeois court system.[67]

The Knights supported equal pay for equal work and helped to organize a number of female unions and strikes. By 1886 there were about 200 women's assemblies and 50,000 female members. The Knights also organized black workers, recording 60,000 black members by 1886. At the 1886 general assembly, the convention set up a women's department to organize women workers, investigate their special problems, and agitate for equal pay. Leonara Barry, an Irish woman who worked in a hosiery mill, became the Knights' General Investigator for women workers, a job that included both education and practical organization. Meanwhile, both the South and the West generated important opposition movements in the 1870s and 1880s: the Granger Movement and Populism. At times these movements seemed on the verge of transcending racism, utilizing the talents of women, and linking up with the industrial working class.

In 1885, the Knights of Labor won a series of strikes in the Southwest and in 1886 they helped to spearhead a national movement for the eight-hour day. In city after city during that year, the working-class 'subculture of opposition' coalesced into stronger organizations, mass marches, huge strikes, and independent political action. Between 1884 and 1886, membership in the Knights of Labor jumped from 50,000 to 700,000. Labor tickets appeared in 189 towns and cities in thirty-four states and four territories, and the Knights claimed to have elected a dozen congressmen in the November election.[68]

Swift and violent repression followed, as the business and middle classes responded in shock and outrage to this evidence of working-class disaffection and potential power. Sean Wilentz has suggested that Haymarket was just the 'beginning of what may some day come to be recognized as the most intense (and probably the most violent) counter-offensive ever waged against any country's organized workers.'[69] The fledgling movement proved unable to withstand the assault. Within a year, membership in the labor movement had dropped precipitously; by 1894, the Knights of Labor were effectively finished. With them went many of the institutions and associations that had nourished class solidarity and opposition. These losses were to have momentous long-range consequences for the evolution of working-class family life.

The reasons for labor's defeat were many: ethnic, craft, and ideological divisions played an important role, as did the gap between small-town labor movements and large-city ones, and the lack of a strong reform wing within the middle class. The ability of the American political system to absorb working-class leaders without adopting working-class programs was also a factor; most of the Knights' political victories involved collaboration with one of the major parties. Leon Fink comments that 'the dominant two parties emerged from this period with a stronger grip than ever on the working class. Ironically, a movement that began by defying the contemporary party system may in the end have left workers even more firmly within its confines.' Mike Davis also directs attention to the emergence of a 'spoils system' for local craft unions within the big-city political machines: 'The overall effect ... was to corrupt labor leadership, substitute paternalism for worker self-reliance, and, through the formation of ethnic patronage monopolies, keep the poorer strata of the working class permanently divided.'[70]

Labor was not wholly crushed. The American Railroad Union led important struggles, culminating in the Pullman strike of 1894; western and southern miners organized; Troy Collar Workers struck successfully; radical German workers in the Midwest and Jewish immigrants in New York built working-class socialist movements; the United Garment Workers was organized; the American Federation of Labor made important gains. There were serious defeats, such as the Homestead and New Orleans strikes of 1892, but important links were forged between the Farmers Alliance and the labor movement, and in 1895 it appeared that a new national coalition between populism and labor might well sweep the country. Yet the coalition was derailed before it had been clearly established. Racism and ethnic divisions were critical determinants of this outcome. The southern elite orchestrated a vicious attack on the Black-white alliance that had begun to emerge in the South, legalizing or extending segregation and whipping up racist fears, while in the North, Law and Order Leagues cooperated with the American Protective Association (founded 1887) to blame immigrants for both economic insecurity and social unrest. At the same time, there was a strong move 'toward depoliticizing reform from above'—'divesting economic decision-making from locally elected officials to appointed bodies (e.g., planning boards, zoning commissions, or insurance and banking commissions) and to the courts.'[71]

The revival of racial segregation in the South, the diversion of western workers' concerns toward Oriental exclusion, the narrowing of political demands to the call for free silver, and (after 1896) a significant increase in farmers' real income tended to dampen discontent, split the movement along racial lines, and divide farmers from industrial workers. The result was that those left out of the capitalist expansion—in the factories, the South, and the West—did not overcome their differences enough to mount a coordinated challenge to the system that so many of them resented. The labor movement divided into a dominant reformist and a minority radical wing (itself split along ethnic and ideological lines), while the Populist Party was compressed into the Free Silver campaign.

The working class splintered electorally, some workers supporting the Republicans in reaction to the agrarian and nativist tone of the Democratic Party, others withdrawing from electoral participation entirely (or, as in the case of southern Blacks, being directly excluded from the polls). While workers remained willing to act militantly and to raise issues of working-class solidarity, 'the responses to such appeals to class solidarity were quite mixed.... Workers were neither consistently class conscious, nor consistently lacking in class consciousness.' Instead, 'as the excitement passed and the reinforcing network of an oppositional subculture atrophied, class loyalties once again had to compete with other alternatives.'[72]

A revival of working-class organization was to come in the twentieth century, though the declining electoral participation of American workers, the split between radicals and reformists, and the growing dominance of incrementalists in the mainstream labor movement were to change the nature of working-class culture and the role of families within it. In the meantime, one immediate legacy of the Great Upheaval was that recognition of class stratification and conflict was forced upon middle-class consciousness. Middle-class readers rediscovered poverty and exploitation as serious issues; their concerns converged with those of far-sighted businessmen and politicians who realized that some of the most pressing grievances had to be met if larger and more successful social explosions were to be averted. Some of the earliest expressions of this new attitude were heard in cities that had experienced the most powerful outbursts during the Great Upheaval. Chicago civic leader Franklin MacVeagh, for example, 'abandoned his 1870s property-based Tory conception of municipal politics and endorsed "the rational demands of the workingmen.... I believe in democracy and democracy is impossible if in the long run workingmen are not a part of its conservative support."'[73]

The attempt to found a conservative support for American democracy in the working class was part of a general transformation of social reproduction that helped to reshape both working-class and middle-class families into forms at once more private and more closely connected to the state. The defeat of the Great Upheaval set the stage for that transformation.

NOTES

1. David Montgomery, 'Labor and the Republic in Industrial America, 1860–1920,' *Mouvement Sociale* 111 (1980), p. 204.
2. Steven Ross, *Workers on the Edge* (New York, 1985), p. xvi; Montgomery, 'Labor and the Republic,' p. 211, and *Beyond Equality: Labor and the Radical Republicans. 1862–72* (New York, 1967).
3. Bruce Laurie and Mark Schmitz, 'Manufacture and Productivity: The Making of an Industrial Base, Philadelphia, 1850–1880,' in Theodore Hershberg, *Philadelphia: A Tale of Three Cities*, pp. 43–92; Michael Katz, *The Social Organization of Early Industrial Capitalism* (Cambridge, MA, 1982), p. 1; Montgomery, *Beyond Equality*, p. 40; Richard Ostreicher, *Solidarity and Fragmentation: Working People and Class Consciousness in Detroit, 1875–1900* (Urbana, 1986), pp. 4–13; Rogers, *Work Ethic*, pp. 24, 161, 163, 171; Berthoff, *Unsettled People*, p. 327.

4. Montgomery, 'Gutman's Nineteenth-Century America,' *Labor History* 19 (1978), pp. 428–9.
5. David Roediger, ' "Not Only the Ruling Classes to Overcome, But Also the So-Called Mob": Class, Skill, and Community in the St. Louis General Strike of 1877,' *Journal of Social History* 19 (1985), p. 227.
6. Leon Fink, *Workingmen's Democracy: The Knights of Labor and American Politics* (Urbana, 1983), p. 57.
7. Ostreicher, *Solidarity and Fragmentation*, p. 60.
8. Lawrence Glasco, 'The Life Cycles and the Structure of American Ethnic Groups,' *Journal of Urban History* 1 (1975); Betsy Caroli, Robert Harney, and Lydio Tomasi, *The Italian Immigrant Woman in North America* (Toronto, 1979); Richard Erlich, ed., *Immigrants in Industrial America, 1850–1920* (Charlortesville, 1977); Charles Mindel and Robert Hubenstein, eds., *Ethnic Families in America* (New York, 1976); Cecyle Neidle, *America's Immigrant Women* (Boston, 1975); Allen Davis and Mark Haller, eds., *The Peoples of Philadelphia: A History of Ethnic Groups and Lower-Class Life, 1790–1940* (Philadelphia, 1973); John Bodnar, *Immigration and Industrialization: Ethnicity in an American Mill Town* (Pittsburgh, 1977); John Bodnar, Roger Simon, and Michael Weber, *Lives of Their Own: Blacks, Italians, and Poles in Pittsburgh, 1900–1960* (Urbana, 1982); Judith E. Smith, 'Our Own Kind: Family and Community Networks in Providence,' in Cott and Pleck, *Heritage of Her Own; Steven Thernstrom, Poverty and Progress* (Cambridge, MA, 1964); Virginia Yans-McLaughlin, *Family and Community: Italian Immigrants in Buffalo* (Ithaca, 1977); Claudia Goldin, 'Family Strategies and the Family Economy in the Late Nineteenth Century,' in Hershberg, *Philadelphia*, p. 293; Mfanwy Morgan and Hilda Golden, 'Immigrant Families in an Industrial City: A Study of Holyoke, 1880,' *Journal of Family History* 4 (1979), p. 62.
9. Morgan and Golden, 'Immigrant Families'; Clyde and Sally Griffen, *Natives and Newcomers*; Davis and Haller, *Peoples of Philadelphia*; Tamara Hareven and Maris Vinovskis, 'Marital Fertility, Ethnicity, and Occupation in Urban Families: An Analysis of South Boston and the South End in 1880,' *Journal of Social History* 8 (1975), p. 84; Micaela di Leonardo, 'The Myth of the Urban Village,' in Susan Armitage and Elizabeth Jameson, eds., *The Women's West* (Norman, 1987), p. 279.
10. Hershberg, *Philadelphia*; Anthony Broadman and Michael Weber, 'Economic Growth and Occupational Mobility in Nineteenth-Century Urban America: A Reappraisal,' *Journal of Social History* 11 (1977), p. 69; Ostreicher, *Solidarity and Fragmentation*; Griffens, *Native and Newcomers*, pp. 259–60; Katz, *Social Organization*, pp. 80–81.
11. John Jentz, 'Bread and Labor; Chicago's German Bakers Organize,' *Chicago History* 12 (1983), pp. 24–35; Edward Bunbys, 'Nativity and the Distribution of Wealth: Chicago 1870,' *Explorations in Economic History* 19 (1982), pp. 101–9; Dirk Hoerder, ed., *'Struggle a Hard Battle': Essays on Working-Class Immigrants* (Dekalb, 1986).
12. John Cumbler, *Working-Class Community in Industrial America: Work, Leisure, and Struggle in Two Industrial Cities, 1880–1930* (Westport, 1979); Francis Couvares, *The Remaking of Pittsburgh: Class and Culture in an Industrializing City, 1877–1919* (Albany, 1984); Roy Rosenzweig, *Eight Hours for What We Will: Workers and Leisure in an Industrial City, 1870–1920* (New York, 1983); Bodnar, *Immigration and Industrialization*; Mike Davis, *Prisoners of the American Dream* (London, 1986), p. 43.

13. Ostreicher, *Solidarity and Fragmentation*, p. 61.
14. Trachtenberg, *Incorporation*, pp. 90–91; Peter Shergold, '"Reefs of Roast Beef": The American Worker's Standard of Living in Comparative Perspective,' in Dirk Hoerder, ed., *American Labor and Immigration History, 1877–1920s: Recent European Research* (Urbana, 1983), p. 101.
15. Michael Haines, 'Industrial Work and the Family Life Cycle, 1889–1890,' *Research in Economic History* 4 (1979), pp. 289–356; Katz, *Social Organization*, p. 280; Ostreicher, *Solidarity*, p. 14.
16. Thernstrom, *Poverty and Progress*; Charles Stephenson, 'A Gathering of Strangers?' in Milton Cantor, ed., *American Workingclass Culture* (Greenwood, 1979); Tamara Hareven, 'The Dynamics of Kin in an Industrial Community,' *American Journal of Sociology* 84 (1978).
17. Cumbler, *Working-Class Community*, p. 118.
18. Francis Early, 'The French-Canadian Family Economy and Standard-of-Living in Lowell, Massachusetts, 1870,' *Journal of Family History* 7 (1982), pp. 184, 188.
19. Katz, *Social Organization*, pp. 336, 343.
20. Haines, 'Industrial Work,' p. 291; Carol Groneman, '"She Earns as a Child; She Pays as a Man": Women Workers in a Mid-Nineteenth-Century New York City Community,' in Milton Canton and Bruce Laurie, eds., *Class, Sex, and the Woman Worker* (Westport, 1977).
21. Boydston, 'Her Daily Bread,' p. 19; Strasser, *Never Done*; Elizabeth Butler, *Women and the Trades, Pittsburgh 1907–1908* (New York, 1909), p. 337; Werrheimer, *We Were There*, p. 214.
22. Robert Smuts, *Women and Work in America* (New York, 1974), pp. 11–12; Susan Strasser, 'An Enlarged Human Existence?' and *Never Done*; Susan Kleinberg, 'Technology and Women's Work: The Lives of Women in Pittsburgh, 1870–1900,' *Labor History* 17 (1976); Margaret Byington, *Homestead: The Households of a Mill Town* (Pittsburgh, 1974), pp. 72–4.
23. Strasser, *Never Done*; Ryan, *Womanhood in America*, p. 214.
24. Robert Bieder, 'Kinship as a Factor in Migration,' *Journal of Marriage and the Family* 35 (1973); A. Gordon Darroch, 'Migrants in the Nineteenth Century; Fugitives or Families in Motion,' *Journal of Family History* 6 (1981); Lawrence Glasco, 'Migration and Adjustment in the 19th Century City,' in Hareven and Vinovskis, *Family and Population*; Eugene Litwach, 'Geographic Mobility and Extended Family Cohesion,' *American Sociological Review* 25 (1960); J.S. and I.D. Macdonald, 'Chain Migration, Ethnic Neighborhood Formation, and Social Networks,' *Millbank Memorial Fund Quarterly* 42 (1964); Virginia Yans-McLaughlin, *Family and Community: Italian Immigrants in Buffalo, 1880–1930* (Ithaca, 1977).
25. Ostreicher, *Solidarity and Fragmentation*, p. 16.
26. Katz, *Social Organization*, p. 131.
27. On the role of upper class women as Sunday school teachers, see Wallace, *Rockdale*; for comments on the acculturation patterns connected to the high percentage of young immigrant females living in the homes of native-born employers, see Lawrence Glasco, 'The Life Cycles and Household Structure of American Ethnic Groups,' in Corr and Pleck, *Heritage of Her Own*.
28. Hans Medick, 'The Proto-Industrial Family Economy,' *Economic History Review* 3 (1976), p. 304. For a discussion of how the peasant immigrant family was susceptible to a special exploitation in American industry, see Bodnar, *Immigration and Industrialization*.
29. Martha May, 'Bread Before Roses: American Workingmen, Labor Unions and

the Family Wage,' in Ruth Milkman, ed., *Women, Work and Protest* (Boston, 1985), pp. 3, 6.

30. Elizabeth Jameson, 'Imperfect Unions: Class and Gender in Cripple Creek, 1894–1904,' in Cantor and Laurie, *Class, Sex, and the Woman Worker*, p. 175; May, 'Bread Before Roses,' pp. 2–21.

31. Linda Schneider, 'The Citizen Striker: Workers' Ideology in the Homestead Strike of 1892,' *Labor History* 23 (1982), p. 63.

32. Nancy Dye, 'The Louisville Wooden Mills Strike of 1887,' *Register of the Kentucky Historical Society* 16 (1982); Carole Turbin, 'Reconceptualizing Family, Work and Labor Organizing: Working Women in Troy, 1860–1890,' *Review of Radical Political Economics* 16 (1984), pp. 9–11.

33. Foner, *Factory Girls*, p. 90.

34. Steven Dubnoff, 'Gender, the Family, and the Problem of Work Motivation in a Transition to Industrial Capitalism,' *Journal of Family History* 4 (1979); Daniel Walkowitz, *Worker City, Company Town: Iron and Cotton-Worker Protest in Troy and Cohoes, Newark, 1855–1884* (Urbana, 1978), pp. 119–20.

35. Kessler-Harris, 'Where are the Women Workers?' p. 356; Ryan, *Womanhood*, p. 207; Louise Odencrantz, *Italian Women in Industry: A Study of Conditions in New York City* (New York, 1919); Smuts, *Woman and Work*, p. 43.

36. May, 'Bread Before Roses,' pp. 7, 8; Jameson, 'Imperfect Unions'; Andrew Dawson, 'The Parameters of Class Consciousness: The Social Outlook of the Skilled Worker, 1890–1920,' in Hoerder, *American Labor and Immigration History*.

37. Rosenzweig, *Eight Hours*, p. 43.

38. Ibid., p. 45; Perry Duis, *The Saloon: Public Drinking in Chicago and Boston, 1880–1920* (Urbana, 1983), p. 2.

39. Ibid., p. 108.

40. Ibid., pp. 148–9; Jon Kingsdale, 'The "Poor Man's Club": Social Functions of the Urban Working-Class Saloon,' in Pleck and Pleck, *The American Man*.

41. Kathy Peiss, *Cheap Amusements: Working Women and Leisure in Turn-of-the-Century New York* (Philadelphia, 1986), p. 26.

42. Zaretsky, 'Place of the Family,' p. 217.

43. John Modell and Tamara Hareven, 'Urbanization and the Malleable Household: An Examination of Boarding and Lodging in American Families,' in Gordon, *Family in Social-Historical Perspective*; Strasser, *Never Done*, pp. 150–52; Hareven, 'Family as Process.'

44. Modell and Hareven, 'Urbanization and the Malleable Household,' pp. 54, 55, 66, n. 10.

45. Sam Bass Warner, *Street Car Suburbs: The Processes of Growth in Boston, 1870–1900* (Cambridge, MA, 1962); Hershberg et al., '"The Journey-to-Work": An Empirical Investigation of Work, Residence and Transportation, Philadelphia, 1850 and 1880,' in Hershberg, *Philadelphia*; Peiss, *Cheap Amusements*, p. 13.

46. Cumbler, *Working-Class Community*, pp. 155–6; Peiss, *Cheap Amusements*, p. 32.

47. Margaret Byington, 'The Mill Town Courts and Their Lodgers,' *Charities and Commons* 21 (1909), pp. 913–20.

48. Robert and Helen Lynd, *Middletown* (New York, 1929), p. 26. For an example of the role of boarding in creating strike support, see Mary Blewett, 'The Union of Sex and Craft in the Haverhill Shoe Strike of 1895,' *Labor History* 20 (1979), p. 360.

49. Stephen Thernstrom, *Poverty and Progress* (Cambridge, MA, 1964); James

Henretta, 'The Study of Social Mobility: Ideological Assumptions and Conceptual Biases,' *Labor History* 18 (1977), p. 175.

50. David Brundage, 'The Producing Classes and the Saloon: Denver in the 1880s,' *Labor History* 26 (1985), p. 39; Leon Fink, *Workingman's Democracy* (Urbana, 1985), p. 12.

51. Montgomery, 'Labor and the Republic,' pp. 204–5.

52. Stanley Elkins, *Slavery: A Problem in American Institutional and Intellectual Life* (Chicago, 1959); Oscar Lewis, 'The Culture of Poverty,' *Scientific American* 215 (1966); Daniel Moynihan, *The Negro Family: The Case for National Action* (Washington, D.C., 1965); Lee Rainwater and W.L. Yancey, *The Moynihan Report and the Politics of Controversy* (Cambridge, MA, 1967); Nathan Glazer and Daniel Moynihan, B*eyond the Melting Pot: The Negroes, Puerto Ricans, Jews, Italians and Irish of New York City* (Cambridge, MA, 1963). A good review of this literature and other perspectives on black families may be found in William Harris, 'Research on the Black Family: Mainstream and Dissenting Perspectives,' *Journal of Ethnic Studies* 6 (1979).

53. Levine, *Black Culture and Consciousness; Gutman, Black Family*; James Borcherr, *Alley Life in Washington: Family, Community, Religion, and Folklife in the City, 1850–1970* (Urbana, 1980), pp. 208, 210.

54. Herbert Gutman, 'Persistent Myths About the Afro-American Family,' *Journal of Interdisciplinary History* 6 (1975); Theodore Hershberg, 'Free Blacks in Antebellum Pennsylvania,' *Journal of Social History* 5 (1971–72); Paul Lammermeier, 'The Urban Black Family of the Nineteenth Century: A Study of Black Family Structure in the Ohio Valley, 1850–1880,' *Journal of Marriage and the Family* 35 (1973), p. 455.

55. Elizabeth Pleck, 'The Two-Parent Household: Black Family Structure in Late Nineteenth-Century Boston,' in Gordon, *American Family*, 1st edn, p. 165; *Pleck, Black Migration and Poverty: Boston 1865–1900* (New York, 1979), pp. 182, 194.

56. Pleck, 'Two-Parent Household'; Hershberg, *Philadelphia*, p. 451; Pleck, *Black Migration.*

57. Gutman, *Black Family*, pp. 448, 452, 521–6, 530; Hershberg, *Philadelphia*, pp. 348, 374.

58. Gutman, 'Persistent Myths,' pp. 205–7; Paul Worthman, 'Working Class Mobility in Birmingham, Alabama, 1880–1914,' in Tamara Hareven, ed., *Anonymous Americans: Explorations in Nineteenth-Century Social History*, (Englewood Cliffs, 1971), p. 197; Ira Berlin and Herberr Gutman, 'Natives and Immigrants, Free Men and Slaves,' *American Historical Review* 88 (1983), p. 1194.

59. Pleck, *Black Migration*, pp. 198–200.

60. Eric Wolf, *Europe and the People Without History* (Berkeley, 1982), p. 381; Hershberg et al., 'A Tale of Three Cities,' pp. 461–91.

61. Carol Stack, *All Our Kin: Strategies for Survival in a Black Community* (New York, 1974); Demetri Shimkin, Edith Shimkin, and Dennis Frare, eds., *The Extended Family in Black Society* (Chicago, 1978); Pleck, *Black Migration*, p. 196; Borchert, *Alley Life*, p. 81; James and Lois Horron, *Black Bostonians: Family Life and Community Struggle in Antebellum Boston* (New York, 1979).

62. Borchert, *Alley Life*, pp. 196, 220 and passim.

63. Eugene Genovese, *Roll, Jordan, Roll: The World the Slaves Made* (New York, 1974), p. 500; Jones, *Labor of Love, Labor of Sorrow.*

64. Elizabeth Pleck, 'A Mother's Wages: Income Earning Among Married Italian

and Black Women, 1896–1911,' in Gordon, *American Family*, 2nd edn, p. 502; Jones, *Labor of Love*; Claudia Goldin, 'Family Strategies and the Family Economy in the Late Nineteenth Century: The Role of Secondary Workers,' in Hershberg, *Philadelphia*, p. 305; E.J. Kahn, *The American People* (New York, 1973); Michael Reich, 'The Economics of Racism,' in Richard Edwards, Michael Reich, and Thomas Weisskopf, eds., *The Capitalist System* (Englewood Cliffs, 1972), p. 314.

65. Pleck, 'A Mother's Wages'; Degler, *At Odds*, pp. 390–91.
66. Robert Wells, *Uncle Sam's Family: Issues in and Perspectives on American Demographic History* (Albany, 1985), p. 50; Jones, *Labor of Love*, p. 114.
67. Davis, *Prisoners*, p. 31.
68. Ostreicher, *Solidarity and Fragmentation*; Fink, *Working Man's Democracy*, pp. 26–7.
69. Sean Wilentz, 'Against Exceptionalism: Class Consciousness and the American Labor Movement, 1790–1920,' *International Labor and Working Class History* 26 (1984), p. 15.
70. Ostreicher, *Solidarity and Fragmentation*; Couvares, *Pittsburgh*; Montgomery, *Beyond Equality*; Fink, *Workingman's Democracy*, p. 226; Davis, Prisoners, p. 33.
71. Fink, *Workingman's Democracy*, pp. 227–8. On the racist counterattack against Black-white alliances, see Joseph Cartwright, *The Triumph of Jim Crow: Tennessee Race Relations in the 1880s* (Knoxville, 1976); Woodward, *Strange Career of Jim Crow and Origins of the New South*; Howard Rabinowitz, *Race Relations in the Urban South, 1865–1900* (New York, 1977); David Gerber, *Black Ohio and the Color Line, 1860–1915* (Urbana, 1976); Davis, *Prisoners*, pp. 38–40.
72. Ostreicher, *Solidarity and Fragmentation*, pp. 222, 230.
73. Richard Schneirov, 'Class Conflict, Municipal Politics, and Governmental Reform in Gilded Age Chicago,' in Harmut Keil and John Jentz, eds., *German Workers in Industrial Chicago: A Comparative Perspective* (Dekalb, 1983), p. 200.

6

EXCERPTS FROM *BECOMING MEXICAN AMERICAN*

ETHNICITY, CULTURE, AND IDENTITY IN CHICANO LOS ANGELES, 1900–1945

George J. Sánchez

FAMILY LIFE AND THE SEARCH FOR STABILITY

As Guadalupe Salazar looked out of her train window, her mind was full of images of the past and questions about the future. Heading from Chicago to Los Angeles, she realized that her life in the United States had not turned out as she had hoped. It was the middle of the Great Depression, and Guadalupe had just ended a marriage that had lasted only a few years. Her ex-husband, Arcadio Yñiguez, had crossed the border in 1913 as a teenager from Nochistlán, Zacatecas, fleeing the violence of the Mexican Revolution. Working at a variety of odd jobs, he finally settled in Chicago during the 1920s, and there met and married Guadalupe. When the two split up, Arcadio returned to Nochistlán, while Guadalupe and their five-year-old son left for California. She was determined to start a new life in Los Angeles, where her father resided, although she had not seen him since his impressment into military service during the revolution twenty years earlier. A single female parent in 1931, Guadalupe Salazar saw her immigrant dream fade into a painful reality of insecurity.[1]

The generation of scholars who wrote during the post–World War II decades about European immigrant family life would not have been surprised by Salazar's experience. Their work emphasized the sharp discontinuities between traditional family relations in Old World peasant villages and the life immigrants encountered in modern, industrial cities after migration. Rooted in an unbending model of modernization, their studies found family disintegration to be an unfortunate, but inevitable consequence of the immigrants' undeniable break with their past. Guadalupe's failed marriage might easily have been portrayed by this school of immigration history as the result of a futile attempt to construct an orthodox union in a new and hostile environment. As Oscar Handlin put it: "Roles once thoroughly defined were now altogether confounded."[2]

Yet Guadalupe's story defied such characterization. Reunited with her father, she built a new life in Los Angeles out of which emerged a remarkable family. Her second husband, Tiburcio Rivera, had been a band musician in Mexico. He knew Guadalupe from Chicago, where he briefly owned a pool hall. They did not court until he too moved to California. In addition to Guadalupe's son, the couple had four daughters, all of whom grew up in East Los Angeles. The family endured the Depression, frequent bouts with overt discrimination, and hazardous work conditions. In spite of these hardships Guadalupe and Tiburcio provided their children a stable working-class family life. Fifty-five years after her arrival in the city, Guadalupe Salazar received the "Mother of the Year" award from the senior citizen clubs in East Los Angeles. Mother of five, grandmother of 28, and great-grandmother of 10, she had become the respected elder of an extended family that totaled more than 200. Asked about her success, she responded: "You have to have family unity."[3]

Critics of the "Handlin school" of immigration history have pointed to the stability and resiliency of immigrant families such as Guadalupe Salazar's. Their depiction of immigrant adaptation stresses the retention of traditional values and the durability and adaptability of social relationships, all of which helped Mexican Americans to withstand the changes wrought by migration, settlement, and adjustment. In particular, these historians understand the critical role of kinship networks which allowed Salazar to reestablish herself in Los Angeles. Her relationship with her father, though strained because of the separation in Mexico, was rebuilt in the United States. In fact, this family was strengthened by Salazar's decision to call upon kin in time of need. As revisionist historian Virginia Yans-McLaughlin has pointed out, "immigrants put their Old World family ties to novel uses in America," essentially putting "new wine in old bottles."[4]

Just as historians of immigration debated the degree of cultural persistence inherent in immigrant family life, Chicano social scientists were examining the dynamics of the Mexican immigrant family. These scholars depicted *la familia* as warm and nurturing, an environment of support and stability in times of stress. They surmised that since roles and expectations continued to be circumscribed in the traditional manner, conflict within the family was kept to a minimum. From this perspective, *machismo* was not so much a maladaptive response which solidified male dominance, but rather represented an appropriate mechanism to insure the continuation of Mexican family pride and respect. Although noted in the literature, the oppression of women within the family was dismissed as a necessary evil in order to maintain family stability and tradition.[5]

Ironically, this approach had much in common with another, older body of sociological literature that depicted the Mexican family as pathological. These psychoanalytically oriented studies were the product of decades of stereotypical accounts examining "the problem" of the Mexican. They viewed Mexican families as authoritarian and *macho-*

dominated, impeding individual achievement and independence while promoting passivity and familial dependence. Thus, the same values that some Chicano scholars characterized as positive were viewed as "a tangle of pathology" by Anglo American social scientists.[6] What both groups shared was a unidimensional view of the Mexican family, a caricature suspended in time and impervious to the social forces acting upon it. Such a perspective found any acculturated family to be atypical.

When placed in historical context, both characterizations of the Mexican immigrant family are problematic. First, and most important, they ignore the great diversity among Mexican immigrant families. Although many Mexicans migrated from rural villages, others came from cities. Many families migrated as entire units, while others were involved in chain migration. Some immigrants settled in largely Mexican communities along the border; others ventured further inland where the Anglo American population dominated. Before 1940, thousands of families and individual family members were in this country only temporarily. Perhaps the majority came as single migrants, and reconstituted their families in the United States. These families were often mixtures of Mexicans born on both sides of the border and occasionally included non-Mexican spouses. Moreover, individual families acculturated and adapted to American life in a multitude of ways.

Second, both conflict and consensus existed within each family. Individual members of a family might disagree over a particular family decision. Over time, positions would reverse themselves as other situations arose. Difficult periods of maturation, like a child's adolescence, could prove to be times of family conflict, while family unity might be invoked during periods of crisis and abrupt change, such as the death of a parent or a new marriage. Moreover, while Mexican family members often gave highest priority to the welfare of the family, specific family decisions could mask the range of compromises made by individuals involved in that resolution.

Finally, every Mexican who came to the United States made adjustments. Though most families did not disintegrate under the weight of changing circumstances, they certainly acclimated. The nature of this acculturation varied, depending on the setting, and different strategies were developed to fit the needs of the historical moment. A new identity was continuously being formed.

To understand the diversity of family experiences among Mexican immigrants in Los Angeles, we must examine critically assumptions regarding family life in turn-of-the-century Mexico in regions that contributed migrants to the United States. Most interpretations characterize Mexican families as hierarchical, rigidly patriarchal, solidified by age-old customs rooted in peasant values and Catholic tradition. Mexicans were characterized as having large, extended family structures in which gender roles were strictly separated, reinforced by stern parental discipline and community pressure. Each individual village usually consisted of a few extended families linked to each other through generations of intermarriage and other kin relationships, including *compadrazgo*, the interlocking bond created by parents and godparents of a child.

Recent studies challenge this interpretation of Mexican family life, depicting much more flexibility within family patterns. By the turn of the century, economic challenges brought about by the penetration of market capitalism into all but the most isolated villages during the Porfiriato forced families to adapt. As land prices were driven up, families were forced to send members, usually adolescent boys and young husbands, into the wage economy. Women were also swept into the cash-based economy. Some marketed surplus food raised on family plots, while others sewed for profit utilizing Singer technology. Central markets in most villages became more active points of economic exchange. A family's own land was increasingly attended to by those outside this cash nexus, usually by women and children closer to home or those who returned from various forms of wage labor in time to complete a harvest.

Rigid gender roles could hardly be maintained under these circumstances. The Mexican family showed that it was capable of flexibility and adaptability, even under the most distressing circumstances. In addition to migration brought about by economic conditions, most villages contained families that had experienced the death of their male heads of household. Widows were often able to maintain a family's well-being, aided by older adolescents or nearby relatives. Female-headed households, the result of either death or desertion, were not uncommon at the turn of the century, although marriage continued to be the preferred societal norm for all adult women.

Most families participated in economic migration in order to maintain a life that they identified as rooted in traditional values. Working for the railroad or in the mines was intended as a short-term solution to an emergency. Yet the Mexican government's economic and social policies around the turn of the century transformed these strategies into a way of life. Porfirian economics demanded a large, growing wage labor pool, as did economic developments in the United States. Families found themselves caught in a cycle of economic uncertainty, necessitating the flexibility of "traditional" roles and norms for survival.

After 1910, the Mexican Revolution only intensified these patterns. Geographic mobility increased, often forcing entire families to flee their native villages to avoid the danger of incoming troops. More often, male family members were sent scurrying, either to avoid conscription or to join one of the military factions. It was common, in the absence of men, for women to perform most day-to-day economic functions related to a family's property and sustenance. If not touched directly by the fighting, families found that destruction of neighboring fields, markets, or transportation could force them to engage in more extensive migration to market their goods or earn wages for their labor.

Mexicans who migrated to the United States generally came from families that had already engaged in years of creative adaptation to adversity. Unlike European immigrant families, whose movement into American society could best be described as chain migration, Mexican families were much more likely to be involved in a pattern of circular migration. Although most European immigrant groups also had high rates of return migration, ranging from 25 to 60 percent, only Mexicans exhibited a pattern of back-and-forth movement that would continue for years.[7] Men ventured north across the border to engage in seasonal labor, then returned south for a period of a few months or a couple of years. If economic circumstances once again necessitated extra cash, the circular pattern began anew. During World War I and up until 1921, the United States government contributed to this pattern by giving entrance visas to temporary workers in order to regulate their movement back into Mexico at the end of a season.

Changes in U.S. immigration policy, however, made it more difficult to engage in this practice after 1921. An enlarged border patrol, enforced literacy tests, and higher visa fees made back-and-forth migration more risky and more expensive during the 1920s. Workers who had grown accustomed to legal, relatively easy passage across the border were now faced with the prospect of venturing north illegally or being held up indefinitely in border cities. Increasingly, Mexicans were forced to decide where they wanted to reside permanently. While many returned to Mexico, the large increase in the Mexican population of Los Angeles during the 1920s suggests that a significant proportion determined to make their homes in the north. For single, independent migrants, the decision meant a reorientation to the experience of working and living in the United States. Heads of households were required to move whole families across the border.

The process of family migration was often tortuous. It was likely to involve careful decision-making concerning which family members should be on which side of the border, taking place over several years. Economic opportunities and emotional attachments had to be weighed. Individual preferences could not always be ignored for the sake of the family good. Others besides immediate family members were often involved in the move; some provided resources while others provided short- and long-term care of minors.

The experience of one family, accessible to us through archived transcripts of the Board of Special Inquiry of the Immigration Service, may serve as an example of the complex process of family migration to Los Angeles.[8] On August 25, 1917, three individuals—María López de Astengo, her twelve-year-old son, José Jr., and Mrs. María Salido de Villa—presented themselves to American immigration authorities in Nogales, Arizona. Mrs. Astengo and her son had ventured north from Rosario, Sinaloa, on the western coast of Mexico. María's husband, José Sr., had fled their ranch two years earlier to avoid the danger associated with the revolution and to earn income for the family. A bookkeeper in Mexico, he used his experience to gain employment as an office clerk in Los Angeles, earning $2.50 a day. Mrs. Astengo did not intend to cross into the United States herself; rather, she was sending her son with a friend of her family, Mrs. Villa, who was going north to visit her own two children who lived in Los Angeles. Mrs. Villa's son had married in the United States and had lived in Los Angeles for the last five years. Her daughter arrived in Los Angeles in 1915. Mrs. Villa intended to return to Mexico in November or December when "the weather gets cold."

The following spring Mrs. Astengo sent Enrique, her next eldest son, to live with his father. He traveled with three other young Mexicans from Rosario, none family members. María Valdez, age twenty-seven, headed the group, guarding everyone's money during the passage. María, accompanied by her fourteen-year-old brother Jesús, came north to see her younger sister Josefina, who had been in the United States for about a year. Josefina was single and supported herself by working as a laundress. She lived in Los Angeles with a widowed second cousin. Josefina had been instructed by her mother in Rosario to put young Jesús in an American public school. María herself intended to stay only for about six months before returning to Rosario.

The fourth member of the group was Jesús Cambreros, a seventeen-year-old girlfriend from Rosario, who came to Los Angeles to live with her married sister Elisa, also a laundress. Elisa's husband, Luis Martinez, worked for Wells Fargo Express, earning seven or eight dollars a week. Since coming to the United States as a boy from Chihuahua, Martinez had also been a baker and a foundry worker. The couple had a baby and lived in a six-room house in the downtown area, renting out space to two other adults.

A few months later, Mrs. Astengo and the rest of her family joined her husband and sons in Los Angeles. But the migration of relatives did not end there. That summer, José Astengo urged his sister in Rosario to send her son to Los Angeles to attend school, rather naïvely noting that the city was "very clean ... perfectly safe and pleasant" with "no saloons, gambling houses, or houses of prostitution." At the beginning of July, Carlos Osuna made the trip through Nogales, accompanied by José's brother. Both planned on living with José's family while attending school. Another brother, Jesús, was also reportedly working in Los Angeles.

These reports of three distinct border crossings suggest the intricate nature of Mexican family migration to the United States. The Astengos first sent their husband north as a temporary measure. Younger male sons followed, once José had established himself in Los Angeles, María Astengo and the youngest children were the last to leave the homeland. Complicating the picture, brothers of José and a nephew also ventured northward when opportunities presented themselves for work or education. The Astengos sent family members north via train, but each trip was facilitated by other relatives or hometown friends who accompanied the travelers. Regular communication between family members on both sides of the border, including periodic visits and oral messages sent through family friends, enabled José to monitor the migration process. It is more difficult to assess the decision-making power of María, since we are not privy to their personal correspondence. One son reported that María maintained a family store in Rosario while José was in the United States, a fact which indicates some level of economic autonomy. Although the Astengos were better off than the average Mexican family, their experiences with immigration characterize many of the ways Mexicans took advantage of economic opportunity.

Other families who emigrated illustrate the many dimensions of familial migration. Older adolescents and young adults formed the bulk of the permanent emigrants. In particular, single men ventured north to find work, often aided by relatives or friends when they arrived. Young women also moved north, but were invariably accompanied by other family members and had relatives waiting for them in Los Angeles. The migration of these young adults' parents was often more problematic, but many visited their children, at least until the tightening of restrictions during the years from 1921 to 1924.

Single male migrants served as initiators of most Mexican migration. Although many European immigrant groups displayed high levels of family migration, the Mexican pattern seems to be similar to that of Italians, whose single migrant rate was around 75 percent. Among male Mexican immigrants who chose to naturalize in Los Angeles, in fact, only 10 percent had first ventured to the United States as married men. As in the Italian case, single Mexican migrants were also more likely to return to their homeland than those who were married and accompanied by their spouses.[9] Single migrants, like those married but traveling alone, generally remained in touch with their families in Mexico. As long as those ties remained strong, a high proportion of single males returned.

For single male migrants through the mid-1920s, the central Plaza area of Los Angeles remained the most important area of introduction to the city. Although this area also contained recently arrived families, single men dominated community life. Theatres, restaurants, bars, dancing clubs, and pool halls nearby catered to this male clientele. The Plaza itself was often used as a employment recruitment site, and on the weekends served as a locus for political discussions. Rental housing, including boarding houses for single men, was the norm in the barrio around the Plaza. Upon arriving in Los Angeles with eight other single men, Arturo Morales, a twenty-eight-year old from Acatlán, Jalisco, remembered being directed to a rooming house run by a woman from his home state. Within a week, all had obtained work, sharing two rooms in the boarding house between the eight of them.[10] Although other ethnic newcomers to Los Angeles increasingly flocked to the Plaza in the 1920s, most notably Italians and Chinese, Mexicans remained the largest group in the historic Mexican pueblo plaza area.

Many, if not most, of these single Mexican men stayed in Los Angeles only temporarily. Often they entered the city with the idea of earning money quickly, then returning to their families in Mexico. Living in the central Plaza area made this plan more possible. A male worker traveling alone could find employment through the various employment agencies with offices near the Plaza, or simply stand around in the early morning and wait for a prospective employer's call. Housing, though crowded and often unsanitary, was relatively cheap in the district and was tolerated by laborers hoping to stay only briefly in the city. With images of loved ones waiting across the border in need, many single men found Los Angeles to be a relatively easy place to find a job and earn extra cash before returning home.

On the other hand, the loosening of ties with the Mexican family of origin was crucial in generating a permanent immigrant population in Los Angeles. Although exact figures are not available, a significant number of single male migrants, who formed the vast majority of the transient Mexican population in the city, reoriented themselves toward permanent residency in the United States. While family considerations were fundamental to Mexicans who contemplated leaving their homeland, breaking those connections was crucial if a migrant was to stay in the United States. This process was aided by the restrictive immigration requirements which originated in 1917. But other factors were also important in solidifying this pattern.

The regional and state origins of immigrants were important factors which determined whether a newcomer planted roots in Los Angeles or not. According to Manuel Gamio's pathbreaking study, migrants from Mexico's agricultural central plateau were much more likely to send money back to their families. Although Los Angeles's Mexican population contained a considerable portion of members from this region, equally significant were migrants from urban areas and northern Mexico. These individuals were less likely to be supporting family members in Mexico. Familiarity with the United States and U.S.-Mexico border communities made it much more likely that single men migrating from northern border areas settled in Los Angeles permanently. Urban migrants were less likely to be involved in the supplemental cash economy which allowed many migrants to retain their agricultural land in Mexico.

The passage of time itself, of course, loosened ties to Mexico. Although many migrants no doubt originally intended a short visit to Los Angeles, thousands never achieved their goals. More often than not, Mexicans could not save much from the meager wages they received. It was easy to postpone a return to Mexico until the ever-elusive extra dollar was earned. As Estanislao Gómez, an immigrant from Guadalajara, put it: "I had always considered returning to Mexico, but the months and years went by, along with the fact that since I earn very little I can't save much."[11] Furthermore, Los Angeles was not a border community, and conditions there made regular contact difficult. Urban jobs, unlike agricultural employment, were less likely to be seasonal and were inflexible in providing time to visit relatives in Mexico. Periodic visits also required surplus cash which many migrants were never able to accrue.

Ironically, it was often the establishment of new family ties which broke a single male's connection to his family of origin. When marriage occurred in the United States, ties to families of origin immediately became secondary. As stays in the United States were lengthened, the likelihood increased dramatically that a young single man would encounter a woman to marry in this country. This turn of events changed the orientation of Mexican men living in the United States from that of expatriates temporarily working here to heads of households formed in the United States.

Unlike men, Mexican migrant women in this period rarely ventured to Los Angeles unattached to their families or unaccompanied by relatives. Even if their family of origin remained in Mexico, they lived in Los Angeles with extended family—siblings, cousins, uncles, or aunts. Most came to the city with their family unit, either as wives or children, directly from Mexico or from another part of the American Southwest. Those single adult women who came north migrated only after some personal or family tragedy. Juana Martínez, for example, migrated from Mazatlán, Sinaloa, with her mother and two sisters only after her divorce and the death of her father. Leova González de López also left Mazatlán, but only to escape the slanderous talk that surrounded her decision to raise her brother's son as a single parent. Tellingly, González was an orphan herself and migrated to Los Angeles under the guidance of her aunt.[12]

From the start, women's orientation toward the United States was formed in the confines of a Mexican family, not as single, independent migrants living alone. Eventually, many of the Chicanas who migrated to Los Angeles as children, whether Mexican or American-born, found employment as young adults to help support their families and often to provide themselves with independent income. A small minority tried to live alone or with girlfriends, away from the watchful eye of intruding relatives.

Perhaps because the largest single concentration of unmarried men lived in the crowded housing around the Plaza, this area was strictly off limits to most women living alone. Instead, the majority lived in the adjacent metropolitan areas to the south and west of the Plaza. Unlike the barrios developing east of the river, housing alternatives to the single-family home emerged. Small apartments, a few boarding houses for women, and households willing to take in a non-related young female were much more common in this part of the city than in other areas populated by Mexican immigrants. Close to downtown, these households provided easy access to both the industrial labor and white-collar employment available to young Mexican women.[13]

The areas west of the river were also home to the communities most integrated with other working-class ethnic groups and, with the exception of the Plaza, least solidly Mexican/Chicano in their cultural orientation. Women and men who lived here were exposed to the cultural practices of myriad ethnic groups, even as they enjoyed the anonymity of living in a big city. "Here no one pays any attention to how one goes about, how one lives," declared Elenita Arce, pleased at the greater freedoms allowed unmarried women.[14] These areas also seemed to provide a haven for immigrants who went against traditional Mexican family practice. Knowledge and use of effective birth control, for example, seemed concentrated in a small group of Mexican women living in these downtown communities.[15] Also, most single Mexican immigrant men and women lived west of the Los Angeles River, while Chicano family life was increasingly centered east of the river during the 1920s. Over three-quarters of all the single migrants sampled lived in the barrios west of the river. Of the single migrants over age twenty-nine—and therefore much less likely to ever marry—most also lived west of the river.[16]

Marriage, however, continued to be part of the expected practice for both Mexican women and men. In Los Angeles, a wide range of possible marriage partners was available. Not only did immigrants from a variety of different Mexican locales reside in the city, but a rapidly growing group of American-born Chicanos provided other potential partners. Non-Mexicans were also potential marriage partners, although prejudice and limited contact kept their numbers relatively small. Still, both native-born Anglo Americans and foreign-born whites were listed among the husbands and wives of Mexican immigrants who applied for naturalization before 1940.

An examination of marriage patterns between Mexican immigrants and other groups reveals figures similar to those offered by earlier historians and social scientists.[17] Almost 83 percent of the marriages involving Mexican immigrants in a sample of 1,214 marriages took place within the Mexican/Chicano community. Some 209 marriages, or 17.2 percent, were between Mexican immigrants and non-Chicanos. Not surprisingly, intermarriage was significantly more prevalent among Mexican immigrant women who chose to naturalize, involving one-third of those in the sample.[18] Marriage to non-Chicanas born outside the United States accounted for only 1.9 percent of the marriages of Mexican men, yet Mexican immigrant women married more foreign-born Anglo American men than American-born ones (see Table 1).

A profile of the Mexican immigrant men who married Anglos uncovers some revealing patterns. Mexican men who married non-Chicanas were more likely to have migrated to the United States before age twenty and to have come from larger urban areas in Mexico. Four-fifths of the Mexican immigrant men who intermarried arrived in this country before age twenty, while men in the sample who married Mexican immigrant women were more likely to have come as adults.[19] Most of the future spouses in intermarried couples came as children to the United States and therefore grew up in similar conditions as American-born Chicanos.

Additionally, urban areas, and to a lesser extent coastal areas, were more likely to produce immigrants who intermarried, largely because they were more familiar with American culture and urban life. Señora

Table 1.
Marriage Patterns of Mexican Immigrants in Los Angeles

Background of spouse	Men		Women		Total	
	Number	Percent	Number	Percent	Number	Percent
Mexican immigrant	670	60.7	47	42.4	717	59.1
Mexican American	261	23.7	27	24.3	288	23.7
Total Chicano	931	84.4	74	66.7	1,005	82.8
Anglo American	151	13.7	18	16.2	169	13.9
Foreign-born Anglo	21	1.9	19	17.1	40	3.3
Total Anglo	172	15.6	37	33.3	209	17.2
Total	1,103	100.0	111	100.0	1,214	100.0

Source: Analysis of naturalization documents, National Archives, Laguna Niguel, California.

María Rovitz Ramos, for example, married a young, bilingual Anglo American. She had grown up in Mazatlán, where her father was owner of a hotel catering to European and American tourists.[20] Immigrants born in Mexico City were particularly likely to intermarry. In fact, the sample revealed that more immigrants from the Mexican capital married Anglo Americans in Los Angeles (38 percent) than married other Mexican immigrants (24 percent).

Non-Chicanos who married Mexican immigrants also shared certain characteristics. Typically, they were also migrants to Los Angeles, often coming as adults. Mexican immigrant women were just as likely to marry foreigners as they were men born in the United States. For Mexican immigrant men, intermarriages most often were made with newcomers from the Midwest or East, although many of these spouses were American-born offspring of Italian or Irish Catholic immigrants.[21] Like Mexican women, these Anglo spouses also tended to marry young—age twenty-two on average. As recent arrivals to Los Angeles, they shared with their Mexican spouses the disruption of family ties and the need to acclimate to life in Los Angeles.

Not surprisingly, intermarried couples were less likely to live in the barrios around the Plaza area and in East Los Angeles. In fact, well over half of all intermarried couples lived in the larger metropolitan area to the south and west of the Plaza, compared to only one-third of the all-Mexican couples in my sample. Many reasons account for this distribution. According to contemporary observers, Mexicans who intermarried were generally lighter-skinned, and thus more easily able to move into areas restricted from dark-skinned Mexicans.[22] Entry was usually eased by a non-Chicano spouse.

Second, many intermarried couples were better off financially and could afford to live outside the barrio. One well-to-do immigrant couple saw three of their Mexican-born children marry Anglo Americans, even though the father felt the spouses "didn't belong to [our] society." The rest of the family, including four other unmarried children, lived in Hollywood, where most of their relations were with Americans. A successful real estate broker, a light-skinned intermarried Mexican woman, admitted: "Although I like my people very much I don't want to live with them, especially on the East Side, because they are very dirty there, there are many robberies and one can't live at ease."[23]

The area west of the river and south of the Plaza provided shelter for Mexican immigrants who were searching for greater cultural freedom, independence from their families, or interaction with other ethnic groups. Still solidly working-class, this community was a secondary one for many different European and Asian groups. It also housed, along Central Avenue, the largest community of blacks in Los Angeles. A substantial number of Mexican immigrants lived here, in more integrated surroundings than in other parts of the city. This integration occurred, however, largely separate from the city's Anglo American middle class. Here was a neighborhood of ethnic mixture, a polyglot zone of working-class people from around the globe.

For Mexicans, this community was more than a haven for intermarried couples and single women living alone. It represented the social freedom found in the United States, especially for women who were caught between the restrictive practices of Mexican families and the more liberal views of Anglo Americans. One representation of this battle within the family was over issues of dress and appearance of young daughters. Angelita V., for example, asserted her independence from her family of origin upon getting married at age nineteen:

> The first thing I did was to bob my hair. My father would not permit it and I have wanted to do [it] for a long time. I will show my husband that he will not boss me the way my father has done all of us.[24]

Other families exhibited tensions over a daughter's refusal to wear a rebozo as head covering or whether makeup would be permitted.[25]

Another aspect of that independence was less supervision over young single women, a situation that provided greater opportunities for young men and women of all nationalities to meet. This greater liberty allowed for more widespread sexual experimentation and subtle changes in sexual mores. Tellingly, almost one-third of the women involved in cross-cultural marriages had conceived a child before marriage, compared with one-fifth of first births among all-Mexican couples. When both partners had been born in Mexico, strict cultural prescriptions against sex before marriage seemed to prevail.[26] On the other hand, more than half the Mexican immigrant women sampled who married American citizens, Chicano or Anglo, had already given birth or were pregnant at marriage (see Table 2).

Despite the increase in premarital sex among women who did not marry Mexican men, widespread cultural values shared in both Chicano and Anglo communities encouraged men and women to marry if pregnancy occurred. In every group, less than 20 percent of births occurred outside of marriage, and only two single women in the sample had children. Many of the Chicano couples who contributed to the 20 percent were probably common-law marriages that were legalized in preparation for naturalization. While American officials and social workers often saw common-law marriages as evidence of moral decay, the Mexican immigrant community viewed these unions as legitimate.[27]

Experimentation among Mexican immigrants living in Los Angeles also led to an increase in married women who worked outside the home. Both Mexican and American cultures designated men as the principal family wage earners. Whether or not a newly married woman worked for wages was often a source of discussion and consternation, although many families found the income generated by wives essential. Among the married women sampled where information concerning employment status was known, about 40 percent were engaged in wage labor outside the home.[28] While this figure is similar to the proportion of married Chicanas found working in other studies of southern California communities in this period, it seems to be a higher rate than that found among married women along the border.[29] This proportion of working Chicana married women is much higher than that of other mar-

Table 2.
Marriage and Conception Among Mexican Immigrants

| Type of marriage (husband/wife) | Outside of marriage | First Birth | | | Total |
		Conceived before marriage	In first 3 years of marriage	After 3 years of marriage	
All-Mexican immigrants	51 (14.5%)	20 (5.7%)	219 (62.2%)	62 (17.6%)	352 (100%)
Mexican/ Mex. Am.	30 (14.9%)	33 (16.3%)	112 (55.4%)	27 (13.4%)	202 (100%)
Mexican/ Anglo	13 (14.9%)	11 (12.7%)	44 (50.6%)	19 (21.8%)	87 (100%)
Mex. Am./ Mexican	4 (20.0%)	7 (35.0%)	9 (45.0%)	0 (0.0%)	20 (100%)
Anglo/ Mexican	3 (20.0%)	6 (40.0%)	6 (40.0%)	0 (0.0%)	15 (100%)
Total	101 (14.9%)	77 (11.4%)	390 (57.7%)	108 (16.0%)	676 (100%)

Source: Analysis of marriage dates and birthdates of eldest children from naturalization documents, National Archives, Laguna Niguel, California.

ried women, including most immigrant women. In 1920 nationwide, only 6.3 percent of married native white women worked for wages outside the home, while 7.2 percent of foreign-born wives were in the work force. Only the proportion of black wives who were paid laborers, 32.5 percent, was similar to that found for Chicanas in Los Angeles.[30]

In contrast to earlier historical arguments, Mexican-born women were more likely to be employed than American-born Chicanas. Almost half of those women were working for wages, as compared with only 20 percent of the American-born Chicana population. These figures call into question Richard Griswold del Castillo's argument for the nineteenth century that Mexican women "had a more traditional frame of reference" and therefore were less likely than native-born women to enter the job market.[31] One reason for this discrepancy may be that different cultural prescriptions were at work during the early twentieth century that made immigrant women more likely to engage in wage labor after marriage. The flexibility demanded of the Mexican immigrant family for survival in a rapidly changing economy overrode "traditional" frames of reference. The shift had begun in Mexico, where women in migrant families were called upon to head households temporarily while men looked for work elsewhere. In Los Angeles, many Mexican immigrant women entered the labor force when their husbands were unable to find employment, were temporarily laid off, or when family expenses became burdensome.[32]

Although much of the changes in women's roles occurred to the west of the Los Angeles River, repercussions were felt throughout Chicano Los Angeles. Young Chicanas living in East Los Angeles with their parents increasingly challenged the elders' notions of dating and courtship, even as they maintained a deferential attitude toward them in other areas. Moreover, many of the skilled workers who bought homes in the east-side neighborhoods of Lincoln Heights and Brooklyn Heights during the 1920s were able to do so because their wives continued to work after marriage, thereby increasing family income.

Family life in the barrios of Los Angeles ranged from conventional to experimental, and often these families lived in close proximity to one another. Even within a family, certain members could exhibit behavior that others might consider inappropriate or "un-Mexican."[33] Freedom could be positive or negative depending on one's position in the family. One Mexican mother, living with her unmarried children west of the Plaza, enjoyed the freedom to go wherever she wanted without restriction. In Mexico, she had felt oppressed by prescriptive social customs. Nevertheless, she did not like the behavior of young women in this country. "Liberty," she stated, had been "contagious" to her daughters, and this bothered her a great deal.[34]

The creation during the 1920s of a more concentrated Mexican community east of the river, however, offered an opportunity to reassert certain family practices deemed traditional in a wholly different setting. The settlement of Mexican families in East Los Angeles implied a permanency which was not characteristic of Mexican communities west of the river. The stability of permanent settlement in the United States, for example, allowed opposition to married women working to regain ascendancy. Married women living east of the river in Belvedere and Boyle Heights were less likely to be employed than those elsewhere. Having achieved a sense of stability through the extra earnings of female employment, many married women left their jobs after moving to an east-side neighborhood.[35]

This process of claiming certain family practices as traditional in a new setting is crucial to understanding Chicano culture. Migration itself inevitably disrupted the family, often forcing members on both sides of the border to adjust to a new constellation of individuals. As migrants reached important life stages, however, they had the opportunity to influence their own "culture"—shaped, of course, by their conception of tradition. This process was influenced by the fact that widespread segregation of Mexicans in the American Southwest kept many cultural practices insulated from those of the Anglo American majority.[36]

Marriage, and the related practice of courtship, was one life stage in which Chicanos were able to alter cultural practices. The age at which men and women married is one indication of this transformation. Migration itself had tended to delay marriage, particularly for women. The average age at marriage for men sampled was approximately 26.3 years. Women married at a substantially younger age, 23. Men who married in Mexico averaged just over 25.7 years of age and women's average age was barely over 21 years. Even more interesting, however, is the fact that those who migrated from Mexico as children married younger than all other groups. Men who had migrated under the age of 15 married at approximately 24.5 years of age, while women who were child migrants married, on the average, under age 20.[37]

These figures suggest that Mexican immigrants did not delay marriage even after being exposed to the American custom of later marriage. The instability of the migratory process itself caused many young adult migrants to postpone marriage until settled. But once established in the new environment, Mexicans who grew up in American society were likely to marry younger than their counterparts in Mexico. Perhaps the erroneous assumption by Mexican parents that Mexicans in the homeland married very young encouraged them to urge their children—particularly the girls—to marry early.[38]

For children seeking greater independence, young marriages provided an escape from strict immigrant parents. Henrietta from Belvedere, age eighteen, expressed anger that "as soon as I was sixteen my father began to watch me and would not let me go anywhere or have my friends come home. He was born in old Mexico but he has been here long enough to know how people do things."[39] This strict discipline could backfire, ironically leading some young women to flee to their own marriage in order to be free of their parents. Concha, also from Belvedere, used her knowledge of Mexican mores to make her own marital decision:

> My father would not let Joe come to the house. He said when it was
> time for me to get married, he would have something to say about
> who my husband would be. So Joe and I fixed that. I ran off with
> him and stayed with his family. We knew that my father would
> make us get married then.[40]

Single migrants who lived west of the river often moved to East Los
Angeles once they were married. This act usually involved a conscious
decision to live in the barrios of the east side, among the growing community of Chicanos. It symbolized the reassertion of community life,
this time in the context of an American barrio. It also signaled the passing from a migrant to a more settled mode of existence. For some, particularly women, it could also mean the surrender of freedoms gained
through work outside the home and living beyond the cultural dictates
of family.

If the communities to the south and west of the Plaza were more conducive to ethnically intermarried couples, Mexican immigrants who married American-born Chicanos congregated in East Los Angeles. These
mixed-nativity couples found the barrios east of the river, particularly
Belvedere and Boyle Heights, particularly appealing. Over one-third of
the families in these two neighborhoods displayed this foreign-
born/native-born marriage pattern, as compared with one-quarter of the
total sample. As these communities grew during the 1920s, they gradually became the locus of Chicano cultural development. Since integration
of the Mexican immigrant population with American-born Chicanos contributed to the creation of a distinctive barrio culture, both Belvedere and
Boyle Heights became important settings for the definition of Chicano life
in California during the twentieth century.

Like those who intermarried, almost all Mexican immigrants who mar-
ried American-born Chicanos arrived in the United States before the age
of twenty. Unlike the intermarried, however, their places of origin in
Mexico were more broadly representative of the entire immigrant group.
Border states consistently produced immigrants who married second-
generation Chicanos, with 40 percent of immigrants from Sonora,
Chihuahua, and Nuevo León engaging in this marriage pattern.
Obviously, the interaction of the Mexican population living along the
American-Mexican border gave immigrants from this area a sense of com-
mon purpose and tradition that fostered intergenerational marriage.

Other immigrants, however, refused to consider marriage to Mexican
Americans. Juana Martínez, who had migrated to Los Angeles with her
sisters and mother after a failed marriage and the death of her father,
worked as a dance-hall employee in the Plaza area. She felt strongly that
if she remarried, it would be with a fellow immigrant. "The Americans
are very dull and very stupid. They let the women boss them. I would
rather marry an American than a *pocho*, however." ("Pocho" refers to

the American offspring of Mexican immigrant parents.) A fellow coworker, Gloria Navas, agreed, saying that she preferred immigrant men because "they know how to behave, they are not as 'rough-neck' as the *pochos*."[41]

Many Mexican immigrant men refused to consider marrying American citizens because American-born Chicanas appeared to exercise greater independence from their husbands. "Here the old women want to run things and the poor man has to wash the dishes while the wife goes to the show," exclaimed thirty-year-old Ignacio Sandoval from Fresnillo, Zacatecas. Another man who had lived in the United States for twenty-five years had remained single because he felt that women in this country were "very unrestrained." He surmised that "they are the ones who control their husband and I nor any other Mexican won't stand for that." He argued that even Mexican women who migrated to the United States took advantage of laws protecting women and became like American women.[42]

Unions between Mexican immigrants and American-born Chicanos, however, did occur often, but could result in continued tensions. One Mexican-born husband expressed resentment that his American-born "wife does not want to stay home and take care of the baby. She learned how to work in a beauty parlor and now she wants to start a beauty parlor and make money."[43] In another cross-generational couple, it was the American-born wife who had complaints:

> My husband is a good man but—too many kids. I am twenty-three years old and I have five. American women do not look old and tired when they are twenty-three. They are still girls. Look at me. My father picked out this husband for me, but he should have sent to Mexico for a girl for him if he wanted to have one.[44]

Although most Mexican immigrants were married to other Mexican immigrants in Los Angeles, only about one-quarter of these marriages involved individuals from the same Mexican state of origin. In light of all the various possible unions in the city, then, no more than 15 percent of Mexican marriages in Los Angeles possibly involved immigrants from the same state in Mexico. Compared with Italians in San Francisco, for example, 65 percent of whom married immigrants from the same commune, the figure for Mexicans is exceedingly low.[45] One possible explanation is that in Los Angeles racism set all Mexicans apart from American society and obfuscated cultural divisions that had existed in Mexico. Sustaining allegiance to a certain area in Mexico became much less important than beginning a new life as an ethnic family in the United States. A more generic form of Chicano identity—different from that of other ethnic groups in America—began to dominate Mexican American cultural life in Los Angeles.[46]

The act of marriage, of course, only began the process of redefining cultural values within the family. The actual nature of the union between husbands and wives varied tremendously, depending on the individuals' perspectives. Recent attempts to describe the Chicano family have portrayed it as an institution closely paralleling that of other immigrant families, something akin to a "father-dominated but mother-centered" family life.[47] Countering the image of the traditional Mexican family as a rigid patriarchy, these interpretations have stressed the flexibility of roles in given social and economic circumstances. Some have begun to place emphasis on the mother-centeredness of the Chicano family, while others have continued to examine the implications of male domination.[48]

One aspect of family life which had profound impact on the relationship between husband and wife was the pattern of childbearing. The number of children a couple had often reflected cultural values regarding family life. However, some immigrant historians have noted substantial variation between immigrant groups from agricultural backgrounds who settled in America's urban centers. For example, Dino Cinel has argued for Italians in San Francisco that "the crucial point is not the transition from rural to urban life, but the way people perceive the transition."[49] Mexican immigrants to Los Angeles exhibited an assortment of birthrate patterns which corroborate Cinel's assertion.

Mexican immigrant families sampled had an average of 2.62 children, with the largest families containing eleven children. The relatively low

Table 3.
Number of Children for Various Types of Marriages

Type of marriage (husband/wife)	No children	1–2 children	3–5 children	6–8 children	Over 8 children	Number (Average)
All-Mexican immigrant	66 (15.8%)	129 (30.9%)	140 (33.5%)	72 (17.2%)	11 (2.6%)	418 (3.17)
Mexican/ Mex. Am.	34 (14.4%)	100 (42.2%)	77 (32.5%)	20 (8.4%)	6 (2.5%)	237 (2.71)
Mexican/ Anglo	44 (33.9%)	59 (45.4%)	25 (19.2%)	2 (1.5%)	0 (0.0%)	130 (1.36)
Mex. Am./ Mexican	7 (25.9%)	15 (55.6%)	5 (18.5%)	0 (0.0%)	0 (0.0%)	27 (1.52)
Anglo/ Mexican	18 (54.5%)	11 (33.3%)	3 (9.1%)	1 (3.0%)	0 (0.0%)	33 (1.00)
Total	169 (20.0%)	314 (37.2%)	250 (29.6%)	95 (11.2%)	17 (2.0%)	845[a] (2.63)

Source: Analysis of naturalization documents, National Archives, Laguna Niguel, California.
[a] 403 marriages in the sample contained no information on children.

average number of children—compared with popular notions of Mexican family size—is undoubtedly a result of the youth of the group which applied for naturalization. Many were couples who had only recently married. Stark differences can be noted in the average number of children, however, when one compares all-Mexican marriages with those involving one non-Mexican immigrant (see Table 3).

Intermarriage with an American-born or foreign-born Anglo resulted in an average of only 1.29 children, as compared with all-Mexican marriages which averaged 3.17 children per family. Marriages involving one Mexican immigrant and an American-born Chicano fell between these two extremes, with 2.59 children per family. Mexican immigrant women who married a man born in the United States, whether a Chicano or an Anglo, were likely to bear substantially fewer children than if they married a man born in Mexico. Mexican immigrant men, on the other hand, were likely to have large families as long as they married within the Chicano community. Only marriages to Anglo women substantially reduced the size of families of Mexican immigrant men.

Not surprisingly, large families were more readily found in East Los Angeles than west of the Los Angeles River. Every barrio east of the river averaged at least 2.8 children per family, while the average west of the river was under 2.5. Given the prevalence of single migrants to the south and west of the Plaza, along with smaller families in these communities, children were a more dominant presence in the barrios on the east side than they had been in the more integrated, working-class neighborhoods around downtown.

Despite variance in the eventual sizes of families, marriage invariably led to childbirth for women in all possible unions in the sample. Between two-thirds and three-quarters of all women had given birth within eighteen months of marriage. Childrearing continued to be the main expectation for married women of this period, even if they continued to work after marriage. The differences that did exist in childbearing practices between families reflect the spacing between births and the curtailment of childbearing among mature unions. The age of marriage and the interval between marriage and first birth were the same for all types of married couples.

As east-side barrios began to grow, the construction of family ties proved a strong basis upon which to promote a sense of community. Powerful religious sanctions against marital breakup kept the numbers of female-headed households low. Despite widespread male migration and the cultural breakdown historians have attributed to both European and black newcomers to the cities, no more than 55 marriages out of 1,249 unions in this sample were affected by divorce or separation. This 4.4 percent rate of divorce is low by American standards in the period, since a 1916 study found one divorce for every five marriages in Los Angeles. More than one-third of these separations occurred between Mexican immigrants who had married Anglos, even though less than 20 percent of the unions in the total sample were intermarriages.[50]

Moreover, three-fourths of these breakups occurred during the 1930s and the instability of the Great Depression. Although it is impossible to know for certain, it does appear that the economic crisis, and the accompanying stress it placed on families, was a direct cause of many of these divorces and desertions. Unemployed men sometimes found it easier to abandon their families than to watch helplessly as their loved ones struggled. Many relief organizations concentrated aid to families with no male head, and perhaps some fathers may have discerned leaving as the best option.

The liberal divorce practices in the United States did provide an alternative generally unavailable in Mexico for women caught in bad marriages. Exercising this option, however, often forced a confrontation with deeply held beliefs concerning proper family relations. Minnie Ortiz, who spent years tolerating her husband's philandering and lack of economic ambition, finally had enough after her husband struck her. A lawyer advised her to apply for a divorce. She did so promptly, but remembered "crying my eyes out, thinking of my shattered home life and of my fatherless girls."[51]

Tellingly, more Chicano families were broken up by death than by divorce or desertion. Sixty-six spouses in my sample were widowed while living in Los Angeles, a rate of 5.3 per 100. Dangerous conditions at work made men more at risk. Some women who lost their husbands moved in with relatives, but most were able to continue as heads of their households. Men who lost their wives often asked relatives to raise their children, since most Chicanos believed that female nurturing was crucial to childrearing. Whatever the situation, family and community networks were called upon in time of family tragedy. As one local Anglo American official acknowledged: "The Mexicans respond to appeals on the basis of their responsibility toward children, on the duties of sisters, aunts, uncles, etc. This is not so in the case of Americans, who are more individualistic."[52]

Many observers who disagree on the strengths and weaknesses of the Chicano family agree that Mexicans are familistic in orientation.[53] Critics of this family orientation accuse the Mexican American family of retarding individual development. These observers blame economic reverses on a family life which encourages members to seek semiskilled jobs with immediate, though circumscribed, rewards. Moreover, familism is often blamed for the lack of a strong sense of public duty, particularly the tendency of Chicanos to dissociate themselves from American politics and public organizations. When emphasis is placed so strongly on the family, they allege that there is little time for contemplating the needs of society.

A strong sense of family, however, enabled Mexican immigrants to survive in a hostile American environment, and contributed to a strengthening of community sentiment inside the barrio. Lack of economic opportunity and outright racial discrimination were at the root of limited mobility, and strong family networks allowed Mexicans to persevere in difficult economic times. As following chapters will make clear, even those who eschewed family solidarity rarely moved up the economic ladder. If anything, familism contributed to slow, but steady, economic advancement, and it was often a family tragedy or widespread economic misfortune which sidetracked Mexican immigrants and Mexican Americans in their quest for greater economic security.

In the period directly following migration, Mexicans were unable to settle down because they could rarely count on the extended family networks available in their native villages. As individuals, they had only their own limited economic resources. Unemployment often led to more migration. Even so, many called upon cousins, distant relatives, and friends from hometowns to aid in this difficult period of transition.[54] As immigrants married, particularly if they married American-born Chicanos, they established roots in a new community which they hoped would bring greater stability to their lives. In time, these barrios came to serve as places which made other newcomers to the city feel welcome.

Creative, adaptative strategies predominated among Mexican immigrants who settled in Los Angeles. Only strong, flexible family ties insured the survival of all members. Certain individuals chose to go it alone, and others left the barrio altogether. Yet, for most immigrants, family and community came together in the emerging neighborhoods east of the river. At times, the barrio was for some a stifling, restrictive environment. Strong cultural norms were enforced which kept the community at least outwardly familiar to most newcomers from Mexico. More often than not, however, the barrio provided a haven for Mexican immigrants and American-born Chicanos. There they could adapt to American society while still retaining in their daily lives much of the flavor of Mexico.

NOTES

1. Marita Hernández and Robert Montemayor, "Mexico to U.S.—a Cultural Odyssey," *Los Angeles Times*, 24 July 1983, pp. 1, 18.
2. Oscar Handlin, *The Uprooted: The Epic Story of the Great Migrations That Made the American People*, 2nd ed., enlarged (1951; Boston: Little, Brown, 1973), 210. Virginia Yans-McLaughlin refers to the body of work portraying immigrant family life in this fashion as a "disorganization" school in *Family and Community: Italian Immigrants in Buffalo, 1880–1930* (Ithaca: Cornell Univ. Press, 1971), 19.
3. Hernández and Montemayor, "Odyssey," 1, 18–21.
4. Yans-McLaughlin, *Family and Community*, 61, 64. For a historical account of the Mexican immigrant family from this perspective, see Mario T. García, "La Familia: The Mexican Immigrant Family, 1900–1930," in *Work, Family, Sex Roles and Language*, Mario Barrera, Alberto Camarillo, and Francisco Hernández, eds. (Berkeley: Tonatiuh-Quinto Sol, 1980), 117–39.
5. David Alvirez and Frank D. Bean, "The Mexican American Family," in *Ethnic Families in America*, Charles H. Mindel and Robert W. Haberstein,

eds. (New York: Elsevier, 1976); Miguel Montiel, "The Social Science Myth of the Mexican American Family," *El Grito: A Journal of Contemporary Mexican American Thought* 3 (1970), 56–63; Nathan Murillo, "The Mexican American Family," in *Chicanos: Social and Psychological Perspectives*, Nathaniel N. Wagner and Marsha J. Haug, eds. (St. Louis: C.V. Mosby, 1971), 97–108; Octavio Ignacio V. Romano, "The Anthropology and Sociology of the Mexican-Americans: The Distortion of Mexican-American History," *El Grito* 2:1 (Fall 1968), 13–26. For an overview of this literature, see Alfredo Mirandé, "The Chicano Family: A Reanalysis of Conflicting Views," *Journal of Marriage and the Family* 39 (1977), 750–51. An excellent summary of various theoretical approaches to family history and their possible application to Chicano history is provided by Richard Griswold del Castillo in chapter 1 of *La Familia: Chicano Families in the Urban Southwest, 1848 to the Present* (Notre Dame: Univ. of Notre Dame Press, 1984), 1–9.

6. Mirandé, "The Chicano Family," 748–51.

7. For a description of widespread European return migration, see John Bodnar, *The Transplanted: A History of Immigrants in Urban America* (Bloomington: Indiana Univ. Press, 1985), 53–54.

8. The following account is derived from transcripts of interviews conducted by a Board of Special Inquiry at Nogales, Arizona, from 25 August 1917 to 1 July 1918, Records of the Immigration and Naturalization Service, RG 85, Box 250, Folder 54281/36B, National Archives, Washington, D.C. These interviews were conducted beginning in 1917 when entrance to the United States was requested by children under the age of sixteen unaccompanied by their parents. Their purpose was to determine whether the child was likely to become a public charge, therefore detailed information regarding the child's family situation in Mexico and the United States was obtained.

9. Dino Cinel, *From Italy to San Francisco: The Immigrant Experience* (Stanford: Stanford Univ. Press, 1982), 168; Naturalization Records, RG 21, National Archives, Laguna Niguel, California.

10. "Interview with Arturo Morales," No. 11, p. 1, interview by Luis Felipe Recinos, 8 April 1927, Biographies & Case Histories III folder, Z-R5, Manuel Gamio collection, Bancroft Library, University of California, Berkeley.

11. "Vida de Estanislao Gómez," 1, interview by Luis Felipe Recinos, 2 April 1927, Biographical & Case Studies II folder, Gamio collection.

12. See "Vida de Leova López," 1, interview by M. Robles, 19 April 1927, Biographies & Case Histories II folder; and "Interview with Juana Martínez," No. 102, p. 1, interview by Luis Felipe Recinos, 6 April 1927, Biographies & Case Histories I folder, Gamio collection.

13. For descriptions of the growth of the central business district and nearby factories, see Robert M. Fogelson, *The Fragmented Metropolis: Los Angeles, 1850–1930* (Cambridge, Mass.: Harvard Univ. Press, 1967), 147–51; Scott L. Bottles, *Los Angeles and the Automobile: The Making of the Modern City* (Berkeley: Univ. of California Press, 1987), 200–201; and Howard J. Nelson, "The Vernon Area, California—A Study of the Political Factor in Urban Geography," *Annals of the Association of American Geographers* 42 (1952), 177–91. For the continuation of these patterns as late as 1940, see Eshref Shevky and Molly Lewin, *Your Neighborhood: A Social Profile of Los Angeles* (Los Angeles: Haynes Foundation, 1949), 24–26.

14. "The Arce (Galván) family," 8, interview by Luis Felipe Recinos, 8 April 1927, Biographies & Case Histories III folder, Gamio collection.

15. See "Interview with Gloria Navas," No. 56, p. 4, interview by Luis Felipe Recinos, 16 April 1927, Biographies & Case Histories I folder; and "Interview with Elisa Morales," No. 53, pp. 3, 5, interview by Luis Felipe Recinos, 16 April 1927, Biographies & Case Histories II folder, Gamio collection. Joanne Meyerowitz describes similar responses to urban environments by these "women adrift" in "Women and Migration: Autonomous Female Migrants to Chicago, 1880–1930," *Journal of Urban History* 13 (1987), 147–68.

16. Analysis of naturalization documents, National Archives, Laguna Niguel, California.

17. Constantine Panunzio found a 17 percent rate of exogamous marriages among Mexicans in "Intermarriage in Los Angeles, 1924–1933," *American Journal of Sociology* 48 (1942), 698, 701. Griswold del Castillo finds similar figures in Familia, 106–7. See Edward Murguia, *Chicano Intermarriage: A Theoretical and Empirical Study* (San Antonio: Trinity Univ. Press, 1982), for comparisons with other regions over time.

18. This figure is skewed by the fact that the number of Mexican immigrant women who naturalized was small—involving only 111 marriages—and that Mexican women who married Mexican men were probably less likely to naturalize than those who married Anglo American men.

19. The pattern is similar for women, although there are many fewer in the sample.

20. "Interview with Sra. María Rovitz Ramos," No. 7, pp. 1, 4, interview by Luis Felipe Recinos, 2 April 1927, Biographies & Case Histories I folder, Gamio collection.

21. From survey of Anglo American spouses in naturalization documents. The argument that ethnic groups tend to intermarry within religious groupings has been made by Milton Gordon in *Assimilation in American Life: The Role of Race, Religion, and National Origins* (New York: Oxford Univ. Press, 1964). Edward Murguia makes a similar argument specifically for Chicanos in *Chicano Intermarriage*, 35. According to at least one local official, Jewish-Mexican intermarriage was rare, despite substantial interaction, because Russian Jews felt that Mexicans were "filthy and godless and without sex morality because of their public courtship." See "Interview with Dr. Miriam Van Waters, Referee of Juvenile Court, Hall of Justice, Los Angeles, California," 2–512, American Officials folder, 74/187c, Paul S. Taylor collection, Bancroft Library, University of California, Berkeley.

22. For examples of lighter-skinned Mexicans intermarrying, see "José Robles," "Sra. Ruhe López," and "Sr. Campos" in Manuel Gamio, *The Life Story of the Mexican Immigrant* (1931; rpt., New York: Dover, 1971), 226–37.

23. "Interview with the Santaella family," No. 45, pp. 2–3, interview by Luis Felipe Recinos, 15 April 1927, Biographies & Case Histories II folder, Gamio collection. "Interview with María Rovitz Ramos," 6. See also Richard Romo, *East Los Angeles: History of a Barrio* (Austin: Univ. of Texas Press, 1983), 85. One quantitative analysis of the 1940 U.S. census suggests that significant rates of intermarriage between Mexican women and non-Mexican men occurred in the Southwest during this period, often leading to relatively higher economic standing for these women. Brian Gratton, F. Arturo Rosales, and Hans DeBano, "A Sample of the Mexican-American Population in 1940," *Historical Methods* 21 (1988), 83–85.

24. Quoted in Mary Lanigan, "Second Generation Mexicans in Belvedere" Master's thesis, University of Southern California, 1932), 20.

25. Ibid., 18–21.

26. Knowledge, let alone use, of effective birth control methods besides abstinence does not appear to have been widespread in the Mexican immigrant community. In addition to strict cultural sanctions against birth control emanating from the Catholic Church, legal restrictions against dispensing birth control information still existed. Mexican women were unlikely to have access to the occasional private physician who might be willing to give such advice. The one exception to this generalization seems to have been the small group of Mexican women who regularly worked as dance hall girls in the Plaza area. See "Interview with Gloria Navas," p. 4; and "Interview with Elisa Morales," No. 53, pp. 3, 5, interview by Luis Felipe Recinos, 16 April 1927, Biographies & Case Histories II folder, Gamio collection.

27. Analysis of birth and marriage dates in naturalization documents, National Archives, Laguna Niguel, California. To place marriage patterns in Los Angeles in a larger historical context, see John D'Emilio and Estelle B. Freedman, *Intimate Matters: A History of Sexuality in America* (New York: Harper and Row, 1988), chap. 5, esp. 89–90.

28. The vast majority of the married couples sampled do not list any information for wives because that question was not asked of husbands applying for naturalization until the second phase of the process. The figures do reflect, however, the labor status of the 142 married women who took out first papers, along with wives of men who got to the second level of the process. This percentage therefore is tentative, as it is based only on 187 total couples in the overall sample of 1,249 (15.0%). In addition, this group would tend to represent those most settled in the United States.

29. Albert Camarillo, *Chicanos in a Changing Society: From Mexican Pueblos to American Barrios in Santa Barbara and Southern California, 1848–1930* (Cambridge: Harvard Univ. Press, 1979), 220; Douglas Guy Monroy, "Mexicanos in Los Angeles, 1930–1941: An Ethnic Group in Relation to Class Forces" (Ph.D. diss., University of California, Los Angeles, 1978), 77; and Mario T. García, *Desert Immigrants: The Mexicans of El Paso, 1880–1920* (New Haven: Yale Univ. Press, 1981), 75, 200.

30. Carl Degler, *At Odds: Women and the Family in America from the Revolution to the Present* (New York: Oxford Univ. Press, 1980), 384. See also Yans-McLaughlin, *Family and Community*, 173; and Bodnar, *Translated*, 78–80.

31. Griswold del Castillo, *Familia*, 63.

32. See Paul S. Taylor, "Mexican Women in Los Angeles Industry in 1928," *Aztlán* 11 (1980), 104–5.

33. See "The Arce (Galván) family," Gamio collection.

34. "Interview with Santaella family," 4, Gamio collection.

35. Analysis of naturalization documents, National Archives, Laguna Niguel, California. See also Taylor, "Industry," 106–8.

36. See Alex M. Saragoza, "The Conceptualization of the History of the Chicano Family," in *The State of Chicano Research in Family, Labor and Migration Studies*, Armando Valdez, Albert Camarillo and Tomás Almaguer, eds. (Stanford: Stanford Center for Chicano Research, 1983), 119–20.

37. Naturalization documents, National Archives, Laguna Niguel, California. Other areas of the Southwest also produced early marriages among more stable populations. Sarah Deutsch reports that from 1860 to 1910, Chicanas married in New Mexico between the ages of 15 and 21, while men tended to marry between age 19 and 26. See "Culture, Class, and Gender: Chicanas and Chicanos in Colorado and New Mexico, 1900–1940" (Ph.D. diss., Yale

University, 1985), 83.

38. See figures for Mascota, Jalisco, in Carlos B. Gil, *Life in Provincial Mexico: National and Regional History Seen from Mascota, Jalisco, 1867–1972* (Los Angeles: UCLA Latin American Studies Center Publications, 1983), 95–98.

39. Lanigan, "Second Generation," 25–26.

40. Ibid., 26.

41. "Interview with Juana Martínez," 3–4; "Interview with Gloria Navas," 7, Gamio collection.

42. "Interview with Ignacio Sandoval," 5; "Interview with Luis Aguiñaga," 1–2, Gamio collection.

43. Lanigan, "Second Generation," 34.

44. Ibid., 33.

45. Cinel, *From Italy*, 177.

46. In contrast, see ibid., 177–78, or Yans-McLaughlin, *Family and Community*, 256–57, for Italians. See Abraham Cahan, *The Rise of David Levinsky* (1917; rpt., New York: Harper and Row, 1960), 106, for Jews.

47. This terminology was first used to describe the southern Italian family by two anthropologists. See Leonard W. Moss and Walter H. Thomson, "The South Italian Family: Literature and Observation," *Human Organization* 18 (1959), 38.

48. See Deutsch, "Culture," 90, for an analysis which stresses the flexibility of the sexual division of labor within the Chicano family. For studies of the contemporary Chicano family which stress flexibility, see Griswold del Castillo, *Familia*, 118–19; Maxine Baca Zinn, "Marital Roles, Marital Power and Ethnicity: A Study of Changing Families" (Ph.D. diss., University of Oregon, 1978); and Lea Ybarra, "Conjugal Role Relationships in the Chicano Family" (Ph.D. diss., University of California, Berkeley, 1977).

49. Cinel, *From Italy*, 188.

50. Analysis of marital status information from naturalization documents, National Archives, Laguna Niguel, California. See Elaine Tyler May, *Great Expectations: Marriage and Divorce in Post-Victorian America* (Chicago: Univ. of Chicago Press, 1980), 9, for comparative data for the rest of Los Angeles.

51. "Manuela 'Minnie' Ortiz," interview by J. Isaac Aceves, 14 June 1937, p. 330, Field Continuity, Mexican Population, San Diego Project, Federal Writers Project collection, Department of Special Collections, University of California, Los Angeles.

52. "Interview with Dr. Miriam Van Waters, Referee of Juvenile Court, Hall of Justice, Los Angeles, California," 1–511, Taylor collection.

53. See Mirandé, "The Chicano Family," 751.

54. See Susan E. Keefe and Amado Padilla, *Chicano Ethnicity* (Albuquerque: Univ. of New Mexico Press, 1987), especially chaps. 9 and 10, for a modern account of this process in southern California.

7

SOUTHERN DIASPORA: ORIGINS OF THE NORTHERN "UNDERCLASS"

Jacqueline Jones

In 1942, when she testified before a congressional committee on national defense migration, Johnnie Belle Taylor was living with her mother and five children in a Farm Security Administration labor camp in the vicinity of Belle Glade, Florida. Born in Talbot County, Georgia, Taylor had spent most of her life near the small town of Dawson in the same state. In 1937, she moved to Florida and began a seasonal pattern of migration, picking beans in the "winter garden," then moving to northern Florida to labor in the corn, lima bean, cucumber, and tobacco fields, until the late-summer cotton-picking season drew her into Georgia. By the late fall of each year she had returned to Belle Glade, ready to repeat the cycle again.[1] To some observers, the way of life followed by this black woman might seem to confirm recent studies of the Southern origins of the Northern "underclass." Taylor was living in a female-headed, extended household within a public housing project, which, along with cotton plantations and coal-mining camps, constituted one of the many Southern prototypes of Northern ghettos. She and her family led a peripatetic existence, performing backbreaking stoop labor under exploitative conditions. Perhaps Taylor might even be seen as a transitional figure of sorts, caught somewhere between the dependency of the sharecropping system in the South and the dependency of the federal welfare system in the North. In any case, in her unsettled life, she seemed to exist outside middle-class or "mainstream" American society, with its devotion to a stable homeplace and to the nuclear family.

For recent observers of the underclass, history is not, or at least not often, "the issue," to paraphrase Charles Murray. Policy implications, and not historical causes or antecedents, stand at the center of the debate over the nature, and future, of concentrated poor inner-city populations. Still, some scholars have addressed the roots of the underclass, and their views can be simply (if rather loosely) categorized according to their emphasis on either the continuity or discontinuity of a Southern-rooted, so-called culture of poverty. For example, in the "continuity" camp stands Nicholas Lemann, a journalist who argues that "every aspect of the underclass culture in the ghettoes is directly traceable to roots in the South—and not the South of slavery but the South of a generation ago ... the nascent underclass of the sharecropper South." In his study of black Chicago in the

1980s, Lemann argues that in the 1950s, a specific group of Mississippi sharecroppers brought north with them "the main characteristics of the underclass—poverty, crime, poor education, dependency, and teenage out-of-wedlock childbearing"—in other words, an "ethic of dependency." He quotes an informant: "Most people on welfare here [in Chicago], they were on welfare there [in Canton, Mississippi], in a sense, because they were sharecroppers. There they were working hard for nothing, now they're not working for nothing. They have been mentally programmed that Mister Charlie's going to take care of them."[2]

In contrast to Lemann's focus on what he perceives as cultural persistence, scholars like William Julius Wilson stress structural aspects of the Northern urban economy in an effort to posit a dramatic break between the neoslave South and the big-city North. In his book *The Truly Disadvantaged: The Inner City, the Underclass, and Public Policy*, Wilson employs the term *historic discrimination* to describe those barriers to equality that black people confronted for the first time in the North (beginning, presumably, during the era of World War II). He argues that Southern migrants did not bring their poverty north with them; rather, discriminatory employment practices, combined with a changing urban economy that had less use for unskilled laborers, placed blacks at a competitive disadvantage with the Eastern European immigrants who had settled in Northeastern cities before them. Wilson draws upon the work of Herbert Gutman in arguing that the "problems of the modern black family ... are a product of more recent social forces," rather than a legacy of either sharecropping or slavery.[3]

The theories of Lemann and Wilson are difficult to compare with one another simply because they deal with different points in time—Wilson, with the post–Great Migration period through the 1960s, when the effects of long-term unemployment on black men began to manifest themselves in high rates of female-headed households; Lemann, with the 1950s, when agricultural mechanization in the Cotton South had lessened the demand for field-workers, and when the Northern urban economy no longer depended on unskilled laborers to any great extent. Nevertheless, both perspectives are striking in their emphasis on the recent past and their lack of attention to Southern society, or African-American culture, during the nineteenth century.

In exploring the Southern origins of the Northern underclass, this essay diverges from the views of both Lemann and Wilson by stressing the historic process of marginalization that engulfed not only freedpeople but also poor whites on the Southern countryside after the Civil War, a process that continues today in the nation's largest cities. Scholars and journalists alike have been too preoccupied with the alleged "pathological" aspects of African-American history, and, together with the popular media, have promoted the idea that the black community constitutes some kind of exotic subculture quite outside the boundaries of "normal," or "mainstream," American life. The claim that, compared to black life in general, ghetto life is "a thousand times more" apart from white society, "with a different language, economy, educational system, and social ethic," not only objectifies the black poor as "others," but also misses larger issues.[4] First, stories of ordinary black people who worked hard and made do with very little in the way of material resources become lost amid generalizations about the "bizarre" quality of inner-city neighborhoods. And second, only a narrow segment of the black community—a predatory youth street culture—holds the attention of whites, who remain fascinated in their own way by sexuality, violence, and substance abuse. In any case, the grip of the black underclass on the American imagination serves to obscure the historical and economic processes that by the late twentieth century produced a multitude of underclasses, people who were neither black nor residents of Northern central cities.

In at least two striking ways, the African-American experience in the United States demonstrates a certain continuity between North and South, agricultural and industrial workers, and rural and urban areas, but not in the ways suggested by Lemann and others. First, in the post–Civil War rural South and the twentieth-century urban North, black folk of all ages and both sexes demonstrated a great deal of resourcefulness in providing for themselves; family members foraged and looked to neighborly cooperation in an effort to resist enforced dependency upon either plantation owners or welfare bureaucrats. Second, regardless of their location, blacks during this period faced overwhelming structural barriers to upward social mobility. Employer discrimination and legal statutes hindered their ability to move from place to place freely, and left them isolated in depressed communities characterized by poor housing and poor schools. Until 1916, most blacks in the rural South remained confined within the plantation economy, a function of the lack of jobs available to them in either the urban South or the North. Northern ghettos were legal creations that prevented Southern migrants from seeking out educational and employment opportunities in suburbs and other outlying areas. At the same time, the post-industrial city has introduced new, corrosive forces into black family life—long-term structural unemployment among black men, the wide availability of firearms, and drugs, and the lure of "the street" for young people. These forces had no literal nineteenth-century rural Southern precedents.

If we return to Johnnie Belle Taylor and flesh out the facts of her life, we learn that she was committed to hard work, to preserving the integrity of her family, and to schooling her children; in other words, that her priorities were not that different from those of poor white Southerners at the time, or members of the industrial working class, or the middle class, for that matter. Taylor was divorced from her first husband, a disabled older man who now lived in a small house on a piece of land in Dawson, Georgia, a place she considered her home; though she spent little time there, she noted, "that's still home, all my things are there." Her current husband was employed on a construction project in Key

West; she said that he was "trying to work down there, so he kind of hated to leave since they needed men so bad on the water line and all. He kind of hated to leave from there." Two of Taylor's children, ages six and seven, were too young to work; they stayed with their grandmother during the day. The next two oldest youngsters labored in the fields some, and attended school some, while the oldest, a daughter, worked as a wage earner along with her mother. During the recent winter months, Johnnie Belle Taylor had used her car, with its balding tires, to shuttle workers to a new construction site in Moultrie, Georgia, not far from Dawson; in this way she was able to make a little cash. Thus a wider, more expansive picture of the Taylor household reveals not a household mired in dependency, but a family that fragmented in the course of a year in an effort to make enough money to provide for itself.

Viewed within concentric circles of historical context, the Taylor household had much in common with households of other-Americans, although the barriers it faced in terms of making a decent living were peculiar, and peculiarly devastating, compared to those faced by other Americans, no matter how poor. By the 1990s, the pressures that forced the Taylors to live apart had exacted a more devastating price from poor families, especially poor black families, throughout the country. Still, the snapshot of a husbandless mother with several small children and a hard lot in life—the stuff of newspaper feature stories and network television documentaries—tends to obscure the more complex histories of these households and their more complex relations between affective and economic ties. The story of the Taylors, then, constitutes not just a chapter in African-American history, but also a chapter placed squarely within the context of American labor and family history.

POLITICAL RESISTANCE AND HOUSEHOLD RESOURCEFULNESS AMONG BLACKS IN THE RURAL SOUTH, 1865–1941

In the South, blacks were marginalized when they were barred, by law or custom, from almost all jobs that were year-round and full-time. As agricultural wage laborers, the vast majority of Southern black men and women fell prey to the annual and seasonal rhythms of the sharecropping system; under that system, the spring planting and fall harvest claimed the energies of all able-bodied blacks, and yet winter and late-summer slack times forced them to scrounge for wages, or otherwise provide for themselves, to compensate for the meager "furnishings" they received from landlord-employers. During the post–Civil War era, black urban artisans found themselves pushed out of the skilled trades; thereafter, Southern cities would systematically deny black men stable employment opportunities, and offer steady work only to black wives and mothers who toiled as ill-paid domestic servants and laundresses. Significantly, the Southern textile industry had virtually no black employees until the mid-1960s; those factory jobs went to poor whites—

men, women, and children who were hardly superior to black people in terms of either formal education or "natural aptitude" for machine work. Not until 1916 did Northern industrial employers show much interest in the vast pool of untapped labor (black and white) that lay to the south of them; until that time they preferred to hire immigrant workers over native-born Americans from the South. In the 1930s, the New Deal legislation that served as the foundation of the modern welfare state quite explicitly excluded from Social Security and worker compensation programs the overwhelming number of blacks in the North as well as the South, including sharecroppers, domestics, the underemployed and chronically unemployed.[5]

The analogy between the Southern plantation and the Northern ghetto springs not from theoretical constructions or statistical models, but from the deeply felt pronouncements of men and women who had experienced both worlds. Interviewed in the late 1960s and 1970s, for example, a group of Southern-born black Northeasterners portrayed Northern society as an extension, or reflection, of the South. Conspicuous in their absence from this set of interviews are references to those themes which implied that migration had involved a radical departure from a caste-bound past—the ability of blacks to vote and participate in party politics, and the transition from sharecropping to industrial wage work. According to John Langston Gwaltney's informants, in the rural South and the urban North, "the business of the white man is to rule": "During all our history here [in the United States] we have been right and they have been wrong and the only man who cannot see that is a fool or a liar." In the end, despite a change of scenery for the grandchildren of slaves, "It just has not changed all that much."[6]

No matter where or when they lived, most black folks could say, "I work. I work hard—you can ask anybody out here—but I don' seem to get nowhere." Though forced to perform the heaviest, hottest jobs—"that plantation thing"—blacks had received from whites only contempt in return: "These lazy Negroes are the ones who dig ditches and build roads and lift heavy pots and things." Ultimately, a black person's class status was irrelevant; "the one fact that we were the children of slaves and the word 'nigger' meant the same thing to [all of] us is very important." In the eyes of whites, blacks remained outside the boundaries of a consumer society that supposedly conferred materialistic aspirations on people in an equal-opportunity way: "See, they do everything to keep us down, and still we got things they think we ain' got no business with!"— the sharecropper with a Model T Ford, the welfare recipient with a color television. A rude cabin in the middle of a cotton field, a tiny apartment in a concrete housing project—it is "*how* you live that's important," and "people need space and they were never meant to be jammed on top of each other." Overcrowded and underfunded schools made a mockery of the ideal of public education, whether in Jim Crow Alabama or in the South Bronx. Despite variations over time and within regions, for slaves as well as for welfare recipients, systems of enforced dependency seemed designed to maximize the humiliation of black people: "I done had all that white folks' help I can use!" And always, a code of racial etiquette rewarded deference and dissembling: "My father used to say, 'Laugh with your friends, but smile with strangers.'"[7]

These comments of Southern migrants suggest a link between the world of the nineteenth-century Southern sharecropper and the late-twentieth-century Northern urban underclass. Both times and places were marked by (to borrow a term from linguistics) "deep structural" forces of economic marginalization. Despite transformations in the national economy from postbellum South to postindustrial North, despite the passage of civil rights legislation of the 1960s, black people faced legal and institutional barriers to their political and economic advancement, barriers remarkable for their persistence and their similarity between regions. The former slaves and their descendants remained confined to temporary, seasonal, unskilled, or domestic work. Trapped within the South's plantation economy or the Northern central city, they lacked access to quality education and to jobs that paid a living wage. As a matter of public policy, implemented by private landowners and employers as well as public institutions, blacks as a group were systematically denied the money and property that would have allowed them to achieve even the modest measure of self-determination enjoyed by the white working class. Proportionately, black women and children always worked for wages to a greater extent than even their poor-white counterparts, a fact that had far-reaching implications for age and gender relations within the black community. Nevertheless, this litany of the structural forces underpinning racial subordination obscures the historic efforts of black people to resist dependence on whites—efforts that, once again, showed striking similarities between rural South and urban North. Whether they were foragers or members of mutual aid societies, participants in an "underground economy" or "scufflers" seeking a better life for their children, black men and women struggled to provide for themselves in defiance of the dictum "The business of white men is to rule."[8]

To explore the efforts of white elites to keep Southern black people literally "in their place," and to understand the efforts of blacks to resist dependency, it is necessary to consider several issues, including the collusion between Southern employers and federal officials to preserve a large black labor force within the region's staple-crop economy; the drive for self-sufficiency in landownership and education on the part of black families and communities; black workers' efforts to earn wages off the plantation in the slack season, to compensate for the promise of payment that rarely materialized at the end of the year; and the migration imperative, which revealed a "restlessness" among Southern sharecroppers determined to seek out a better way of life, and unwilling to give themselves over totally to an oppressive labor and political system.

The exploitative Southern sharecropping system was not necessarily an aberration within an industrializing society; indeed, the federal government helped to create and preserve this system as a means of producing a staple crop marketed worldwide throughout the nineteenth and twentieth centuries. Too often, scholars and modern commentators assume that employment in the private sector differs in a complete and fundamental way from reliance on government largesse in any form. In fact, historically, the private and public dimensions of black enforced dependency were not mutually exclusive categories. For the first two or three crucial years after the Civil War, the United States Bureau of Refugees, Freedmen, and Abandoned Lands enforced a labor contract system that mandated agricultural labor as the only legitimate form of employment for the newly freed slaves. Each contract covered a calendar year, an anomaly of sorts in the staple-crop South, where labor was deployed according to various crop-growing seasons, which each lasted less than twelve months. Still, bureau contracts bound individual workers (and eventually, under share-cropping, their families) to year-long residence on a single plantation, so that planters would not have to renegotiate for hands during the busy harvest season. In this way the Freedmen's Bureau provided a federal stamp of approval to a system that kept blacks tied to a single planter whether or not that employer had work enough to keep his workers occupied—and compensated—on a year-round basis.[9]

In the 1930s, the introduction of federal welfare programs blurred clear distinctions between local, private labor markets and patterns of public relief. On the one hand, cotton planters, like those in the Mississippi Delta, might remain "fearful of any governmental program [like a public-works project] that promises to bring independence to the sharecroppers." Labor contracts often prohibited families from keeping livestock or tending gardens, and many employers kept their workers in perpetual debt, a custom that was difficult to challenge, given the physical isolation of most plantations and the complicity of law-enforcement agents in routine employer fraud. More often than not, federal aid programs reinforced a Southern political economy that relegated almost all blacks to seasonal work on the countryside. In some cases, planters and administrators agreed among themselves (of course the two groups overlapped in many locales in any case) that needy families should qualify for aid only during the slack season; in this way the Federal Emergency Relief Administration (for example) shored up the furnishing system (whereby landlords extended credit and advanced supplies to their workers). A 1934 FERA survey, "Landlord-Tenant Relations and Relief in Alabama," found that, although the "conventional attitude" was that the landlord "is expected to 'take care of' the tenant when the latter needs aid ... now ... many landlords are shifting the responsibility to the relief agencies." The fact that landlords at times took the initiative to get their workers on relief rolls meant that, over the long run, federal programs enabled employers to retain a reserve army of agricultural laborers without assuming year-long responsibility for them. Moreover, in a break with tradition, some planters took advantage of relief programs and "split" households by furnishing only able-bodied workers, instead of entire household units that invariably included young, ill, and elderly members. In this way too, planters and government officials might collude to keep workers neither fully employed nor permanently on relief; the result was a system of enforced dependency that represented a linear progression from slavery through sharecropping, culminating in overtly political federal welfare policies.[10]

The case of federal relief reveals that certain attitudes about the appropriate role of blacks in the Southern economy were not peculiar to the descendants of Southern slaveholders; rather, these views were part of a national system of white hegemony dominated by men of property. Northerners who went South after the Civil War were struck by the efforts of the newly freed slaves to establish for themselves a modest self-sufficiency, as hunters, fishers, gardeners, and foragers. Yet neither the victorious Yankees nor the vanquished Rebels considered such forms of productive labor "work" at all, since they had no place within a staple-crop economy dominated by white employers. During the 1866 slack season, Freedmen's Bureau agent Edward F. O'Brien observed that the black people near Mount Pleasant, South Carolina, were subsisting on green corn, pond lily beans, and alligator meat. He went on to describe the "idle, vicious vagrants, whose sole idea consists in loafing without working.... Being so close to the city of Charleston they find plenty temptation there to cause them to become idlers and they return to this parish only to plunder for the purpose of indulging their vicious practices.... Lead pipes taken from wells and sisterns, Harness from stables, cotton from the fields and even the iron from the cotton Gins and engines." Whatever their other shortcomings, Christ Church Parish blacks were hardly "idle." Like their slave parents who considered roast pig a delicacy, especially when pilfered from the master's hogpen, and their Northern ghetto grandchildren who earned wages "under the table," the freedpeople sought to provide for themselves outside labor systems controlled exclusively by whites.[11]

Within an agricultural economy, only property conferred independence; rather than embracing a pathetic dependence upon their employers, black families throughout the postbellum period adhered to an ideal of landownership, though relatively few were able to achieve it. Around 1915, the percentage of black landowners in the South peaked at 20 percent; most were concentrated in eastern Virginia, the South Carolina Sea Islands, and northeastern Texas, on poor land and small plots. First-generation owners won hard-earned reputations as "strivers." For example, W. L. Bost and his wife, Mamie, purchased "a little piece of ground" for $125 near Newton, North Carolina, in 1895. By buying lumber "a little at a time," they built a house for their family of three children. Forty-two years later, the Bosts still occupied the land, and could note with some satisfaction, "It's been a good home for us and the children."[12]

The rise of black-owned banks helps to account for at least some of the relatively few black farm owners during the early twentieth century; historians have documented the refusal of white-owned financial institutions throughout the South to grant credit to aspiring black home owners. In addition, in many areas of the South, propertied whites agreed among themselves not to sell land to blacks who desperately desired release from the plantation staple-crop economy. Nevertheless, the withholding of land and credit from blacks seemed almost moot in a place and at a time when the vast majority of workers were at the mercy of employers who paid them or not, just as they pleased, without fear of legal repercussion. Within such a society, otherwise normal forms of economic activity—accumulating and spending money— assumed ominous overtones when carried out by black people. Those black men and women who scrimped and saved what little they had during the last decades of the nineteenth century could hardly have been oblivious to the fact that they would be the likely victims of white resentment—lynch mobs and law enforcement agents seeking bodies for chain gangs. In the words of one woman, "You know, black folks who had money had to be kind of careful then."[13]

Just as Southern black landowners battled the odds in order to do better by themselves, so black communities all over the South invested in schools for their children, despite the violent objections of white people, rich and poor. For example, in the early 1920s, the people of Bexar in Marion County, Alabama, managed to overcome their initial shock when informed that a new schoolhouse (to replace their "little old dingy" one) would cost seven hundred dollars. They set about building the school themselves: "Men went to the woods, cut down trees, hauled them to the saw mill and had them cut into lumber. Others cleared away the grounds, and even women worked carrying water, and feeding the men while they labored until enough material was placed on the grounds for the two-teacher building."[14]

The case of education is but one illustration of the way in which blacks could work together to advance the interests of their own race; after the Civil War, a flurry of institution building among the freedpeople, who started their own churches, burial societies, neighborhood and mutual-aid associations, workers' groups, and fraternal orders testified to their determination to provide for themselves. Viewed from a long-term, historic perspective, these groups in the rural South (and later the urban North)—some well funded and enduring, others makeshift and short-lived, gender- or class-based, secular or denominational— attempted to meet the same needs. They aimed to fill the gap left by the discriminatory policies of craft unions and public and private welfare agencies; to provide places of worship or study where black people could come together, apart from degrading Jim Crow policies, North and South; and to press for black civil rights in the courts, the workplace, and in the schools. Whether sponsored by the African Methodist Episcopal Church, a black college, a segregated YMCA, ad hoc neighborhood groups, the National Association for the Advancement of Colored People, the Congress of Racial Equality, or a lone, inspired individual, these groups reveal a tradition of resourcefulness, a corporate ethos that originated in the slave quarters, persisted in the postbellum

South, and found a new, if similarly harsh, home in the urban North.

This emphasis on the struggles of black families and communities to provide for themselves, and to resist the debilitating dependency forced upon them by white men of property, diverges from the "conventional wisdom" that informs the current underclass debate. Whether organized in nuclear families, kin groups, or formal organizations, black women and men expressed in no uncertain terms their unwillingness to capitulate to the expectations of landlords and employers. Embedded in the historical record of ordinary families, then, is a powerful refutation of the culture of poverty or culture of dependency thesis.

LABOR MOBILITY IN THE PLANTATION SOUTH AND ITS COROLLARY, NORTHWARD MIGRATION

Black people, then, were hardly the passive victims of white hegemony. Even the poorest families often demonstrated a great deal of energy and ingenuity in piecing together a living for themselves. In households like the Holtzclaws' of Alabama, the mother found work for white folks as a cook while the youngsters gathered hog potatoes, persimmons, nuts, and muscadines and the father and older son went off to search for temporary employment in sawmills and railroad camps. This patchwork family economy did not preclude work in the cotton fields, but since landlords routinely curtailed furnishings during the slack season, family members had to work together, and sometimes apart, to keep "body and soul together during those dark days."[15]

An extensive network of rural nonagricultural enterprises, including turpentine orchards, phosphate mines, and lumber and sawmill camps, relied on the manpower of blacks who left their sharecropper cabins once the crop had been laid by (in the early summer) and after harvest (in the winter months). The heavy work associated with the construction, extractive, and processing industries favored the employment of able-bodied men. Nevertheless, other family members found ways to add to the household income in the course of the year. When grudgingly granted the opportunity by planters, wives earned "patch" money by marketing small surpluses of vegetables and dairy products. They took in laundry and served as midwives, at times for their poor white neighbors as well as their landlords. Children of all ages helped their fathers cut firewood and fat pine to sell, and hired themselves out as cotton pickers on nearby farms once they had fulfilled harvesttime duties at home. Local truck farms employed women and children to pick berries and vegetables during the cotton slack season.[16]

Paradoxically, as black people tried to preserve their families in an economic sense, they were often forced to depart from the family homeplace for indeterminate periods, either regularly or sporadically. The efforts of fathers, husbands, and older sons to seek out wage work stemmed from both their resourcefulness as breadwinners and from financial necessity borne of their chronic underemployment within the sharecropping system. Thus the household economy mandated the physical separation of family members, especially at certain times of the year; it is quite possible that Herbert Gutman's data on the prevalence of late-nineteenth-century rural black two-headed households underestimates these forces of fragmentation, since federal census takers usually made their appointed rounds in April, when everyone was bound to be at home for planting time. These economic imperatives, and not some ill-defined predisposition toward a "disorganized" family life, help to account for stresses on black households in the rural South.

In myriad ways over time, and in various places, the exigencies of making a living deprived black Southern fathers and mothers, husbands and wives, parents and children, of the opportunity to live together. For example, in the 1920s, after the cotton harvest, some black men from Georgia began to venture south to Florida's winter garden (just south of Lake Okeechobee) to pick beans for wages before returning home in time for the beginning of the planting season. By World War II, thousands of black families from the Lower South were moving into the East Coast migratory labor stream on a more or less permanent basis. In the process, individual households devised survival strategies calculated to take advantage of wage-earning opportunities and the needs of family members, though as we have seen in the case of Johnnie Belle Taylor, these strategies might not always permit cohabitation. In general, throughout the Southern countryside, a mother who found herself without a husband or older sons had little choice but to move in with her kinfolk or to migrate to a nearby town or city and find work as a domestic servant. Moreover, although many of the South's rural industrial enterprises continued to rely heavily on fathers who refused to abandon their farms altogether, some sons felt compelled to take up residence in mining or phosphate camps, or in the transient sawmills or turpentine camps, and live apart from their families for months, if not years, at a time. Employees of the Armour Fertilizer Works (a phosphate mine) in Bartow, Florida, faced the trade-offs familiar to rural-industrial commuters; by renting homes in nearby villages, they might avoid the dirty, crowded company quarters, but the four- to eight-mile walk to work and back each day, plus the "long working hours[,] make their homes only a place for sleep."[17]

Pressures on the black family economy in the rural South during the Great Depression indicate that first, long-term structural underemployment was not unique to the urban North, and second, two-parent black households failed to enjoy a "golden age" of sorts between slavery and Northern migration. In the late 1930s and on into the World War II period, government construction of factories and army installations hastened the process by which agricultural workers lost their ties to the land; at the same time, these building projects spurred much interregional mobility among male wage seekers, many of whom left their families behind. Army construction projects like the Triangular Division

Camp near Ozark, Alabama, could put 18,000 men on its payroll during its peak season; but half of these employees fell into the category of unskilled, and they had to move on once the work was completed—in this case in 120 days. Housing was so scarce around some of the larger projects that employees had to make do with the most primitive of conditions—about 3,000 of the 19,400 construction workers at Florida's Camp Blanding set up tents in the nearby woods southwest of Jacksonville. In Newport News, Virginia, inadequate housing for black male workers led to high turnover rates among husbands and fathers who quit in order to go home and visit their families periodically, prompting white employers to denounce blacks as "irresponsible" war workers.[18]

Crop reduction programs sponsored by the Agricultural Adjustment Administration (beginning in 1933), plus large government public-works projects, pushed croppers off the plantations and forced families to regroup somehow, either as squatters nearby or as casual wage workers clustered on the fringes of major Southern cities. Family members dispersed throughout the South, their traditional way of life, based as much on foraging as on cotton culture, shattered forever. Though released in 1942, and dealing specifically with the Huntsville, Alabama, area, a study of the impact of national defense on various rural communities applied equally to households throughout the years of the Great Depression and earlier: "The family which worked at odd jobs, tilling a few acres in a haphazard manner, and augmenting earnings through scouring the woods for sassafrass roots, picking dallas green seed, trapping coons and skunks, snaring fish in baskets, and poaching on game reservations, etc., could not be dumped into another community with the expectation that the resourcefulness of the family would enable it to get by."[19]

The problem of worker mobility and migration highlights the struggle between labor-hungry rural employers on the one hand and employees resistant to exploitative conditions on the other. In particular, the phenomenon of "shifting" sharecroppers was ultimately a political issue that helped to shape labor relations on plantations throughout the Cotton South from 1865 until the large-scale replacement of agricultural wage earners with tractors in the 1940s and 1950s. Deprived of the ability to move up the agricultural tenure ladder (through the accumulation of land or cash), or to make a living wage in Southern cities or textile mill villages, black families engaged in an annual form of lateral geographical movement that took them down the road to a neighboring plantation every couple of years or so, without the benefit of much (apparent) gain in the way of material resources or labor contract provisions. Shifting had an urban industrial counterpart in the high rates of job turnover among wage earners in the lowest paid jobs, a characteristic of poor white and black, immigrant and native-born workers alike. The phenomenon resulted from several factors—the impulse on the part of landlords, or employers, to evict or fire "troublesome" workers; and the desire on the part of employees to search for something better elsewhere, and to deny an exploitative boss complete control over one's labor. In the words of one Southern white man, "If he [the worker] doesn't trust you he is not going to stay long, not if he can get some place else to go."[20]

Too often Southern employers confused "shifting" with "shiftlessness" or irresponsibility on the part of croppers. In reality, households calculated their various interests, both economic and affective, on a year-to-year basis. Black families found that, over time, their needs—in terms of housing, proximity to a town or school—changed in response to household composition and size; consequently, a move to another employer might result in incremental benefits, like a better chimney or a closer spring of water, but not a noticeably higher standard of living or fairer deal at the end of the year. Too, croppers routinely fled from abusive or cheating planters, and the pervasiveness of state-sanctioned fraud practiced by rural-South employers kept many families perpetually on the move. A Georgia sharecropper, Ed Brown, likened himself to a rabbit: "Zigzag, zigzag, dodgin one hunter then the next." In the words of one contemporary observer, "[croppers'] one outstanding means of asserting freedom is mobility, although within an extremely narrow range." Together, in family groups, the former slaves institutionalized the practice of running away, though they could deprive only one particular white man (a current employer), but not whites in general, of their labor.[21]

On the other hand, planters as a matter of course dismissed or violently expelled workers who during the year defiantly kept a little garden spot, stole chickens, or appropriated wood for their own use, or spent too much time grubbing for wild potatoes before the crop lien was satisfied. When Southern planters complained about a "shortage" of labor between the Civil War and the Second World War, they had in mind a particular kind of laborer, one sufficiently skillful at picking time and sufficiently tractable at "reckoning" (that is, end-of-year settlement) time; according to this standard, then, most planters despaired of ever securing an "assured tenantry." In the words of one United States Department of Agriculture official, planters used a constant process of "selection and elimination." "Reliable tenants" were those who were "public-spirited and loyal to the planter and who exercise a good influence over those inclined to become dissatisfied." Still, employers could always count on hiring their neighbors' former hands, black men and women fleeing from the same kind of abuses that their new employer had committed against his previous workers.[22]

When blacks rejected the sedentary form of labor demanded of them in the rural South, they reacted in ways not unlike those of other dispossessed groups in history, the urban poor and colonized peoples who led transient lives, scavenged for a living, and participated in a "moral economy" outside the boundaries of the paid labor force. At the same time, within the context of American history, African Americans were a unique group by virtue of the political and legal restraints imposed on their mobility, restraints based on race and not on class. During the antebellum period, slave and free black alike moved around the Southern country-side, and across state lines, only at the behest of whites; after the war, the notorious "black codes" passed by Southern legislatures (and resurrected later through vagrancy statutes) made it a crime for black people to travel for reasons not directly related to the needs of a white employer. A lack of economic opportunities in other areas of the country effectively kept blacks bound to the land worked by their slave grandparents. By the late 1800s, it was clear that Northern industrial employers would continue to favor unskilled, non-English-speaking Eastern European immigrants, to the detriment of the large black population languishing in the South. In 1916, when immigration slowed and the need for defense workers intensified in Northern cities, black people eagerly left the South, an impulse that one migrant to Chicago compared to shifting: "Before the North opened up with work all we could do was to move from one plantation to another in the hope of finding something better." A black man who eventually moved to Newark, New Jersey, also recalled. "After a time we moved 'round, you know, to see if we could find a better place. That's the nature of farmin'."[23]

Indeed, the very act of migration out of the South belies the theory of black "dependency." Had black people as a group embraced a hopeless and fatalistic view of the world, they probably would have avoided the considerable exertion necessary to make complicated relocation arrangements, which included keeping in touch with friends already in the North, scraping together the fare for the train ride north, selling precious belongings, and in some instances engineering an exceedingly daring late-night departure, children and chickens in tow, from a Delta plantation.

There is little evidence to indicate that blacks left the South for the explicit purpose of receiving higher welfare payments in the North during any period. Most migrants necessarily relinquished what little aid they might have received in the South in exchange for the chance to work in the North; in any case, Northern communities' residency requirements could prevent migrants from qualifying for assistance for any number of months or for as many as five years. Families like the Moshers of Russell County, Alabama, could confound welfare workers who assumed that blacks would automatically and unquestionably react to either the offer or the withdrawal of relief, no matter how meager. Left behind by large numbers of their kind and neighbors who moved to Chicago during World War I, in 1933 the Moshers (a family of ten) decided that they too should relocate when they found that they could not live on the small amount of public aid allotted them. After Mrs. Mosher traveled with two of the children to Chicago the following year, to attend the funeral of her brother, she remained in the city, and by September 1935 six of her other offspring had followed her there. Alarmed Chicago social workers informed the mother that she would not receive any public assistance, assuming that the threat would dissuade her husband and the two other children from coming North.

Instead, the recent migrants determined "to try not only to stay in Chicago but also to bring the rest of the family North to join them." The Mosher's household strategy signaled their eagerness to move North, to preserve family ties, and to scorn local and federal efforts to confine them to one area of the country or another through the manipulation of various public-assistance programs.[24]

To some observers, black migration northward represented an irrevocable break with a distinctive way of life mired in the South's regional peculiarities of slavery, and then postbellum neoslavery. But for one family that had to "scuff around" for day work in Virginia, and then "scuff around" for day work in Newark, New Jersey, in the early 1960s, the way north seemed a less dramatic move than most "detached" observers might have imagined. To some degree, the issue turned on gender issues and on timing; for example, in the 1920s, Charlottesville, Virginia, domestics bound for New York City would find few other kinds of jobs open to them. On the other hand, male wartime migrants might experience a more drastic break with their past jobs, as they began to "leave off tending green growing things to tending iron monsters." Nevertheless, chronic underemployment would continue to plague black husbands and fathers in the North as well as in the South, though a modern industrial economy would present fewer alternatives for foraging and day work compared to life on the nineteenth-century countryside.[25]

THE CREATION OF THE BLACK GHETTO: THE HISTORY OF WHITE APPALACHIAN MIGRANTS AS A COUNTEREXAMPLE

In order to unravel the class and racial factors that converged to produce the black ghetto in the North, it is fruitful to examine the fate of poor-white Southerners (here the focus is on men and women from the southern Appalachian area), and the way their experiences diverged from those of black migrants to Northern cities. From World War I until the end of the Great Depression, 1.5 million black people left the South for the North. Between 1940 and 1970, about 5 million more blacks abandoned the South, and approximately 3.2 million people migrated out of the southern Appalachian region. (In the decade of the 1950s alone, Kentucky lost 35 percent of its total population through outmigration; West Virginia suffered comparable losses, of 25 percent.) Some historians and social scientists have compared Southern-born blacks with Eastern European immigrants and argued that black people found themselves at a disadvantage in the urban North as a result of transformations in the Northern economy that (beginning in the 1920s) gradually eliminated the need for large numbers of unskilled workers.[26] However, if that had been the major reason for the growth of poor black inner-city communities, then Appalachian white migrants, who started their northward trek in earnest in the 1940s and had comparable (that is, comparably low) levels of schooling and job status compared to blacks, would have fared even worse in the race for good jobs and decent housing. In fact, as a group, southern Appalachians prospered early, and steadily, in their host communities, Midwestern towns and cities. These migrants were relatively successful primarily because they gained easy access to semi-skilled jobs, and they had the freedom to move around within urban areas, or at least as far as their fortunes and kin ties would take them.

This comparison, which holds class factors (strictly defined) constant, and highlights the issue of race, is not without its difficulties. On the one hand, it is possible to draw some compelling, if unexpected, parallels between the two groups; blacks and poor whites adhered to a "traditional," rural way of life that valued kin connections and neighborly cooperation over an ethos of wage-based capital accumulation or individual "success." Neither black sharecroppers nor white mountain people could claim much in the way of either formal education or work experience outside the agricultural or extractive sectors. Though they came from different cultures, historically defined, members of both groups adhered to Protestant fundamentalism, and they nourished grievances (some more long-standing than others) toward planters or coal-mining companies who set in motion the forces of displacement that deprived them of homesteads and caused them to assume a semi-nomadic existence. When mountain folk deferred to their betters, they practiced a kind of deference ritual that blacks had perfected under slavery. Even musical forms considered the core of a "pure" Appalachian culture included elements of Southern black influence (blues and gospel music) and changed rapidly over the generations.[27]

In sum, social workers and scholars alike have spent much time and effort trying to define a distinctive Appalachian culture without realizing that many of the traits ascribed to this group were common to rural folk in general. The effort on the part of white households to combine wage work with patch farming, and to rely on kin for financial support in good times and bad, was less a "Kentucky way" than a rural way of life. Once in the North, southern Appalachians exhibited few of the collective or associational impulses that would qualify them as an ethnic group; their extended families, rather than precisely defined cultural bonds, served as their primary reference point. And finally, the "backwardness" of Appalachian life was belied by the strenuous efforts of a considerable proportion of the population to leave it, at least temporarily. Commented Rosalie Van Houton, a Kentucky native who had moved with her husband to Detroit during World War II, "They [that is, Northerners] think we're dumb just because we come from outside. They're a whole lot dumber than we are. They've never been outside their own little community."[28]

Most Appalachian migrants headed for the Midwest, where they were soon stereotyped in terms similar to those used to describe black people. Municipal officials considered Southern whites as a group to be lazy, promiscuous, rapidly proliferating welfare seekers, a drain on the public treasury, a stain on the city's image. Educational officials tracked their children for failure in the public schools, and medical authorities decried their persistent superstitions in all manner of ailments, like rinsing out a child's mouth with urine to cure a rash called thrush. Employers expressed mixed feelings; the migrants provided cheap labor, but they were (in the eyes of some bosses and plant foremen) unreliable, inept at machine work, slow on the job, and unambitious. Landlords told them that they need not apply, citing their large families, allegedly deplorable housekeeping practices, and violent proclivities (with the knife as the weapon of choice). Their neighbors native to the North soon developed a repertoire of jokes that focused on the migrants' so-called ignorance of city ways, their primitive Southern origins, their slovenly appearance and demeanor. Condemned as shiftless, evasive, and untrustworthy, they squandered their weekly paychecks on trinkets and drink (or so it was charged). Social workers believed that in their new home, as in their old, the migrants remained willing and able to tolerate the most degraded living and working conditions, "immune to discomforts that sorely try other Americans." This last point, in particular, echoed the convictions of Southern cotton planters who justified furnishing black croppers at a bare subsistence level because of the former slaves' (reported) remarkable ability to survive on so little in the way of material resources.[29]

And yet, despite their poverty and the hostility they encountered from Northerners, Appalachian whites did not come from or adhere to a distinctive folk culture comparable (at least for analytic purposes) to Afro-American culture. The whites hailed from a variety of local economies—subsistence farming, commercial tobacco production, coal mining, or some combination of the three—and not until they arrived in the North did (some) people from the region begin to think of themselves as a homogeneous group. Even then, any sense of cultural loyalty or identification could be fleeting. For the upwardly mobile of either sex, it was possible to leave the "ridgerunner" and "briarhopper" taunts behind forever by losing their accents, adopting Northern dress fashions, and switching the radio dial from Hank Williams to Frank Sinatra. Predictably, many of the children of migrants saw little reason to tout themselves as the kin of "hillbillies."

Southern Appalachians migrated both to the largest cities in the Midwest, where they won favor over blacks in direct competition for unskilled and semiskilled jobs, and to the small towns of southern Ohio, where they effectively kept black people from migrating in large numbers at all, so tight was their hold over manufacturing jobs at every level. To cite an example of the process as it affected workers of both races in Detroit (known as the "capital city of Hell" for its racial and ethnic tensions and its shortage of housing during World War II and later): Waiting in line for a job in a Detroit defense plant in April 1943, a black man named Charles Denby found himself standing next to a white migrant from Tennessee. The two struck up a conversation. The white man, who had "never been North before or in a plant," mentioned that he had no idea what kinds of jobs were available. Denby, though raised on a cotton farm in Lowndes County, Alabama, had had considerable factory work experience—in a Detroit auto plant, a Pittsburgh steel mill, an Anniston, Alabama, foundry, and a Memphis machine supply company. Denby had heard from a friend that "the best job was riveting," and that it paid $1.16 an hour. When it came time for him to talk to the employment officer, Denby said he knew all about riveting ("I was lying to him but I wanted to get the job"). The officer replied that Denby's "experience wouldn't apply," and offered him the choice of attending riveting school, which paid 60 cents an hour, or taking a "laboring job" that paid 27 cents an hour more. With a family to support, Denby decided to accept the latter position. Shortly thereafter he learned that the Tennessean had also asked for the riveting job, but that no one had inquired about his work history or insisted that he undergo a period of low-paid training. Denby later recalled, "He said they had given him a job, riveting." The white man marveled, "And I just come in from the fields." In contrast, Denby was assigned to the dope room, where "the odor of glue made the average person sick," and labor turnover was high; gradually, black men took the places of white men who departed, but in the course of the war, black women came to predominate in the small, suffocating space.[30]

In Detroit and Chicago (for example), racial conflicts over jobs and housing were explicit, and bloody. In contrast, southern Appalachians who migrated to Ohio's Miami Valley established an early and exclusive foothold in the heavy industries of that region, then as a group perpetuated their predominance through kin networks eagerly exploited by employment officers. In Middletown, Ohio, in the early 1950s, one-half of all employees of the Inland Container Corporation hailed from Wolfe County, Kentucky, the home of a company superintendent who combined job recruitment with periodic visits to kin back home. In the same town, the Armco Steel Corporation as a matter of policy granted hiring preference to the children and relatives of workers; as a result, migrants from certain Kentucky counties came to predominate in individual departments. Asked about the prejudice of southern Ohioans against mountain folk, one migrant said that he had encountered "no trouble" in his entry-level job, because almost all his workers shared the same roots and "there weren't no buckeyes [that is, Ohio-born people] to get along with." Clearly, manufacturing jobs in this area of the country went to southern Appalachian whites not because they possessed superior skills or training compared to blacks (they did not), but because they were part of a chain migration that sustained itself over the generations, aided and abetted by Northern employers. Thus throughout the Midwest, Southern whites benefited from racially exclusionary hiring practices, from their kin connections, and from most businesses' policy of upgrading and providing on-the-job training for current employees who aspired to semiskilled and operative positions. The wives and daughters who migrated from Appalachia might supplement the wages of their menfolk through factory or clerical work, positions closed to most black women through the 1960s. Indeed, until that time, most black female migrants, and Northern black women in general, remained confined to domestic and institutional service.[31]

Discriminatory housing policies in the urban North—policies achieved through the redlining practices of banks, suburban zoning restrictions and restrictive covenants, and the segregationist imperative as implemented by city councils and the Federal Housing Administration—have been described in detail elsewhere, and well. For our purposes, it is necessary to consider the residential patterns of southern Appalachian migrants to the North, for those patterns exhibited a variety and fluidity that set them apart from the process of ghettoization that affected blacks of all classes. For example, over the generations, Appalachian migrants and their children established for themselves a number of different kinds of communities in Ohio. East Dayton, Cincinnati's Over-the-Rhine and Lower Price Hill, and Hamilton's Armondale and Peck's Addition represented classic port-of-entry communities for the first migrants and for some of those who followed. Yet these poor neighborhoods were characterized by high rates of residential turnover, as migrants and their relatively successful offspring explored other housing options—stable working-class or lower-middle-class areas like Mill Creek, near Cincinnati, or Wrightview, outside of Dayton; or small towns like South Lebanon, where families could tend some corn and fish a nearby stream; and finally, pleasant suburbs where well-to-do whites might quickly blend into the middle-American landscape. A migrant family might logically progress from Peck's Addition to a better area of the working-class Belmont district, and finally move out to Fairfield Township, where they could enjoy "at least superficially some of the isolation of the hollow ... set up a vegetable patch and ... find some of the [ethnic and racial] homogeneity still preserved in the Kentucky hills." On the other hand, other white migrants, depending on their own background and the location of their Northern kin, might move directly from the South to a stable suburb and stay there.[32]

Because of their physical proximity to their Southern homes, and their fondness for a "farm freedom" characteristic of the Appalachian region in the past (if not in the present or future), the poorest white migrants found it difficult to commit themselves wholeheartedly to Northern life; in accounting for the lack of associational activity among this group (in striking contrast to collective-minded ghetto residents), observers noted the ease with which poor whites might move between South and North, never fully here nor there. Unlike blacks, the poorest whites retained a fondness for the historic tradition represented by their Southern homes, and the story of their migration northward had a mournful, elegiac quality. By the 1960s, a white underclass (proportionately much smaller than the concentrated poor black population) had developed in scattered migrant communities throughout the North—families like that of Charlotte and Harold Gibson, who spent years in transit between their home in Logan, West Virginia, and Chicago's

Uptown neighborhood, and were worn down by a series of round-trips to despair. An abusive man unable to hold a steady job, Harold would disappear for months at a time, leaving thirty-two-year-old Charlotte to rear their ten children in rat-infested apartments and to beg for help from disapproving landlords, truant officers, welfare bureaucrats, and private charity agencies. Many of the family's moves between West Virginia and Chicago reflected Charlotte's efforts to follow the whims of Harold's job quests. Bad luck seemed to dog his every step—a sudden layoff, a repossessed car. One promising stint as a coal miner in Logan came to an abrupt end soon after creditors started to garnish his wages; he quit out of spite. The welfare officials who considered Charlotte Gibson's case saw only an irresponsible white woman unable to maintain steady contact with any agency or keep her children in school for any length of time. At least as long as the Gibson family resided in Uptown's slums, they were part of Chicago's white underclass. Though characterized by all those indexes of social pathology normally associated with blacks in big-city ghettos, poor whites in the North were more dispersed throughout metropolitan regions and so more difficult to count and study. Therefore, most experts on the underclass ignored them altogether.[33]

The case of Appalachian migrants reveals that, in Northern cities, plain white folk from the rural South were afforded advantages in jobs and housing not because of some putative superiority (to blacks) in formal education, in "factory sense," or in personal values, but because of the color of their skin. In southern Ohio, for example, when men and women from the hills and hollows of Kentucky received promotions that lifted them out of unskilled and into semiskilled work, and when they decided to move out of depressed port-of-entry communities and into stable working-class neighborhoods, they profited from the pervasive racial discrimination against Deep South black migrants. Thus the emergence of the black ghetto was not a foregone conclusion, or an unfortunate but inevitable result of migration and settlement patterns among the rural Southern poor; rather, the ghetto was a product of Jim Crow discrimination, Northern style, and Chicago offered only a variation of the forces that had beleaguered the freedpeople and their descendants in Mississippi.

By the late twentieth century, the political and economic forces that had dispossessed Southern black people of their homes and the living they wrung from the soil, displaced them from the Southern countryside, and finally, rendered their labor superfluous within a postindustrial society, culminated in the distressed inner-city populations of the urban North. By this time the poorest black citizens lacked one of the most basic resources available to their parents and their grandparents— the hope for a better life elsewhere. And yet it would be misleading to interpret those forces of dispossession in exclusively racial terms. The United States consisted of a number of underclasses, marginalized groups that shared the same symptoms of poverty—high rates of unemployment, female-headed households, crime and substance abuse—but differed from one another in terms of culture, skin color, and regional identification. In the Midwest, the collapse of heavy industry in the 1970s left in its wake the seeming paradox of impoverished homeowners and car owners, men and women now forced to seek out menial service jobs that carried no benefits or union card. In the depressed coal regions of Appalachia, and in the backwoods of rural New England, rural folk pieced together a living by fishing and foraging, looking for odd jobs, and relying on the goodwill of more fortunate kin and neighbors. In the barrios of Los Angeles and in the decaying mill towns of Massachusetts, Hispanic youth became caught up in a violent street culture and suffered from higher school dropout rates than did black students throughout the nation. New immigrants from Southeast Asia, from the Carribbean and Latin America, desperately sought out work in the East Coast agricultural migratory labor stream and in fly-by-night sweatshops in El Paso and New York City.

Black people arrived in Northern ghettos via a path that was historically unique, a path that began in the slave South, a path pockmarked by racial prejudice and political oppression. And yet the problems that plagued their neighborhoods in the 1990s were not unique, but rather common to other poor groups scattered throughout the nation—lack of access to quality education, decent jobs, and affordable health care. America was a country not only of radical economic inequality among persons, but also of radically unequal places. Still, black ghettos seemed to attract more than their fair share of pity, or scorn, for reasons that reflected contemporary middle-class American values and priorities. More particularly, sensational stories about the underclass (a shorthand term for poor blacks in general, and a predatory youth culture in particular) brought to real life the mainstream vices of violence and misogyny glorified by Hollywood, the popular media, and commercial advertisers. Moreover, this preoccupation with a drug and street culture seemed to confirm traditional American beliefs that poverty in the countryside was somehow cleaner, healthier, more wholesome, and less degrading than its inner-city counterpart.[34]

In the 1860s, black people emerged from slavery, landless and confined within a plantation economy that barred them from meaningful lateral or upward mobility. In the twentieth century, black migrants arrived in the urban North, only to find themselves confined within ghettos. Throughout these transformations, from emancipation to the sharecropping plantation and then to industrial and postindustrial society, black Americans struggled to cope with the forces of dislocation, not by embracing a slavish dependence on whites, but by providing for themselves in ways that few whites could abide or even comprehend. Though the external configuration of her household failed to conform to certain middle-class notions of what that household should look like, Johnnie Belle Taylor worked to preserve the integrity of her family, and her own self-respect. And yet when present-day observers continue to scrutinize her struggles, and those of family members in Northern ghettos, through a lens of racial exclusivity, we relegate Taylor, and all African Americans, to the fringes of American social history, without appreciating the aspirations they shared with other American workers regardless of class, race, or region. Thus does a society conceived in slavery perpetuate itself; in its devotion to a politics based on race, late-twentieth-century America remains the postbellum South writ large.

NOTES

The author would like to acknowledge the helpful suggestions of other members of the SSRC Historical Origins of the Underclass group, and especially those of Michael Katz, Clayborne Carson, Kathryn Neckerman, and Thomas Sugrue.

1. Testimony of Johnnie Belle Taylor, in *Hearings before the Select Committee Investigating National Defense Migration*, House of Representatives, 77th Cong., 2d Sess., pt. 33, pp. 12627–28 (hereafter *National Defense Migration Hearings*, with part no.).
2. Charles Murray, *Losing Ground: American Social Policy, 1950–1980* (New York: Basic Books, 1984), p. 31; Nicholas Lemann, "The Origins of the Underclass, Pt. I," *Atlantic Monthly* 257 (June 1986): 35, 41, 47; and Nicholas Lemann, *The Promised Land: The Great Black Migration and How It Changed America* (New York: Random House, 1991).
3. William Julius Wilson, *The Truly Disadvantaged: The Inner City, the Underclass, and Public Policy* (Chicago: University of Chicago Press, 1987), pp. 30, 32; Herbert Gutman, *The Black Family in Slavery and Freedom, 1750–1920* (New York: Pantheon, 1976). For a highly idiosyncratic view stressing a degree of continuity between slavery and the modern underclass, see Orlando Patterson, "Toward a Study of Black America: Notes on the Culture of Racism." *Dissent* (Fall 1989): 476–86. Patterson makes the rather remarkable assertion that "we can trace the underclass, as a persisting social phenomenon," back to "a distinct underclass of slaves" that included "incorrigible blacks of whom the slaveholder class was forever complaining" (p. 480).
4. Lemann, "The Origins of the Underclass, Pt. II," *Atlantic Monthly* (July 1986): 59.
5. Roger Ransom and Richard Sutch, *One Kind of Freedom: The Economic Consequences of Emancipation* (New York: Cambridge University Press, 1977); Allen H. Stokes, Jr., "Black and White Labor for the Development of the Southern Textile Industry, 1800–1920" (Ph.D. diss., University of South Carolina, 1977); Raymond Wolters, *Negroes and the Great Depression: The Problem of Economic Recovery* (Westport, Conn.: Greenwood, 1970); Gavin Wright, *Old South, New South: Revolutions in the Southern Economy Since the Civil War* (New York: Basic Books, 1986).
6. Interviews with Jackson Jordan, Jr., and Ruth Shays, in John Langston Gwaltney, *Drylongso: A Self-Portrait of Black America* (New York: Vintage Books, 1980), pp. 98, 101, 31.
7. Interviews with Seth Bingham, Ella Turner Surry, Nancy White, Gordon Etheridge, Bernard Vanderstell, Jon Oliver, Janet McCrae, Mabel Lincoln, ibid., pp. 226, 239, 144, 235, 115, 18, 124, 234, 69.

8. "the business": interview with Jackson Jordan, Jr., ibid., p. 98.

9. For examples of labor contracts, see the archives of the Bureau of Refugees, Freedmen, and Abandoned Lands (Record Group 105, National Archives, Washington, D.C. [available on microfilm]). See also Gerald Jaynes, *Branches without Roots: Genesis of the Black Working Class in the American South, 1862–1882* (New York: Oxford University Press, 1986).

10. "fearful" and "conventional": Harold C. Hoffsomer, "Landlord-Tenant Relations and Relief in Alabama," Federal Emergency Relief Administration Confidential Research Bulletin 2738 (July 10, 1934), summary, np. in vol. 4. Works Progress Administration Collection (Record Group 69, National Archives, Washington, D.C.); "split": A. R. Mangus, "The Rural Negro on Relief, Feb., 1935," FERA Research Bulletin 6950 (October 17, 1935), p. ii (Record Group 69, National Archives). On sharecropping in the Delta, see, for example, E. L. Langsford and B. H. Thibodeaux, "Plantation Organization and Operation in the Yazoo-Mississippi Delta Area," Department of Agriculture Technical Bulletin No. 682 (Washington, D.C., May 1939).

11. Edward F. O'Brien to A. M. Crawford, Mount Pleasant, South Carolina, September 5, 1866, M869 (S.C.), Reel 34, BRFAL, RG 105, NA.

12. W. L. Bost interview, George Rawick, ed., *The American Slave: A Composite Autobiography*, vol. 14 (N.C. Narratives), pt. 1 (Westport, Conn.: Greenwood Press, 1972–79), p. 146. See also Lewis C. Gray et al., "Farm Ownership and Tenancy," Department of Agriculture, *Agricultural Yearbook, 1923* (Washington, D.C.: GPO, 1924); Elizabeth Rauh Bethel, *Promiseland: A Century of Life in a Negro Community* (Philadelphia: Temple University Press, 1981); Kevern J. Verney, "Trespassers in the Land of Their Birth: Blacks and Landownership in South Carolina and Mississippi during the Civil War and Reconstruction," *Slavery and Abolition* 4 (1983): 64–78; Loren Schweninger, *Black Property Owners in the South, 1790–1915* (Urbana: University of Illinois Press, 1990).

13. "you know": James P. Comer, *Maggie's American Dream: The Life and Times of a Black Family* (New York: New American Library, 1988), p. 19; Ransom and Sutch, *One Kind of Freedom*; Manning Marable, "The Politics of Black Land Tenure, 1877–1915," *Agricultural History* 53 (1979): 142, 147–48.

14. Rosenwald Building Fund agent quoted in James D. Anderson, *The Education of Blacks in the South, 1860–1935* (Chapel Hill: University of North Carolina Press, 1988), p. 165. The story of the Savannah Education Association is recounted in Jacqueline Jones, *Soldiers of Light and Love: Northern Teachers and Georgia Blacks, 1865–1873* (Chapel Hill: University of North Carolina Press, 1980), pp. 73–76. See also Robert C. Morris, *Reading, 'Riting and Reconstruction: The Education of Freedmen in the South, 1861–1870* (Chicago: University of Chicago Press, 1981); Vincent P. Franklin and James D. Anderson, eds., *New Perspectives on Black Educational History* (Boston: G. K. Hall, 1978).

15. William H. Holtzclaw, *The Black Man's Burden* (New York: Neale Publishing Co., 1915), pp. 17–18, 20–25, 27, 31. See also Theodore Rosengarten, *All God's Dangers: The Life of Nate Shaw* (New York: Knopf, 1974).

16. These points are developed more fully in chap. 5 of Jacqueline Jones, *The Dispossessed: America's Underclasses from the Civil War to the Present* (New York: Basic Books, 1992).

17. *Employees v. Armour Fertilizer Works*, Bartow, Florida (Docket no. 689,

1918, Entry 4, File no. 0112, National War Labor Board, Record Group 2, National Archives, Washington, D.C.); Jacqueline Jones, *Labor of Love, Labor of Sorrow: Black Women, Work and the Family from Slavery to the Present* (New York: Basic Books, 1985), pp. 110–51.

18. James G. Maddox, "The Role of Low-Income Farm Families in the War Effort," *National Defense Migration Hearings*, pt. 28, p. 10786; testimony of Roberta C. Williams, Florida Travellers' Aid, *Hearings before the Select Committee to Investigate the Interstate Migration of Destitute Citizens*, House of Representatives, 77th Cong., 3d Sess. (hereinafter *Interstate Migration Hearings*), pt. 9 (1940), p. 3619; Frank S. Horne, "War Homes in Hampton Roads," *Opportunity* 20 (July 1942): 200–202.

19. Pete Daniel, *Breaking the Land: The Transformation of Cotton, Tobacco, and Rice Cultures since 1880* (Urbana: University of Illinois Press, 1985); Jack Temple Kirby, *Rural Worlds Lost: The American South, 1920–1960* (Baton Rouge: Louisiana State University Press, 1987); "the family": E. S. Morgan, "Displacement of Farm Families Caused by National Defense Activities in Alabama, Georgia, South Carolina, and Florida," *National Defense Migration Hearings*, pt. 32, p. 12082.

20. Testimony of Luther Jones, *National Defense Migration Hearings*, pt. 33, p. 12667.

21. "zigzag": Jane Maguire, *On Shares: Ed Brown's Story* (New York: Norton, 1975), p. 63; "one": John Lee Coulter, "The Rural Life Problem of the South," *South Atlantic Quarterly* 12 (1913): 64.

22. "assured": Alfred Holt Stone, *Studies in the American Race Problem* (New York: Doubleday, Page, 1908), p. 127; "selection": C. O. Brannen, "Relation of Land Tenure to Plantation Organization," Department of Agriculture Bulletin no. 1269 (October 18, 1924), p. 50. See also W. J. Spillman and E. A. Goldenweiser, "Farm Tenantry in the United States," Department of Agriculture, *Agriculture Yearbook for 1916* (Washington, D.C.: GPO, 1917), p. 345.

23. "before": quoted in James Grossman, *Land of Hope: Chicago, Black Southerners, and the Great Migration* (Chicago: University of Chicago Press, 1989). p 18; "after": "The Master Called Me to Preach the Bible," in Audrey Olsen Faulkner et al., *When I Was Comin' Up: An Oral History of Aged Blacks* (Hamden, Conn.: Archon Books, 1982), p. 84. See also Eric Foner, *Reconstruction: America's Unfinished Revolution, 1863–1877* (New York: Harper and Row, 1988); Oscar Zeichner, "The Legal Status of the Agricultural Laborer in the South," *Political Science Quarterly* 55 (September 1940): 412–28; William Cohen, "Negro Involuntary Servitude in the South, 1865–1940: A Preliminary Analysis," *Journal of Southern History* 42 (February 1976): 31–60.

24. John N. Webb and Malcolm Brown, "Migrant Families," Works Progress Administration Research Monograph 18 (Washington, D.C.: GPO, 1938), pp. 23–24. See also Larry H. Long, "Poverty Status and Receipt of Welfare among Migrants and Nonmigrants in Large Cities," *American Sociological Review* 39 (February 1974): 46–56. William Julius Wilson reviews the literature on the transferral of poverty and welfare dependency from South to North in *The Truly Disadvantaged*, pp. 177–80.

25. "scuff": "Nine Luzianne Coffee Boxes," in Faulkner et al., *When I Was Comin' Up*, p. 60; Marjorie Felice Irwin, "The Negro in Charlottesville and Albermarle County" (Phelps-Stokes Fellowship Paper, University of Virginia, 1929), pp. 24–29; "leave off": William Attaway, *Blood on the Forge* (1941; reprint, New York: Monthly Review Press, 1987), p. 64.

26. See, for example, Stanley Lieberson, *A Piece of the Pie: Blacks and White Immigrants since 1880* (Berkeley: University of California Press, 1980).

27. Ronald D. Eller, *Miners, Millhands, and Mountaineers: Industrialization of the Appalachian South, 1880–1930* (Knoxville: University of Tennessee Press, 1982); Allen Batteau, "Rituals of Dependence in Appalachian Kentucky," in Allen Batteau, ed., *Appalachia and America: Autonomy and Regional Dependence* (Lexington: University Press of Kentucky, 1983), pp. 142–67; D. K. Wilgus, "Country-Western Music and the Urban Hillbilly," *Journal of American Folklore* 83 (April–June 1970): 157–79. See also Patricia D. Beaver, *Rural Community in the Appalachian South* (Lexington: University Press of Kentucky, 1986), pp. 56–78.

28. Rhoda Halperin, *The Livelihood of Kin: Making Ends Meet "The Kentucky Way"* (Austin: University of Texas Press, 1990); "they": T. E. Murphy. "The Orphans of Willow Run," *Saturday Evening Post*, August 4, 1945, p. 110. See also William W. Philliber, *Appalachian Migrants in Urban America: Cultural Conflict or Ethnic Group Formation?* (New York: Praeger, 1981).

29. "immune": E. Russell Porter, "Where Cultures Meet: Mountain and Urban," Nursing Outlook 2 (June 1963): 418. See also Ellen J. Stekert, "Focus for Conflict: Southern Mountain Medical Beliefs in Detroit," *Journal of American Folklore* 83 (April–June 1970): 115–47; Lewis M. Killian, "Southern White Laborers in Chicago's West Side," (Ph. D. diss., University of Chicago, 1949); Staff of the *Cincinnati Enquirer*, *Urban Appalachians* (Cincinnati, Ohio: *Cincinnati Enquirer*, 1981); James S. Brown and George A. Hillery, Jr., "The Great Migration, 1940–1960," in Thomas R. Ford, ed., *The Southern Appalachian Region* (Lexington: University of Kentucky Press, 1962), pp. 54–78.

30. "capital": "Mountain Dreams," in Robert Coles and Jane Hallowell Coles, *Women of Crisis: Lives of Struggle and Hope* (New York: Delta/Seymour Lawrence, 1978), p. 80; Charles Denby, *Indignant Heart: Testimony of a Black American Worker* (London: Pluto Press, 1978), pp. 87–89.

31. John Leslie Thompson, "Industrialization in the Miami Valley: A Case Study of Interregional Labor Migration" (Ph.D. diss., University of Wisconsin, 1955), p. 132; "no trouble": quoted in Martin J. Crowe, "The Occupational Adaptation of a Selected Group of Eastern Kentuckians in Southern Ohio" (Ph.D. diss., University of Kentucky, 1964), p. 134. See also Gene B. Peterson, Laure M. Sharp, and Thomas F. Drury, *Southern Newcomers to Northern Cities: Work and Social Adjustment to Cleveland* (New York: Praeger, 1966); Barbara Zigli, "Dream of Moving Up Becomes True for Many," in Staff of *Chicago Enquirer*, *Urban Appalachians*, pp. 16–17.

32. "at least": Stanley B. Greenberg, *Politics and Poverty: Modernization and Response in Five Poor Neighborhoods* (New York: John Wiley, 1974), p. 53; Grace G. Leybourne, "Urban Adjustments of Migrants from the Southern Appalachian Plateau," *Journal of Social Forces* 16 (December 1937): 238–46; Gary Fowler, "The Residential Distribution of Urban Appalachians," in William W. Philliber and Clyde B. McCoy, eds., *Invisible Minority: Urban Appalachians* (Lexington: University Press of Kentucky, 1981), pp. 81–94. On housing segregation, see, for example, Arnold E. Hirsch, *Making the Second Ghetto: Race and Housing and Chicago, 1940–1960* (New York: Cambridge University Press, 1983); Dorothy Newman et al., *Protest, Politics, and Prosperity: Black Americans, White Institutions, 1940–1975* (New York: Pantheon, 1978).

33. Todd Gitlin and Nanci Hollander, *Uptown: Poor Whites in Chicago* (New

York: Harper and Row, 1970), pp. 239–54 (the quotation is on p. 253); Ronald Mincy, "Is There a White Underclass?" (Washington, D.C.: Urban Institute Discussion Paper, 1988); Erol R. Ricketts and Isabel V. Sawhill, "Defining and Measuring the Underclass," *Journal of Policy Analysis and Management* 7 (1988): 316–25. In her article "The Underclass: An Overview" (*Public Interest* 96 [Summer 1989]), Sawhill states, "Underclass neighborhoods are often thought of as 'inner-city areas,' or 'ghettos.' Our data indicate that they are, indeed, distinctly urban places; we find almost none in rural America" (p. 6).

34. But see, for example, United States Congress, Office of Technology Assessment, Health Care in Rural America, OTA-H-434 (Washington, D.C.: GPO, September 1990), and a summary of a study by the Center on Budget and Policy Priorities, Washington, D.C., showing that the rural poor lack health insurance, medical coverage, and access to physicians in greater proportion than do urban residents ("Study Finds Medical Care Wanting in Rural U.S.," *New York Times*, March 13, 1991).

Part II

Integrating Race, Class, and Gender into Family Theory

8

FAMILY AND CLASS IN CONTEMPORARY AMERICA: NOTES TOWARD AN UNDERSTANDING OF IDEOLOGY*

Rayna Rapp

This paper is grounded in two contexts, one political and one academic. The political context is that of the Women's Movement, in which a debate seems always to be raging concerning the future of the family. Many of us have been to an archetypical meeting in which someone stands up and asserts that the nuclear family ought to be abolished because it is degrading and constraining to women. Usually, someone else (often representing a Third World position) follows on her heels, pointing out that the attack on the family represents a White, middle-class position, and that other women need their families for support and survival. Evidently both speakers are, in some senses, right. And just as evidently they aren't talking about the same families.

The archetypical political debaters arguing over the meaning of the family aren't talking about the same families. Neither are the social scientists. We need to make a distinction between families and households, and to examine their relation to one another. The entities in which people actually live are not families, but households (as any census-taker, demographer, or fieldworking anthropologist will tell you). Households are the empirically measurable units within which people pool resources and perform certain tasks. Goody analyzes them as units of production, reproduction and consumption.[1] They are residential units within which personnel and resources get distributed and connected. Households may vary in their membership composition, and also in their relation to resource allocation, especially in a system such as our own. That is, they vary systematically in their ability to hook into, accumulate, and transmit wealth, wages, or welfare. This seems a simple unit to define.

Families, on the other hand, are a bit more slippery. In English we tend to gloss "family" to mean household. But analytically, the concept means something else. For all classes of Americans, the word has at least two levels of meaning.[2] One is normative: husbands, wives and children are a set of relatives who should live together (that is, the nuclear family). The other meaning includes a more extended network of kin relations which people may activate selectively. That is, the American family includes the narrower and broader webs of kin ties that are "the nuclear family" and all relations by blood and marriage. The concept of family is presumed in America to carry a heavy load of affect. We say, "blood is thicker than water," "till death do us part," "you can choose your friends, but not your relatives," etc. What I will argue in this paper is that the concept of family also carries a heavy load of ideology.

The reason for this is that the family is the normative, correct way in which people get recruited into households. It is through families that people enter into productive, reproductive, and consumption relations. The two genders enter them differently. Families organize households, and it is within families that people experience the absence or presence, the sharing or witholding, of basic poolable resources. "Family" (as a normative concept in our culture) reflects those material relations; it also distorts them. As such, the concept of family is a socially necessary illusion which simultaneously expresses and masks recruitment to relations of production, reproduction and consumption—relations that condition different kinds of household resource bases in different class sectors. Our notions of family absorb the conflicts, contradictions and tensions that are actually generated by those material, class-structured relations that households hold to resources in advanced capitalism. "Family," as we understand (and misunderstand) the term, is conditioned by the exigencies of household formation, and serves as a shock-absorber to keep households functioning. People are recruited and kept in households by families in all classes, yet the families they have (or don't have) are not the same.

Having asserted that households and families vary by class, we now need to consider that third concept, class. If ever a concept carried a heavy weight of ideology, it is the concept of class in American social science. We have a huge and muddled literature which attempts to reconcile objective and subjective criteria, to sort people into lowers, uppers and middles, to argue about the relation of consciousness to material reality.[3] I will say only the following: "social class" is a shorthand for a process, and not a thing. That process is the one by which different social relations to the means of production are inherited and reproduced under capitalism. As the concept is developed by Marx, the process of capital accumulation generates and constantly deepens relations between two categories of people: those who are both available and forced to work for wages because they own no means of production, and those who control those means of production. The concept of class expresses a historical process of expanding capital. In the process, categories of people get swept up at different times and places, and deposited into different relations to the means of production, and to one another. People then get labeled "blue-collar" or "white-collar"; they may experience their social existence as mediated by ethnicity or the overwhelming legacy of slavery and racism. Yet all of these categories must be viewed in the light of the historic process of capitalist accumulation in the United States. To a large extent, what are actually being accumulated are changing categories of proletarians. Class formation and composition is always in flux; what gets accumulated in it are relationships. Under advanced capitalism, there are shifting frontiers which separate poverty, stable wage-earning, affluent salaries, and inherited wealth. The frontiers may be crossed by individuals, and in either direction. That is, both upward and downward mobility are real processes. The point is, "class" isn't a static place which individuals inhabit. It is a process determined by the relationships set up in capital accumulation.

Returning to the initial distinction between family and household, I want to explore how these two vary among differing class sectors in contemporary America and to draw a composite picture of the households formed around material relations by class, and the families which organize those households. I will argue that those families mean different things by class, and by genders as well, because classes and genders stand in differing material relations to one another. I'll further argue that their meanings are highly ideological.

I'd like to begin with a review and interpretation of the studies done on the working-class family. There are studies which span the post-war decades from the late 1940s to the present. They are regionally diverse, and report on both cities and suburbs. The data provided by researchers such as Berger, Gans, Komarovsky, Howell, Rubin, and others reveal a composite portrait.[4] The most salient characteristic of household organization in the working class is dependency on hourly wages. Stable working-class households participate in relations of production, reproduction and consumption by sending out their labor-power in exchange for wages. "Sending out" is important: there is a radical split between household and workplace, yet the resources upon which the household depends come from participation in production outside of itself. How much labor-power a working-class household needs to send out is determined by many things: the cost of reproducing (or maintaining) the household, the work careers and earning trajectories of individual members, and the domestic cycle (that is, the relations between the genders and the generations, which specify when and if wives and adolescent children are available to work outside the home). Braverman[5] estimates that the average working-class household now sends out 1.7 full-time equivalent workers. That figure tells us that a high percentage of married women and teenaged children are contributing their wages to the household. In many ways, the work patterns for 19th century European capitalism described by Tilly and Scott[6] still leave their mark on the contemporary American working class household: it is not only male heads of household upon whom survival depends.

What the working class sends out in exchange for basic resources is labor-power. Labor-power is the only commodity without which there can be no capitalism. It is also the only commodity for which the working class controls its own means of production.[7] Control over the production of labor-power undoubtedly affected women's experiences historically, as it still does today.[8] In the early stages of industrialization, it appears that working-class households literally produced a lot of babies (future labor-power) as their strategy for dealing with a market economy.[9] Now workers produce fewer children, but the work of servicing them (social reproduction) is still a major process that goes on in the household. Households are the basic units in which labor-power is reproduced and maintained. This takes place in a location radically removed from the workplace. Such relations therefore appear as autonomous from capital, but of course they are not: without wages, households are hard to form and keep functioning; without the production of a disciplined labor force, factories cannot produce and profit.

The work that gets done in households (primarily by women) is not simply about babies. Housework itself has recently been rediscovered as work, and its contribution to arenas beyond the household is clear.[10] At the very least, housework cuts the reproduction costs of wage-workers. Imagine if all those meals had to be bought at restaurants, those clothes cleaned at laundry rates, those beds made by hotel employees! Housework is also what women do in exchange for access to resources which are bought by their husbands' wages. As such, it is a coin of exchange between men and women. As housework is wageless, it keeps its workers dependent on others for access to commodities bought with wages. It makes them extremely vulnerable to the work conditions of their men. When women do work (as increasingly they do), their primary definition as houseworkers contributes to the problems they encounter in entering the paid labor force. They are available for part-time (or full-time) work in the lowest paid sectors of the labor market, in jobs which leave them less economically secure than men. Participation in the "sexregated" labor market then reinforces dependency upon the earnings of other household members, and the continued importance of women's domestic labor.[11]

Of course, these rather abstract notions of "household participation" in the labor market or in housework are experienced concretely by family members. Working-class families are normatively nuclear. They are formed via marriage, which links men and women "for love" and not "for money."[12] This relation is of course both real, and a socially necessary illusion. As such, it is central to the ideology of the family. The cultural distinction between love and money corresponds to the distinction between private family life in the home, and work life outside the home. The two are experienced as opposite; in fact they are interpenetrating. The seeming autonomy to exchange love at home expresses something ideological about the relation between home and work: one must work for the sake of the family, and having a family is the "pay-off" for leading a good life. Founding a family is what people do for personal gratification, for love and for autonomy. The working-class family literature is full of life-histories in which young women saw "love" as the way to get out of their own, often difficult families. Rubin's interviews, for example, are full of teenaged girls who said, "When I grow up, I'll marry for love, and it will be better than my parents' marriage." You may marry for love, but what you mainly get is babies; 40–60 percent of teenaged pregnancies are conceived premaritally, and approximately 50 percent of working-class women marry in their teen years.[13] It's a common experience to go from being someone's child to having someone's child in under a year. This is not exactly a situation which leads to autonomy.

For men, the situation is complementary. As one of the young working class men in Rubin's study puts it:

> I had to work from the time I was thirteen and turn over most of my pay to my mother to help pay the bills. By the time I was nineteen, I had been working for all those years and I didn't have anything— not a thing. I used to think a lot about how when I got married, I would finally get to keep my money for myself. I guess that sounds a little crazy when I think about it now because I have to support the wife and kids. I don't know *what* I was thinking about, but I never thought about that then.[14]

What you get from the romance of love and marriage is in fact not simply a family, but a household, and that's quite another matter. Romance is implicated in gender identity and ideology. We are all aware of the cultural distinction made between the sexual identity of a good and a bad girl; a good girl is one who accumulates her sexual resources for later investment. Autonomy means escaping your childhood family to become an adult with your own nuclear family. For young men, the identity process includes the cultural role of wild boy—one who "sows some wild oats," hangs out on street corners, perhaps gets in trouble with the police, and drinks.[15] Ideally, the good girl domesticates the wild boy; she gives him love, and he settles down and goes out to work. Autonomy means becoming an adult with your own nuclear family as an escape. But of course, autonomy is illusive. The family is classically seen as an escape from production, but in fact it is what sends people into relations of production, for they need to work to support their families. The meaning of production is simultaneously denied and experienced through family relations; working-class wives say of a good husband that he works steadily, provides for the kids, and never harms anyone in the family. The complementary statement is uttered by working-class husbands, who define a good wife as one who keeps the kids under control when he comes home from a hard day's work, and who runs the household well.[16] To exchange love is also to underwrite both the necessity and the ability to keep on working. *This* is the heritage that working class families pass on, in lieu of property, to their children.

The family expresses ideology in another sense as well—the distinction between norms and realities. The norms concerning families are that people should be loving and sharing within them, and that they should be protective. The reality is too often otherwise, as the recent rising consciousness of domestic violence indicates. Even without domestic violence, there are more commonplace stresses to which families are often subjected. Rubin found in her study that 40 percent of the adults she interviewed had an alcoholic parent.[17] Fifty percent had experienced parental desertion or divorce in their childhood. National statistics con-

firm these figures.[18] About half the adults in her study had seriously destabilizing experiences within their families. The tension generated by relations to resource base can often tear households apart. Under these conditions, to label the working class personality "authoritarian" seems a
cruel hoax. When the household is working, it expresses work discipline.

Ideology is expressed in gender role in families in another sense as
well. Throughout the urban kinship literature, across classes and ethnic
groups, the work of reproducing families is in part undertaken by larger kinship groups (the family in the broader sense of relatives). Family
networks in this larger sense are women-centered and tend to be ser-
viced by women. There exists a large literature on women-centered kinship networks in which it is usually assumed that women minister to
kinship because they minister to families in general. Sylvia Yanagisako
suggests that there is also a symbolic level to the kinship work which
women do: ideologically, women are assigned to "inside, home, private" domains, while men are seen to represent the outside world.[19]
Nuclear families are under cultural constraints to appear as autonomous
and private. Yet they are never as private in reality as such values might
indicate. The ideal autonomy of an independent nuclear family is constantly being contradicted by the realities of social need, in which
resources must be pooled, borrowed, shared. It is women who bridge
the gap between what a household's resources really are, and what a
family's position is supposed to be. Women exchange babysitting, share
meals, lend small amounts of money. When a married child is out of
work, his (or her) nuclear family turns to the mother, and often moves
in for a while. The working-class family literature is filled with examples of such pooling.[20] To the extent that women "represent" the family,
they facilitate the pooling which is needed at various points in the
domestic cycle. Men maintain, at least symbolically, the autonomy of
their families. Pooling is a norm in family behavior, but it's a hard norm
to live with, to either meet or ignore. To comply with the demands of
the extended family completely is to lose control over material and
emotional resources; to refuse is very dangerous, as people know they
will need one another. The tightrope act which ensues is well characterized in the classic mother-in-law story, which usually concerns a
young wife and her husband's mother. The two women must figure out
a way to share the small services, the material benefits, and the emotional satisfactions which one man brings to them both in their separate
roles of mother and wife. The autonomy of the younger woman is often
compromised by the elder's needs; the authority of the mother is sometimes undermined by the demands of the wife. Women must constantly test, strain, and repair the fibers of their kinship networks.

Such women-centered networks are implicated in a process which
has not yet been discussed. We have spoken of production and reproduction as they affect the working-class household and family. We
ought briefly to mention consumption as well. As a household function,
consumption includes turning an amount of wages into commodities so

that labor-power may be reproduced. This is often women's work. And work it really is. Weinbaum and Bridges tell us that the centralization and rationalization of services and industry under advanced capitalism may be most efficient from the point of view of capital, but it leaves a lot of unrewarding, technical work to be done by women in supermarkets, in paying bills, in dealing with huge bureaucracies.[21] Women experience the pay packet in terms of the use values it will buy. Yet their consumption work is done in the world of exchange value. They mediate the tension between use and exchange, as exemplified in the classic tales concerning domestic quarrels over money in which the man blames the woman for not making his pay check stretch far enough. In stable working-class neighborhoods, the consumption work is in part done by women united by family ties who exchange services, recipes, sales information, and general lifestyle skills. Kinship networks are part of "community control" for women. As Seifer notes, working class women become involved in political issues that threaten the stability of their neighborhoods.[22] Perhaps one reason is that their neighborhoods are the locus of extended families within which both work needs and emotional needs are so often met.

When everyone submits to the conditions described here "for the sake of the family," we see the pattern that Howell labels "settled living."[23] Its opposite, in his words, is "hard living," a family lifestyle which includes a lot of domestic instability, alcohol, and rootlessness. I want to stress that I am here departing from a "culture of poverty" approach. The value of a label like "hard living" is that it stresses a continuum made up of many attributes. It is composed of many processes with which the working class has a lot of experience. Given the national statistics on alcoholism, desertion, divorce, premarital pregnancy, etc., everyone's family has included such experiences, either in its own domestic cycle, or in the wider family network.[24] Everyone had a wild brother, or was a bad girl, or had an uncle who drank too much, or cousins who got divorced. In each of such cases, everyone experienced the pooling of resources (or the lack of pooling) as families attempted to cope with difficult, destabilizing situations. In a sense, the hard livers keep the settled livers more settled: the consequences of leaving the normative path are well-known and are not appealing. This, too, is part of the working class heritage. In studies by Seifer, Howell and Rubin, young women express their hopes of leaving a difficult family situation by finding the right man to marry. They therefore marry young, with little formal education, possibly about to become parents, and the cycle begins again.

Of course, hard living is most consistently associated with poverty in the urban family literature. For essentially political reasons, Black poverty has more frequently been the subject of social science analysis than has white poverty, but the pattern is found across races. Black Americans have survived under extremely difficult conditions; many of their household and family patterns have evolved to deal with their specific history, while others are shared with Americans of similar class and regional backgrounds. The problems of household formation under poverty conditions are not unique to any group of people; some of the specific, resilient solutions to those problems may be. Because we know far more about Black families in poverty than we do about whites, I'll draw a composite picture of households and families using studies that are primarily Black.[25] Even when talking about very poor people, analysts such as Liebow, Hannerz, Valentine, and Stack note that there are multiple household types, based on domestic cycles and the relative ability to draw on resources. Hannerz, for example, divides his Black sample into four categories.[26] Mainstreamers live in stable households composed of husband, wife and children. The adults are employed, and either own their own homes or aspire to do so. Their households don't look very different from the rest of the working class. Swingers (Hannerz' second type) are younger, single persons who may be on their way into mainstream life, or they may be tending toward street-families (type three), whose households are headed by women. It is this type which is most important for our study. The fourth category is composed of street men who are peer-oriented, and predominantly hard-core unemployed or underemployed. They are similar to the men of *Tally's Corner*.[27] While Hannerz and Liebow both give us a wealth of information about what men are doing, they don't analyze these men's domestic arrangements in detail. It is Carol Stack,[28] who did her field work from the perspective of female-centered households, who most clearly analyzes household formation of the very poor. She presents us with domestic networks: extremely flexible and fluctuating groups of people committed to resource pooling, to sharing, to mutual aid, who move in and out from under one another's roofs.

Given the state of the job market, welfare legislation, and segregated slum housing, households are unstable. These are people essentially living below socially necessary reproduction costs. They therefore reproduce themselves by spreading out the aid and the risks involved in daily life. For the disproportionally high numbers who are prevented from obtaining steady employment, being part of what Marx called the floating surplus population is a perilous endeavor. What this means in human terms is not only that the poor pay more (as Caplowitz tells us),[29] but that the poor share more as well. Stack's monograph contains richly textured descriptions of the way that food, furniture, clothing, appliances, kids, and money make the rounds between individuals and households. She subtitles one chapter, "What Goes Round Comes Round," and describes the velocity with which pooling takes place. People try to give what they can and take what they need. Meeting consumption requirements is hard work under these conditions, and domestic networks get the task done. The pleasures and pressures of such survival networks are predominantly organized around the notion of family.

Meyer Fortes tells us that "domestic groups are the workshops of social reproduction."[30] Whatever else they do, the families that organize domestic networks are responsible for children. As Ladner and Stack[31] remind us, poverty, low levels of formal education, and early age for first pregnancy are highly correlated: a lot of young girls have children while they are not fully adults. Under these circumstances, at least among Black families, there is a tremendous sharing of the children themselves. On the whole, these are not kids who grow up in "isolated nuclear families." Stack, for example, found that 20 percent of the A.D.C. (Aid to Dependent Children) children in her study were being raised in a household other than that which contained the biological mother. In the vast majority of cases, the household was related through the biological mother's family. Organizing kinship networks so that children are cared for is a primary function of families. Men, too, often contribute to child-rearing. Like women, they share out bits and pieces of whatever they have. While some men make no contribution, others may be simultaneously contributing to sisters, to a mother and aunt, as well as to wives or lovers. They may sleep in one household, but bring groceries, money, and affection to several others.[32] Both Stack and Ladner analyze the importance of a father's recognition of his children, by which act he links the baby to his own kinship network. It is family in the broader sense of the term that organizes social reproduction.

Family may be a conscious construction of its participants. Liebow, Stack, Ladner and others describe fictive kinship, by which friends are turned into family. Since family is supposed to be more reliable than friendship, "going for brothers," "for sisters," "for cousins," increases the commitment of a relationship, and makes people ideally more responsible for one another. Fictive kinship is a serious relationship. Stack (who is white) describes her own experience with Ruby, a Black woman with whom she "went for sisters." When Ruby's child was seriously ill, Stack became deeply involved in the crisis. When the baby was admitted to the hospital, she and Ruby rushed over for visiting hours. They were stopped by a nurse, who insisted that only the immediate family could enter. Ruby responded, "Caroline here is my sister, and nothing's stopping her from visiting this baby." And they entered, unchallenged. Ruby was correct; under the circumstances, white Caroline was her sister.[33]

Liebow notes that fictive kinship increases the intensity of relationships to the point where they occasionally explode: the demands of brothers and sisters for constant emotional and material aid may lead to situations that shatter the bonds. Fictive kinship is a prime example of family-as-ideology. In this process, reality is inverted. "Everybody" gets a continuous family, even though the strains and mobility associated with poverty may conspire to keep biological families apart. The idiom of kinship brings people together despite centrifugal circumstances.

It is important not to romanticize this pattern. It has enormous benefits, but its participants also pay high costs. One of the most obvious costs is leveling: resources must be available for all, and none may get ahead. Variations in the chance for survival are smoothed out in domestic networks via sharing. Stack tells the story of a couple, Calvin and Magnolia, who unexpectedly inherit a sum of money. While the money might have enabled them to insure their own security, it is gone within a few months. It disappears into the network, of which Calvin and Magnolia are the central couple, to pay off bills, buy clothing for children, allow people to eat better.[34] Similar stories are told by Hannerz, Liebow, and Howell. No one gets ahead because individual upward mobility can be bought only at the price of cutting off the very people who have contributed to one's survival. Upward mobility becomes a terribly scarring experience under these circumstances. To get out, a person must stop sharing, which is unfamilial, unfriendly, and quite dangerous. It also requires exceptional circumstances. Gans[35] speaks of the pain which working class children face if they attempt to use school as a means to achieve mobility, for they run into the danger of being cut off from their peer-group. The chance for mobility may occur only once or twice in a lifetime—for example, at specific moments in a school career, or in marriage. People rarely get the occasion, and when they do, to grasp it may simply be too costly. The pressures to stay in a supportive and constraining network, and to level out differences may be immense. These pressures contribute to the instability of marriage and the normative nuclear family, for the old networks compete with the new unit for precious resources.

The family as an ideological construction is extremely important to poor people. Many studies show that the poor don't aspire to less "stable families," if that term is understood as nuclear families. They are simply much more realistic about their life-chances. Ties to family, including fictive family, are the lifelines that simultaneously hold together and sustain individuals. My guess is that among the poor, families do not exhibit the radical split between "private, at home" and "public, at work" which is found in families of the stable working class. Neither work relations nor household relations are as continuous, or as distinct. What is continuous is the sharing of reproduction costs throughout a network whose resources are known to all. There can be no privatization when survival may depend on rapid circulation of limited resources. In this process, women don't "represent" kinship to the outside world. They become the nodal points in family nets which span whatever control very poor people have over domestic and resource-getting arrangements. Families are what make the huge gap between norm and reality survivable.

It is particularly ironic that the ideology of family, so important to poor people, is used by ruling class ideologues to blame the poor for their own condition. In a society in which *all* Americans subscribe to some version of the normative nuclear family, it is cruelty to attack "the Black family" as pathological. Mainstream culture, seeing the family as "what you work for" (and what works for you), uses "family language" to stigmatize those who are structurally prevented from accumulating stable resources. The very poor have used their families to cement and patch tenuous relations to survival; out of their belief in "family" they have invented networks capable of making next-to-nothing go a long way.[36] In response, they are told that their notion of family is inadequate. It isn't their notion of family that is deficient, but the relationship between household and productive resources.

If we now return to the political debate which opened this paper, I believe we can see that there are two different concepts of family at work. To achieve a normative family is something many categories of Americans are prevented from doing because of the ways that their households plug into tenuous resource bases. And when normative families are achieved, it is at substantial and differential costs to both men and women.

Having considered the meaning of family and household among class sectors with regular or unstable relations to wages, we should now consider those sectors with more affluent resource bases. Analyzing the family and household life of the middle class is a tricky business. The term "middle class" is ambiguous; a majority of Americans identify themselves as part of it whenever they answer questionnaires, and the category obviously carries positive connotations. Historically, we take the notion from the Marxian definition of the petty bourgeoisie: that category of people who own small amounts of productive resources, and have control over their working conditions in ways that proletarians do not. The term signifies a stage in proletarianization in which small-scale entrepreneurs, tradesfolk, artisans, and professionals essentially stand outside the wage-labor/capital relation. That stage is virtually over: there are ever fewer small-scale proprietors or artisans working on their own account in post–World War II America. We now use the term to refer to a different sector—employees in corporate management, government and organizational bureaucrats of various kinds, and professionals, many of whom work directly or indirectly for big business, the state and semi-public institutions. On the whole, this "new middle class" is dependent on wages; as such, it bears the mark of proletarianization. Yet the group lives at a level that is quite different from the wage levels of workers.[37] Such a category is obviously hard to define; like all class sectors, it must be historically situated, for the middle class of early 20th century America differs markedly from that of our own times. To understand what middle class means for the different groups, we need to know not only their present status, but also the ethnic and regional variations in class structure within which their families entered America.

In a sense, the middle class is a highly ideological construction which pervades American culture; it is, among other things, the perspective from which mainstream social scientists approach the experiences of all the other sectors they attempt to analyze. To analyze the middle class's household formations and family patterns, we have to examine not only the data available on all the people who claim to be middle class, but also explore the biases inherent in much of social science. This is a task beyond the scope of the present paper. Instead, I merely suggest a few tentative ideas as notes toward future research.

Households among the middle class are obviously based on a stable resource base which allows for some amount of luxury and discretionary spending. When exceptional economic resources are called for, nonfamilial institutions usually are available in the form of better medical coverage, expense accounts, pension plans, credit at banks, etc. Such households may maintain their economic stability at the cost of geographical instability; male career choices may move households around like pieces on a chessboard. When far from family support networks, such households may get transitional aid from professional moving specialists, or institutions like the Welcome Wagon.[38] Middle-class households probably are able to rely on commodity-forms rather than on kinship processes to ease both economic and geographic transitions.

The families which organize such households are commonly thought to be characterized by egalitarian marriages.[39] Rubin comments that "egalitarian marriage" may be a biased gloss for a communication pattern in which the husband's career is in part reflected in the presentation of his wife.[40] To entertain intelligently, and instill the proper educational and social values in the children, women may need to know more about the male world. They represent the private credentials of family to the public world of their men at work. If this is the case, then "instrumental communication" might be a more appropriate term.

I am not prepared at this point to offer an analysis of middle-class kinship patterns, but I have a few hunches to present:

1) At this level, kinship probably shifts from the lateral toward the lineal. That is, resources (material and economic) are invested lineally, between parents, children, and grandchildren, and not dispersed into larger networks, as happens with working-class and poor families. Such a pattern would of course vary with geographical mobility, and possibly with ethnicity. There is usually a greater investment across generations, and a careful accumulation within them. This kind of pattern can be seen, for example, in the sums invested in children's educations, setting up professional practices, wedding gifts (in which major devolvement of property may occur), etc.

2) Perhaps friendship, rather than kinship, is the nexus within which the middle class invests its psychic and "familial" energies. Friendship allows for a great deal of affective support and exchange, but usually does not include major resource pooling. It is a relation which is consistent with resource accumulation, rather than dispersal. If the poor convert friendship into kinship to equalize pooling, it seems to me that the middle class does the converse: it reduces kinship exchanges, and replaces them with friendship, which protects them from pooling and leveling.[41]

There is one last sector of the American class system whose household and family patterns would be interesting to examine—the upper class, sometimes identified as the ruling class, or the very rich. Once again, I limit myself to a few tentative observations. As one sociologist (either quite naive or quite sardonic) commented, "We know so little about the very wealthy because they don't answer our questionnaires." Indeed! They fund them, rather than answer them. The few studies we do have (by authors such as Domhoff, Amory, Baltzell, Veblen) are highly suggestive. The upper class, they tell us, appears to hang together as a cultural phenomenon. They defend their own interests corporately, and have tremendous ideological importance.

We know very little about the household structure of the very rich. They are described as having multiple households which are recomposed seasonally[42] and filled with service workers, rather than exclusively with kin and friends. While there is a general tendency toward "conspicuous consumption," we have no basic information on the relation of their resource bases to domestic arrangements.

When we turn to the family structure of the very rich, some interesting bits and pieces emerge (which may possibly be out of date). Families are described as extremely lineal, and concerned with who they are, rather than what they do. People have access to one another through their control of neighborhoods, schools, universities, clubs, churches, and ritual events. They are quite ancestor-oriented, and conscious of the boundaries which separate the "best" families from all others. Families are obviously the units within which wealth is accumulated and transmitted. Yet the link between wealth and class is not so simple; some of the "best" families lose fortunes but remain in the upper class. Mobility is also possible. According to Baltzell,[43] under certain circumstances it is possible for nonmembers to enter the class via educational and work-related contacts. What emerges from the literature is a sketch of a group which is perhaps the only face-to-face subculture that America contains.

Women serve as gatekeepers of many of the institutions of the very rich.[44] They launch children, serve as board members at the private schools, run the clubs, and facilitate the marriage pools through events like debuts and charity balls. Men also preside over exclusive clubs and schools, but different ones. The upper class appears to live in a world which is very sex-segregated. Domhoff mentions several other functions that very rich women fulfill. These include: (1) setting social and cultural standards, and (2) softening the rough edges of capitalism by doing charity and cultural work. While he trivializes the cultural standards that women establish for things like dress and high art, I think he has alerted us to something more important. In the upper class, women "represent" the family to the outside world. But here, it is an outside world that is in many senses created by their own class (in the form of high cultural institutions, education, social welfare, and charity). Their public presence is an inversion of reality: they appear as wives and mothers, but it is not really their family roles but their class roles which dictate those appearances. To the extent that "everyone else" either has a wife/mother or is a wife/mother, upper-class women are available to be perceived as something both true and false. What they can do because of their families (and ultimately, for their families) is utterly, radically different from what other women who "represent" their families can do. Yet what everyone sees is their womanness as family members, rather than as class members. They influence our cultural notions of what feminine and familial behavior should be. They simultaneously become symbols of domesticity and of public service to which others may aspire. The very tiny percentage of very wealthy women who live in a sex-segregated world and have no need to work are thus perceived as benevolent and admirable by a much larger group of women whose relation to sex-role segregation and work is not nearly so benign. "Everybody" can yearn for a family in which sex-role segregation is valued; nobody else can have a family in which it is valued quite as highly as theirs. In upper-class families, at least as they present themselves to "the public," we see a systematic confusion of cultural values with the values of family fortunes. We have here an excellent illustration of how the ideas of the ruling class become part of the ruling ideas of society.

• • •

At each level of American society, households vary systematically as to resource base, and their ability to tap wealth, wages, and welfare. Households are organized by families (which means relatives both distant and close, imaginary and real). Families both reflect and distort the material relations within which households are embedded. The working-class and middle-class household may *appear* isolated from the arenas in which production takes place. But in fact, their families are formed to generate and deepen relations to those work processes that underwrite their illusion of autonomy. Women's experience with "the family" varies systematically by class because class expresses the material and social relations upon which their household bases rest. We need to explore their transformative potential as well as the constraints that differential family patterns provide.

Women have structurally been put in the position of representing the contradictions between autonomy and dependence, between love and money, in the relations of families to capitalism. The ideological role that women have played needs to be demystified as we struggle toward a future in which consumption and reproduction will not be determined by capitalist production, in which households will have access to more even resource bases, and in which women will neither symbolically nor in their real relations be forced to bridge the gap between affective norms and contradictory realities under the name of love. To liberate the notion of voluntary relations which the normative family is supposed to represent, we have to stop paying workers off in a coin called love.**

New School for Social Research

NOTES

*Social analysis is always a collective endeavor, even when individually presented. This paper builds quite directly on the published work of many people cited in the text, and the unpublished work and discussion of many others. The University of Michigan's Women Studies Program called this paper into being, gave it a first airing, and contributed a stimulating set of discussions. Subsequent presentation of these ideas at the New School for Social Research, the URPE. Spring conference on Public Policy, and the Anthropology Department of the University of Northern Colorado provided invaluable feedback. I especially want to thank Jill Cherneff, Ingelore Fritsch, Susan Harding, Mike Hooper, Janet Siskind, Deborah Jay Stearns, Batya Weinbaum and Marilyn Young for their comments. The women of Marxist-Feminist Group II posed the questions which led me to write this paper; they supplied, as always, the supportive context within which the meaning of my work has been discussed. Above all, Gayle Rubin deserves my thanks for her general intellectual aid, and the specific editorial work she did in turning my primary process into a set of written ideas.

**This paper was first presented to the University of Michigan's Women's Studies Research on Women Seminar sponsored by Grant #E.H. 2-5643-76-772 from the National Endowment for the Humanities. It is reprinted with grateful acknowledgement from the Special Issue of the University of Michigan Papers in Women's Studies, June 1978.

1. Jack Goody, "The Evolution of the Family," in *Household and Family in Past Time*, Peter Laslett and Richard Wall, eds. (Cambridge, 1972).

2. Ibid. Also see David M. Schneider and Raymond T. Smith, *Class Differences and Sex Roles in American Kinship and Family Structure* (Englewood Cliffs, 1973).

3. There is a vast literature on this subject. Its mainstream interpretations in relation to family research are reviewed in Luther B. Otto, "Class and Status in Family Research," *Journal of Marriage and the Family*, 1975, 37: 315–332. Marxist perspectives are presented in Charles H. Anderson, *The Political Economy of Social Class* (Englewood Cliffs, 1974); Anderson, *Toward a New Sociology*, revised edition (Homewood, Ill., 1974); Alfred Szymanski, "Trends in the American Class Structure," *Socialist Revolution*, July–August 1972, No. 10; and Harry Braverman, *Labor and Monopoly Capital: The Degradation of Work in the Twentieth Century* (New York, 1974).

4. This composite is drawn from the works of Bennett Berger, *Working Class Suburb: A Study of Auto Workers in Suburbia* (Berkeley, 1968); Herbert J. Gans, *The Urban Villagers* (New York, 1962); Gans, *The Levittowners* (New York, 1967); Louise Kapp Howe, ed., *The White Majority: Between Poverty and Affluence* (New York, 1970); Joseph Howell, *Hard Living on Clay Street* (New York, 1973); Mirra Komarovsky, *Blue Collar Marriage* (New York, 1962); Lillian Rubin, *Worlds of Pain* (New York, 1976); Joseph A. Ryan, ed., *White Ethnics: Life in Working Class America* (Englewood Cliffs, 1973); Nancy Seifer, "Absent From the Majority: Working Class Women in America," Middle America Pamphlet Series, National Project on Ethnic America; *American Jewish Committee*, 1973; Seifer, *Nobody Speaks for Me: Self-Portraits of American Working Class Women* (New York, 1976); Arthur B. Shostak, *Blue Collar Life* (New York, 1969); Richard Sennett and Jonathan Cobb, *The Hidden Injuries of Class* (New York, 1972); Patricia Cayo Sexton

and Brendan Sexton, *Blue Collars and Hard Hats* (New York, 1971); and Studs Terkel, *Working* (New York, 1972).

5. Braverman, *Labor and Monopoly Capital.*
6. Louise Tilly and Joan Scott, "Women's Work in Nineteenth Century Europe." *Comparative Studies in Society and History*, 1975, 17: 36–64.
7. See Ira Gerstein, "Domestic Work and Capitalism," *Radical America*, 1973, 7: 101–130.
8. Linda Gordon, *Women's Body, Women's Right: A Social History of Birth Control in America* (New York, 1976).
9. Louise Tilly, "Reproduction, Production and the Family among Textile Workers in Roubaix, France," paper presented at the Conference on Social History, February 1977.
10. The economic value of housework has been the subject of vigorous debate in Marxist literature in recent years. The debate was begun with the publication of Mariarosa Dalla Costa, "Women and the Subversion of the Community," *Radical America*, 1972, 6: 67–102; and continued by Wally Secombe, "The Housewife and Her Labour Under Capitalism," *New Left Review*, 1974, 83: 3–24; Jean Gardiner, "Women's Domestic Labour," *New Left Review*, 1975, 89: 47–71; Lise Vogel, "The Earthly Family," *Radical America*, 1973, 7: 9–50; Gerstein, "Domestic Work and Capitalism"; and others. See also Heidi I. Hartmann, "Capitalism and Women's Work in the Home, 1900–1930." Ph.D. dissertation, Yale University, 1974; and Joann Vanek, "Time Spent in Housework," *Scientific American*, November 1974: 116–20, for American case historical materials, and Nona Glazer-Malbin, "Review Essay: Housework," *Signs*, 1: 905–922, for a review of the field.
11. For historical, sociological and political-economic analyses of women's economic position in the labor market, see the special issue of *Signs*, Barbara B. Reagan and Martha Blaxall, eds., "Women and the Workplace," 1976, 1: 3, part 2. See also U.S. Bureau of the Census, *Statistical Abstract of the U.S.*, 1974, for statistical data on demography and workforce participation rates of women.
12. Schneider and Smith, *Class Differences and Sex Roles in American Kinship and Family Structure*, Ch. 5.
13. Rubin, *Worlds of Pain*, Ch. 4.
14. Ibid., 56f.
15. See ibid.; also Shostak, *Blue Collar Life* and Howell, *Hard Living on Clay Street.*
16. See Rubin, *Worlds of Pain;* Shostak, *Blue Collar Life*; Sennett and Cobb, *The Hidden Injuries of Class*; and Terkel, *Working.*
17. Rubin, *Worlds of Pain.*
18. U.S. Bureau of Census, *Statistical Abstract of the U.S.*, 1974, 221f.
19. Sylvia Junko Yanagisako, "Women-Centered Kin Networks in Urban, Bilateral Kinship," *American Ethnologist*, 1977.
20. This literature is reviewed in Yanagisako, op. cit. Further instances are found in the sources listed in note 4. The pattern is given much attention in Peter Wilmott and Michael Young, *Family and Kinship in East London* (London, 1957), and in Elizabeth Bott, *Family and Social Network* (New York, 1971).
21. Batya Weinbaum and Amy Bridges, "The Other Side of the Paycheck: Monopoly Capital and the Structure of Consumption," *Monthly Review*, 1976, 28: 88–103.
22. Seifer, "Absent From the Majority: Working Class Women in America," and

Seifer, *Nobody Speaks For Me: Self-Portraits of American Working Class Women.*

23. Howell, *Hard Living on Clay Street.*
24. Throughout her work, Rubin (*Worlds of Pain*) is especially sensitive to this issue, and provides an excellent discussion of individual lifecycles in relation to domestic cycles. She explains why the labeling issue is such a critical one (p. 223, note 5).
25. Howell's study (*Hard Living on Clay Street*) provides important and sensitive insights into the domestic lives of poor and working white families, collected in the style of Oscar Lewis. Composite Black family studies include Ulf Hannerz, *Soulside: Inquiries into Ghetto Culture and Community* (New York, 1969); Joyce Ladner, *Tomorrow's Tomorrow: The Black Woman* (New York, 1971); Elliot Liebow, *Tally's Corner* (Boston, 1967); Lee Rainwater, *Behind Ghetto Walls: Black Families in a Federal Slum* (Chicago, 1970); John Scanzoni, *The Black Family in Modern Society* (Rockleigh, N.J., 1971); Carol B. Stack, *All Our Kin: Strategies for Survival in a Black Community* (New York, 1974); Charles Valentine, *Culture and Poverty: Critique and Counter-Proposals* (Chicago, 1968); and Valentine, "Black Studies and Anthropology: Scholarly and Political Interests in Afro-American Culture," *McCaleb Module in Anthropology*, No. 15.
26. Hannerz, *Soulside: Inquiries into Ghetto Culture and Community.*
27. Liebow, *Tally's Corner.*
28. Stack, *All Our Kin: Strategies for Survival in a Black Community.*
29. David Caplowitz, *The Poor Pay More* (New York, 1967).
30. Meyer Fortes, "Introduction," in *The Development Cycle in Domestic Groups*, Jack Goody, ed. (Cambridge, 1972).
31. Ladner, *Tomorrow's Tomorrow: The Black Woman*, and Stack, *All Our Kin: Strategies for Survival in a Black Community.*
32. Stack, *All Our Kin: Strategies for Survival in a Black Community*, Ch. 7.
33. Ibid., 21.
34. Ibid., 105–107.
35. Gans, *The Urban Villagers.*
36. It is easier to make this point given the consciousness-raising works of Alex Haley, *Roots* (New York, 1976), and Herbert Gutman, *The Black Family in Slavery and Freedom, 1750–1925* (New York, 1976), which point out—in popular and scholarly language respectively—the historical depth and importance of this pattern.
37. Braverman, *Labor and Monopoly Capital*, Ch. 18.
38. Vance Packard, "Mobility: Restless America," *Mainliner Magazine*, May 1977.
39. Schneider and Smith, *Class Differences and Sex Roles in American Kinship and Family Structure*, Ch. 4.
40. Rubin, *Worlds of Pain.*
41. I know of no substantial work describing the uses of friendship versus kinship in the middle class. Ingelore Fritsch is currently conducting research on the networks of families in a suburban middle-class East coast community; her results should add to this discussion.
42. William Hoffman, *David: Report on a Rockefeller* (Secanous, N. J., 1971); E. Digby Baltzell, *Philadelphia Gentlemen: The Making of a National Upper Class* (New York, 1958).
43. Baltzell, *Philadelphia Gentlemen: The Making of a National Upper Class.*
44. G. William Domhoff, *The Higher Circles* (New York, 1971).

9

SHIFTING THE CENTER: RACE, CLASS, AND FEMINIST THEORIZING ABOUT MOTHERHOOD

Patricia Hill Collins

I dread to see my children grow, I know not their fate. Where the white boy has every opportunity and protection, mine will have few opportunities and no protection. It does not matter how good or wise my children may be, they are colored.

an anonymous African-American mother in 1904,
reported in Lerner 1972, p. 158.

For Native American, African-American, Hispanic, and Asian-American women, motherhood cannot be analyzed in isolation from its context. Motherhood occurs in specific historical situations framed by interlocking structures of race, class, and gender, where the sons and daughters of white mothers have "every opportunity and protection," and the "colored" daughters and sons of racial ethnic mothers "know not their fate." Racial domination and economic exploitation profoundly shape the mothering context, not only for racial ethnic women in the United States, but for all women.[1]

Despite the significance of race and class, feminist theorizing routinely minimizes their importance. In this sense, feminist theorizing about motherhood has not been immune to the decontextualization of Western social thought overall.[2] While many dimensions of motherhood's context are ignored, the exclusion of race and/or class from feminist theorizing generally (Spelman 1988), and from feminist theorizing about motherhood specifically, merit special attention.[3]

Much feminist theorizing about motherhood assumes that male domination in the political economy and the household is the driving force in family life, and that understanding the struggle for individual autonomy in the face of such domination is central to understanding motherhood (Eisenstein 1983).[4] Several guiding principles frame such analyses. First, such theories posit a dichotomous split between the public sphere of economic and political discourse and the private sphere of family and household responsibilities. This juxtaposition of a public, political economy to a private, noneconomic and apolitical, domestic household allows work and family to be seen as separate institutions. Second, reserving the public sphere for men as a "male" domain leaves the private domestic sphere as a "female" domain. Gender roles become tied to the dichotomous constructions of these two basic societal institutions—men work and women take care of families. Third, the public/private dichotomy separating the family/household from the paid labor market shapes sex-segregated gender roles within the private sphere of the family. The archetypal white, middle-class nuclear family divides family life into two oppositional spheres—the "male" sphere of economic providing and the "female" sphere of affective nurturing, mainly mothering. This normative family household has, as its ideal head, a working father who earns enough to allow his spouse and dependent children to withdraw from the paid labor force. Due in large part to their superior earning power, men as workers and fathers exert power over women in the labor market and in families. Finally, the struggle for individual autonomy in the face of a controlling, oppressive, "public" society, or the father as patriarch, comprises the main human enterprise.[5] Successful adult males achieve this autonomy. Women, children, and less successful males, namely those who are working-class or from racial ethnic groups, are seen as dependent persons, as less autonomous, and therefore as fitting objects for elite male domination. Within the nuclear family, this struggle for autonomy takes the form of increasing opposition to the mother, the individual responsible for socializing children by these guiding principles (Chodorow 1978; Flax 1978).

Placing the experiences of women of color in the center of feminist theorizing about motherhood demonstrates how emphasizing the issue of father as patriarch in a decontextualized nuclear family distorts the experiences of women in alternative family structures with quite different political economies. While male domination certainly has been an important theme for racial ethnic women in the United States, gender inequality has long worked in tandem with racial domination and economic exploitation. Since work and family have rarely functioned as dichotomous spheres for women of color, examining racial ethnic women's experiences reveals how these two spheres actually are interwoven (Glenn 1985; Dill 1988; Collins 1990).

For women of color, the subjective experience of mothering/motherhood is inextricably linked to the sociocultural concern of racial ethnic communities—one does not exist without the other. Whether because of the labor exploitation of African-American women under slavery and its ensuing tenant farm system, the political conquest of Native American women during European acquisition of land, or exclusionary immigration policies applied to Asian-Americans and Hispanics, women of color have performed motherwork that challenges social constructions of work and family as separate spheres, of male and female gender roles as similarly dichotomized, and of the search for autonomy as the guiding human quest. "Women's reproductive labor—that is, feeding, clothing, and psychologically supporting the male wage earner and nurturing and socializing the next generation—is seen as work on behalf of the family as a whole, rather than as work benefiting men in particular," observes Asian-American sociologist Evelyn Nakano Glenn

(1986, p. 192). The locus of conflict lies outside the household, as women and their families engage in collective effort to create and maintain family life in the face of forces that undermine family integrity. But this "reproductive labor" or "motherwork" goes beyond ensuring the survival of one's own biological children or those of one's family. This type of motherwork recognizes that individual survival, empowerment, and identity require group survival, empowerment, and identity.

In describing her relationship with her "Grandmother," Marilou Awiakta, a Native American poet and feminist theorist, captures the essence of motherwork:

> Putting my arms around the Grandmother, I lay my head on her shoulder. Through touch we exchange sorrow, despair that anything really changes.

Awiakta senses the power of the Grandmother and of the motherwork that mothers and grandmothers do:

> But from the presence of her arms I also feel the stern, beautiful power that flows from all the Grandmothers, as it flows from our mountains themselves. It says, "Dry your tears. Get up. Do for yourselves or do without. Work for the day to come." (1988, p. 127)

Awiakta's passage places women and motherwork squarely in the center of what are typically seen as disjunctures, the places between human and nature, between private and public, between oppression and liberation. I use the term "motherwork" to soften the existing dichotomies in feminist theorizing about motherhood that posit rigid distinctions between private and public, family and work, the individual and the collective, identity as individual autonomy and identity growing from the collective self-determination of one's group. Racial ethnic women's mothering and work experiences occur at the boundaries demarking these dualities. "Work for the day to come," is motherwork, whether it is on behalf of one's own biological children, or for the children of one's own racial ethnic community, or to preserve the earth for those children who are yet unborn. The space that this motherwork occupies promises to shift our thinking about motherhood itself.

SHIFTING THE CENTER: WOMEN OF COLOR AND MOTHERWORK

What themes might emerge if issues of race and class generally, and understanding of racial ethnic women's motherwork specifically, became central to feminist theorizing about motherhood? Centering feminist theorizing on the concerns of white, middle-class women leads to two problematic assumptions. The first is that a relative degree of economic security exists for mothers and their children. The second is that all women enjoy the racial privilege that allows them to see themselves primarily as individuals in search of personal autonomy, instead of as members of racial ethnic groups struggling for power. It is these assumptions that allow feminist theorists to concentrate on themes such as the connections among mothering, aggression, and death, the effects of maternal isolation on mother-child relationships within nuclear family households, maternal sexuality, relationships among family members, all-powerful mothers as conduits for gender oppression, and the possibilities of an idealized motherhood freed from patriarchy (Chodorow and Contratto 1982; Eisenstein 1983).

While these issues merit investigation, centering feminist theorizing about motherhood in the ideas and experiences of African-American, Native American, Hispanic, and Asian-American women might yield markedly different themes (Andersen 1988; Brown 1989). This stance is to be distinguished from one that merely adds racial ethnic women's experiences to preexisting feminist theories, without considering how these experiences challenge those theories (Spelman 1988). Involving much more than simply the consulting of existing social science sources, the placing of ideas and experiences of women of color in the center of analysis requires invoking a different epistemology. We must distinguish between what has been said about subordinated groups in the dominant discourse, and what such groups might say about themselves if given the opportunity. Personal narratives, autobiographical statements, poetry, fiction, and other personalized statements have all been used by women of color to express self-defined standpoints on mothering and motherhood. Such knowledge reflects the authentic standpoint of subordinated groups. Therefore, placing these sources in the center and supplementing them with statistics, historical material, and other knowledge produced to justify the interests of ruling elites should create new themes and angles of vision (Smith 1990).[6]

Specifying the contours of racial ethnic women's motherwork promises to point the way toward richer feminist theorizing about motherhood. Themes of survival, power, and identity form the bedrock and reveal how racial ethnic women in the United States encounter and fashion motherwork. That is, to understand the importance of working for the physical survival of children and community, the dialectical nature of power and powerlessness in structuring mothering patterns, and the significance of self-definition in constructing individual and collective racial identity is to grasp the three core themes characterizing the experiences of Native American, African-American, Hispanic and Asian-American women. It is also to suggest how feminist theorizing about motherhood might be shifted if different voices become central in feminist discourse.

Motherwork and Physical Survival

When we are not physically starving we have the luxury to realize psychic and emotional starvation. (Cherrie Moraga 1979, p. 29)

Physical survival is assumed for children who are white and middle-class. The choice to thus examine their psychic and emotional well-being and that of their mothers appears rational. The children of women of color, many of whom are "physically starving," have no such choices however. Racial ethnic children's lives have long been held in low regard: African-American children face an infant mortality rate twice that for white infants; and approximately one-third of Hispanic children and one-half of African-American children who survive infancy live in poverty. In addition racial ethnic children often live in harsh urban environments where drugs, crime, industrial pollutants, and violence threaten their survival. Children in rural environments often fare no better. Winona LaDuke, for example, reports that Native Americans on reservations often must use contaminated water. And on the Pine Ridge Sioux Reservation in 1979, 38 percent of all pregnancies resulted in miscarriages before the fifth month, or in excessive hemorrhaging. Approximately 65 percent of all children born suffered breathing problems caused by underdeveloped lungs and jaundice (1988, p. 63).

Struggles to foster the survival of Native American, Hispanic, Asian-American, and African-American families and communities by ensuring the survival of children comprise a fundamental dimension of racial ethnic women's motherwork. African-American women's fiction contains numerous stories of mothers fighting for the physical survival both of their own biological children and of those of the larger Black community.[7] "Don't care how much death it is in the land, I got to make preparations for my baby to live!" proclaims Mariah Upshur, the African-American heroine of Sara Wright's 1986 novel *This Child's Gonna Live* (p. 143). Like Mariah Upshur, the harsh climates which confront racial ethnic children require that their mothers "make preparations for their babies to live" as a central feature of their motherwork.

Yet, like all deep cultural themes, the theme of motherwork for physical survival contains contradictory elements. On the one hand, racial ethnic women's motherwork for individual and community survival has been essential. Without women's motherwork, communities would not survive, and by definition, women of color themselves would not survive. On the other hand, this work often extracts a high cost for large numbers of women. There is loss of individual autonomy and there is submersion of individual growth for the benefit of the group. While this dimension of motherwork remains essential, the question of women doing more than their fair share of such work for individual and community development merits open debate.

The histories of family-based labor have been shaped by racial ethnic women's motherwork for survival and the types of mothering relationships that ensued. African-American, Asian-American, Native American and Hispanic women have all worked and contributed to family economic well-being (Glenn 1985; Dill 1988). Much of their experiences with motherwork, in fact, stem from the work they performed as children. The commodification of children of color, starting with the enslavement of African children who were legally "owned" as property, to the subsequent treatment of children as units of labor in agricultural work, family businesses, and industry, has been a major theme shaping motherhood for women of color. Beginning in slavery and continuing into the post–World War II period, Black children were put to work at young ages in the fields of Southern agriculture. Sara Brooks began full-time work in the fields at the age of eleven, and remembers, "we never was lazy cause we used to really work. We used to work like men. Oh, fight sometime, fuss sometime, but worked on" (Collins 1990, p. 54).

Black and Hispanic children in contemporary migrant farm families make similar contributions to their family's economy. "I musta been almost eight when I started following the crops," remembers Jessie de la Cruz, a Mexican-American mother with six grown children. "Every winter, up north. I was on the end of the row of prunes, taking care of my younger brother and sister. They would help me fill up the cans and put 'em in a box while the rest of the family was picking the whole row" (de la Cruz 1980, p. 168). Asian-American children spend long hours working in family businesses, child labor practices that have earned Asian Americans the dubious distinction of being "model minorities." More recently, the family-based labor of undocumented racial ethnic immigrants, often mother-child units doing piecework for the garment industry, recalls the sweatshop conditions confronting turn-of-the-century European immigrants.

A certain degree of maternal isolation from members of the dominant group characterizes the preceding mother-child units. For women of color working along with their children, such isolation is more appropriately seen as reflecting a placement in race- and class-stratified labor systems than as a result of a patriarchal system. The unit may be isolated, but the work performed by the mother-child unit closely ties the mothering experiences to wider political and economic issues. Children, too, learn to see their work and that of their mother not as isolated from wider society, but as essential to their family's survival. Moreover, in the case of family agricultural labor or family businesses, women and children work alongside men, often performing the same work. If isolation occurs, the family, not the mother-child unit, is the focus of such isolation.

Children working in close proximity to their mothers receive distinctive types of mothering. Asian-American children working in urban family businesses, for example, report long days filled almost exclusively with work and school. In contrast, the sons and daughters of African-American sharecroppers and migrant farm children of all backgrounds have less access to educational opportunities. "I think the longest time I went to school was two months in one place," remembers Jessie de la Cruz. "I attended, I think, about forty-five schools. When my parents or my brothers didn't find work, we wouldn't attend school because we weren't sure of staying there. So I missed a lot of school" (de la Cruz 1980, pp. 167–8). It was only in the 1950s, in fact, that Southern school districts stopped the practice of closing segregated Black schools during certain times of the year so that Black children could work.

Work that separated women of color from their children also framed the mothering relationship. Until the 1960s, large numbers of African-American, Hispanic, and Asian-American women worked in domestic service. Even though women worked long hours to ensure their children's physical survival, that same work ironically denied mothers access to their children. Different institutional arrangements emerged in these mothers' respective communities to resolve the tension between maternal separation due to employment and the needs of dependent children. The extended family structure in African-American communities endured as a flexible institution that mitigated some of the effects of maternal separation. Grandmothers are highly revered in Black communities, often because grandmothers function as primary caretakers of their daughters' and daughter-in-laws' children (Collins 1990). In contrast, exclusionary immigration policies that mitigated against intergenerational family units in the United States led Chinese-American and Japanese-American families to make other arrangements (Dill 1988).

Some mothers are clearly defeated by the demands for incessant labor that they must perform to ensure their children's survival. The magnitude of their motherwork overwhelms them. But others, even while appearing to be defeated, manage to pass on the meaning of motherwork for survival to their children. African-American feminist June Jordan remembers her perceptions of her mother's work:

> As a child I noticed the sadness of my mother as she sat alone in the kitchen at night.... Her woman's work never won permanent victories of any kind. It never enlarged the universe of her imagination or her power to influence what happened beyond the front door of our house. Her woman's work never tickled her to laugh or shout or dance. (Jordan 1985, p. 105)

But Jordan also sees her mother's work as being essential to individual and community survival:

> She did raise me to respect her way of offering love and to believe that hard work is often the irreducible factor for survival, not something to avoid. Her woman's work produced a reliable home base where I could pursue the privileges of books and music. Her

woman's work invented the potential for a completely new kind of work for us, the next generation of Black women: huge, rewarding hard work demanded by the huge, different ambitions that her perfect confidence in us engendered. (Jordan 1985, p. 105)

MOTHERWORK AND POWER

Jessie de la Cruz, a Mexican-American migrant farm worker, experienced firsthand the struggle for empowerment facing racial ethnic women whose daily motherwork centers on issues of survival:

> How can I write down how I felt when I was a little child and my grandmother used to cry with us 'cause she didn't have enough food to give us? Because my brother was going barefooted and he was cryin' because he wasn't used to going without shoes? How can I describe that? I can't describe when my little girl died because I didn't have money for a doctor. And never had any teaching on caring for sick babies. Living out in labor camps. How can I describe that? (de la Cruz 1980, p. 177)

A dialectical relationship exists between efforts of racial orders to mold the institution of motherhood to serve the interests of elites, in this case, racial elites, and efforts on the part of subordinated groups to retain power over motherhood so that it serves the legitimate needs of their communities (Collins 1990). African-American, Asian-American, Hispanic, and Native American women have long been preoccupied with patterns of maternal power and powerlessness because their mothering experiences have been profoundly affected by this dialectical process. But instead of emphasizing maternal power in dealing with father as patriarch (Chodorow 1978; Rich 1986), or with male dominance in general (Ferguson 1989), women of color are concerned with their power and powerlessness within an array of social institutions that frame their lives.

Racial ethnic women's struggles for maternal empowerment have resolved around three main themes. First is the struggle for control over their own bodies in order to preserve choice over whether to become mothers at all. The ambiguous politics of caring for unplanned children has long shaped African-American women's motherwork. For example, the widespread institutionalized rape of Black women by white men, both during slavery and in the segregated South, created countless biracial children who had to be absorbed into African-American families and communities (Davis 1981). The range of skin colors and hair textures in contemporary African-American communities bears mute testament to the powerlessness of African-American women in controlling this dimension of motherhood.

For many women of color, choosing to become a mother challenges institutional policies that encourage white, middle-class women to reproduce, and discourage or even penalize low-income racial ethnic women from doing so (Davis 1981). Rita Silk-Nauni, an incarcerated Native American woman, writes of the difficulties she encountered in trying to have additional children. She loved her son so much that she only left him to go to work. "I tried having more after him and couldn't," she laments.

> I went to a specialist and he thought I had been fixed when I had my son. He said I would have to have surgery in order to give birth again. The surgery was so expensive but I thought I could make a way even if I had to work 24 hours a day. Now that I'm here, I know I'll never have that chance. (Brant 1988, p. 94)

Like Silk-Nauni, Puerto Rican and African-American women have long had to struggle with issues of sterilization abuse (Davis 1981). More recent efforts to manipulate the fertility of women dependent on public assistance speaks to the continued salience of this issue.

A second dimension of racial ethnic women's struggles for maternal empowerment concerns the process of keeping the children that are wanted, whether they were planned for or not. For mothers like Jessie de la Cruz, whose "little girl died" because she "didn't have money for a doctor," maternal separation from one's children becomes a much more salient issue than maternal isolation with one's children within an allegedly private nuclear family. Physical and/or psychological separation of mothers and children, designed to disempower individuals, forms the basis of a systematic effort to disempower racial ethnic communities.

For both Native American and African-American mothers, situations of conquest introduced this dimension of the struggle for maternal empowerment. In her fictional account of a Native American mother's loss of her children in 1890, Brant explores the pain of maternal separation:

> It has been two days since they came and took the children away. My body is greatly chilled. All our blankets have been used to bring me warmth. The women keep the fire blazing. The men sit. They talk among themselves. We are frightened by this sudden child-stealing. We signed papers, the agent said. This gave them rights to take our babies. It is good for them, the agent said. It will make them civilized. (1988, p. 101)

A legacy of conquest has meant that Native American mothers on "reservations" confront intrusive government institutions such as the Bureau of Indian Affairs in deciding the fate of their children. For example, the long-standing policy of removing Native American children from their homes and housing them in reservation boarding schools can be seen as efforts to disempower Native American mothers. For African-American women, slavery was a situation where owners controlled numerous dimensions of their children's lives. Black children could be sold at will, whipped, or even killed, all without any recourse by their mothers. In such a situation, getting to keep one's children and raise them accordingly fosters empowerment.

A third dimension of racial ethnic women's struggles for empowerment concerns the pervasive efforts by the dominant group to control the children's minds. In her short story, "A Long Memory," Beth Brant juxtaposes the loss felt by a Native American mother in 1890 whose son and daughter had been forcibly removed by white officials, to the loss that she felt in 1978 upon losing her daughter in a custody hearing. "Why do they want our babies?" queries the turn-of-the-century mother. "They want our power. They take our children to remove the inside of them. Our power" (Brant 1988, p. 105). This mother recognizes that the future of the Native American way of life lies in retaining the power to define that worldview through the education of children. By forbidding children to speak their native languages, and in other ways encouraging children to assimilate into Anglo culture, external agencies challenge the power of mothers to raise their children as they see fit.

Schools controlled by the dominant group comprise one important location where this dimension of the struggle for maternal empowerment occurs. In contrast to white, middle-class children, whose educational experiences affirm their mothers' middle-class values, culture, and authority, the educational experiences of African-American, Hispanic, Asian-American and Native American children typically denigrate their mothers' perspective. For example, the struggles over bilingual education in Hispanic communities are about much more than retaining Spanish as a second language. Speaking the language of one's childhood is a way of retaining the entire culture and honoring the mother teaching that culture (Morago 1979; Anzaldua 1987).

Jenny Yamoto describes the stress of continuing to negotiate with schools regarding her Black-Japanese sons:

> I've noticed that depending on which parent, Black mom or Asian dad, goes to school open house, my oldest son's behavior is interpreted as disruptive and irreverent, or assertive and clever.... I resent their behavior being defined and even expected on the basis of racial biases their teachers may struggle with or hold.... I don't have the time or energy to constantly change and challenge their teachers' and friends' misperceptions. I only go after them when the children really seem to be seriously threatened. (Yamoto 1988, p. 24)

In confronting each of these three dimensions of their struggles for empowerment, racial ethnic women are not powerless in the face of racial and class oppression. Being grounded in a strong, dynamic, indigenous culture can be central to these women's social constructions of motherhood. Depending on their access to traditional culture, they invoke alternative sources of power.[8]

"Equality, per se, may have a different meaning for Indian women and Indian people," suggests Kate Shanley. "That difference begins with personal and tribal sovereignty–the right to be legally recognized as people empowered to determine our own destinies" (1988, p. 214). Personal sovereignty involves the struggle to promote the survival of a social structure whose organizational principles represent notions of family and motherhood different from those of the mainstream. "The nuclear family has little relevance to Indian women," observes Shanley. "In fact, in many ways, mainstream feminists now are striving to redefine family and community in a way that Indian women have long known" (p. 214).

African-American mothers can draw upon an Afrocentric tradition where motherhood of varying types, whether bloodmother, othermother, or community othermother, can be invoked as a symbol of power. Many Black women receive respect and recognition within their local communities for innovative and practical approaches not only to mothering their own "blood" children, but also to being othermothers to the children in their extended family networks, and those in the community overall. Black women's involvement in fostering Black community development forms the basis of this community-based power. In local African-American communities, community othermothers can become identified as powerful figures through their work in furthering the community's well-being (Collins 1990).

Despite policies of dominant institutions that place racial ethnic mothers in positions where they appear less powerful to their children, mothers and children empower themselves by understanding each other's position and relying on each other's strengths. In many cases, children, especially daughters, bond with their mothers instead of railing against them as symbols of patriarchal power. Cherrie Moraga describes the impact that her mother had on her. Because she was repeatedly removed from school in order to work, by prevailing standards Moraga's mother would be considered largely illiterate. But she was also a fine storyteller, and found ways to empower herself within dominant institutions. "I would go with my mother to fill out job applications for her, or write checks for her at the supermarket," Moraga recounts.

> We would have the scenario all worked out ahead of time. My mother would sign the check before we'd get to the store. Then, as we'd approach the checkstand, she would say—within earshot of the cashier—"oh, honey, you go 'head and make out the check," as if she couldn't be bothered with such an insignificant detail. (1979, p. 28)

Like Cherrie Moraga and her mother, racial ethnic women's motherwork involves collaborating to empower mothers and children within structures that oppress.

MOTHERWORK AND IDENTITY

> *Please help me find out who I am. My mother was Indian, but we*
> *were taken from her and put in foster homes. They were white and*
> *didn't want to tell us about our mother. I have a name and maybe*
> *a place of birth. Do you think you can help me?* (Brant 1988, p. 9)

Like this excerpt from a letter to the editor, the theme of lost racial ethnic identity and the struggle to maintain a sense of self and community
pervade many of the stories, poetry and narratives in Beth Brant's volume, *A Gathering of Spirit*. Carol Lee Sanchez offers another view of the
impact of the loss of self. "Radicals look at reservation Indians and get
very upset about their poverty conditions," observes Sanchez.

> But poverty to us is not the same thing as poverty is to you. Our
> poverty is that we can't be who we are. We can't hunt or fish or
> grow our food because our basic resources and the right to use them
> in traditional ways are denied us. (Brant 1988, p. 165)

Racial ethnic women's motherwork reflects the tensions inherent in
trying to foster a meaningful racial identity in children within a society
that denigrates people of color. The racial privilege enjoyed by white,
middle-class women makes unnecessary this complicated dimension of
the mothering tradition of women of color. While white children can be
prepared to fight racial oppression, their survival does not depend on
gaining these skills. Their racial identity is validated by their schools,
the media, and other social institutions. White children are socialized
into their rightful place in systems of racial privilege. Racial ethnic
women have no such guarantees for their children; their children must
first be taught to survive in systems that oppress them. Moreover, this
survival must not come at the expense of self-esteem. Thus, a dialectical relationship exists between systems of racial oppression designed to
strip subordinated groups of a sense of personal identity and a sense of
collective peoplehood, and the cultures of resistance extant in various
racial ethnic groups that resist the oppression. For women of color,
motherwork for identity occurs at this critical juncture (Collins 1990).

"Through our mothers, the culture gave us mixed messages," observes
Mexican-American poet Gloria Anzaldua. "Which was it to be—strong or
submissive, rebellious or conforming?" (1987, p. 18). Thus women of
color's motherwork requires reconciling contradictory needs concerning
identity. Preparing children to cope with and survive within systems of
racial oppression is extremely difficult because the pressures for children
of racial ethnic groups to assimilate are pervasive. In order to compel
women of color to participate in their children's assimilation, dominant
institutions promulgate ideologies that belittle people of color. Negative
controlling images infuse the worlds of male and female children of color

(Tajima 1989; Collins 1990; Green 1990). Native American girls are encouraged to see themselves as "Pocahontases" or "squaws"; Asian-American girls as "geisha girls" or "Suzy Wongs"; Hispanic girls as "Madonnas" or "hot-blooded whores"; and African-American girls as "mammies," "matriarchs," and "prostitutes." Girls of all groups are told that their lives cannot be complete without a male partner, and that their educational and career aspirations must always be subordinated to their family obligations.

This push toward assimilation is part of a larger effort to socialize racial ethnic children into their proper, subordinate places in systems of racial and class oppression. Since children of color can never be white, however, assimilation by becoming white is impossible despite the pressures. Thus, a second dimension of the mothering tradition involves equipping children with skills to confront this contradiction and to challenge systems of racial oppression. Girls who become women believing that they are only capable of being maids and prostitutes cannot contribute to racial ethnic women's motherwork.

Mothers make varying choices in negotiating the complicated relationship of preparing children to fit into, yet resist, systems of racial domination. Some mothers remain powerless in the face of external forces that foster their children's assimilation and subsequent alienation from their families and communities. Through fiction, Native American author Beth Brant again explores the grief felt by a mother whose children had been taken away to live among whites. A letter arrives giving news of her missing children:

> This letter is from two strangers with the names Martha and Daniel. They say they are learning civilized ways. Daniel works in the fields, growing food for the school. Martha is being taught to sew aprons. She will be going to live with the schoolmaster's wife. She will be a live-in girl. What is live-in girl? I shake my head. The words sound the same to me. I am afraid of Martha and Daniel. These strangers who know my name. (Brant 1988, pp. 102–103)

Other mothers become unwitting conduits of the dominant ideology. Gloria Anzalduce (1987, p. 16) asks:

> How many time have I heard mothers and mothers-in-law tell their sons to beat their wives for not obeying them, for being *hociconas* (big mouths), for being *callajeras* (going to visit and gossip with neighbors), for expecting their husbands to help with the rearing of children and the housework, for wanting to be something other than housewives?

Some mothers encourage their children to fit in, for reasons of survival. "My mother, nursed in the folds of a town that once christened its black babies Lee, after Robert E., and Jackson, after Stonewall, raised me on a dangerous generation's old belief," remembers African-American author Marita Golden.

> Because of my dark brown complexion, she warned me against wearing browns or yellow and reds ... and every summer I was admonished not to play in the sun "cause you gonna have to get a light husband anyway, for the sake of your children." (Golden 1983, p. 24)

To Cherrie Moraga's mother:

> On a basic economic level, being Chicana meant being "less." It was through my mother's desire to protect her children from poverty and illiteracy that we became "anglocized"; the more effectively we could pass in the white world, the better guaranteed our future. (1979, p. 28)

Despite their mothers' good intentions, the costs to children taught to submit to racist and sexist ideologies can be high. Raven, a Native American woman, looks back on her childhood:

> I've been raised in white man's world and was forbade more or less to converse with Indian people. As my mother wanted me to be educated and live a good life, free from poverty. I lived a life of loneliness. Today I am desperate to know my people. (Brant 1988, p. 221)

To avoid poverty, Raven's mother did what she thought best, but ultimately, Raven experienced the poverty of not being able to be who she was.

Still other mothers transmit sophisticated skills to their children, enabling them to appear to be submissive while at the same time to be able to challenge inequality. Willi Coleman's mother used a Saturday-night hair-combing ritual to impart a Black women's standpoint to her daughters:

> Except for special occasions mama came home from work early on Saturdays. She spent six days a week mopping, waxing and dusting other women's houses and keeping out of reach of other women's husbands. Saturday nights were reserved for "taking care of them girls'" hair and the telling of stories. Some of which included a recitation of what she had endured and how she had triumphed over "folks that were lower than dirt" and "no-good snakes in the grass." She combed, patted, twisted and talked, saying things which would have embarrassed or shamed her at other times. (Coleman 1987, p. 34)

Historian Elsa Barkley Brown captures this delicate balance that racial ethnic mothers negotiate. Brown points out that her mother's behavior demonstrated the "need to teach me to live my life one way and, at the same time, to provide all the tools I would need to live it quite differently" (1989, p. 929).

For women of color, the struggle to maintain an independent racial identity has taken many forms: All reveal varying solutions to the dialectical relationship between institutions that would deny their children their humanity and institutions that would affirm their children's right to exist as self-defined people. Like Willi Coleman's mother, African-American women draw upon a long-standing Afrocentric feminist worldview, emphasizing the importance of self-definition, self-reliance, and the necessity of demanding respect from others (Terborg-Penn 1986; Collins 1990).

Racial ethnic cultures, themselves, do not always help to support women's self-definition. Poet and essayist Gloria Anzaldua, for example, challenges many of the ideas in Hispanic cultures concerning women. "Though I'll defend my race and culture when they are attacked by non-*mexicanos*,... I abhor some of my culture's ways, how it cripples its women, *como burras*, our strengths used against us" (1987, p. 21). Anzaldua offers a trenchant analysis of the ways in which the Spanish conquest of Native Americans fragmented women's identity and produced three symbolic "mothers." *La Virgen de Guadalupe*, perhaps the single most potent religious, political and cultural image of the Chicano people, represents the virgin mother who cares for and nurtures an oppressed people. *La Chingada (Malinche)* represents the raped mother, all but abandoned. A combination of the other two, *La Llorona* symbolizes the mother who seeks her lost children. "Ambiguity surrounds the symbols of these three 'Our Mothers,'" claims Anzaldua.

> In part, the true identity of all three has been subverted—*Guadalupe*, to make us docile and enduring, *la Chingada*, to make us ashamed of our Indian side, and *la Llorona* to make us a long-suffering people. (1987, p. 31)

For Anzaldua, the Spanish conquest, which brought racism and economic subordination to Indian people, and created a new mixed-race Hispanic people, simultaneously devalued women:

> No, I do not buy all the myths of the tribe into which I was born. I can understand why the more tinged with Anglo blood, the more adamantly my colored and colorless sisters glorify their colored culture's values—to offset the extreme devaluation of it by the white culture. It's a legitimate reaction. But I will not glorify those aspects of my culture which have injured me and which have injured me in the name of protecting me. (Anzaldua 1987, p. 22)

Hispanic mothers face the complicated task of shepherding their children through the racism extant in dominant society, and the reactions to that racism framing cultural beliefs internal to Hispanic communities.

Many Asian American mothers stress conformity and fitting in as a way to challenge the system. "Our parents are painted as hard workers who were socially uncomfortable and had difficulty expressing even the smallest opinion," observes Japanese-American Kesaya Noda, in her autobiographical essay "Growing Up Asian in America" (1989, p. 246). Noda questioned this seeming capitulation on the part of her parents: "'Why did you go into those camps,' I raged at my parents, frightened by my own inner silence and timidity. 'Why didn't you do anything to resist?'" But Noda later discovers a compelling explanation as to why Asian-Americans are so often portrayed as conformist:

> I had not been able to imagine before what it must have felt like to be an American—to know absolutely that one is an American—and yet to have almost everyone else deny it. Not only deny it, but challenge that identity with machine guns and troops of white American soldiers. In those circumstances it was difficult to say, "I'm a Japanese-American." "American" had to do. (1989, p. 247)

Native American women can draw upon a tradition of motherhood and woman's power inherent in Native American cultures (Allen 1986; Awiakta 1988). In such philosophies, "water, land, and life are basic to the natural order," claims Winona LaDuke.

> All else has been created by the use and misuse of technology. It is only natural that in our respective struggles for survival, the native peoples are waging a way to protect the land, the water, and life, while the consumer culture strives to protect its technological lifeblood. (1988, p. 65)

Marilou Awiakta offers a powerful summary of the symbolic meaning of motherhood in Native American cultures. "I feel the Grandmother's power. She sings of harmony, not dominance," offers Awiakta. "And her song rises from a culture that repeats the wise balance of nature: the gender capable of bearing life is not separated from the power to sustain it" (1988, p. 126). A culture that sees the connectedness between the earth and human survival, and sees motherhood as symbolic of the earth itself, holds motherhood as an institution in high regard.

CONCLUDING REMARKS

Survival, power, and identity shape motherhood for all women. But these themes remain muted when the mothering experiences of women of color are marginalized in feminist theorizing. Feminist theorizing about motherhood reflects a lack of attention to the connection between ideas and the contexts in which they emerge. While such decontextualization aims to generate universal "theories" of human behavior, in actuality, it routinely distorts, and omits huge categories of human experience.

Placing racial ethnic women's motherwork in the center of analysis recontextualizes motherhood. While the significance of race and class in shaping the context in which motherhood occurs remains virtually invisible when white, middle-class women's mothering experiences assume prominence, the effects of race and class on motherhood stand out in stark relief when women of color are accorded theoretical primacy. Highlighting racial ethnic mothers' struggles concerning their children's right to exist focuses attention on the importance of survival. Exploring the dialectical nature of racial ethnic women's empowerment in structures of racial domination and economic exploitation demonstrates the need to broaden the definition of maternal power. Emphasizing how the quest for self-definition is mediated by membership in different racial and social class groups reveals how the issues of identity are crucial to all motherwork.

Existing feminist theories of motherhood have emerged in specific intellectual and political contexts. By assuming that social theory will be applicable regardless of social context, feminist scholars fail to realize that they themselves are rooted in specific locations, and that the specific contexts in which they are located provide the thought-models of how they interpret the world. While subsequent theories appear to be universal and objective, they actually are partial perspectives reflecting the white, middle-class context in which their creators live. Large segments of experience, specifically those of women who are not white and middle-class, have been excluded (Spelman 1988).

Feminist theories of motherhood are thus valid as partial perspectives, but cannot be seen as *theories* of motherhood generalizable to all women. The resulting patterns of partiality inherent in existing theories, such as, for example, the emphasis placed on all-powerful mothers as conduits for gender oppression, reflect feminist theorists' positions in structures of power. These theorists are themselves participants in a system of privilege that rewards them for not seeing race and class privilege as being important.

Theorizing about motherhood will not be helped by supplanting one group's theory with that of another; for example, by claiming that women of color's experiences are more valid than those of white, middle-class women. Varying placement in systems of privilege, whether race, class, sexuality, or age, generates divergent experiences with motherhood; therefore, examination of motherhood and mother-as-subject from multiple perspectives should uncover rich textures of difference. Shifting the center to accommodate this diversity promises to recontextualize motherhood and point us toward feminist theorizing that embraces difference as an essential part of commonality.

Notes

1. In this essay, I use the terms "racial ethnic women" and "women of color" interchangeably. Grounded in the experiences of groups who have been the targets of racism, the term "racial ethnic" implies more solidarity with men involved in struggles against racism. In contrast, the term "women of color" emerges from a feminist background where racial ethnic women committed to feminist struggle aimed to distinguish their history and issues from those of middle-class, white women. Neither term captures the complexity of African-American, Native American, Asian-American and Hispanic women's experiences.

2. Positivist social science exemplifies this type of decontextualization. In order to create scientific descriptions of reality, positivist researchers aim to produce ostensibly objective generalizations. But because researchers have widely differing values, experiences, and emotions, genuine science is thought to be unattainable unless all human characteristics except rationality are eliminated from the research process. By following strict methodological rules, scientists aim to distance themselves from the values, vested interests, and emotions generated by their class, race, sex, or unique situation. By decontextualizing themselves, they allegedly become detached observers and manipulators of nature. Moreover, this researcher decontextualization is paralleled by comparable efforts to remove the objects of study from their contexts (Jaggar 1983).

3. Dominant theories are characterized by this decontextualization. Boyd's (1989) helpful survey of literature on the mother-daughter relationship reveals that while much work has been done on motherhood generally, and on the mother-daughter relationship, very little of it tests feminist theories of motherhood. Boyd lists two prevailing theories, psychoanalytic theory and social learning theory, that she claims form the bulk of feminist theorizing. Both of these approaches minimize the importance of race and class in the context of motherhood. Boyd ignores Marxist-feminist theorizing about motherhood, mainly because very little of this work is concerned with the mother-daughter relationship. But Marxist-feminist analyses of motherhood provide another example of how decontextualization frames feminist theories of motherhood. See, for example, Ann Ferguson's *Blood at the Root: Motherhood, Sexuality, and Male Dominance* (1989), an ambitious attempt to develop a universal theory of motherhood that is linked to the social construction of sexuality and male dominance. Ferguson's work stems from a feminist tradition that explores the relationship between motherhood and sexuality by either bemoaning their putative incompatibility or romanticizing maternal sexuality.

4. Psychoanalytic feminist theorizing about motherhood, such as Nancy Chodorow's groundbreaking work, *The Reproduction of Mothering* (1978), exemplifies how decontextualization of race and/or class can weaken what is otherwise strong feminist theorizing. Although I realize that other feminist approaches to motherhood exist—see Eisenstein's (1983) summary, for example—I have chosen to stress psychoanalytic feminist theory because the work of Chodorow and others has been highly influential in framing the predominant themes in feminist discourse.

5. The thesis of the atomized individual that underlies Western psychology is rooted in a much larger Western construct concerning the relation of the individual to the community (Hartsock 1983). Theories of motherhood based on

the assumption of the atomized human proceed to use this definition of individual as the unit of analysis, and then construct theory from this base. From this grow assumptions based on the premise that the major process to examine is that of freely choosing, rational individuals engaging in bargains (Hartsock 1983).

6. The narrative tradition in the writings of women of color addresses this effort to recover the history of mothers. Works from African-American women's autobiographical tradition, such as Ann Moody's *Coming of Age in Mississippi*, Maya Angelou's *I Know Why the Caged Bird Sings*, Linda Brent's *Narrative in the Life of a Slave Girl*, and Marita Golden's *The Heart of a Woman* contain the authentic voices of Black women centered on experiences of motherhood. Works from African-American women's fiction include Sarah Wright's *This Child's Gonna Live*, Alice Walker's *Meridian*, and Toni Morrison's *Sula and Beloved.* Asian-American women's fiction, such as Amy Tan's *The Joy Luck Club* and Maxine Kingston's *Woman Warrior*, and autobiographies such as Jean Wakatsuki Houston's *Farewell to Manzanar* offer a parallel source of authentic voice. Connie Young Yu (1989) entitles her article on the history of Asian-American women "The World of Our Grandmothers," and proceeds to recreate Asian-American history with her grandmother as a central figure. Cherrie Moraga (1979) writes a letter to her mother as a way of coming to terms with the contradictions in her racial identity as a Chicana. *In Borderlands/La Frontera*, Gloria Anzaldua (1987) weaves autobiography, poetry and philosophy together in her exploration of women and mothering.

7. Notable examples include Lutie Johnson's unsuccessful attempt to rescue her son from the harmful effects of an urban environment in Ann Petry's *The Street*; and Meridian's work on behalf of the children of a small Southern town after she chooses to relinquish her own child, in Alice Walker's *Meridian.*

8. Noticeably absent from feminist theories of motherhood is a comprehensive theory of power and explanation of how power relations shape theories. Firmly rooted in an exchange-based marketplace, with its accompanying assumptions of rational economic decision-making and white, male control of the marketplace, this model of community stresses the rights of individuals, including feminist theorists, to make decisions in their own self-interests, regardless of the impact on larger society. Composed of a collection of unequal individuals who compete for greater shares of money as the medium of exchange, this model of community legitimates relations of domination either by denying they exist or by treating them as inevitable but unimportant (Hartsock, 1983).

REFERENCES

Allen, Paula Gunn. 1986. *The Sacred Hoop: Recovering the Feminine in American Indian Traditions.* Boston: Beacon.

Andersen, Margaret. 1988. "Moving Our Minds: Studying Women of Color and Reconstructing Sociology." *Teaching Sociology* 16 (2), pp. 123–132.

Anzaldua, Gloria. 1987. *Borderlands/La Frontera: The New Mestiza.* San Francisco: Spinsters.

Awiakta, Marilou. 1988. "Amazons in Appalchia." In Beth Brant, ed., *A*

Gathering of Spirit. Ithaca, NY: Firebrand, pp. 125–130.

Boyd, Carol J. 1989. "Mothers and Daughters: A Discussion of Theory and Research." *Journal of Marriage and the Family* 51, pp. 291–301.

Brant, Beth, ed. 1988. *A Gathering of Spirit: A Collection by North American Indian Women.* Ithaca, NY: Firebrand.

Brown, Elsa Barkley. 1989. "African-American Women's Quilting: A Framework for Conceptualizing and Teaching African-American Women's History." *Signs* 14 (4), pp. 921–929.

Chodorow, Nancy. 1978. *The Reproduction of Mothering.* Berkeley, CA: University of California Press.

———, and Susan Contratto. 1982. "The Fantasy of the Perfect Mother." In Barrie Thorne and Marilyn Yalom, eds., *Rethinking the Family: Some Feminist Questions.* New York: Longman, pp. 54–75.

Coleman, Willi. 1987. "Closets and Keepsakes." *Sage: A Scholarly Journal on Black Women* 4 (2), pp. 34–35.

Collins, Patricia Hill. 1990. *Black Feminist Thought: Knowledge, Consciousness and the Politics of Empowerment.* New York: Unwin Hyman/Routledge.

de la Cruz, Jessie. 1980. "Interview." In Studs Terkel, ed., *American Dreams: Lost and Found.* New York: Ballantine.

Davis, Angela Y. 1981. *Women, Race, and Class.* New York: Random House.

Dill, Bonnie Thornton. 1988. "Our Mothers' Grief: Racial Ethnic Women and the Maintenance of Families." *Journal of Family History* 13 (4), pp. 415–431.

Eisenstein, Hester. 1983. *Contemporary Feminist Thought.* Boston: G. K. Hall.

Ferguson, Ann. 1989. *Blood at the Root: Motherhood, Sexuality, and Male Dominance.* New York: Unwin Hyman/Routledge.

Flax, Jane. 1978. "The Conflict between Nurturance and Autonomy in Mother-Daughter Relationships and within Feminism." *Feminist Studies* 4 (2), pp. 171–189.

Glenn, Evelyn Nakano. 1985. "Racial Ethnic Women's Labor: The Intersection of Race, Gender and Class Oppression." *Review of Radical Political Economics* 17 (3), pp. 86–108.

———. 1986. *Issei, Nisei, War Bride: Three Generations of Japanese American Women in Domestic Service.* Philadelphia: Temple University Press.

Green, Rayna. 1990. "The Pocahontas Perplex: The Image of Indian Women in American Culture." In Ellen Carol DuBois and Vicki Ruiz, eds., *Unequal Sisters.* New York: Routledge, pp. 15–21.

Hartsock, Nancy. 1983. *Money, Sex and Power.* Boston: Northeastern University Press.

Jordan, June. 1985. *On Call.* Boston: South End Press.

LaDuke, Winona. 1988. "They always come back." In Beth Brant, ed., *A Gathering of Spirit.* Ithaca, NY: Firebrand, pp. 62–67.

Lerner, Gerda. 1972. *Black Women in White America.* New York: Pantheon.

Moraga, Cherrie. 1979. "La Guera." In Cherrie Moraga and Gloria Anzaldua, eds., *This Bridge Called My Back: Writings By Radical Women of Color.* Watertown, MA: Persephone Press, pp. 27–34.

Noda, Kesaya E. 1989. "Growing Up Asian in American." In Asian Women United of California, eds., *Making Waves: An Anthology of Writings By and About Asian American Women.* Boston: Beacon, pp. 243–50.

Rich, Adrienne. 1986 [1976]. *Of Woman Born: Motherhood as Institution and Experience.* New York: W. W. Norton.

Shanley, Kate. 1988. "Thoughts on Indian Feminism." In Beth Brant, ed., *A Gathering of Spirit.* Ithaca, NY: Firebrand, pp. 213–215.

Smith, Dorothy E. 1990. *The Conceptual Practices of Power: A Feminist Sociology of Knowledge.* Boston: Northeastern University Press.

Spelman, Elizabeth V. 1988. *Inessential Woman: Problems of Exculsion in Feminist Thought.* Boston: Beacon Press.

Tajima, Renee E. 1989. "Lotus Blossoms Don't Bleed: Images of Asian Women." In Asian Women United of California, eds., *Making Waves: An Anthology of Writings By and About Asian American Women.* Boston: Beacon, pp. 308–317.

Terborg-Penn, Rosalyn. 1986. "Black Women in Resistance: A Cross-Cultural Perspective." In Gary Y. Okhiro, ed., *In Resistance: Studies in African, Caribbean and Afro-American History.* Amherst: University of Massachusetts Press, pp. 188–209.

Wright, Sarah. 1986. *This Child's Gonna Live.* Old Westbury, NY: Feminist Press.

Yamoto, Jenny. 1988. "Mixed Bloods, Half Breeds, Mongrels, Hybrids ..." In Jo Whitehorse Cochran, Donna Langston, and Carolyn Woodward, eds., *Changing Our Power: An Introduction to Women's Studies.* Dubuque, IA: Kendall/Hunt, pp. 22–24.

Yu, Connie Young. 1989. "The World of Our Grandmothers." In Asian Women United of California, eds., *Making Waves: An Anthology of Writings By and About Asian American Women.* Boston: Beacon, pp. 33–41.

10

Toward a Unified Theory
of Class, Race, and Gender

Karen Brodkin Sacks

Racial/Ethnic and Gender Diversity

Capitalism has specifically recruited workers on the basis of race, and of gender and family relations within specific racial-ethnic communities. But this is part of a historical dialectic whose other pole was the age/marital status and gender of those who were "expendable" in a particular culture's division of labor—as for example, the contrast between male-centered farming systems in Euroamerica with "expendable" farm daughters, and female-centered farming in Africa with "expendable" sons. The "value" of such expendable laborers seems to have been set by an interaction of the social relations and expectations of domestic production with employers' demands for cheap labor, where sons' and daughters' wages were not expected to support them. Recognizing the influence of peasant or agrarian family organization on the age, race, and gender makeup of wage labor forces further highlights continuities among family, community, and workplace for the experience and interpretation of class (Sacks 1984).

The long-term workings out of this dialectic throughout the capitalist world—which began with capitalists' eternal search for cheap labor and nonproletarian communities' turning loose only their less "valuable" laborers—has been a major contributor to racial/ethnic segregation of working-class communities and racial/ethnic and sex segregation. This dialectic operated historically when industrialists sought out specifically white, Yankee daughters in nineteenth-century New England textiles and twentieth-century Southeast Asian daughters in apparel (Dublin 1979; Ong 1983); pre-married African boys and men in colonial East and Southern Africa in domestic work as well as mining (Hansen 1989); white mothers in contemporary front office work, and young black women for back offices (Glenn and Feldberg 1977; Machung 1984); black families in pre–World War II agriculture (Jones 1985); white rural daughters in Appalachian textiles before World War II, and black southerners more recently (Frankel 1984; Hall et al. 1987); European young women as live-in maids and then black women in pre–WWII domestic day work (Katzman 1978; Rollins 1985); teenagers in today's fast food shops; European immigrants in mining and heavy industry, and so on (see Glenn 1985 for a summary of the changing historical patterns of job segregation for black, Latina, and Chinese-American women in the United States).

It is important not to lose sight of women's history of struggles to break through race and gender occupational patterns, but even victories have been eroded through new forms of occupational segregation. Recent work has documented women's gains in the auto industry (Milkman 1987); in the pre-deregulation phone company (Hacker 1982); hospitals (Sacks 1988a); and in heavy industry during World War II (Anderson 1981; Gluck 1987). However, even when women do win battles, they may still face an "up the down escalator" phenomenon—when women and minorities gain access to a job it is redefined as less skilled, becomes intensely supervised, and, at the same time typed as women's/minority's. Thus Carter and Carter (1981) show that women's recent progress in professions like medicine and law are largely into an emergent second-class track characterized by lower pay, less professional autonomy, and fewer opportunities for advancement. The subtitle of their article, "Women Get a Ticket to Ride After the Gravy Train Has Left the Station" is especially apt for the professions, but Hacker (1982) documents a similar down side for women's victory in access to skilled craft jobs in the Bell phone system—except here those jobs were eliminated by more advanced technology shortly after women entered them. Remy (1984) shows the ways in which company and union in meatpacking have manipulated new technologies and job design to eliminate high-seniority women workers. Sacks (1988a), Glenn (1985), and Glenn and Feldberg (1977) deal with minority women's progress in clerical work in the 1960s, but also show these women being simultaneously tracked into an emergent factory-like back office sector.

There has been considerable recent attention devoted to women's work culture in work-places where women predominate, such as department stores, offices, hospitals, and garment factories (Benson 1978, 1986; Feldberg and Glenn 1983; Glenn and Feldberg 1977; Machung 1984; Sacks 1988a; Westwood 1985). It is becoming clear that occupational segregation results in different experiences and consciousness of class for women and men, racial-ethnic and white workers. The concomitant is that "working class-consciousness" has multiple shapes (Eisenstein 1983; Goldberg 1983; Sacks 1988b). It would also appear that women's ways of expressing class consciousness are as often as not drawn from their community- and family-based experiences of being working class. And, because working-class communities in the United States have been segregated, the experience and expressions of class consciousness have also been embedded in ethnically specific forms (Collins 1989; Davis 1981). To some degree, women have used family-based metaphors and values to share these consciousnesses across racial/ethnic lines (see especially Bookman and Morgen 1988; Lamphere 1984; Westwood 1985).

The point of all this is that one should not expect to find any generic worker or essential worker, or for that matter, working-class consciousness; that not only is class experienced in historically specific ways, but it is also experienced in racially specific, gender-specific, and kinship-specific ways.

The big issue is how to go about finding the unities and commonalities of class and class consciousness while being attentive to specificity. Critiques of white feminism by women of color and critiques by socialist feminists of male Marxist views of class offer parallel solutions about how to conceptualize unity in diversity. Both criticize implicit and privileged norms against which "others" are measured, and urge instead taking "the other" as the subject in conceptualizing womanhood, and class.

For example, bell hooks (1984) urges placing women of color at the center of feminist analysis, while Bettina Aptheker (1982) suggests "pivoting the center." Along with Deborah King (1988) they argue for theory that stems directly from the experiences of women of color—in contrast to theory that is generated from comparisons that interpret those experiences with reference to a norm or modal woman, who, in feminist theory, has been white and middle class. As Bonnie Dill (1979) suggested in indicating the importance of understanding the "dialectics of black womanhood," doing so offers the possibility of a more inclusive sisterhood for all American women. Such statements about how to construct theory underlie the concrete analyses cited earlier about racially specific conceptualizations of domestic labor, women's economic dependence, and the sexual stereotypes. In these analyses commonalities emerged from the process of resolving conflicts. I will return to the issue of commonalities underlying racial and class-specific gender stereotypes later.

We have seen parallel socialist feminist critiques of traditional, white, male-centered notions of class, which have asked how women relate to a wage-based class structure. Socialist feminists have answered that women's unwaged domestic labor is a necessary condition for the existence of waged labor. When working-class women are the subjects and narrative voices of case studies, class membership, gender and kinship organization, class-based mobilization, and class consciousness look very different from the way they have been portrayed in nonfeminist Marxist analyses. Feminist theorists, as Martha Acklesberg put it so trenchantly, "talk of the need to unite workplace and community. But women's lives have done that—and do it—on a daily basis, although perhaps without the consciousness that that is what they are about!" (1984:256).

Feminist theory applied to the study of working-class women's lives has birthed questions like: What are the social relations by which the working class sustains and reproduces itself? How do women conceptualize their unwaged labor and community-building activities? How—and where—do working-class women organize to struggle against capital? What are the issues that women find are worth fighting about? What are we learning about the persistence of unwaged labor and the ways it changes forms? What are the experiential sources and metaphors by which working-class women express class consciousness? How do women's constructions of their sexuality relate to issues of class and kinship?

Embedded in these questions, I would suggest, is a definition of the working class in which membership is not determinable on an individual basis, but rather as membership in a community that is dependent upon waged labor, but that is unable to subsist or reproduce by such labor alone. This then is the economic basis of class as a relationship to the means of capitalist production. Following on this, it is not surprising that women of many ethnicities, times, and regions share a broader conception of class struggle than men. In part this results from women's socially assigned responsibility for unwaged domestic labor and their consequent centrality in confrontations with the state over family and community welfare issues (Bookman and Morgen 1988; Hall et al. 1987; Susser 1982; Zavella 1987a). This has led to suggestions that working-class women in general, and women of color in particular, are likely to develop the most radical demands for social change (Giddings 1984; hooks 1984; Kaplan 1982; Kessler-Harris and Sacks 1987).

Many new case studies describe the ways in which women's unwaged work creates community-based and class-based social ties of interdependence that are key to neighborhood and household survival. Many of these build on older understandings that working-class kin networks are important resources for coping with economic adversity (Bott 1957; Young and Willmott 1962). Some show women as central economic and political actors in these kinship networks, and suggest that these networks create and carry parts of what tends to be called working-class culture in European literature (Humphries 1977; Scott and Tilly 1978; Tilly 1981; but see Eisenstein 1983 for an early feminist class analysis in the United States); black culture in Afro-American communities (Day 1982; Gilkes 1980; Jones 1985; Reagon 1986; Stack 1974); Chicana or Latina culture (Zavella 1987a, 1987b); Third World culture (Caulfield 1974); or Southern working-class culture among Southern whites (Hall et al. 1987). Others show the ways in which women use languages and values of kinship to create unity and community in the waged workplace (Lamphere 1984, 1987; Sacks 1988a, 1988b; Westwood 1985).

Although the bulk of these studies focus on the social history of daily life (Westwood 1985; Zavella 1987a), some show the way these ties become the infrastructure of large-scale class protests, whether classic strikes (Cameron 1985; Frankel 1984; Hall et al. 1987; Milkman 1985; Tax 1980) or community-based movements, which make demands on the state for civil rights, housing, health care, education, or welfare (Bookman and Morgen 1988; Kaplan 1982; West 1981). They analyze women's centrality in organizing and sustaining labor unions, civil rights, and community-based movements (Giddings 1984; Gilkes 1980; MacLean 1982; Robinson 1987; Ruiz 1987).

Two "findings" regarding social structure and working-class culture are embedded in this new literature. One is the contributions made by working-class women through household economies and community-based cultures to notions of social justice and entitlement (Acklesberg 1984; Bookman and Morgen 1988). The other is the prevalence of institutions, networks, and cultures that women generate outside family life, in public space in working-class communities (see Zagarell 1988 for an analysis of "novels of community" as a women's literary genre). In short, this literature does more than counter theories of the workplace as the sole source for generating political mobilization around economic issues. It provides the beginnings of a gender-based construction of class that is somewhat attentive to racial/ethnic diversity.

A third set of "findings" about working-class women's conceptions of womanhood is emerging from some very diverse studies that explore long-hidden histories of (mainly) working-class women's challenges to bourgeois ideals of domesticity, femininity, compulsory heterosexuality, motherhood, and reproduction. For example, Emily Martin's (1987) wonderful exploration of how American women understand menstruation, birth, and menopause shows middle-class women tending to accept the dominant, medicalized views of women as ruled by their reproductive organs, while working-class, especially black working-class, women do not see these as ruling events, nor does the medical view of their bodies have much hegemony in their consciousnesses.

In a similar vein, studies of conflicts between Progressive-era reformers' notions of proper domesticity and those of working-class women (Ehrenreich and English 1978; Kessler-Harris 1982) have shown overt and covert resistance to submissive domesticity on the latter's part. They resonate with theoretical suggestions made by Mies (1986) that "housewifization" is historically a relatively new and middle-class-specific organization of women's unwaged labor. Mies argues that the privatization of women's work, and the cult of domesticity surrounding and sustaining it, were and are resisted by working-class women (though not by working-class men, who benefited from these constructions), who struggle to keep their work "socialized," or collectively organized. Bennholdt-Thomsen (1988) illustrates one such form this struggle takes: in the Isthmus of Tehuantepec, Mexico, women sustain a regional marketing and food preparation system with an elaborate division of labor, interdependence among women, and no subordination to men. Similar arguments are implicit in discussions about women's marketing and subsistence production in Africa (Leis 1974; Mbilinyi 1988), and in the economies of taking in boarders, laundry, and so on—widely described for European-American working-class pre–World War II urban neighborhoods, although the power dynamics of gender need to be explored further (Cott and Pleck 1979; Ewen 1985; Kessler-Harris 1982; see also Kessler-Harris and Sacks 1987; Sacks 1984).

We are also beginning to learn some of the ways in which young working-class women, past and present, white and black, have independently appropriated and refashioned some of the conventional images of sexiness to convey the sense of themselves as autonomous, independent, and assertive adult women, and to challenge—often at high risk to themselves—our culture's insistence on submissive femininity for women (Hall 1986; Ladner 1970; Myerowitz 1988; Peiss 1985;

Petchesky 1985; Stansell 1986; Westwood 1985; see also Vance 1984 and Snitow, Stansell, and Thompson 1983). Hall's study, "Disorderly Women," is perhaps the most dramatic discussion of how women used their sexuality as a metaphor of class strength and confrontation, how such use of sexuality was understood in that way by other men and women of their working-class Appalachian community, but how it was seen in conventional "bad women" terms by both employers and outside union representatives.

Just as heterosexuality has been a language of working-class women's resistance to a combined class and gender subordination, so too has lesbian sexual identity and community provided a historically specific tradition of resistance to submissive domesticity. Following Adrienne Rich's (1983) insights on the politics of homophobia and Carol Smith-Rosenberg's work on 19th-century women's worlds of love and ritual (1985), D'Emilio and Freedman (1988), as well as Rapp and Ross (1983), argue that stigmatization of homosexuality (and its complement, celebration of companionate marriages for compulsory heterosexuality), developed about the same time that it became possible for a significant number of women to be able to live on their own earnings, without domestic dependence on men. Davis and Kennedy's (1986) oral history of Buffalo's working-class lesbian community, as well as D'Emilio and Freedman's (1988), Katz's (1976) and D'Emilio's (1983) analyses of the creation of specifically gay and lesbian social identities in the mid-twentieth century show some of these forms of resistance as well as the creation of alternate institutions, roles, and identities.

SUMMARY

As Martha Acklesberg has noted, when "we take seriously the 'relatedness' that seems to characterize the lives of many women," we also challenge "the assumption central to the Marxist paradigm that the development of a truly radical consciousness requires the transcendence, or abandonment, of all sources of community feeling other than class (in particular, those feelings based in racial, ethnic, national, or—we might add—sexual identity).... In fact, rather than acting as a 'drag' on radical consciousness, communities—and the network of relationships that they nurture and on which they are based—have been, and can be, important contexts for politicization" (Acklesberg 1988:306).

This essay has reviewed some of the theoretical consequences of socialist feminist critiques of the political economy of "personal life." Its focus has been on efforts to comprehend class, race, and gender oppression as parts of a unitary system, as opposed to analyses that envision capitalism and patriarchy as separate systems. More specifically, I have interpreted analyses of the relations of waged and unwaged labor, work and family in such a way as to expand the meaning of working class to encompass both waged and unwaged workers who are members of a community that is dependent upon waged labor but that is unable to reproduce itself on those wages alone. The implications of such a reading are fairly radical, and each one requires a great deal of further exploration. First and most apparent, it significantly alters conventional Marxist understandings of class and of contemporary social movements. Second, it does so in such a way as to make visible the centrality of people of color and white working-class women to the direction of world history. Third, for feminist theory, it suggests the fruitfulness of recognizing that women's gender identities are not analytically separable from their racial and class identities. Fourth, class emerges as a relation to the means of production that is collective rather than individual, a relation of communities to the capitalist state more than of employees to employers. Fifth, this embeds a critique of the ideology of liberal individualism, and links it to the shapes of post–World War II resistance to capitalism, which have generated the pluralistic visions behind efforts to develop a unified feminist theory that encompasses race and class as well as gender and sexuality.

Acknowledgments: Ancestors and earlier versions of this paper were presented at the Conference on Family and Production at Duke University in 1985, the American Ethnological Society meetings in 1985, and the Center for the Study of Women's Faculty Research Seminar at UCLA and the Los Angeles Chapter of Sociologists for Women in Society in 1988. I have benefited greatly from discussions at each of these forums. In addition, I would like to thank Sharon Bays, Kathleen Gough, Patricia Gumport, Sondra Hale, Nicky Hart, Louise Lamphere, Carol Lasser, Sandra Morgen, Tom Patterson, Rayna Rapp, and "Red Wednesday" for their supportive critiques as this paper evolved.

References

Acklesberg, Martha. 1984. "Women's Collaborative Activities and City Life: Politics and Policy." In *Political Women: Current Roles in State and Local Government*, J. Flammang, ed, pp.242–259. Beverly Hills, CA: Sage.

———. 1988. "Communities, Resistance, and Women's Activism: Some Implications for a Democratic Polity." In *Women and the Politics of Empowerment*, Bookman and Morgen, eds., pp. 297–313. Philadelphia: Temple University Press.

Anderson, Karen. 1981. *Wartime Women*. Westport, CT: Greenwood.

Aptheker, Bettina. 1982. *Women's Legacy: Essays in Race, Sex and Class in American History*. Amherst: University of Massachusetts Press.

Barkley-Brown, Elsa. 1989. "African-American Women's Quilting: A Framework for Conceptualizing and Teaching African-American Women's History." *Signs* 14(4):921–929.

Beneria, Lourdes, ed. 1982. *Women and Development*. New York: Praeger.

Bennholdt-Thomsen, Veronika. 1981. "Subsistence Production and Extended Reproduction." In *Of Marriage and the Market*, K. Young, C. Wolkowitz, and

R. McCullagh, eds., pp. 16–29. London: CSE Books.

———. 1984. "Towards a Theory of the Sexual Division of Labor." In *Households and the World Economy*, Joan Smith, I. Wallerstein, and H. D. Evers, eds., pp. 252–271. Beverly Hills, CA: Sage.

———. 1988. "Women's Dignity Is the Wealth of Juchitan" (Oax., Mexico). Paper presented at 12th International Congress of Anthropological and Ethnological Sciences, Zagreb, Yugoslavia, July 24–31.

Benson, Susan Porter. 1978. "The Clerking Sisterhood: Rationalization and the Work Culture of Saleswomen." *Radical America* 12:41–55.

———. 1986. *Counter Cultures: Saleswomen, Managers, and Customers in American Department Stores 1890–1940*. Urbana: University of Illinois Press.

Benston, Margaret. 1969. "The Politic Economy of Women's Liberation." *Monthly Review* 21(4):13–27.

Bookman, Ann, and Sandra Morgen, eds. 1988. *Women and the Politics of Empowerment*. Philadelphia: Temple University Press.

Boris, Eileen, and Peter Bardaglio. 1983. "The Transformation of Patriarchy: The Historic Role of the State." In *Families, Politics and Public Policy: A Feminist Dialogue on Women and the State*, I. Diamond and M. L. Shanley, eds., pp. 70–91. New York: Longman.

Bott, Elizabeth. 1957. *Family and Social Network*. London: Tavistock Publications.

Brecher, Jeremy. 1972. *Strike: The True History of Mass Insurgency from 1877 to the Present*. San Francisco: Straight Arrow.

Brenner, Johanna, and Maria Ramas. 1984. "Rethinking Women's Oppression." *New Left Review* 144:33–71.

Cameron, Ardis. 1985. "Bread and Roses Revisited: Women's Culture and Working-Class Activism in the Lawrence Strike of 1912." In *Women, Work and Protest*, Milkman, ed., pp. 42–61. Boston: Routledge and Kegan Paul.

Cantarow, Ellen, and Sharon O'Malley. 1980. "Ella Baker: Organizing for Civil Rights." In *Moving the Mountain: Women Working for Social Change*, Cantarow, ed., pp. 52–93. Old Westbury, NY: Feminist Press.

Carter, Susan B., and Michael Carter. 1981. "Women's Recent Progress in the Professions, or Women Get a Ticket to Ride After the Gravy Train Has Left the Station." *Feminist Studies* 7:477–504.

Caulfield, Mina Davis. 1974. "Imperialism, the Family and Cultures of Resistance." *Socialist Revolution* 20:76–85.

Collins, Patricia Hill. 1989. "The Social Construction of Black Feminist Thought." *Signs* 14(4):745–773.

Cott, Nancy, and Elizabeth Pleck, eds. 1979. *A Heritage of Her Own: Toward a New Social History of American Women*. New York: Simon and Schuster.

Dalla Costa, Mariarosa, and Selma James. 1972. *The Power of Women and the Subversion of the Community*. Montpelier, England: Falling Wall Press.

Davis, Angela Y. 1981. *Women, Race and Class*. New York: Random House.

Davis, Madeline, and Elizabeth L. Kennedy. 1986. "Oral History and the Study of Sexuality in the Lesbian Community: Buffalo, New York, 1940–1960." *Feminist Studies* 12(Spring):7–26.

Day, Kay. 1982. "Kinship in a Changing Economy: A View from the Sea Islands." In *Holding onto the Land and the Lord*, C. Stack and R. Hall, eds. Athens: University of Georgia Press.

D'Emilio, John. 1983. *Sexual Politics, Sexual Communities: The Making of a Homosexual Minority in the United States, 1940–1970*. Chicago: University of Chicago Press.

D'Emilio, John, and Estelle B. Freedman. 1988. *Intimate Matters: A History of*

Sexuality in America. New York: Harper and Row.

Dill, Bonnie Thornton. 1979. "The Dialectics of Black Womanhood." *Signs* 4:543–555.

Dublin, Thomas. 1979. *Women at Work: The Transformation of Class and Community in Lowell, Massachussetts 1826–1860*. New York: Columbia University Press.

Edholm, Felicity, Olivia Harris, and Kate Young. 1977. "Conceptualising Women." *Critique of Anthropology* 3(9–10):101–130.

Ehrenreich, Barbara, and Dierdre English. 1978. *For Her Own Good*. New York: Pantheon.

Eisenstein, Sarah. 1983. *Give Us Bread, but Give Us Roses Too*. Boston: Routledge and Kegan Paul.

Eisenstein, Zillah, ed. 1979. *Capitalist Patriarchy and the Case for Socialist Feminism*. New York: Monthly Review Press.

Evans, Sara. 1980. *Personal Politics: The Roots of Women's Liberation in the Civil Rights Movement*. New York: Random House.

Ewen, Elizabeth. 1985. *Immigrant Women in the Land of Dollars*. New York: Monthly Review Press.

Feldberg, Roslyn, and Evelyn Nakano Glenn. 1983. "Technology and Work Degradation: Effects of Office Automation on Women Clerical Workers." In *Machina ex Dea: Feminist Perspectives on Technology*, J. Rothschild, ed., pp. 59–78. New York: Pergamon.

Frankel, Linda. 1984. "Southern Textile Women: Generations of Struggle and Survival." In *My Troubles Are Going to Have Trouble with Me*. Sacks and Remy, eds., pp. 39–60. New Brunswick, NJ: Rutgers University Press.

Giddings, Paula. 1984. *When and Where I Enter*. New York: Bantam.

Gilkes, Cheryl. 1980. "'Holding Back the Ocean with a Broom:' Black Women and Community Work." In *The Black Woman*, LaFrances Rodgers-Rose, ed., pp. 217–231. Beverly Hills, CA: Sage.

———. 1988. "Building in Many Places: Multiple Commitments and Ideologies in Black Women's Community Work." In *Women and the Politics of Empowerment. Bookman and Morgen*, eds., pp. 53–76. Philadelphia: Temple University Press.

Glenn, Evelyn Nakano. 1985. "Racial Ethnic Women's Labor: The Intersection of Race, Gender and Class Oppression." *Review of Radical Political Economics* 17(3):86–108.

———. 1986. *Issei, Nissei, War Bride: Three Generations of Japanese American Women in Domestic Service*. Philadelphia: Temple University Press.

Glenn, Evelyn Nakano, and Roslyn Feldberg. 1977. "Degraded and Deskilled: The Proletananization of Clerical Work." *Social Problems* 25(1):52–64.

Gluck, Sherna B. 1987. *Rosie the Riveter Revisited: Women, the War, and Social Change*. Boston: Twayne Publishers.

Goldberg, Roberta. 1983. *Organizing Women Office Workers: Dissatisfaction, Consciousness and Action*. New York: Praeger.

Hacker, Sally. 1982. "Sex Stratification, Technology and Organizational Change: A Longitudinal Case Study of AT&T." In *Women and Work*, R. Kahn-Hut, A. Daniels, and R. Colvard, eds., pp. 248–266. New York: Oxford University Press.

Hall, Jacqueline D. 1986. "Disorderly Women: Gender and Labor Militancy in the Appalachian South." *Journal of American History* 73(2):354–382.

Hall, Jacqueline D., J. Leloudis, R. Korstad, M. Murphy, L. Jones, and C. Daly. 1987. *Like a Family: The Making of a Southern Mill World*. Chapel Hill: University of North Carolina Press.

Hansen, Karen T. 1989. *Distant Companions: Servants and Employers in Zambia, 1900–1985.* Ithaca, NY: Cornell University Press.

Hartmann, Heidi I. 1976. "Capitalism, Patriarchy and Job Segregation by Sex." *Signs* 1(1)pt. 2:137–170.

hooks, bell. 1984. *Feminist Theory from Margin to Center.* Boston: South End Press.

Homphoes, Jane. 1977. "Class Struggle and the Persistence of the Working Class Family." *Cambridge Journal of Economics* 1:241–248.

Jaggar, Alison. 1983. *Feminist Politics and Human Nature.* Sussex: Rowman and Allenheld.

Jones, Jacqueline. 1985. *Labor of Love, Labor of Sorrow.* New York: Basic Books.

Kaplan, Temma. 1982. "Female Consciousness and Collective Action: The Case of Barcelona, 1910–1918." *Signs* 7(3):545–567.

Katz, Jonathan, ed. 1976. *Gay American History: Lesbians and Gay Men in the U.S.A.* New York: Thomas Crowell.

Katzman, David. 1978. *Seven Days a Week: Women and Domestic Service in Industrializing America.* New York: Oxford University Press.

Kessler-Harris, Alice. 1982. *Out to Work.* New York: Oxford University Press.

Kessler-Harris, Alice, and Karen Brodkin Sacks. 1987. "The Demise of Domesticity." In *Women, Households and the Economy*, L. Beneria and C. Stimpson, eds., pp. 65–84. New Brunswick, NJ: Rutgers University Press.

King, Deborah. 1988. "Multiple Jeopardy, Multiple Consciousness: The Context of a Black Feminist Ideology." *Signs* 14(1) 42–72.

Ladner, Joyce. 1970. *Tomorrow's Tomorrow.* New York: Doubleday Anchor.

Lamphere, Louise. 1984. "On the Shop Floor: Multi-Ethnic Unity against the Conglomerate." In *My Troubles Are Going to Have Trouble with Me*, K. Sacks and D. Remy, eds., pp. 247–263. New Brunswick, NJ: Rutgers University Press.

———. 1987. *From Working Daughters to Working Mothers: Immigrant Women in a New England Industrial Community.* Ithaca, NY: Cornell University Press.

Leis, Nancy. 1974. "Women in Groups. Ijaw Women's Associations." In *Woman, Culture and Society*, M. Rosaldo and L. Lamphere, eds., pp. 223–242. Stanford, CA: Stanford University Press.

Machung, Anne. 1984. "Word Processing: Forward for Business, Backward for Women." In *My Troubles Are Going to Have Trouble with Me*, K. Sacks and D. Remy, eds., pp. 124–139. New Brunswick, NJ: Rutgers University Press.

MacLean, Nancy. 1982. "The Culture of Resistance: Female Institution-Building in the Ladies Garment Workers' Union 1905–1925." *Occasional Papers in Women's Studies*, University of Michigan.

Mainardi, Pat. 1970. "The Politics of Housework." In *Sisterhood Is Powerful*, R. Morgan, ed., pp. 447–454. New York: Random House.

Martin, Emily. 1987. *The Woman in the Body.* Boston: Beacon.

Mbilinyi, Marjorie. 1988. "Runaway Wives in Colonial Tanganyika: Forced Labour and Forced Marriage in Rungwe District 1919–1961." *International Journal of the Sociology of Law* 16:1–29.

Meillassoux, Claude. 1981. *Maidens, Meal and Money: Capitalism and the Domestic Community.* Cambridge: Cambridge University Press.

Mies, Maria. 1986. *Patriarchy and Accumulation on a World Scale: Women and the International Division of Labour.* London: Zed Books.

Milkman, Ruth, ed. 1985. *Women, Work and Protest.* Boston: Routledge and Kegan Paul.

————. 1987. *Gender at Work: The Dynamics of Job Segregation by Sex During World War II.* Urbana: University of Illinois Press.

Mitchell, Juliet. 1966. "Women—The Longest Revolution." *New Left Review* 40:11–37.

————. 1971. *Woman's Estate.* Baltimore: Penguin Books.

Myerowitz, Joanne J. 1988. *Women Adrift: Independent Wage Earners in Chicago, 1880–1930.* Chicago: Chicago University Press.

Nash, June, and Maria Patricia Fernandez-Kelly, eds. 1983. *Women, Men and the International Division of Labor.* Albany: SUNY Press.

Ong, Aihwa. 1983. "Global Industries and Malay Peasants in Peninsular Malaysia." In *Women, Men and the International Division of Labor*, Nash and Fernandez-Kelly, eds., pp. 426–439. Albany: SUNY Press.

Palmer, Phyllis M. 1983. "White Women/Black Women: The Dualism of Female Identity and Experience in the United States." *Feminist Studies* 9:151–170.

————. 1984. "Housework and Domestic Labor: Racial and Technological Change." In *My Troubles Are Going to Have Trouble with Me*. K. Sacks and D. Remy, eds., pp. 80–94. New Brunswick, NJ: Rutgers University Press.

Peiss, Kathy. 1985. *Cheap Amusements: Working Women and Leisure in Turn-of-the-Century New York.* Philadelphia: Temple University Press.

Petchesky, Rosalind P. 1985. *Abortion and Woman's Choice.* Boston: Northeastern University Press.

Rapp, Rayna. 1978. "Family and Class in Contemporary America: Notes Toward an Understanding of Ideology." *Science and Society* 42(3):278–300.

Rapp, Rayna, and Ellen Ross. 1983. "The Twenties' Backlash: Compulsory Heterosexuality, the Consumer Family and the Waning of Feminism." In *Class, Race and Sex*, A. Swerdlow and H. Lessinger, eds., pp. 93–107. Boston: G. K. Hall.

Reagon, Bernice Johnson. 1986. "African Diaspora Women: The Making of Cultural Workers." *Feminist Studies* 12(1):77–90.

Remy, Dorothy, and Larry Sawers. 1984. "Economic Stagnation and Discrimination." In *My Troubles Are Going to Have Troubles with Me*, K. Sacks and D. Remy, eds., pp. 95–112. New Brunswick, NJ: Rutgers University Press.

Rich, Adrienne. 1983. "Compulsory Heterosexuality and Lesbian Existence." In *Powers of Desire: The Politics of Sexuality*, Snitow, Stansell, and Thompson, eds., pp. 177–205. New York: Monthly Review Press.

Robinson, Jo Ann Gibson. 1987. *The Montgomery Bus Boycott and the Women Who Started It.* David J. Garrow, ed. Knoxville: University of Tennessee Press.

Rollins, Judith. 1985. *Between Women.* Philadelphia: Temple University Press.

Romero, Mary. 1987. "Domestic Service in the Transition from Rural to Urban Life: The Case of La Chicana." *Women's Studies* 13(3):199–222. (Special issue, "As the World Turns," K. B. Sacks and N. Scheper-Hughes, eds.)

Ruiz, Vicki L. 1987. *Cannery Women Cannery Lives: Mexican Women, Unionization and the California Food Processing Industry, 1930–1950.* Albuquerque: University of New Mexico Press.

Sacks, Karen Brodkin. 1974. "Engels Revisited." In *Woman, Culture, and Society*, M. Rosaldo and L. Lamphere, eds., pp. 207–222. Stanford, CA: Stanford University Press.

————. 1979. *Sisters and Wives.* Westport, CT: Greenwood Press.

————. 1984. "Generations of Working Class Families." In *My Troubles Are Going to Have Trouble with Me*, K. Sacks and D. Remy, eds., New Brunswick,

NJ: Rutgers University Press.

———. 1988a. *Caring by the Hour.* Urbana: University of Illinois Press.

———. 1988b. "Gender and Grassroots Leadership." In *Women and the Politics of Empowerment*, Bookman and Morgen, eds., pp. 77–96. Philadelphia: Temple University Press.

Sargent, Lydia, ed. 1981. *Women and Revolution: A Discussion of the Unhappy Marriage of Marxism and Feminism.* Boston: South End Press.

Scott, Joan W., and Louise Tilly. 1978. *Women, Work and Family.* New York: Holt, Rinehart and Winston.

Smith-Rosenberg, Carol. 1985. "The Female World of Love and Ritual: Relations Between Women in Nineteenth-Century America." Reprinted in *Disorderly Conduct: Visions of Gender in Victorian America*, Carol Smith-Rosenberg. New York: Oxford University Press.

Snitow, Ann, Christine Stansell, and Sharon Thompson, eds. 1983. *Powers of Desire: The Politics of Sexuality.* New York: Monthly Review Press.

Stack, Carol. 1974. *All Our Kin.* New York: Harper Colophon.

Stansell, Christine. 1986. *City of Women: Sex and Class in New York, 1789–1860.* New York: Knopf.

Stolcke, Verena. 1981. "Women's Labours: The Naturalisation of Social Inequality and Women's Subordination." In *Of Marriage and the Market*, K. Young, C. Wolkowitz, and R. McCullagh, eds., pp. 30–48. London: CSE Books.

Susser, Ida. 1982. *Norman Street.* New York: Oxford University Press.

Tax, Meredith. 1980. *The Rising of the Women: Feminist Solidarity and Class Conflict 1880–1917.* New York: Monthly Review Press.

Tilly, Louise A. 1981. "Paths of Proletarianization: Organization of Production, Sexual Division of Labor, and Women's Collective Action." *Signs* 7(2):400–417.

Vance, Carol. 1984. *Pleasure and Danger.* Boston: Routledge and Kegan Paul.

Vogel, Lise. 1983. *Marxism and the Oppression of Women: Toward a Unitary Theory.* New Brunswick, NJ: Rutgers University Press.

West, Guida. 1981. *The National Welfare Rights Movement: The Social Protest of Poor Women.* New York: Praeger.

Westwood, Sallie. 1985. *All Day Every Day.* Urbana: University of Illinois Press.

Wolfe, George C. 1988. *The Colonization of American Culture, or, One playwright(of color)'s not-so-humble opinion.* Performing Arts Westwood Playhouse, Los Angeles.

Young, Michael, and Peter Willmott. 1962. *Family and Kinship in East London.* Baltimore: Penguin Books.

Zagarell, Sandra. 1988. "The Narrative of Community: The Identification of a Genre." *Signs* 13(3):498–527.

Zavella, Patricia. 1987a. "'Abnormal Intimacy': The Varying Work Networks of Chicana Cannery Workers." *Feminist Studies* 11(3):541–558.

———. 1987b. *Women's Work and Chicano Families: Cannery Workers of the Santa Clara Valley.* Ithaca, NY: Cornell University Press.

11

Social Science Theorizing for Latino Families in the Age of Diversity

Maxine Baca Zinn

In the last two decades of the 20th century, the United States has once again become a nation of immigrants. This population transition is taking place in a historical context that has included the restructuring of the U.S. economy and the advent of a more conservative political climate. Immense changes in American life, together with a great influx of people from around the world, have created a nation of diversity.

The flux of these changes has a special bearing on families. In a highly charged intellectual climate, social critics lamenting the state of the family often assert that the emerging array of alternatives weakens and undermines society (Briemelow, 1992; Popenoe, 1988; Whitehead, 1993). Diverse family arrangements now place a special spotlight on racial/ethnics[1] and non-European immigrants (Fukuyama, 1993). As minorities become an ever larger share of the U.S. population, the ability to understand the new social diversity will become a central task within family studies.

Latinos are at the epicenter of several transformations that are changing our conceptions of the family. This chapter addresses some pressing theoretical issues for studying Latino families in light of the demographic shift from an Anglo-European society to a multiracial, multicultural society. Although research of the past two decades has disputed many distortions of the past, the social and political changes now sweeping the country pose new intellectual challenges. Current social changes require renewed efforts to dislodge dominant thinking about Latino families.

This chapter identifies ongoing currents in social science thinking about Latino families. The following questions are posed:

1. What social science themes in family studies have shaped our visions?
2. To what extent has the re-visioning of the Latino family during the past two decades touched the mainstream of family studies?
3. Why are certain troublesome themes about Latinos and other racial/ethnic families resurfacing today?
4. How can we avoid the pitfalls of earlier theories in understanding various Hispanic groups?
5. What further changes does the ongoing re-construction of Latino families face?
6. How can we apply our new knowledge about Latinos and other racial/ethnics where it belongs—at the core of family theory?

CONVENTIONAL SOCIAL SCIENCE FRAMEWORKS

The formal academic study of Latino families in the United States originated in the context of immigration and social problems. Much of our thinking about Latino families today is muddled by concepts and ideas that emerged during the late nineteenth and early twentieth centuries. During this time, sociologists concluded that Mexican immigration, settlement, and poverty created problems in developing U.S. urban centers. The new field of "family study" emerged out of a deep, fundamental belief in the need to document and ameliorate social problems (Thomas & Wilcox, 1987). The field of family studies has a tradition of being heavily normative, moralistic, and mingled with social policy and the social objectives of various action groups. Furthermore, it lacks a strong tradition of theory (Morgan, 1975).

The underlying assumptions in mainstream family scholarship produced a deeply flawed framework that misrepresented the family experiences of Latinos and other racial/ethnics by using a dominant family form as the normative experience for all. This framework was fused with and embedded in prevailing theories of race relations. Both fields were strongly influenced by the Chicago School of Sociology. The dominant paradigms of assimilation and modernization guided and shaped research. Race relations' preoccupation with "traditional" and "modern" forms of social organization joined family sociology's preoccupation with the nuclear family, its wage-earner father and domestic-earner mother. This explained the different family arrangements of Latinos and other immigrants. Compared to mainstream families, they were analyzed as traditional *cultural forms.* Studies of Mexican immigrants highlighted certain *ethnic lifestyles* that were said to produce social disorganization. Structural conditions were rarely a concern. Instead, researchers examined (a) their foreign patterns and habits, (b) the moral quality of their family relationships, and (c) the prospects for their Americanization (Bogardus, 1934).

As transplants from traditional societies, the immigrants and their children were thought to be at odds with social requirements in new industrial settings. Their family arrangements were treated as cultural exceptions to the rule of standard family development. Their slowness to acculturate and take on Western patterns of family development left them behind, as other families in American society modernized. They were peripheral to the standard family model and viewed as problems because of their failure to adopt the family patterns of the mainstream (Baca Zinn, 1990). Social reforms of the times favored the "modern" family (nuclear in form, with women in the home), as a way of combating social problems. (Even today, conservatives uphold this family ideal.)

In family studies, the twin pillars of modernization and assimilation influenced the main currents of thought and types of preoccupations through the 1950s, when functionalist theories came to prevail. Using a framework that took one type of family (by no means the only form, even then) and making it "the normal family" (Boss & Thorne, 1989), functionalism intensified the social science misinterpretation of Latino families. With its emphasis on fixed boundaries and a fixed division of labor, this normal family type presented a stark contrast with the familistic and traditional Mexican family of anthropological research (Heller, 1966; Madsen, 1964; Rubel, 1966).

RETHINKING LATINO FAMILIES

An extensive body of revisionist scholarship has reshaped our thinking about Latino families. The new research developed with two major objectives. The first was reinterpreting Mexican-origin family life by uncovering new information about the history of these people and by analyzing their experiences with an "insider's" perspective. The second, an outgrowth of the first, has involved correcting social science generalizations about Latino families and ultimately about various aspects of family life in general.

Beginning with a critique of functionalist accounts of Mexican-heritage families as dysfunctional units that acted as barriers to individual and group mobility (Heller, 1966; Madsen, 1964; Rubel, 1966; Staples & Mirandé, 1980), scholars produced studies showing that alternative family patterns do not reflect deviance, deficiency, or disorganization. Instead of representing outmoded cultural forms handed down from generation to generation, Mexican family lifestyles often reflect adaptive responses to social and economic conditions. What were once labeled culturally deficient family patterns may now be viewed as family strategies that serve as solutions to constraints imposed by economic and social structures in the wider society.

Although the long-standing interest in cultural patterning in family life continues alongside a "social adaptation" approach, greater attention is now given to the social situations and contexts that affect Latino families (Vega, 1990). Structural approaches explore the close connections between the internal dynamics of family life and external conditions, such as changing labor markets and political systems. In the 1980s the frameworks shifted

> from a stereotypic model of family life, characterized by rigidity, authoritarianism, and a patriarchal structure, to a social adaptation perspective based on themes of family metamorphoses, resilience, flexibility, and cohesion in the face of changing social environments and economic circumstances. (Berardo, 1991, p. 6)

CONNECTING THE NEW BODY OF RESEARCH ON LATINO FAMILIES WITH OTHER REVISIONIST TRADITIONS

Latino family studies should be recognized as a vital thread in the overall family re-visioning effort because the field has developed within and alongside other emergent social science discourses. Social history, feminism, and race and ethnic studies have offered unique challenges to past traditions of family thought. All together, these bodies of scholarship have produced new descriptions of family dynamics and identified new topics for investigation. Central to all of the scholarship is the strategy of "moving beneath and around the family as a unit of analysis" (Thorne, 1992, p. 12). Like other revisionist strands, this strategy has generated a proliferation of studies showing that Latino families are shaped by social and economic forces of particular times and particular places. As Zavella (1991) puts it, "household arrangements originate in the transition of larger social forces" (p. 318). This has produced a notable shift from earlier preoccupations with culture to the contemporary investigation of families and their encompassing social conditions.

The following themes capture some of the most important thinking in revisionist family scholarship and its infusion in Latino family studies.

1. *Conventional social science frameworks have falsely universalized the family.* What has long been upheld as normal was, in fact, only one of many family forms produced by uneven social and economic patterns of development occurring in society. Although long defined as the rule, the standard family was never the norm nor the dominant family type. It was, however, the measure against which other families were judged (Baca Zinn & Eitzen, 1993).

2. *Families are socially constructed.* This means that they are not merely biological arrangements; nor are they the products of ethnic culture alone. Instead, families are shaped by specific historical, social, and material conditions. In challenging the assumption that minority family arrangements are merely the result of cultural or ethnic variations, researchers have discovered that many Latino family patterns are distinctive because their social settings produce and may even require diverse arrangements.

3. *Families are closely connected with other structures and institutions in society.* Rather than being separate spheres, they cannot be understood in isolation from outside structures. This has directed attention to basic social divisions and structures of power. Whereas the importance of economic factors in making a living and hence shaping family life has long been acknowledged in family research, other structural forces have been invisible. Along with social class, gender and race are structured inequalities producing widely varying experiences

of family life (Thorne, 1992).

4. *Gender is a basic organizing principle of society that shapes families in historically specific ways.* Making gender a basic category of analysis has profoundly altered family studies in general, and it has advanced research on Latino families as well. Latino family research has long been preoccupied with women's and men's differentiated family experiences. No assumption about Latino families is more deeply ingrained than that of male dominance. But cultural frameworks explained male dominance as traditional patriarchy; that is, an ethnic or machismo family dynamic. Although gender inequality remains an important theme, two developments have provided new explanations of male dominance. The first wave of studies conducted in the 1970s and 1980s challenged the distorted descriptions of macho-dominated Mexican-origin families (Baca Zinn, 1980; Ybarra, 1982). Often referred to as the "revisionist works" (Zavella, 1987), these studies found that Mexican American families exhibited many different patterns of marital decision making, including a patriarchal, role-segregated pattern and egalitarian patterns, with many combinations in between. In that early period, our engagement with questions about gender in Chicano families was very different from later approaches; nevertheless, the questions we engaged were feminist.

The second wave of feminist research on Latino families was strongly influenced by the shift from the study of *sex roles* to the study of *gendered institutions* (Acker, 1992). This line of analysis has led Latina feminists, in dialogue with other branches of feminist thinking, to investigate how women's family lives are bound up with a broader system of gender inequality. Latinas' subordination, like that of other women, is rooted in the "pervasive social ordering of human activities, practices, and social structures in terms of differentiation between women and men" (Acker, 1992, p. 567). In conjunction with class and race inequalities, this ubiquitous gender order produces Latino family arrangements that constrain women in particular ways. Zavella's (1991) study of Chicano families is exemplary in its exploration of the close connections between women's family lives and economic conditions as they are bound up with a broader system of inequality. Others, too, have offered new insights about how specific structural inequalities make the family experiences of Latinas and Latinos different from other women and men. From motherhood (Segura & Pierce, 1993) to household decision making (Pesquera, 1993) to migration (Hondagneu-Sotelo, 1992), gender inequalities intersect with race, ethnicity, and social class to shape family life.

5. *Racial stratification is a powerful shaper of family life.* Like the class and gender hierarchies, racial stratification is a fundamental organizing principle of social relationships in U.S. society (Omi & Winant, 1986). Although social science has tended to treat race as fixed, we now have a better understanding of how racial categories change over time. New patterns of immigration are making the end of the twentieth cen-

tury a period in which our conceptions of racial categories are being dramatically transformed. Omi and Winant (1986) call this "racial formation," meaning that society assigns different worth and unequal treatment to groups on the basis of its definition of race. Racial formation touches people throughout society, not just those who are subordinated. This racial formation perspective offers important insights and challenging avenues for studying Latino families, because Latinos are not simply an ethnic group but an integral component within the U.S. racial hierarchy. Racial inequalities place families in different social locations, giving some greater access to resources and rewards and denying or limiting access to these same conditions for others.

I have pushed for a reconstruction of family theory through incorporating race as a dimension of social structure rather than merely an expression of cultural differences (Baca Zinn, 1990, 1994). Several formidable problems remain in applying this perspective to Latinos. In conventional thought and even in much social science, race is treated as if it were the property only of African Americans, or of African Americans and Whites. This biracial or dichotomous thinking (Collins, 1990) is one of the reasons for the long-standing invisibility of Latinos in social science. Bonilla (1990, p. 215) has called this "The American Dilemma of Latinos." In Gunnar Myrdal's classic on the sociology of race, *An American Dilemma*, Bonilla found practically no references to Latinos. The four decades following publication of that classic have continued to see Latinos left out of the race relations analysis.

The perspective of Latinos as an ethnic group—simply another variant of standard ethnic immigrants—has long held sway in mainstream sociology. Despite the fact that "the single biggest change facing the United States is the increasing racial and ethnic diversity of its population" (Landry, 1991, p. 206), public discussions about "the new politics of race" (as well as the pervasive images in mainstream family theory) remain couched in images of Black and White.

To be sure, mainstream scholarship on race and ethnicity acknowledges that Latinos are structurally denied those opportunities that are available to White people. In other words, scholars know that Latinos fare poorly in the social order, that dramatic shifts in the population will render Latinos the largest minority in only half a decade, and that these trends portend new forms of social inequality and ethnic conflict.

Federal data sources classify Latinos as an ethnic category, not a race. However, classifying information by "race and Hispanic-origin" does not help us think about Latinos as being situated in a changing racial hierarchy. The U.S. Bureau of the Census has recently acknowledged the limitations of a White/non-White division and the need to move beyond this division. The current system of classifying information on Hispanics is in need of reassessment and refinement in order to more accurately reflect a diverse society (Lott, 1993). Current shifts in the composition of the U.S. population are producing a multiracial society that bears little resemblance to the way things once were. Race is not just about tensions, conflicts, and negotiations between Black and White; rather, racial politics entail further hierarchies of domination and subordination.

Applying the racial formation perspective to Latinos is complicated. Latinos are "racially heterogeneous populations made up of a variety of racial ancestries: Europeans, Africans, Amerindians, Asians, and various mixtures thereof" (Massey, 1993, p. 8). Latinos do not possess a single unifying racial identity. Nevertheless, they are distinguished as a social category and dominated within a racial hierarchy. This last point is important because the crucial aspect of any racial category is that the distinguishing characteristics are *socially* defined.

The racial order works with and through the class system to determine opportunities for making a living, and hence for family well-being. Of course, we cannot speak of Latino families as a universal category. Not only do Latinos represent a diverse collection of national origin groups, they occupy many social statuses. Latinos are divided along the same lines that divide all families. Race, class, gender, nationality, and sexual orientation intersect with each other to produce a variety of Latino family experiences. Still, within these hierarchies, most Latinos are forced to acquire their life necessities in locations that are far removed from society's opportunity structures. One of the most important ways racial stratification penetrates and shapes households is in determining the kind of work people do and the wages they receive. Racialized economic contexts have created similar opportunities for people of color. Composite portraits of people of color show them to have family configurations that differ from those of White Americans. Although each group is distinguishable from the others, Latinos, African Americans, and Asians share some important commonalities (Glenn & Yap, 1993). These include an extended kinship structure and informal support networks spread across multiple households.

How Re-visioning Traditions Can Enlarge Family Studies

Using macrostructural inequalities to contextualize family life has given us new understanding of why Latino families exhibit distinctive configurations. We know that race, class, and gender inequalities create varied patterns in the way families and individuals are located and embedded in different social environments. Those environments structure social opportunities differently, and they position groups in systematic ways. Such findings and insights are not limited to Latino families. Instead the family experiences of Latinos and other racial/ethnics require a rethinking of family life in general.

Stratifying forces in U.S. society structure family life in fundamentally different ways. Today we have the analytic frameworks to reshape the basic assumptions and concepts of family studies by showing how all families are affected by interconnected systems of social inequality. The family that mainstream social science has upheld as standard is no less a product of social structure and culture; it emerged as a result of social and economic conditions that are no longer operative for most Americans and that never were operative for many poor Americans and racial/ethnics. From the original settlement of the American colonies through the mid-twentieth century, families of European descent often received economic and social supports to establish and maintain families (Dill, Baca Zinn, & Patton, 1993).

Rather than being an expression of group-specific differences alone, family diversity in the United States is an outgrowth of distinctive patterns in the way families and their members are embedded in environments with varying opportunities, resources, and rewards. (The following is adapted from Baca Zinn & Eitzen, 1993.) These differences have enormous effects on the quality of marital relations, on the size of families, on lifestyles and life chances. Social locations, not cultural differences, are the key to understanding family differences. Favored positions in the racial and class hierarchies offer advantages and supports that are unavailable to those in less favorable social locations. Although the structures of race, class, and gender create disadvantages for some, they provide unacknowledged benefits for those who are at the top of their hierarchies—non-Hispanic Whites, members of the upper classes, and males. In addition, the availability of privilege for those at the top of their hierarchy is dependent on those at the bottom. This approach decenters and problematizes advantaged families rather than treating them as the norm.

Establishing a critical perspective in which systems of race, class, and gender differently shape families will make other contributions to family theory. For example, an important theme within several bodies of revisionist scholarship is that women and men create meaningful lives for themselves and their families. Despite severe structural constraints, they forge strategies that help them survive, resist, and cope. The study of Latinos offers fertile ground to explore not only *pathogenic* but *salutogenic* responses (Portes & Rumbaut, 1990, p. 144) of individuals and their families to limited opportunities. This is not meant to create mythical images of family life among subordinated peoples. Poor immigrant and racial minority families were and are found in contradictory settings of conflict as well as survival.

Excluding Latinos and other racial/ethnics from the mainstream of society has important consequences for family theory. Ultimately, such exclusion prevents a full understanding of the relationship between family and society. The failure to make racial/ethnic families a vital building block of family theory will cost the field the ability to provide a broad and comprehensive analysis of family life and social organization. It will render family theory incomplete and incorrect.

THE DANGERS OF A CONVENTIONAL DIVERSITY MODEL

Although these revisions offer family studies several transformative directions, we should not anticipate an imminent mainstreaming of the new themes within family studies. Two developments could severely forestall the intellectual contributions produced by revisionist studies of Latino families. The first is the marginalization of racial/ethnic families. The second is the increase of new immigration within a historical context that includes the restructuring of the U.S. economy and the advent of a more conservative political climate characterized by growing immigrant backlash.

Intellectual Marginalization

Family scholars now routinely note the importance of diversity: of race, class, gender, and other differences in family study. Although the field of family studies is expanding to include a discussion of various kinds of difference, such differences do not inform the core of thinking about family dynamics in general. Like the earlier ghettoization of gender studies in the discipline of sociology (Stacey & Thorne, 1985), the study of family diversity remains contained within a "cultural diversity" category. Of course, most mainstream perspectives have dropped the cultural deviant perspective. However, they still treat family diversity as if it were the intrinsic property of groups that are "different" rather than as the product of forces that affect all families but in varying ways.

Instead of asking how cross-cutting systems of structural inequality shape families differently, most explanatory frameworks treat difference culturally, just as they did seventy-five years ago. Family studies research remains remarkably unstructural in theorizing family diversity. By stripping diversity from the social and political contexts shaping all families, cultural diversity has come to mean "others." Fundamentally, mainstream family thought has failed to transcend the cultural legacy of the past. Until it does, the intellectual revisioning of the past two decades will relegate Latinos and other racial/ethnic families to the rubric of special interest topics.

The Demographic Transformation

An intellectual climate that marginalizes racial/ethnic families breeds a far more dangerous possibility. Current demographic upheavals pose the risk that mainstream family thinking will fall back on the false analytic strategies of earlier generations.

There are striking parallels between the current turn-of-the-century transitions and the changes that swept the world in the late eighteenth century, when conventional thinking about families took hold (Baca Zinn & Eitzen, 1993). The social science produced then was rooted in structural transformations that are once again sweeping the world: massive immigration, political and economic systems in flux, political unrest, ethnic and racial solidarity and strife, and restorative and transformative social movements (Baca Zinn & Eitzen, 1993).

As population shifts produce a new demographic profile and U.S. institutions seem more and more unsettled, many family scholars regard family diversity with renewed anxiety (Popenoe, 1988; Whitehead, 1993). Conservative rhetoric is fueling a growing social and ideological cleavage between traditional family forms and the emerging alternatives (Gerson, 1991). This polarized climate threatens many of the advances produced by revisionist scholarship. Whereas the rhetoric of "family values" was at one time a conservative theme that blamed social decay on bad people doing bad things, that theme has now entered the political mainstream. Even President Clinton has recently echoed the conservative claim that the breakup of the two-parent family is a primary source of social disarray.

As racial and ethnic minorities become an ever larger share of the United States population, and forge their family lives within widely varying settings of structured opportunity, the themes of family diversity and family values will surely escalate. We must rigorously oppose all thinking that measures family difference against a false universal standard. Immigration is undoubtedly creating alternative family patterns. However, we must not allow mainstream family thinking to dredge up cultural reductionist theories in which immigrant families are made the scapegoats for society's problems. Even well-meaning pleas for "culturally sensitive" approaches to the study of minority and immigrant families can be problematic because they unwittingly keep the family ensnared in a normative model. The great challenge facing us now is to press for greater understanding of family diversity, not in group-specific terms, but as part of a socially constructed system. The demographic transformation now occurring in the United States poses new opportunities for us to move beyond the hollow theories of the past and toward a richer understanding of family life.

NOTE

1. The term *racial/ethnic* refers to groups that are socially and legally subordinated and remain culturally distinct within U.S. society. It is meant to include: (a) the systematic discrimination of socially constructed racial groups, and (b) their distinctive cultural arrangements. Historically, the categories of African American, Latino, Asian American, and Native American were constructed as both racially and culturally distinct. Each group has a common culture and shares a common heritage within a larger society that subordinates them. The racial characteristics of these groups have become meaningful within a society that continues to change (Baca Zinn & Dill, 1994).

REFERENCES

Acker, J. (1992). Gendered institutions: From sex roles to gendered institutions. *Contemporary Sociology* 21, 565–69.

Baca Zinn, M. (1980). Employment and education of Mexican American women: The interplay of modernity and ethnicity in eight families. *Harvard Educational Review* 50, 47–62.

———. (1990). Family, feminism, and race in America. *Gender and Society.* 4(1), 68–82.

Baca Zinn, M., & Dill, B. T. (1994). Difference and domination. In M. Baca Zinn & B. T. Dill (eds.), *Women of color in U.S. society* (pp. 3–12). Philadelphia: Temple University Press.

Baca Zinn, M., & Eitzen, D. S. (1993). *Diversity in families.* New York: HarperCollins College Publishers.

Berardo, F. M. (1991). Family research in the 1980s: Recent trends and future directions. In A. Booth (ed.), *Contemporary families: Looking forward, looking back* (pp. 1–11). Minneapolis, MN: National Council on Family Relations.

Bogardus, A. (1934). *The Mexican in the United States.* Los Angeles: University of Southern California Press.

Bonilla, F. (1990). Poverty and inequality in the 1990s. In H. D. Romo (ed.), *Latinos and Blacks in the cities* (pp. 213–19). Austin: University of Texas Press.

Boss, P., & Thorne, B. (1989). Family sociology and family therapy. In M. McGoldrick, C. M. Anderson, & F. Walsh (eds.), *Women in families* (pp. 78–96). New York: W. W. Norton.

Briemelow, P. (1992). Time to rethink immigration. *National Review*, June 22, pp. 30–46.

Collins, P. H. (1990). *Black feminist thought: Knowledge, consciousness, and the politics of empowerment.* Boston: Unwin Hyman.

Dill, B. T., Baca Zinn, M., & Patton, S. (1993). Feminism, race, and the politics of family values. *Philosophy and Public Policy* 13(3), 13–18.

Fukuyama, F. (1993). Immigrants and family values. *Commentary*, May, pp. 26–32.

Gerson, K. (1991). Coping with commitment: Dilemmas and conflicts of family life. In A. Wolfe (ed.), *In America at century's end* (pp. 35–57). Berkeley: University of California Press.

Glenn, E. N., & Yap, S. H. (1993). Chinese American families. In R. L. Taylor (ed.), *Minority families in the United States: Comparative perspectives* (pp. 115–45). Englewood Cliffs, NJ: Prentice Hall.

Heller, C. (1996). *Mexican-American youth: Forgotten youth at the crossroads.* New York: Random House.

Hondagneu-Sotelo, P. (1992). Overcoming patriarchal constraints: The reconstruction of gender relations among Mexican immigrant women and men. *Gender & Society* 6(3), 393–415.

Landry, B. (1991). The enduring dilemma of race in America. In A. Wolfe (ed.), *America at century's end* (pp. 185–207). Berkeley: University of California Press.

Lott, J. T. (1993). Do United States racial/ethnic categories still fit? *Population Today* 21(1), 6–9.

Madsen, W. (1964). *The Mexican-Americans of South Texas.* New York: Holt, Rinehart & Winston.

Massey, D. S. (1993). Latino poverty research: An agenda for the 1990s, *Items* (Social Science Research Council Newsletter) 47(1), 7–11.

Morgan, D. H. (1975). *Social theory and the family.* London: Routledge & Kegan Paul.

Omi, M., & Winant, H. (1986). *Racial formation in the United States.* London: Routledge & Kegan Paul.

Pesquera, B. M. (1993). In the beginning he wouldn't even lift a spoon: The division of household labor. In A. de la Torre & B. M. Pesquera (eds.), *Building with our hands: New directions in Chicana studies* (pp. 181–95). Berkeley: University of California Press.

Popenoe, D. (1988). *Disturbing the nest: Family change and decline in modern societies.* New York: Aldine de Gruyter.

Portes, A., & Rumbaut, R. G.(1990). *Immigrant America: A portrait.* Berkeley: University of California Press.

Rubel, A. (1966). *Across the tracks: Mexican Americans in a Texas city.* Austin: University of Texas Press.

Segura, D.A., & Pierce, J.L. (1993). Chicana/o family structure and gender personality: Chodorow, familism, and psychoanalytic sociology revisited. *Signs: Journal of Women in Culture and Society* 19(1), 62–91.

Stacey, J., & Thorne, B. (1985). The missing feminist revolution in sociology. *Social Problems* 32(4), 301–15.

Staples, R., & Mirandé, A. (1980). Racial and cultural variations among American families: A decennial review of the literature on minority families. *Journal of Marriage and the Family* 42(4), 887–903.

Thomas, D. L., & Wilcox, J. E. (1987). The rise of family theory. In M. B. Sussman & S. Steinmetz (eds.), *Handbook of marriage and the family* (pp. 81–102). New York: Plenum.

Thorne, B. (1992). Feminism and the family: Two decades of thought. In B. Thorne & M. Yalorn (eds.), *Rethinking the family: Some feminist questions* (pp. 3–30). Boston: Northeastern University Press.

Vega, W. A. (1990). Hispanic families in the 1980s: A decade of research. *Journal of Marriage and the Family* 52, 1015–24.

Whitehead, B. D. (1993). Dan Quayle was right. *Atlantic* 271(4), 47–84.

Ybarra, L. (1982). When wives work: The impact on the Chicano family. *Journal of Marriage and the Family* 44, 169–78.

Zavella, P. (1991). Mujeres in factories: Race and class perspectives on women, work, and family. In M. de Leonardo (ed.), *Gender at the crossroads of knowledge* (pp. 312–336). Berkeley: University of California Press.

Part III

WORKING-CLASS AND INNER-CITY FAMILIES UNDER ECONOMIC STRESS

12

Poor Families in an Era of Urban Transformation: The "Underclass" Family in Myth and Reality

Thomas J. Sugrue

Isolated by class and race, the families of the urban poor increasingly must scrape together a meager existence in areas left behind by investors and denounced or ignored by politicians. One such place is North Philadelphia's Badlands. Home to thousands of black and Hispanic poor people, it is now one of hundreds of neighborhoods around the country identified as "high poverty areas"—places where poverty rates exceed 40 percent and where a majority of the adult population is unemployed. Ringing the once-bustling neighborhood are the shells of abandoned factories, grim reminders of the economic depredations that have reshaped the city. The ghost of a prosperous industrial past hovers over debris-strewn vacant lots and haunts the lives of area residents who remember the days when union-wage industrial jobs were plentiful. Abandoned houses mar virtually every block, graffiti scars the ubiquitous red-brick building facades, and crack vials and hypodermic needles lie scattered among broken bottles and shattered car glass along the streets. On the horizon, only a few miles away, is Philadelphia's glimmering downtown, more closely connected to New York's stock exchanges, to the money markets of London and Paris, to the courtrooms of Chicago and Washington, than to the gritty postindustrial neighborhoods in its shadow.[1]

Prevailing explanations of the decline of places like the Badlands focus on the behavior and culture of poor people. In current political discourse, urban poverty is the consequence of dysfunctional families, parents who lack the motivation to work, and children who engage in crime and sexual libertinism, all subsidized by government welfare expenditures that snare the poor in a debilitating culture of "dependency." But the plight of families in the Badlands and other urban centers cannot be understood outside of the context of two generations of economic dislocation, political marginalization, and massive capital disinvestment. Residents of America's countless badlands have found themselves increasingly superfluous to the high-tech global labor market. In a suburban-dominated political order, their needs (from education to social services) are increasingly peripheral to the national political agenda.[2]

Urban poverty and family stress have tangled roots in the interaction of

profound economic and demographic changes that began in the seemingly prosperous 1940s and 1950s. American cities lost millions of entry-
level jobs, largely in manufacturing, over the last fifty years. Between
1947 and 1977 alone, twelve of the largest Northeastern and Midwestern
cities lost 2.1 million manufacturing, wholesale, and retail jobs, while
gaining only 316,000 service jobs. The hemorrhage began at the very same
time that millions of Southern blacks were pushed out of the South by
disruptions in the agricultural economy. The promise of steady, secure,
and relatively well-paid employment in the North for Southern black
migrants proved to be illusory. Major employers increasingly relocated
production to suburban areas, small towns, and even to sites outside the
United States, benefiting whites at the expense of young African
Americans who flocked to the cities seeking work.[3]

In recent decades, most new jobs that have opened up in major cities
have been in the service sector. These jobs fall into two distinct categories: high-tech and information-dependent firms like finance, real
estate, and the law, attracting highly educated professionals, and menial
employment where wages remain low and benefits are virtually nonex-
istent. The leading area of job growth since 1980 has been temporary
work, often part-time and usually without benefits.[4]

Meanwhile, the transformation of the labor market continues to worsen
the persistent income inequality that has plagued American cities. Over
the last twenty-five years, the gap between rich and poor has widened. For
the poorest segment of the American population, wages have stagnated
and declined. In 1992, the average yearly income for the poorest fifth of
families in the country was a mere $9,708, in contrast to a remarkable and
rising $99,252 for the richest fifth. As economists Sheldon Danziger and
Daniel Weinberg have shown, the income share of the poorest fifth of the
population fell during the 1970s and 1980s, from a post–World War II high
of 5.6 percent in 1969 to a low of 4.4 percent in 1992. The top fifth of the
population, by contrast, made between 40 to 45 percent of the national
income between 1947 and 1992, and almost all the income gains of the
past twenty years have gone directly into their pockets.[5]

Workplace discrimination, despite the three decades of civil rights legislation and litigation, also remains a pressing problem. Affirmative
action has improved opportunities for many blacks and women, but has
been least effective in helping those with little education and few skills.
Recent interviews with Detroit, Boston, Atlanta, and Los Angeles–area
employers show that inner-city blacks face much suspicion in the hiring
office, and are regularly turned away by employers who are skeptical
about their work skills, motivation, and intellectual ability.[6] And research
by anthropologist Katherine Newman finds that the competition for
inner-city jobs is extremely stiff, even for poor-paying, insecure employment in fast-food chains. A McDonald's in Harlem, for example, has an
average of fourteen people applying for every job opening.[7]

Exacerbating the plight of urban minorities has been the persistence
of residential racial segregation. After World War II, urban blacks and

the growing Latin American immigrant population found themselves trapped in rapidly expanding yet increasingly isolated urban ghettos. The real estate market, combined with the legal and extralegal activities of white neighborhood associations, subdivided cities racially and magnified racial tensions. Zoning restrictions kept minorities and the poor out of most suburban communities.[8] Federal and local governments—by placing public housing in older, predominantly poor sections of cities, and by bankrolling white suburbanization through racially discriminatory housing subsidies—further perpetuated racial divisions in major metropolitan areas.[9]

The interaction of economic restructuring and racial discrimination has devastated the lives of the urban poor. A growing number of poor families are entrapped in neighborhoods bereft of economic and social institutions that help to mitigate poverty. In addition, residence in the inner city has become a self-perpetuating stigma, as employers often use place of residence as a means of screening potential workers. Further complicating the situation is the uneven economic growth of metropolitan areas. The lion's share of new jobs have been created in outlying suburban communities. But most poor people cannot commute to distant suburbs: They often do not have access to reliable automobile transportation. And public transportation has seldom penetrated the suburbs with any degree of effectiveness. It is also increasingly difficult for the urban poor to gain access to information about jobs in suburban locales.[10]

Economic insecurity, underemployment, and joblessness, on top of years of defeats and dashed hopes, have proven devastating to poor families. Young men find it more and more difficult to find steady, well-paying jobs, particularly at the entry level. Reviewing the evidence on black youth unemployment, labor economists Richard Freeman and Harry Holzer have noted that black youth "are out of work for very long periods of time and that, once non-employed, they have great difficulty securing another job." Between 1950 and 1985, the proportion of black men age sixteen to twenty-four who were employed fell from about 70 percent to under 45 percent. By contrast, rates of employment increased steadily among African-American women, but primarily in low-paying, insecure jobs, often without health and child-care benefits. The jobs that provided the bedrock of economic security for masses of Americans forty years ago have largely disappeared.[11]

In the hostile environment of the inner city, in a shrinking labor market dominated by mediocre jobs, maintaining enough income for mere subsistence has grown difficult. The wages of a single breadwinner are often insufficient to pay for adequate housing, food, child care, and health insurance. And the percentage of households with more than one worker still living in poverty has risen. The wages of two underemployed workers barely pull families above the poverty line. As dozens of ethnographic studies have noted, it is difficult for families with few resources to cope with the emotional costs of long-term joblessness, irregular employment, and financial uncertainty, whatever their values or original intentions, and no matter how strong their love. In poor, inner-city communities devoid of supportive communal institutions to help families cope and move forward, the strains of dislocation are all the greater.[12]

The street corners and porch stoops in Philadelphia's Badlands, as in other cities, are full of men and women who no longer have access to the security and relatively stable wages and benefits that their neighborhood's industries once provided. Those who are lucky enough to find work in a still-shrinking labor market are usually trapped in mediocre service-sector jobs, cleaning up attorneys' offices, making hotel beds, working as hospital orderlies, or working behind the counters in fast-food restaurants. Vulnerable to layoffs and firing, usually without day-care or health benefits, North Philadelphia residents rely on unemployment benefits, food stamps, and welfare when they lose their insecure jobs. Welfare is an important part of the survival strategy for Badlands' poor families. Still, it is impossible to pay monthly rents, utility bills, and basic food, clothing, and other expenses on a meager welfare check, and welfare is hardly a stable source of income. Applicants face long lines, hostile administrators, probing and personal questions, and arbitrary cutoffs. Furthermore, welfare reaches only a portion of the poor. The vast majority of welfare recipients are women with children. Very few men receive American Families with Dependent Children monies, and Pennsylvania, like many other penurious states, has virtually eliminated its General Assistance program, cutting off all single adults deemed to be "able-bodied." Many welfare recipients hold minimum-wage jobs surreptitiously, to avoid losing their benefits and falling even further into poverty. Men tinker with broken-down cars on vacant lots, trading parts and labor, to save expenses. Some women operate unlicensed day care out of their homes, to remain with their children, to assist family members who cannot afford commercial child care, and to make enough money to survive. Others rely on the unreported income of lovers, sons, and brothers who work the crack cocaine trade, one of the neighborhood's few well-paying employment opportunities. Survival is difficult in such troubled neighborhoods. Yet as poor people grapple with the consequences of a harsh reality over which they have little control, a discussion of economic change remains at the margins of the public debate about poverty today.[13]

The tragedy of current welfare debates is that they fail to grapple with the wrenching structural changes that have created persistent, concentrated urban poverty. Instead, as the political spectrum in the United States drifted rightward in the 1980s, behavioral and cultural explanations of poverty moved into the mainstream. A growing number of social scientists and policy makers argued that a new urban "underclass" had emerged whose poverty was rooted in antisocial attitudes and actions. The causes of contemporary poverty, they argued, could be found in family breakdown, out-of-wedlock childbearing (the old-fashioned term illegitimacy moved back into popular currency), welfare dependence, and a new, violent youth culture. At the root of arguments about the "underclass" was an assumption that female-headed households in the inner city were the primary source of poverty and related social ills. In the hands of scholars and pundits, the term "underclass" has become a powerfully evocative metaphor. Allowing these commentators to ignore a reality far more diverse than they care to admit, the term has become a shorthand way of bundling together America's poor under a label that conjures up images of racial inferiority, violence, family breakdown, and uncontrolled sexuality. In a single word, the term "underclass" encapsulates middle-class Americans' most intimate fears and reaffirms their sense of social and moral superiority.[14]

The emphasis on culture and behavior in American poverty scholarship and public policy constitutes both a reprise of old themes of morality, virtue, and vice, and a new agenda on the cutting edge of scholarly research. Profound skepticism about the moral capacity of the poor has a long history in Anglo-American political discourse, which is informed by an ethic of self-help and a republican theory of citizenship that emphasizes virtue and responsibility. Reagan-era conservatives advocated a sort of scholarly Calvinism, which presumed the inherent moral depravity of the poor, and their susceptibility to the sins of sloth (not working), lust (promiscuous sex and out-of-wedlock pregnancy), and greed (grasping for government handouts).[15] Charles Murray and George Gilder argued that "the perverse incentives of welfare" created laziness, dependency, and promiscuity among the poor, all subsidized by taxpayers' money.[16]

Recent conservative arguments about poverty have integrated old racial and ethnic biases into a new emphasis on a fearsome underclass created by postwar welfare policy. In his influential study of poverty and public policy, conservative political scientist Lawrence Mead argues that blacks have a "deep conviction that they have to 'get things from white people' if they are to live a decent life." In Mead's view, residential segregation is the fault of blacks: "If poor blacks functioned better, whites would show less resistance to living among them." Mead also believes blacks have abandoned the work ethic of their grandparents' generation. "In that era, working hard and going to church were much of what black culture meant. Today, tragically, it is more likely to mean rock music or the rapping of drug dealers on ghetto street corners. That change rather than any change in the surrounding society seems to lie at the origin of the underclass." New Latin American immigrants are, according to Mead, equally at fault for their impoverishment: They are "less interested in economic progress, suspicious of individual striving, and slower to change."[17]

Somewhat contradictorily, Richard Herrnstein and Charles Murray, authors of the runaway best-seller, *The Bell Curve,* attribute family breakdown and impoverishment not to the abandonment of ancestral values but to the inheritance of intellectual deficiencies. The poor—particularly blacks and Hispanics—are simply less intelligent and thus more likely to be at the bottom of the economic ladder.[18]

The right, then, casts arguments in terms of moral defects and innate deficiencies: Poor people are poor because of their lack of motivation, their unwillingness to work, and their propensity to sexual libertinism. Conservative academics and policymakers offer a romantic evocation of the two-parent nuclear family as the exemplar of hard work, sexual restraint, and responsibility. This idealized past stands in sharp contrast to their dire picture of the current single-parent family as the breeder of crime, promiscuity, and laziness. They ignore the two-parent families that still exist in the inner cities and suffer from many of the same problems that plague single-parent households. They downplay the practical difficulties of forming or maintaining families under conditions of high unemployment. They overlook the actual diversity (including the success stories) among many single-parent families. And they argue, with little evidence, that government policies have actively encouraged the destruction of the "traditional family" by rewarding women for bearing children outside of marriage. In their final analysis, poverty is not rooted in the economy, but instead is a manifestation of family breakdown. If only we had strong, independent, male-headed families, they argue, they would instill in children the values of hard work and self-motivation, breaking the cycle of poverty. The free market, with abundant jobs, conservatives assume, would readily absorb poor people.[19]

But the political right has not been the only group to revive a moral and behavioral analysis of poverty in recent years. Joining the conservatives have been prominent liberal social scientists, most notably William Julius Wilson, Paul Peterson, David Ellwood, Mary Jo Bane, and Christopher Jencks, and journalists such as Ken Auletta and Nicholas Lemann. These liberals have offered some qualifications to the dominant conservative framework. They concede, at least in principle, that poverty is rooted in a changing labor market and that poor people, especially minorities, face barriers to equal opportunity. But as conservatives began to dominate the debate over poverty, liberals also put increasing emphasis on the behavior of the poor. Wilson, for example, combined a thorough analysis of urban industrial decline and joblessness with a discussion of the "pathologies" of the black urban poor such as out-of-wedlock childbearing.[20] Auletta and Lemann wrote moving pseudo-ethnographic accounts of poor families that included alarming depictions of family dysfunctionality, violence, and substance abuse—reinforcing popular beliefs that antisocial behaviors generated poverty.[21] Peterson acknowledged the impact of discrimination and technological change on the poor, but also focused increasingly on the "perverse incentives" of welfare.[22]

The work of influential sociologist Christopher Jencks is representative of a new generation of liberal poverty scholars who have imported conservative ideas into mainstream policy debates. Jencks's work combines rigorous statistical analysis of economic causes of poverty with a self-described "cultural conservatism" that focuses on poor people who do not "follow norms of behavior that most of society endorses."[23] Ignoring the fact that most children of unwed mothers in the inner cities would be poor even if their parents were married, Jencks suggests that permissive sexuality, rather than unemployment for men and discriminatory wages paid to women, is the ultimate problem. "Poor children," he claims, "have suffered most from our newly permissive approach to reproduction. Shotgun weddings and lifetime marriages caused adults a lot of misery, but they ensured that every child had a claim on some adult male's earnings unless his father died. That is no longer the case. This change is, I think, a byproduct of growing individualism and commitment to personal freedom."[24]

Similarly, David Ellwood and Mary Jo Bane, prominent liberal academics who worked in the Clinton administration, base their vision of welfare reform on a contrast between "long-term dependency" that they believe characterized the American poor and the "independence and self-support" that they believe should be the goal of government policy.[25] Thus right and left alike have refocused the debate over poverty onto values and culture, shunting aside rigorous analyses of inequality and laying blame instead on individual characteristics. The new liberal emphasis on the behavioral origins of poverty came to fruition in the Clinton administration's attempts to "end welfare as we know it."

Both the conservative and the liberal frameworks share a number of fundamental assumptions. The most important include an emphasis on personal responsibility, the belief that family structure is a cause rather than a symptom of poverty, and a preoccupation with dependence. In the end both liberals and conservatives believe that policies need to be reformulated "to reinforce our values of work, family, independence, and responsibility." The desired goal of liberal welfare reform, like that of its conservative kin, is moral rather than economic, resting on an ideological celebration of "self-reliance" and "independence."

But as Nancy Fraser and Linda Gordon have persuasively argued, the dichotomy between dependency and independence is false, resting on the erroneous assumption that "the normal human condition is independence and that dependence is deviant." The new bipartisan orthodoxy on poverty assumes that in the past, most poor people were self-reliant, ignoring the countless ways that families in the past have survived only through a bundle of government support, charitable assistance, and mutual support.[26] In fact, other groups in American society are far more dependent on the state than the poor, yet manage to escape moral condemnation. Middle-class homeowners benefit from government-backed loans, mortgage guarantees, and tax deductions; they travel to malls (built with the assistance of tax abatements) on government-subsidized highways. Government insurance programs protect people from the consequences of building homes on flood plains or eroding sea cliffs. Returning veterans have been beneficiaries of a form of affirmative action through the GI Bill and through the VA housing program. Scientists, defense contractors, agribusinesses, lumber and mining firms, and savings and loan associations survive because of government handouts. Yet no one labels white suburbanites, the elderly, veterans, the military-industrial complex, or bankers as pathological victims of a culture of dependency. No cries about "perverse incentives" fill the air. The largest group to benefit from federal largesse in the last half century has been the elderly, because of Social Security and Medicare. But the resulting decline in the work force participation of able-bodied elderly people has been a source of celebration rather than outrage.

Yet despite these widely accepted and highly effective government subsidies for the nonpoor, the conventional wisdom is that government assistance to the poor has created or at least exacerbated poverty. One of the most influential right-wing critics of welfare, Charles Murray, has made a now-widely accepted argument that Johnson's Great Society programs of the 1960s sapped the initiative of poor people by discouraging them from working and by subsidizing family breakup. The result, Murray contended, was the emergence of a new, pernicious form of poverty bankrolled by the state. Murray and other conservatives argue that more people are poor now than in the 1960s, not because of changes in the job market, a restructuring of the global economy, or the persistence of racial discrimination, but because generous government programs have permitted poor people to live indolently. Welfare payments, in this view, set into motion a dangerous cycle of intergenerational dependency that saps individual initiative, discourages responsible parenting, and contributes to rising rates of crime, adolescent pregnancy, and school dropouts.[27]

This damning interpretation of the Great Society is based on ignorance or misrepresentation of the history of welfare and of recent trends among the poor. First, it overlooks the fact the War on Poverty was a short-lived and incomplete attempt to expand the safety net—an effort that has been under attack for twenty-five years. Given the small funding of the program in comparison to expenditures such as those for the military, it was quite effective when it was in place: Rates of child poverty reached their lowest point in 1970, when the Great Society programs were at their height. But an unheralded war on welfare began under Richard Nixon and has gathered momentum since. The proportion of female household heads with children receiving AFDC declined from 63 percent in 1972 to 45 percent in 1988, at the same time that the mean payment of AFDC diminished from $435 per month in 1970 to $350 a month in 1980. States have also harshly cut back on welfare payments. In 1993, the average AFDC benefit in Connecticut, the third-highest-paying state, was a meager $2,400 per year; in Mississippi, the stingiest state, it was only $504 per year. The real value of welfare benefits has fallen dramatically because AFDC payments, unlike Social Security installments, are not indexed to inflation. Thus median AFDC payments in 1992 were 43 percent lower than they were in 1970. By 1990, AFDC payments for a family of four were lower, in constant dollars, than they were in 1960.[28]

One unintended consequence of the dramatic reduction of welfare benefits is that a rising number of poor people must rely on outside, unreported sources of income to make ends meet each month. In one of the most detailed studies of welfare recipients, sociologist Kathryn Edin found that 86 percent of AFDC recipients in four major cities relied on income from unreported jobs and additional support from parents, relatives, and partners. Welfare payments were simply insufficient to meet monthly food, rent, and living expenses. As in previous periods in American history, the poor have ingeniously cobbled together resources—working, borrowing, and bartering—to survive. Such statistics testify both to the resilience and interdependence of poor families and to the absurdity of abstract notions of "dependency."[29]

The attack on welfare policy has been fueled by growing moral outrage directed against the poor. Beginning in the 1970s, for example, politicians evoked the specter of an "epidemic" of teenage pregnancy, supposedly made possible by the easy access that unmarried mothers had to AFDC benefits. But the rate of teenaged motherhood actually declined during the 1960s and 1970s (when welfare grants were more generous), and has remained more or less constant since 1980. The rate of births to unmarried mothers has increased since the 1970s, but this has occurred in all segments of American society, not simply among the poor or among nonwhites. Indeed, many of the behaviors we associate with the inner-city poor are manifestations of changes that affect all members of American society. Furthermore, studies of the relationship between welfare receipt and the rate of children living in single-parent homes have found an inverse correlation. States with the lowest welfare payments have the highest rates of children born to unmarried mothers; those with the highest AFDC payments have the lowest.[30]

Politicians have also blamed the supposedly generous welfare system for family breakdown, alarming school dropout rates, and an increase in crime. But the best social scientific research has found little or no correlation between joblessness, education levels, family structure, race, welfare receipt, and crime. On each count, the statistical record offers no proof for pessimistic arguments about the emergence of a growing, threatening "underclass." For example, black high school dropout rates have fallen steadily, from 28 percent in 1970 to 15 percent in 1988; white rates have barely changed, from 11 to 9.5 percent over the same period. Crime rates have leveled off and, in many instances, even fallen, since the early 1970s. American cities are by no means uniformly safe places, but overall they are somewhat safer than they were twenty-five years ago.[31]

Yet while politicians debate how to encourage abstinence among poor teenage girls or to reinvigorate a work ethic among the poor by cutting back on already meager welfare payments, structural changes in the economy continue to wreak havoc on poor people's lives. The deficiency of most recent poverty scholarship and welfare policy is that it rests on grand theories about human behavior rather than on an understanding of the real experience of the poor themselves. Few scholars and fewer policymakers have any sense of the day-to-day struggles of poor families. The run-down apartments, boarded-up houses and vacant lots, crumbling schools, pothole-ridden streets, and the abandoned factories that stand in virtually every inner city offer a powerful explanation for the persistence of poverty. They also explain why some people find themselves in situations where behaviors that might seem pathological in a middle-class suburb may be a temporary survival mechanism, not a cultural value. The obsession with personal morality, values, and behavior has blinded observers to the bleak reality that most poor people face, as well as to the lack of options they have in coping with this reality.

The current debate over family policy and welfare flattens the complex lives and strategies of poor people to a few simple buzzwords: "underclass," "dependence," "laziness," "children having children," "crime," "drugs." The precarious existence of poor people is forgotten inside the Beltway, in the corridors of state capitols, on the green lawns of suburbia, as policymakers shape programs that are firmly rooted in unreality. While Congress debates the impact of AFDC cutoffs on teen mothers, the rate of teen motherhood has stabilized. While Republicans advocate block grants to states, poor people, already reeling from state and local budget cuts, scrape together a living on the rough streets. While Democrats and Republicans quibble over the merits of two- or five-year cutoffs for welfare beneficiaries, poor mothers lose their minimum-wage jobs because they have to spend time at home with sick children. Poor people struggle to survive in a hostile environment in which political leaders ignore their plight or blame it on the poor themselves, in an economy from which textile jobs have fled to Mexico and Haiti, from which electronics jobs have vanished to Korea and Singapore, and from which machinery jobs have been lost to a new generation of exploited third-world laborers.

Any discussion of today's urban crisis worth telling must confront the awful reality of the profound transformation of American cities over the past forty years. Instead, the emphasis on race, culture, behavior, and values allows elected officials to avoid grappling with the difficult, seemingly intractable structural problems at the root of contemporary urban poverty while they earn easy political points by denouncing the poor for their deviance. But poverty is an economic problem, not a cultural problem. Until public policy contends with the consequences of massive job loss, persistent racial segregation and discrimination, and growing income inequality, poverty will only grow as a social problem, families will only suffer more, and young people will only grow more and more desperate.

NOTES

Thanks to Dana Barron, Stephanie Coontz, and Alice O'Connor for their advice and assistance with this essay.

1. For context, see Carolyn Adams, David Bartelt, David Elesh, Ira Goldstein, Nancy Kleniewski, and William Yancey, *Philadelphia: Neighborhoods, Division, and Conflict in a Postindustrial City* (Philadelphia: Temple University Press, 1991). On the growth of high poverty areas in Philadelphia and elsewhere, see Paul Jargowsky and Mary Jo Bane, "Neighborhood Poverty: Basic Questions," in Laurence E. Lynn, Jr. and Michael G.H. McGeary, eds., *Inner City Poverty in the United States* (Washington, D.C.: National Academy Press, 1990), 16–67.
2. Kenneth T. Jackson, *Crabgrass Frontier: The Suburbanization of the United States* (New York: Oxford University Press, 1985); William Schneider, "The Suburban Century Begins," *Atlantic* 270 (July 1992), 33–44; Margaret Weir, "Urban Poverty and Defensive Localism," *Dissent* (Summer 1994), 337–342.
3. For a historical overview of the process of economic change, see Thomas J. Sugrue, "The Structures of Urban Poverty: The Reorganization of Space and Work in Three Periods of American History," in Michael B. Katz, ed., *The "Underclass" Debate: Views From History* (Princeton: Princeton University Press, 1993), 85–117. See also William Julius Wilson and Loic J.D. Wacquant, "The Cost of Racial and Class Exclusion in the Inner City," *Annals of the American Academy of Political and Social Science* 501 (January 1989), 26–47; Barry Bluestone and Bennett Harrison, *The Deindustrialization of America: Plant Closings, Community Abandonment, and the Dismantling of Basic Industry* (New York: Basic Books, 1982). For statistical overviews of urban labor market restructuring, see John D. Kasarda, "Urban Change and Minority Opportunities," in Paul E. Peterson, ed., *The New Urban Reality* (Washington, D.C.: The Brookings Institution, 1985), 33–67, figures on job loss from Table 1. See also John D. Kasarda, "Structural Factors Affecting the Location and Timing of Urban Underclass Growth," *Urban Geography* 11 (1990), esp. 242.
4. On temporary work, see Chris Tilly, *Short Hours, Short Shrift: Causes and Consequences of Part-Time Work* (Washington, D.C.: Economic Policy Institute, 1990); Polly Callaghan and Heidi Hartmann, *Contingent Work: A Chart Book on Part Time and Temporary Employment* (Washington, D.C.: Economic Policy Institute, 1991).
5. Sheldon H. Danziger and Daniel H. Weinberg, "The Historical Record: Trends in Family Income, Inequality, and Poverty," in Danziger, et al., *Confronting Poverty*, 22–24.
6. See especially the reports from the ongoing Multi-City Study of Urban Inequality, sponsored by the Ford and Russell Sage Foundations, which integrates household and employer survey data from Detroit, Los Angeles, Boston, and Atlanta. Summaries include Joleen Kirschenmann, Philip Moss, and Chris Tilly, "Space as a Signal, Space as a Barrier: How Employers Map and Use Space in Four Metropolitan Labor Markets," Russell Sage Foundation Working Paper 89; Philip Moss and Chris Tilly, "Raised Hurdles for Black Men: Evidence From Interviews With Employers," Russell Sage Foundation Working Paper 81. See also Harry Holzer, *What Employers Want: Job Prospects for the Less Educated* (New

York: Russell Sage Foundation, 1996).

7. "Take this Job: Up From Welfare, It's Harder and Harder," *New York Times* (April 16, 1995), Section 4, p. 1; "A Long Line for Fast Food Jobs," *Business Week* (July 31, 1995), 30.

8. Arnold Hirsch, *Making the Second Ghetto: Race and Housing in Chicago, 1940–1960* (Cambridge: Cambridge University Press, 1983); Thomas J. Sugrue, *The Origins of the Urban Crisis: Race and Inequality in Postwar Detroit* (Princeton: Princeton University Press, 1996), chapters 2, 8, 9; Michael Danielson, *The Politics of Exclusion* (New York: Columbia University Press, 1976).

9. Kenneth T. Jackson, "Race, Ethnicity, and Real Estate Appraisal: The Home Owners Loan Corporation and the Federal Housing Administration," *Journal of Urban History* 6 (1980), 419–452; John Bauman, *Public Housing, Race, and Renewal: Urban Planning in Philadelphia, 1920–1974* (Philadelphia: Temple University Press, 1987); Hirsch, *Making the Second Ghetto*, 212–275. For an overview, see Raymond Mohl, "Shifting Patterns of American Urban Policy Since 1900," in Arnold Hirsch and Raymond Mohl, eds., *Urban Policy in Twentieth-Century America* (New Brunswick: Rutgers University Press, 1993), 1–45.

10. Douglas Massey and Nancy Denton, *American Apartheid: Residential Segregation and the Making of the Underclass* (Cambridge: Harvard University Press, 1992); Loic J.D. Wacquant, "Urban Outcasts: Stigma and Division in the Black American Ghetto and the French Urban Periphery," *International Journal of Urban and Regional Research* 17 (1993), 366–383. On employers' use of residence as a means of excluding potential workers, see Joleen Kirschenman and Kathryn M. Neckerman, "'We'd Love to Hire Them, But ...': The Meaning of Race for Employers," in Jencks and Peterson, eds., *The Urban Underclass*, 203–234.

11. The most prominent discussion of the phenomenon is in Charles Murray, *Losing Ground: American Social Policy 1950–1980* (New York: Basic Books, 1984), 69–82. Murray, however, does not consider the relationship of youth unemployment to the decline in entry-level manufacturing jobs in the center cities. An important scholarly examination of the problem is John Cogan, "The Decline in Black Teenage Employment, 1950–1970," *American Economic Review* 72 (1982), 621–638, but Cogan emphasizes the decline in agricultural employment, an issue not relevant to the labor force participation of black youth in major cities. The best overview is Richard B. Freeman and Harry J. Holzer, eds., *The Black Youth Employment Crisis* (Chicago: University of Chicago Press, 1986), quote from 9. See also Troy Duster, "Postindustrialism and Youth Employment: African Americans as Harbingers," in Katherine McFate, Roger Lawson, and William Julius Wilson, eds., *Poverty, Inequality, and the Future of Social Policy: Western States in the New World Order* (New York: Russell Sage Foundation, 1995), 466–473. On the changing fortunes of women, see Lourdes Benaria and Catherine Stimpson, eds., *Women, Households, and the Economy* (New Brunswick: Rutgers University Press, 1988). Figures from Gerald David Jaynes and Robin M. Williams, Jr., eds., *A Common Destiny: Blacks and American Society* (Washington, D.C.: National Academy Press, 1989), 301–302.

12. For a few examples of studies of the impact of economic dislocation, see E.W. Bakke, *The Unemployed Worker* (New Haven: Yale University Press, 1940); Gregory Pappas, *The Magic City: Unemployment in a Working-Class Community* (Ithaca: Cornell University Press, 1989); Katherine Newman,

Falling From Grace: The Experience of Downward Mobility in the American Middle Class (New York: Free Press, 1988).

13. The literature on the post–World War II black migration is slim. See Nicholas Lemann, *The Promised Land: The Great Black Migration and How It Changed America* (New York: Random House, 1991). An implicit critique of Lemann is Jacqueline Jones, *The Dispossessed: America's Underclasses From the Civil War to the Present* (New York: Basic Books, 1992), 205–265. On the economic history of the urban poor since World War II, especially blacks after the migration, see Sugrue, *The Origins of the Urban Crisis*, especially chapters 4–6.

14. The most prominent critiques of the term "underclass" include Michael B. Katz, "The 'Underclass' as a Metaphor of Social Transformation," chapter 1 in Katz, ed., *The "Underclass" Debate: Views From History* (Princeton: Princeton University Press, 1993), 3–23; Herbert Gans, *The War Against the Poor* (New York: Basic Books, 1995); Adolph Reed, "The Underclass as Myth and Symbol," *Radical America* 24 (1992), 21–40.

15. Michael B. Katz, *In the Shadow of the Poorhouse: A Social History of Welfare in America* (New York: Basic Books, 1986). On Britain, see Gertrude Himmelfarb, *The Idea of Poverty: England in the Early Industrial Age* (New York: Knopf, 1983). On attitudes toward work, see Daniel Rodgers, *The Work Ethic in Industrial America, 1850–1920* (Chicago: University of Chicago Press, 1978). On notions of virtue and responsibility in republican thought, see Drew R. McCoy, *The Elusive Republic: The Political Economy of Jeffersonian America* (Chapel Hill: University of North Carolina Press, 1980).

16. George Gilder, *Wealth and Poverty* (New York: Basic Books, 1981). Gilder is a prominent advocate of "supply-side economics" who enjoyed great influence in the early Reagan years. Charles Murray, *Losing Ground: American Social Policy, 1950–1980* (New York: Basic Books, 1984). Murray, affiliated with conservative think tanks such as the Manhattan Institute and the American Enterprise Institute, set the antiwelfare state agenda with his widely cited *Losing Ground*; he has also played a major role reinvigorating scientific racism. See Charles Murray and Richard Herrnstein, *The Bell Curve: Intelligence and Class Structure in American Life* (New York: The Free Press, 1994).

17. Lawrence Mead, *The New Politics of Poverty: The Nonworking Poor in America* (New York: Basic Books, 1992), 57, 151 (emphasis added); see also Mead's earlier book, *Beyond Entitlement: The Social Obligations of Citizenship* (New York: The Free Press, 1985). For a critique of Mead, see Thomas J. Sugrue, "The Impoverished Politics of Poverty," *Yale Journal of Law and the Humanities* 6 (1994), esp. 169–179. For a wide-ranging discussion of poverty politics in the twentieth century, see James T. Patterson, *America's Struggle Against Poverty, 1900–1994* (Cambridge, Mass.: Harvard University Press, 1995).

18. Murray and Herrnstein, *The Bell Curve*.

19. Mead, *The New Politics of Poverty*, 12.

20. William Julius Wilson, *The Truly Disadvantaged: The Inner City, the Underclass, and Public Policy* (Chicago: University of Chicago Press, 1987). Wilson, a University of Chicago sociologist and director of the multiyear Chicago Poverty and Family Life project, has influenced a whole generation of recent scholarship on urban poverty.

21. Ken Auletta, *The Underclass* (New York: Random House, 1982); Nicholas Lemann, "The Origins of the Underclass," *Atlantic* 257 (June 1986);

Lemann, *The Promised Land: The Great Black Migration and How It Changed America* (New York: Knopf, 1991). Auletta and Lemann, liberal journalists, played a key role in bringing the issue of the urban "underclass," the fear of ominous changes in American urban life, and the findings of poverty scholars into the public agenda.

22. Paul Peterson, ed., *The New Urban Reality* (Washington, D.C.: The Brookings Institution, 1985); Paul Peterson and Mark Rom, *Welfare Magnets: A New Case for a National Standard* (Washington, D.C.: The Brookings Institution, 1990). Peterson, former head of governmental studies at the Brookings Institution, and professor of government at Harvard, has shaped the poverty research agenda through his books and his role as leader of the Social Science Research Council's Committee on the Urban Underclass.

23. Christopher Jencks, *Rethinking Social Policy: Race, Poverty, and the Underclass* (Cambridge: Harvard University Press, 1992).

24. Jencks, *Rethinking Social Policy*, 135.

25. David T. Ellwood and Mary Jo Bane, *Welfare Realities: From Rhetoric to Reform* (Cambridge: Harvard University Press, 1994), esp. 67–123, quote from 161. Compare with David T. Ellwood, *Poor Support: Poverty in the American Family* (New York: Basic Books, 1987); David T. Ellwood, "The Spatial Mismatch Hypothesis: Are There Teenage Jobs Missing in the Ghetto," in Richard Freeman and Harry Holzer, eds., *The Black Youth Unemployment Problem* (Chicago: University of Chicago Press, 1986).

26. The most prominent liberal evocation of "dependency" is Bane and Ellwood, *Welfare Realities*, a powerful critique of the politics of dependency is Nancy Fraser and Linda Gordon, "'Dependency' Demystified: Inscriptions of Power in a Keyword of the Welfare State," *Social Politics* 1 (Spring 1994), 4–31, quote from 24. See also Stephanie Coontz, *The Way We Never Were: American Families and the Nostalgia Trap* (New York: Basic Books, 1992); Kathryn M. Neckerman, "The Emergence of 'Underclass' Family Patterns, 1900–1940" in Katz, ed., *The "Underclass" Debate*, 194–219.

27. Murray, *Losing Ground*. For an especially forceful version of this argument, see Myron Magnet, *The Nightmare and the Dream: The Sixties Legacy to the Underclass* (New York: William Morrow, 1993). For a popularization of it, see "Personal Responsibility Act," in Ed Gillespie and Bob Schellhas, eds., *Contract With America* (New York: Times Books, 1994), 65–77.

28. On the limitations of the Great Society, see Hugh Heclo, "Poverty Politics," in Sheldon H. Danziger, Gary D. Sandefur, and Daniel H. Weinberg, eds., *Confronting Poverty: Prescriptions for Change* (Cambridge: Harvard University Press, 1994), 407–412; Thomas F. Jackson, "The State, the Movement, and the Urban Poor: The War on Poverty and Political Mobilization in the 1960s," in Katz, ed., *The "Underclass" Debate*, 403–439; Jill Quadagno, *The Color of Welfare: How Racism Undermined the War on Poverty* (New York: Oxford University Press, 1994). For a comprehensive overview, see Michael B. Katz, *The Underserving Poor: From the War on Poverty to the War on Welfare* (New York: Pantheon, 1989). Figures from Jencks, *Rethinking Social Policy*, 77. See also Rebecca M. Blank, "The Employment Strategy: Public Policies to Increase Work and Earnings," in Danziger et al., *Confronting Poverty*, 179–180. For figures on statewide payments, see R. Kent Weaver and William T. Dickens, eds., *Looking Before We Leap: Social Science and Welfare Reform* (Washington, D.C.: The Brookings

Institution, 1995), table 3–6.

29. Kathryn J. Edin, "The Myths of Dependence and Self-Sufficiency: Women, Welfare, and Low-Wage Work," *Focus* 17:2 (Fall/Winter 1995), 1–9. The cities were San Antonio, Chicago, Boston, and Charleston, South Carolina. See also Edin and Christopher Jencks, "Reforming Welfare," in Jencks, *Rethinking Social Policy*, 204–235. For studies of the strategies of poor people in the past, see Michael B. Katz, *Improving Poor People: The Welfare State, the "Underclass," and Urban Schools as History* (Princeton: Princeton University Press, 1995), 144–172; Jacqueline Jones, *The Dispossessed: America's Underclasses From the Civil War to the Present* (New York: Basic Books, 1992); Carol B. Stack, *All Our Kin: Strategies for Survival in a Black Community* (New York: Harper and Row, 1974).

30. On growing concerns about unwed motherhood in the 1970s, see Maris Vinovskis, *An "Epidemic" of Adolescent Pregnancy: Some Historical and Policy Considerations* (New York: Oxford University Press, 1988), 23–37; figures from Jencks, *Rethinking Social Policy.* On the relationship between welfare receipt and rates of children living in single-parent homes, see David T. Ellwood and Lawrence H. Summers, "Poverty in America: Is Welfare the Answer or the Problem?" in Sheldon H. Danziger and Daniel H. Weinberg, eds., *Fighting Poverty: What Works and What Doesn't* (Cambridge: Harvard University Press, 1986), 94–96; Ellwood, *Poor Support*, 61–62.

31. For figures on dropout rates and crime, see Jencks, *Rethinking Social Policy*, 173–174, 185. For a detailed study of crime, see Elliot Currie, *Confronting Crime* (New York: Pantheon Books, 1985).

13

No Good Choices: Teenage Childbearing, Concentrated Poverty, and Welfare Reform

Gabrielle Raley

Teenage pregnancy provides just the stuff good tabloid sales are made of: babies for profit; lust and deception; an over-sexed community of women laughing in the face of fatherhood and family and deciding to go it on their own—that is, as long as they have the backing of welfare checks for which they won't have to work. To many people, this is what teenage childbearing looks like: Unsupervised girls irresponsibly yet deliberately get pregnant, the government gives them money for it, and financially strapped taxpayers foot the bill. In large part, these images fueled passage of the 1996 welfare-reform bill, which set lifetime limits on the receipt of public assistance for poor women and their children and even stricter restrictions on teen mothers.

When one gets beyond the stereotypes surrounding teenage child-bearing and begins to wade through the data, however, a very different story emerges. Less marketable than the tabloid version, this story shows poor girls growing up in neighborhoods with a generations-long history of limited access to adequate schools and interesting jobs, looking for a measure of control in their lives. In this context, it is not that teenage motherhood represents a *good* choice, but that it is an often *understandable* one, given the lack of better options.

Teenage childbearing is the result of a many-stranded fusion of socioeconomic constraints with racism, an unequal educational system, and gender-influenced expectations and opportunities. Added to this are the conflicting messages adolescents receive about responsible sex in a cultural economy that rewards sexualized consumption with social status. What teenage childbearing is decidedly *not* is the result of a racial-ethnic disposition, as is commonly assumed, or the supposed incentive of welfare dollars. In fact, the greatest rise in unwed teen births occurred during a period when welfare benefits declined sharply; the recent drop in teen births occurred before the replacement of Aid to Families with Dependent Children (AFDC) with the state-controlled Temporary Assistance to Needy Families (TANF) in 1996.[1]

Sociologist Mark Robert Rank studied 3,000 AFDC recipients over eight years and found that, contrary to popular stereotype, women who received public assistance had dramatically lower birth rates than women in the general population. Controlling for race, education, num-ber of children, employment status, and age, Rank found that the birth rate among the welfare recipients he studied was approximately 45.8 births per 1,000 women, compared to 71.1 births per 1,000 women for the country as a whole. Most researchers agree that welfare has an insignificant effect on the rate of unwed teen births: The few studies that have found any relation between the two have found it only for white women.[2]

Recently, politicians have been cracking down on how much monetary assistance teen mothers and their children receive, arguing that welfare gives teens the incentive and means to carelessly bear children while unmarried. Some states have experimented with "family cap" policies to this end, arguing that if mothers on welfare don't receive increased benefits following the birth of a child, they will have fewer children. But independent researchers who have recently evaluated control-group data from states with family cap policies find no difference in births between women subject to the family cap policy and women eligible to continue to receive benefits. As Barbara Vobejda and Judith Havemann of the *Washington Post* point out, "... the threat of losing out on $90 a month in extra benefits doesn't get much notice in the chaotic lives of many women on welfare. It must compete with an often chronic state of crisis, with frequent moves from one tenuous household to another, with a constant struggle to pay the bills, and with neighborhoods wracked by violence and crime...." Rank's respondents laughed at the suggestion that they would have additional children in order to collect what amounts to an extra $60–90 a month in benefits.[3]

In fact, as many scholars have noted, the data support the reverse correlation than assumed by most welfare "reformers": There is a strong association between *low* welfare benefit levels and a high incidence of unmarried teenage pregnancy. For instance, the states boasting the five highest rates of unmarried teenage childbearing offer welfare payments that are among the seven lowest in the country. Furthermore, if welfare encourages teens to bear children out of wedlock, many European countries offering more generous and less punitive social welfare should be overrun with the children of unmarried teen parents by now. Instead the opposite is true: American teenagers have birth rates up to six-and-a-half times greater than those of their European counterparts. Rather than encouraging teens to suddenly "develop character," lack of investment in lower-income families means that members of these families are less able to obtain the education and opportunities that would allow them to avoid poverty and plan their childbearing more carefully.[4]

The evidence suggests that poverty is more a cause of unwed childbearing than its effect. Women who receive public assistance not only have fewer children than most people believe, but the disadvantage their kids inherit in terms of future welfare dependence is less than commonly assumed. Although children who receive welfare are somewhat more likely than others to collect welfare as adults, this is largely explained by the fact that lower-income families have a more difficult time providing their children with the economically based assets and opportunities that will help them escape poverty in the future. Children of lower-income families are also more likely to experience the same discrimination and lack of opportunity that led to their parents' poverty in the first place. But the "cycle of disadvantage" has been greatly exaggerated. As the Center on Social Welfare Policy and Law reported in 1996, only 9 percent of AFDC recipients also received aid consistently as children. The overwhelming majority of recipients collected no public assistance in their youth, with a full 75 percent of recipients receiving no aid as children and an additional 16 percent receiving aid infrequently in their youth. The fact that a greater percentage of those who receive welfare as children go on to collect aid as adults is, as historian Stephanie Coontz argues, more likely the result of too little investment in welfare support and meaningful job training rather than of too much.[5]

Frank Furstenberg, Jr., the author of several longitudinal studies of teenage mothers and their children, argues that the vast majority of teenage mothers who rely on public assistance to offset the economic hardship of early parenthood enter the labor force when their youngest children reach school age. Rather than signaling a self-perpetuating cycle of dependency, this pattern of welfare utilization demonstrates the need for high-quality subsidized child care in conjunction with education and useful job training to help adolescent mothers rise out of poverty.[6]

One factor routinely ignored in discussions of the relation between teen motherhood, welfare dependency, and child outcomes is the socioeconomic background of teenage mothers prior to their pregnancies. We know teenage childbearing entails economic and social setbacks. What is less well known is that the consequences associated with teenage childbearing diminish dramatically when the social background of adolescent parents is truly accounted for. Lower-income adolescents, who experience much higher rates of childbearing than their more affluent counterparts, are also much more likely to reside in areas of concentrated poverty. Here they encounter limited access to good schools and decent jobs, making it difficult for them to rise out of poverty whether or not they wait until their twenties to have children. To be sure, their chances are better if they wait, but not significantly so, and not for all segments of the population. For example, Nan Marie Astone found that while delaying birth until age twenty-five or later appears to have a positive effect on the future economic standing of white women, this effect does not hold true for African-American women. Though the evidence regarding the actual disadvantage associated with adolescent childbearing is complex and often contradictory, it is clear that efforts to depict teenage childbearing as the main determinant of future economic status do not take sufficient account of the prior socioeconomic standing of many adolescent parents.[7]

The socioeconomic status of adolescent parents is also ignored in arguments that link teenage childbearing to a supposed "culture of poverty." Cultural explanations of teenage childbearing are, all too often, thinly disguised appeals to racial and ethnic prejudices. As

Thomas J. Sugrue argues (this volume), the emphasis on an independent causal role of values ignores the matrix of economic isolation and discrimination in which people absorb and modify generally held social values on the basis of practical experience. Politically, the culture-of-poverty thesis systematically ignores social class, appealing to racial-ethnic prejudice to justify parsimonious social spending on the grounds that anti-poverty spending will be a waste of time until inner-city residents acquire the right values.[8]

Those who argue that values explain teen pregnancy and inner-city poverty often claim to "control," for income or education in their studies. But there is no way to control for the structural and economic forces that have consigned people of color to economically disadvantaged and socially isolated neighborhoods over long periods of time, subjecting them to the material (and class) consequences of racial-ethnic discrimination. The relationship between race-ethnicity and class can be difficult to see accurately, as we tend to think of class in individual terms, defining class position by a person's income or education at a certain time. Under this definition, it makes sense to think that if a person simply works harder or gets an education, they are already on their way to middle-class security.[9]

But class is first a *social* relationship that places one group of people in a certain pattern of interaction with other groups and gives group members a set of shared experiences, expectations, problem-solving habits, vulnerabilities, and privileges. It is a set of long-term options, not just a particular income or job that determines class status. This is why a broke college student is in a higher and more secure class, with completely different dynamics, than a resident of America's inner cities, even one who is currently flush. In our country, class has been constructed not just by economic processes but by racial exclusion and ethnic stratification over a long period of time.

Louise Lamphere and her colleagues argue that class is best understood as a social location. In their study of Chicana and white female factory workers, they define social location as operating on two planes: "At one level the term denotes the location of women in a particular political economy.... At a second level, the term refers to a woman's social location not in a strictly spatial sense, but within a social structure where socially constructed categories—gender, class, race, ethnicity, sexual orientation—are linked to positions that in turn shape experience." The idea of class as a social location must inform our understanding of why teenage childbearing occurs disproportionately among some segments of the population. It is true, for instance, that African-American teens experience higher rates of childbearing than their white counterparts. But this fact demonstrates first of all the embedded relationship of race ethnicity and class in our country, not the notion that racially or ethnically derived values cause poverty, as the "culture of poverty" argument so often puts forth.[10]

Contrary to the history most people are raised on, the historical oppression of African Americans did not end with slavery. Ever since the 1820s, and continuing into the 1950s, African Americans were the frequent target of organized mob actions and riots. In the late nineteenth century, they were driven out of skilled trades, exploited in Southern agriculture, confined to the oldest, most dilapidated sections of Northern cities, and excluded from industrial jobs and union work. After World War II, thousands of African Americans moved North to seek work. While they faced continuing violence and segregation, some managed to find footholds in manufacturing fields. These occupational gains, combined with the struggle for civil rights, opened up new employment and educational opportunities in the 1960s. These gains were, however, offset by losses in "foothold industries" and the simultaneous transition of goods-based to service-based industries, technological advances, and the division of the labor market into low-wage and high-wage sectors.[11]

African Americans have also been particularly hard hit by the relocation of many industries from central-city locations to more remote suburban sites. In one example, sociologist William Julius Wilson reports that the relocation of over 2,300 companies from Illinois cities to suburbs in the 1970s resulted in an African-American employment rate decrease of 24.3 percent; the white employment rate declined by only 9.8 percent. African Americans have also been heavily represented in the automobile, rubber, and steel industries most affected by recent plant closings. In the 1970s, these factors combined with racially biased housing regulations to form poor segregated neighborhoods in which there were few connections to job networks. Most middle- and working-class families relocated during this time period, leaving inner-city residents few tangible examples of the economic system working, of neighbors experiencing successful employment or economic security.[12]

These economic factors have combined to shape today's inner cities. Due to a mutually reinforcing cycle of discrimination and economic inequality, people of color are not only more likely to be poor than whites, but also more likely to reside in areas of particularly concentrated poverty. While only 7 percent of all poor whites live in what are termed "extreme poverty areas," 32 percent of all poor Chicanos and 39 percent of all poor African Americans reside in these areas. Here residents face substandard housing, ill-funded schools, and social isolation, though they do get more than their fair share of liquor stores and hazardous waste-dump sites.[13]

Applying these economically based perspectives to teen childbearing allows us to recognize historically constructed patterns in different racial-ethnic groups without ignoring the ultimately determining role of class. Naomi Farber's qualitative study of the reasons many African-American and white teens from lower-, working-, and middle-class backgrounds elect not to marry the fathers of their children is useful in further understanding the class components of racial-ethnic differences. Farber points out that both African-American and white teen mothers from nonpoor backgrounds expect to marry in the future. When they

decide not to marry the fathers of their children, it is for the same reasons: because it might compromise their future educational goals or
because they did not believe their baby's father constituted a suitable
marriage partner, not because they see marriage as an unrealistic or
undesirable goal. The primary racial variance Farber notes among these
middle-class teens is the support they receive from their families.
Middle-class African-American teens know they can usually count on
their families for support if they become pregnant; white teens are generally surprised at the help their families provide.[14]

The case is much different for lower-class teens, who rightly see few
advantages in marrying their partners, who are often unemployed and in
similar financial straits themselves. This observation is most applicable
to the African-American teens Farber studied: "A perception that is more
common and explicit among the black lower-class teens is that marriage
as actually experienced by the people they know offers no real advantage
over single motherhood." States one lower-class African-American teen:
".... I was walking home from school with one of my friends, and she was
like, 'Why don't you go and talk to that guy?' I said, 'He got a job? Do he
keep money?' She said, 'No.' I said, 'Bye.'"[15]

Marriage seldom improves the life prospects of poor teen mothers or
their children, as the father most often experiences the same lack of
opportunity and job prospects. In a 1992 ethnographic study of teen
fathers from three poor and working-class neighborhoods (respectively
composed of predominantly African-American, Chicano, and white residents), Mercer Sullivan found that ethnic values do make a difference in
marriage rates: Chicano teen fathers were more likely than their African-
American or white counterparts to marry their girlfriends, to share a
house with them, or to willingly establish paternity after the birth of a
child. Ironically, however, rather than placing teen mothers and their
children at an advantage, marriage and cohabitation may create additional economic and psychological stresses. First, as Sullivan points out,
many teen mothers in the poor and predominantly Chicano neighborhood he studied needed governmental assistance to help them raise their
children. Because Chicano teens were more likely to marry after the birth
of a child than African-American or white adolescents, these teens could
not pursue strategies in which the mother collected welfare and the father
supplemented this income from work when he was able to find it.
Coresidence proved equally challenging. Because these teens did not
have the financial resources to set up households of their own, coresidence most often necessitated one teen moving into the other's family
home. Here conflicts between the teen parents or between one teen and
the family were common and resulted in frequent shifts of residence.
Such conflicts and disruptions can be harder on children than what they
face growing up in a single-parent home.[16]

There may be some historically conditioned cultural values making
single motherhood more acceptable in African-American communities
(see Crosbie-Burnett and Lewis, this volume, for an argument that the

African-American community retains traces of a child-centered tradition that is less concerned about "legitimacy"), while encouraging low rates of abortion and high rates of marriage in Chicano neighborhoods. But several studies have documented the salience of class over race and ethnicity in determining the incidence of teenage childbearing. For instance, Lisbeth Schorr found that in Washington, D.C., the rate of teenage births was more strongly associated with poor households than with African-American households, and she argues that poverty is a more definitive predictor than race in determining whether an adolescent is sexually active and uses contraceptives. Christopher Jencks and Susan Mayer found that, controlling for race and family background, sixteen- to eighteen-year-old girls were considerably more likely to bear children while unmarried if they lived in poor neighborhoods than if they lived in economically average neighborhoods. Casting further doubt on the notion of a racialized "culture of poverty," Jonathan Crane found that the few white teens living in the poorest areas of the largest cities demonstrated patterns of teenage childbearing that were "more like [those of] black teens than other whites in terms of childbearing."[17]

Class, culture, and family background interact in complicated ways. In many studies, poor academic skills and low prospects for educational attainment rank with poverty in determining incidence of adolescent childbearing. According to Schorr, educational aspirations and socioeconomic status rank as the two most important factors in using contraception effectively and postponing sex, and she found that the higher a teenage female's educational prospects, the more likely she is to avoid pregnancy. Linda Waite and her colleagues at the Rand Corporation found that teen birth rates were highest among girls who had the greatest economic disadvantage and the lowest academic ability. Again however, educational attainment is difficult to disentangle from the historical influence of class status, enforced through systematic racial-ethnic discrimination. Though terms such as "academic ability" and "educational aspirations" sound neutral enough, they are factors highly tempered by social privilege.[18]

Most people think that able and committed children will automatically stay in school, and that their efforts will pay off in a fair shot at an economically stable future. But the social location of the poorest of the poor produces neighborhoods with few connections to the job market and few opportunities to get a decent education. To be sure, the occasional gifted student can, with a little luck, get an education; but other intelligent students run into dead ends, while average students, or ones who would have succeeded with extra help in more affluent communities, fall farther and farther behind. Schools do much more than prepare kids for future jobs or education. In neighborhoods and schools, both rich and poor, children are instilled with a sense of the opportunities available to them, of their place in the social order. Children who attend poor, segregated schools soon learn to doubt their capabilities as well as their opportunities, giving them little incentive to engage in what middle-class Americans would consider rational planning for the future.

The correlation between attending a poor school and bearing a child in one's teens is extraordinary. Inner-city schools in Chicago, New York, Cincinnati, and San Antonio, composed of predominantly African-American and Chicano student bodies, have dropout rates of approximately 50 to 60 percent; high school dropouts are six times more likely than their contemporaries who remain in school to become unmarried parents. A high school teacher in a poor school in East St. Louis makes the connection between schooling and teen childbearing this way:

> I have four girls right now in my senior home room who are pregnant or have just had babies. When I ask them why this happens, I am told, 'Well, there's no reason not to have a baby. There's not much for me in public school.' The truth is, that's a pretty honest answer. A diploma from a ghetto high school doesn't count for much in the United States today. So, if this is really the last education that a person's going to get, she's probably perceptive in that statement.[19]

Just how little does a diploma from an inner-city high school count? Designs for Change, a Chicago-based research center, found in a survey of the eighteen poorest schools in the country that only 3.5 percent of the students both graduate and can read at the national level. In other words, if 6,700 students enter the ninth grade in these eighteen schools every year, only 300 will make it out with both a diploma and adequate reading skills.[20]

Due to inequitable and antiquated systems of school funding, most inner-city schools do not possess the funds to offer college preparatory or advanced classes, even though inner-city residents often tax themselves at higher rates than those in the suburbs (residents of impoverished East St. Louis have the highest property tax rate in the state of Illinois, for example). Instead, as Johnathon Kozol, author of some of the most incisive work on economic inequity in public schools, asserts: "Job-specific courses such as 'cosmetology' ... are a common item in the segregated high schools and are seen as realistic preparation for the adult roles that sixteen-year-old black girls may expect to fill." Wilson argues that most inner-city schools "train minority youth so that they feel and appear capable of only performing jobs in the low-wage sector," while Samuel Bowles and Herbert Gintis, in a study of the history of education in America, argue that the education students receive in inner-city schools helps solidify a bleak economic standing in the future.[21]

Children in inner-city schools are well aware of the inequity of their situation. Students in suburban schools, they realize, don't have to put up with regular sewage and heating disasters or severe shortages of books and supplies. Nor do suburban elementary schools exist in former roller-skating rinks where there is no playground or even windows in the classrooms (after lunch these kids sit and wait until it's time to go back to class because there is no place for them to play). They get the message quite quickly about society's assessment of their relative worth.[22]

A Puerto Rican student at a poor high school in New York calls attention to the racism and economic disadvantage that characterize these circumstances. He states:

> If you threw us into some different place, some ugly land, and put white children in this building in our place, this school would start to shine.... They'd fix it fast, no question. People on the outside may think that we don't know what it is like for other students, but we *visit* other schools, and we have eyes and we have brains. You cannot hide the differences. You see it and compare....[23]

The differences are shocking. For instance, in 1988–89 the spending disparity in New Jersey public schools reached $4,187 per pupil. Students in the wealthy and predominantly white suburban district of Princeton received $7,725 per pupil during this school year, while students in the nearby and predominantly African-American and Chicano district of Camden received $3,538 per pupil. Where economically disadvantaged students should be getting high-quality and amply funded schooling to help assuage the deficits of poverty, they are getting less than half of what wealthy white kids are thought to so obviously deserve.[24]

Poverty, racial-ethnic discrimination, unfair school funding, and inadequate job training are great enough burdens for any child or adolescent to attempt to live with and fight back against. But teens must also make decisions about sex in a culture that inundates them with sexual commodification at every turn yet allows them few acceptable ways to engage in responsible sex while unmarried.

In some respects, all adolescents face grossly conflicting messages about sex, responsibility, and future goals. Laurence Steinberg argues that contemporary adolescents have gained access to adult consumption patterns but have lost access to responsible adult roles, a condition he terms "adolescent rolelessness." Steinberg states:

> Owing to age segregation, contemporary teenagers are given a relatively high degree of freedom to pursue adolescent activities ... but owing to their rolelessness, they have relatively less autonomy to pursue societally valued adult activities (it is more difficult for a young person today to secure full-time employment than it was early in this century, for example).[25]

Furthermore, as Kristin Luker and others have pointed out, teens become physically mature much earlier than in the past (menarche occurs at an average twelve-and-a-half years of age currently) while the average age at first marriage has risen to almost twenty-four years of age for women and to over twenty-five years of age for men. This presents adolescents with a dilemma in simple time management. Most will face a decade or more in which they are both sexually mature and unmarried.[26]

Social rolelessness makes the gap between sexual and economic maturation especially hard to manage. Steinberg argues that because teens are privy to adult consumption expectations without access to fulfilling, adult roles, teen consumption patterns take on a narrow focus that is not informed by an expectation of adult responsibility. In this way, teens become remarkably sexualized consumers: greater discretionary consumption and leisure are seen as ends in themselves. With a lower age of sexual maturation but higher age of marriage, a ubiquitously sexualized market economy but no education for responsible sex outside of marriage, contemporary adolescence, even in the best of circumstances, is, as Luker remarks, a "reproductive minefield."[27]

Systematic discrimination and lack of economic or educational opportunity make it difficult for impoverished teens to successfully negotiate this minefield and resist the temptations (or pressures) of unprotected sex. Most young women do not try to become pregnant: 86.7 percent of all teen pregnancies are unintended. However, when a teen lacks other options for the future, there is often little reason to wait to have a baby. In this context of extraordinary deprivation and lack of control, there are some conditions that even encourage a teenage girl to bear a child, though these are completely different from the "incentives" so often, and as we have seen, misguidedly, attributed to welfare.[28]

Most pregnancies among impoverished teens are unintended, yet with opportunities for continued education and future employment seriously limited, carrying a baby to term is often the one societally valued avenue through which lower-income girls can assert their grown-up status and attempt to change some aspect of their lives. Anthropologist Elijah Anderson, who has studied African-American inner-city neighborhoods for more than twenty years, argues that teen mothers may be attempting to take part in what seems like grown-up middle-class behavior. Pregnancy, he reasons, brings hope to a teenager, however fleetingly, of a stable future complete with mate, children, and home.[29]

This hope is frustrated more often than not. Having a baby as a teenager can perpetuate educational disadvantage for the mother and pose added risks to her child. But bearing a child in one's teens is not always a self-destructive act. According to a 1990 study of 2,000 youths, teenage mothers showed significantly lower rates of substance abuse, depression, stress, and suicide than their childless peers. Says one teen mother, "Having a baby saved my life. Otherwise I'd still be on the streets—maybe dead." And as Mike Males and others have pointed out, poor teens garner much needed attention from professionals and social services when they become pregnant and can no longer be safely ignored.[30]

While it is important to recognize the complex motivations and personal agency of teens who have babies, we cannot deny the oppressive situations in which they make their choices. This oppression is not only economic, but often sexual. In two out of three births to unmarried teen mothers, the father is not a teen at all but twenty years of age or older, often much older than the mother. One factor at play here may be the association of older men with more maturity and stability than young women witness in their young male counterparts. A group of teen mothers attending two public schools for adolescent mothers described older men as "more controlling and possessive than teenage boys, but they unanimously described younger men as worse: self-centered and immature, more interested in their clothes than the children they fathered." On the other hand, it is highly probable that many of these relationships involved some measure of sexual exploitation or coercion for young teen mothers: nearly three quarters of women who had intercourse before age fourteen said they had at some point been forced to have sex.[31]

The complex mix of causes and motives driving teenage childbearing requires an equally complex and multistranded response. Instead, commentators of all political bents tend to advocate a simplistic and one-dimensional solution: getting teens to postpone childbearing until their twenties. But as Frank Furstenberg and others have noted, women from socioeconomically disadvantaged backgrounds face long odds against doing well later in life whether or not they bear children in their teens. Richard Wertheimer and Kristin Moore have estimated that if we could somehow decrease the teen birthrate by half, actual welfare costs would decline by only 20 percent rather than 50 percent, because many women would require public assistance for children born to them later in life.[32]

Luker further complicates the issue. As she points out, in the absence of social and economic reforms to change their life prospects, a large number of these women will *never* be economically ready to have children. Behind the paternalistic concern for teenage mothers may lie a more stark point of view. Our society doesn't seem to think that poor women deserve to have children at all.[33]

This would certainly seem to be the thinking behind the 1996 welfare reform law. Under the former AFDC program, states received from $1 to $4 from the federal government for every dollar they contributed to welfare, the higher rates going to poorer states. Now all states, rich or poor, are given a fixed block grant to meet the needs of poor children and their families. If a state requires more funding than the block grant provides, it will have to make up the difference itself or fail to provide benefits. On the other hand, as Christopher Jencks points out, if a state finds ways to save on its welfare expenses, either through strict time limits, stiff eligibility requirements or other measures, it gets to keep the difference—not an insignificant incentive for cutbacks in a climate where race and class prejudices translate into hostility toward impoverished women and children.[34]

In addition to removing the federal safety net for poor mothers with young children, the law sets stringent work requirements: 50 percent of each state's welfare caseload must have jobs by 2002, though again, many states have set even stricter work requirements. The law also sets a five-year maximum lifetime limit for the receipt of federal aid, though many states have already opted for shorter two-year limits. Both taxpayers and politicians have breathed public sighs of relief at these stipulations: no more free handouts for mothers who refuse to work. There are a few problems, however, with the idea that this kind of welfare legislation will solve the problem.[35]

How mothers with limited skills and experience will find jobs, what they will do with their kids when they are working and federal childcare subsidies have run out, and what will happen when they cannot find or keep steady jobs and have reached their lifetime assistance limits are critical questions still unanswered at this point. Most mothers on welfare have limited skills and job experience, qualifying them for only the most menial and unstable work in the service sector. Welfare recipients will flood the low-wage service sector, depressing low wages there even further. Some workers are likely to be pushed even further to the bottom when state caseworkers and trainers do not have the language skills necessary to communicate with non-English-speaking welfare recipients.[36]

As researchers have pointed out, there are sure to be a significant numbers of women whom no one wants to hire or who cannot work because of physical or psychological disabilities, either their own or their children's. Without the creation of a substantial number of government-funded jobs and an increase in Supplemental Social Security payments for those women who are unable to work, many families will undoubtedly fall through the cracks, splitting up or ending up in shelters when they have exhausted other options.[37]

It is also uncertain whether mothers will earn enough through low-wage work to support their families. Women incur a host of additional expenses when they leave welfare for work that often outweigh actual wage gains. Working mothers have to pay for child care and transportation, necessitating a working, maintained car. At the same time that mothers are scrambling to find ways to afford these expensive items on minimum wages, they also eventually lose Medicaid benefits while facing severe reductions in food-stamp allotments and housing subsidies. Low-wage working mothers live in a more precarious position that might be immediately apparent: one severely sick child or major car repair can easily threaten basic subsistence or job security. It is uncertain where these mothers will now turn in the face of crisis.[38]

As this book goes to press, support for the welfare reform law is high, with some states reporting declines in caseloads and former welfare recipients finding jobs. But these gains are more likely a result of the robust economic expansion since 1992 than of welfare law changes. What will become of these mothers and their families when the next recession hits and low-wage jobs are the first to be cut? Also unknown at this point is the effect of a large influx of low-wage workers into an economy where many lower-income workers are barely managing to survive. Many economists worry that an influx of this magnitude will drive meager wages even lower and make crucial housing and child-care subsidies even harder to come by.[39]

It would be foolish to romanticize the old welfare system, which often trapped women into behaviors and habits that were necessary in order to subsist on below-poverty incomes and within tangled eligibility rules, but made it impossible to move forward. If states take advantage of good economic times to invest in child care, steady jobs, and home-assistance programs, there are many innovative and helpful things that can be done under the new law. Unfortunately, the new law also offers states the easy option of cutting benefits, paying nominal fines rather than meeting federal guidelines, and continuing to penalize teen mothers and their children. After all the talk about the shortsighted values of welfare recipients and teen mothers, perhaps political and economic leaders should question their own inability to defer short-run tax-refund gratification in favor of planning seriously for the future.

NOTES

Thanks to Nathan Woods, Maya Parson, Jessica Raley, and Quata Coty for their comments on drafts of this work, and to Todd Smith for his kind support. Thanks especially to Stephanie Coontz for our conversations on African-American history, for her careful editing of every draft, and for her constant demand for clarity and relevance.

1. Stephanie Coontz, *The Way We Really Are: Coming to Terms With America's Changing Families* (New York: Basic Books, 1997).
2. Richard Morin, "The Tooth Fairy, the Easter Bunny, and the Welfare Mom," *Washington Post National Weekly Edition*, 25 April–1 May 1994; Barbara Vobejda, "Gauging Welfare's Role in Motherhood," *Washington Post*, 2 June 1994.
3. Vobejda, "Gauging Welfare's Role in Motherhood"; Barbara Vobejda and Judith Havemann, "Social Policy vs. Human Nature," *Washington Post National Weekly Edition*, 7 April 1997.
4. Morin, "The Tooth Fairy, the Easter Bunny, and the Welfare Mom"; Kevin Ryan and Jill Chaifetz, "Cutting Welfare Won't Reduce Teen-Age Births," *New York Times*, 21 April 1995. On U.S. and European abortion and birth rates see Diane Scott-Jones, "Adolescent Childbearing: Whose Problem? What Can We Do?" *Kappan Special Report*, November 1993, p. K5; Stephen J. Caldas, "Teen Pregnancy: Why It Remains a Serious Social, Economic and Educational Problem in the U.S." *Phi Delta Kappan*, January 1994, p. 404.
5. Center on Social Welfare Policy and Law, "Welfare Myths: Fact or Fiction?" *Welfare News*, 3 June 1996, pp. 10–11; Stephanie Coontz, *The Way We Never Were: American Families and the Nostalgia Trap* (New York: Basic Books, 1992).
6. Frank F. Furstenberg Jr., Jeanne Brooks-Gunn, and Lindsay Chase-Lansdale, "Teenaged Pregnancy and Childbearing," *American Psychologist* 44,

February 1989, p. 315.

7. Arline Geronimus and Sanders Korenman, "The Socioeconomic Consequences of Teen Childbearing Reconsidered," *Quarterly Journal of Economics* CVII, 1992. Nan Marie Astone, "Are Adolescent Mothers Just Single Mothers?" *Journal of Research on Adolescence* 3 (4), 1993, p. 367. On rates of poverty by race and ethnicity see Laurence E. Lynn Jr. and Michael G.H. McGeary, eds., *Inner-City Poverty in the United States* (Washington, D.C.: National Academy Press, 1990), p. 10; William Julius Wilson, *The Truly Disadvantaged* (Chicago: University of Chicago Press, 1987); Mervin L. Oliver and Thomas M. Shapiro, *Black Wealth/White Wealth* (New York: Routledge, 1995). For adolescent rates of poverty by race and ethnicity see Andrew M. Sum and W. Neal Fogg, "The Adolescent Poor and the Transition to Early Adulthood," in Peter B. Edelman and Joyce Ladner, eds., *Adolescence & Poverty: Challenge for the 1990s* (Washington, D.C.: Center for National Policy Press, 1991), p. 43. On the connection between poverty and teenaged childbearing see Lisbeth Schorr, *Within Our Reach: Breaking the Cycle of Disadvantage* (Garden City, N.Y.: Anchor Press/Doubleday, 1988).

8. Thomas J. Sugrue, "Poor Families in an Era of Urban Transformation: The 'Underclass' Family in Myth and Reality," in the present volume.

9. Thank you to Stephanie Coontz for clarification of these points.

10. Louise Lamphere, Patricia Zavella, Felipe Gonzales, with Peter B. Evans, *Sunbelt Working Mothers: Reconciling Family and Factory* (New York: Cornell University Press, 1993).

11. Wilson, *The Truly Disadvantaged.*

12. Wilson, *The Truly Disadvantaged*, pp. 50–56, 135.

13. Wilson, *The Truly Disadvantaged*, p. 58. On conditions of inner cities see Jonathan Kozol, *Savage Inequalities: Children in America's Schools* (New York: Crown Publishers, 1991).

14. Naomi Farber, "The Significance of Race and Class in Marital Decisions among Unmarried Adolescent Mothers," *Social Problems*, Vol. 37, No. 1, February 1990.

15. Farber, "The Significance of Race and Class in Marital Decisions," pp. 58–59.

16. Mercer L. Sullivan, "Culture and Class as Determinants of Out-of-Wedlock Childbearing and Poverty During Late Adolescence," *Journal of Research on Adolescence*, Vol. 3, No. 3, 1993.

17. Margaret Crosbie-Burnett and Edith A. Lewis "Use of African-American Family Structures and Functioning to Address the Challenges of European-American Postdivorce Families" in the present volume; Lisbeth Schorr, *Within Our Reach: Breaking the Cycle of Disadvantage*, p. 60; Christopher Jencks and Susan E. Mayer, "The Social Consequences of Growing Up in a Poor Neighborhood," in Laurence E. Lynn Jr. and Michael G.H. McGeary, eds., *Inner-City Poverty in the United States*, p. 167; Jonathan Crane, "Effects of Neighborhoods on Dropping Out of School and Teenage Childbearing," in Christopher Jencks and Paul E. Peterson, eds., *The Urban Underclass* (Washington, D.C.: Brookings Institution, 1991), p. 311.

18. Schorr, *Within Our Reach*, p. 62; Luker, "Dubious Conceptions: The Controversy Over Teen Pregnancy," p. 169.

19. Kozol, *Savage Inequalities*; Schorr, *Within Our Reach*, quote from p. 9.

20. Kozol, *Savage Inequalities*, pp. 58–59.

21. Kozol, *Savage Inequalities*, p. 76; Wilson, *The Truly Disadvantaged*, p. 103.

22. Kozol, *Savage Inequalities*.
23. Ibid., p. 104.
24. Ibid., p. 236.
25. Laurence Steinberg, "The Logic of Adolescence," in Peter B. Edelman and Joyce Ladner, eds., *Adolescence & Poverty: Challenge for the 1990s*, p. 30.
26. Luker, "Dubious Conceptions," p. 171.
27. Steinberg, "The Logic of Adolescence"; Luker, "Dubious Conceptions," p. 171.
28. Laurie Schwab Zabin, Nan Marie Astone, and Mark R. Emerson, "Do Adolescents Want Babies? The Relationship Between Attitudes and Behavior," *Journal of Research on Adolescence* 3 (1), 1993.
29. Elijah Anderson, "Neighborhood Effects on Teenage Pregnancy," in Jencks and Peterson, eds., *The Urban Underclass*, p. 382.
30. Elizabeth Gleick et al., "The Baby Trap," *Time*, 24 October 1994, p. 43; Mike Males, "In Defense of Teenaged Mothers," *The Progressive*, August 1994, pp. 22–23.
31. Mireya Navarro, "Teen-Age Mothers Viewed as Abused Prey of Older Men," *New York Times*, 19 May 1996; Barbara Vobejda, "Teens Improve on Prevention of Pregnancy: Study Contradicts Widely Held Beliefs About Adolescent Sex," *Washington Post*, 7 June 1994.
32. Frank F. Furstenberg Jr., "As the Pendulum Swings: Teenage Childbearing and Social Concern," *Family Relations* 40, April 1991, p. 132; Luker, "Dubious Conceptions," p. 173.
33. Luker, "Dubious Conceptions."
34. Christopher Jencks, "The Hidden Paradox of Welfare Reform," *The American Prospect*, No. 32, May–June 1997, pp. 33–40.
35. Kathryn Edin and Laura Lein, "Work, Welfare, and Single Mothers' Economic Strategies," *American Sociological Review*, Vol. 62, No. 2, April 1997, pp. 253–266.
36. Evelyn Nakano Glenn, "From Servitude to Service Work: Historical Continuities in the Racial Division of Paid Productive Labor," in Vicki L. Ruiz and Ellen Carol DuBois, eds., *Unequal Sisters: A Multicultural Reader in U.S. Women's History*. 2d. ed., quote by Bibiana Andrade in Laura Flanders and Janine Jackson, "Reforming Welfare Coverage," *EXTRA!*, Vol. 10, No. 3, May–June 1997, pp. 6–10.
37. Jencks, "The Hidden Paradox of Welfare Reform."
38. Edin and Lein, "Work, Welfare, and Single Mothers." For an excellent discussion of coping strategies of women in low-wage work and welfare, see Edin and Lein, *Making Ends Meet: How Single Mothers Survive Welfare and Low Wage Work* (S.L. Russell Sage Foundation, 1997).
39. Jencks, "The Hidden Paradox of Welfare Reform."

14

EXCERPTS FROM *FAMILIES ON THE FAULT LINE:*

AMERICA'S WORKING CLASS SPEAKS ABOUT THE FAMILY, THE ECONOMY, RACE, AND ETHNICITY

Lillian B. Rubin

"They're letting all these coloreds come in and soon there won't be any place left for white people," broods Tim Walsh, a thirty-three-year-old white construction worker. "It makes you wonder: Is this a white country, or what?"

It's a question that nags at white America, one perhaps that's articulated most often and most clearly by the men and women of the working class. For it's they who feel most vulnerable, who have suffered the economic contractions of recent decades most keenly, who see the new immigrants most clearly as direct competitors for their jobs.

It's not whites alone who stew about immigrants. Native-born blacks, too, fear the newcomers nearly as much as whites do—and for the same economic reasons. But for whites the issue is compounded by race, by the fact that the newcomers are primarily people of color. For them, therefore, their economic anxieties have combined with the changing face of America to create a profound uneasiness about immigration.

While there's little doubt that racial anxieties are at the center of white concerns, our historic nativism also plays a part in escalating white alarm. The new immigrants bring with them languages and ethnic cultures that are vividly expressed wherever they congregate. And it's this also, the constant reminder of an alien presence from which whites are excluded, that's so troublesome to them.

The nativist impulse isn't, of course, given to the white working class alone. But for those in the upper reaches of the class and status hierarchy—those whose children go to private schools, whose closest contact with public transportation is the taxicab—the immigrant population supplies a source of cheap labor, whether as nannies for their children, maids in their households, or workers in their businesses. They may grouse and complain that "nobody speaks English anymore," just as working-class people do. But for the people who use immigrant labor, legal or illegal, there's a payoff for the inconvenience—a payoff that doesn't exist for the families in this study but that sometimes costs them dearly.[1] For while it may be true that American workers aren't eager for many of the jobs immigrants are willing to take, it's also true that the presence of a large immigrant population—especially of those who come from developing countries where living standards are far below our own—helps to make these jobs undesirable by keeping wages depressed well below what most American workers are willing to accept.[2]

Indeed, the economic basis of our immigration policies too often gets lost in the lore that we are a land that says to the world, "Give me your tired, your poor, your huddled masses, yearning to breathe free."[3] I don't mean to suggest that our humane impulses are a fiction, only that the reality is far more complex than Emma Lazarus's poem suggests. The massive immigration of the nineteenth and early twentieth centuries didn't just happen spontaneously. America may have been known as the land of opportunity to the Europeans who dreamed of coming here—a country where, as my parents once believed, the streets were lined with gold. But they believed these things because that's how America was sold by the agents who spread out across the face of Europe to recruit workers—men and women who were needed to keep the machines of our developing industrial society running and who, at the same time, gave the new industries a steady supply of hungry workers willing to work for wages well below those of native-born Americans.

The enormous number of immigrants who arrived during that period accomplished both those ends. In doing so, they set the stage for a long history of antipathy to foreign workers. For today, also, one function of the new immigrants is to keep our industries competitive in a global economy. Which is simply another way of saying that they serve to depress the wages of native-born American workers.

It's not surprising, therefore, that working-class women and men speak so angrily about the recent influx of immigrants. They not only see their jobs and their way of life threatened, they feel bruised and assaulted by an environment that seems suddenly to have turned color and in which they feel like strangers in their own land. So they chafe and complain: "They come here to take advantage of us, but they don't really want to learn our ways," Beverly Sowell, a thirty-three-year-old white electronics assembler, grumbles irritably. "They live different than us; it's like another world how they live. And they're so clannish. They keep to themselves, and they don't even *try* to learn English. You go on the bus these days and you might as well be in a foreign country; everybody's talking some other language, you know, Chinese or Spanish or something. Lots of them have been here a long time, too, but they don't care; they just want to take what they can get."

But these complaints reveal an interesting paradox, an illuminating glimpse into the contradictions that beset native-born Americans in their relations with those who seek refuge here. On the one hand, they scorn the immigrants; on the other, they protest because they "keep to themselves." It's the same contradiction that dominates black-white relations. Whites refuse to integrate blacks but are outraged when they stop knocking at the door, when they move to sustain the separation on their own terms—in black theme houses on campuses, for example, or in the newly developing black middle-class suburbs.

I wondered, as I listened to Beverly Sowell and others like her, why the same people who find the lifeways and languages of our foreign-born population offensive also care whether they "keep to themselves."

"Because like I said, they just shouldn't, that's all," Beverly says stubbornly. "If they're going to come here, they should be willing to learn our ways—you know what I mean, be real Americans. That's what my grandparents did, and that's what they should do."

"But your grandparents probably lived in an immigrant neighborhood when they first came here, too," I remind her.

"It was different," she insists. "I don't know why; it was. They wanted to be Americans; these here people now, I don't think they do. They just want to take advantage of this country."

She stops, thinks for a moment, then continues, "Right now it's awful in this country. Their kids come into the schools, and it's a big mess. There's not enough money for our kids to get a decent education, and we have to spend money to teach their kids English. It makes me mad. I went to public school, but I have to send my kids to Catholic school because now on top of the black kids, there's all these foreign kids who don't speak English. What kind of an education can kids get in a school like that? Something's wrong when plain old American kids can't go to their own schools.

"Everything's changed, and it doesn't make sense. Maybe you get it, but I don't. We can't take care of our own people and we keep bringing more and more foreigners in. Look at all the homeless. Why do we need more people here when our own people haven't got a place to sleep?"

"Why do we need more people here?"—a question Americans have asked for two centuries now. Historically, efforts to curb immigration have come during economic downturns, which suggests that when times are good, when American workers feel confident about their future, they're likely to be more generous in sharing their good fortune with foreigners. But when the economy falters, as it did in the [early] 1990s, and workers worry about having to compete for jobs with people whose standard of living is well below their own, resistance to immigration rises. "Don't get me wrong; I've got nothing against these people," Tim Walsh demurs. "But they don't talk English, and they're used to a lot less, so they can work for less money than guys like me can. I see it all the time; they get hired and some white guy gets left out."

It's this confluence of forces—the racial and cultural diversity of our new immigrant population; the claims on the resources of the nation now being made by those minorities who, for generations, have called America their home; the failure of some of our basic institutions to serve the needs of our people; the contracting economy, which threatens the mobility aspirations of working-class families—all these have come together to leave white workers feeling as if everyone else is getting a piece of the action while they get nothing. "I feel like white people are left out in the cold," protests Diane Johnson, a twenty-eight-year-old white single mother who believes she lost a job as a bus driver to a black woman. "First it's the blacks; now it's all those other colored people, and it's like everything always goes their way. It seems like a white person doesn't have a chance anymore. It's like the squeaky wheel gets the grease, and they've been squeaking and we haven't," she concludes angrily.

Until recently, whites didn't need to think about having to "squeak"— at least not specifically as whites. They have, of course, organized and squeaked at various times in the past—sometimes as ethnic groups, sometimes as workers. But not as whites. As whites they have been the dominant group, the favored ones, the ones who could count on getting the job when people of color could not. Now suddenly there are others— not just individual others but identifiable groups, people who share a history, a language, a culture, even a color—who lay claim to some of the rights and privileges that formerly had been labeled "for whites only." And whites react as if they've been betrayed, as if a sacred promise has been broken. They're white, aren't they? They're *real* Americans, aren't they? This is their country, isn't it?

The answers to these questions used to be relatively unambiguous. But not anymore. Being white no longer automatically assures dominance in the politics of a multiracial society. Ethnic group politics, however, has a long and fruitful history. As whites sought a social and political base on which to stand, therefore, it was natural and logical to reach back to their ethnic past. Then they, too, could be "something"; they also would belong to a group; they would have a name, a history, a culture, and a voice. "Why is it only the blacks or Mexicans or Jews that are 'something'?" asks Tim Walsh. "I'm Irish, isn't that something, too? Why doesn't that count?"

In reclaiming their ethnic roots, whites can recount with pride the tribulations and transcendence of their ancestors and insist that others take their place in the line from which they have only recently come. "My people had a rough time, too. But nobody gave us anything, so why do we owe them something? Let them pull their share like the rest of us had to do," says Al Riccardi, a twenty-nine-year-old white taxi driver.

From there it's only a short step to the conviction that those who don't progress up that line are hampered by nothing more than their own inadequacies or, worse yet, by their unwillingness to take advantage of the opportunities offered them. "Those people, they're hollering all the time about discrimination," Al continues, without defining who "those people" are. "Maybe once a long time ago that was true, but not now. The problem is that a lot of those people are lazy. There's plenty of opportunities, but you've got to be willing to work hard."

He stops a moment, as if listening to his own words, then continues, "Yeah, yeah, I know there's a recession on and lots of people don't have jobs. But it's different with some of those people. They don't really want to work, because if they did, there wouldn't be so many of them selling drugs and getting in all kinds of trouble."

"You keep talking about 'those people' without saying who you mean," I remark.

"Aw c'mon, you know who I'm talking about," he says, shifting uneasily in his chair. "It's mostly the black people, but the Spanish ones, too."

In reality, however, it's a no-win situation for America's people of color, whether immigrant or native born. For the industriousness of the Asians comes in for nearly as much criticism as the alleged laziness of other groups. When blacks don't make it, it's because, whites like Al Riccardi insist, their culture doesn't teach respect for family; because they're hedonistic, lazy, stupid, and/or criminally inclined. But when Asians demonstrate their ability to overcome the obstacles of an alien language and culture, when the Asian family seems to be the repository of our most highly regarded traditional values, white hostility doesn't disappear. It just changes its form. Then the accomplishments of Asians, the speed with which they move up the economic ladder, aren't credited to their superior culture, diligence, or intelligence—even when these are granted—but to the fact that they're "single-minded," "untrustworthy," "clannish drones," "narrow people" who raise children who are insufficiently "well-rounded."[4]

True, the remarkable successes of members of the Asian immigrant community have engendered grudging, if ambivalent, respect. "If our people were as hard working and disciplined as the Asians, we'd be a lot better off," says Doug Craigen, a thirty-two-year-old white truck driver.

But the words are barely out of his mouth before the other side surfaces and he reaches for the stereotypes that are so widely accepted. "I'm not a racist, but sometimes they give me the creeps. You've got to watch out for them because they'll do anything for a buck, anything. I guess the thing that bothers me most is you can't get away from them," he explains, as if their very presence is somehow menacing. "They're all over the place, like pushy little yellow drones. You go to the bank, they're working there. You go to a store, they're behind the counter. It's like they're gobbling up all the jobs in town."

The job market isn't the only place where Asians are competing successfully with whites. From grade school to college, Asian students are taking a large share of the top honors, leaving white parents in a state of anxious concern.[5] "I don't know if our kids can compete with those Chinese kids," worries Linda Hammer, a thirty-year-old white beautician who hopes to see her children in college one day. "My kids aren't bad students, but those Asian kids, that's all they live for. I don't think it's good to push kids so hard, do you? I mean, I hear some of those people beat their kids if they don't get A's. They turn them into little nerds who don't do anything but study. How can American kids compete with that?"

Whites aren't alone in greeting Asian successes so ambivalently. Like Doug Craigen, Lurine Washington, a black thirty-year-old nurse's aide, speaks admiringly of the accomplishments of her Asian neighbors. "I could get killed for saying this, but I don't care. The Asians are a lot more disciplined than blacks as a whole. That's not a racist statement;

it's a fact because of their culture. Saying that doesn't mean I don't like my people, but I'm not blind either. All I know is if our kids worked as hard in school as theirs do, they could make something of themselves, too. And those families, all of them working together like that. You've got to respect that, don't you?"

Moments later, however, Lurine complains, "If we don't watch out, they'll take over everything. I mean, they already own half the country, even Rockefeller Center. You know what I mean. They're like ants; there's so many of them, and they're so sneaky and everything. And they think they're better than other people; that's what really makes me mad."

Not surprisingly, as competition increases, the various minority groups often are at war among themselves as they press their own particular claims, fight over turf, and compete for an ever shrinking piece of the pie. In several African-American communities, where Korean shopkeepers have taken the place once held by Jews, the confrontations have been both wrenching and tragic. A Korean grocer in Los Angeles shoots and kills a fifteen-year-old black girl for allegedly trying to steal some trivial item from the store.[6] From New York City to Berkeley, California, African-Americans boycott Korean shop owners who, they charge, invade their neighborhoods, take their money, and treat them disrespectfully.[7] But painful as these incidents are for those involved, they are only symptoms of a deeper malaise in both communities—the contempt and distrust in which the Koreans hold their African-American neighbors, and the rage of blacks as they watch these new immigrants surpass them.

Latino-black conflict also makes headlines when, in the aftermath of the riots in South Central Los Angeles, the two groups fight over who will get the lion's share of the jobs to rebuild the neighborhood. Blacks, insisting that they're being discriminated against, shut down building projects that don't include them in satisfactory numbers. And indeed, many of the jobs that formerly went to African-Americans are now being taken by Latino workers. In an article entitled, "Black vs. Brown," Jack Miles, an editorial writer for the *Los Angeles Times*, reports that "janitorial firms serving downtown Los Angeles have almost entirely replaced their unionized black work force with non-unionized immigrants."[8]

On their side of the escalating divide, the Latino community complains bitterly that they always take second place to black demands. "Nobody pays attention to us like they do to the blacks," protests Julio Martinez, a thirty-year-old Latino warehouseman. "There's a saying in Spanish: You scratch where it itches. There's plenty of problems all around us here," he explains, his sweeping gesture encompassing the Latino neighborhood where he lives, "but they don't pay attention because we don't make so much trouble. But people are getting mad. That's what happened in L.A.; they got mad because nobody paid attention."

But the disagreements among America's racial minorities are of little interest or concern to most white working-class families. Instead of conflicting groups, they see one large mass of people of color, all of them making claims that endanger working-class whites' own precarious place in the world. It's this perception that has led some white ethnics to believe that reclaiming their ethnicity alone is not enough, that so long as they remain in their separate and distinct groups, their power will be limited. United, however, they can become a formidable countervailing force, one that can stand fast against the threat posed by minority demands. But to come together solely as whites would diminish their impact and leave them open to the charge that their real purpose is simply to retain the privileges of whiteness. A dilemma that has been resolved, at least for some, by the birth of a new entity in the history of American ethnic groups—the "European-Americans."[9]

At the University of California at Berkeley, for example, white students and their faculty supporters insisted that the recently adopted multicultural curriculum include a unit of study on European-Americans. At Queens College in New York City, where white ethnic groups retain a more distinct presence, Italian-American students launched a successful suit to win recognition as a disadvantaged minority and gain the entitlements accompanying that status, including special units of Italian-American studies.

White high school students, too, talk of feeling isolated and, being less sophisticated and wary than their older sisters and brothers, complain quite openly that there's no acceptable and legitimate way for them to acknowledge a white identity. "There's all these things for all the different ethnicities, you know, like clubs for black kids and Hispanic kids, but there's nothing for me and my friends to join," Lisa Marshall, a sixteen-year-old white high school student explains with exasperation. "They won't let us have a white club because that's supposed to be racist. So we figured we'd just have to call it something else, you know, some ethnic thing, like Euro-Americans. Why not? They have African-American clubs."

Ethnicity, then, often becomes a cover for "white," not necessarily because these students are racist but because racial identity is now such a prominent feature of the discourse in our social world. In a society where racial consciousness is so high, how else can whites define themselves in ways that connect them to a community and, at the same time, allow them to deny their racial antagonisms?

Ethnicity and race—separate phenomena that are now inextricably entwined. Incorporating newcomers has never been easy, as our history of controversy and violence over immigration tell us.[10] But for the first time, the new immigrants are also people of color, which means that they tap both the nativist and racist impulses that are so deeply a part of American life. As in the past, however, the fear of foreigners, the revulsion against their strange customs and seemingly unruly ways, is only part of the reason for the anti-immigrant attitudes that are increasingly being expressed today. For whatever xenophobic suspicions may arise in modern America, economic issues play a critical role in stirring them up.

"This Country Don't Owe Nobody Nothing!"

Two decades ago, when I began the research for *Worlds of Pain*, we were living in the immediate aftermath of the civil rights revolution that had convulsed the nation since the mid-1950s. Significant gains had been won. And despite the tenacity with which this headway had been resisted by some, most white Americans were feeling good about themselves. No one expected the nation's racial problems and conflicts to dissolve easily or quickly. But there was also a sense that we were moving in the right direction, that there was a national commitment to redressing at least some of the worst aspects of black-white inequality.

In the intervening years, however, the national economy buckled under the weight of three recessions, while the nation's industrial base was undergoing a massive restructuring. At the same time, government policies requiring preferential treatment were enabling African-Americans and other minorities to make small but visible inroads into what had been, until then, largely white terrain. The sense of scarcity, always a part of American life but intensified sharply by the history of these economic upheavals, made minority gains seem particularly threatening to white working-class families.

It isn't, of course, just working-class whites who feel threatened by minority progress. Wherever racial minorities make inroads into formerly all-white territory, tensions increase. But it's working-class families who feel the fluctuations in the economy most quickly and most keenly. For them, these last decades have been like a bumpy roller coaster ride. "Every time we think we might be able to get ahead, it seems like we get knocked down again," declares Tom Ahmundsen, a forty-two-year-old white construction worker. "Things look a little better; there's a little more work; then all of a sudden, boom, the economy falls apart and it's gone. You can't count on anything; it really gets you down."

This is the story I heard repeatedly: Each small climb was followed by a fall, each glimmer of hope replaced by despair. As the economic vise tightened, despair turned to anger. But partly because we have so little concept of class resentment and conflict in America, this anger isn't directed so much at those above as at those below. And when whites at or near the bottom of the ladder look down in this nation, they generally see blacks and other minorities.

True, during all of the 1980s and into the 1990s, white ire was fostered by national administrations that fanned racial discord as a way of fending off white discontent—of diverting anger about the state of the economy and the declining quality of urban life toward the foreigners and racial others in our midst. But our history of racial animosity coupled with our lack of class consciousness made this easier to accomplish than it might otherwise have been.

The difficult realities of white working-class life not withstanding, however, their whiteness has accorded them significant advantages—

both materially and psychologically—over people of color. Racial discrimination and segregation in the workplace have kept competition for the best jobs at a minimum. Obviously, working-class whites have to compete with each other for the resources available. But that's different. It's a competition among equals; they're all white. They don't think such things consciously, of course; they don't have to. It's understood, rooted in the culture and supported by the social contract that says they are the superior ones, the worthy ones. Indeed, this is precisely why, when the courts or the legislatures act in ways that seems to contravene that belief, whites see themselves as victims.

From the earliest days of the republic, whiteness has been the ideal, and freedom and independence have been linked to being white. "Republicanism," writes labor historian David Roediger, "had long emphasized that the strength, virtue and resolve of a people guarded them from enslavement."[11] And it was whites who had these qualities in abundance, as was evident, in the peculiarly circuitous reasoning of the time, in the fact that they were not slaves.

By this logic, the enslavement of blacks could be seen as stemming from their "slavishness" rather than from the institution of slavery. Slavery is gone now, but the reasoning lingers on in white America, which still insists that the lowly estate of people of color is due to their deficits, whether personal or cultural, rather than to the prejudice, discrimination, and institutionalized racism that has barred them from full participation in the society.

This is not to say that culture is irrelevant, whether among black Americans or any other group in our society. The lifeways of a people develop out of their experiences—out of the daily events, large and small, that define their lives; out of the resources that are available to them to meet both individual and group needs; out of the place in the social, cultural, and political systems within which group life is embedded. In the case of a significant proportion of blacks in America's inner cities, centuries of racism and economic discrimination have produced a subculture that is both personally and socially destructive. But to fault culture or the failure of individual responsibility without understanding the larger context within which such behaviors occur is to miss a vital piece of the picture. Nor does acknowledging the existence of certain destructive subcultural forms among some African-Americans disavow or diminish the causal connections between the structural inequalities at the social, political, and economic levels and the serious social problems at the community level.

In his study of "working-class lads" in Birmingham, England, for example, Paul Willis observes that their very acts of resistance to middle-class norms—the defiance with which these young men express their anger at class inequalities—help to reinforce the class structure by further entrenching them in their working-class status.[12] The same can be said for some of the young men in the African-American community, whose active rejection of white norms and "in your face" behavior consigns them to the bottom of the American economic order.

To understand this doesn't make such behavior, whether in England or the United States, any more palatable. But it helps to explain the structural sources of cultural forms and to apprehend the social processes that undergird them. Like Willis's white "working-class lads," the hip-hoppers and rappers in the black community who are so determinedly "not white" are not just making a statement about black culture. They're also expressing their rage at white society for offering a promise of equality, then refusing to fulfill it. In the process, they're finding their own way to some accommodation and to a place in the world they can call their own, albeit one that ultimately reinforces their outsider status.

But, some might argue, white immigrants also suffered prejudice and discrimination in the years after they first arrived, but they found more socially acceptable ways to accommodate. It's true—and so do most of today's people of color, both immigrant and native-born. Nevertheless, there's another truth as well. For wrenching as their early experiences were for white ethnics, they had an out. Writing about the Irish, for example, Roediger shows how they were able to insist upon their whiteness and to prove it by adopting the racist attitudes and behaviors of other whites, in the process often becoming leaders in the assault against blacks. With time and their growing political power, they won the prize they sought—recognition as whites. "The imperative to define themselves as white," writes Roediger, "came from the particular 'public and psychological wages' whiteness offered to a desperate rural and often preindustrial Irish population coming to labor in industrializing American cities."[13]

Thus does whiteness bestow its psychological as well as material blessings on even the most demeaned. For no matter how far down the socioeconomic ladder whites may fall, the one thing they can't lose is their whiteness. No small matter because, as W. E. B. DuBois observed decades ago, the compensation of white workers includes a psychological wage, a bonus that enables them to believe in their inherent superiority over nonwhites.[14]

It's also true, however, that this same psychological bonus that white workers prize so highly has cost them dearly. For along with the importation of an immigrant population, the separation of black and white workers has given American capital a reserve labor force to call upon whenever white workers seemed to them to get too "uppity." Thus, while racist ideology enables white workers to maintain the belief in their superiority, they have paid for that conviction by becoming far more vulnerable in the struggle for decent wages and working conditions than they might otherwise have been.

Politically and economically, the ideology of white supremacy strips from white workers the ability to make the kind of interracial alliances that would benefit all of the working class. Psychologically, it leaves them exposed to the double-edged sword of which I spoke earlier. On one side, their belief in the superiority of whiteness helps to reassure them that they're not at the bottom of the social hierarchy. But their insistence that their achievements are based on their special capacities and virtues, that it's only incompetence that keeps others from grabbing a piece of the American dream, threatens their precarious sense of self-esteem. For if they're the superior ones, the deserving ones, the ones who earned their place solely through hard work and merit, there's nothing left but to blame themselves for their inadequacies when hard times strike.

In the opening sentences of *Worlds of Pain* I wrote that America was choking on its differences. If we were choking then, we're being asphyxiated now. As the economy falters, and local, state, and federal governments keep cutting services, there are more and more acrimonious debates about who will share in the shrinking pie. Racial and ethnic groups, each in their own corners, square off as they ready themselves for what seems to be the fight of their lives. Meanwhile, the quality of life for all but the wealthiest Americans is spiraling downward—a plunge that's felt most deeply by those at the lower end of the class spectrum, regardless of color.[15]

As more and more mothers of young children work full-time outside the home, the question of who will raise the children comes center stage. Decent, affordable child care is scandalously scarce, with no government intervention in sight for this crucial need. In poor and working-class families, therefore, child care often is uncertain and inadequate, leaving parents apprehensive and children at risk. To deal with their fears, substantial numbers of couples now work different shifts, a solution to the child-care problem that puts its own particular strains on family life.

In families with two working parents, time has become their most precious commodity—time to attend to the necessary tasks of family life; time to nurture the relationships between wife and husband, between parents and children; time for oneself, time for others; time for solitude, time for a social life.[16] Today more than ever before, family life has become impoverished for want of time, adding another threat to the already fragile bonds that hold families together.

While women's presence in the labor force has given them a measure of independence unknown before, most also are stuck with doing two days' work in one—one on the job, the other when they get home at night. Unlike their counterparts in the earlier era, today's women are openly resentful about the burdens they carry, which makes for another dimension of conflict between wives and husbands.

Although the men generally say they've never heard of Robert Bly or any of the other modern-day gurus of manhood, the idea of men as victims has captured their imagination.[17] Given the enormous amount of publicity these men's advocates have garnered in the last few years, it's likely that some of their ideas have filtered into the awareness of the men in this study, even if they don't know how they got there. But their belief in their victimization is also a response to the politics of our time, when so many different groups—women, gays, racial minorities, the handicapped—have demanded special privileges and entitlements on the basis of past victimization. And once the language of victimization enters the political discourse, it becomes a useful tool for anyone wanting to resist the claims of others or to stake one of their own.

As the men see it, then, if their wives are victims because of the special burdens of womanhood, the husbands, who bear their own particular hardships, can make the claim as well. If African-American men are victims because of past discrimination, then the effort to redress their grievances turns white men into victims of present discrimination.

To those who have been victimized by centuries of racism, sexism, homophobia, and the like, the idea that straight white men are victims, too, seems ludicrous. Yet it's not wholly unreal, at least not for the men in this study who have so little control over their fate and who so often feel unheard and invisible, like little more than shadows shouting into the wind.

Whether inside the family or in the larger world outside, white men keep hearing that they're the privileged ones, words that seem to them like a bad joke. How can they be advantaged when their inner experience is that they're perched precariously on the edge of a chasm that seems to have opened up in the earth around them? It's this sense of vulnerability, coupled with the conviction that their hardships go unseen and their pain unattended, that nourishes their claim to victimhood.

Some analysts of family and social life undoubtedly will argue that the picture I've presented here is too grim, that it gives insufficient weight to both the positive changes in family life and the gains in race relations over these past decades. It's true that the social and cultural changes we've witnessed have created families that, in some ways at least, are more responsive to the needs of their members, more democratic than any we have known before.[18] But it's also true that without the economic stability they need, even the most positive changes will not be enough to hold families together.

Certainly, too, alongside the racial and ethnic divisions that are so prominent a part of American life today is the reality that many more members of these warring groups than ever before are living peaceably together in our schools, our factories, our shops, our corporations, and our neighborhoods. And, except for black-white marriages, many more are marrying and raising children together than would have seemed possible a few decades ago.

At the same time, there's reason to fear. The rise of ethnicity and the growing racial separation also means an escalating level of conflict that sometimes seems to threaten to fragment the nation. In this situation, ethnic entrepreneurs like Al Sharpton in New York and David Duke in Louisiana rise to power and prominence by fanning ethnic and racial discord. A tactic that works so well precisely because the economic pressures are felt so keenly on all sides of the racial fissures, because both whites and people of color now feel so deeply that "it's not fair."

As I reflect on the differences in family and social life in the last two decades, it seems to me that we were living then in a more innocent age—a time, difficult though it was for the working-class families of our nation, when we could believe that anything was possible. Whether about the economy, race relations, or life inside the family, most Americans believed that the future promised progress, that the solution to the social problems and inequities of the age were within our grasp, that sacrifice today would pay off tomorrow. This is perhaps the biggest change in the last twenty years: The innocence is gone.

But is this a cause for mourning? Perhaps only when innocence is gone and our are eyes unveiled will we be able to grasp fully the depth of our conflicts and the sources from which they spring.

We live in difficult and dangerous times, in a country deeply divided by class, race, and social philosophy. The pain with which so many American families are living today, and the anger they feel, won't be alleviated by a retreat to false optimism and easy assurances. Only when we are willing to see and reckon with the magnitude of our nation's problems and our people's suffering, only when we take in the full measure of that reality, will we be able to find the path to change. Until then, all our attempts at solutions will fail. And this, ultimately, will be the real cause for mourning. For without substantial change in both our public and our private worlds, it is not just the future of the family that is imperiled but the very life of the nation itself.

NOTES

1. Zoë Baird, the first woman ever to be nominated to be attorney general of the United States, was forced to withdraw when it became known that she and her husband had hired an illegal immigrant as a nanny for their three-year-old child. The public indignation that followed the revelation came largely from people who were furious that, in a time of high unemployment, American workers were bypassed in favor of cheaper foreign labor.
2. This is now beginning to happen in more skilled jobs as well. In California's Silicon Valley, for example, software programmers and others are being displaced by Indian workers, people who are trained in India and recruited to work here because they are willing to do so for lower wages than similarly skilled Americans (*San Francisco Examiner*, February 14, 1993).
3. From Emma Lazarus's "The New Colossus," inscribed at the base of the Statue of Liberty in New York's harbor, the gateway through which most of the immigrants from Europe passed as they came in search of a new life.
4. These were, and often still are, the commonly held sterotypes about Jews. Indeed, the Asian immigrants are often referred to as "the new Jews."
5. In the fall 1992 freshman class at the University of California at Berkeley, Asians accounted for 37 percent of the students, the largest single group admitted; at the university's Los Angeles campus, they were nearly 40 percent of incoming freshmen; and at Irvine, Asian students made up just under half the first-year class. Final admission figures for the 1993–94 academic year are not available at this writing, but it's already clear that the proportion of Asians will increase substantially.

6. Soon Ja Du, the Korean grocer who killed fifteen-year-old Latasha Harlins, was found guilty of voluntary manslaughter, for which she was sentenced to four hundred hours of community service, a $500 fine, reimbursement of funeral costs to the Harlins family, and five years' probation.

7. The incident that incited the Berkeley boycott didn't happen in the black ghetto, as most of the others did. There, the Korean grocery store is near the University of California campus, and the African-American involved in the incident is a female university student who was Maced by the grocer after an argument over a penny.

8. Jack Miles, "Blacks vs. Browns," *Atlantic Monthly* (October 1992), 41–68.

9. For an interesting analysis of what he calls "the transformation of ethnicity," see Richard D. Alba, *Ethnic Identity* (New Haven: Yale University Press, 1990).

10. In the past, many of these who aggitated for a halt to immigration were immigrants or native-born children of immigrants. The same is often true today. As anti-immigrant sentiments grows, at least some of those joining the fray are relatively recent arrivals. One man in this study, for example—a fifty-two-year-old immigrant from Hungary—is one of the leaders of an anti-immigration group in the city where he lives.

11. David R. Roediger, *Wages of Whiteness* (New York: Verso, 1991), 35.

12. Paul Willis, *Learning to Labour* (New York: Columbia University Press, 1977).

13. Roediger, *Wages of Whiteness*, 137. For a full discussion of this issue, see chapter 7, 133–163, "Irish-American Workers and White Racial Formation in the Antebellum United States."

14. W. E. B. DuBois, *Black Reconstruction in the United States, 1860–1880* (New York: Harcourt Brace, 1935).

15. When adjusted for inflation, the average after-tax income of the one hundred million Americans who make up the bottom two-fifths of the income spectrum has fallen sharply since 1977. The average of the middle fifth of households has edged up 2–4 percent. But the average after-tax income of upper middle-income households has climbed more than 10 percent. And among the wealthiest 5 percent of taxpayers—those with incomes of $91,750 and more—after-tax income rose more than 60 percent during this period (Robert Greenstein, "The Kindest Cut," *The American Prospect* [Fall 1991]: 49–57).

16. Juliet B. Schor, *The Overworked American* (New York: Basic Books, 1992), shows that Americans now work 140 more hours a year than they did twenty years ago. Partly at least this is because most people need every dollar they can earn, so they're reluctant to give up any part of their income for leisure. In fact, large numbers of working-class people forego their vacation time and take the money instead while continuing to work, thereby earning double wages for the vacation period.

17. Robert Bly, *Iron John* (Reading, Mass.: Addison-Wesley, 1990). See also Sam Keen, *Fire in the Belly* (New York: Bantam Books, 1991).

18. See, for example, Judith Stacey, *Brave New Families* (New York: Basic Books, 1990); Stephanie Coontz, *The Way We Never Were: American Families and the Nostalgia Trip* (New York: Basic Books, 1992); and Arlene Skolnick, *Embattled Paradise: The American Family in an Age of Uncertainty* (New York: Basic Books, 1991).

Part IV

GLOBALIZATION AND TODAY'S IMMIGRANT FAMILIES

15

WOMEN AND CHILDREN FIRST: NEW DIRECTIONS IN ANTI-IMMIGRANT POLITICS

Pierrette Hondagneu-Sotelo

In November 1994, California voters passed Proposition 187, which, if implemented, will deny public school education, health care, and other public benefits to undocumented immigrants and their children. I believe that the rhetoric animating support for this proposition reflects a distinctive shift from anti-immigrant hysteria of recent decades, and is approximated perhaps only by the allegations targeting Mexicans and Mexican Americans during the Great Depression. Unlike the xenophobia of recent decades, the current rhetoric focuses on public resource usage and targets immigrant women, relying on both racist and misogynist imagery.

This current wave of xenophobia is fostered by multiple trends: historically constructed and politically deployed racism, the contemporary national fervor against public welfare, and the fiscal crises facing state and local governments in California. But a look at recent shifts in xenophobic narratives—in particular the new emphasis on women and tax-supported public resources—suggests that 187 can be read as a reaction to changing patterns of Mexican immigration to California. The second half of the twentieth century has witnessed a transformation from a predominantly sojourner or cyclical pattern of Mexican migration to the widespread establishment of Mexican immigrant families and communities throughout California. As increasingly well-established Mexican immigrant communities have proliferated throughout the state, media-orchestrated portrayals of the "Mexicanization" or "Latinization" of California have helped fuel and sustain hostile reactions to this permanent settlement. I argue that contemporary xenophobia targets women and children because they are central to making settlement happen. Viewed in this manner, the 187 campaign is less about "illegal immigration" and more about rejecting Mexican—and more generally Latino—immigrants and their U.S.-born family members as permanent members of U.S. society.

I begin by examining the narrative devices that framed and fueled the 187 campaign. This detour illuminates some of the similarities that the current wave of anti-immigrant politics shares with the expulsion campaigns directed at Mexicans in the early 1930s. Next, I contrast sojourner and settler patterns of Mexican immigration and examine coercive systems of labor and their implications for family organization. Under slavery and systems of contract labor in the United States, family life was, in effect, legislatively outlawed. In my view, contemporary xenophobic rhetoric is animated in part by the assumption that Mexican immigrant work life should be severed from family and community life.

ANTI-IMMIGRANT NARRATIVES

Anti-immigrant anxieties are constructed at multiple levels, but they are primarily provoked by changes in immigration patterns and by the way these changes are perceived. In a media-driven society, anti-immigrant expressions are conveyed through the images and "stories" that saturate experience and funnel perceptions of everyday life. In some cases, these stories may in fact become "more real" than either experience or documentary evidence, allowing people to reinterpret their own lived experience in ways that are framed by the dominant narratives. These narratives, however, do not appear out of thin air. In an admittedly distorted fashion, they reflect contemporary political and economic reconfigurations.

Historically, xenophobic narrative in the United States has revolved around three claims. Though the three claims or stories are typically used in tandem, within particular anti-immigrant campaigns, one of these narratives usually rises to the foreground. The stories are constantly rewritten, and they contain elements of good and bad. The assignment of positive and negative attributes—drawn from heroic imagery of European immigrants of the past as well as the "social problem" imagery of third-world immigrants of the present—lends these stories a veneer of veracity and plausibility. This pastiche also allows for the submergence of racialized texts. Before examining the principal narrative devices used in the 187 campaign in California, I will retell these generic stories.[1]

The economic story goes like this: immigrants are impoverished in their poor, preindustrial, backwards countries, where they are oppressed and exploited by a small, merciless elite. The poor, however, are hungry and willing to work hard, and so they come to the land of opportunity—the United States—to work long hours at back-breaking jobs, forfeiting comforts to better their lives. The problematic in this story line emerges when the immigrant workers take the jobs that "rightfully" belong to U.S. citizens and when their willingness to work for low pay depresses the wages of U.S.-citizen workers. Unfair economic competition is the central motif, with immigrant workers raising unemployment rates and dragging standards down for everyone.

In the cultural differences story, immigrants again originate in poor, backwards countries, usually rural areas. Here the focus is on the cultural traditions, foreign languages, religious beliefs and practices, and, perhaps, distinctive racial features and skin colors. In this assimilationist dream gone awry, the melting pot turns sour when these newcomers don't learn English, neglect to pick up the new society's ways, or simply fail to blend. When they remain distinctive and unassimilable, they threaten to tear apart the whole.

Finally, in the story of government resource drain, immigrants once again hail from impoverished places. They come to the United States planning to make a better life for themselves, but they are ill-equipped to do so. Lacking discipline, moral values, proper education, and perhaps literacy skills, their only alternative is to make do with what the system offers. And it offers them plenty. The women bear many children, secure in the knowledge that their obstetrical care will be covered and that their children will get free vaccinations and go to good schools with hot breakfasts and no tuition fees. They do not pay taxes. Their children clog the school system but eventually drop out. Their daughters get pregnant, and their sons fill the jails. Notice that it is not merely generic immigrants, but immigrant women—racialized and gendered—who, together with their children, drain the government coffers fed by U.S.-citizen taxpayers.

These are caricature-like renditions, but such xenophobic claims succeed in galvanizing support precisely because of their simplicity. The three narratives feature different story lines, but they share a common and clear-cut villain. The demonization and removal of this villain promises unequivocal resolution. The narrative of anti-immigrant rhetoric has changed dramatically in the last decade. As recently as the early 1980s, the principal claim fueling immigration restriction was based on the allegation that undocumented immigrants steal jobs from U.S. citizens and depress wages. These allegations of job competition intensified during the recession of the early 1980s, when plant closures, unemployment, and the declining number of manufacturing jobs were foremost in the public's eye. From the late 1970s, when employer sanction measures were first proposed, until passage of the Immigration Reform and Control Act (IRCA) in 1986, the stories of job displacement and diminishing wages fueled anti-immigrant sentiment and restrictionist legislation. During the recession of the early 1980s, politicians and newspaper editorials commonly scapegoated immigrants for causing the economy to lag. Anti-immigrant groups such as the Federation of Americans for Immigration Reform and the Immigration and Naturalization Service (INS), never neutral voices in these national discussions, fueled the fires. One of the INS's more memorable efforts occurred when then western regional director David Ilchert orchestrated "Operation Jobs," a series of workplace raids followed by sensationalistic press conferences announcing the number of jobs—and the corresponding hourly rates—opened due to the deportations.

During this era, restrictionist lobby groups achieved national prominence, and their leaders warned that new immigrants and refugees were causing a hodgepodge of social problems, including high taxes, crime, and even California's notorious traffic jams and air pollution. Arguments based on cultural difference and public resource drainage were also vocalized, but they did not predominate. Of the two, the "cultural differences" story, with its focus on literacy and linguistic abilities, succeeded more in mobilizing anti-immigrant sentiment. The well-funded national organization, "U.S. English," campaigned against the implementation of bilingual education programs and election ballots. Mimicking the allegations voiced by their predecessors about Southern and Eastern European immigrants in the early 20th century, these immigration restrictionists argued that the new immigrants from Asia and Latin America were after all "too different," that they were ultimately unassimilable. Continuing immigration signaled, as Senator Alan K. Simpson, a major proponent of restrictionist legislation, put it, the cultural and linguistic "Quebecization" of the United States. These narratives, principally the economic and cultural stories, peaked in November 1986, when IRCA was signed by the President and when California voters made English the official language in their state.

By the early 1990s, with the 187 campaign the dominant narrative shifted to public resource depletion, muffling rather than silencing the claims about jobs, language, or culture. Replacing the hardworking but impoverished immigrant workers and the culturally and linguistically "different" newcomers as the protagonists in this scenario were poor, pregnant immigrant women and their children. In this scenario, poor immigrant women come to the United States to give birth in publicly financed county hospitals, allowing their children to be born as U.S. citizens and subsequent recipients of taxpayer-supported medical care, public assistance, and education. Immigrants and their children constitute a growing underclass, draining education and medical resources in the United States. As Harold Ezell, the former INS commissioner and coauthor of 187 put it in his Jesse Jackson–inspired parlance, "How many illegals can we educate, medicate, compensate, and incarcerate before California goes bankrupt?"[2]

The campaign's focus on welfare dependency and the targeting of women and children says less about immigrant usage of public assistance than it does about the anxieties arising from popular recognition of the growing Latino immigrant population in California. Latino settlements are inescapably etched throughout California and visible to the casual observer. In Los Angeles, one of the most widely listened to radio stations draws on a primarily Mexican immigrant audience and plays the newly popular *banda* music, a Mexican "cowboy" style that dates back to 19th-century German polka influences in the state of Sinaloa. The expansion of Spanish-language marketing, mass media, and (bilingual) education and the reapportionment of voting districts all testify to the flourishing Latino immigrant communities, many of which are primarily Mexican.

The contemporary xenophobic narrative departs from recent twentieth-century anti-immigrant narrative, approaching arguments not heard so vociferously since the Great Depression, when the public resources claims added to the economic claims a rationale for deportation. A brief review here identifies points of similarity with the current campaign.

PARALLELS WITH THE 1920S AND 1930S

The Great Depression prompted the expulsion of half a million people to Mexico, a group that included Mexican undocumented immigrants, legal permanent residents, and U.S. citizens of Mexican descent.[3] Anti-immigrant citizens groups, allegations about Mexicans' use of public relief, and the active intervention of social workers and relief agencies played important parts in this euphemistically titled "repatriation."

Beginning in 1931, local government and relief agencies threatened to cut Mexican families' public relief and sometimes paid for the families' return transportation to Mexico. Like the 187 campaign, these efforts were concentrated in Southern California. In Los Angeles, local welfare agencies aggressively promoted the repatriation of men, women, and children.[4] Thousands of Mexican families with their accumulated possessions loaded automobiles and boarded trains bound for the border.

While deportation was not formally organized, both state and non-state entities worked toward its implementation. Camille Guerin-Gonzalez recounts how the director of the Los Angeles Citizens' Committee on Coordination of Unemployment Relief worked to organize the removal of Mexicans from California during the early 1930s.[5] This citizens' group implemented raids with police and federal immigration agents, and they also worked toward expulsion with social workers and public relief agencies. For example, working with the Los Angeles Department of Public Charities, the group tried to persuade those legal Mexican immigrants and U.S. citizens of Mexican heritage receiving public assistance to repatriate. (Repatriation would be a misnomer for the removal of those U.S.-born citizens who had never been in Mexico.) The Department of Charities deployed social workers to urge families to leave voluntarily, and they also threatened Mexican families receiving public aid with deportation. According to Guerin-Gonzalez, their efforts particularly targeted settled immigrants and Mexican Americans.[6] The deportees, reflecting the increase in family migration during the 1920s, included substantial numbers of women and children. In fact, Mercedes Carrerras reports that between 1931 and 1933, two-thirds of the deportees were women.[7] So successful was the campaign that by 1940, the Mexican population in the United States had declined to about half of what it had been in 1930.[8]

What is interesting about that 1930s case is that the expulsion campaign followed a period in which a significant component of Mexican migration consisted of Mexican families settling in the United States. In the 1920s, family immigration made up a larger portion of Mexican immigration than it had in prior decades. The economic disruption and violence of the Mexican revolution (1910–1919), and of the Cristero Rebellion in the central-western area of Mexico (1926–1929), prompted the migration of people with a strong motivation to remain in the

United States. During this period the booming U.S. economy provided both urban and rural jobs, and Mexican families settled into the growing barrios of Los Angeles, El Paso, and San Antonio. These urban-based, segregated settlement communities served as labor-distribution centers for Mexican workers who were recruited for agricultural work and for jobs in growing urban centers.[9]

There are at least four points of congruity between the present and the events of the Great Depression. First, the 1930s expulsion program came on the heels of the 1920s, a period of Mexican migration characterized by increased permanent settlements of families. Second, the "draining public resources" narrative was effectively used to rationalize expulsion, with social workers and relief agencies taking an active role in enforcement, targeting women and families. Third, the activism of civilian anti-immigrant groups, not just government agents, played a key role in the campaign. Last, the 1930s repatriation occurred during a period of national economic reorganization, just as contemporary events correspond to capitalist realignments at a global level.

BACK TO THE FUTURE: TRYING TO UNDO THE SETTLEMENT THAT WOMEN CONSTRUCT

In the early 1990s, proponents of immigration restriction successfully switched the anti-immigrant narrative from the "job displacement" and "linguistic and cultural deficiency" arguments to the "draining public resources" argument. What explains the rather abrupt switch in xenophobic rhetoric? On the one hand, the switch reflects exhaustion and the ineffectiveness of the old anti-immigrant narratives. By the early 1990s, California voters readily acknowledged that most jobs held by Mexican immigrants—in the lower end of garment manufacturing, food processing, construction, services, and agriculture—were not desirable ones. Politicians recognized that the job displacement platform could no longer assure reelection. Similarly, the issues of cultural and linguistic homogeneity, as much as they had inspired patriotism and righteous exclusionist sentiment, were not salient enough to animate restrictionist drives or expulsion (or perhaps these arguments appeared to be too blatantly racist). Viewed from the context of national politics, 187 can be seen as part of a more general racialized attack on the welfare system, one which demonizes poor women of color. For these various reasons, the contemporary rationale behind immigration restriction is no longer jobs and language but the resources needed to sustain everyday family life.

The switch in rhetoric reflects more than expedient ploys by political consultants and desperate politicians. It reflects, I believe, a profound historical moment and a muted acknowledgment that there has been a transformation from a predominantly sojourner or temporary pattern of Mexican undocumented migration to a pattern that is reflected in the widespread establishment of Mexican immigrant families and permanent settlement communities throughout California. As Latino immigrant neighborhoods multiplied and expanded beyond rural areas and urban enclaves, growing even in suburban locales, local city councils, business leaders, and the media registered their anxieties with the 187 campaign.

Certainly Mexican immigrant settlement is not a new occurrence. As many as 80,000 to 100,000 Mexicans were well established in the Mexican territory conquered and claimed by the United States in 1848. But Mexican workers who migrated north for work in the late nineteenth century and later in the first half of the twentieth century often did not settle down permanently. The prevailing "ebb and flow" or "revolving door" pattern of labor migration was calibrated by seasonal labor demands, economic recessions, and mass deportations.[10] Although some employers encouraged the immigration of Mexican women and entire families in order to stabilize and expand an available, exploitable work force, many other employers, assisted at times by government-sponsored "bracero programs," recruited only men for an elastic, temporary labor supply, a reserve army of labor that could be discarded when redundant. Employers did not absolutely command the movement of Mexican workers, but employers' needs constructed a particular structure of opportunities that shaped migration.

The end of the contract-labor program in 1964 heralded a new era of growth in legal and in undocumented Mexican immigration, characterized by the establishment of permanent settlement communities in geographically dispersed areas, and more diversified uses of Mexican labor.[11] By the 1970s, both undocumented and legal Mexican immigrants had established a significant number of permanent settlement communities in the United States. These have been referred to as "settling-out" processes, as "daughter communities," and by the unfortunate, but perhaps illustrative, term "sediment" communities.[12] Women and their families played a key part in building these communities. Research conducted during the 1970s and 1980s recorded a significant presence of women among the population of Mexican undocumented immigrants.[13] While Mexican women participate in seasonal or sojourner undocumented immigration, they concentrate in the settler portion of the undocumented population, where they are evenly represented with men.[14]

Since the late 1960s, increasing numbers of undocumented immigrant Mexican men, women, and children have challenged a historical pattern of sojourner migration, and have found themselves, through their daily activities, increasingly committed to building family and community life in the United States. Contemporary nativism exhibited in the 187 campaign mobilized support not against immigrant workers or illegal immigration but against the permanent integration of Mexican immigrants into U.S. society. Here, it is worthwhile to analytically contrast sojourner and settler patterns.

Marxist-informed studies of sojourner migration have noted that this pattern is characterized by the physical separation of employment and family home residence as well as by the separation of the costs of maintaining and reproducing labor.[15] These arrangements allow for the maximum exploitation of immigrant workers, who receive the resources necessary for their daily maintenance in the country of destination, but the costs of sustaining and bringing up new generations of workers (or reproduction costs) are borne in their country of origin.

Settlement, as defined by the unification in the new society of family residence and employment, and of the maintenance and reproduction of labor, reverses this arrangement, since it hinges on the presence of immigrant women and entire families. In settlement, the children of immigrant workers—the next generation of workers—are now raised in the United States. The resources for daily sustenance derive from the United States, and immigrant families discover that they must purchase those materials necessary to sustain daily family maintenance and reproduction in an economy with prices higher than in the one from which they came.

It is important to bring women to the foreground of the settlement discussion by examining how they facilitate—on a daily basis—the joining of labor reproduction and maintenance. Although some scholarship has highlighted the major contributions that women make to urban settlements in Latin American cities, women have an understated presence in the literature on Mexican immigration and settlement. Putting women and their activities at the center of analysis highlights their contributions in three arenas that are key to settlement: creating and helping to sustain permanent, year-round employment; building community life; and provisioning resources for daily family maintenance and reproduction.[16] Below, I draw on research that I conducted in a northern California Mexican immigrant barrio to suggest women's participation in constructing settlement. Because of the focus of this essay, I devote most of the following discussion to the provisioning of resources and the use of public assistance.

First, urban, metropolitan areas are conducive to settlement, because they offer a diverse array of relatively stable, nonseasonal job opportunities, especially for immigrant women.[17] Immigrant women contribute to settlement through their own employment as well as through their physical presence, which allows immigrant men to work at stable jobs without interruptions caused by visits to see their families in Mexico.

Second, women build community through their interaction with one another, and indirectly through the activities of their families, which spawns a multiplicity of ties to other families, friends, and institutions. These strong community ties both emerge from and foster family settlement, since individuals who regularly interact with organizations and other individuals in the United States are more likely to remain for an extended period of time. Women are also central to the establishment of family connections with secondary associations and organizations. Many long-term-resident, undocumented immigrants are directly involved with some formal community or volunteer organization, usually ones associated with schools and churches, or self-help groups.

Third, the provisioning of resources necessary to sustain daily life also plays an important role in settlement. Undocumented immigrant families with young children face particularly high living costs, since mothers and their infants require pre- and postnatal care, and children need medical attention, child care, and schooling.[18] The initial stages of settlement require substantial investment, since renting a place and acquiring a minimal amount of furniture, clothing, and utensils are expensive projects.[19] The burden of supporting non-income-earning dependents and unexpected breaks in employment can quickly lead to poverty.

To cope with these circumstances, undocumented immigrant families combine strategies. They try to cover expenses by employing as many wage earners as possible, by sharing residences with other families, or by taking in boarders and lodgers who sleep in living rooms and garages. Individuals and families share and borrow resources with close friends, relatives, or *comadres* and *compadres* (co-godparents) in their social network, and they may rely on older women kin for relatively inexpensive child care.

Immigrants share resources, but they live in a consumer-oriented, capitalist market economy. The basic package of necessities—housing, clothing, medical attention, transportation, and household goods—is available primarily on a cash basis. Reciprocity among immigrant kin and friends may stretch scarce resources, but it does not produce all of a family's needed resources. These must be purchased in a capitalist economy. Due to undocumented immigrant workers' low wages, the high cost of living in the United States, and the burden of supporting non-income-earning dependents, family settlement sometimes requires reliance on institutional forms of public and private resources. I have grouped these resources into three categories: credit and installment purchases, assistance from private charities, and public assistance. Through my research I found, as have other researchers, that it is primarily women who become adept at seeking out and utilizing these resources in the United States, and I argue that this is one of the ways that women advance settlement.[20]

Immigrants are considerably less likely than the native-born to receive public assistance. This is especially true of undocumented immigrants, who are excluded as beneficiaries from most programs and who fear apprehension and deportation.[21] Until passage of proposition 187, undocumented immigrants were technically eligible to receive restricted Medi-Cal coverage for emergency and pregnancy services, and Women, Infants, and Children (WIC) services. Under the WIC program, some undocumented immigrant women have received supplemental food and nutrition counseling for their families as well as health-care referrals while pregnant, postpartum, or breast-feeding. Some undocumented immigrant parents, who were themselves ineligible for public assistance, lawfully solicited assistance for their U.S.-born children to receive Aid to Families with Dependent Children (AFDC), food stamps, and Supplemental

Security Income (SSI).[22] Douglas Massey and his collaborators have shown that Mexican immigrants' public-service utilization generally increases with years of migrant experience, but their study did not reveal the gendered nature of this use.[23]

As I assisted Latino immigrants through the amnesty-legalization procedure in the late 1980s, various individuals "confessed" to me that they had at one time—and, almost always, temporarily—received public assistance. Many of them used it as a last resort, and yet they spoke of receiving public benefits with shame and stigma. In almost all instances, these resources were used by women and children. Families with infants and small children are most likely to be in need of assistance, and families with U.S.-citizen children are eligible for some public programs. Because of the sensitive nature of public benefits usage, I did not systematically collect information on the use of public assistance, but I did learn of past instances of the utilization of public resources by families headed by undocumented immigrant parents, usually women. One woman, for example, had accepted AFDC for her young infant during a time when she was not receiving money from her husband and when she herself was unable to work due to illness immediately after the birth of her child.

That undocumented immigrants sometimes utilize public assistance first came to my attention during the early months of 1987 when I worked in the San Francisco Bay Area with a grassroots, neighborhood-based group that organized a public informational forum on IRCA and the amnesty-eligibility provisions. After a basic presentation, we divided the more than 350 people in attendance into different elementary school classrooms where attorneys addressed special eligibility problems encountered by agricultural workers, by persons with criminal records, and by prior recipients of public-cash assistance. This last group risked being denied legalization, as immigration adjudicators might determine they would be likely to become "public charges." The session for past recipients of public assistance was attended by about thirty women, most of whom came with young children. Not one man was in attendance. These are uncomfortable truths but ones that deserve acknowledgment. I believe they also deserve wide broadcast in a new narrative of immigrant rights.

The 187 campaign targets the use of public resources by Latina immigrant women and children, but the implications of the proposition go further, I believe, than the expulsion of well-established Mexican and Latino families and communities. Ultimately, the proposition promises to reinstate a more coercive system of labor, one that rests on a more restrictive family life for Mexican and Latino immigrant workers.[24] There is certainly a strong historical legacy of U.S. state interventions to maintain limited family life for workers of African, Asian, and Mexican heritage. As Bonnie Thornton Dill observes in her historical overview, "race has been a fundamental criterion determining the kind of work people do ... and [the] social support provided for their families."[25] And in an essay on family, feminism and race, Maxine Baca Zinn notes that in the United States, "groups subordinated in the racial hierarchy are often deprived of access to social institutions that offer supports for family life."[26] These analyses, and a brief historical disgression, provide important points of departure for understanding the implications of the new xenophobia.

Unlike European immigrants, most people of color in the United States were historically incorporated into the nation through coercive systems of labor. These systems—principally slavery and contract labor—were organized in ways that maximized economic productivity. Maximizing labor productivity meant that few supports were made available for sustaining family life. In some cases family life was legislatively denied.

Under the brutality of plantation slavery, African slaves were encouraged to form families as long as they stayed under the control and surveillance of the master. Slave women were regarded as breeders of future slave workers, so they were encouraged to form families. These families, however, faced disruption due to sale or death, and marriages among slaves were not legally recognized. Sexual violence perpetuated by slave owners on African-American slave women went unpunished; parents struggled to see their babies survive childhood (and when those children did survive, they were prohibited from inheriting the personal belongings of their parents).

Both Chinese and Japanese men were initially brought to work in western agriculture as contracted laborers, and exclusion laws were deliberately set in place to restrict the migration of women and entire families. Although male Chinese workers began coming to the United States during the mid-nineteenth century for work, it was more than a century before the second generation formed. Although many of these Chinese men in fact hoped to earn and save enough money to return home to China, the 1882 Chinese Exclusion Act and antimiscegenation laws effectively denied them the right to form families in the United States. For years, the only Chinese women allowed to enter the United States were the wives of wealthy merchants, and prostitutes, who the dominant society counted on to help keep order in the Chinese "bachelor" communities. Writing about the Chinese case, Evelyn Nakano Glenn notes that the profitability of coercive systems of labor rests, in part, on the separation of family life from work life: "The split household form makes possible maximum exploitation of the workers.... The labor of prime-age male workers can be bought relatively cheaply, since the cost of reproduction and family maintenance is borne partially by unpaid subsistence work of women and old people in the home village."[27]

This analysis has tremendous relevance for understanding Proposition 187. Although the Mexican presence in California precedes the establishment of today's U.S.-Mexico border, one need only step back a few decades to appreciate the significance of Proposition 187. For Mexican workers in the U.S., the Bracero Program, a contract labor system in effect from 1942 until 1964, institutionalized both sojourner migration and the denial of family life. During those twenty-two years, nearly five million labor contracts were issued to Mexican agricultural workers (most of them men), while many other Mexican men without contracts found seasonal work in the fields. These work stints required long family separations, ranging from months to years to even decades, interspersed with brief visits. Eventually, these men used their developing social contacts to seek jobs in the growing cities and suburbs of postwar California. They were subsequently joined in commercial and residential areas by Mexican women, who also found jobs in diverse economic niches. Today, Mexican women and men are rejecting the long-distance, long-term separation of work life from family and community life. In this process, it is primarily women's daily activities that are making this more seamless life possible.

The proponents of 187 seem to be operating on the belief that this pattern can and should be reversed. This is like wanting a labor force without human beings. Today, many undocumented immigrant workers and their families have developed strong personal, social, and economic ties in the United States. These families are firmly integrated and rooted here. When they're not working, they go to PTA meetings, root for their kids' sports teams, get together with extended family, and participate in various church and civic organizations. Moreover, the California economy is not just dependent on the labor of one sex—as it was during the tenure of temporary contract-labor programs—but rather, California appears to be about equally dependent on the labor of Mexican and other Latina immigrant women as it is on men. The remuneration of this labor remains substandard, especially for the purpose of sustaining family life, and this is why public supports are necessary.

While the outcome of 187 remains gridlocked in the courts, the facility with which it passed in the California ballot has rejuvenated anti-immigrant politics at a national level. Proposition 187's passage prompted national proposals to deny public benefits to legal permanent residents and to strike out the 14th Amendment to the Constitution.[28] Proponents of these measures argue that the 14th Amendment, initially introduced to reverse the Dred Scott decision and to guarantee citizenship to the children of slaves, now serves as a magnet for "illegals" to come give birth in the United States. Ironically, drawing from my research, activist work, and job experiences, I can think of only one Mexican immigrant woman who told me she was satisfied with her childbirth experience in the United States. Mexican immigrant women give birth in the United States because this is where they work and live. However, this is beside the point, as the proposals against the 14th Amendment are less about addressing the motivating factors behind migration and more about enforcing coercive labor that disenfranchises immigrant workers and their family members. Like Proposition 187, the proposals to deny public benefits to already legalized immigrants or to deny birth-right citizenship—*jus solis*—to the

U.S.-born children of undocumented immigrant workers are fundamentally about further circumscribing as "outsiders" those who are of Latin American, Caribbean, or Asian heritage.

Nations often change the way they define who belongs, but programmatic efforts to exclude membership may lead to countercurrents. Latino immigrant workers in California continue to fuel the ranks of militant trade unions. In Los Angeles, the Hotel Employees and Restaurant Employees Union Local 11 is well-known for its creative actions, and Justice for Janitors, a component of the Service Employees International Local 399, claims 8,000 members and recently won a major victory with janitorial contractors.[29] Latinos were already the fastest growing group of voters in California, but the immigrant bashing has apparently helped to fuel the ranks of future Latino voters, as legal immigrants rush to become naturalized U.S. citizens.[30] And the backers of 187 have also unwittingly inspired a new corps of progressive, activist, Latino college and high school students.

Thwarting future anti-immigrant assaults and discrimination requires new political narratives and leadership to bring together fragmented activists into broad-based coalitions. The immigrant rights movement, rejuvenated by protest against the Simpson-Rodino bills in the 1980s, is today sustained by the efforts of a committed, hardworking core of legal-service providers, labor organizers, and church and community groups. The obstacles to organizing an effective proactive movement are daunting and too numerous to list here, but one important, missing link that has not been introduced into the debate is the moral issue of mandating the transnational separation of work and family life. We need new immigrant-rights narratives that acknowledge and embrace some of the "uncomfortable truths" about undocumented-immigrant usage of public school education and public resources, that stake a claim to these health and educational resources, and that advocate for the right to other, very basic human entitlements, such as the right to live with one's family and community. We also need analysis that counters not only the racist but also the misogynist imagery used in the contemporary anti-immigrant campaign. Passage of Proposition 187 codifies an attack on Mexican and other immigrant families, but these people aren't going home. California is home, and you can't sunder these roots.

NOTES

I am grateful to Michael Messer for tolerating our daily discussions on the topic of this paper, and I thank Edward Park for inspiring the title. This paper was initially prepared for the conference "Immigration and Ethnic Communities: A Focus on Latinos," held at the Julian Samora Research Institute at Michigan State University, April 28, 1995. A shorter version will appear in the conference proceedings.

1. My conceptualization of xenophobic claims as a series of "stories" is

inspired by a talk delivered by Judith Stacey at the Department of Sociology, U.S.C, on March 9, 1995, where she interpreted the family values debate as a series of projected fables. See her paper "Virtual Post-Familism: Social Science and the Campaign for Family Values," in *New Locations*, ed. George Marcus (Santa Fe, NM: School of American Research Press, forthcoming).

2. Harold Ezell, "Enough Is More than Enough: We Can't Afford Illegal Immigration," *Los Angeles Times*, Oct. 23, 1994, M5.

3. Abraham Hoffman, *Unwanted Mexican Americans in the Great Depression: Repatriation Pressures, 1929–1939* (Tucson: University of Arizona Press, 1974), 126.

4. Mexicans did not respond passively to these attacks. Mexican communities organized mutual-aid societies that provided assistance and that protested the massive raids and the boycotts against hiring Mexicans. Mexican government officials, under the leadership of President Lazaro Cardenas (1934–1940), welcomed the *repatriados* by granting land and tools to help them reestablish themselves. Still, in establishing themselves in Mexico, the *repatriados'* departure encountered prejudice and financial and emotional difficulties. See Francisco Balderrama, *In Defense of La Raza: The Los Angeles Mexican Consulate and the Mexican Community, 1929–1936* (Tucson: University of Arizona Press, 1982); George C. Kiser and Martha Woody Kiser, eds., *Mexican Workers in the United States* (Albuquerque: University of New Mexico Press, 1976); and Hoffman.

5. Camille Guerin-Gonzalez, *Mexican Workers and American Dreams: Immigration, Repatriation, and California Farm Labor, 1900–1939* (New Brunswick, NJ: Rutgers University Press, 1994).

6. In his book, *Becoming Mexican American* (New York: Oxford University Press, 1993), George Sánchez offers a divergent or qualified view of the *repatriados* departing from Los Angeles. He claims that "the single male migrants to the city were among the first to leave, since they had fewer familial obligations and generally had not invested in real estate.... Those that remained in the city in 1933 tended to be members of a family unit, to be property owners, and to be residents in the city for at least a decade." (221) Sánchez states that well-established families were among the most anchored of Mexicans in Los Angeles, but this does not necessarily contradict the conclusion that entire families and women were well-represented among the *repatriados*. On this point see Mercedes Carrerras, *Los Mexicanos que devolvio a ala crisis, 1929–1932* (Mexico City: Secretaria de Relaciones Exteriores, 1974); Hoffman; and Guerin-Gonzalez, 83.

7. Carrerras.

8. Rosalinda M. Gonzalez, "Chicanas and Mexican Immigrant Families, 1920–1940." in *Decades of Discontent: The Women's Movement 1920–1940*, ed. Lois Scharf and Joan M. Jensen (Westport, CT: Greenwood, 1983), 59–83.

9. Ricardo Romo, *East Los Angeles: History of a Barrio* (Austin: University of Texas Press, 1983).

10. Jorge Bustamante, *Espaldas mojadas: Materia prima para le expansion del capital norteamericano, Cuadernos del Centro de Estudios Sociologicos, no. 9* (Mexico City: Colegio de Mexico, 1975); Manuel Garcia y Griego, "The Importation of Mexican Contract Laborers to the United States, 1942–64: Antecedents, Operation, and Legacy," in *The Border That Joints: Mexican Migrants and U.S. Responsibility*, ed. Peter G. Brown and Henry Shue (Totowa, NJ: Rowman and Littlefield, 1983), 49–98; and Alejandro Portes

and Robert L. Bach, *Latin Journey: Cuban and Mexican Immigrants in the United States* (Berkeley: University of California Press, 1985).

11. Between 1960 and 1980, over 1 million Mexicans legally immigrated to the U.S., exceeding earlier numbers. The biggest increments, however, were shown in records of apprehensions of the undocumented. During the 1960s, the INS recorded 1 million, and in the 1970s over 7 million, arrests of undocumented Mexican immigrants (see *1980 Statistical Yearbook of the Immigration and Naturalization Service* [Washington, DC: U.S. Government Printing Office, 1983]). INS figures for apprehensions and deportations do not precisely enumerate undocumented persons, as the figures signify events, not persons. By 1986, when the Immigration Reform and Control Act made legalization available for a segment of the population, demographers estimated that there were approximately 3.1 million undocumented Mexican immigrants in the U.S. For these figures see Jeffrey S. Passel and Karen A. Woodrow, "Change in the Undocumented Alien Population in the United States, 1979–83," *International Migration Review* 21 (1987): 304–323.

12. Harley L. Browning and Nestor Rodriguez, "The Migration of Mexican Indocumentados as a Settlement Process: Implications for Work," in *Hispanics in the U.S. Economy*, ed. G.J. Borjas and M. Tienda (New York: Institute for Research on Poverty Monograph Series, Academic Press, 1985), 277–297; Wayne Cornelius, "From Sojourners to Settlers: The Changing Profile of Mexican Immigration to the United States," in *U.S.-Mexico Relations: Labor Market Interdependence*, ed. J.A. Bustamante, C.W. Reynolds, and R.A. Hinojosa Ojeda (Stanford, CA: Stanford University Press, 1992); Douglas Massey, Rafael Alarcon, Jorge Durand, and Hector Gonzalez, *Return to Aztlan: The Social Process of International Migration from Western Mexico* (Berkeley: University of California Press, 1987); and Portes and Bach.

13. See, for example, Gilberto Cardenas and Estevan T. Flores, *The Migration and Settlement of Undocumented Women* (Austin: Center for Mexican American Studies, University of Texas Press, 1986); Julia E. Curry-Rodriguez, "Labor Migration and Familial Responsibilities: Experiences of Mexican Women," in *Mexicanas at Work in the United States*, ed. Margarita B. Melville (Houston, TX: Mexican American Studies Monograph No. 5., University of Houston, 1988); Pierrette Hondagneu-Sotelo, *Gendered Transitions: Mexican Experiences of Immigration* (Berkeley: University of California Press, 1994); and Rita James Simon and Margo Corona DeLey, "Undocumented Mexican Women: Their Work and Personal Experiences," in *International Migration: The Female Experience*, ed. Rita James Simon and Caroline B. Brettell (Totowa, NJ: Rowman and Allanheld, 1986), 113–132.

14. On sojourner migration see Sylvia Guendelman and Auristela Perez-Itriago, "Double Lives: The Changing Role of Women in Seasonal Migration," *Women's Studies* 13 (1987): 249–271; Sherrie A. Koussodji and Susan I. Ranney, "The Labor Market Experience of Female Migrants: The Case of Temporary Mexican Migration to the U.S.," *International Migration Review* 18 (1984): 1120–1143; and Adela de la Torre, "Hard Choices and Changing Roles among Mexican Migrant Campesinas," in *Building with Our Hands: New Directions in Chicana Studies*, ed. Adela de la Torre and Beatriz M. Pesquera (Berkeley: University of California Press, 1993), 168–180. On women's concentration among settlers see Cardenas and Flores; and Jeffrey

S. Passel, "Undocumented Immigration," *Annals of the American Academy of Political and Social Science* (1986): 487.

15. Michael Burawoy, "The Functions and Reproduction of Migrant Labor: Comparative Material from Southern Africa and the United States," *American Journal of Sociology* 81 (1976): 1050–1087; and Evelyn Nakano Glenn, *Issei, Nisei, Warbride: Three Generations of Japanese American Women in Domestic Service* (Philadelphia: Temple University Press, 1986).

16. Some of these ideas and portions of this article are taken from my *Gendered Transitions*, and "Beyond The Longer They Stay (and Say They Will Stay): Women and Mexican Immigrant Settlement," *Qualitative Sociology* 18 (Jan. 1995): 21–43.

17. Browning and Rodriguez; and Massey et al.

18. Browning and Rodriguez.

19. Leo Chavez, "Settlers and Sojourners: The Case of Mexicans in California," *Human Organization* 47 (1988): 95–108.

20. A. Chavira, "Tienes Que Ser Valiente: Mexican Migrants in a Midwestern Farm Labor Camp," in *Mexicanas at Work in the United States*, ed. M. B. Melville (Houston, TX: Mexican American Studies Monograph No. 5., University of Houston, 1988).

21. F. Blau, "The Use of Transfer Payments by Immigrants," *Industrial and Labor Relations Review* 37 (1984): 222–239; Marta Tienda and Leif Jensen, "Immigration and Social Program Participation: Dispelling the Myth of Dependency," *Social Science Research* 15 (1985): 372–400; and Leif Jensen, "Patterns of Immigration and Public Assistance Utilization, 1970–1980," *International Migration Review* 22 (1988): 51–83.

22. National Immigration Law Center, *Guide to Alien Eligibility for Federal Programs*, 2d ed. (Los Angeles: National Immigration Law Center, 1993).

23. Massey et al.

24. In an analysis of the 1986 Immigration Reform and Control Act's public charge exclusions and five-year ban on social services and public benefits, Grace Chang argues that these provisions were formulated to keep Latina immigrant women available for employment in subordinate jobs, principally as nannies and domestic employees (see Grace Chang, "Undocumented Latinas: Welfare Burdens or Beasts of Burden?" *Socialist Review* 23, no. 3 [1994]: 151–185). While this analysis is relevant to the 187 campaign, I believe that the primary impulse toward coercive work hinges on the denial of family life for Mexican and other Latino immigrant workers. In fact, as Chang points out, this denial is exactly what live-in domestic employment requires.

25. Bonnie Thornton Dill, "Our Mothers' Grief: Racial-Ethnic Women and the Maintenance of Families," *Journal of Family History* 13 (1988): 415–431.

26. Maxine Baca Zinn, "Family, Feminism, and Race in America," *Gender and Society* 4 (1990): 68–82.

27. Evelyn Nakano Glenn, "Split Household, Small Producer, and Dual Earner: An Analysis of Chinese-American Family Strategies," *Journal of Marriage and the Family* 45 (1983): 35–46.

28. Anti-immigrant campaigns do not always succeed in producing their desired effect. Anti-immigrant hysteria and national proposals to restrict the legal rights of permanent legal residents have fueled a mad rush to naturalization, especially among Mexicans who are traditionally recalcitrant to naturalize. In the wake of 187's passage, citizenship applications rose throughout the U.S. but most acutely in Los Angeles. During April 1995, the *Los*

Angeles Times reported that INS offices in Los Angeles were "receiving about 2,500 citizenship applications daily, a tenfold increase from the rate just 18 months ago" (see Patrick J. McDonnell, "Applications for Citizenship Soar in L.A.," *Los Angeles Times*, Apr. 10, 1995, A1, A14). According to one commentator, some people were "being scared into becoming a U.S. citizen" (see George Ramos, "The Fright Factor as an Incentive to Seek Citizenship," *Los Angeles Times*, Apr. 10, 1995, B3).

29. Eric Mann, "Janitors Win a Measure of Justice," *Los Angeles Times*, Apr. 11, 1995, 117.

30. Harry Pachon, "A Flirtation with the GOP Turns Cold," *Los Angeles Times*, Nov. 6, 1994, M5.

16

GLOBAL EXCHANGE: THE WORLD BANK, "WELFARE REFORM," AND THE GLOBAL TRADE IN FILIPINA WORKERS

Grace Chang

Armed with little more than enormous optimism and pluck, more than 1,300 migrants a day leave the Philippines to escape crushing poverty and carve out a better future for their families.... [T]hey travel halfway around the world to work as nannies and house-keepers for middle-class working couples in New York, Hong Kong, Vancouver, or Toronto.
> —*Toronto Globe and Mail*, January 20, 1996

We take care of everybody else's weaker members of society, while we let our own society go to hell.
> —Ninotschka Rosca of Gabriela Network USA, on Filipinas working in the U.S. health-care industry

These two accounts paint very different pictures of the motivations for, and consequences of, women's migration from the Third World. The first statement reflects the prevailing attitude in wealthy nations that women find "golden opportunities" by leaving their homes and families to work as caregivers and service workers abroad. The second asserts that Third World countries sacrifice their women to care for privileged employers overseas while their own families go neglected. For millions of Third World women, migration is not a matter of individual choice but a response to poverty created historically by imperialism and by the continued extraction of capital and human resources from the Third World by First World nations. Many governments of Third World indebted nations participate in the exportation of women migrant work-ers, commodifying women in the futile effort to keep up with debt pay-ments. These women arrive in their "host" countries through a series of international finance and trade agreements, and work in private house-holds under conditions of debt bondage mirroring the relationship between the women's home countries and the host countries that receive them.

Since the 1980s, the World Bank, International Monetary Fund, and other international financial institutions (IFIs) based in the First World, have routinely prescribed structural adjustment policies (SAPs) to the governments of indebted countries as preconditions for loans. These prescriptions have included cutting government expenditures on social programs, slashing wages, liberalizing imports, opening markets to foreign investment, expanding exports, devaluing local currency, and privatizing state enterprises. While SAPs are ostensibly intended to promote efficiency and sustained economic growth in the "adjusting" country, in reality they function to open up developing nations' economies and peoples to imperialist exploitation.

SAPs strike women in these nations the hardest and render them most vulnerable to exploitation both at home and in the global labor market. At the Fourth World Conference on Women and the Nongovernmental Organizations Forum in China in 1995, poor women of color from Africa, Latin America, the Middle East, and Asia spoke of increasing poverty and rapidly deteriorating nutrition, health, and work conditions that have emerged for women in their countries as a result of SAPs. When wages and food subsidies are cut, women as wives and mothers adjust household budgets, often at the expense of their own and their children's nutrition. As public health care and education vanishes, women suffer from lack of prenatal care and become nurses to ill family members at home, while girls are the first to be kept from school to help at home or go to work. When export-oriented agriculture is encouraged, indeed coerced, peasant families are evicted from their lands to make room for corporate farms, and women become seasonal workers in the fields or in processing areas. Many women are forced to find work in the service industry, in manufacturing, or in their homes producing garments for export.[1]

When women take on these extra burdens and are still unable to sustain their families, many have no other viable option but to leave their families and migrate in search of work. At the NGO Forum, Asian women organizers in particular pointed to the massive migration from their countries as a consequence of SAP-driven poverty. Asian women migrate by the millions each year to work as servants, service workers, and sex workers in the United States, Canada, Europe, the Middle East, and Japan. Not coincidentally, the demand for service workers and especially for private household caregivers and domestic workers is exploding in wealthy nations of the First World undergoing their own versions of adjustment.

For example, in the United States, domestic forms of structural adjustment, including cutbacks in health care and the continued lack of subsidized child care, contribute to an expanded demand among dual-career middle-class households for workers in child care, elderly care, and housekeeping. The slashing of benefits and social services under "welfare reform" helps to guarantee that this demand is met by eager migrant women workers. The dismantling of public supports in the United States in general, and the denial of benefits and services to immigrants in particular, act in tandem with structural adjustment abroad to force migrant women into low-wage labor in the United States. Migrant women workers from indebted nations are kept pliable not only by the dependence of their home countries and families on remittances, but also by stringent restrictions on immigrant access to almost all forms of assistance in the United States. Their vulnerability is further reinforced by U.S. immigration policies, designed to recruit migrant women as contract laborers or temporary workers ineligible for the protections and rights afforded to citizens.[2]

Both in their indebted home countries and abroad, women suffer the most from the dismantling of social programs under structural adjustment. In the Third World, women absorb the costs of cuts in food subsidies and health care by going hungry and foregoing proper medical care. Ironically, these same women continue to take up the slack for vanishing social supports in the First World, by nursing the elderly parents and young children of their employers for extremely low wages. Thus, there is a transferral of costs from the governments of both sending and receiving countries to migrant women workers from indebted nations. In both their home and "host" countries, and for both their own and their employers' families, these women pay most dearly for "adjustment."

TESTIMONIES OF WOMEN LIVING UNDER SAPs: LIVING WITHOUT BASIC NEEDS

At the Women's NGO Forum of 1995, women from the Third World gave first-hand testimony on the impacts of SAPs on their daily lives and struggles for survival. The women's testimony demonstrates their clear recognition that they bear the brunt of hardships under structural adjustment, while their nations' governments and elites reap fat rewards in the form of women's cheap or unpaid labor, and remittances from migrant women workers abroad. The phenomenon consistently reported is that overall standards of living, and conditions for women and girls in particular, have deteriorated dramatically since the onset of SAPs. Often this has occurred after periods of marked improvement in women's employment, health, education, and nutrition following national independence movements and prior to the institution of SAPs.

Peasant women from the Philippines, for example, testified that under SAPs, they have had to relinquish all the profits of their labor to landlords, and that lands once used to grow staples such as rice and corn for local consumption have been converted to growing orchids and "other exotic flowers that you can't eat" for export.[3] Filipina rural women also reported going without power for four to eight hours of every day and coping with little or no water.[4] Urban women from the Philippines reported working an average of eighteen hours a day doing domestic work, laundry work outside their homes, and begging, while men face increasing unemployment. Their children are most often on the street, rather than in school, and many families are becoming homeless as a result of the high price of housing or the demolition of their houses to make room for development. Families may eat only once or twice a day because they can't afford more, and most go without any health care as the public hospitals demand payment up front and prescription medicines are prohibitively expensive.[5]

EXPORTING WOMEN—THE "NEW HEROES"

Each day, thousands of Filipinas leave their homes and families in search of work abroad. The Philippine government estimates that more than four percent of the country's total population are contract workers overseas. About 700,000 Filipinas/os were deployed through a government agency, the Philippine Overseas Employment Administration (POEA), in each of the past two years.[6] In 1991, women constituted a larger proportion of the country's overseas workforce (41 percent) than its domestic workforce (36 percent). Of those overseas, approximately 70 percent are women working as domestic servants in middle- and upper-class homes in the United States, the United Kingdom, Europe, Japan, and the Middle East. Many of the others work as nurses, sex workers, and entertainers.[7] Such massive migrations of women have led to public outcries that the Philippine government is selling or trafficking in women.

Indeed, this massive migration is no mere coincidence of individual women's choices to leave the Philippines. The Philippine government receives huge sums of remittances from its overseas workers each year. In 1993, overseas contract workers' remittances were estimated at 3.4 percent of the Gross Domestic Product, which is the equivalent of 30 percent of the trade deficit or the entire interest payments on the country's foreign debt. "Host" country governments and private employers welcome the migrant women workers for the cheap labor they do. These governments and employers accrue savings not only by paying extremely low wages, but by not providing public benefits or social services to these temporary workers. Finally, recruiting agencies and other entrepreneurs on each end of the trade route reap tremendous profits from providing employers in host countries with ready and willing service workers and caregivers of all kinds.

Host countries are eager to receive these female mercenaries, as they bolster their economies, too. As many countries of the First World undergo downsizing and the dismantling of public supports, migrant women workers offer the perfect solution. The steady flow of migrant women provides an ideal source of cheap, highly exploitable labor. These women are channeled directly into the service sector, where they do every form of care work for a pittance and no benefits. Ironically, immigrant domestic workers, nannies, in-home caregivers, and nurses pick up the slack for cuts in government services and supports that pervade the First World as well as the Third World. Overseas, they provide care for the ill, elderly, and children, while their own families forego this care because of the economic restructuring that drives them overseas.

As the Freedom From Debt Coalition, a Philippines-based NGO fighting against SAPs, described this trade in migrant women workers: "Indeed, what the country cannot achieve through export of goods, it compensates for through the export of human resources."[8] A Philippines ambassador to Canada attempted to promote the trade in romantic terms, proclaiming: "The migrant workers are our heroes because they sustain our economy."[9]

Nurses and Home-Care Workers

Currently, there are 100,000 registered nurses in the Philippines, but almost none actually reside in the country. Similarly, 90 percent of all Filipina/o medical-school graduates do not live in their country. Since the 1970s, the United States has imported women from the Philippines to work as nurses, ostensibly in response to domestic shortages in trained nurses. This importation system became institutionalized with the H-1 nursing visa, which enables a hospital or nursing home to sponsor or bring a nurse with a professional license from abroad to work in the United States for two years.

Under the H-1 program, the woman must take the U.S. nurses' licensing exam. If she passes, she can gain permanent residency after two years. During those two years, she is almost captive to her original sponsoring employer. If she fails the exams, she loses her sponsorship and must, technically, leave the country. More often, such women go underground until they can take the exams again. Sometimes they work in nursing homes, where they are underpaid at $5 an hour, or buy green-card marriages.

Mayee Crispin, a Filipina nurse, who organizes H-1 nurses at the St. Bernard's Hospital in Chicago, suggests that importing nurses from the Philippines is a money-making venture for both the hospitals and the nursing recruiters with whom they contract. According to Crispin, a hospital typically gets workers from overseas by making an official certification that it can not find U.S. workers to fill its nursing positions. This is usually because the hospital offers wages that no U.S. workers are willing to accept. The hospital is then free to contract a recruiter to go to the Philippines in search of nurses. A nurse must pay, on average, between $7,000 and $9,000 (U.S.) to the recruiter. Ostensibly, a portion of this fee goes to the recruiter's salary, and a portion goes to a lawyer to arrange the woman's visa. Since most women can not afford this fee, they agree to have it deducted from their wages. After paying off such fees and sending roughly 25 to 30 percent of their wages to their families at home, their monthly wages quickly disappear. In essence, most of these women live in a situation much like indentured servitude or debt bondage for at least two years.

HOME-CARE WORKERS

Home health care is another industry in which immigrant women are highly concentrated and fall prey to both profit-seeking agencies and the cost-cutting U.S. government. Many home-care workers are employees of the state, under a state-funded program called "in-home support services" (IHSS). Some of these women are registered nurses while others are not trained as nurses at all. The program provides no training, no regulations, and no monitoring of the work, which includes everything from performing medical procedures such as giving enemas and insulin shots, changing bandages, and hooking up dialysis machines, to cleaning, preparing meals, and assisting elderly or ill clients, which may include bathing them and washing out their bedpans.[10] To keep costs down, the state pays workers a minimum wage of $4.50 an hour and provides no benefits, including no sick leave, family leave, overtime pay, compensation for injuries on the job, or reimbursement for bus fares or gasoline to run errands for patients or to take them to the doctor.[11] In California, there are 170,000 of these workers statewide, of whom approximately 80 percent are women, 60 to 70 percent are people of color, and 40 percent are immigrants.

Employing an IHSS worker saves taxpayers approximately $30,000 a year, the difference between the cost of keeping a patient in a nursing home and the typical salary of $7,000 a year earned by an IHSS worker who works thirty hours a week. This savings is reaped by the county, state, and (through Medicaid) federal governments which share the program's annual cost. Robert Barton, manager of the adult-services branch of the California Department of Social Services overseeing the program, commented: "It's a good deal for the government." The union's director of organizing in Washington, David Snapp, retorts: "It's a scam."[12] The IHSS program provides perhaps the best illustration available of the tremendous savings to local, state, and federal governments through the low-wage labor of migrant care workers. Other savings to the state and employers have not been measured, such as those from not providing public benefits, services, and protections to these workers.

In the private sector, the situation is no better, with agencies and companies turning a profit from placing these workers instead of the state saving money by underpaying workers. Home-care agencies, just like hospitals, make huge profits from recruiting and placing home-care workers. For example, an agency will typically contract out a live-in caregiver to a client for $120–200 a day, of which the worker herself receives only $80.

DOMESTIC WORKERS AND NANNIES

The majority of migrant Filipina workers are domestic workers and nannies. Many of them work in Canada, which has had a "live-in caregiver program" since 1992 to facilitate the importation of these migrants. Through this program, a Canadian employer (either an individual or employment agency) may apply through the Canadian Employment Office for a prospective employee. The employer must show that it first tried to find a Canadian to do the job. The prospective employee must have six months of formal training or twelve months experience in caregiving work and be in good health. If approved, the employee can gain temporary employment authorization for one year, and this can be extended for an additional year. A nanny must undergo a personal interview with Canadian consular officials and a security clearance. Once matched with an employer, she must notify the Ministry of Citizenship and Immigration if she wishes to change employers. After two years of live-in work, a nanny can apply for landed-immigrant status. She can then sponsor immediate family members to join her if they can prove that they have a source of steady income. Three years after applying for landed-immigrant status, she can become a Canadian citizen.[13]

The film *Brown Women, Blonde Babies*, produced by Marie Boti, documents the conditions for Filipina migrant women working as domestics and nannies in Canada. Typically, these women work round-the-clock, from 7 A.M. to 10 P.M. and beyond, and are always considered to be on-call. They earn an average of $130 (U.S.) a month after taxes. Women who wish to leave their employers must persuade an immigration officer to let them. In response to one woman's pleas for release from an employer, an immigration officer said coldly, "You didn't come here to be happy."

Women's Resistance

In 1988, on a state visit to Hong Kong, President Aquino declared migrant women the new heroes of the Philippine economy.[14] A spokeswoman from the Freedom From Debt Coalition countered: "Because of their economic contributions, migrant workers are hailed by the administration as the new heroes and labor export is elevated into a national policy, the appalling social costs and the prevalence of abuses notwithstanding."[15] Migrant women workers have mobilized worldwide to expose the abuses they face and to fight for protection of their rights. Women in many "host" countries, including Canada, Japan, Britain, and the United States, have organized grassroots groups to offer support and legal advocacy and to lobby for the protection of Filipina and other migrant workers abroad. For example, the activist pro-migrant group Kalayaan lobbies to change British law to allow migrant workers to change employers freely and to continue working in the country while pursuing legal action against former employers. INTERCEDE is a similar organization, based in Toronto, doing research and advocacy for Filipina and Caribbean migrant domestic-worker rights.

A study by Kalayaan reveals that abuse of overseas domestic workers in Britain is widespread. Between 1992 and 1994, Kalayaan interviewed 755 workers from the Philippines, Sri Lanka, India, Ghana, Nigeria, Colombia, and Brazil: a full 60 percent had received no regular food, 42 percent had no bed, and 51 percent had no bedroom and were forced to sleep in a hallway, kitchen, bathroom, or storeroom. Thirty-four percent reported being imprisoned or not allowed to leave the house. Ninety-one percent reported working for an average of seventeen hours a day with no time off. Fifty-five percent were not paid regularly, and 81 percent were paid less than was agreed upon in their contracts, with an average monthly wage of $105 (U.S.). Eighty-eight percent had experienced psychological abuse, including name-calling, threats, and insults, and 38 percent had endured physical abuse of some form. Eleven percent had experienced attempted, threatened, or actual sexual assault or rape.

Sarah Balabagan, a fifteen-year-old Filipina working as a maid in the United Arab Emirates (UAE), was raped at knifepoint by her employer in July 1994. Balabagan's case sparked one of the largest campaigns for justice for migrant domestic workers worldwide. Balabagan had stabbed and killed her rapist/employer in self-defense, yet was sentenced to seven years imprisonment. In response to protests, Balabagan was retried but was then sentenced to death. In outrage, many overseas Filipinas joined protests staged by Gabriela Network USA in front of the UAE mission and the Philippine government consulate in the United States. Again, Balabagan's sentence was revised. This time, she was sentenced to one year in prison and 100 lashes, and ordered to pay her deceased employer's family 150,000 dirhams or the equivalent of (U.S.) $41,995. Gabriela's Ninotschka Rosca speculates that the main reason the UAE government rescinded the death sentence was fear of a walkout by the approximately 75,000 Filipinas/os working in the UAE—a walkout that would have paralyzed the country. The Philippine government's agreement to this final sentence over continued protests reinforced outrage that the Philippine government refuses to protect its overseas people and is clearly willing to sacrifice women's lives in order to maintain good relations with its chief trading partners.[16]

In the United States, organized labor has also begun to address the particular issues confronting a growing force of migrant women workers. For example, health-care workers, many of whom are migrant women, are the fastest-growing service industry and a prime target for unions as some of the most exploited and, until recently, least-organized workers.[17] A recent victory by the Service Employees International Union (SEIU) against the California state government represents the fruits of a five-year struggle for the unionization of over 50,000 home-care workers in the state. In 1994, SEIU brought a class-action suit against the state of California (*Caldman* v. *California*) on behalf of more than 10,000 IHSS workers whose paychecks were delayed up to two months during the budget crises of 1990 and 1992.[18] SEIU's success in the lawsuit represents a dramatic victory over a government that all too easily evades responsibility for the well-being and basic rights of both its impoverished and ill citizens and the migrant workers it actively recruits to care for them.

Josie Camacho, organizer for Local 250 of SEIU, points to the ongoing challenges of organizing home-care workers: First, there is no central workplace, with workers scattered among as many as 6,000 different work sites in a country. Second, some immigrant workers feel indebted to their employers and are not only reluctant to join the union but have reported other workers who do. Finally, the union has had to identify an "employer" from which to make its demands in collective bargaining, as the state is unwilling to identify as such.

The union has had to create an employer, called the "public authority," which is made up of disability advocates, clients currently receiving In-home Support Services, and seniors. This need to create an employer illustrates a central challenge in organizing for migrant workers' rights. No party is willing to admit responsibility, or can be held accountable, for the rights and protection of these workers. All parties, including both the sending and receiving countries' governments, employers, and employment agencies, evade or completely disclaim responsibility. Yet all benefit immensely from these workers' labor, extracting foreign currency, profits, savings, and care services.

This challenge also hinders efforts to rally mainstream U.S. feminists' support around the issue of the trade in women and migrant women workers' rights. When the National Organization of Women (NOW) was called upon to put the issue of the global trafficking of women on its agenda, its leadership declined to do so, stating that NOW does not deal with international issues.[19] Perhaps the real issue is that privileged women of the First World, even self-avowed feminists, may be some of the primary consumers and beneficiaries in this trade. Middle- and upper-class professional women generally have not joined efforts to improve wages or conditions for care workers in the United States, since they have historically relied on the "affordability" of women of color and migrant women working in their homes, day-care centers, and nursing homes.

For example, major U.S. women's groups were conspicuously absent or silent during the Zoë Baird controversy, when the attorney general nominee was found to have employed two undocumented migrant workers as baby-sitter and gardener. Shortly after the Baird scandal, proposals for a "home-care worker" or "nanny visa," modeled after the Canadian Live-in Caregiver program, were discussed at the Immigration Reform Commission hearings. Only a few individuals from NOW attended the hearings, but they were not representing NOW. It appears that U.S. women's groups with mainly white, middle-class memberships have little interest in regulating the care work that women of color and immigrant women do. Or, more to the point, they may have a vested interest in keeping these professions unregulated.

Even among grassroots organizations fighting for justice for migrant women workers, it may prove difficult to develop a unified position or strategy. The effectiveness and viability of one strategy, imposing a ban on recruitment of Filipinas for migrant work, has been debated since such a ban was imposed by the Aquino administration in 1988. A coalition of twenty-two migrant worker groups in Hong Kong formed to press the Aquino government to repeal the ban, arguing that it hindered Filipinas' ability to secure employment, actually debilitating rather than protecting them.[20]

Almost ten years later, debate over the tactic of the ban continues. Felicita Villasin, executive director of INTERCEDE and former executive board member of the National Action Committee on the Status of Women (NAC) in Canada, says that she does not embrace the strategy of calling for a reduction in or stop to labor migration. She sees this as an impractical measure that will only drive women to face greater danger and abuses as illegal migrants. Instead, she calls for structural changes in the Philippine economy that will make migration a choice, and not a necessity. At least on this last point, Villasin asserts, there seems to be consensus among the women's groups involved in Filipina migrant worker struggles.

Since before the NGO Forum, INTERCEDE has done popular education among its members and the public about the connections between labor migration and the SAPs imposed on indebted countries of Asia and the Caribbean, exposing the structural reasons many of its members have had to leave their families to migrate for work. INTERCEDE is a member organization of NAC, a coalition of 600 women's groups who, according to Villasin, "seek our counterparts in the South to work not just toward solidarity or sympathy but toward strategy on an international level."[21]

Asian, Pacific Islander, and other women-of-color feminists in the First World would do well to take the lead from groups like INTERCEDE and from our Third World sisters who have been mobilizing around the issues of SAPs and the traffic in women for years now. At the NGO Forum, many First World women remarked that they were the least well-informed or organized on global economic issues. Many First World feminists of color came home from the Forum resolved to undertake or redouble efforts to understand and expose the links between economic restructuring in the First World, SAPs in the Third World, and the global trade in women.

In Canada, NAC and the Canadian Labour Congress cosponsored a month-long, nationwide Women's March Against Poverty in May and June 1996. The march culminated in a rally at the nation's capital to bring to Parliament the demands for measures to redress women's poverty both in Canada and globally. The call to action included the need to strengthen employment conditions and opportunities for women, to reinforce social services and to adopt "as a foreign-policy objective" the elimination of women's poverty.[22]

In the United States, Miriam Ching Louie and Linda Burnham of the

Women of Color Resource Center returned from the NGO Forum committed to designing an education project, Women's Education in the Global Economy (WEdGE). The project includes a curriculum and set of trainings focused on a broad range of global economic issues and trends impacting women: the global assembly line; SAPs; women's unpaid contingent and informal work; welfare; environmental justice; women's human rights, sex trafficking, and migration; and organizing around these issues.[23]

• • •

The goal in each of these efforts is to educate women broadly about global restructuring as a complex of interconnected systems that bolster patriarchy, racism, capitalism, and imperialism in oppressing poor women of color worldwide. In the United States, for example, more needs to be done to expose how the Contract with America, Proposition 187 and its imitations at the federal level, and SAPs in the Third World all contribute to the channeling and entrapment of migrant women and women of color in exploitative, low-wage service work.

SAPs and other economic restructuring policies affect Third World women in similar ways the world over: making survival more precarious, women's unpaid labor burdens heavier, and exacerbating women's exploitation as low-wage workers both at home and abroad. First World variations of structural adjustment bring consequences that are less well-known but no less insidious. Walden Bello, author of *Dark Victory: The United States, Structural Adjustment and Global Poverty*, describes the effects of "welfare reform" as the domestic version of SAPs in the United States: In 1992, by the end of the Republicans' assault on social-welfare programs, the living standards of many Americans had deteriorated to Third World levels. Approximately 20 million U.S. residents lived in hunger, and infant-mortality rates among poor African Americans reached rates higher than those of countries such as Jamaica, Trinidad, and Cuba.[24]

Bello says that the original intentions of SAPs were: first, to resubordinate the Third World—particularly those nations threatening to become developed—by crippling the authority of their governments, and second, to repress labor globally in order to free corporate capital from any hindrances to maximum profits. Clearly SAPs in the Philippines have been an uncontested success by these measures. The Philippine government has been unable to protect its own female citizens abroad and apparently has given up any intention of doing so. The trade in women from the Philippines has proven immensely profitable to the Philippine government and entrepreneurs, and highly "economical" to the governments that recruit Filipinas and the elite who employ them. Yet the struggles and triumphs of women like Balabagan and Tristan, and groups such as Kalayaan, INTERCEDE, Gabriela, and SEIU stand as testament to the ability of women to resist this global assault on Third World women workers.

NOTES

This article is extracted from a chapter in my forthcoming book, *Gatekeeping and Housekeeping,* and from *Dragon Ladies: Asian-American Feminists Breathe Fire* (South End Press, 1997). I would like to thank Luisa Blue, Josie Camacho, Mayee Crispin, Ninotchka Rosca, Carole Salmone, and Felicita Villasin for sharing their great insights, expertise, and time to interview with me. I am also indebted to Miriam Ching Louie and Linda Burnham for bravely leading the WCRC delegation to Huairou, and for their pioneering work on WEDGE since we returned. I am grateful to Nathaniel Silva for his insights and comments in developing this piece.

1. Pamela Sparr, *Mortgaging Women's Lives: Feminist Critiques of Structural Adjustment* (London and New Jersey: Zed Books Ltd., 1994).
2. See Grace Chang, "Disposable Nannies: Women's Work and the Politics of Latina Immigration," *Radical America* 26, No. 2 (October 1996), 5–20.
3. Gabriela Workshop, September 3, 1995.
4. Testimony of Merceditas Cruz, Migration and the Globalizing Economy workshop, September 6, 1995.
5. Testimony of Carmen, Organization of Free & United Women under Gabriela.
6. This number does not include women who are trafficked, illegally recruited, migrate for marriage, students, or tourists who eventually become undocumented workers (compiled by Kanlungan Center Foundation from Philippine Overseas Employment Administration (POEA) and Department of Labor and Employment (DOLE) statistics).
7. Isabel Vincent, "Canada Beckons Cream of Nannies: Much-sought Filipinas Prefer Work Conditions," *The Globe and Mail*, January 20, 1996, A1, A6. Other authors more extensively address trafficking in women for the sex work, entertainment, and mail-order bride industries. See, e.g., Ninotchka Rosca, "The Philippines' Shameful Export," *The Nation*, April 17, 1995, 523–525; Elaine Kim, "Sex Tourism in Asia: A Reflection of Political and Economic Equality," *Critical Perspectives of Third World America* 2, No. 1 (Fall 1984), 215–231; video produced by Chela Blitt, "Sisters and Daughters Betrayed: The Trafficking of Women and Girls and the Fight to End It," Global Fund for Women.
8. Editorial: "Flor Contemplacion: Victim of Mismanaged Economy," *PAID! (People Against Immoral Debt),* newsletter of Freedom From Debt Coalition, April 1995, 7.
9. Video produced by Marie Boti, *Brown Women, Blonde Babies,* Multimonde Productions, Montreal, Canada.
10. Ibid.
11. Peter T. Kilborn, "Union Gets the Lowly to Sign Up: Home Care Aides Are Fresh Target," *New York Times*, November 21, 1995.
12. Kilborn.
13. Interview with Ms. Greenhill of the Canadian Consulate in Los Angeles, Calif. December 1993; Vincent, A1.
14. Interview with Ninotchka Rosca, April 29, 1996.
15. Freedom From Debt Coalition, statement prepared for NGO Forum 1995.
16. *Kapihan Sa Kanlungan: A Quarterly Digest of Migration News*, newsletter produced by Kanlungan Center Foundation, April–June 1995; Interview with Ninotchka Rosca; Vincent, A6.

17. Kilborn.
18. SEIU press release, May 30, 1995, "Delayed Payment Case for Home Care Workers Settled With State for $4 Million."
19. Interview with Rosca.
20. Enloe, 188. Slowly, the Aquino government exempted one government after another from its requirements and by 1989, twenty-two countries enjoyed exemption from the ban.
21. Interview with Felicitas Villasin, May 6, 1996.
22. NAC bulletins concerning the Women's March Against Poverty, Canada, May–June 1996.
23. For information, contact: Women of Color Resource Center, 2288 Fulton Street, Suite 103, Berkeley, CA 94704.
24. Walden Bello with Shea Cunningham and Bill Rau, *Dark Victory: The United States, Structural Adjustment and Global Poverty* (London: Pluto Press with Food First and Transnational Institute, 1994).

17

MIGRATION AND VIETNAMESE AMERICAN WOMEN: REMAKING ETHNICITY

Nazli Kibria

Ethnicity is a gender-contested realm. It is an arena of conflict between men and women and one over which they struggle to gain control. Recent feminist scholarship has emphasized the utility of ethnic[1] bonds and institutions for immigrant women. Thus immigrant families and communities are seen as vehicles by which immigrant women resist and cope with their disadvantaged status as racial-ethnics in the dominant society, rather than as sources of gender oppression. The focus on the role of ethnicity as a mode of resistance has provided important insights into the dynamics of racial-ethnic oppression in immigrant lives. However, by making secondary the ongoing gender struggles within the immigrant community, this perspective has also given rise to an overemphasis on the consensual character of ethnic ties.

Drawing on data from my study of family life and gender relations in an urban Vietnamese American community, this chapter attempts to capture both the constraints faced by immigrant women and the resistances they offer to oppressive forces in the immigrant community as well as the dominant society.

WOMEN AND IMMIGRANT TIES: OPPRESSION AND RESISTANCE

One of the most important and dominant frameworks on immigrant adaptation in the United States is the assimilationist perspective (Gordon 1964; Hirschman 1983; Park and Burgess 1969).[2] A central assumption of this perspective is that immigrant groups gradually become Americanized, that is, they shed their loyalties and connections with the traditional immigrant culture and community and become assimilated into the "melting pot" of America. In this process, women have been seen in two capacities. On the one hand, immigrant women, viewed as staunch supporters of immigrant traditions and culture, have been viewed as barriers to assimilation. Alternatively, they have been seen as important intermediaries or vehicles of integration into the dominant society (see Deutsch 1987:719–720). But regardless of the particular role into which immigrant women are cast, assimilation is viewed as synonymous with greater gender equality. Since immigrant ties are seen as a source of patriarchal oppression—as the group assimilates into American culture, immigrant women are expected to be freed from the shackles of tradition and male authority.

The assimilation model has been subject to a series of sharp and wide-ranging attacks in recent decades (Hirschman 1983; Morawska 1985). One of the fundamental criticisms has been that the characterization of the immigrant assimilation process as one of unilineal, progressive development from the "traditional" to the "modern" is far too simplistic. Instead, scholars have argued for a perspective that recognizes the uneven quality of modernization processes, and the ability of traditional values and institutions to coexist with modern ones. But perhaps the most serious criticism of the assimilation model is that it fails to take into account the distinct situation and experience of people of color within American society. The assimilation model was formulated with reference to the experiences of White European immigrants in the United States. As a result, it neglects the ways in which race shapes the adaptation of minority groups to the dominant society.

Feminist scholarship has both shared and contributed to the critique of the assimilation model. For example, the model's dichotomous characterization of migration as a movement from the "traditional" to the "modern" has been brought under question by studies which show that migration may be detrimental rather than favorable to women's status. In fact, rather than leading to greater gender equality, migration, like economic development, may result in losses for women, in terms of traditional sources of support and power in the domestic sphere as well as access to production processes and thus economic resources (Beneria and Sen 1981; Deutsch 1987). Feminist scholars have also been sensitive to the assimilation model's neglect of racial oppression and its role in shaping the experience of minority groups.

In fact, much recent scholarship on immigrant women has focused not on assimilation processes but on the disadvantaged status of immigrant women within the dominant society. Terms such as "multiple jeopardy" and "triple oppression," signifying the complex intertwining of class, racial-ethnic, and gender oppression, increasingly dominate discussions of racial-ethnic women's experience (Brettell and Simon 1986:10; King 1988). As women, as racial-ethnics, and as inhabitants of the lower rungs of the social class ladder, racial-ethnic women experience multiple disadvantages in the dominant society. This emphasis on the marginal location of racial-ethnic women within dominant society structures has been accompanied by a shift in how scholars view the relationship of racial-ethnic women to their families and communities. These "traditional" institutions are not simply sources of patriarchal oppression. Rather, family and community represent modes of resistance to dominant society constraints, or vehicles by which the minority group struggles to survive (Caulfield 1974; Glenn 1986; Dill 1988). While immigrant women may struggle against the oppression they experience as women within the immigrant family and community, the oppression they experience from the dominant society as members of a racial-ethnic group generates needs and loyalties of a more immediate and pressing nature. Thus, immigrant women may remain attached to, and indeed support, traditional patriarchal family and community structures. This is due not simply to the entrenched cultural beliefs or cultural conservatism of the women, but also to the benefits that they gain from retaining these structures, given the multiple disadvantages they face in the dominant society. In short, for immigrant women, the traditional family and community are ways of surviving and maintaining cultural autonomy in the "new" society. The need to sustain family and community may take priority over the internal struggles against male dominance in the immigrant family and community.

In general, this view of ethnic affiliation—that it is a resource for coping with the dominant society—has become increasingly important in the scholarship on immigration, including studies that are not explicitly concerned with the gendered dimensions of the racial-ethnic experience. Thus many contemporary studies of ethnicity focus on the persistence and adaptive relevance of "traditional" immigrant affiliations (see, for example, Kim 1981; Morawska 1985; Portes and Bach 1985). These studies suggest that immigrant ties may actually be a vehicle for or a product of individual and collective modernization, rather than an impediment or barrier to modernity (Morawska 1985; See and Wilson 1988). Ethnic boundaries are seen as dynamic and situational, and there is an emphasis on the active part played by the immigrant group in generating and shaping group membership. To summarize, from varied and diverse currents in social science scholarship on immigrants, there has emerged a theoretical consensus of sorts about immigrant institutions, one that is critical of the assimilation model. For immigrant women and men, the immigrant family and community are sources of economic, political, and cultural resistance, vehicles for adaptation to the dominant society.

The emphasis on the notion of adaptation that has come to dominate much of the literature on the immigrant experience does, however, raise some critical questions. For one thing, the focus on the adaptive quality of the immigrant family and community has led to a neglect of the divisions and conflicts within these institutions. To see ethnic institutions only as vehicles of resistance to dominant society oppression implies a uniformity and consensuality of experience within the ethnic group. But to what extent is this true—do all participants benefit in the same way from ethnic solidarities? In recent years feminist scholarship has become increasingly critical of the concept of the family or household economy, which assumes that families act in unison and agreement on their economic strategies (Beneria and Roldan 1987). This emphasis on consensus serves to whitewash the conflictual aspects of family life (Beneria and Roldan 1987). However, this critique of familial consensus has not been fully and adequately extended to the study of ethnic ties and institutions. This is so, despite the existence of many studies that document the conflicts and tensions between men and women that have been a part of the political struggles and social movements of racial-ethnic groups (Chow 1987; King 1988; Baca Zinn 1975). In general, it seems essential to acknowledge that women and men may gain vastly different kinds of benefits and rewards from ethnic resources, given the different statuses and powers of women and men in the immigrant family and community. There is evidence, for example, that the ethnic enclave economy, which has been celebrated by scholars as an example of how ethnic ties may function as a resource, confers quite different economic rewards on men and women (Zhou and Logan 1989).

Both sources of oppression—those within and those without—are important in an understanding of immigrant women's experience. But a perspective that acknowledges both the oppressive and the supportive dimensions of the family and community leaves certain questions unanswered. How do immigrant women respond to this division, the "double-edged" quality and meaning of ethnic family and community in their lives? I suggest that it is important to see the immigrant family and community as contested and negotiated arenas. Immigrants play an important part in actively shaping and constructing their ethnic institutions. But these institutions are also gender-contested, that is, arenas of conflict and struggle between men and women. The processes by which the ethnic family and community are shaped and negotiated thus ultimately reflect gender divisions, as men and women clash over the question of how to define and construct family and community. In their struggles, they attempt to gain control of and shape the resources of family and ethnicity, in ways that enhance their interests both as members of the family and community, and as men or women.

The struggle between men and women to shape immigrant institutions will vary in its strength and visibility, depending on the balance of power between women and men in the group. This balance of power is deeply shaped by the comparative access of the immigrant men and women to economic, political, and social resources in the dominant society. Particularly when migration is concurrent with a drastic shift in the resources of women and men relative to each other, the gender-based struggle to control family and community may become especially visible. While men and women jockey to control family and community, to redefine it on their terms, they are also, of course, engaged in a conflict over gender relations—the place and power of men and women within the family and community. As family and community life are reorganized by men and women, their roles and relations also undergo change. Thus the study of change in immigrant family life, gender relations, and ethnic organizations must approach these spheres as deeply intertwined rather than as separate aspects of immigrant life. In my research on Vietnamese Americans, I found the impact of migration on family life and the status of women to be issues of major debate in the ethnic community. For Vietnamese Americans, the future of their family and gender relations has been tied to cultural identity—what it means "to be Vietnamese in America." In other words, the importance and fervor of the debate about family and gender stems in part from the implications of these debates for the core of ethnic identity and meaning itself.

VIETNAMESE AMERICANS AND THE RISE IN WOMEN'S POWER

My research on the adaptive strategies of a community of Vietnamese refugees in Philadelphia revealed some of the ways in which women and men struggled and clashed with each other in efforts to shape the social organization of family and community life. From 1983 to 1985, I gathered information on family life and gender relations through participant observation in household and community settings, as well as in-depth interviews with women and men in the ethnic community.

The Vietnamese of the study were recent immigrants who had arrived in the United States during the late 1970s and early 1980s. Most were from urban, middle-class backgrounds in southern Vietnam. At the time of the study, over 30 percent of the adult men in the households of study were unemployed. Of the men who were employed, over half worked in low-paying, unskilled jobs in the urban service sector or in factories located in the outlying areas of the city. Women tended to work periodically, occupying jobs in the informal economic sector as well as in the urban service economy. Eight of the twelve households had members who collected public assistance. Both the family economy and informal community exchange networks were important means by which the households dealt with economic scarcities. Family and community were of tremendous economic salience to the group, as they were important resources for survival in the face of a rather inhospitable economic and social environment.

As suggested by the high rate of the men's unemployment, settlement in the United States had generated some shifts in power in favor of the women in the group. Traditional Vietnamese family and gender relations were modeled on Confucian principals, which placed women in subordination to men in every aspect of life. A key aspect of the social and economic oppression of women in traditional Vietnamese life was the patrilineal extended household. Its organization dictated that women married at a young age, following which they entered the household of their husband's father. This structure ensured the concentration of economic resources in the hands of men and men's control of women through the isolation of women from their families of origin.[3]

It is important to note the deep-seated changes in traditional family and gender structures in Vietnam during this century. War and urbanization eroded the structure of the patrilineal extended household. While unemployment was high in the cities, men from middle-class backgrounds were able to take advantage of the expansion of middle-level positions in the government bureaucracy and army. Such occupational opportunities were more limited for women: the women study participants indicated that they engaged in seasonal and informal income-generating activities or worked in low-level jobs in the growing war-generated service sector in the cities. The transition from rural to urban life had generated a shift in the basis of men's control over economic and social resources. However, families relied on men's income to maintain a middle-class standard of living. Thus women remained in a position of economic subordination to men, a situation that served to sustain the ideals of the traditional family system and men's authority in the family. Restrictions on women's sexuality were important for middle-class families seeking to distinguish themselves from the lower social strata. My data suggest that families were especially conscious of the need to distance themselves from poorer "fallen" women who had become associated with the prostitution generated by the American military presence.

Within the Vietnamese American community of study, I found several conditions that were working to undermine the bases on which male authority had rested in Vietnam. Most important, for the Vietnamese men, the move to the United States had involved a profound loss of social and economic status. Whereas in pre-1975 Vietnam the men held middle-class occupations, in the United States they had access to largely unskilled, low-status, and low-paying jobs. Also, because of their difficulties with English and their racial-ethnic status, the men found themselves disadvantaged within social arenas of the dominant society. Compounding these problems was the dearth of strong formal ethnic organizations in the community that could have served as a vehicle for the men's political assertion into the dominant society.

As a result of these losses, the comparative access of men and women to the resources of the dominant society had to some extent become equalized. In contrast to the experiences of the men, migration had not significantly altered the position of the women in the economy. As in Vietnam, the women tended to work sporadically, sometimes in family businesses or, more commonly, in temporary jobs in the informal and service-sector economies of the city. However, the economic contributions of women to the family budget had risen in proportion to those of the men. I have suggested that in modern, urban South Vietnam the force and legitimacy of male authority had rested heavily on the ability of men to ensure a middle-class status and standard of living for their families. In the United States, the ability of men to fulfill this expectation had been eroded. Among the men, there was widespread concern about the consequences of this situation for their status in the family, as is revealed by the words of a former lieutenant of the South Vietnamese army: "In Vietnam, the man earns and everyone depends on him. In most families, one or two men could provide for the whole family. Here the man finds he can never make enough money to take care of the family. His wife has to work, his children have to work, and so they look at him in a different way. The man isn't strong anymore, like he was in Vietnam."

Such changes had opened up the possibilities for a renegotiation of gender relations, and were the cause of considerable conflict between men and women in the family and community. The shifts in power had also enhanced the ability of women to construct and channel familial and ethnic resources in ways that they chose. Previously I suggested that the changes in the balance of power between men and women generated by migration are crucial to understanding the manner and degree to which immigrant family and community reveal themselves to be gender contested. How, then, did the fairly drastic shift in the gender balance of power among the Vietnamese Americans reflect itself in the ability of the men and women in this group to influence family and community life? In the following section, I describe some of the ways in which gender interests and conflict shaped family and community life for the Vietnamese Americans.

FAMILY AND ETHNICITY AS GENDER-CONTESTED

One of the most intriguing and important strategies of Vietnamese American adaptation that I observed was the rebuilding of kinship networks. Family ties had undergone tremendous disruption in the process of escape from Vietnam and resettlement in the United States. Despite this, the households of the group tended to be large and extended. The process by which household growth occurred was one in which the study participants actively worked to reconstruct family networks by building kin relationships. In order for this to take place, the criteria for inclusion in the family had become extremely flexible. Thus close friends were often incorporated into family groups as fictive kin. Also, relationships with relatives who were distant or vaguely known in Vietnam were elevated in importance. Perhaps most important for women, the somewhat greater significance traditionally accorded to the husband's kin receded in importance.[4] Given the scarcity of relatives in the United States, such distinctions were considered a luxury, and the demands of life made the rebuilding of family a valuable, if not a necessary, step in the process of adaptation to the dominant society.

While important for the group as a whole, the reconstruction of kinship as it took place had some special advantages for women. One consequence of the more varied and inclusive nature of the kinship network was that women were rarely surrounded exclusively by the husband's relatives and/or friends. As a result, they were often able to turn to close fictive kin and perhaps members of their families of origin for support during conflicts with men in the family. Another condition that enhanced the power of married women in the family was that few had to deal with a mother-in-law's competing authority in the household, because elderly women have not been among those likely to leave Vietnam.

The reconstruction of kinship thus had important advantages for women, particularly as it moved the Vietnamese perhaps even further from the ideal model of the patrilineal extended household than they had been in the past. But women were not simply passive beneficiaries of the family rebuilding process. Rather, they played an active part in family reconstruction, attempting to shape family boundaries in ways that were to their advantage. I found women playing a vital part in creating fictive kin by forging close ties. And women were often important, if not central, "gatekeepers" to the family group and household. Thus the women helped to decide such matters as whether the marriage of a particular family member was a positive event and could be taken as an opportunity to expand kinship networks. At other times the women passed judgment on current or potential family members, as to whether they had demonstrated enough commitment to such important familial obligations as the sharing of economic and social resources with kin.

Although women undoubtedly played an important part in family reconstruction, their control over decisions about family membership was by no means exclusive or absolute. In fact, the question of who was legitimately included in the family group was often a source of tension within families, particularly between men and women. The frequency of disputes over this issue stemmed in part from the fluidity and subsequent uncertainty about family boundaries, as well as the great pressures often placed on individuals to subordinate their needs to those of the family collective. Beyond this, I also suggest that disputes over boundaries arose from the fundamental underlying gender divisions in the family. That is, the different interests of women and men in the family spurred efforts to shape the family in ways that were of particular advantage to them. For the reasons I have previously discussed, the Vietnamese American women had greater influence and opportunity in the shaping of family in the United States than they had in the past. The women tended to use this influence to construct family groups that extended their power in the family.

In one case that I observed, considerable tension developed between a couple named Nguyet and Phong concerning the sponsorship[5] of Nguyet's nephew and his nephew's family from a refugee camp in Southeast Asia. Nguyet and Phong had been together with their three children (two from Nguyet's previous marriage) for about seven years, since they had met in a refugee camp in Thailand. Phong remained married to a woman who was still living in Vietnam with his children, a fact that was the source of some stress for Nguyet and Phong. The issue of the nephew's sponsorship seemed to exacerbate tensions in the relationship. Phong did not want to undertake the sponsorship because of the potentially heavy financial obligations it entailed. He also confessed that he was worried that Nguyet would leave him after the nephew's arrival, a threat often made by Nguyet during their quarrels. Finally, he talked of how Nguyet's relationship with the nephew was too distant to justify the sponsorship. Nguyet had never even met the nephew, who was the son of a first cousin rather than of a sibling.

Confirming some of Phong's fears, Nguyet saw the presence of the nephew and his family as a potentially important source of support for herself. She spoke of how she had none of "my family" in the country, in comparison with Phong, whose sister lived in the city. She agreed that she did not know much about her nephew, but nonetheless felt that his presence would ease her sense of isolation and also would provide a source of aid if her relationship with Phong deteriorated. Eventually she proceeded with the sponsorship, but only after a lengthy dispute with Phong.

While the issue of sponsorship posed questions about kinship in an especially sharp manner, there were other circumstances in which women and men clashed over family boundaries. When kin connections could not be questioned (for example, in the case of a sibling), what came under dispute was the commitment of the particular person involved to familial norms and obligations. One of my woman respondents fought bitterly with her older brother about whether their male cousin should live with them. Her brother objected to the cousin's presence in the household on the grounds that he had not responded to their request for a loan of money two years ago. The woman respondent wanted to overlook this breach of conduct because of her extremely close relationship with the cousin, who had been her "best friend" in Vietnam.

Regardless of the particular circumstances, gender conflict seemed an important part of the family reconstruction process. Women and men shared an interest in creating and maintaining a family group that was large and cohesive enough to provide economic and social support. However, their responses to the family reconstruction process were framed by their differing interests, as men and women, within the family. Men and women attempted to channel family membership in ways that were to their advantage, such that their control over the resources of the family group was enhanced.

Gender divisions and conflicts also entered into the community life of the group. The social networks of the Vietnamese American women were central to the dynamics and organization of the ethnic community. They served to organize and regulate exchange between households. While "hanging out" at informal social gatherings, I observed women exchanging information, money, goods, food, and tasks such as child care and cooking. Given the precarious economic situation of the group, these exchanges played an important role in ensuring the economic survival and stability of the households. The women's centrality to these social networks gave them the power not only to regulate household exchange but also to act as agents of social control in the community in a more general sense. I found that women, through the censure of gossip and the threat of ostracism, played an important part in defining community norms. In short, the relative rise in power that had accrued to the Vietnamese American women as a result of migration expressed itself in their considerable influence over the organization and dynamics of the ethnic community. Like kinship, community life was a negotiated arena, one over which women and men struggled to gain control.

The gender-contested quality of ethnic forms was also apparent in the efforts of women to reinterpret traditional Vietnamese familial ideologies on their own terms. In general, the Vietnamese American women continued to espouse and support traditional ideologies of gender relations as important ideals. For example, when asked during interviews to describe the "best" or ideal roles of men and women in the family, most of my respondents talked of a clear division of roles in which women assumed primary responsibility for maintaining the home and taking care of the children, and men for the economic support of the family. Most felt that household decisions should be made jointly, although the opinion of the man was seen to carry more weight. About half of those interviewed felt that a wife should almost always obey her husband. Even more widespread were beliefs in the importance of restrictions on female (but not male) sexuality before marriage.

While women often professed such beliefs, their relationship to traditional ideologies was active rather than passive and inflexible. In other words, the women tended to emphasize certain aspects of the traditional familial ideology over others. In particular, they emphasized parental authority and the obligation of men to sacrifice individual needs and concerns in order to fulfill the needs of the family, traditional precepts they valued and hoped to preserve in the United States. The women's selective approach to Vietnamese "tradition" emerged most clearly in situations of conflict between men and women in the family. In such disputes, women selectively used the traditional ideologies to protect themselves and to legitimate their actions and demands (Kibria 1990). Thus, husbands who beat their wives were attacked by other women in the community on the grounds that they (the husbands) were inadequate breadwinners. The women focused not on the husband's treatment of his wife but on his failure to fulfill his family caretaker role. Through this selective emphasis, the women managed to condemn the delinquent husband without appearing to depart from "tradition." In short, for the Vietnamese American women, migration had resulted in a greater ability to shape family and community life.

CONCLUSION

For immigrant women, ethnic ties and institutions may be both a source of resistance and support, and of patriarchal oppression. Through an acknowledgment of this duality we can arrive at a fuller understanding of immigrant women's lives: one that captures the multifaceted constraints as well as the resistances that are offered by immigrant women to the oppressive forces in their lives. In patterns similar to those noted in studies of other racial-ethnic groups (Stack 1976; Baca Zinn 1975), the Vietnamese Americans presented here relied on family and community for survival and resistance. Their marginal status made the preservation of these institutions an important priority.

Like other racial-ethnic women, the ability of the Vietnamese American women to shape ethnicity was constrained by their social-structural location in the dominant society. These women saw the traditional family system as key to their cultural autonomy and economic security in American society. Migration may have equalized the economic resources of the men and women, but it had not expanded the economic opportunities of the women enough to make independence from men an attractive economic reality. The Vietnamese American women, as is true for other women of color, were especially constrained in their efforts to "negotiate" family and community in that they faced triple disadvantages (the combination of social class, racial-ethnic, and gender statuses) in their dealings with the dominant society.

Recognition of the role of ethnic institutions in facilitating immigrant adaptation and resistance is essential. However, it is equally important not to lose sight of gender divisions and conflicts, and the ways in which these influence the construction of ethnic institutions. Feminist scholars have begun to explore the diverse ways in which immigrant women manipulate family and community to enhance their own power, albeit in ways that are deeply constrained by the web of multiple oppressions that surround them (Andezian 1986; Bhachu 1986; Kibria 1990). Such work begins to suggest the complexity of immigrant women's relationship to ethnic structures, which is informed by both strength and oppression.

NOTES

1. I define "ethnicity" as a collective identity based on culture or nationality. I reserve the term "racial-ethnic" to refer to the subordinate status of the group (stemming from racial and ethnic oppression) in the dominant society. The simultaneous use of these terms is somewhat awkward but necessary in order to convey the multiple statuses occupied by many immigrant groups. For example, the Vietnamese share an ethnic identity and status as Vietnamese, based on a common nationality and culture. At the same time, they hold a racial status in the dominant society as Asian Americans.
2. My definition of the assimilationist model includes its subvariations, such as "cultural pluralism" and "Anglo conformity."
3. Some scholars stress the fact that the reality of women's lives was far different from that suggested by these Confucian ideals. Women in traditional Vietnam also had a relatively favorable economic position in comparison with Chinese women due to Vietnamese women's rights of inheritance as well as their involvement in commercial activities (see Hickey 1964; Keyes 1977). Despite these qualifications, there is little to suggest that the economic and social subordination of women was not a fundamental reality in Vietnam.
4. Hy Van Luong (1984) has noted the importance of two models of kinship in Vietnamese life, one that is patrilineal in orientation and another in which bilateral kin are of significance. Thus the flexible, encompassing conceptions of family that I found among the study group were not entirely new, but had their roots in Vietnamese life; however, they had acquired greater significance in the context of the United States.

5. Refugee resettlement in the United States involves a system of sponsorship by family members or other interested parties who agree to assume part of the responsibility for taking care of those sponsored for a period of time after their arrival.

REFERENCES

Andezian, Sossie. 1986. "Women's Roles in Organizing Symbolic Life: Algerian Female Immigrants in France." Pp. 254–266 in *International Migration: The Female Experience*, edited by R. J. Simon and C. B. Brettell. Totowa, N.J.: Rowman and Allenheld.

Baca Zinn, Maxine. 1975. "Political Familism: Toward Sex Role Equality in Chicano Families." *Aztlan* 6, no. 1: 13–26.

Beneria, Lourdes, and Martha Roldan. 1987. *The Crossroads of Class and Gender*. Chicago: University of Chicago Press.

Beneria, Lourdes, and Gita Sen. 1981. "Accumulation, Reproduction and Women's Role in Economic Development: Boserup Revisited." *Signs* 7, no. 2 (Winter): 279–298.

Bhachu, Parminder K. 1986. "Work, Dowry and Marriage Among East African Sikh Women in the U.K." Pp. 241–254 in *International Migration: The Female Experience*, edited by R. J. Simon and C. B. Brettell. Totowa, N.J.: Rowman and Allenheld.

Brettell, Caroline B., and Rita J. Simon. 1986. "Immigrant Women: An Introduction." Pp. 3–21 in *International Migration: The Female Experience*, edited by Rita J. Simon and Caroline B. Brettell. Totowa, N.J.: Rowman and Allenheld.

Caufield, Mina D. 1974. "Imperialism, the Family, and Cultures of Resistance." *Socialist Review* 4, no. 2: 67–85.

Chow, Esther Ngan-Ling. 1987. "The Development of Feminist Consciousness Among Asian American Women." *Gender and Society* 1, no. 3: 284–299.

Deutsch, Sarah. 1987. "Women and Intercultural Relations: The Case of Hispanic New Mexico and Colorado." *Signs* 12: 719–740.

Dill, Bonnie Thornton. 1988. "Our Mothers' Grief: Racial-Ethnic Women and the Maintenance of Families." *Journal of Family History* 13, no. 4: 415–431.

Glenn, Evelyn Nakano. 1986. *Issei, Nissei, War Bride*. Philadelphia: Temple University Press.

———. 1987. "Gender and the Family." Pp. 348–381 in *Analyzing Gender: A Handbook of Social Science Research*, edited by Beth B. Hess and Myra M. Ferree. Newbury Park, Calif.: Sage.

Gordon, Milton. 1964. *Assimilation in American Life*. New York: Oxford University Press.

Hickey, Gerald C. 1964. *Village in Vietnam*. New Haven: Yale University Press.

Hirschman, Charles. 1983. "America's Melting Pot Reconsidered." *Annual Review of Sociology* 9: 397–423.

Keyes, Charles F. 1977. *The Golden Peninsula*. New York: Macmillan.

Kibria, Nazli. 1990. "Power, Patriarchy and Gender Conflict in the Vietnamese Immigrant Community." *Gender and Society* 4, no. 1 (March): 9–24.

Kim, Ill Soo. 1981. *New Urban Immigrants: The Korean Community in New York*. Princeton: Princeton University Press.

King, Deborah H. 1988. "Multiple Jeopardy, Multiple Consciousness: The

Context of a Black Feminist Ideology." *Signs* 14, no. 1: 42–72.

Luong, Hy Van. 1984. " 'Brother' and 'Uncle': An Analysis of Rules, Structural Contradictions and Meaning in Vietnamese Kinship." *American Anthropologist* 86, no. 2: 290–313.

Morawska, Ewa. 1985. *For Bread with Butter.* Cambridge: Cambridge University Press.

Park, Robert, and Ernest Burgess. 1969. *Introduction to the Science of Society.* Student ed. abridged by Morris Janowitz. Chicago: University of Chicago Press.

Portes, Alejandro, and Robert L. Bach. 1985. *Latin Journey: Cubans and Mexican Immigrants in the U.S.* Berkeley: University of California Press.

See, Katherine O'Sullivan, and William J. Wilson. 1988. "Race and Ethnicity." Pp. 223–243 in *Handbook of Sociology*, edited by Neil J. Smelser. Newbury Park, Calif.: Sage.

Stack, Carol. 1974. *All Our Kin.* New York: Harper & Row.

Zhou, Min, and John R. Logan. 1989. "Returns on Human Capital in Ethnic Enclaves: New York City's Chinatown." *American Sociological Review* 54 (October): 809–820.

Part V

WORK-FAMILY ISSUES

18

Management by Stress: The Reorganization of Work Hits Home in the 1990s

Sarah Ryan

When 185,000 United Parcel Service workers went on strike in August 1997 they may have been prepared to win their wage and pension demands. What they were not prepared for was the outpouring of public support that greeted them. While hundreds of union members and community supporters joined picket lines and rallies, they had also joined rallies for many losing strikes in the 1980s and 1990s, when the public consensus seemed to be against organized labor. This time, a Cable News Network poll showed solid support for the striking UPS workers—55 percent of those surveyed supported the union, while 27 percent supported the company position. Other polls showed similar results. For the first time in over two decades, a major strike succeeded in winning wage gains and job security and captured the public's imagination as well.

The problems of UPS workers sounded all too familiar to millions of American families, and they identified with the goals of the strike. The Teamsters Union members at UPS wanted to create 10,000 new full-time jobs from the tens of thousands of low-wage part-time jobs at the company that controlled 80 percent of the nation's package deliveries. About 57 percent of UPS's 185,000 Teamster workers labored part time—in many terminals two-thirds or even three-quarters of the employees. They made up 80 percent of new hires since 1993. The part-time workers' problems mirrored those of many Americans: They earned as little as $8 per hour as opposed to about $20 for full-timers; they often worked almost full time at their part-time wage; many needed a second job to get by; and few had any prospects for stable employment.[1] As more and more families have found themselves insecure about jobs and benefits, the dilemmas faced by part-time workers have grown.

In large part because of visible public support, the strikers won wage increases for part-timers totaling $4.10 per hour over the contract's term, raised the full-time wage by about 3 percent, and preserved the quality of their pension and medical plans. For the first time in many years, the public caught a glimpse of an alternative to the lean-and-mean workplace faced by so many. It was a glimmer of hope that was sorely needed.

An almost constant sense of insecurity haunts American families in the 1990s. Nearly half the population worries that someone in their household will be out of work in the next year. Parents no longer expect their children to have a higher standard of living than themselves. Most expect large-scale layoffs to be a permanent feature of the modern economy; meanwhile, they experience more stress while at work and are contributing more and more hours to the job.[2] No wonder nostalgia for more prosperous and predictable times is a recurring theme in politics and the arts, even among young people who have embraced the technology and values of the 1990s.

"Exiles in the promised land," Elizabeth Gilbert called them in 1996. A young reporter for a rock-music magazine, she described a sense of betrayal felt by many of her peers. There was supposed to be a reward for hard work in America—a rising standard of living based on growing productivity. Home ownership. The assurance that your children would have a better life than you had. "When my parents were young, America was unchallenged, cars looked great, a wife could raise her children safely, a husband could buy a home on a laborer's wage," Gilbert wrote, describing what many considered America's post–World War II social contract. While millions of African Americans and other United States minority populations were, for the most part, not included in the bargain, the contract has now been broken even for white families. A generation of workers is learning the hard lesson of the 1990s: Technology and the reengineering of work have changed almost every aspect of jobs, lowering compensation and expectations, increasing work hours, and deeply impacting family life.[3]

A fundamental reorganization of work has taken place in the last two decades. What the *Wall Street Journal* has labeled "the reengineering movement"[4] is not an accidental byproduct of technology or global competition. It is the result of a corporate political and economic strategy to abandon the old tactic of ensuring social peace by guaranteeing special privileges and security to some groups of workers. This has paid off on the stock market, as stock indexes hit record highs in 1996 and wealth distribution was dramatically altered.[5] Individual strategies for "coping with stress" have emerged, but social policy has not seriously addressed the nature of work reengineering or attempted to ameliorate its effects.

Consultants and psychologists retained by employers to help people cope with job and family stress usually deny the extent to which fear of job loss or overwork is engineered into workers' lives by real changes in the structure of the economy. They tell people that if they can change their attitudes, they can solve their problems. "People think of stress as something external," said Joel Haber, a White Plains, N.Y., clinical psychologist. "It's really our reaction to the events, rather than the events themselves, that causes stress." The president of the American Institute of Stress, a nonprofit research group, is quoted as advising: "The feeling of being out of control is always stressful, but very often that's a matter of perception. If you can't fight and you can't flee, you have to learn how to flow."[6]

The truth, however, is that very few workers have the resources or maneuvering room to either flee or flow. Corporate CEOs and highly paid professionals have the option of "downshifting"—cashing in their stock options or investments and seeking a simpler life. Underpaid and overworked production and service workers, male or female, cannot find relief in similar individual coping strategies.

The Families and Work Institute conducted a survey of 3,000 wage and salary workers in 1993 and found that 75 percent felt used up at the end of the workday, while 70 percent were still tired when they awoke to face another day on the job. Researcher Deborah Holmes explained: "One of the results of downsizing is that people are having heavier workloads. Not surprisingly, workers with heavier workloads report more job burnout."

What are the major aspects of work reengineering today?

1. *Lowering of worker compensation.* Real (adjusted for inflation) weekly earnings for nonsupervisory workers declined by 19 percent from 1972 to 1995.[7] When discussed as a "fall" or "decline" in wages, the use of the passive voice obscures the active attack on workers' living standards that has been underway for almost three decades. The grinding down of compensation levels represents a successful campaign by major businesses to avoid wage increases, hire new workers at lower pay levels, roll back previous gains, and defeat or restrain labor unions. Even over the past two years of rapid economic recovery and job growth, incomes continued to fall for the bottom sixty percent of households, while the gap between rich and poor did not narrow.[8]

Lower wages are not due to lack of worker productivity. Real Gross Domestic Product (a measure of how much each worker produces and a reliable index of the productivity of the average worker) *rose* by 19 percent per capita from 1970 through 1994.[9] In an unusually frank discussion of macroeconomic trends published in a February 1996 issue of the *New York Times*, Stephen Roach of Morgan Stanley, a Wall Street brokerage firm, acknowledged that corporations "have gone too far in squeezing the worker to boost corporate profitability and competitiveness.... Pay rates have now been squeezed so that they are running below the productivity curve and economic theory suggests that workers should be paid their marginal productivity contribution."[10]

Falling wages necessitate that families send more of their members into the work force, spend more hours working, or get second or third jobs just to barely maintain their previous living standards. Or, of course, they must cope with economic hardship.

2. *Automation of production, information, and service work.* Technologies of the "information age" and automation of production have eliminated millions of jobs, and technology-based layoffs are feared by telephone workers and machinists alike. The steel industry is a prime example of the dramatic effect of technology on production and employment. U.S. Steel (now USX), the nation's largest steel company, employed 120,000 in 1980. By 1990, it produced roughly the same output with 20,000 workers.[11] Employment in the telephone industry, the economy's automation pacesetter, declined by 179,800 from 1981 to

1988.[12] AT&T alone announced 40,000 layoffs in early 1996.[13] While laid-off employees generally found other jobs, they most often received lower pay, and the insecurity generated by such experience clouds the lives of remaining workers.

3. *Internationalization of production, with manufacturing exported to low-wage areas.* Trade agreements like the North American Free Trade Agreement (NAFTA) and the Global Agreement on Tariffs and Trade (GATT) have loosened government restrictions and sped up the rate at which industries are moving production to countries like Mexico, where wages are about one-tenth of U.S. averages. The "maquiladora" program—the establishment of production factories along the U.S.-Mexican border—began in 1965. By 1992, half a million workers were employed on the Mexican side of the border in over 2,000 low-wage plants. Labor economist Harley Shaiken estimates that U.S. auto manufacturers could save $100 million annually in wages per plant, as Mexican automobile workers' total compensation averages $2 per hour as compared with U.S. auto workers' $30.[14] Thousands of Americans have watched their jobs head across the Mexican border in recent years.

4. *Corporate mergers and reorganization, with workforce "downsizing."* It became common for corporate CEOs in the 1990s to find their bonuses and stock prices increasing after the announcement of mass layoffs. Nearly three-quarters of all households have had a close encounter with layoffs since 1980. The *New York Times*' 1996 feature series (and, later, book) "The Downsizing of America," examined the chaos, insecurity, and destruction in peoples' lives resulting from corporate downsizing. Workers who had staked their futures on the idea that their loyalty to the company would be returned told of their sense of loss and betrayal. One in ten adults said a lost job had precipitated a major crisis in their lives.[15]

Since 1979, 43 million jobs have been "extinguished." While manufacturing jobs have typically been thought of as those most vulnerable to layoffs, the *Times* researchers found that white-collar work was just as insecure in the 1990s. Workers typically find it difficult or impossible to replace their lost jobs with anything that would pay similar wages. The median pay drop in 1994 was $85 per week when new jobs were found.

5. *Newly created jobs are part-time and temporary as companies shift to "no-commitment" hiring.* "It's really a revolution," was how Gary Burtless, a labor economist with the Brookings Institution, described things in 1995. Temporary employment had tripled in only one decade, rising to include 2.1 million workers by May 1995.[16] Perhaps no statistic speaks as dramatically as this: Manpower Temporary Services, with 767,000 "employees," is now the nation's largest civilian employer, displacing the rapidly downsizing General Motors from the top spot.[17] Even government agencies have increased temporary employment. The U.S. Postal Service alone has over 70,000 contingent workers who have no

job security, lower wages, and no health-care insurance.

Corporations face no additional cost or penalty for downsizing their permanent workforce and replacing long-term employees with temporaries, and they can hire and fire rapidly when business demands change. Temporary workers earn lower wages, usually have no benefits, and never know from one day to the next if they will be working. A Bureau of Labor Statistics (BLS) survey found that "most firms reported that less than ten percent of their temporary workers participated in a company-sponsored health-insurance program." Additionally, BLS found that temporary workers' real wages are declining. Between 1989 and 1994, wages for the employees of temporary agencies that employ twenty or more workers rose only 2 percent—before inflation.[18]

6. *Increased use of overtime and rotating shifts, particularly in manufacturing.* If you work for a major industrial employer, it's hard to "flee or flow" from management demands. While economic pressures sometimes compel workers to seek overtime, often there is nothing voluntary about longer work weeks. Workers may face firings or other disciplinary actions for refusing overtime to take care of their children. Bell Atlantic telephone, for example, after cutting 4,000 jobs in recent years, has been suspending workers who refuse overtime. Joe Bryant, a single father of two children, had worked overtime on weekends but was unable to put in extra hours during the week due to child-care problems. He was given a suspension for refusing weekday overtime so that he could pick up his children at school. Another Bell Atlantic technician had worked sixty-nine of the previous seventy-three days and was suspended for three days for refusing additional overtime.[19]

In Decatur, Illinois, a corn-products plant, a tire factory, and a tractor manufacturer all demanded twelve-hour rotating schedules from their workers. In manufacturing operations like the A.E. Staley plant, twelve-hour days, with three days on and three days off, were imposed, and workers were switched from days to nights every thirty days. Staley workers Dick and Sandy Schable explained how their family life was severely disrupted by these schedules: "After the first day on twelve hours you were pretty much shot. The other problem was each week you'd have a different day off. And you could be called in during your time off at any shift at any time they deemed it necessary."

Some workers, unable to flee or flow, have been able to fight. In March 1996, twenty-six of General Motors Corporation's twenty-nine North American automobile manufacturing plants were idled as a result of a 3,000-person strike. The workers at a brake plant in Dayton, Ohio, had been required to work fifty-six-hour weeks. GM was demanding additional overtime, or it would contract the parts to low-wage shops. The strike, lasting seventeen days, won the hiring of 417 new workers.[20] GM had been a pioneer in "alternative work schedules," and excessive overtime has caused other recent strikes in GM plants.

7. *Team-concept and "total quality" management systems.* Worker/management cooperation plans swept the corporate world in the 1980s

and 1990s. A 1992 survey of Fortune 1000 corporations found that 80 percent used management techniques such as Quality of Work Life, Quality Circles, or Employee Involvement.[21] While these techniques were initially presented as signs of a "new respect for the worker," they were accompanied by wage cutting, downsizing, and a new, intense pressure for more production, often applied by a worker's peers in addition to management. The Nissan Corporation was an early team concept, "lean production" leader. While company literature claimed the system was built on teamwork, cooperation and trust, declaring that "people are our most valued resource," workers described the job as "eight-hour aerobics. You feel like you've done three days' work at the end of the shift."

A former Nissan manager has described the long range results of such aerobics: "We hired exceptionally good people, people we thought we could keep for the rest of their working lives. I ran into one of them at the pharmacy the other day. He looked like he was dead.... He said to me, 'I think they've got us on a four- or five-year cycle. They'll wear us out and then hire new blood.' I think he may be right."[22]

While seemingly contradictory, team concept and high-pressure cost-cutting strategies are two sides of the same coin, according to labor journalists Jane Slaughter and Mike Parker, who say that the function of participation programs is to introduce management by stress.[23]

United Parcel Service, the target of the fifteen-day strike in 1997, calls itself "the tightest ship in the shipping business" and is well-known for a demanding and injurious work atmosphere. The rate of lost-time injuries in 1994 was 15 per 100 workers, compared to a shipping-industry average of eight or nine.[24] At the parcel sorting hubs, the system is designed to push the individual workers beyond normal capacity, as mechanized belt and box lines are operated at speeds with which virtually no worker can keep pace. When workers loading trucks inevitably fall behind, packages pile up, and extra "floaters" make rounds helping them catch up.[25] Work hours are often long for drivers. When a 1995 *Wall Street Journal* piece referred to UPS drivers as America's new sex symbol, the wife of a UPS driver wrote to the *Detroit Free Press*, "We are glad that someone has reminded us of what our husbands look like because, with the hours they work, you don't see a whole lot of them. That would also explain why they're being called 'Fantasy Men.' ... No UPS wife has ever had an ache or tiredness that couldn't be topped by her husband."[26]

CONSEQUENCES FOR FAMILY LIFE

The reengineering of work occurs at the same time that family work patterns and gender roles are changing. Such work changes both accelerate these family changes and often deform their previously liberating possibilities for men and women. Few families fit the single-earner "Ozzie and Harriet" stereotype today, as more and more are supported by dual earner couples. In 1950, only 33.9 percent of working-age females were in the labor force; by 1993, 57.9 percent were working. By 1993, just over one-fifth of couples fit the single–male-earner model.[27] The rest were dual-earner couples or single-parent families, struggling to get by on one income in an economy that increasingly requires two.

Past generations of workers fought for a "family wage" and the eight-hour workday as policy solutions that would help them live with the industrial world. While the family wage was never paid to many workers, particularly African Americans, Latinos, and women, it was perceived as a reachable goal for many. The demand for a family wage was based on the assumption that every family could afford and would prefer to have a male full-time wage worker with a full-time, stay-at-home wife to tend to child care, housework, and family comfort. Many commentators feel that workers should fight to revive this family-wage system.

But social changes in recent decades have made the family-wage concept obsolete. Women do not want to, and often cannot be forced to, choose between work or family, even though they find that family life often turns into a "second shift" when housework and care of others is added to a demanding job schedule. Men also do not want to be forced into choosing between work and home. "I wish I could work part time," a male postal worker commented; "for men, it seems there's only a choice between full time or overtime."

Social solutions to the converging needs of men and women will not come out of the male-breadwinner–female-homemaker model. New solutions are being sought by labor organizations, women's groups, and others. While a consensus does not yet exist, ideas like shorter work time, business-tax penalties or incentives, corporate-shareholder activism, and militant labor organizing are being discussed. The very technologies that allow us to produce so much should allow us to have a richer life, not just a higher Dow Jones average. The quality of life in the future depends not on our ability to adapt our families to work, but to adapt work to our family, community, and individual needs.

A shorter work week with no pay cut is among the most promising solutions to the new realities of the work world. Shorter work time addresses the work, leisure, and family needs of both men and women. Proponents argue that since fewer workers are now needed to produce needed goods and services, the available work, income, and leisure should be shared by reducing the number of hours in a "full-time" job. Europe has had an active shorter-hours movement, and European countries have reduced work time through lengthened paid vacations and holidays. In the United States, we work about 200 hours more per year than workers do in Europe.[28]

In early 1995, a conference at the University of Iowa entitled "Our Time Famine: A Critical Look at the Culture of Work and a Reevaluation of 'Free' Time" drew together scholars, political leaders, labor activists, policy analysts, writers, business consultants, simple-living advocates, and exhausted workers in a search for solutions. The conference brought pioneering feminist writer Betty Friedan together with "war-zone" labor strategist Jerry Tucker. Former Senator and presidential candidate Eugene McCarthy conferred with Juliet Schor, author of *The Overworked American*.

The "Iowa City Declaration" adopted by the conference said that "the maldistribution of work and free time, with attendant inequality of incomes, has created a growing social problem.... We therefore urge the national governments of Canada and the United States to put in place before the year 2000 the legal arrangements to ensure that a thirty-two hour workweek will become the norm for full-time workers in the first decade of the new millennium."[29]

Betty Friedan expressed the feelings of most participants when she commented that "it is obscene to continue in a culture of greed where the only people who benefit are the top 2 percent." Friedan's home town of Peoria, Illinois, was the site of a bitter strike against Caterpillar Tractor's wage cutting and work reengineering. Seeing the results of falling wages, she warned that "a 20 percent drop in male income" could sow the seeds of political backlash against women's gains. To avoid such a counterproductive response, she argued, "it is necessary for women and men to work together to restructure work and restructure home." Such a backlash has already rolled back the gains that African-American and other workers made in the 1970s, and here too the shorter-work-week movement represents a promising alternative to attempts to reassert white privilege in order to gain a larger share of a shrinking pie. The conference, Friedan commented, was "part of a paradigm shift—which I can say with some authority, having been a part of one before."[30]

European unions and political bodies have adopted the goal of shortening work time and have negotiated twenty-seven- to thirty-four-hour work weeks with corporations like Volkswagen, Hewlett-Packard, and Digital Equipment.[31] "Time for living, loving, and laughter ... that's what we want for our Saturdays," read a German strike banner at Volkswagen. The U.S. shorter-work-time movement is just beginning to revive after a decades-long sleep. In fits and spurts, progress toward a shorter work week is being made in some large American corporations. Oddly, it is in the course of fighting forced overtime, massive layoffs, and speedup that workers have proposed, and won, shorter hours with no cuts in pay.

In St. Louis, autoworkers producing top-selling minivans were faced with Chrysler demands for a ten-hour day. The union members voted down the company's schedule and proposed an alternative that would keep production going around-the-clock and create jobs: They won three thirty-four-hour shifts at forty hours pay and were able to recall 1,200 laid-off workers. "There was less stress, attendance was better, attitude was better," commented a local union officer.

Steelworkers at National Steel's Granite City, Illinois, mill had worked five eight-hour shifts a week for years. When the company demanded "alternative work schedules" involving up to sixteen hours per day with rotating shifts, the workers struck and shut down the mill.

Their "Cold Mill Committee for a Decent Schedule" held public rallies involving spouses and children, claiming that the company's alternative schedule was "a family wrecker." The union proposed its own four-crew schedule and won a thirty-six-hour workweek with forty hours pay and no forced overtime.[32]

The paradigm shift Betty Friedan referred to is happening in some labor struggles and in the individual choices of workers. It has not yet been reflected in social policy, but the emerging shorter-hours movement and the new energy among some labor unions make it possible to envision a future where families control their work, not the other way around.

NOTES

1. David Bacon, "The UPS Strike—Unions Win When They Take the Offensive," August 24, 1997. "Polls Show UPS Strikers Have Wide Public Support," August 14, 1997, *Wall Street Journal Interactive Edition.*
2. "The Downsizing of America," *New York Times*, March 3, 1996, 16.
3. Elizabeth Gilbert, "Exiles in the Promised Land," *New York Times*, January 7, 1996, E19.
4. Al Ehrbahr, " 'Reengineering' Gives Firms New Efficiency, Workers the Pink Slip," *Wall Street Journal*, March 16, 1993, 1.
5. For more background on wealth redistribution, social and tax policy, see: Donald L. Bartlett and James B. Steele, *America: What Went Wrong?* (Kansas City: Andrews and McMeel, 1992); Thomas Byrne Edsall, *The New Politics of Inequality*, (New York: W. W. Norton, 1984); Thomas Ferguson and Joel Rogers, *Right Turn: The Decline of the Democrats and the Future of American Politics* (Hill and Wang, 1986); U.S. Department of Labor, "Fact-finding Report: Commission on the Future of Worker-Management Relations," 1994.
6. Tim Donahue, "Workplace is becoming more stressful," *Seattle Times*, July 24, 1995, D4.
7. Labor Research Association, "Economic Notes," March 1996.
8. "The Tide Is Not Lifting Everyone," *New York Times*, October 2, 1997, A2.
9. "Rising Output, Falling Incomes," *Dollars and Sense*, May–June 1995, 43.
10. Floyd Norris, "Three Views, No Agreement," *New York Times,* February 4, 1996, F5.
11. Drucker, Peter, *Post Capitalist Society* (New York: Harper Collins, 1993).
12. "Outlook for Technology and Labor in Telephone Communications," U.S. Department of Labor, Bureau of Labor Statistics, July 1990, Bulletin 2357, 1, 11–12.
13. Louis Uchitelle and N.R. Kleinfield, "The Downsizing of America: A National Heartache," *New York Times*, March 3, 1996, 15.
14. LaBotz, Dan, "The Team in Mexico," Working Smart, Labor Education and Research Project, 1994, 239–240.
15. "The Downsizing of America," *New York Times*, March 3, 1996, 1.
16. "Job Insecurity: A Special Report," *New York Times*, July 3, 1995, 1.
17. "The Downsizing of America," *New York Times*, March 3, 1996, 16.
18. Labor Research Association, "Economic Notes," December 1995.

19. "Overtime Tyrant Gets Tough," *CWA News*, vol. 55, no. 9, October 1995, 7.
20. Keith Bradsher, "Showdown at GM Leaves Big Issues Still Unresolved," *New York Times*, March 23, 1996, 1.
21. Adrienne Eaton, "New Production Techniques, Employee Involvement and Unions," *Labor Studies Journal*, vol. 20, no. 3, Fall 1995.
22. John Junkerman, "Nissan, Tennessee: It Ain't What It's Cracked Up to Be," *The Progressive*, June 1987, 16–20.
23. Mike Parker and Jane Slaughter, "Working Smart: Guide to Participation Programs and Reengineering," Labor Education and Research Project, Detroit, Mich., 1994, Chapter 1, 1.
24. "In the Productivity Push, How Much Is Too Much?" *New York Times*, December 17, 1995, sec. 3, 1.
25. Interview with Tom Bernard, Business Agent, Teamsters local 174, Seattle, May 1, 1996.
26. Letter to *Detroit Free Press* reproduced in a flyer by Teamsters Local 174, Seattle.
27. "Fact-Finding Report," Commission on the Future of Worker-Management Relations, U.S. Department of Labor, 1994, 10–11.
28. Ibid., 19.
29. "Iowa City Declaration," available from William McGaughey, 1702 Glenwood Ave., N. Minneapolis, MN 55405. Also, Shorter Work Time Group, 69 Dover Street #1, Somerville, MA 02144.
30. Betty Friedan, remarks to "Our Time Famine" conference, University of Iowa, March 10, 1996.
31. Jeremy Rifkin, *The End of Work* (New York: GB Putnam, 1995), 224–226.
32. Kim Moody and Simone Sagovac, "Time Out!" Labor Education and Research Project, Detroit, Mich., 1995, 40–42.

19

Gender Displays and Men's Power: The "New Man" and the Mexican Immigrant Man

Pierrette Hondagneu-Sotelo
Michael A. Messner

In our discussions about masculinity with our students (most of whom are white and upper-middle class), talk invariably turns to critical descriptions of the "macho" behavior of "traditional men." Consistently, these men are portrayed as "out there," not in the classroom with us. Although it usually remains an unspoken subtext, at times a student will actually speak it: Those men who are still stuck in "traditional, sexist, and macho" styles of masculinity are black men, Latino men, immigrant men, and working-class men. They are not us; we are the New Men, the Modern, Educated, and Enlightened Men. The belief that poor, working-class, and ethnic minority men are stuck in an atavistic, sexist "traditional male role," while white, educated middle-class men are forging a more sensitive egalitarian "New," or "Modern male role," is not uncommon. Social scientific theory and research on men and masculinity, as well as the "men's movement," too often collude with this belief by defining masculinity almost entirely in terms of gender display (i.e., styles of talk, dress, and bodily comportment), while ignoring men's structural positions of power and privilege over women and the subordination of certain groups of men to other men (Brod, 1983–1984). Our task in this chapter is to explore and explicate some links between contemporary men's gender displays and men's various positions in a social structure of power. Scott Coltrane's (1992) comparative analysis of gender display and power in ninety-three non-industrial societies provides us with an important starting point. Coltrane found that men's "fierce public displays and denigration of women ... competitive physical contests, vociferous oratory, ceremonies related to warfare, exclusive men's houses and rituals, and sexual violence against women" are common features in societies where men control property and have distant relations with young children (Coltrane, 1992, p. 87). By contrast, "in societies in which women exercise significant control over property and men have close relationships with children, men infrequently affirm their manliness through boastful demonstrations of strength, aggressiveness, and sexual potency" (p. 86). This research suggests that men's public gender displays are not grounded in some essential "need" men have to dominate others but, instead, tend to vary according to the extent of power and privilege that men hold vis-à-vis women. Put another way, the micropolitics of men's and women's daily gender displays and interactions both reflect and reconstruct the macropolitical relations between the sexes (Henley, 1977).

But in modern industrial societies, the politics of gender are far more complex than in nonindustrial societies. Some men publicly display verbal and physical aggression, misogyny, and violence. There are public institutions such as sports, the military, fraternities, and the street where these forms of gender display are valorized (Connell, 1991a, 1992b; Lyman, 1987; Martin & Hummer, 1989; Messner, 1992; Sabo, 1985). Other men, though, display more "softness" and "sensitivity," and this form of gender display has been recently lauded as an emergent "New Masculinity."

In this chapter, we will contrast the gender display and structural positions of power (in both public and domestic spheres of life) of two groups of men: class-privileged white men and Mexican immigrant men. We will argue that utilizing the concepts of Modern (or New) and Traditional men to describe these two groups oversimplifies a complex reality, smuggles in racist and classist biases about Mexican immigrant men, and obscures the real class, race, and gender privileges that New Men still enjoy. We will argue that the theoretical concepts of hegemonic, marginalized, and subordinated masculinities best capture the dynamic and shifting constellation of contemporary men's gender displays and power (Brod, 1987; Connell, 1987; Kaufman, 1987; Segal, 1990). We will conclude by arguing that a critical/feminist sociology of men and masculinity should decenter and problematize hegemonic masculinity by proceeding from the standpoint of marginalized and subordinated masculinities.

THE "NEW MAN" AS IDEOLOGICAL CLASS ICON

Today there is a shared cultural image of what the New Man looks like: He is a white, college-educated professional who is a highly involved and nurturing father, "in touch with" and expressive of his feelings, and egalitarian in his dealings with women. We will briefly examine two fragments of the emergent cultural image of the contemporary New Man: the participant in the mythopoetic men's movement and the New Father.[1] We will discuss these contemporary images of men both in terms of their larger cultural meanings and in terms of the extent to which they represent any real shift in the ways men live their lives vis-à-vis women and other men. Most important, we will ask if apparent shifts in the gender displays of some white, middle-class men represent any real transformations in their structural positions of power and privilege.

Zeus Power and the Mythopoetic Men's Movement

A recently emergent fragment of the cultural image of the New Man is the man who attends the weekend "gatherings of men" that are at the heart of Robert Bly's mythopoetic men's movement. Bly's curious interpretations of mythology and his highly selective use of history, psychology, and anthropology have been soundly criticized as "bad social science" (e.g., Connell, 1992a; Kimmel, 1992; Pelka, 1991). But perhaps more important than a critique of Bly's ideas is a sociological interpretation of why the mythopoetic men's movement has been so attractive to so many predominantly white, college-educated, middle-class, middle-aged men in the United States over the past decade. (Thousands of men have attended Bly's gatherings, and his book was a national best-seller.) We speculate that Bly's movement attracts these men not because it represents any sort of radical break from "traditional masculinity" but precisely because it is so congruent with shifts that are already taking place within current constructions of hegemonic masculinity. Many of the men who attend Bly's gatherings are already aware of some of the problems and limits of narrow conceptions of masculinity. A major preoccupation of the gatherings is the poverty of these men's relationships with their fathers and with other men in workplaces. These concerns are based on very real and often very painful experiences. Indeed, industrial capitalism undermined much of the structural basis of middle-class men's emotional bonds with each other as wage labor, market competition, and instrumental rationality largely supplanted primogeniture, craft brotherhood, and intergenerational mentorhood (Clawson, 1989; Tolson, 1977). Bly's "male initiation" rituals are intended to heal and reconstruct these masculine bonds, and they are thus, at least on the surface, probably experienced as largely irrelevant to men's relationships with women.

But in focusing on how myth and ritual can reconnect men with each other and ultimately with their own "deep masculine" essences, Bly manages to sidestep the central point of the feminist critique—that men, as a group, benefit from a structure of power that oppresses women as a group. In ignoring the social structure of power, Bly manages to convey a false symmetry between the feminist women's movement and his men's movement. He assumes a natural dichotomization of "male values" and "female values" and states that feminism has been good for women in allowing them to reassert "the feminine voice" that had been suppressed. But, Bly states (and he carefully avoids directly blaming feminism for this): "the masculine voice" has now been muted—men have become "passive ... tamed ... domesticated." Men thus need a movement to reconnect with the "Zeus energy" that they have lost. "Zeus energy is male authority accepted for the good of the community" (Bly, 1990, p. 61).

The notion that men need to be empowered *as men* echoes the naïveté of some 1970s men's liberation activists who saw men and women as "equally oppressed" by sexism (e.g., Farrell, 1975). The view that everyone is oppressed by sexism strips the concept of oppression of its political meaning and thus obscures the social relations of domination and subordination. Oppression is a concept that describes a relationship between social groups; for one group to be oppressed, there must be an oppressor group (Freire, 1970). This is not to imply that an oppressive relationship between groups is absolute or static. To the contrary, oppression is characterized by a constant and complex state of play: Oppressed groups both actively participate in their own domination and actively resist that domination. The state of play of the contemporary gender order is characterized by men's individual and collective oppression of women (Connell, 1987). Men continue to benefit from this oppression of women, but, significantly, in the past twenty years, women's compliance with masculine hegemony has been counterbalanced by active feminist resistance.

Men do tend to pay a price for their power: They are often emotionally limited and commonly suffer poor health and a life expectancy lower than that of women. But these problems are best viewed not as "gender oppression," but rather as the "costs of being on top" (Kann, 1986). In fact, the shifts in masculine styles that we see among some relatively privileged men may be interpreted as a sign that these men would like to stop paying these costs, but they do not necessarily signal a desire to cease being "on top." For example, it has become commonplace to see powerful and successful men weeping in public—Ronald Reagan shedding a tear at the funeral of slain U.S. soldiers, basketball player Michael Jordan openly crying after winning the NBA championship. Most recently, the easy manner in which the media lauded U.S. General Schwartzkopf as a New Man for shedding a public tear for the U.S. casualties in the Gulf War is indicative of the importance placed on *styles of masculine gender display* rather than the institutional *position of power* that men such as Schwartzkopf still enjoy.

This emphasis on the significance of public displays of crying indicates, in part, a naïve belief that if boys and men can learn to "express their feelings," they will no longer feel a need to dominate others. In fact, there is no necessary link between men's "emotional inexpressivity" and their tendency to dominate others (Sattel, 1976). The idea that men's "need" to dominate others is the result of an emotional deficit overly psychologizes a reality that is largely structural. It does seem that the specific type of masculinity that was ascendent (hegemonic) during the rise of entrepreneurial capitalism was extremely instrumental, stoic, and emotionally inexpressive (Winter & Robert, 1980). But there is growing evidence (e.g., Schwartzkopf) that today there is no longer a neat link between class-privileged men's emotional inexpressivity and their willingness and ability to dominate others (Connell, 1991b). We speculate that a situationally appropriate public display of sensitivity such as crying, rather than signaling weakness, has instead become a legitimizing sign of the New Man's power.[2]

Thus relatively privileged men may be attracted to the mythopoetic men's movement because, on the one hand, it acknowledges and validates their painful "wounds," while guiding them to connect with other men in ways that are both nurturing and mutually empowering.[3] On the other hand, and unlike feminism, it does not confront men with the reality of how their own privileges are based on the continued subordination of women and other men. In short, the mythopoetic men's movement may be seen as facilitating the reconstruction of a new form of hegemonic masculinity—a masculinity that is less self-destructive, that has revalued and reconstructed men's emotional bonds with each other, and that has learned to feel good about its own Zeus power.

The New Father

In recent years Western culture has been bombarded with another fragment of the popular image of the New Man: the involved, nurturant father. Research has indicated that many young heterosexual men do appear to be more inclined than were their fathers to "help out" with housework and child care, but most of them still see these tasks as belonging to their wives or their future wives (Machung, 1989; Sidel, 1990). Despite the cultural image of the "new fatherhood" and some modest increases in participation by men, the vast majority of child care, especially of infants, is still performed by women (Hochschild, 1989; La Rossa, 1988; Lewis, 1986; Russell, 1983).

Why does men's stated desire to participate in parenting so rarely translate into substantially increased involvement? Lynn Segal (1990) argues that the fact that men's apparent attitudinal changes have not translated into widespread behavioral changes may be largely due to the fact that men may (correctly) fear that increased parental involvement will translate into a loss of their power over women. But she also argues that increased paternal involvement in child care will not become a widespread reality unless and until the structural preconditions—especially economic equality for women—exist. Indeed, Rosanna Hertz (1986) found in her study of upper-middle class "dual career families" that a more egalitarian division of family labor sometimes developed as a rational (and constantly negotiated) response to a need to maintain his career, her career, and the family. In other words, career and pay equality for women was a structural precondition for the development of equality between husbands and wives in the family.

However, Hertz notes two reasons why this is a very limited and flawed equality. First, Hertz's sample of dual-career families in which the women and the men made roughly the same amount of money is still extremely atypical. In two-income families, the husband is far more likely to have the higher income. Women are far more likely than men to work part-time jobs, and among full-time workers, women still earn about sixty-five cents to the male dollar and are commonly segregated in lower paid, lower status, dead-end jobs (Blum, 1991; Reskin & Roos,

1990). As a result, most women are not in the structural position to be able to bargain with their husbands for more egalitarian divisions of labor in the home. As Hochschild's (1989) research demonstrates, middle-class women's struggles for equity in the home are often met by their husbands' "quiet resistance," which sometimes lasts for years. A woman is left with the choice of either leaving the relationship (and suffering not only the emotional upheaval, but also the downward mobility, often into poverty, that commonly follows divorce) or capitulating to the man and quietly working her "second shift" of family labor.

Second, Hertz observes that the roughly egalitarian family division of labor among some upper-middle-class dual-career couples is severely shaken when a child is born into the family. Initially, new mothers are more likely than fathers to put their careers on hold. But eventually many resume their careers, as the child care and much of the home labor is performed by low-paid employees, almost always women, and often immigrant women and/or women of color. The construction of the dual-career couple's "gender equality" is thus premised on the family's privileged position within a larger structure of social inequality. In other words, some of the upper-middle-class woman's gender oppression is, in effect, bought off with her class privilege, while the man is let off the hook from his obligation to fully participate in child care and housework. The upper-middle-class father is likely to be more involved with his children today than his father was with him, and this will likely enrich his life. But given the fact that the day-to-day and moment-to-moment care and nurturance of his children is still likely to be performed by women (either his wife and/or a hired, lower-class woman), "the contemporary revalorisation of fatherhood has enabled many men to have the best of both worlds" (Segal, 1990, p. 58). The cultural image of the New Father has given the middle-class father license to choose to enjoy the emotional fruits of parenting, but his position of class and gender privilege allow him the resources with which he can buy or negotiate his way out of the majority of second shift labor.

In sum, as a widespread empirical reality, the emotionally expressive, nurturant, egalitarian New Man does not actually exist; he is an ideological construct, made up of disparate popular images that are saturated with meanings that express the anxieties, fears, and interests of relatively privileged men. But this is not to say that some changes are not occurring among certain groups of privileged men (Segal, 1990). Some men are expressing certain feelings that were, in the past, considered outside the definition of hegemonic masculinity. Some men are reexamining and changing their relationships with other men. Some men are participating more—very equitably in some cases, but marginally in many others—in the care and nurturance of children. But the key point is that when examined within the context of these men's positions in the overall structure of power in society, these changes do not appear to challenge or undermine men's power. On the contrary, the cultural image of the New Man and the partial and fragmentary empirical changes that this image represents serve to file off some of the rough edges of hegemonic masculinity in such a way that the possibility of a happier and healthier life for men is created, while deflecting or resisting feminist challenges to men's institutional power and privilege. But because at least verbal acceptance of the "New Woman" is an important aspect of this reconstructed hegemonic masculinity, the ideological image of the New Man requires a counterimage against which to stand in opposition. Those aspects of traditional hegemonic masculinity that the New Man has rejected—overt physical and verbal displays of domination, stoicism and emotional inexpressivity, overt misogyny in the workplace and at home—are now increasingly projected onto less privileged groups of men: working-class men, gay body-builders, black athletes, Latinos, and immigrant men.

MEXICAN IMMIGRANT MEN

According to the dominant cultural stereotype, Latino men's "machismo" is supposedly characterized by extreme verbal and bodily expressions of aggression toward other men, frequent drunkenness, and sexual aggression and dominance expressed toward normally "submissive" Latinas. Manuel Peña's (1991) research on the workplace culture of male undocumented Mexican immigrant agricultural workers suggests that there is a great deal of truth to this stereotype. Peña examined the Mexican immigrant male's participation in the *charritas coloradas* (red jokes) that characterize the basis of his workplace culture. The most common basis of humor in the *charritas* is sexualized "sadism toward women and symbolic threats of sodomy toward other males" (Paredes, 1966, p. 121).

On the surface, Peña argues, the constant "half-serious, half-playful duels" among the men, as well as the images of sexually debased "perverted wenches" and "treacherous women" in the *charritas*, appear to support the stereotype of the Mexican immigrant male group as being characterized by a high level of aggressive masculine posturing with shared antagonisms and hatred directed toward women. But rather than signifying a fundamental hatred of women, Peña argues that these men's public displays of machismo should be viewed as a defensive reaction to their oppressed class status:

> As an expression of working-class culture, the folklore of machismo can be considered a realized signifying system [that] points to, but simultaneously displaces, a class relationship and its attendant conflict. At the same time, it introduces a third element, the gender relationship, which acts as a mediator between the signifier (the folklore) and the signified (the class relationship). (Peña, 1991, p. 40)

Undocumented Mexican immigrant men are unable to directly confront their class oppressors, so instead, Peña argues, they symbolically displace their class antagonism into the arena of gender relations. Similar arguments have been made about other groups of men. For instance, David Collinson (1988) argues that Australian male blue-collar workers commonly engage in sexually aggressive and misogynist humor as an (ultimately flawed) means of bonding together to resist the control of management males (who are viewed, disparagingly, as feminized). Majors and Billson (1992) argue that young black males tend to embody and publicly display a "cool pose," an expressive and often sexually aggressive style of masculinity that acts as a form of resistance to racism. These studies make important strides toward building an understanding of how subordinated and marginalized groups of men tend to embody and publicly display styles of masculinity that at least symbolically resist the various forms of oppression that they face within hierarchies of intermale dominance. These studies all share the insight that the public faces of subordinated groups of men are *personally and collectively constructed performances of masculine gender display*. By contrast, the public face of the New Man (his "sensitivity," etc.) is often assumed to be one-and-the-same as who he "is," rather than being seen as a situationally constructed public gender display.

Yet in foregrounding the oppression of men by men, these studies risk portraying aggressive, even misogynist, gender displays primarily as liberatory forms of resistance against class and racial oppression (e.g., Mirandé, 1982). Though these studies view microlevel gender display as constructed within a context of structured power relations, macrolevel gender relations are rarely viewed as a constituting dynamic within this structure. Rather gender is commonly viewed as an epiphenomenon, an effect of the dominant class and/or race relations. What is obscured, or even drops out of sight, is the feminist observation that masculinity itself is a form of domination over women. As a result, women's actual experiences of oppression and victimization by men's violence are conspicuously absent from these analyses, thus leaving the impression that misogyny is merely a symbolic displacement of class (or race) antagonism. What is needed, then, is an examination of masculine gender display and power within the context of intersecting systems of class, race, and gender relations (Baca Zinn, Cannon, Higginbotham, & Dill, 1986; Collins, 1990). In the following section we will consider recent ethnographic research on Mexican immigrant communities that suggests that gender dynamics help to constitute the immigration process and, in turn, are reconstituted during and following the immigrant settlement process.

The Rhetoric of Return Migration as Gender Display

Mexican immigrant men who have lived in the United States for long periods of time frequently engage in the rhetoric of return migration. These stated preferences are not necessarily indicative of what they will do, but they provide some telling clues to these men's feelings and per-

ceptions about their lives as marginalized men in the United States.
Consider the following statements:[4]

> I've passed more of my life here than in Mexico. I've been here for
> thirty-one years. I'm not putting down or rejecting this country, but
> my intentions have always been to return to Mexico ... I'd like to
> retire there, perhaps open a little business. Maybe I could buy and
> sell animals, or open a restaurant. Here I work for a big company,
> like a slave, always watching the clock. Well I'm bored with that.

> I don't want to stay in the U.S. anymore. [Why not?] Because here
> I can no longer find a good job. Here, even if one is sick, you must
> report for work. They don't care. I'm fed up with it. I'm tired of
> working here too. Here one must work daily, and over there with
> my mother, I'll work for four, maybe five months, and then I'll have
> a four- or five-month break without working. My mother is old and
> I want to be with the family. I need to take care of the rancho. Here
> I have nothing. I don't have my own house, I even share the rent!
> What am I doing here?

> I would like to return, but as my sons are born here, well that is
> what detains me here. Otherwise, I would go back to Mexico ...
> Mexico is now in a very inflationary situation. People come here
> not because they like it, but because the situation causes them to do
> so, and it makes them stay here for years and years. As the song
> says, this is a cage made of gold, but it is still a cage.

These statements point to disappointments with migration. In recent
years, U.S.-bound migration has become institutionalized in many areas
of Mexico, representing a rite of passage for many young, single men
(Davis, 1990; Escobar, Gonzalez de la Rocha, & Roberts, 1987). But once
in the United States the accomplishment of masculinity and maturity
hinges on living up to the image of a financially successful migrant. If a
man returns homes penniless, he risks being seen as a failure or a fool.
As one man explained: "One cannot go back without anything, because
people will talk. They'll say 'oh look at this guy, he sacrificed and suffered to go north and he has nothing to show for it.'"

Although most of these men enjoyed a higher standard of living in
the United States than in Mexico, working and settling in the United
States significantly diminished their patriarchal privileges. Although
the men compensated by verbally demonstrating their lack of commitment to staying in the United States, most of these men realized that
their lives remained firmly anchored in the United States and that they
lacked the ability to return. They could not acquire sufficient savings in
the public sphere to fund return migration, and in the domestic sphere,
they did not command enough authority over their wives or children,
who generally wished to remain in the United States, to coerce the
return migration of their families. Although Mexican immigrant men

blamed the terms of U.S. production as their reason for wanting to return to Mexico, we believe that their diminished patriarchal privileges significantly fueled this desire to return.[5] Here, we examine the diminution of patriarchy in three arenas: spatial mobility, authority in family decision-making processes, and household labor.

Mexican immigrant men, especially those who were undocumented and lacked legal status privileges, experienced limited spatial mobility in their daily lives and this compromised their sense of masculinity (Rouse, 1990). As undocumented immigrants, these men remained fearful of apprehension by the Immigration Naturalization Service and by the police.[6] In informal conversations, the men often shared experiences with police harassment and racial discrimination. Merely "looking Mexican," the men agreed, was often cause for suspicion. The jobs Mexican immigrant men commonly took also restricted their spatial mobility. As poor men who worked long hours at jobs as gardeners, dishwashers, or day laborers, they had very little discretionary income to afford leisure activities. As one man offered, "Here my life is just from work to the home, from work to the home."

Although the men, together with their families, visited parks, shops, and church, the public spaces open to the men alone were typically limited to street corners and to a few neighborhood bars, pool halls, and doughnut shops. As Rouse (1990) has argued, Mexican immigrant men, especially those from rural areas, resent these constrictions on their public space and mobility and attempt to reproduce public spaces that they knew in Mexico in the context of U.S. bars and pool halls. In a California immigrant community Rouse observed that "men do not come to drink alone or to meet with a couple of friends ... they move from table to table, broadening the circuits of information in which they participate and modulating social relationships across the widest possible range." Although these men tried to create new spaces where they might recapture a public sense of self, the goal was not so readily achieved. For many men, the loss of free and easy mobility signified their loss of publicly accorded status and recognition. One man, a junkyard assembler who had worked in Mexico as a rural *campesino* (peasant), recalled that in his Mexican village he enjoyed a modicum of public recognition: "I would enter the bars, the dances, and when I entered everyone would stand to shake my hand as though I were somebody—not a rich man, true, but I was famous. Wherever you like, I was always mentioned. Wherever you like, everyone knew me back there." In metropolitan areas of California, anonymity replaced public status and recognition.

In Mexico many of these men had acted as the undisputed patriarchs in major family decision-making processes, but in the United States they no longer retained their monopoly on these processes. When families were faced with major decisions—such as whom to seek for legal help, whether or not to move to another town, or the decision to lend money or make a major purchase—spousal negotiation replaced patriarchal exertions of authority. These processes did not go uncontested, and some of the decision-making discussions were more conflictual than harmonious, but collaboration, not domination, characterized them.

This trend toward more egalitarian patterns of shared authority often began with migration. In some families, men initially migrated north alone, and during their absences, the women acted decisively and autonomously as they performed a range of tasks necessary to secure family sustenance. Commentators have referred to this situation as one in which "thousands of wives in the absence of their husbands must 'take the reigns'" (Mummert, 1988, p. 283) and as one in which the wives of veteran migrants experience "a freedom where woman command (*una libertad donde mujeres mandan*)" (Baca & Bryan, 1985). This trend toward more shared decision making continued after the women's migration and was also promoted by migration experiences as well as the relative increase in women's and the decrease in men's economic contributions to the family (Hondagneu-Sotelo, 1992). As the balance of relative resources and contributions shifted, the women assumed more active roles in key decision-making processes. Similar shifts occurred with the older children, who were now often reluctant to subordinate their earnings and their autonomy to a patriarchal family hierarchy. As one man somewhat reluctantly, but resignedly, acknowledged: "Well, each person orders one's self here, something like that ... Back there [Mexico], no. It was still whatever I said. I decided matters."

The household division of labor is another arena that in some cases reflected the renegotiation of patriarchal relations. Although most families continued to organize their daily household chores along fairly orthodox, patriarchal norms, in some families—notably those in which the men had lived for many years in "bachelor communities" where they learned to cook, iron, and make tortillas—men took responsibility for some of the housework. In these cases, men did part of the cooking and housework, they unselfconsciously assumed the role of hosts in offering guests food and beverages, and in some instances, the men continued to make tortillas on weekends and special occasions. These changes, of course, are modest if judged by ideal standards of feminist egalitarianism, but they are significant when compared to patriarchal family organization that was normative before immigration.

This movement toward more egalitarian divisions of labor in some Mexican immigrant households cannot be fully explained by the men's acquisition of household skills in bachelor communities. (We are reminded, for instance, of several middle-class male friends of ours who lived in "bachelor" apartments during college, and after later marrying, conveniently "forgot" how to cook, wash clothes, and do other household chores.) The acquisition of skills appears to be a necessary, but not a sufficient, condition for men's greater household labor participation in reunited families.

A key to the movement toward greater equality within immigrant families was the change in the women's and men's relative positions of power and status in the larger social structure of power. Mexican immigrant men's public status in the United States is very low, due to racism, insecure and low-paying jobs, and (often) illegal status. For those families that underwent long periods of spousal separation, women often engaged in formal- or informal-sector paid labor for the first time, developed more economic skills and autonomy, and assumed control over household affairs. In the United States nearly all of the women sought employment, so women made significant economic contributions to the family. All of these factors tend to erode men's patriarchal authority in the family and empower women to either directly challenge that authority or at least renegotiate "patriarchal bargains" (Kandiyoti, 1988) that are more palatable to themselves and their children.

Although it is too soon to proclaim that gender egalitarianism prevails in interpersonal relations among undocumented Mexican immigrants, there is a significant trend in that direction. This is indicated by the emergence of a more egalitarian household division of labor, by shared decision-making processes, and by the constraints on men's and expansion of women's spatial mobility. Women still have less power than men, but they generally enjoy more than they previously did in Mexico. The stereotypical image of dominant macho males and submissive females in Mexican immigrant families is thus contradicted by actual research with these families.

MASCULINE DISPLAYS AND RELATIVE POWER

We have suggested that men's overt public displays of masculine bravado, interpersonal dominance, misogyny, embodied strength, and so forth are often a sign of a lack of institutional power and privilege, vis-à-vis other men. Though it would be a mistake to conclude that Mexican immigrant men are not misogynist (or, following Peña, that their misogyny is merely a response to class oppression), there is considerable evidence that their actual relations with women in families—at least when measured by family divisions of labor and decision-making processes—are becoming more egalitarian than they were in Mexico. We have also argued that for more privileged men, public displays of sensitivity might be read as signs of class/race/gender privilege and power over women and (especially) over other men (see Table 1 for a summary comparison of these two groups).

Coltrane (1992) argues that in nonindustrial societies, "men's displays of dominance confirm and reinforce existing property relations rather than compensate for a lack of control over valued resources" (pp. 102–103). His claim that men's *control* (rather than lack of control) of resources is correlated with more extreme microdisplays of masculinity seems, at first, to contradict findings by Peña, Collinson, and Billson and Majors, who claim that in industrial societies, *lack* of access to property and other material resources by Mexican immigrant, working-

Table 1.
Comparison of Public and Domestic Gender Displays of White,
Class-Privileged Men and Mexican Immigrant Men

| | *Public* | | *Domestic* | |
	Power/Status	*Gender Display*	*Power/Status*	*Gender Display*
White, class-privileged men	High, built into position	"Sensitive," little overt misogyny	High, based on public status/ high income	"Quiet control"
Mexican immigrant men	Low (job status, pay, control of work, legal rights, public status)	"Hombre": verbal misogyny, embodied toughness in work/ peer culture	Contested, becoming more egalitarian	Exaggerated symbols of power and authority in family

class, and black males correlates with more overt outward displays of
aggressive, misogynist masculinity. The key to understanding this
apparent contradiction is that Coltrane is discussing societies where
women enjoy high social status, where men are highly involved in child
care, and where women have a great deal of control over property and
other material resources. In these types of societies, men do not "need"
to display dominance and masculine bravado. But in complex, stratified
societies where the standards of hegemonic masculinity are that a man
should control resources (and other people), men who do not have
access to these standards of masculinity thus tend to react with displays
of toughness, bravado, "cool pose," or "hombre" (Baca Zinn, 1982).

Marginalized and subordinated men, then, tend to overtly display exaggerated embodiments and verbalizations of masculinity that can be read as
a desire to express power over others within a context of relative powerlessness. By contrast, many of the contemporary New Man's highly celebrated public displays of sensitivity can be read as a desire to project an
image of egalitarianism within a context where he actually enjoys considerable power and privilege over women and other men. Both groups of
men are "displaying gender," but the specific forms that their masculine
displays take tend to vary according to their relative positions in (a) the
social structure of men's overall power relationship to women and (b) the
social structure of some men's power relationships with other men.

CONCLUSION

We have argued for the importance of viewing microlevel gender displays of different groups of men within the context of their positions in
a larger social structure of power. Too often critical discussions of mas-

culinity tend to project atavistic, hypermasculine, aggressive, misogynist masculinity onto relatively powerless men. By comparison, the masculine gender displays of educated, privileged New Men are too often uncritically applauded, rather than skeptically and critically examined. We have suggested that when analyzed within a structure of power, the gender displays of the New Man might best be seen as strategies to reconstruct hegemonic masculinity by projecting aggression, domination, and misogyny onto subordinate groups of men. Does this mean that all of men's changes today are merely symbolic and ultimately do not contribute to the types of changes in gender relations that feminists have called for? It may appear so, especially if social scientists continue to collude with this reality by theoretically framing shifts in styles of hegemonic masculinity as indicative of the arrival of a New Man, while framing marginalized men as Other—as atavistic, traditional men. Instead, a critical/feminist analysis of changing masculinities in the United States might begin with a focus on the ways that marginalized and subordinated masculinities are changing.

This shift in focus would likely accomplish three things: First, it would remove hegemonic masculinity from center stage, thus taking the standpoints of oppressed groups of men as central points of departure. Second, it would require the deployment of theoretical frameworks that examine the ways in which the politics of social class, race, ethnicity, and sexuality interact with those of gender (Baca Zinn, Cannon, Higginbotham, & Dill, 1986; Collins, 1990; Harding, 1986; Hondagneu-Sotelo, 1992; Messner, 1990). Third, a sociology of masculinities that starts from the experience of marginalized and subordinated men would be far more likely to have power and politics—rather than personal styles or lifestyles—at its center. This is because men of color, poor and working-class men, immigrant men, and gay men are often in very contradictory positions at the nexus of intersecting systems of domination and subordination. In short, although they are oppressed by class, race, and/or sexual systems of power, they also commonly construct and display forms of masculinity as ways of resisting other men's power over them, as well as asserting power and privilege over women. Thus, to avoid reverting to the tendency to view masculinity simply as a defensive reaction to other forms of oppression, it is crucial in such studies to keep women's experience of gender oppression as close to the center of analysis as possible. This sort of analysis might inform the type of progressive coalition building that is necessary if today's changing masculinities are to contribute to the building of a more egalitarian and democratic world.

NOTES

The authors thank Harry Brod, Scott Coltrane, and Michael Kaufman for help-ful comments on earlier versions of this chapter.

1. This section of the chapter is adapted from Messner (1993).
2. It is significant, we suspect, that the examples cited of Reagan, Jordan, and Schwartzkopf publicly weeping occurred at moments of *victory* over other men in war and sport.
3. Our speculation on the class and racial bias of the mythopoetic men's move-ment and on the appeal of the movement to participants is supported, in part, by ongoing (but as yet unpublished) research by sociologist Michael Schwalbe. Schwalbe observes that the "wounds" of these men are very real, because a very high proportion of them are children of alcoholic parents and/or were victims of childhood sexual abuse or other forms of violence. Many are involved in recovery programs.
4. Material in this section is drawn from Hondagneu-Sotelo's study of long-term undocumented immigrant settlers, based on 18 months of field research in a Mexican undocumented immigrant community. See Hondagneu-Sotelo (1994). *Gendered Transitions: Mexican Experiences of Immigrants.* Berkelely: University of California Press.
5. For a similar finding and analysis in the context of Dominican immigrants in New York City, see Pessar (1986).
6. This constraint was exacerbated by passage of the Immigration Reform and Control Act of 1986, which imposed employer sanctions and doubly crimi-nalized undocumented immigrants' presence at the workplace.

REFERENCES

Baca, R., & Bryan, D. (1985). Mexican women, migration and sex roles. *Migration Today, 13,* 14–18.

Baca Zinn, M. (1982). Chicano men and masculinity. *Journal of Ethnic Studies, 10,* 29–44.

Baca Zinn, M., Cannon, L. W., Higginbotham, E., & Dill, B. T. (1986). The costs of exclusionary practices in women's studies. *Signs: Journal of Women in Culture and Society, 11,* 290–303.

Blum, L. M. (1991). *Between feminism and labor: The significance of the com-parable worth movement.* Berkeley: University of California Press.

Bly, R. (1990). *Iron John: A book about men.* Reading, MA: Addison-Wesley.

Brod, H. (1983–1984). Work clothes and leisure suits: The class basis and bias of the men's movement. *Changing Men, 11* (Winter), 10–12, 38–40.

Brod, H. (Ed.) (1987). *The making of masculinities: The new men's studies.* Boston: Allen & Unwin.

Clawson, M. A. (1989). *Constructing brotherhood: Class, gender, and fraternal-ism.* Princeton, NJ: Princeton University Press.

Collins, P. H. (1990). *Black feminist thought: Knowledge, consciousness, and the politics of empowerment.* Boston: Unwin Hyman.

Collinson, D. L. (1988). "Engineering humor": Masculinity, joking and conflict in shop-floor relations. *Organization Studies, 9,* 181–199.

Coltrane, S. (1992). The micropolitics of gender in nonindustrial societies.

Gender & Society, 6, 86–107.

Connell, R. W. (1987). *Gender and power.* Stanford, CA: Stanford University Press.

Connell, R. W. (1991a). Live fast and die young: The construction of masculinity among young working-class men on the margin of the labor market. *Australian & New Zealand Journal of Sociology, 27,* 141–171.

Connell, R. W. (1991b). *Men of reason: Themes of rationality and change in the lives of men in the new professions.* Unpublished paper.

Connell, R. W. (1992a). Drumming up the wrong tree. *Tikkun, 7,* 517–530.

Connell, R. W. (1992b). Masculinity, violence, and war. In M. S. Kimmel & M. A. Messner (Eds.), *Men's lives* (2nd ed., pp. 176–182). New York: Macmillan.

Davis, M. (1990). *Mexican voices, American dreams: An oral history of Mexican immigration to the United States.* New York: Henry Holt.

Escobar, A. L., Gonzales de la Rocha, M., & Roberts, B. (1987). Migration, labor markets, and the international economy: Jalisco, Mexico and the United States. In J. Eades (Ed.), *Migrants, workers, and the social order* (pp. 42–64). London: Tavistock.

Farrell, W. (1975). *The liberated man.* New York: Bantam.

Freire, P. (1970). *Pedagogy of the oppressed.* New York: Herder & Herder.

Harding, S. (1986). *The science question in feminism.* Ithaca, NY: Cornell University Press.

Henley, N. M. (1977). *Body politics: Power, sex, and nonverbal communication.* Englewood Cliffs, NJ: Prentice Hall.

Hertz, R. (1986). *More equal than others: Women and men in dual career marriages.* Berkeley: University of California Press.

Hochschild, A. (1989). *The second shift: Working parents and the revolution at home.* New York: Viking.

Hondagneu-Sotelo, P. (1992). Overcoming patriarchal constraints: The reconstruction of gender relations among Mexican immigrant women and men. *Gender & Society, 6,* 393–415.

Kandiyoti, D. (1988). Bargaining with patriarchy. *Gender & Society, 2,* 274–290.

Kann, M. E. (1986). The costs of being on top. *Journal of the National Association for Women Deans, Administrators, & Counselors, 49,* 29–37.

Kaufman, M. (Ed.). (1987). *Beyond patriarchy: Essays by men on pleasure, power, and change.* Toronto: Oxford University Press.

Kimmel, M. S. (1992). Reading men: Men, masculinity, and publishing. *Contemporary Sociology, 21,* 162–171.

La Rossa, R. (1988). Fatherhood and social change. *Family Relations, 37,* 451–457.

Lewis, C. (1986). *Becoming a father.* Milton Keynes, UK: Open University Press.

Lyman, P. (1987). The fraternal bond as a joking relation: A case study of the role of sexiest jokes in male group bonding. In M. Kimmel (Ed.), *Changing men: New directions in research on men and masculinities* (pp. 148–163). Newbury Park, CA: Sage.

Machung, A. (1989). Talking career, thinking job: Gender differences in career and family expectations of Berkeley seniors. *Feminist Studies, 15.*

Majors, R., & Billson, J. M. (1992). *Cool pose: The dilemmas of black manhood in America.* New York: Lexington.

Martin, P. Y., & Hummer, R. A. (1989). Fraternities and rape on campus. *Gender & Society, 3,* 457–473.

Messner, M. A. (1990). Men studying masculinity: Some epistemological questions in sport sociology. *Sociology of Sport Journal, 7,* 136–153.

Messner, M. A. (1992). *Power at play: Sports and the problem of masculinity.* Boston: Beacon.

Messner, M. A. (1993). "Changing men" and feminist politics in the U.S. *Theory & Society, 22,* 723–737.

Mirandé, A. (1982). Machismo: Rucas, chingasos y chagaderas. *De Colores: Journal of Chicano Expression and Thought, 6*(1/2), 17–31.

Mummert, G. (1988). Mujeres de migrantes y mujeres migrantes de Michoacán: Nuevos papeles para las que se quedan y para las que se van. In T. Calvo & G. Lopez (Eds.), *Movimientos de población en el occidente de Mexico* (pp. 281–295). Mexico, DF: Centre de'etudes mexicaines et centroamericaines and El colegio de Mexico.

Paredes, A. (1966). The Anglo-American in Mexican folklore. In R. B. Browne & D. H. Wenkelman (Eds.), *New voices in American studies.* Lafayette, IN: Purdue University Press.

Pelka, F. (1991). Robert Bly and Iron John: Bly romanticizes history, trivializes sexist oppression and lays the blame for men's "grief" on women. *On the Issues, 19,* 17–19, 39.

Peña, M. (1991). Class, gender and machismo: The "treacherous women" folklore of Mexican male workers. *Gender & Society, 5,* 30–46.

Pessar, P. (1986). The role of gender in Dominican settlement in the United States. In J. Nash & H. Safa (Eds.), *Women and change in Latin America* (pp. 273–294). South Hadley, MA: Bergin & Garvey.

Reskin, B. F., & Roos, P. A. (1990). *Job queues, gender queues: Explaining women's inroads into male occupations.* Philadelphia: Temple University Press.

Rouse, R. (1990). *Men in space: Power and the appropriation of urban form among Mexican migrants in the United States.* Paper presented March 14 at the Residential College, University of Michigan, Ann Arbor.

Russell, G. (1983). *The changing role of fathers.* London: University of Queensland Press.

Sabo, D. F. (1985). Sport, patriarchy, and male identity: New questions about men and sport. *Arena Review, 9,* 1–30.

Sattel, J. W. (1976). The inexpressive male: Tragedy or sexual politics? *Social Problems, 23,* 469–477.

Segal, L. (1990). *Slow motion: Changing masculinities, changing men.* New Brunswick, NJ: Rutgers University Press.

Sidel, R. (1990). *On her own: Growing up in the shadow of the American dream.* New York: Penguin.

Tolson, A. (1977). *The limits of masculinity: Male identity and women's liberation.* New York: Harper & Row.

Winter, M. F., & Robert, E. R. (1980). Male dominance, late capitalism, and the growth of instrumental reason. *Berkeley Journal of Sociology, 25,* 249–280.

20

CHILD-CARE DILEMMAS IN CONTEMPORARY FAMILIES

Tamara Anderson
Beth Vail

In fall 1997, Americans were transfixed and divided by the murder trial of a British au pair, Louise Woodward, on charges of murdering an infant under her care by shaking him to death. The trial was a micro-cosm of the complex issues and emotions raised by the issue of child care in America. Class and gender resentments surfaced in indictments of the child's mother (a physician who could presumably have "afford-ed to stay home") for putting her career above her children, while the father's parenting actions and motivations were unquestioned. Yet few of the people who attacked the dead child's mother for working three days a week said anything about the recent forced influx of welfare mothers into the workforce, often at jobs with such long commutes that their children spend up to ten hours a day in child care. And while many questioned the mother's judgment for hiring an untrained teenag-er who was away from her social support networks, few said much about the need of isolated and impoverished teenage mothers for sup-port services and parenting education.

Another issue that surfaced in the trial was the role of financial vest-ed interests in decisions about child care. The expensive lawyers hired by the au pair agency gambled that a jury would not convict the young-ster of murder, and rejected the possibility of a lesser manslaughter charge. Many observers wondered if this was connected to the legal fact that the only verdict that would have made the au pair agency liable for damages was manslaughter. A murder conviction would have absolved them of responsibility, as would, of course, an acquittal.

The jury found Woodward guilty of murder, telling the press that they thought she'd done something and therefore couldn't acquit her entirely, but wished they had had a lesser charge to consider. At this point, the judge overturned the decision, reduced the charge to manslaughter, and counted her 279 days already spent in jail as sufficient penalty. But this act of compassion raised other issues of racial fairness. Only one radio commentary pointed out that Lacresha Murray, a 12-year-old African-American girl in Texas, had without any comparable fanfare just begun serving a twenty-five year sentence for causing the death of an infant while helping her mother in an at-home day-care center.[1]

The extraordinary attention and emotion lavished on Woodward's trial reflect the tensions that have accompanied the influx of mothers into the workforce, but also the deformed character of a debate in which, as columnist Ellen Goodman explains: "There is no child care good enough to justify the middle-class mother seeking a career but no child care poor enough to justify the welfare mother staying at home."[2]

Over the last quarter of a century, women have entered the workplace in unprecedented numbers. By 1993, 67 percent of all mothers of children under eighteen were in the labor force, a figure 20 percentage points higher than in 1975. Seventy percent of employed mothers with children under six worked full-time. Today, women with children under the age of six are currently the fastest-growing segment of the labor force. It has become the norm for women to hold down a forty-hour-week job even when they retain the primary responsibility for child raising. These dual roles are now shared by women of all racial-ethnic groups and classes. It is no longer just minority or impoverished mothers who work outside the home.[3]

As women's job hours have expanded, one might assume that men's, or at least fathers', have decreased, in order to balance family/work pressures. But in the 1980s, a third of fathers with children under the age of eighteen were putting in fifty hours or more at their jobs. Although a growing minority of displaced or contingent workers face what author Juliet Schor calls "enforced idleness," the majority of workers, both male and female, have seen their work hours lengthen, while many have had to respond to declining wages or job demotions by moonlighting.[4]

The growing work involvement of mothers, combined with the time pressures on all workers, has created an immense need for child care. The Census Bureau estimates that in 1993 there were 9.9 million children under five who needed full-time care while their mothers worked and an additional 21.2 million school children, aged five to fourteen, who needed supplemental care before or after school. The welfare reform act of 1996, designed to move mothers of young children into the workforce, has already swollen the demand for child-care slots, while the number of children needing subsidized care is expected to triple by 2000. Many of the mothers now being told to leave welfare to work are single and without husbands to help with child care. The entry-level, low-wage jobs available to them usually consist of inflexible schedules, changing or nonstandard hours, and few fringe benefits such as sick days or personal days. They face urgent needs for child-care programs that operate nontraditional hours, take mildly ill children, and are conveniently located to public-transportation systems.[5]

How do parents meet their expanding and diverse needs for child care? Despite longer work hours for men and women, many parents try to keep child care within the family. This is especially true for infants and toddlers, whom parents realize require intensive, sensitive, and responsive care—something not always available or affordable outside the family. As female employment has risen, fathers have significantly increased their role in the care of children. By 1993, fathers took care of children about 20 percent of the time their wives were working. Low-

and middle-income two-earner families often share care by what is known as "tag teaming," where parents work different shifts in order to have one on child-care duty at all times. This method keeps child-care costs down and meets desires to minimize care by strangers, but it can be very stressful on a marriage. Tag teaming is especially common in families where the parents are under thirty.[6]

Nevertheless, shared care does not usually cover a mother's entire work schedule, especially if she works forty hours or more, so reliance on father care must be coordinated with other arrangements. One such arrangement is informal child care, usually performed by extended family members or neighbors in a home setting. African-American and Hispanic families are almost twice as likely to rely on relatives for child care as are white families. In general, low-income families are the most likely to rely on relatives, with grandparents being the most frequent caregivers. Fewer than one-half of low-income children are cared for by nonfamily members, compared to two-thirds of upper-income children.[7]

Other arrangements include family day care and in-home care. In 1993, parents used family day care for 17 percent of the time that mothers worked; in-home care accounted for just 5 percent. However, the use of in-home care is widespread in the life cycles of families with upper-income, professional women. Almost a third of parents who have advanced degrees have used in-home care at some point in their lives.[8]

"Family day care," despite its name, refers to care by a nonrelative in her (very seldom his) home. Often the day-care provider combines care of her own children with paid care for others' kids. In-home care involves hiring a provider to come to the family's home and provide day care there, sometimes performing other household tasks as well. Some in-home caregivers are found privately by parents; others may be provided by agencies. The average cost of family day care was $50 per week in 1993, while the cost of in-home care was about $65.[9]

Obviously, expense and availability help shape many of the differences in care choices, but cultural values also play a role. While many parents place preschool children in formal center care because they see it as providing social and developmental skills necessary for school readiness, others perceive formal child-care institutions as embodying a set of values from which they want to protect their children. Low-income parents in particular may fear for their children's safety, especially if they had harsh experiences in institutional settings themselves. Parents from ethnic-racial subgroups or minority religious and cultural traditions may disagree with the standards and methods of mainstream child development theory, as these are practiced by many centers.

For instance, African-American parents have been found to value programs with strong discipline and heavy academics, rather than the informal play groups and free exploration valued by white middle-class parents. This preference may reflect the fact that African-American parents cannot count on their children having easy access to good schools or jobs, or even, in many cases, to safe neighborhoods. For Latino parents, and likely for many immigrant groups, language usage and religious or cultural hegemony of mainstream values may pose problems in sending children to formal child-care centers. These cultural preferences or concerns may be reinforced by economic issues, as the low-income status of many ethnic-racial minorities means they sometimes have access only to centers that have low staff-to-child ratios and high staff turnover.[10]

As family income rises, dependence on care outside the family increases, despite the temporary use of in-home care by many affluent professional families. Usually this means organized child-care centers: day care, nursery school, and preschool. These are characterized by set hours and fees, and possibly by a formal curriculum. The staff have certain levels of training, though this varies greatly. Organized child-care centers were used by families about 30 percent of the time in 1993, at an average cost of $65 per week.[11]

The costs and benefits of each arrangement differ. Informal child care offers the possibility of flexible arrangements with a trusted, familiar caregiver who may develop a personal relationship with the child and parents. On the other hand, such arrangements may lack structure, effective regulation, and safeguards for child treatment and safety. The Families and Work Institute in New York reports that relative care is not more likely to be better than nonrelative care in these settings, unless the relatives genuinely want to be with the children, rather than doing it to meet family obligations or earn a little money off the books. Informal care may also be unreliable, with illness or family emergencies of caregivers interrupting care.

Parents who use organized child-care centers generally report fewer problems with reliability of caregivers. Centers may provide more structure and more predictable standards. However, the fixed hours of operation tend to pose problems for parents who work nonstandard hours. Although this is often seen as a problem for high-powered career workers (and it does explain why many attorneys and executive women seek in-home care), it is even more of a problem for low-income workers. Almost half of employed poor parents work rotating shifts. One-third of working poor mothers are employed on weekends, and another 9 percent work evenings and nights. These figures will likely increase as welfare recipients enter the labor force and are forced to accept nonstandard hours. Only 10 percent of centers and 6 percent of family day cares operate on weekends.[12]

The availability of organized care has been increasing in response to the burgeoning demands of working parents. In 1978, only 110 companies offered some kind of child-care assistance. By 1990, there were 5,400 such companies. "Family-friendly" policies such as flextime, job-sharing, telecommuting, homeworking, compressed workweeks, and even subsidies to purchase home computers have been instituted. Many companies offer sick-child-care days off, on-site care centers, after-school and summer programs, and more. It has been shown that such policies produce lower turnover rates and higher productivity, even when workers are under pressure to work longer hours.[13]

Yet the availability of such centers remains very small in comparison to the need. Only 13 percent of all companies employing 100 or more employees have such policies, and this actually understates how many families are helped, since most women work in smaller companies. Even women who work in larger companies with employee child care may face problems of affordability. For instance, John Hancock Insurance Company has a showcase child-care center on site and two off-site centers serving 230 children, with sliding fees ranging from $94 to $266 a week as of 1995. But even $94 is high for a clerk or secretary.[14]

Women continue to bear the overwhelming responsibility for arranging as well as providing child care. This means working women scramble to recruit baby-sitters from networks of family, friends, and neighbors, or they interview paid child-care workers, compare centers, and set up formal care. Women not only make the arrangements, struggle to fill in gaps, and shoulder the guilt for inadequate care, but they must constantly balance their earnings against the cost of child care. In most families, it is the woman's wages rather than the couple's that are seen as the source of child-care payments.[15]

Because women are responsible for child care in most families, and because they earn less than men, they are under tremendous pressure to find an exploitable, cheap labor force to care for their children, and they may utilize race or class privileges to do so. Child-care workers, whether in centers or home care, are among the worst-paid employees in America. Often these jobs are held by women with few other options. Illegal immigrants are especially vulnerable to being trapped in the low pay and stretched-out hours of informal care. Thus we find, on the one hand, a typical pattern where race, ethnicity, and class cut across seeming universals in the lives of women, such as child care and domestic responsibilities, with white and upper-income women using class or race advantages to pass their gender burdens on to lower-income workers.[16] But there are, on the other hand, some interesting variations and crosscutting dilemmas in these relationships. They complicate the question in surprising ways, suggesting that in the long run, using class and racial-ethnic hierarchies to organize child care is not in the interests even of more privileged women.

Undoubtedly, the best-positioned working mothers are those highly skilled, well-paid workers employed by the 13 percent of large corporations who have decided to invest in child care. The overwhelming majority of working mothers whose employers do not provide child care must look elsewhere. And the hierarchies of privilege that they can draw upon in doing so are not always so clear-cut as one might suppose. For example, there has been a rapid rise in for-profit day-care chains, primarily marketed to the suburban working and middle classes. These centers are often physically appealing and follow state regulations on safety, but the fact that their affordability has been largely achieved by holding down wages adversely affects the quality and continuity of the care offered by staff. In fact, one of the ironies of America's child-care system is that researchers have found the "most uniformly poor quality of care ... in the predominantly middle-class centers."[17]

The finding that the "most uniformly poor quality of care" occurs in middle-class centers is counterintuitive and needs explanation. The reason for this stems from the fact that the average among centers for low-income and impoverished families is raised by the presence of a few experimental or well-funded government programs for the poor. These high-quality programs, such as Head Start or the Perry Preschool Program, have been extremely successful, demonstrating that government programs can work very well. Comprehensive, developmental, culturally sensitive programs for impoverished children have been shown to significantly improve their social, motor, and cognitive skills. These programs also enhance parenting skills, as mothers become more responsive to their children and less critical. There is even evidence that such child-care programs facilitate maternal education and employment, an important element in building parental resources, both financial and emotional.[18]

But lower middle-class families cannot afford such quality care on their own and do not get significant subsidies allowing them to take advantage of it. As a result, lower middle-class women in particular may settle for poor quality child care. They may also experience extreme discontinuity in care arrangements, as they struggle to conserve an adequate ratio between their own earnings and their child-care costs, while feeling obliged to "make up" for their lower net returns (child care deducted from wages) by taking on extra hours or by shifting care arrangements.

The subsidies for impoverished parents and welfare recipients may fuel class and race resentments when middle- and low-income working parents see a small minority of targeted families receiving higher-quality child care than they can afford. Several states have already reported that an early effect of welfare reform has been the removal of working-poor families from subsidized child-care slots in order to make room for the children of women who are just getting off welfare. However, it is important to point out that only a small minority of low-income and impoverished families benefit from such programs. On average, child-care centers in working-class and poor communities run at 102 percent of capacity, with long waiting lists. Most programs designed to help low-income mothers purchase child care are inadequate. Because they fund only 75 percent of the market rate, parents must scramble to make up the rest. Centers are reluctant to accept children at the funded rate, and feel they cannot rely on the tenuous extra income that parents try to use to make up the difference. Thus many otherwise qualified low-income parents are forced to make do with unregulated, uninspected care, missing out on the comprehensive health and food programs available to regulated providers who serve low-income populations. Meanwhile, the high ratio of child-care costs to the wages of poorly educated women is a major reason that women cannot stay off welfare.[19]

Thus, while low-income families who receive subsidies and use center care may actually be getting comparable care to higher-income families, this camouflages severe inequalities within the low-income population, since the working poor and lower middle class are least likely to receive subsidies from either employers or the government. Head Start, for example, reached only 36 percent of those eligible for it in 1995. Such programs, furthermore, often operate only for part of a day and for part of the year, making them unmanageable for full-time working parents.[20]

Nevertheless, it is both interesting and potentially significant for future political action that the dilemmas of child care sometimes disrupt the ordinary hierarchies of race and class privilege. Working-class and middle-class families may hold racially charged resentments of child-care subsidies for the lower class, but unlike in the case of welfare, they are more likely to call for the extension of such subsidies rather than their abolition. They can see both the effectiveness of such government programs and their potential benefits for themselves.

Other contradictions also cut across customary class and race alignments. For example, even when there is social class congruity between working mothers and family day-care providers, there is an undercurrent of resentment and ideological distance that in the long run gives working mothers an incentive to cease seeking private, class-based solutions to child-care needs and to call for universally regulated formal centers. Margaret Nelson points out that most family day-care providers choose this job as a way of avoiding going to work outside the home. They are thus in the strange position of depending for their livelihood on women engaging in activities of which they disapprove. The blurred boundaries of paid work and informal care in such settings create many ambiguities and stresses. Caregivers implicitly criticize working mothers for shirking their mothering responsibilities, but they also feel very keenly the low status, low pay, and lack of respect for their work in society as a whole. They want to be valued for their "mothering," but they also wish to receive payment for what they do. The parents of their charges, on the other hand, want the caregivers to relate as friends to them rather than as substitute mothers. Though they value the personal attention their children get, they also want to pay as little as possible for extra services, preferring to define these as coming out of friendship.[21]

These willful misunderstandings and conflicting interests breed frustrations on both sides. In this situation, Nelson says, both providers and working mothers often perceive themselves as the powerless ones in the relationship. Indeed, the structure does in fact disempower both parties. Resentments build up and get personalized, without any formal mechanisms for resolving them. Such conflicts often result in the mother removing a child from the provider's care, or the provider deciding to look for more formal work, where boundaries are easier to maintain. Either way, the outcome can be painful for everyone involved.

The case of in-home care illustrates why child-care dilemmas cannot be satisfactorily resolved through the maintenance of class and race privileges, even for the beneficiaries of privilege. Much in-home care involves upper-income women using the services of poor, minority, or immigrant women. At the deepest level, of course, this is a traditional dynamic where upper-class women gain a degree of gender equality not by sharing their family responsibilities with their husbands but by passing those responsibilities on to women who are lower than they in the economic and social hierarchy. The most obvious victims of this process are the providers. They have few ways of improving their working conditions, especially when they are illegal immigrants, or even legal ones without good English skills. Such providers work long hours for low pay. They are isolated in their employers' homes, face severe restrictions on their personal freedom, and are often the recipients of humiliating "charity," expected to accept old clothes and dinner leftovers in lieu of extra pay.[22]

But class privilege always entails class resistance, and when this takes place within the home, especially with children present, even the upper-class employers face disturbing predicaments. Unlike their husbands, they cannot compartmentalize their family life and exert class or race privilege through impersonal, "objective" channels. Nor can they protect their children from seeing what goes on. It is one thing to have exploited workers hidden away in sweatshops making the garments that affluent women wear; it is another thing entirely to have exploited and resentful workers in their homes, taking care of their kids. Class and race resentments between mothers and providers may be played out in front of children, either distressing the children or destroying their naïveté.

There is also the possibility that providers will resist by cutting back on their care for the children. Since child care, unlike housework, is not easily measured at the end of the day, there is little employers can do to guarantee this does not happen. Accordingly, even wealthy women sometimes feel disempowered by child-care arrangements. Their class and race privileges do not protect them from the anxieties of mothers who must work outside the home; indeed, sometimes those class and race privileges make them feel such anxieties all the more keenly.

Recent research provides good and bad news for worried mothers. The latest long-term study to date, conducted by the National Institute of Child Health and Human Development, found that the age at which a child enters day care, the hours spent there, and the formal training of the providers made no average difference to child outcomes or mother-child attachment. Only when a mother was already insensitive to her child's cues and then placed the child in poor-quality care for long hours was mother-child attachment at risk. Good child care and good parenting, by contrast, actively enhance a child's well-being. The bad news, however, is that poor mothering and poor child care can interact to increase risks for children, poor-quality child care is extremely widespread, and it is very difficult for parents to get accurate information and referrals for high-quality care. Furthermore, these studies continue to focus on mothers and children, leaving fathers out of the picture. So far, growing paternal responsibilities have been ignored in studies looking at the relation between day care, parent/child bonding, child development, and outcomes.[23]

Ultimately, helpful though it may be to get fathers involved, child care must be a public, not a private responsibility. As a bank president from Colorado commented at the 1997 White House conference on child care, "when it comes to child care, Adam Smith's invisible hand is all thumbs." The problems are especially acute when it comes to the transition from welfare to work for former AFDC mothers. If America is serious about reducing welfare roles by providing employment, poor parents must have affordable child care that will not harm their children or jeopardize their employment. Universal child-care programs are necessary to ensure uniform standards of quality and availability. Subsidization of workers' salaries is also necessary. Studies show that "children's experience [in child care] is directly related to the well-being of their caregivers."[24]

Government support and subsidy are critical for the provision of decent child care. Employer-mandated benefits are also essential, whatever the size of the firm. But it is also true that government and employers cannot do it all. Children are not created to standard specifications, and child care cannot be mass-produced in the way we manufacture products. While the provision of well-designed center-care programs with clear universalist minimum standards is of the utmost importance, there is also a need for flexible and informal child-care arrangements. Communities, employers, the government, and parents must work out a range of options, from subsidized parental leaves during the first six months after childbirth to tax credits for providing child care, to subsidies for community centers. This is one area where class and race privileges are ultimately in no child's best interests, because they prevent all parents from developing the humane and effective arrangements that are needed.

Our society needs to recognize and incorporate a sense of collective responsibility for children. To do this we must begin to value caregiving work for both men and women, while activists must insist that production be reorganized so that it can be made compatible with reproduction. This is a need and a desire that reaches across economic and cultural divisions; it is a potential area for alliances across race, ethnicity, and class lines.

NOTES

1. George Cole, George Washington University Law Center, National Public Radio, November 14, 1997.
2. *The Olympian*, November 15, 1997, A8.
3. Deborah A. Phillips (1989). "Future Directions and Need for Child Care in the United States." in *Caring for Children: Challenge to America* (Lawrence Erlbaum Associates Inc., Hillsdale, N.J.), p. 258; Nicole Poersh, Gina Adams, Jodi Sandfort (1994) *Child Care and Development, Key Facts* (Children's Defense Fund, Washington, D.C.), p. 1.
4. Juliet B. Schor (1993). *The Overworked American: The Unexpected Decline of Leisure* (Basic Books, New York, N.Y.), p. 21.
5. Bureau of the Census (1994). *Who's Minding the Kids? Child Care Arrangements: Fall 1991* (U.S. Dept. of Commerce, Washington, D.C.), p. 1; "Ending Welfare: Were We Wrong?" *The Progressive*, October 1997, pp. 8–9.
6. Anne Mitchell, Emily Cooperstein, and Mary Larner (1992). *Child Care Choices, Consumer Education, and Low-Income Families* (National Center for Children in Poverty, Columbia University, New York, N.Y.), p. 19; Marian Wright-Edelman (1994). "Vanishing Dreams of America's Young Families," *Race and Gender in the American Economy, Views From Across the Spectrum* (Prentice Hall, Englewood Cliffs, N.J.), p. 204; Bureau of the Census (1995) "Current Population Reports: What Does It Cost to Mind Our Preschoolers?" (U.S. Dept. of Commerce, Washington, D.C.), p. 2.
7. Mitchell, Cooperstein, and Larner (1992). *Child Care Choices, Consumer Education and Low-Income Families* (National Center for Children in Poverty, Columbia University, New York, N.Y.), p. 29. Also see Karen Fox Folk and Yunae Yi, "Piecing Together Child Care—Study of Multiple Arrangements: Crazy Quilt or Preferred Pattern" in *Journal of Marriage and the Family*, 56 (August 1994): pp 669–680.
8. Bureau of the Census (1995), "Current Population Reports: What Does It Cost to Mind Our Preschoolers?" (U.S. Dept. of Commerce, Washington, D.C.); Julia Wrigley (1995), *Other People's Children* (Basic Books, New York, N.Y.), p. 147.
9. Bureau of the Census (1995), "Current Population Reports: What Does It Cost to Mind Our Preschoolers?" (U.S. Dept. of Commerce, Washington, D.C.), p. 2.
10. Mitchell, Cooperstein, and Larner (1992). *Child Care Choices, Consumer Education, and Low-income Families*, p. 19; Karen Hill-Scott (1989), "No Room at the Inn: The Crisis in Child Care Supply," in *Caring for Children: Challenge to America*, p. 210.
11. Bureau of the Census (1995). "Current Population Reports: What Does It Cost to Mind Our Preschoolers?" (U.S. Dept. of Commerce, Washington, D.C.), p. 2; Mitchell, Cooperstein, and Larner (1992), *Child Care Choices, Consumer Education, and Low-Income Families,* p. 29; Deborah A. Phillips and Anne Bridgman, eds. (1995). "New Findings on Children, Families, and Economic Self-Sufficiency: Summary of a Research Briefing" (National Academy Press, Washington, D.C.), p. 14.
12. Phillips and Bridgman, "New Findings on Children," 10–11.
13. Dayle M. Smith (1991). "Kincare and the American Corporation: Solving the Work/Family Dilemma" (Business One Irwin, Homewood, Ill.), p. 217; Margery L. Sher, Madeline Fried (1994). "Child Care Options: A Workplace Initiative for the 21st Century" (Oryx Press, Phoenix, Ariz.); Families and

Work Institute. An Evaluation of Johnson and Johnson's Work-Family Initiative (1993), New York, N.Y.

14. Milton Moskowitz and Carol Townsend, "100 Best Companies for Working Mothers," *Working Mother*. October 1995 (Lang Communications, New York, N.Y.) 61; Bureau of the Census (1995), "Current Population Reports: What Does It Cost to Mind Our Preschoolers?" (U.S. Dept. of Commerce, Washington, D.C.) p. 2.

15. Gail Wilson (1987). *Give and Take in Families* (Allen and Uwin, London), 86; Arlie Hochschild (1989), *The Second Shift* (Avon Books, N.Y.) See also Philip Blumenstein and Pepper Schwartz (1983), *American Couples: Money, Work, and Sex* (Morrow, New York, N.Y.) For a recent comparison of a particular groups' gendered obligation to household duties as relates to single status, marriage/cohabitation and parenthood, see H. Wesley Perkins and Debra K. DeMeis, "Gender and Family Effects on the 'Second-Shift' Domestic Activity of College-Educated Young Adults" in *Gender & Society*, Vol. 10, No. 1, Feb. 1996, pp. 78–93. Researchers found that these women's "second shift" and sense of obligation to household tasks increased with marriage/cohabitation and parenthood, while the men's sense of obligation for domestic work remained constant as "helping out," regardless of parental status or a partner's employment.

16. Wrigley (1995) *Other People's Children*; Judith Rollins (1985), *Between Women: Domestics and Their Employers* (Temple University Press, Penn.).

17. Whitebook et al. (1989), "Who Cares? Child Care Teachers and the Quality of Care in America: Executive Summary National Child Care Staffing Study," Oakland, Calif. Child Care Employee Project; William Goodman, "Boom in Day Care Industry" in *Monthly Labor Review*, August 1995, p. 3; Phillips et al., "Child Care for Children in Poverty: Opportunity or Inequity?" in *Child Development* 1994, p. 65. Society for Research in Child Development, Inc. p. 489.

18. Deborah A. Phillips (1995), *Child Care for Low-Income Families: Summary of Two Workshops* (National Academy Press, Washington, D.C.), p. 13; Jeanne Brooks-Gunn, "Strategies for Altering the Outcomes of Poor Children and Their Families" in *Escape From Poverty: What Makes a Difference for Children* (1995), (Cambridge University Press, Cambridge), pp. 100–104; Hedy Nai-Lin Chang and Denise De La Rosa Salazer, *Drawing Strength From Diversity: Effective Services for Children, Youth and Families* (San Francisco: California Tommorrow Research and Policy Report, 1994).

19. Karen Hill-Scott (1989), "No Room at the Inn: The Crisis in Child Care Supply" in *Caring for Children: Challenge for America* (Lawrence Erlbaum Associates, Inc., Hillsdale, N.J.) p. 205; Susan Chira, "Working-Class Parents Face Shortage of Day Care Centers, a Study Finds," *New York Times*, September 14, 1993: A13; Children's Defense Fund, Helen Blank (1994) "Protecting Our Children: State and Federal Policies for Exempt Child Care Settings" (Washington, D.C.) pp. 10–11; Sandra L. Hofferth and Ellen Eliason Kisker "Comprehensive Services in Child Care Settings: Prevalence and Correlates" in *Pediatrics* 1994 (6): 1088–1090; Chris Tilly and Randy Albelda, "It's Not Working: Why Many Single Mothers Can't Work Their Way Out of Poverty" in *Dollars and Sense* November–December 1994, 8; Robert Imrie, "As Welfare Recipients Go to Work, Child Care Pinched," *The Olympian*, August 12, 1997; Sara Rimer, "Children of Working Poor Are Daycare's Forgotten," *New York Times*, November 25, 1997.

20. Deborah A. Phillips (1995), *Child Care for Low-Income Families*, p. 22; Children's Defense Fund, *The State Of America's Children* (Washington, D.C.: 1996).

21. Margaret K. Nelson (1989), "Negotiating Care: Relationships Between Family Day Care Providers and Mothers" in *Feminist Studies*, Vol. 15 No. 1.

22. Julia Wrigley (1995), *Other People's Children* and Rollins (1985); Rollins, *Between Women* (Temple University Press, Philadelphia, Penn.).

23. Sue Shellenbarger, "Impact of Child Care Mixed, Study Says," *The Wall Street Journal*, April 4, 1997; "Study Says Day Care Okay," *The Olympian*, April 4, 1997; "Child Care and the Family," The NICHD Early Child Care Research Network, Spring 1996; NICHD Early Child Care Research Network, "Characteristics of Infant Child Care: Factors Contributing to Positive Caregiving," *Early Childhood Research Quarterly*, 11 (1996).

24. Quote from Lynet Uttal (1994). *Racial Safety, Cultural Competence and Cultural Maintenance: The Child Care Concerns of Employed Mothers*, Center for Research on Women (University of Memphis, Memphis, Tenn.) p. 31; David Whitman, "Waiting For Mary Poppins," *U.S. News & World Report*, November 24, 1997, p. 10.

25. Nancy Folbre (1994), "Children as Public Goods" in *American Economic Review*, 84 (2): 86. See also Susan Chira, "Study Says Babies in Child Care Keep Secure Bonds to Mothers" April 21, 1996, *New York Times*.

Part VI

NEW FORMS
OF FAMILY DIVERSITY

21

GAY AND LESBIAN FAMILIES ARE HERE; ALL OUR FAMILIES ARE QUEER; LET'S GET USED TO IT![1]

Judith Stacey

> In 1992 in Houston, I talked about the cultural war going on for the soul of America. And that war is still going on! We cannot worship the false god of gay rights. To put that sort of relationship on the same level as marriage is a moral lie.
>
> —Pat Buchanan, February 10, 1996

> Homosexuality is a peculiar and rare human trait that affects only a small percentage of the population and is of little interest to the rest.
>
> —Jonathan Rauch, 1994

> I came to Beijing to the Fourth World Conference of Women to speak on behalf of lesbian families. We are part of families. We are daughters, we are sisters, we are aunts, nieces, cousins. In addition, many of us are mothers and grandmothers. We share concerns for our families that are the same concerns of women around the world.
>
> —Bonnie Tinker, *Love Makes a Family*, September 1995

Until but a short time ago, gay and lesbian families seemed quite a queer concept, even preposterous, if not oxymoronic, not only to scholars and the general public, but even to most lesbians and gay men. The grass roots movement for gay liberation that exploded into public visibility in 1969, when gays resisted a police raid at the Stonewall bar in New York City, struggled along with the militant feminist movement of that period to liberate gays and women *from* perceived evils and injustices represented by the family, rather than *for* access to its blessings and privileges. During the early 1970s, marches for gay pride and women's liberation flaunted provocative, countercultural banners, like "Smash The Family" and "Smash Monogamy." Their legacy is a lasting public association of gay liberation and feminism with family subversion. Yet how "queer" such antifamily rhetoric sounds today, when gays and lesbians are in the thick of a vigorous profamily movement of their own.

Gay and lesbian families are indisputably here. In June of 1993, police chief Tom Potter joined his lesbian police officer daughter in a Portland, Oregon gay pride march for "family values." By the late 1980s an astonishing "gay-by boom" had swelled the ranks of children living with gay and lesbian parents to between six and fourteen million.[2] *Family Values* is the title of a popular 1993 book by and about a lesbian's successful struggle to become a legal second mother to one of these "turkey-baster" babies, the son she and his biological mother have co-parented since his birth.[3] In 1989 Denmark became the first nation in the world to legalize a form of gay marriage, termed "registered partnership," and its Nordic neighbors Norway and Sweden soon followed suit. In 1993, thousands of gay and lesbian couples participated in a mass wedding ceremony on the Washington Mall during the largest demonstration for gay rights in U.S. history. Three years later, on March 25, 1996, Mayor of San Francisco Willie Brown proudly presided over a civic ceremony to celebrate the domestic partnership of nearly 200 same-sex couples. "We're leading the way here in San Francisco," the mayor declared, "for the rest of the nation to fully embrace the diversity of people in love, regardless of their gender or sexual orientation."[4] By then, thousands of gay and lesbian couples across the nation were eagerly awaiting the outcome of *Baehr v. Lewin*, cautiously optimistic that Hawaii's Supreme Court would soon order the state to become the first in the United States, and in the modern world, to grant full legal marriage rights to same-sex couples. As this article went to press in May 1996, the Republican party had just made gay marriage opposition a wedge issue in their presidential campaign.

Gay and lesbian families are undeniably here, yet they are not queer, if one uses the term in the sense of "odd" to signify a marginal or deviant population.[5] It is nearly impossible to define this category of families in a manner that could successfully distinguish all of their members, needs, relationships, or even their values, from those of all other families. In fact, it is almost impossible to define this category in a satisfactory, substantive way at all. What should count as a gay or lesbian family? Even if we bracket the thorny matter of how to define an individual as gay or lesbian and rely on self-identification, we still face a jesuitical challenge. Should we count only families in which every single member is gay? Clearly there are not very many, if even any, of these. Or does the presence of just one gay member color a family gay? Just as clearly, there are very many of these, including those of Ronald Reagan, Colin Powell, Phyllis Schlafly and Newt Gingrich.[6] More to the point, why would we want to designate a family type according to the sexual identity of one or more of its members? No research, as we will see, has ever shown a uniform, distinctive pattern of relationships, structure, or even of "family values," among families that include self-identified gays. Of course, most nongays restrict the term "gay family" to units that contain one or two gay parents and their children. However, even such families that most commonsensically qualify as gay or lesbian are as diverse as are those which do not.

Gay and lesbian families come in different sizes, shapes, ethnicities, races, religions, resources, creeds, and quirks, and even engage in diverse sexual practices. The more one attempts to arrive at a coherent, defensible sorting principle, the more evident it becomes that the category "gay and lesbian family" signals nothing so much as the consequential social fact of widespread, institutionalized homophobia.[7] The gay and lesbian family label marks the cognitive dissonance, and even emotional threat, that much of the nongay public experiences upon recognizing that gays can participate in family life at all. What unifies such families is their need to contend with the particular array of psychic, social, legal, practical, and even physical challenges to their very existence that institutionalized hostility to homosexuality produces. Paradoxically, the label "gay and lesbian family" would become irrelevant if the nongay population could only "get used to it."

In this chapter I hope to facilitate such a process of normalization, ironically, perhaps, to allow the marker "gay and lesbian" as a family category once again to seem queer—as queer, that is, as it now seems to identify a *family*, rather than an individual or a desire, as heterosexual. I conclude this book with an extensive discussion of this historically novel category of family, not only because of its inherent interest, but to suggest how it crystallizes the general processes of family diversification and change that characterize what I have been describing as the postmodern family condition.[8] Gay and lesbian families represent such a new, embattled, visible and necessarily self-conscious genre of postmodern kinship, that they more readily expose the widening gap between the complex reality of postmodern family forms and the simplistic modern family ideology that still undergirds most public rhetoric, policy and law concerning families.[9] In short, I hope to demonstrate that, contrary to Jonathan Rauch's well-meaning claim in the second epigraph above, the experience of "homosexuals"[10] should be of immense interest to everyone else. Nongay families, family scholars and policymakers alike can learn a great deal from examining the experience, struggles, conflicts, needs, and achievements of contemporary gay and lesbian families.

Brave New Family Planning

History rarely affords a social scientist an opportunity to witness during her own lifetime the origins and evolution of a dramatic, and significant, cultural phenomenon in her field. For a family scholar, it is particularly rare to be able to witness the birth of an historically unprecedented variety of family life. Yet the emergence of the genus gay and lesbian family as a distinct social category, and the rapid development and diversification of its living species, have occurred during the past three decades, less than my lifetime. Of course, same-sex desire and behavior have appeared in most human societies, including all Western ones, as well as among most mammalian species; homosexual relationships, identities, and communities have much longer histories than most Western heterosexuals imagine; and historical evidence documents the practice of sanctioned and/or socially visible same-sex unions in the West, as well as elsewhere, since ancient times.[11] Nonetheless, the notion of a gay or lesbian family is decidedly a late twentieth-century development, and several particular forms of gay and lesbian families were literally inconceivable prior to recent developments in reproductive technology.

Indeed, before the Stonewall rebellion, the family lives of gays and lesbians were so invisible, both legally and socially, that one can actually date the appearance of the first identifiable species of gay family life—a unit that includes at least one self-identified gay or lesbian parent and children from a former, heterosexual marriage. Only one child custody case in the United States reported before 1950 involved a gay or lesbian parent, and only five more gays or lesbians dared to sue for custody of their children between 1950 and 1969. Then, immediately after Stonewall, despite the predominantly anti-family ethos of the early gay liberation period, gay custody conflicts jumped dramatically, with fifty occurring during the 1970s and many more since then.[12] Courts consistently denied parental rights to these early pioneers, rendering them martyrs to a cause made visible by their losses. Both historically and numerically, formerly married lesbian and gay parents who "came out" after marriage and secured at least shared custody of their children represent the most significant genre of gay families. Such gay parents were the first to level a public challenge against the reigning cultural presumption that the two terms—gay and parent—are antithetical. Their family units continue to comprise the vast majority of contemporary gay families and to manifest greater income and ethnic diversity than other categories of gay parents. Moreover, studies of their "care and feeding habits" provide nearly the entire data base of the extant research on the effects of gay parenting on child development.

It was novel, incongruous, and plain brave for lesbian and gay parents to struggle for legitimate family status during the height of the anti-natalist, anti-maternalist, anti-family fervor of grass-roots feminism and gay liberation in the early 1970s. Fortunately for their successors, such fervor proved to be quite short-lived. Within very few years many feminist theorists began to celebrate women's historically developed nurturing capacities, not coincidentally at a time when aging, feminist baby-boomers had begun producing a late-life boomlet of our own.[13] During the middle to late seventies, buoyed by the legacy of sexual revolution and feminist assertions of female autonomy, inspired by the "Black matriarchs" who had been turned into political martyrs by Daniel Patrick Moynihan's mid-sixties attack,[14] and abetted by the popularization of alternative reproductive technologies and strategies, a first wave of "out" lesbians began to join the burgeoning ranks of women actively choosing to have children outside of marriage.

Fully intentional childbearing outside of heterosexual unions represents one of the only new, truly original, and decidedly controversial genres of family formation and structure to have emerged in the West during many centuries. While lesbian variations on this cultural theme include some particularly creative reproductive strategies, they nonetheless represent not deviant, but vanguard manifestations of much broader late twentieth century trends in Western family life. Under postmodern conditions, processes of sexuality, conception, gestation, marriage, and parenthood, which once appeared to follow a natural, inevitable progression of gendered behaviors and relationships, have come unhinged, hurtling the basic definitions of our most taken-for-granted familial categories—like mother, father, parent, offspring, sibling, and, of course, "family" itself—into cultural confusion and contention.

A peculiar melange of contradictory social forces, from the conservative turn to profamily and postfeminist sensibilities of the Reagan-Bush era to the increased institutionalization, visibility, and confidence of gay and lesbian communities, helped to fuel the "gay-by" boom that escalated rapidly during the 1980s. It seems more accurate to call this a "lesbaby boom," because lesbians vastly outnumber the gay men who can, or have chosen to, become parents out of the closet. Lesbian planned parenthood strategies have spread and diversified rapidly during the past two decades. With access to customary means to parenthood denied or severely limited, lesbians must necessarily construct their chosen family forms with an exceptional degree of reflection and intentionality. Accordingly lesbians have been choosing motherhood within a broad array of kinship structures. Like infamous Murphy Brown, some become single moms, but more often lesbians choose to share responsibility for rearing children with a lover and/or with other co-parents, such as sperm donors, gay men, and other friends and relatives. New Hampshire and Florida categorically prohibit adoptions by lesbians or gay men, and most adoption agencies actively discriminate against prospective gay parents. Consequently, independent adoption provided the first, and remains the most traveled, route to lesbian maternity, but increasing numbers of lesbians have been choosing to bear children of their own. In pursuit of sperm, some lesbians have resorted quite instrumentally to heterosexual intercourse, but most prefer alternative insemination strategies, locating known or anonymous donors through personal networks or through private physicians or sperm banks.

In the very period when the right-wing, profamily war against abortion has commanded center-ring priority in feminist struggles for reproductive rights, lesbians have had to apply considerable pluck and ingenuity in their own profamily efforts to procreate. Institutionalized heterosexism and married couple biases pervade the medically mediated fertility market. Most private physicians and many sperm banks in the United States, as well as Canadian and most European health services, refuse to inseminate unmarried women in general, and lesbians particularly. More than 90 percent of U.S. physicians surveyed in 1979 denied insemination to unmarried women, and a 1988 federal government survey of doctors and clinics reported that homosexuality was one of their top four reasons for refusing to provide this service.[15] Thus, the first wave of planned lesbian pregnancies depended primarily upon donors located through personal networks, frequently involving gay men or male relatives who might also agree to participate in childrearing, in varying degrees. Numerous lesbian couples solicit sperm from a brother or male relative of one woman to impregnate her partner, hoping to buttress their tenuous legal, symbolic, and social claims for shared parental status over their "turkey-baster babies."

Despite its apparent novelty, "turkey-baster" insemination for infertility dates back to the late eighteenth century, and, as the nickname implies, is far from a high-tech procedure requiring medical expertise.[16] Nonetheless, because the AIDS epidemic and the emergence of child custody conflicts between lesbians and known sperm donors led many lesbians to prefer the legally sanitized, medical route to anonymous donors, feminist health care activists mobilized to meet this need. In 1975 the Vermont Women's Health Center added donor insemination to its services, and in 1980 the Northern California Sperm Bank opened in Oakland expressly to serve the needs of unmarried, disabled, or non-heterosexual women who want to become pregnant. The clinic ships frozen semen throughout North America, and more than two-thirds of the clinic's clients are not married.[17]

The absence of a national health system in the United States commercializes access to sperm and fertility services, introducing an obvious class bias into the practice of alternative insemination. Far more high-tech, innovative, expensive, and therefore, uncommon, is a procreative strategy some lesbian couples now are adopting in which an ovum is extracted from one woman, fertilized with donor sperm, and then implanted in her lover's uterus. The practical and legal consequences of this still "nascent" practice have not yet been tested, but the irony of deploying technology to assert a biological, and thereby a legal, social and emotional claim to maternal and family status throws the contemporary instability of all the relevant categories—biology, technology, nature, culture, maternity, family—into bold relief.

While the advent of AIDS inhibited joint procreative ventures between lesbians and gay men, the epidemic also fostered stronger social and political solidarity between the two populations and stimulated gay men to keener interest in forming families. Their ranks are smaller and newer than those of lesbian mothers, but by the late 1980s gay men were also visibly engaged in efforts to become parents, despite far more limited opportunities to do so. Notwithstanding Arnold Schwarzenegger's 1994 celluloid pregnancy in *Junior*,[18] not only do men still lack the biological capacity to derive personal benefits from most alternative reproductive technologies, but social prejudice also severely restricts gay male access to children placed for adoption, or even into foster care. Ever since Anita Bryant led a "Save the Children" campaign against gay rights in 1977, right-wing mobilizations in diverse states, including Florida, New Hampshire, and Massachusetts, have successfully cast gay men, in particular, as threats to children and families and denied them the right to adopt or foster the young. Wishful gay fathers have persevered against these odds, resorting to private adoption and surrogacy arrangements, accepting the most difficult-to-place adoptees and foster children, or entering into shared social parenting arrangements with lesbian couples or single women.

Compelled to proceed outside conventional cultural and institutional channels, lesbian and gay male planned parenthood has become an increasingly complex, diverse, creative, and politicized self-help enterprise. Because gays forge kin ties without established legal protections or norms, relationships between gay parents and their children suffer heightened legal and social risks. If the shock troops of gay parenthood were the formerly married individuals who battled for child custody during the 1970s, by the mid-1980s many lesbians and gays were shocked to find themselves battling each other, as custody conflicts between lesbian co-parents or between lesbian parents and sperm donors and/or other relatives began to reach the dockets and to profoundly challenge the judicial doctrinal resources of family courts.[19] Despite a putative "best interests of the child" standard, "normal" heterosexual family prejudices instead guided virtually all the judges who heard these early cases. Biological claims of kinship nearly always trumped those of social parenting, even in heartrending circumstances of custody challenges to bereaved lesbian "widows" who, with their deceased lovers, had jointly planned for, reared, loved and supported children since their birth.[20] Likewise, judges routinely honored fathers' rights arguments by favoring parental claims of donors who had contributed nothing more than sperm to their offspring over those of lesbians who had coparented from the outset, *even when these men had expressly agreed to abdicate paternal rights or responsibilities*. The first, and still rare, exception to this rule involved a donor who did not bring his paternity suit until the child was ten years old.[21] And while numerous sperm donors have reneged on their prenatal agreements, thus far no lesbian mother has sued a donor to attain parental terms different from those to which he first agreed. On the other hand, in the one case in which a lesbian biological mother has sought financial support from her former lesbian partner, a New York court found the non-biological co-parent to be a parent. Here, the state's fiduciary interest, rather than gay rights, governed the decision.[22]

Perhaps the most poignant paradox in gay and lesbian family history concerns the quiet heroism displayed by gays compelled to struggle for family status precisely when forces mobilized in the name of "the family" conspire to deny this to them. The widely publicized saga of the Sharon Kowalski case, in which the natal family of a lesbian who had been severely disabled in a car crash successfully opposed the guardianship claim made by her chosen life-companion, proved particularly galvanizing in this cause, perhaps because all of the contestants were adults. After eight years of legal and political struggle, Sharon's lover, Karen Thompson, finally won a reversal, in a belated, but highly visible, landmark victory for gay family rights.[23]

Gay family struggles have achieved other significant victories, like the 1989 *Braschi* decision by New York state's top court, which granted a gay man protection against eviction from his deceased lover's rent-controlled apartment by explicitly defining family in inclusive, social terms:

> the exclusivity and longevity of the relationship, the level of emotional and financial commitment, the manner in which the parties have conducted their everyday lives and held themselves out to society, and the reliance placed upon one another for daily family services ... it is the totality of the relationship as evidenced by the dedication, caring, and self-sacrifice of the parties which should, in the final analysis, control.[24]

Currently, one of the most active fronts in the gay family rights campaign is the struggle for second-parent adoption rights, which enable a lesbian or gay man to adopt a lover's children without removing the legal parent's custody rights. Numerous lesbian couples (including former undersecretary of Housing and Urban Development and 1995 San Francisco mayoral candidate Roberta Achtenberg and her partner) as well as a handful of gay male couples, have won this form of legal parenthood, which has been granted at the state court level in Vermont, Massachusetts, and New York, and at local levels in several additional states. Curiously, this particular struggle is more advanced in the United States than in Canada, Europe, or even in the Nordic countries—where legislatures explicitly excluded adoption rights when they legalized a form of gay marriage.[25] Probably the decentralized character of family law in the U.S. accounts for this anomaly.

Of course, even in the United States, very few jurisdictions grant second-parent adoptions, which, in any case, provide only a second-class route to parenthood for lesbian or gay co-parents, because they require a home study conducted after a child is born. No jurisdiction allows gay couples to legally parent a child together from its birth.[26] Moreover, the highly politicized character of family change in the United States renders even this second-class option painfully vulnerable to unfavorable political winds. For example, during his unsuccessful bid for the 1996 Republican presidential nomination, California's Governor Pete Wilson courted his party's right-wing, profamily factions by reimposing state barriers to lesbian and gay second-parent adoptions that had recently been dismantled. The National Center for Lesbian Rights considers this right to be so crucial to the lesbian "profamily" cause that it revoked its former policy of abstaining from legal conflicts between lesbians over this issue. Convinced that the long-term, best interests of gay and lesbian parents and their children depend upon defining parenthood in social, rather than biological, terms, the Center decided to represent lesbian parents who are denied custody of their jointly reared children when their former lovers exploit the biological and homophobic prejudices of the judiciary.[27]

Here again, gay family politics telescope, rather than stray from, pervasive cultural trends. Gay second-parent adoptions, for example, trek a kin trail blazed by court responses to families reconstituted after divorce and remarriage. Courts first allowed some stepparents to adopt their new spouses' children without terminating the custody rights of the children's former parents. Gay family rights law bears a kind of second cousin tie to racial kin case law. Gay and lesbian custody victories rely heavily on a milestone race custody case, *Palmore v. Sidoti* (1984), which restored the custody rights of a divorced, white mother who lost her children after she married a black man. Even though *Palmore* was decided on strict legal principles governing race discrimination which do not yet apply to gender or sexual discrimination, several successful gay and lesbian custody decisions rely on its logic by refusing to interpret discrimination against their parents as serving "the best interests" of children. The first successful second-parent adoption award to a lesbian couple actually was a "third-parent" adoption on the model of stepparent adoption after divorce. The court granted co-parent status to the nonbiological mother without withdrawing it from the sperm donor father, a Native American, in order to honor the shared desires of all three parents to preserve the child's bicultural inheritance.[28]

As tabloid and talk show fare testify daily, culturally divisive struggles over babies secured or lost through alternative insemination, in vitro fertilization, ovum extraction, frozen embryos, surrogacy, transracial adoption, not to mention mundane processes of divorce and remarriage are not the special province of a fringe gay and lesbian minority. We now inhabit a world, however unwittingly, in which technology has up-ended the basic premises of the aged nature-nurture debate by rendering human biology more amenable to intervention than human society. Inevitably, therefore, contests between biological and social definitions of kinship, such as the notorious battles over "Baby M," involving surrogacy, and adopted baby Jessica DuBoer, will continue to proliferate and to rub social nerves raw. By their very existence, gay and lesbian families thwart potent cultural impulses to deny this unwelcome reality. Perhaps that is one source of the irrational hostility they elicit.

While one can discern a gradual political and judicial trend toward granting parental and family rights to gays, the legal situation in the fifty states remains starkly discriminatory, uneven, volatile, and replete with major setbacks for gay and lesbian parents, like the ongoing Sharon Bottoms case in Virginia in which a lesbian mother is fighting to regain custody of her young son.[29] The crucial, and chilling, fact remains that twenty-one states still criminalize sodomy with impunity, because in 1986 the U.S. Supreme Court in *Bowers v. Hardwick* upheld the constitutionality of this most basic impediment to civil rights or even survival for gay relationships. Gay and lesbian families certainly have come a long way since Stonewall, but a much longer road, studded with formidable stone walls, remains for them to traverse.

A MORE, OR LESS, PERFECT UNION?

Much nearer at hand than most ever dared to imagine, however, has come the momentous prospect of legal gay marriage. The idea of same-sex marriage used to draw nearly as many jeers from gays and lesbians as from nongays. As one lesbian couple recalls, "In 1981, we were a very, very small handful of lesbians who got married. We took a lot of flak from other lesbians, as well as heterosexuals. In 1981, we didn't know any other lesbians, not a single one, who had had a ceremony in Santa Cruz, and a lot of lesbians live in that city. Everybody was on our case about it. They said, What are you doing, How heterosexual. We really had to sell it."[30]

Less than a decade later, gay and lesbian couples could proudly announce their weddings and anniversaries, not only in the gay press, which now includes specialized magazines for gay and lesbian couples, like *Partners Magazine*, but even in such mainstream, Midwestern newspapers as the Minneapolis *Star Tribune*.[31] Jewish rabbis, Protestant ministers, Quaker meetings, and even some Catholic priests regularly perform gay and lesbian wedding or commitment ceremonies. This phenomenon is memorialized in cultural productions within the gay community, like *Chicks In White Satin*, a documentary about a Jewish lesbian wedding which won prizes at recent gay film festivals, but it has also become a fashionable pop culture motif. In December 1995, the long-running TV sitcom program *Roseanne* featured a gay male wedding in a much-hyped episode called "December Bride." Even more provocative, however, was a prime-time lesbian wedding that aired one month later on *Friends*, the highest rated sitcom of the 1995–1996 television season. Making a cameo appearance on the January 18, 1996 episode, Candice Gingrich, the lesbian half-sister of right-wing Speaker of the House Newt Gingrich, conducted a wedding ceremony which joined the characters who play a lesbian couple on the series "in holy matrimony" and pronounced them "wife and wife."

When the very first social science research collection about gay parents was published in 1987, not even one decade ago, its editor concluded that however desirable such unions might be, "it is highly unlikely that marriages between same-sex individuals will be legalized in any state in the foreseeable future."[32] Yet, almost immediately thereafter, precisely this specter began to exercise imaginations across the political spectrum. A national poll reported by the *San Francisco Examiner* in 1989 found that 86 percent of lesbians and gay men supported legalizing same-sex marriage.[33] However, it is the pending *Baehr v. Lewin* court decision concerning same-sex marriage rights in Hawaii that has thrust this issue into escalating levels of front-page and prime-time prominence. Amidst rampant rumors that thousands of mainland gay and lesbian couples were stocking their hope chests with Hawaiian excursion fares, poised to fly to tropical altars the instant the first gay matrimonial bans falter, right-wing Christian groups began actively mobilizing resistance. Militant antiabortion leader Randall Terry of Operation Rescue flew to Hawaii in February 1996 to fight "queer marriage," and right-wing Christian women's leader and radio broadcast personality Beverly LaHaye urged her "Godly" listeners to fight gay marriage in Hawaii.[34]

Meanwhile, fearing that Hawaii will become a gay marriage mecca, state legislators have rushed to introduce bills that exclude same-sex marriages performed in other states from being recognized in their own, because the "full faith and credit" clause of the U.S. Constitution obligates interstate recognition of legal marriages. While fourteen states had rejected such bills by May 1995, eight others had passed them, and contests were underway in numerous others, including California.[35] On May 8, 1996, gay marriage galloped onto the nation's center political stage when Republicans introduced the Defense of Marriage Act (DOMA), which defines marriage in exclusively heterosexual terms, as "a legal union between one man and one woman as husband and wife."[36] The last legislation that Republican presidential candidate Bob Dole cosponsored before he resigned from the Senate to pursue his White House bid full throttle, DOMA exploited homophobia in an attempt to defeat President Clinton and the Democrats in November 1996. With Clinton severely bruised by the political debacle incited by his support for gay rights in the military when he first took office, but still dependent upon the support of his gay constituency, the President indeed found himself "wedged" between a rock and a very hard place. Unsurprisingly, he tried to waffle. Naming this a "time when we need to do things to strengthen the American family." Clinton publicly opposed same-sex marriage at the same time that he tried to reaffirm support for gay rights and to expose the divisive Republican strategy.[37]

Polemics favoring and opposing gay marriage rights now proliferate in editorial pages and legislatures across the nation, and mainstream religious bodies find themselves compelled to confront the issue. In March 1996 the Vatican felt called upon not merely to condemn same-sex marriage as a "moral disorder," but also to warn Catholics that they would themselves risk "moral censure" if they were to support "the election of the candidate who has formally promised to translate into the law the homosexual demand."[38] Just one day after the Vatican published this admonition, the Central Conference of American Rabbis, which represents the large, generally liberal wing of Judaism, took a momentous action in direct opposition. The Conference resoundingly endorsed a resolution to "support the right of gay and lesbian couples to share fully and equally in the rights of civil marriage." Unsurprisingly, Orthodox rabbis immediately condemned the action as prohibited in the Bible and "another breakdown in the family unit."[39] One week later, in another historic development, a lead editorial in the *New York Times* strongly endorsed gay marriage.[40]

As with child custody, the campaign for gay marriage clings to legal footholds carved by racial justice pioneers. It is startling to recall how recently it was that the Supreme Court finally struck down antimiscegenation laws. Not until 1967, that is, only two years before Stonewall, did the high court, in *Loving vs. Virginia*, find state restrictions on interracial marriages to be unconstitutional. (Twenty states still had such restrictions on the books in 1967, only one state fewer than the twenty-one which currently prohibit sodomy.) A handful of gay couples quickly sought to marry in the 1970s through appeals to this precedent, but until three lesbian and gay male couples sued Hawaii in *Baehr v. Lewin* for equal rights to choose marriage partners without restrictions on gender, all U.S. courts had dismissed the analogy. In a historic ruling in 1993, the Hawaiian State Supreme Court remanded this suit to the state, requiring it to demonstrate a "compelling state interest" in prohibiting same-sex marriage, a strict scrutiny standard that few believe the state will be able to meet. Significantly, the case was neither argued nor adjudicated as a gay rights issue. Rather, just as ERA opponents once had warned and advocates had denied, passage of an equal rights amendment to Hawaii's state constitution in 1972 paved the legal foundation for *Baehr*.[41]

Most gay activists and legal scholars anticipate a victory for gay marriage when *Baehr* is finally decided early in 1997, but they do not all look forward to this prospect with great delight. Although most of their constituents desire the right to marry, gay activists and theorists continue to vigorously debate the politics and effects of this campaign. Refining earlier feminist and socialist critiques of the gender and class inequities of marriage, an articulate, vocal minority seeks not to extend the right to marry, but to dismantle an institution they regard as inherently and irredeemably hierarchical, unequal, conservative, and repressive. Nancy Polikoff, one of the most articulate lesbian legal activist-scholars opposed to the marriage campaign, argues that

> Advocating lesbian and gay marriage will detract from, and even contradict, efforts to unhook economic benefits from marriage and make basic health care and other necessities available to all. It will also require a rhetorical strategy that emphasizes similarities between our relationships and heterosexual marriages, values long-term monogamous coupling above all other relationships, and denies the potential of lesbian and gay marriage to transform the gendered nature of marriage for all people. I fear that the very process of employing that rhetorical strategy for the years it will take to achieve its objective will lead our movement's public representatives, and the countless lesbians and gay men who hear us, to believe exactly what we say.[42]

A second perspective supports legal marriage as one long-term goal of the gay rights movement, but voices serious strategic objections to making this a priority before there is sufficient public support to sustain a favorable ruling in Hawaii or the nation. Such critics fear that a premature victory will prove pyrrhic, because efforts to defend it against the

vehement backlash it has already begun to incite are apt to fail, after sap-
ping resources and time better devoted to other urgent struggles for gay
rights. Rather than risk a major setback for the gay movement, they advise
an incremental approach to establishing legal family status for gay and
lesbian kin ties through a multifaceted struggle for family diversity.[43]

However, the largest, and most diverse, contingent of gay activist
voices now supports the marriage rights campaign, perhaps because gay
marriage can be read to harmonize with virtually every hue on the gay
ideological spectrum. Pro-gay marriage arguments range from profoundly conservative to liberal humanist to radical and deconstructive.
Conservatives, like those radicals who still oppose marriage, view it as
an institution that promotes monogamy, commitment, and social stability, along with interests in private property, social conformity, and
mainstream values. They likewise agree that legalizing gay marriage
would further marginalize sexual radicals by segregating counter-cul-
tural gays and lesbians from the "whitebread" gay couples who could
then choose to marry their way into Middle America. Radicals and conservatives, in other words, envision the same prospect, but regard it
with inverse sentiments.[44]

Liberal gays support legal marriage, of course, not only to affirm the
legitimacy of their relationships and help sustain them in a hostile
world, but as a straightforward matter of equal civil rights. As one long-
coupled gay man expresses it: "I resent the fact that married people get
lower taxes. But as long as there is this institution of marriage and heterosexuals have that privilege, then gay people should be able to do it
too."[45] Liberals also recognize that marriage rights provide access to the
social advantages of divorce law. "I used to say, 'Why do we want to get
married? It doesn't work for straight people,'" one gay lawyer comments. "But now I say we should care: They have the privilege of
divorce and we don't. We're left out there to twirl around in pain."[46]

Less obvious or familiar, however, are cogent arguments in favor of
gay marriage that some feminist and other critical gay legal theorists
have developed in response to opposition within the gay community.
Nan Hunter, for example, rejects feminist legal colleague Nancy
Polikoff's belief that marriage is an unalterably sexist and heterosexist
institution. Building upon critical theories that reject the notion that
social institutions or categories have inherent, fixed meanings apart
from their social contexts, Hunter argues that legalized same-sex marriage would have "enormous potential to destabilize the gendered definition of marriage for everyone."[47]

Evan Wolfson, director of the Marriage Project of the gay legal rights
organization Lambda Legal Defense, who has submitted a brief in support of *Baehr*, pursues the logic of "anti-essentialism" even more consistently. The institution of marriage is neither inherently equal nor
unequal, he argues, but depends upon an everchanging cultural and
political context.[48] (Anyone who doubts this need only consider such
examples as polygamy, arranged marriages, or the same-sex unions in

early Western history documented by the late Princeton historian, John Boswell.) Hoping to use marriage precisely to change its context, gay philosopher Richard Mohr argues that access to legal marriage would provide an opportunity to reconstruct its meaning by serving "as a nurturing ground for social marriage, and not (as now) as that which legally defines and creates marriage and so precludes legal examination of it." For Mohr, social marriage represents "the fused intersection of love's sanctity and necessity's demands," and does not necessarily depend upon sexual monogamy.[49]

Support for gay marriage, not long ago anathema to radicals and conservatives, gays and nongays, alike, now issues forth from ethical and political perspectives as diverse, and even incompatible, as these. The cultural and political context has changed so dramatically since Stonewall that it now seems easier to understand why marriage has come to enjoy overwhelming support in the gay community than to grasp the depth of resistance to the institution that characterized the early movement. Still, I take seriously many of the strategic concerns about the costly political risks posed by a premature campaign. Although surveys and electoral struggles suggest a gradual growth in public support for gay rights, that support is tepid, uneven and fickle, as the debacle over Clinton's attempt to combat legal exclusion of gays from the military made distressingly clear. Thus, while 52 percent of those surveyed in a 1994 *Time* magazine/CNN poll claimed to consider gay lifestyle acceptable, 64 percent did not want to legalize gay marriages or to permit gay couples to adopt children.[50]

Gay marriage, despite its apparent compatibility with mainstream family values sentiment, raises far more threatening questions than does military service about gender relations, sexuality, and family life. Few contemporary politicians, irrespective of their personal convictions, display the courage to confront this contradiction, even when urged to do so by gay conservatives. In *Virtually Normal: An Argument About Homosexuality*, *New Republic* editor Andrew Sullivan develops the "conservative case for gay marriage," that he earlier published as an op-ed, which stresses the contribution gay marriage could make to a conservative agenda for family and political life. A review of Sullivan's book in the *New Yorker* points out that "here is where the advocates of gay rights can steal the conservatives' clothes."[51] The epigraph to this chapter by Jonathan Rauch about the insignificance of the homosexual minority comes from a *Wall Street Journal* op-ed he wrote to persuade Republicans that they should support legal gay marriage, not only because it is consistent with conservative values, but to guard against the possibility that gay rights advocates will exploit the party's inconsistency on this issue to political advantage.[52]

The logic behind the conservative case for gay marriage strikes me as compelling. Most importantly, gay marriage would strengthen the ranks of those endangered two-parent, "intact," married-couples families whose praises conservative, "profamily" enthusiasts never seem to tire of singing. Unsurprisingly, however, the case has won few nongay conservative converts to the cause. After all, homophobia is a matter of passion and politics, not logic. The religious right regards homosexuality as an abomination, and it has effectively consolidated its influence over the Republican Party. For example, in 1994, Republicans in the Montana state senate went so far as to pass a bill that would require anyone convicted of homosexual acts to register for life as a violent offender. They reversed their vote in response to an outpouring of public outrage.[53] It was not long afterward, however, that Republican presidential contender Robert Dole returned a thousand-dollar campaign contribution from the gay Log Cabin Republicans in the name, of course, of family values. Nor have figures prominent in the centrist, secular neo-family-values campaign or the communitarian movement, whose professed values affirm both communal support for marital commitment and for tolerance, displayed much concern for consistency.[54] And even when, in the 1995 fall pre-election season, President Clinton sought to "shore up" his standing among gays and lesbians by announcing his administration's support of a bill to outlaw employment discrimination against gays, he specifically withheld his support from gay marriage.[55] First Lady Hillary Rodham Clinton's recent book, *It Takes a Village*, ostensibly written to challenge "false nostalgia for family values," fails even to mention gay marriage or gay families, let alone to advocate village rights and resources for children whose parents are gay.[56]

Despite my personal political baptism in the heady, anti-family crucible of early second wave feminism, I, for one, have converted to the long-term cause. A "postmodern" ideological stew of discordant convictions enticed me to this table. Like Wolfson, Mohr, and Hunter, I have come to believe that legitimizing gay and lesbian marriages would promote a democratic, pluralistic expansion of the meaning, practice, and politics of family life in the United States. This could help to supplant the destructive sanctity of *the family* with respect for diverse and vibrant *families.*

To begin with, the liberal implications of legal gay marriage are far from trivial, as the current rush by the states and Congress to nullify them should confirm. The Supreme Court is certain to have its docket flooded far into the next century with constitutional conflicts that a favorable decision in Hawaii, or elsewhere, will unleash. Under the "full faith and credit" provision of the Constitution, which requires the fifty states to recognize each other's laws, legal gay marriage in one state could begin to threaten anti-sodomy laws in all the others. Policing marital sex would be difficult to legitimate, and differential prosecution of conjugal sex among same-sex couples could violate equal protection legislation. Likewise, if gay marriages were legalized, the myriad state barriers to child custody, adoption, fertility services, inheritance, and other family rights that lesbians and gay men currently suffer could also become subject to legal challenge. Moreover, it seems hard to overestimate the profound cultural implications of the struggle against the pernicious effects of legally condoned homophobia that would ensue were lesbian and gay relationships to be admitted into the ranks of legitimate kinship. In a society that forbids most public school teachers and counselors even the merest expression of tolerance for homosexuality, while lesbian and gay youth attempt suicide at rates three to five times greater than other youth,[57] granting full recognition to even just whitebread lesbian and gay relationships could have dramatic, and salutary, consequences.

Of course, considerations truer to some of my earlier, more visionary feminist convictions also invite me to join the gay wedding procession. For while I share some of Polikoff's disbelief that same-sex marriage can in itself dismantle the patterned gender and sexual injustices of the institution, I do believe it could make a potent contribution to those projects, as the research on gay relationships I discuss below seems to indicate. Moreover, as Mohr suggests, admitting gays to the wedding banquet invites gays and nongays alike to consider the kinds of place settings that could best accommodate the diverse needs of all contemporary families.

Subjecting the conjugal institution to this sort of heightened democratic scrutiny could help it to assume varied creative forms. If we begin to value the meaning and quality of intimate bonds over their customary forms, there are few limits to the kinds of marriage and kinship patterns people might wish to devise. The "companionate marriage," a much celebrated, but less often realized, ideal of modern sociological lore, could take on new life. Two friends might decide to marry without basing their bond on erotic or romantic attachment, as Dorthe, a prominent Danish lesbian activist who had initially opposed the campaign for gay marriage, fantasized after her nation's parliament approved gay registered partnerships: "If I am going to marry it will be with one of my oldest friends in order to share pensions and things like that. But I'd never marry a lover. That is the advantage of being married to a close friend. Then, you never have to marry a lover!"[58] Or, more radical still, perhaps some might dare to question the dyadic limitations of Western marriage and seek some of the benefits of extended family life through small-group marriages arranged to share resources, nurturance, and labor. After all, if it is true that "The Two-Parent Family Is Better"[59] than a single-parent family, as family-values crusaders like David Popenoe tirelessly proclaim, might not three-, four-, or more-parent families be better yet, as many utopian communards have long believed?

While conservative advocates of gay marriage surely would balk at such radical visions, they correctly realize that putative champions of committed relationships and of two-parent families who oppose gay marriage can be charged with gross hypocrisy on this score. For access to legal marriage not only would promote long-term, committed intimacy among gay couples, but also would afford invaluable protection to the children of gay parents, as well as indirect protection to closeted gay youth who reside with nongay parents. Clearly, only through a process of massive denial of the fact that millions of children living in gay and lesbian families are here, and here to stay, can anyone genuinely concerned with the best interests of children deny their parents the right to marry.

In the face of arguments for legalizing gay marriage as compelling and incongruent as these, it is hard to dispute Evan Wolfson's enthusiastic claim that, "The brilliance of our movement's taking on marriage is that marriage is, at once and truly, both conservative and transformative, easily understood in basic human terms of equality and respect, and liberating in its individual and social potential."[60]

IN THE BEST INTERESTS OF WHOSE CHILDREN?

The most cursory survey of the existing empirical research on gay and lesbian families reveals the depth of sanctioned discrimination such families continue to suffer and the absence of evidence to justify this inequity. To be sure, substantial limitations mar the social science research on this subject, which is barely past its infancy. For openers, mainstream journals, even those specializing in family research, warmed to this subject startlingly late and little, relegating the domain primarily to sexologists, clinicians and a handful of movement scholars and their sympathizers and opponents. A recent survey of the three leading journals of family research in the United States found only twelve of the 2,598 articles published between 1980 and 1993—less than .05 percent—focused on the families of lesbians and gay men, which, even by conservative estimates, make up at least 5 percent of U.S. families.[61] The research that does exist, however, has deficiencies that skew results so as to exaggerate, rather than understate, any defects of gay and lesbian families. Until very recently, most investigators began with a deviance perspective, seeking, whether homophobically or defensively, to test the validity of the popular prejudice that gay parenting is harmful to children. In other words, the reigning premise has been that gay and lesbian families are dangerously, and *prima facie*, "queer" in the pejorative sense, unless proven otherwise. Taking children reared by nongay parents as the unquestioned norm, most studies asymmetrically ask whether lesbian and gay parents hinder their children's emotional, cognitive, gender, and sexual development. Because lesbian and gay planned parenthood is so new, and its progeny so young, nearly all of the studies to date sample the ranks of formerly married parents who had children before they divorced and came out of the closet. The studies are generally small-scale and draw disproportionately from urban, white, middle-class populations. Frequently they make misleading comparisons between divorced lesbian and nongay, single-mother households by ignoring the presence or absence of lesbian life partners or other caretakers in the former.[62]

Despite such limitations, psychologists, social psychologists, and sociologists have by now conducted dozens of studies which provide overwhelming support for the "proven otherwise" thesis. Almost without exception they conclude, albeit in defensive or patronizing tones, that lesbian and gay parents do not produce inferior, or even particularly different, kinds of children than do other parents. Studies generally find no significant differences in school achievement, social adjustment, mental health, gender identity, or sexual orientation between the two groups of children. As Joan Laird's overview of research on lesbian and gay parents summarizes:

> a generation of research has failed to demonstrate that gays or lesbians are any less fit to parent than their heterosexual counterparts. Furthermore, a substantial number of studies on the psychological and social development of children of lesbian and gay parents have failed to produce any evidence that children of lesbian or gay parents are harmed or compromised or even differ from, in any significant ways along a host of psychosocial developmental measures, children raised in heterosexual families.[63]

Research to date finds lesbian and gay parents to be at least as effective, nurturant, responsible, loving and loved, as other parents. The rare small differences reported tend to favor gay parents, portraying them as somewhat more nurturant and tolerant, and their children, in turn, more tolerant and empathic, and less aggressive than those reared by nongay parents.[64] In April 1995, British researchers published the results of their unusual sixteen-year-long study which followed twenty-five children brought up by lesbian mothers and twenty-one brought up by heterosexual mothers from youth to adulthood. They found that the young adults raised in lesbian households had better relationships with their mothers' lesbian partners than the young adults brought up by heterosexual single mothers had with their mothers' male partners.[65] Published research to date seems to vindicate one ten-year-old girl who, rather apologetically, deems herself privileged to be the daughter of two lesbian parents: "But I think you get more love with two moms. I know other kids have a mom and a dad, but I think that moms give more love than dads. This may not be true, but it's what I think." Her opinion is shared by a six-old-girl from another lesbian family: "I don't tell other kids at school about my mothers because I think they would be jealous of me. Two mothers is better than one."[66]

In light of the inhospitable, often outrightly hostile climate which gay families, by their very existence, encounter, this seems a remarkable achievement. One sign that mainstream social scientists are beginning to recognize the achievement is the inclusion of Laird's chapter on "Lesbian and Gay Families" in the 1993 edition of a compendium of research, *Normal Family Processes*, the first edition of which (1982) ignored the subject.[67] Researchers have begun to call for, and to initiate, a mature, creative, undefensive approach to studying the full range of gay and lesbian families. Coming to terms with the realities of the postmodern family condition, such studies begin with a pluralistic premise concerning the legitimacy and dignity of diverse family structures. They ask whether and how gay and lesbian families differ, rather than "deviate," from nongay families; they attend as much to the differences between such families as to those that divide them from nongays; and they explore the particular benefits as well as the burdens such families bestow on their members.[68]

I am confident that this kind of research will discover more advantages of gay and lesbian family life for participants and "the rest of us" than have yet been explored. Most obvious, certainly, are mental-health rewards for gay and lesbian youth fortunate enough to come of age in such families. Currently most youth who experience homosexual inclinations either conceal their desires from their immediate kin or risk serious forms of rejection. State hostility to gay parents can have tragic results. In 1994, for example, the Nebraska Department of Social Services adopted a policy forbidding lesbian or gay foster homes, and the next day a seventeen-year-old openly gay foster child committed suicide, because he feared he would be removed from the supportive home of his gay foster parents.[69]

Of course, this speaks precisely to the heart of what homophobes most fear, that public acceptance of lesbian and gay families will spawn an epidemic of gay youth. As Pat Robertson so crudely explained to a Florida audience, "That gang of idiots running the ACLU, the National Education Association, the National Organization of Women, they don't want religious principles in our schools. Instead of teaching the Ten Commandments, they want to teach kids how to be homosexuals."[70] Attempting to respond to such anxieties, most defenders of gay families to date have stressed the irrelevance of parental sexual identity to that of their children. Sympathetic researchers repeatedly, and in my view wrongheadedly, maintain that lesbian and gay parents are no more likely than nongay parents to rear lesbian and gay children. Laird, for example, laments: "One of the most prevalent myths is that children of gay parents will themselves grow up gay; another that daughters will be more masculine and sons more feminine than normal children. A number of researchers have concluded that the sexual orientations/preferences of children of gay or lesbian parents do not differ from those whose parents are heterosexual."[71]

I find this claim illogical, unlikely and unwittingly anti-gay. Ironically, it presumes the very sort of fixed, "essentialist" definition of sexuality that the best contemporary gay and lesbian scholarship has challenged. Although it is clearly true that, until now, nearly all homosexuals, like almost everyone else, have been reared by nongays, it is equally clear that sexual desire and identity do not represent a singular fixed trait that expresses itself free of cultural context. However irresolvable eternal feuds over the relative weight of nature and nurture may forever prove to be, historical and anthropological data leave no doubt that culture profoundly influences sexual meanings and practices.[72] Homophobes are quite correct to believe that environmental conditions incite or inhibit expressions of same-sex desire, no matter its primary source. If culture had no influence on sexual identity, there would not have emerged the movement for gay and lesbian family rights that inspired me to write this chapter.

Contrary to what most current researchers claim, public acceptance of gay and lesbian families should, in fact, slightly expand the percentage of youth who would dare to explore their same-sex desires. In fact, a careful reading of the studies does suggest just this. Children reared by lesbian or gay parents feel greater openness to gay or bisexuality. In January 1996, the researchers who conducted the long-term British study conceded this point, after issuing the obligatory reassurance that, "the commonly held assumption that children brought up by lesbian mothers will themselves grow up to be lesbian or gay is not supported by the findings." Two of the twenty-five young adults in the study who were reared by lesbians themselves grew up to identify as lesbians, but none of the twenty-one who were reared in the comparison group of heterosexual mothers identify as lesbian or gay. More pertinent, in my view, five daughters and one son of lesbian mothers, but none of the children of heterosexual mothers, reported having had a same-sex erotic experience of some sort, prompting the researchers to acknowledge that, "It seems that growing up in an accepting atmosphere enables individuals who are attracted to same sex partners to pursue these relationships."[73] This prospect should disturb only those whose antipathy to homosexuality derives from deeply held religious convictions or irrational prejudice.

The rest of us could benefit from permission to explore and develop sexually free from the rigid prescriptions of what Adrienne Rich memorably termed "compulsory heterosexuality."[74] Currently, lesbian and gay parents grant their children such permission much more generously than do other parents. Not only do they tend to be less doctrinaire or phobic about sexual diversity than heterosexual parents, but, wishing to spare their children the burdens of stigma, some gay parents actually prefer that their youngsters do not become gay. Indeed, despite the ubiquity of Pat Robertson's sort of alarmist, propagandistic warnings, "advice on how to help your kids turn out gay," as cultural critic Eve Sedgwick sardonically puts it, "is less ubiquitous than you might think."[75]

Heterosexual indoctrination is far more pervasive and far the greater danger. Contemporary adolescent culture is even more mercilessly homophobic, or perhaps less hypocritically so, than most mainstream adult prejudices countenance. Verbal harassment, ridicule, hazing, and ostracism of "faggots," "bull-dykes," and "queers"—quotidian features of our popular culture—are particularly blatant among teens. "Sometimes I feel like no one really knows what I'm going through," one fifteen-year-old daughter of a lesbian laments: "Don't get me wrong. I really do love my mom and all her friends, but being gay is just not acceptable to other people. Like at school, people make jokes about dykes and fags, and it really bothers me.

I mean I bite my tongue, because if I say anything, they wonder, Why is she sticking up for them?"[76] In a recent survey, nearly half the teen victims of reported violent physical assaults identified their sexual orientation as a precipitating factor. Tragically, family members inflicted 61 percent of these assaults on gay youth.[77]

Little wonder such disproportionate numbers of gay youth commit suicide. Studies attribute one-third of teen suicide attempts to gay youth.[78] To evade harassment, most of the survivors suffer their clandestine difference in silent isolation, often at great cost to their esteem, social relationships, and to their very experience of adolescence itself. One gay man bought his life partner a Father's Day card, because he "realized that in a lot of ways we've been brother and father to each other since we've had to grow up as adults. Because of homophobia, gay people don't have the same opportunity as heterosexuals to be ourselves when we are teenagers. A lot of times you have to postpone the experiences until you're older, until you come out."[79]

The increased social visibility and community building of gays and lesbians has vastly improved the quality of life for most gay adults. Ironically, however, Linnea Due, author of a recent book about growing up gay in the 1990s, was disappointed to find that the visible movement has had contradictory consequences for gay teens. Due expected to find conditions much better for gay youth than when she grew up in the "silent '60s." Instead, many teens thought their circumstances had become more difficult, because, as one young man put it, "Now they know we're here."[80]

While most youth with same-sex desires will continue to come of age closeted in nongay families into the forseeable future, they would surely gain some emotional comfort from greater public acceptance of gay and lesbian families. Yet in 1992, when the New York City board of education tried to introduce the Rainbow multicultural curriculum guide, which advocated respect for lesbian and gay families in an effort "to help increase the tolerance and acceptance of the lesbian/gay community and to decrease the staggering number of hate crimes perpetrated against them," public opposition became so vehement that it contributed to the dismissal of School Chancellor Joseph Fernandez.[81]

Indeed, the major documented special difficulties that children in gay families experience derive directly from legal discrimination and social prejudice. As one otherwise well-adjusted, sixteen-year-old son of a lesbian puts it: "If I came out and said my mom was gay, I'd be treated like an alien."[82] Children of gay parents are vicarious victims of rampant homophobia and institutionalized heterosexism. They suffer all of the considerable economic, legal and social disadvantages imposed on their parents, sometimes even more harshly. They risk losing a beloved parent or co-parent at the whim of a judge. They can be denied access to friends by the parents of playmates. Living in families that are culturally invisible or despised, the children suffer ostracism by proxy, and are forced continually to negotiate conflicts between loyalty to home, mainstream authorities and peers.

However, as the Supreme Court belatedly concluded in 1984, when it repudiated discrimination against interracial families in *Palmore v. Sidoti*, and as should be plain good sense, the fact that children of stigmatized parents bear an unfair burden provides no critique of their families, and the social cloud that confronts them has its silver lining. The sad *social* fact of prejudice and discrimination indicts the family values of the bigoted society, not the stigmatized family. In the words of the Court: "private biases may be outside the reach of the law, but the law cannot, directly or indirectly, give them effect."[83] Although the strict scrutiny standards that now govern race discrimination do not apply to sexual orientation discrimination, several courts in recent years have relied on the logic of Palmore in gay custody cases. These decisions have approved lesbian and gay custody awards while explicitly acknowledging that community disapproval of their parents' sexual identity would require "greater than ordinary fortitude" from the children, but that in return they might more readily learn that "people of integrity do not shrink from bigots." A New Jersey appellate court enumerated potential benefits children might derive from being raised by lesbian or gay parents that could serve as child-rearing ideals for a democracy: "emerge better equipped to search out their own standards of right and wrong, better able to perceive that the majority is not always correct in its moral judgments, and better able to understand the importance of conforming their beliefs to the requirements of reason and tested knowledge, not the constraints of currently popular sentiment or prejudice."[84] The testimony of one fifteen-year-old daughter of a lesbian mother and gay father indicates just this sort of outcome: "I think I am more open-minded than if I had straight parents. Sometimes kids at school make a big deal out of being gay. They say it's stupid and stuff like that. But they don't really know, because they are not around it. I don't say anything to them, but I know they are wrong. I get kind of mad, because they don't know what they are talking about."[85]

In fact, literature suggests that parents and children alike who live in fully closeted lesbian and gay families tend to suffer more than members of "out" gay families who contend with stigma directly.[86] Of course, gay parents who shroud their families in closets do so for compelling cause. Many judges make the closet an explicit condition for awarding custody or visitation rights to gay or lesbian parents, at times imposing direct restrictions on the parents' participation in gay social or political activity.[87] Or, fearing judicial homophobia, some parents live in mortal terror of losing their children, like one divorced lesbian in Kansas City whose violent ex-husband has threatened an ugly custody battle if anyone finds out about her lesbianism.[88] Should not the special burdens of the closet that gay families bear indict the "don't ask, don't tell" values of a society that treats gay families like cultural skeletons rather than those of the families denied the light and air of social respect?

Heroically, more and more brave new "queer" families are refusing the clandestine life. If a comprehensive recent survey article, "The Families of Lesbians and Gay Men: A New Frontier in Family Research,"[89] is correctly titled, then research on fully planned lesbian and gay families is its vanguard outpost. Researchers estimated that by 1990, between five and ten thousand lesbians in the United States had given birth to chosen children,[90] and the trend has increased visibly in the 1990s. Although this represents a small fraction of the biological and adopted children who live with lesbian parents, planned lesbian births, as Kath Weston suggests, "began to overshadow these other kinds of dependents, assuming a symbolic significance for lesbians and gay men disproportionate to their numbers."[91] Lesbian "turkey-baster" babies are equally symbolic to those who abhor the practice. National Fatherhood Initiative organizer David Blankenhorn, for example, calls for restricting sperm bank services to infertile married couples in order to inhibit the production of such "radically fatherless children," and similar concerns have been expressed in such popular publications as *U.S. News and World Report* and *Atlantic Monthly*.[92] (Interestingly, restrictions that limit access to donor sperm exclusively to married women are widespread in Europe, even in the liberal Nordic nations.) Because discrimination against prospective gay and lesbian adoptive parents leads most to conceal their sexual identity, it is impossible to estimate how many have succeeded in adopting or fostering children, but this too has become a visible form of gay planned parenthood.[93]

Research on planned gay parenting is too young to be more than suggestive, but initial findings give more cause for gay pride than alarm. Parental relationships tend to be more cooperative and egalitarian than among heterosexual parents, childrearing more nurturant, children more affectionate.[94] On the other hand, lesbian mothers do bear some particular burdens. Like straight women who bear children through insemination, they confront the vexing question of how to negotiate their children's knowledge of and relationship to sperm donors. As Hollywood's 1994 romantic comedy *Made in America* spoofed, some progeny of unknown donors, like many adopted children, certainly do quest for contact with their genetic fathers. One ten-year-old girl conceived by private donor insemination explains why she was relieved to find her biological father: "I wanted to find my dad because it was hard knowing I had a dad but not knowing who he was. It was like there was a missing piece."[95]

Lesbian couples planning a pregnancy contend with some unique questions and challenges concerning the relationship between biological and social maternity. They must decide which woman will try to become pregnant and how to negotiate feelings of jealousy, invisibility, and displacement that may be more likely to arise between the two than between a biological mother and father. Struggling to equalize maternal emotional stakes and claims, some lesbian couples decide to alternate the childbearing role, others attempt simultaneous pregnancies, and some, as we have seen, employ reproductive technology to divide the genetic and gestational components of procreation. Sometimes a nongestational lesbian mother jointly breastfeeds the baby her partner bears. Some of these lesbian mothers assume disproportionate responsibility for child care to compensate for their biological "disadvantage," and others give their surnames to their partner's offspring.

Planned lesbian and gay families, however, most fully realize the early Planned Parenthood goal, "every child a wanted child," as one twelve-year-old son of a lesbian recognized: "I think that if you are a child of a gay or lesbian, you have a better chance of having a great parent. If you are a lesbian, you have to go through a lot of trouble to get a child, so that child is really wanted."[96] Disproportionately, "queer" families choose to reside in and construct communities that support family and social diversity. Partly because fertility and adoption services are expensive and often difficult to attain, intentional gay parents are disproportionately better educated and more mature than other parents. Preliminary research indicates that these advantages more than offset whatever problems their special burdens cause their children. Clearly, it is in the interest of all our children to afford their families social dignity and respect.

If we exploit the research with this aim in mind, deducing a rational wish list for public policy is quite a simple matter. A straightforward liberal equal rights agenda for lesbians and gays would seem the obvious and humane course. In the best interests of all children, we would provide lesbian and gay parents equal access to marriage, child custody, adoption, foster children, fertility services, inheritance, employment, and all social benefits. We would adopt "rainbow" curricula within our schools and our public media that promote the kind of tolerance and respect for family and sexual diversity that Laura Sebastian, an eighteen-year-old reared by her divorced mother and her mother's lesbian lover, advocates: "A happy child has happy parents, and gay people can be as happy as straight ones. It doesn't matter what kids have—fathers, mothers, or both—they just need love and support. It doesn't matter if you are raised by a pack of dogs, just as long as they love you! It's about time lesbians and gays can have children. It's everybody's right as a human being."[97] We would expand support groups for gay youth and teen suicide prevention programs. In the name of our children, we would do all this and more, were there a rational relationship between empirical social science and public rhetoric and policy. Yet in a world so much the captive of virtual social science and virtual family values, how hopelessly utopian such an agenda appears!

IF WE COULD ONLY GET USED TO IT

Far from esoteric, the experiences of diverse genres of gay and lesbian "families we choose" bear on many of the most feverishly contested issues in contemporary family politics. They can speak to our mounting cultural paranoia over whether fathers are expendable, to nature-nurture controversies over sexual and gender identities and the gender division of labor, to the meaning and purpose of voluntary marriage, and most broadly, to those ubiquitous family values contests over the relative importance for children of family structure or process, of biological or psychological parents.

From the African-American Million Man March in October 1995, the ecstatic mass rallies currently attended by hundreds of thousands of Christian male Promise Keepers, and Blankenhorn's National Fatherhood Initiative pledge campaign, to California governor Pete Wilson's 1996 state of the state address and President Clinton's 1996 state of the union address, the nation seems to be gripped by cultural obsession over the decline of dependable dads. Of course, feminists like myself heartily welcome men's efforts to assume their full share of responsibility for the children they intentionally sire, as well as the ones they acquire.[98] After all, feminists spearheaded struggles coaxing fathers to share equally the drudgery and divinity of childrearing, at times with paradoxical costs to maternal self-interest.[99] This is quite a different matter, however, from nostalgic, reactionary moves to reify genetic paternity or stereotypical masculinity as crucial to the welfare of children and the nation alike.

Here is where research on lesbian families, particularly on planned lesbian couple families, could prove of no small import. Thus far, as we have seen, such research offers no brief for Blankenhorn's angst over "radically fatherless children," nor does research on other types of families without fathers justify such paternalistic alarm. For example, a careful, comprehensive study of eighth-graders living in single-parent households found that boys derived no benefits from living with fathers rather than mothers: "of the 35 social psychological and educational outcomes studied, we cannot find even one in which both males and females benefit significantly from living with their same-sex parent."[100] Even more challenging to those who seem to believe that the mere presence of a father in a family confers significant benefits on his children are surprising data reported in a recent study of youth and violence conducted by Kaiser Permanente and Children Now. The study of 1,000 eleven- to seventeen-year-olds and of 150 seven- to ten-year-olds found that, contrary to popular belief, 68 percent of the "young people exposed to higher levels of health and safety threats" were from conventional two-parent families. Moreover, rather poignantly, fathers were among the last people that troubled teens would turn to for help, even when they lived in conventional two-parent families. Only 10 percent of the young people in such two-parent families said they would seek their father's advice first, compared with 44 percent who claimed they would turn first to their mothers, and 26 percent who would first seek help from friends. Many more youth were willing to discuss concerns over their health, safety, and sexuality with nurses or doctors.[101] Thus, empirical social science to date, like the historical record, gives us sound cause to regard either fathers or mothers alike as "expendable." It is the quality, commitment, and character of parents, rather than their gender, that truly matter.

Similarly, research on the relationships of gay male and lesbian couples depicts diverse models for intimacy from which others could profit. "Freed" from normative conventions and institutions that govern heterosexual gender and family relationships, self-consciously "queer" couples and families, by necessity, have had to reflect much more seriously on the meaning and purpose of their intimate commitments. Studies that compare lesbian, gay male, and heterosexual couples find intriguing contrasts in their characteristic patterns of intimacy. Gender seems to shape domestic values and practices more powerfully than sexual identity, so that same-sex couples tend to be more compatible than heterosexual couples. For example, both lesbian and straight women seem to be more likely than either gay or straight men to value their relationships over their work. Yet both lesbian and gay male couples agree that both parties should be employed, while married men are less likely to agree with wives who wish to work. Predictably, same-sex couples share more interests and time together than married couples. Also unsurprisingly, lesbian couples tend to have the most egalitarian relationships, and married heterosexual couples the least. Lesbian and gay male couples both share household chores more equally and with less conflict than do married couples, but they share them differently. Lesbian couples tend to share most tasks while gay males more frequently assign tasks "to each according to his abilities," schedules, and preferences.[102]

Gender differences in sexuality are particularly striking and intriguing, because in this arena married women may be imposing more of their preferences on their husbands than conventional lore might predict. Gay male couples tend to have much more active, nonexclusive, and casual sex lives than either lesbian or married couples. Nearly two-thirds of the gay male couples studied by sociologists Blumstein and Schwartz in 1983, before AIDS had reached visibly epidemic proportions, practiced open relationships, but the clear majority of both lesbian and married couples were monogamous. While sexual frequency was lowest among lesbian couples, they considered themselves more compatible sexually than did either married couples or gay men. Husbands and wives disagreed the most about their sexual compatibility (with husbands claiming greater compatibility than wives reported), but gay men were the least troubled by sexual incompatibility, because they generally invested sex with fewer possessive, romantic, or emotional meanings than did most women or married men.[103]

Each of these modal patterns for intimacy and sexuality has its particular strengths and vulnerabilities. Gender conventions and gender fluidity alike have advantages and limitations, as Blumstein and Schwartz and other researchers have discussed. For example, gay men who seek sexual monogamy can have as much trouble achieving it as many heterosexual men have in trying to escape its restrictions.[104] Getting used to queer families would not mean converting to any characteristic patterns of intimacy, but coming to terms with the collapse of a monolithic cultural regime governing our intimate bonds. It would mean embracing a genuinely pluralist understanding that there are diverse, valid ways to form and sustain these which could benefit us all. In the end, Jonathan Rauch may be right in one respect, after all. If we reserve the term homosexuality to signify the expression of same-sex desire, it should indeed be of little public concern. "The rest of us," however, share a great interest in becoming so used to the presence of gay and lesbian families among us that the very label will once again come to seem embarrassingly queer.

If there is anything truly distinctive about lesbian and gay families, it is how unambiguously the substance of their relationships takes precedence over their form, their emotional and social commitments over genetic claims. Compelled to exercise "good old-fashioned American" ingenuity in order to fulfill familial desires, gays and lesbians improvisationally assemble a patchwork of blood and intentional relations—gay, straight, and other—into creative, extended kin bonds.[105] Gay communities more adeptly integrate single individuals into their social worlds than does mainstream heterosexual society, a social skill quite valuable in a world in which divorce, widowhood, and singlehood are increasingly normative. Because queer families must continually, self-consciously migrate in and out of the closet, they also hone bicultural skills particularly suitable for life in a multicultural society.[106] Self-identified queer families serve on the pioneer outpost of the postmodern family condition, confronting most directly its features of improvisation, ambiguity, diversity, contradiction, self-reflection, and flux.

Even the distinctive, indeed the definitional, burden that pervasive homophobia imposes on lesbian and gay families does not fully distinguish them from other contemporary families. Unfortunately, prejudice, intolerance, and disrespect for "different" or "other" families is all too commonplace in the contemporary world, and it diminishes us all. Ethnocentric and intolerant familism harms the families of many immigrants, interracial couples, single mothers (be they unwed or divorced, impoverished or affluent), remarried couples, childless "yuppie" couples, bachelors and "spinsters," house-husbands and working mothers, and the homeless, and it even places that vanishing, once-hallowed breed of full-time homemakers on the ("I'm just-a-housewife") defensive.

Gay and lesbian families simply brave intensified versions of widespread contemporary challenges. Both their plight and their pluck unequivocally expose the dangerous disjuncture between our family rhetoric and policy, on the one hand, and our family and social realities, on the other. Stubbornly denying the complex, pluralist array of contemporary families and kinship, most of our legal and social policies atavistically presume to serve a singular, "normal" family structure—the conventional, heterosexual, married-couple, nuclear family. In the name of children, politicians justify decisions that endanger them, and in the name of "the Family," they cause great harm to our families. It is time to get used to the postmodern family condition we all now inhabit. In the name of our families, and of democracy, we must move forward, not backward, to address the great social threats that imperil us all.

EPIGRAPH SOURCES

1. Buchanan quoted in Susan Yoachum and David Tuller, "Right Makes Might in Iowa," *San Francisco Chronicle*, February 12, 1996, A1, 11.
2. Jonathan Rauch, "A Pro-Gay, Pro-Family Policy," *Wall Street Journal*, November 29, 1994, A22.
3. Bonnie Tinker, "Love Makes a Family," Presentation to 1995 United Nations International Women's Conference, Beijing, September 14, 1995.

NOTES

1. With all due credit and apologies to Queer Nation and ACT-UP for adapting their slogan: "We're Here, We're Queer, Get Used to It!"
2. The estimate that at least six million children were living in households with at least one gay parent by 1985 appeared in Schulenberg, *Gay Parenting*, and has been accepted or revised upwards by most scholars since then. See, for example, Bozett, 39; Patterson; Allen and Demo.
3. Burke.
4. Goldberg.
5. Many gay activist groups and scholars, however, have begun to reclaim the term "queer" as a badge of pride, in much the same way that the Black Power movement of the 1960s reclaimed the formerly derogatory term for blacks.
6. Reagan and Schlafly both have gay sons, Powell has a lesbian daughter, and Gingrich has a lesbian half-sister.
7. For a sensitive discussion of the definitional difficulties involved in research on gay and lesbian families, see Allen and Demo, 112–13.
8. See the introduction and chapters one and two of All Our Families (see Permissions Acknowledgments, p. 501) for a direct discussion of the postmodern family condition. In Stacey, *Brave New Families*, I provide a book-length, ethnographic treatment of postmodern family life in the Silicon Valley.
9. I explain my use of the term "modern" family above in the introduction, pp. 6–8, chapter one, pp. 18–19, and chapter two, pp. 38–43 of *All Our Families*.
10. Most gay and lesbian scholars and activists reject the term "homosexual" because it originated within a medical model that classified homosexuality as a sexual perversion or disease and because the term emphasizes sexuality as at the core of the individual's identity. In this chapter, I follow the generally preferred contemporary practice of using the terms "lesbians" and "gay men," but I also occasionally employ the term "gay" generically to include both women and men. I also play with the multiple, and currently shifting, meanings of the term "queer," by specifying whether I am using the term in its older pejorative sense, in its newer sense of proudly challenging fixed notions of gender and sexuality, or in its more colloquial sense of simply "odd."
11. For historical and cross-cultural treatments of same-sex marriages, relationships, and practices in the West and elsewhere, see Boswell, and Eskridge .
12. Rivera.

13. Among the influential feminist works of this genre were: Chodorow, *The Reproduction of Mothering*; Gilligan, *In a Different Voice*; and Ruddick, *Maternal Thinking*.

14. See Introduction, p. 5, chapter 3, p. 53, and chapter 4, pp. 83–85.

15. See Rosenbloom, 226, (fn 22); and Benkov, 117.

16. Wikler and Wikler, 10.

17. Ibid.

18. In "Junior," a 1994 Christmas season "family film" release, Schwarzenneger plays a research scientist who becomes pregnant as part of experimental fertility research.

19. The first known custody battle involving a lesbian couple and a sperm donor was *Loftin v. Flournoy* in California. For a superb discussion of the relevant case law, see Polikoff.

20. Polikoff provides detailed discussion of the most significant legal cases of custody contests after death of biological lesbian co-mother. In both the most prominent cases, higher courts eventually reversed decisions that had denied custody to the surviving lesbian parent, but only after serious emotional harm had been inflicted on the children and parents alike. See Polikoff, pp. 527–32.

21. Henry, 297.

22. Ibid., 300; and Polikoff, 492.

23. Griscom.

24. See Rubenstein, 452.

25. For a fascinating discussion of the political compromises involved in the Danish case, see Miller, chap. 12.

26. However, the highest courts in Vermont, Massachusetts and New York now allow unmarried couples, including lesbian and gay male couples, to jointly adopt a child. In November 1995 the highly divided NY top court reached this decision which explicitly acknowledged "fundamental changes" in U.S. family life and its significance for gay parents. See Dao, A11.

27. National Center for Lesbian Rights, "Our Day in Court—Against Each Other," in Rubenstein, 561–2.

28. de Lamadrid, p. 178.

29. In 1994 Sharon Bottoms lost custody of her two-year-old son because the trial court judge deemed her lesbianism to be immoral and illegal. In April 1995 the Virginia state supreme court upheld the ruling, which at this writing is being appealed to the U.S. Supreme Court.

30. Quoted in Sherman, 191.

31. Ibid., 173.

32. Bozett, 232.

33. Cited in Sherman, 9, fn 6. A more recent poll conducted by *The Advocate* suggests that the trend of support for gay marriage is increasing. See Wolfson, 583.

34. Terry announced his plans January 24, 1996 on *Randall Terry Live*, and LaHaye made her pitch the next day, January 25, 1996 on *Beverly LaHaye Live*.

35. Dunlap, "Some States Trying to Stop Gay Marriages before They Start," A18; Dunlap, "Fearing a Toehold for Gay Marriage, Conservatives Rush to Bar the Door," A7. Lockhead, "GOP Bill Targets Same-Sex Marriages," *San Francisco Chronicle*, May 9, 1996, A1, 15.

36. Ibid., A1.

37. Press Briefing by Mike McCurry, White House, May 14, 1996, Office of the

Press Secretary.

38. "Vatican Denounces Gay-Marriage Idea." *New York Times*, March 29, 1996, A8.

39. Dunlap, "Reform Rabbis Vote to Back Gay Marriage," A8.

40. "The Freedom to Marry." *New York Times*, April 7, 1996, Editorials/Letters, p. 10.

41. The decision stated that the sexual orientation of the parties was irrelevant, because same-sex spouses could be of any sexual orientation. It was the gender discrimination involved in limiting one's choice of spouse that violated the state constitution. See Wolfson, 573.

42. Polikoff.

43. Law Professor, Thomas Coleman, who is executive director of the "Family Diversity Project" in California, expresses these views in Sherman, 128–9.

44. Sullivan; Rauch.

45. Tede Matthews in Sherman, 57.

46. Kirk Johnson quoted in Wolfson, 567.

47. Hunter, 12.

48. Wolfson.

49. Mohr, 48, 41, 50.

50. "Some Progress Found in Poll on Gay Rights," *San Francisco Chronicle*, June 20, 1994.

51. Ryan, 90. Sullivan.

52. Rauch.

53. Herscher, A2.

54. See chap. 3, pp. 69–71 above.

55. Clinton, according to his senior adviser George Stephanopoulos, "thinks the proper role for the government is to work on the fight against discrimination, but he does not believe we should support (gay) marriage." Quoted in Sandalow and Tuller, A2.

56. Clinton, book jacket copy.

57. Remafedi.

58. Quoted in Miller, 350.

59. This is the title and central argument of Popenoe's *New York Times* op-ed discussed above in the Introduction, p. 8 and chapter 3, pp. 53–57.

60. Wolfson, 599.

61. The three journals were *Journal of Marriage and the Family, Family Relations*, and *Journal of Family Issues*. Allen and Demo, 119.

62. For overviews of the research, see Patterson; Laird; and Allen and Demo.

63. Laird, 316–17.

64. Ibid., 317; Demo and Allen, 26; Patterson; Tasker and Golombok.

65. Tasker and Golombok.

66. Quoted in Raskin, 34.

67. Laird.

68. See, for example, Patterson; Demo and Allen; Benkov; Weston; and Peplau.

69. Minton, "U.S.A.," in Rosenbloom, 219.

70. Quoted in Maralee Schwartz and Kenneth J. Cooper, "Equal Rights Initiative in Iowa Attacked," *Washington Post*, August 23, 1992, A15.

71. Laird, 315–16.

72. See, for example, Williams.

73. As Tasker and Golombok concede, "Young adults from lesbian homes tended to be more willing to have a sexual relationship with someone of the same gender if they felt physically attracted to them. They were also more

likely to have considered the possibility of developing same-gender sexual attractions or relationships. Having a lesbian mother, therefore, appeared to widen the adolescent's view of what constituted acceptable sexual behavior to include same-gender sexual relationships," 212.

74. Rich.
75. Sedgwick, 76.
76. Quoted in Raskin, 64–5.
77. Shannon Minter, "United States," in Rosenbloom, 222.
78. Remafedi.
79. Quoted in Sherman, 70.
80. Due.
81. See Irvine, "A Place in the Rainbow: Theorizing Lesbian and Gay Culture," 232.
82. Quoted in Raskin, 24.
83. Quoted in Polikoff, 569–70.
84. Quoted in Polikoff, 570.
85. Quoted in Raskin, 81.
86. Benkov, chap. 8.
87. Kurdek and Schmitt; Lynch, "Nonghetto Gays: An Ethnography of Suburban Homosexuals" in Herdt, ed., *Gay Culture in America.*
88. Raskin, 39.
89. Allen and Demo.
90. Polikoff, "This Child Does Have Two Mothers," 461 (fn. 2).
91. Weston, "Parenting in the Age of AIDS," 159.
92. Blankenhorn, 233; Leo, 26; Seligson, 28.
93. Bozett, p. 4 discusses gay male parenthood strategies.
94. Demo and Allen, 26. Also see Laird.
95. Quoted in Raskin, 33.
96. Ibid., 53.
97. Ibid., 174.
98. See Newton, A6; Segal; Ehrensaft.
99. Shared parenting between women and men was a favored political goal that many feminists deduced from such 1970s works of feminist theory as Dinnerstein, *The Mermaid and the Minotaur*, and Chodorow, *Reproduction of Mothering*. Ehrensaft, *Parenting Together*, provides a balanced treatment of some of the paradoxes, difficulties and achievements of shared parenting efforts. Joint custody, however, which many feminists first favored, has often been used to reduce child support and financial settlements.
100. Downey and Powell.
101. Fairbank, Maslin, Maullin & Associates, 8, 10.
102. Kurdek; Blumstein and Schwartz; Peplau, 193.
103. Peplau, 193; Blumstein and Schwartz.
104. Blumstein and Schwartz; Peplau; Laird.
105. See Weston for an ethnographic treatment of these chosen kin ties.
106. As Allen and Demo suggest, "an aspect of biculturalism is resilience and creative adaptation in the context of minority group oppression and stigma," and this "offers a potential link to other oppressed groups in American society" 122.

REFERENCES

Allen, Katherine R., and David H. Demo. "The Families of Lesbians and Gay Men: A New Frontier in Family Research." *Journal of Marriage and the Family* 57 (February 1995): 111–27.

Benkov, Laura. *Reinventing the Family: Lesbian and Gay Parents.* New York: Crown, 1994.

Blankenhorn, David. *Fatherless America: Confronting Our Most Urgent Social Problem.* New York: Basic Books, 1995.

Blumstein, Philip, and Pepper Schwartz. *American Couples.* New York: William Morrow, 1983.

Boswell, John. *Same-Sex Unions in Premodern Europe.* New York: Villard Books, 1994.

Bozett, Frederick W., ed. *Gay and Lesbian Parents.* New York: Praeger, 1987.

Burke, Phyllis. *Family Values: A Lesbian Mother's Fight for Her Son.* New York: Random House, 1993.

Chodorow, Nancy. *The Reproduction of Mothering.* Berkeley and Los Angeles: University of California Press, 1978.

Clinton, Hillary Rodham. *It Takes A Village: And Other Lessons Children Teach Us.* New York: Simon & Schuster, 1996.

Dao, James. "Ruling Lets Unwed Couples Adopt," *New York Times*, November 3, 1995, A11.

Demo, David H., and Katharine R. Allen. "Diversity Within Lesbian and Gay Families: Challenges and Implications for Family Theory and Research." *Journal of Social and Personal Relationships* 13 (1996), n.3.

Dinnerstein, Dorothy. *The Mermaid and the Minotaur: Sexual Arrangements and Human Malaise.* New York: Harper & Row, 1976.

Downey, Douglas B., and Brian Powell. "Do Children in Single-Parent Households Fare Better Living With Same-Sex Parents?" *Journal of Marriage and the Family* 55 (February 1993): 55–71.

Due, Linnea. *Joining the Tribe: Growing Up Gay and Lesbian in the '90s.* New York: Doubleday, 1996.

Ehrensaft, Diane. *Parenting Together: Men and Women Sharing the Care of Their Children.* New York: Free Press, 1987.

Eskridge, Jr. William N., "A History of Same-Sex Marriage." *Virginia Law Review* 79 (1993):1419–1513.

Fairbank, Maslin, Maullin & Associates. "National Health and Safety Study: Summary of Results." Santa Monica and San Francisco, CA: October 1995.

Gilligan, Carol. *In a Different Voice: Psychological Development and Woman's Psychology.* Cambridge, MA: Harvard University Press, 1982.

Goldberg, Carey. "Virtual Marriages for Same-Sex Couples." *New York Times*, March 26, 1996, A8.

Griscom, Joan. "The Case of Sharon Kowalski and Karen Thompson." In P.S. Rothenberg, ed., *Race, Class, and Gender in the United States: An Integrated Study.* New York: St. Martin's Press, 1992.

Henry, Vickie L. "A Tale of Three Women: A Survey of the Rights and Responsibilities of Unmarried Women Who Conceive by Alternate Insemination and a Model for Legislative Reform," *American Journal of Law & Medicine* XIX, n.3 (1993):297.

Herscher, Elaine. "After Reconsidering, Montana Junks Gay Sex Bill," *San Francisco Chronicle*, March 24, 1995.

Kurdek, Lawrence. "The Allocation of Household Labor in Gay, Lesbian, and Heterosexual Married Couples," *Journal of Social Issues* 49, n.3 (1993):127–39.

Kurdek, L. A., and J. P. Schmitt. "Relationship Quality of Gay Men in Closed or Open Relationships," *Journal of Homosexuality* 12, n.2 (1985):85–99.

Laird, Joan. "Lesbian and Gay Families." In Froma Walsh, ed., *Normal Family Processes*, Second edition. New York: Guilford Press, 1993.

Leo, John. "Promoting No-Dad Families," *U.S. News and World Report*, 118, n.19 May 15, 1995, 26.

Miller, Neil. *Out in the World: Gay and Lesbian Life from Buenos Aires to Bangkok*. New York: Random House, 1992.

Mohr, Richard. *A More Perfect Union. Why Straight American Must Stand Up for Gay Rights*. Boston: Beacon, 1994.

Newton, Judith. "A Feminist Among Promise Keepers," *Davis Enterprise*, October 8, 1995, A6.

Patterson, Charlotte J. "Children of Lesbian and Gay Parents." *Child Development* 63 (1992):1025–42.

Peplau, Letitia. "Research of Homosexual Couples: An Overview." In John P. De Cecco, ed., *Gay Relationships*. New York: Haworth Press, 1998.

Polikoff, Nancy. "This Child Does Have Two Mothers: Redefining Parenthood to Meet the Needs of Children in Lesbian-Mother and Other Nontraditional Families." *Georgetown Law Journal* 78 (1990).

Polikoff, Nancy. "We Will Get What We Ask For: Why Legalizing Gay and Lesbian Marriage Will Not 'Dismantle the Legal Structure of Gender in Every Marriage'," *Virginia Law Review* 79 (1993): 1549–50.

Raskin, Lousie, ed. *Different Mothers: Sons and Daughters of Lesbians Talk About Their Lives*. Pittsburgh: Cleis Press, 1990.

Rauch, Jonathan. "A Pro-Gay, Pro-Family Policy," *Wall Street Journal*, November 29, 1994, A22.

Remafedi, Gary, ed. *Death by Denial*. Boston: Alyson Publications, 1994.

Rich, Adrienne. "Compulsory Heterosexuality and Lesbian Existence." *Signs* 5, n.2 (Summer 1980).

Rivera, Rhonda R. "Legal Issues in Gay and Lesbian Parenting." In Frederick W. Bozett, ed., *Gay and Lesbian Parents*. New York: Praeger, 1987.

Rosenbloom, Rachel, ed. *Unspoken Rules: Sexual Orientation and Women's Human Rights*. San Francisco: International Gay and Lesbian Human Rights Commission, 1995.

Rubenstein, William B. ed. *Lesbians, Gay Men, and the Law*. New York: New Press, 1993.

Ruddick, Sarah. *Maternal Thinking: Toward a Politics of Peace*. Boston: Beacon Press, 1989.

Ryan, Alan. "No Easy Way Out," *New Yorker* (September 11, 1995): 90.

Sandalow, Marc and David Tuller. "White House Tell Gays It Backs Them," *San Francisco Chronicle*, October 21, 1995, A2.

Schulenberg, John. *Gay Parenting*. New York: Doubleday, 1985.

Sedgwick, Eve. "How to Bring Your Kids Up Gay." In Michael Warner, ed., *Fear of a Queer Planet: Queer Politics and Social Theory*. Minneapolis: University of Minnesota Press, 1993.

Segal, Lynne. *Slow Motion: Changing Masculinities, Changing Men*. London: Virago, 1990.

Seligson, Susan. "Seeds of Doubt," *Atlantic Monthly* (March 1995), 28.

Sherman, Suzanne, ed. *Lesbian and Gay Marriage: Private Commitments, Public*

Ceremonies. Philadelphia: Temple University Press, 1992.

Stacey, Judith. *Brave New Families: Stories of Domestic Upheaval in Late Twentieth Century America.* New York: Basic Books, 1990.

Sullivan, Andrew. "Here Comes the Groom: A (Conservative) Case for Gay Marriage." *New Republic* v. 201, 19 (August 28, 1989): 20–21.

Tasker, Fiona, and Susan Golombok. 1995. "Adults Raised as Children in Lesbian Families," *American Journal of Orthopsychiatry* 65, n.2 (April): 203–215.

Weston, Kath. *Families We Choose: Lesbians, Gays, Kinship.* New York: Columbia University Press, 1991.

Wikler, Daniel, and Norma J. Wikler. "Turkey-baster Babies: The Demedicalization of Artificial Insemination." *Milbank Quarterly* 69, n. 1 (1991):5–40.

Williams, Walter L. *The Spirit and the Flesh: Sexual Diversity in American Indian Culture.* Boston: Beacon Press, 1986.

Wolfson, Evan. "Crossing the Threshold: Equal Marriage Rights For Lesbians and Gay Men and the Intra-Community Critique," *Review of Law & Social Change* XXI, n.3 (1994–95).

22

AFRICAN AMERICAN LESBIANS: ISSUES IN COUPLES THERAPY

Beverly Greene
Nancy Boyd-Franklin

TRIPLE JEOPARDY: RACISM, SEXISM, HOMOPHOBIA

African American lesbians live in triple jeopardy; that is, they are vulnerable to the social discrimination and internalization of all the negative stereotypes traditionally aimed at African Americans, women, and lesbians. A therapist's understanding of what it means to be an African American lesbian requires careful examination of race, gender, and sexual orientation issues at multiple systems levels including: (1) *American Society:* racism, sexism, and homophobia in the society as a whole; (2) *African American Culture*: racial identity, gender roles, and homophobia within the African American community; (3) *Couples/Families:* the interactions among partners' and family members' racial identities, gender-role attitudes, and attitudes toward lesbianism; and (4) *Individuals*: the dynamic interactions within the individual or racial, gender, and sexual orientation component of identity. Most important is to grasp how ethnosexual myths, superimposed by the larger society, have affected African American cultural views of women and lesbianism which, in turn, have affected the particular family relationships of African American lesbians. Thus, before we examine therapy, the psychohistorical context of African American lesbians' lives must be understood.

GENDER ROLES AND ETHNOSEXUAL MYTHS

From a historical perspective, African Americans are a diverse group, with cultural origins primarily in the tribes of West Africa, who were brought to the United States as slaves. The tribal legacy includes strong family ties encompassing nuclear and extended family members in complex networks of mutual obligation and support (Boyd-Franklin, 1989; Greene, 1986, 1994a, 1994c, 1996; Icard, 1986). Traditional African culture involves more flexible gender roles than those found in European and other ethnic groups, due in part to values stressing interdependence and a greater egalitarianism in precolonial Africa.

In African American culture, flexible family structures and lack of rigid gender-role stratification were also responses to racism in the

United States. Lack of employment opportunities made it difficult for African American men to conform to the Western ideal of male-as-provider and required women to work full-time outside the home. Notwithstanding this greater gender-role flexibility in African American culture, sexism continues to exist in African American communities (Greene, 1994a, 1994c).

In addition, historically oppressed groups that have faced racist genocidal practices, specifically African Americans and Native Americans, have accorded reproductive sexuality greater importance than other groups in order to continue their presence in the world. Thus African Americans sometimes look upon nonreproductive sexual practices as another threat to group survival, a view Kanuha (1990) terms "fears of extinction" (p. 176). Although a lesbian sexual orientation does not preclude having children, particularly among lesbians of color, the internalization of this view may make it harder for a lesbian of color and her family to accept affirmatively her sexual orientation.

Because they arrived in America as objects of the United States slave trade, African American women were considered to be property, and forced sexual relationships with African males and White slavemasters were the norm. Afro-Caribbean women not of Latin descent often possess cultural values and practices reflective of the colonization of their islands, particularly by Great Britain or France. The sexual objectification of African Americans during slavery was reinforced by the public images propagated about this population, feeding stereotypes of sexual promis-·cuity and moral looseness (Clarke, 1983; Collins, 1990; Greene, 1986, 1990a, 1990b, 1990c; Icard, 1986; Loiacano, 1989). Such ethnosexual myths are relevant in terms of self-image and how the larger family and African American community view gay or lesbian members.

It is useful to explore the relationship of such ethnosexual beliefs to an African American's attitudes about lesbian sexual orientation. These myths, perpetrated by the dominant culture, often represent a complex combination of racial and sexual stereotypes designed to objectify women of color, isolate them from their idealized White counterparts, and promote their sexual exploitation and control (Collins, 1990; Greene, 1994a, 1994c; hooks, 1981). The symbolism of these racial and sexual stereotypes and their interactions with other stereotypes held about lesbians can be central areas of clinical inquiry in family therapy.

Ethnosexual stereotypes about African American women have their roots in images created by White society. African American and Caribbean women clearly did not fit the traditional stereotypes of women as fragile, weak, and dependent, as they were never allowed to be this way. The "Mammy" figure is the historical antecedent to the stereotype of African American women as assertive, domineering, and strong. Such traits were applauded in a woman as long as those qualities were put to the caregiving service of her master and mistress.

Popular images of African American women as "castrating" were created in the interest of maintaining the social power hierarchy in which

African American men and women were subordinate to Whites and women were subordinate to men. These images of the so-called "castrating woman" were used to stigmatize any woman who wanted to work outside the home or cross the gender-role stereotypes of a patriarchal culture (hooks, 1981). Today's stereotypes are a product of those myths and depict African American women as not sufficiently subordinate to African American men, inherently sexually promiscuous, morally loose, assertive, matriarchal, and as castrating or masculinized when compared to their White counterparts (Christian, 1985; Clarke, 1983; Collins, 1990; Greene, 1986, 1990b, 1990c, 1994a, 1994c; hooks, 1981; Icard, 1986; Silvera, 1991). Stereotypes of lesbians as masculinized females coincide with racial stereotypes of African American and Afro-Caribbean women. Both are depicted as defective females who want to be or act like men and are sexually promiscuous.

Institutional racism plays a prominent role in the development of myths and distortions regarding the sexuality of African American and Afro-Caribbean lesbians. Males in the culture are encouraged to believe that strong women, rather than racist institutions, are responsible for their oppression. Racism, sexism, and heterosexism combine to cast the onus upon African American women for family problems in the African American population. The ideas that African American women are at fault for the problems of African American families and men's oppression imply that the remedy for liberating people of African descent is to reinforce male dominance and female subordination.

Many African American and Afro-Caribbean women, including lesbians, have internalized these myths about strong, independent women, which compromises their ability to obtain support from the larger African American and Caribbean communities (Collins, 1990; Greene, 1994a, 1994c). Thus the legacy of gendered racism plays a role in the response of many African Americans to lesbians in their families or as visible members of their communities. African American men and women who have internalized the racism and sexism inherent in the patriarchal values of Western culture may scapegoat any strong, independent woman. Lesbians are easy targets for such scapegoating.

These false stereotypes include the notions that lesbians typically are: wishing to be men; mannish in appearance (Taylor, 1983); unattractive or less attractive than heterosexual women (Dew, 1985); less extroverted (Kite, 1994); unable to get a man; victims of traumatic relationships with men that presumably turned them against men; or defective females (Christian, 1985; Collins, 1990; Greene, 1994a, 1994c; Kite, 1994). In African American communities, the assumption that sexual attraction to men is intrinsic to being a normal woman often leads to a range of equally inaccurate conclusions, such as the notion that reproductive sexuality is the only normal and morally correct form of sexual expression (Garnets & Kimmel, 1991; Glassgold, 1992), or the myth that there is a direct relationship between sexual orientation and conformity to traditional gender roles within the culture (Kite & Deaux, 1987; Newman, 1989; Whitley, 1987).

The latter idea presumes that women who do not conform to traditional gender-role stereotypes must be lesbian, whereas women who do conform must be heterosexual. These assumptions are used to threaten women with the stigma of being labeled "lesbian" if they do not adhere to traditional gender-role stereotypes about males being dominant and females being submissive (Collins, 1990; Gomez & Smith, 1990; Smith, 1982). This pressure to conform occurs in African American communities despite their history and traditions of greater flexibility for women in family decision making and work roles.

Being labeled a lesbian can prevent women, whether they are lesbian or not, from seeking nontraditional roles or engaging in nontraditional behaviors. Some scholars who are women of color may feel that simply writing about or acknowledging lesbian themes will raise questions about their own sexual orientation and that they will be viewed negatively as a result (Clarke, 1991). Such an atmosphere leads many scholars to refrain from focusing on lesbian themes, further contributing to the invisibility of African American lesbians. In a society wherein male dominance and female subordination have been viewed as normative, the fears of being labeled lesbian, with its negative consequences, may serve to further perpetuate patriarchy.

HOMOPHOBIA

It is important to explore how sexuality and gender interrelate with culture. Espin (1984) suggests that in most cultures, a *range* of sexual behaviors is tolerated. The clinician needs to determine where the client's behavior fits within the spectrum for her particular culture (Espin, 1984). In exploring the range of sexuality tolerated by the woman's culture, it is helpful to know whether *formally* forbidden practices are tolerated, as long as they are not discussed or labeled. As with their ethnic-majority counterparts, the strength of African American family ties often mitigates against outright rejection of gay and lesbian family members.

Nevertheless, the African American community is viewed by gay and lesbian members as extremely homophobic, generating the pressure to remain closeted (Clarke, 1983; Croom, 1993; Gomez & Smith, 1990; Greene, 1990c, 1994a, 1994c, 1996; Icard, 1986; Loiacano, 1989; Mays & Cochran, 1988: Poussaint, 1990; Smith, 1982). Homophobia among African Americans and Afro-Caribbeans is multiply determined. These cultures often have strong religious and spiritual orientations. For adherents to Western Christianity, selective interpretations of Biblical scripture may be used to reinforce homophobic attitudes (Claybourne, 1978; Greene, 1994a, 1994c, 1996; Icard, 1986; Moses & Hawkins, 1982). Silvera (1991) writes that when her grandmother discovered that Silvera was a lesbian, she took out her Bible and explained: "This was a 'ting only people of mixed blood was involved in" (p. 16). Certain non-Christian African American sects view homosexuality as a decadent Western practice.

Clarke (1983), Silvera (1991), and Smith (1982) cite heterosexual privilege as another factor in the homophobia of African American and Afro-Caribbean women. Because of sexism in both dominant and African American cultures and racism in the dominant culture, *African American women may find heterosexuality the only privileged status they can possess* (Greene, 1994a, 1994c). As such, they may be reluctant to jeopardize the privileges associated with this status by explicitly coming out.

Internalized racism is another determinant of homophobia among African Americans and Afro-Caribbeans. For those who have internalized the negative stereotypes about African Americans constructed by the dominant culture, sexual behavior outside societal norms may be viewed as a negative reflection on all African Americans (Greene, 1996; Poussaint, 1990). Lesbianism may be experienced as a particular embarrassment to African Americans who most strongly identify with the dominant culture. Hence, there may be an exaggerated desire among some African Americans to model normalcy to the dominant culture and a related antipathy toward lesbians and gay men (Clarke, 1983; Monteflores, 1986; Gomez, 1983; Greene, 1986, 1994a, 1994c, 1996; Wyatt, Strayer, & Lobitz, 1976).

Indeed, the only colloquial names for lesbians in the African American community—"funny women" or "bulldagger women"—are derogatory (Jeffries, 1992, p. 44; Omosupe, 1991). Silvera (1991) writes of her childhood in Jamaica:

> The words used to describe many of these women would be "Man royal" and/or "Sodomite." Dread words. So dread that women dare not use these words to name themselves. The act of loving someone from the same sex was sinful, abnormal—something to hide. (pp. 15–16)

She explains that the word *sodomite*, derived from the Old Testament, is used in Jamaica to brand any strong, independent woman: "Now all you have to do is not respond to a man's call to you and dem call you sodomite or lesbian" (p. 17).

Clarke (1983) and Jeffries (1992) observe that there was a greater tolerance for gay men and lesbians in some poor African American communities in the 1940s through the 1950s, which Clarke explains as "seizing the opportunity to spite the white man," and Jeffries attributes to the empathy African Americans felt, as oppressed people, toward members of another oppressed group. However, a strong component of this tolerance may have been the relative invisibility of homosexuals within the African American community and the dominant culture. The recent heightened visibility of lesbians may challenge the denial that permitted this tolerance in earlier times. Lesbians may not be tolerated as easily in the African American community to the extent that they no longer are viewed as helpless and silent victims of oppression who exist only in small numbers.

Despite the homophobia in the African American community, African American lesbians claim a strong attachment to their cultural heritage and cite their identity as African Americans as *primary*, compared to their identity as lesbians (Acosta, 1979; Croom, 1993; Mays et al., 1993). Therefore, they often experience a sense of conflicting loyalties between the African American community and the mainstream lesbian community. Most are unwilling to jeopardize their ties to the African American community, despite realistic concerns about rejection or ridicule if they openly disclose their lesbian sexual orientation (Dyne, 1980; Greene, 1990a, 1990c, 1994a, 1994c, 1996; Icard, 1986; Mays & Cochran, 1988; Mays et al., 1993). Another factor adding to the sense of conflicting loyalties is the racial discrimination African American lesbians face in the broader, predominantly White, lesbian community, including discrimination in admission to lesbian bars, employment, and advertising (Greene, 1994a, 1994c, 1996; Gutierrez & Dworkin, 1992; Mays & Cochran, 1988).

In analyzing the history of discrimination of an ethnic group, the group members' own understandings of their oppression and coping strategies must be incorporated. Accepting the dominant culture's perspectives on such groups may only reinforce ethnocentric, heterocentric, and androcentric biases. Thus, rather than making assumptions, it is important to explore with each couple in therapy how the partners perceive the constraints they and their family members are under from the larger culture and from their specific communities and neighborhoods.

FAMILY OF ORIGIN

In therapy with African American lesbian clients, many questions about the family of origin need to be explored, especially: (1) How much do parents or other family of origin members continue to control or influence adult children and grandchildren?; and (2) How important is the extended family as a source of economic, emotional, and practical support (Mays & Cochran, 1988)? Other factors to be explored include: (1) the degree to which procreation and continuation of the family line are valued; (2) the closeness of ties to the ethnic community; (3) the degree of acculturation or assimilation of the client and whether it is significantly different from that of other family members; (4) the family's religious beliefs; and (5) the oppression the family group has faced and continues to face within the dominant culture.

Historically, the African American family has functioned as a refuge to protect group members from the racism of the dominant culture. Villarosa (interviewed in Brownworth, 1993) observes that the importance of African American family and community as a survival tool makes the coming-out process for African American lesbians much different than that of their White counterparts:

> It is harder for us to consider being rejected by our families.... All we have is our families, our community. When the whole world is racist and against you, your family and your community are the only people who accept you and love you even though you are black. So you don't know what will happen if you lose them ... and many black lesbians (and gay men) are afraid that's what will happen. (p. 18)

Because of the strength of family ties, there is a reluctance to expel a lesbian from the family despite an undisputed rejection of a lesbian sexual orientation. This may result from varying levels of tolerance for nonconformity, denial of the person's sexual orientation, or even culturally distinct ways of conveying negative attitudes about a family member's sexual orientation. In African American families, lesbians are not "disowned," as Villarosa observes, because of the importance of family members to one another; rather, they "keep you around to talk you out of it" (Brownworth, 1993, p. 18).

The clinician should not interpret apparent tolerance as approval (Acosta, 1979), as the family's tolerance is usually contingent on a lesbian's silence. Serious conflicts may occur once a family member openly discloses, labels herself, or discusses being a lesbian. For example, a lesbian family member's lover *may* have been treated well until the relationship is labeled openly as "lesbian" or until the lesbian family member seeks her family's support or direct acknowledgment of her lesbian sexual orientation, relationship, or partner. Even when family members are accepting and supportive, the broader African American or Caribbean community may not be.

COUPLES ISSUES AND THERAPY

There is great diversity among couples within the African American lesbian community, which we will illustrate with clinical case examples. It is crucial for the reader to first understand that the race or ethnicity of the partner of an African American lesbian can greatly affect the dynamics of the relationship, as well as its degree of visibility and therefore how it is perceived and received by the African American family and community.

Many African American lesbians' relationships are largely unsupported outside the lesbian community. These women encounter unique challenges in relationships, given that their partners have the same gender socialization in a culture that conspicuously devalues their person and devalues their relationships on many levels. Moreover, the culture provides few open, healthy models of such relationships. Those in lesbian relationships may find tacit support for their relationship within the African American community; however, this support is often marked by a collusion of silence, ambivalence, and denial. African

American lesbians who have received family support for their struggles with racism, and perhaps sexism, cannot presume that this support will extend to their romantic relationships or that their families will empathize with their distress if the relationship is troubled. This lack of understanding is compounded upon seeking professional assistance, only to find few, if any, therapists of color who have training in addressing issues in lesbian relationships (Greene, 1994a, 1994b, 1994c).

INTERRACIAL LESBIAN COUPLES

Compared with White lesbians, African American lesbians and lesbians of color in general have a higher proportion of relationships with women who are not members of their same ethnic group (Croom, 1993; Greene, 1995; Mays & Cochran, 1988; Tafoya & Rowell, 1988). This has been attributed in part to the larger numbers of White lesbians in the United States (Tafoya & Rowell, 1988). While heterosexual interracial relationships often lack the support of each member's family and community, lesbian interracial relationships face even greater challenges to a situation already fraught with difficulty.

An interracial lesbian couple may be more publicly visible and thus more readily identifiable as a couple than two women of the same ethnic group, which may exacerbate homophobic reactions from the outside world. In addition, the White partner may be forced to experience the realities of racism for the first time in her life. Clunis and Green (1988) observe that racism does not disappear from relationships because women have "worked on" the issue. Because racism is an ever present reality and stressor for lesbians of color, they often wear a protective psychological armor (Sears, 1987) and usually have developed a variety of coping strategies using it. A White partner who has never confronted racism may be unprepared to deal with it (Clunis & Green, 1988). For example, a White partner may be oblivious to slights that are racist in origin and experience her partner's anger as inappropriate; she may overreact and criticize her partner for complacency; or she may even take on the protective role of "rescuer," which her partner may find presumptuous, unwanted, unneeded, and even patronizing (Greene, 1994a, 1994c).

A White partner may also feel guilty about racism. Unable to distinguish between her personal behavior in the relationship and the racism in the outside world, a White partner may attempt to compensate her African American partner for the racism the partner faces in the world— a task the White partner cannot do successfully and that will ultimately leave her feeling angry and frustrated. Neither partner in such relationships should rely on the White person's politics or intentions as a realistic predictor that she is free of racism (Clunis & Green, 1988; Garcia, Kennedy, Pearlman, & Perez, 1987). Also, the African American lesbian partner may need to be alert to her own jealousy or resentment of her lover's privileged status in the dominant culture and in the lesbian community. Both partners may be perceived by others as lacking loyalty to their own ethnic or racial group and may even feel ashamed of their involvement with a person of a different group (Clunis & Green, 1988; Falco, 1991; Greene, 1994c, 1995, 1996). This both complicates the resolution of issues within the relationship and intensifies the complex web of loyalties and estrangements for lesbian women of color.

While interracial issues and cultural differences offer realistic challenges to lesbian relationships, they are not the source of every problem within them. However, couples sometimes overinterpret these highly visible differences as causal explanations for their problems. Attributing the source of difficulties to racial differences may allow the couple to avoid looking at more complex, often painful personal issues in their relationship (Greene, 1994c, 1995). Therapists should be aware that although racial differences are often the cause of significant difficulties, other problems arising out of conflicts over intimacy, internalized homophobia, or character issues and symptoms may be "racialized," that is, experienced as if they are about the couple's racial or ethnic differences.

Choices of partners and feelings about those choices may, but do not automatically, reflect an individual's personal conflicts about racial and ethnic identity. Such conflicts may be enacted by African American lesbian women who choose or are attracted to White women exclusively or who devalue lesbians of color, viewing them as unsuitable partners. African American lesbians who experience themselves as racially or culturally deficient or ambiguous may seek a partner from their own ethnic group to compensate for their perceived deficiency or demonstrate their cultural loyalty. An African American lesbian in an interracial relationship with a non–African American lesbian of color may tend to presume a greater level of similarity of experiences or worldviews than is realistically warranted. While their common oppression as women of color and as lesbians may be similar and important in the early development of their relationship, their views on their respective roles in a relationship, maintaining a household, and the role of other family members in their lives may be very different (Greene, 1994c, 1995).

African American lesbians may be appropriately sensitive to what Sears (personal communication, 1992) refers to as "pony stealing" and to what Clunis and Green (1988, p. 140) describe as "ethnic chasing." These terms are used to describe White women who seek out lesbians of color as partners to assuage their own guilt about being White, their lack of a strong ethnic identity, or as proof of their liberal attitudes. In addition, the belief in ethnosexual stereotypes of African American lesbians as less sexually inhibited than their White counterparts may serve to motivate this behavior (Greene, 1994c). An ethnic chaser may seek, usually unconsciously, to gain from an African American lesbian whatever they perceive to be lacking in themselves. This attempt at self-repair is doomed to fail, and the White partner may respond by feeling angry, resentful, and somehow betrayed by her partner. In treatment, it is helpful to clarify such women's expectations about being in *any* relationship. Beyond this general assessment, the kinds of assumptions held about ethnic or White women within an intimate relationship should be explored (Greene, 1994a, 1994c).

Exclusive choices in this realm may also reflect a woman's tendency to idealize people who are like her and devalue those who are not, or vice versa. When this is the case, the reality often does not live up to the fantasy, resulting in disappointment and self-denigration. It is important to remember that such decisions and preferences have many different determinants and that these are often made outside the woman's conscious awareness.

A therapist should not presume that participation in an interracial lesbian relationship is an expression of cultural or racial self-hate in the African American lesbian. Similarly, the therapist cannot accurately presume that her client's presence in a relationship with another African American woman is anchored in either loyalty or respect for that culture. The aforementioned problematic premises may not be present at all. Therapists simply need to be aware of a wide range of clinical possibilities and be prepared to explore them accordingly.

A case example of an interracial lesbian relationship is presented below, followed by discussion of the therapeutic issues involved.

Case 1: Interracial Couples

JoAnn is a thirty-eight-year-old White lesbian from a Midwestern Presbyterian background who has lived for the last five years in the urban Northeast. At the age of twenty, she came out to her parents during a visit home from college. Both rejected and essentially disowned her. She has had no meaningful contact with them for the past ten years or with her only sibling, an older sister who is married and has two children. Her partner, Marion, whom she met in graduate school, is a thirty-five-year-old African American lesbian who is part of a large, enmeshed African American extended family, most of whom live in the same urban Northeastern city in which she was born and raised and currently resides.

Marion has never told any member of her family of her sexual orientation but assumes that they know. The couple has entered treatment because of the exclusion JoAnn experiences from Marion's intense involvement with her family. It became apparent as therapy progressed that there was not only a sense of lack of family in JoAnn's life but an absence of ethnic identity as well. JoAnn used the term vanilla when asked to describe her ethnic identity, as this word clearly evoked the White homogeneity of her Midwestern upbringing.

Marion grew up as the oldest and parental child of four siblings in a large, extremely close African American extended family. She has a very intense relationship with her maternal grandmother, who is unambivalently nurturing. Her relationship with her mother, while intense, can be both loving and painfully critical. Her parents divorced after a brief marriage, and Marion has had no contact with her father since early childhood.

In the first session, the partners explained that they had been a couple for four years, although they lived in separate apartments. The discussion of moving in together precipitated a crisis in the relationship. In subsequent sessions, the therapist helped both members of the couple to express their conflicts and concerns about the move and the escalation of their involvement.

For JoAnn, the most painful issue is her perception of Marion's exclusion of her from her "other life." Marion sees, interacts with, or speaks by telephone to members of her extended family several times a week; JoAnn has been included in family gatherings on only two occasions. As JoAnn angrily describes this experience of being left out, Marion for the first time in their relationship begins to explain her fears about her family's response to disclosure of her sexual orientation.

The therapist explored Marion's assumption that some members knew she was a lesbian, despite the fact that she has never actually told anyone. The therapist also explored Marion's fears about disclosure. Marion's response, which is not unusual, was that she anticipated total rejection from her family. The therapist helped Marion construct a genogram and inquired about the responses of specific family members. During this process, Marion expressed her desire to stop leading a double life. The therapist then explored whether or not JoAnn was willing to support Marion in what might be a slow and difficult process of disclosure. JoAnn agreed. The couple decided it would be easier for JoAnn to enter the family system by attending holiday celebrations. Over a period of the next few months, Marion included JoAnn at Thanksgiving dinner, the exchange of presents on Christmas morning, and finally and most significantly, Mother's Day. The couple discussed each occasion with the therapist and the feelings that were aroused. In the final phases of therapy, the therapist helped Marion decide who would be the safest members of her family to come out to. It was important to include JoAnn in supporting Marion's process.

Marion identified her grandmother, whom she felt would love her no matter what, and her next oldest sister, whom she described as "pretty hip." The grandmother's response, "Honey, I've known for some time," was particularly gratifying. Disclosure was more difficult with her sister, Velma, who was very concerned about their mother's reaction and thus was less supportive than Marion had anticipated. In addition, Velma's concerns emphasized the interracial aspect of the relationship by characterizing JoAnn as "that White woman who made you this way." Marion was unprepared for this reaction, which created a crisis in the couple relationship.

Marion withdrew somewhat from JoAnn and became more silent in treatment sessions, while JoAnn became increasingly angry. The therapist apologized to both for not raising the possibility of this response sooner and explored the concept of ambivalence. The therapist also noted the importance of assisting the couple in identifying possible allies within the family before disclosing to family members who are less likely to be allies. The therapist had to work with the couple on giving up their fantasy of the happy ending outcome in which everyone is satisfied, and instead emphasized the importance of JoAnn and Marion nurturing their own relationship, particularly by developing gay-affirmative networks of friends and ultimately developing a family of choice. Marion expressed her preference that this process be extended to include lesbians of color, because their current circle of friends consisted primarily of White lesbians.

Over the next year, Marion continued the process of gradual disclosure to specific members of her extended family, and JoAnn continued to attend an increasing number of family gatherings. Finally, at Christmastime, Marion came out to her mother. As anticipated in the therapeutic role play, her mother was initially rejecting and used her fundamentalist religious beliefs to tell Marion that homosexuality in their religion was a sin. She chastised Marion for not fulfilling her role as a Black woman by having children. As Velma had done, Marion's mother disparaged the interracial aspect of Marion's relationship by referring to JoAnn as "that White woman." "She put you up to this," Marion's mother said. "She is coming between you and your family and your people."

Although Marion was hurt and angry during and after this discussion, the therapeutic rehearsal had precluded the emotional devastation that might otherwise have resulted. Initially, Marion's mother banned both JoAnn and Marion from family gatherings. The therapist offered to meet with Marion and her family during this period, but the family rejected the therapist's suggestion. Marion's mother relented somewhat and allowed Marion to come to her family's home alone. Many months later, Marion took the chance of bringing JoAnn again.

Approximately one year later, Marion and JoAnn moved in together, having strengthened their relationship through the therapeutic process. Marion remained engaged with her extended family; JoAnn participated on certain occasions. They had learned as a couple how to anticipate some of the responses they would receive and how to compromise on their fantasy of perfect acceptance. Marion was out to all of her significant family members, and JoAnn was included in important family gatherings, albeit grudgingly, and the issue of their lesbian relationship was never discussed openly in Marion's family, despite a great deal of therapeutic work and discussion of this issue.

It is not unusual for a member of a couple who is essentially cut off from her own family to be attracted to a partner who is intensely involved with her own family of origin. This can be problematic in the couple relationship in that it often conceals an unexpressed fantasy of being included in the partner's close involvement with her family. When this fantasy is not realized, feelings of exclusion and rejection can result. The exclusion by the partner's family reactivated preexisting feelings of loss, abandonment, envy, and jealousy in JoAnn.

When discussing disclosure issues, it is important that therapists explore the responses of specific individuals and not accept the expectation of blanket rejection or acceptance from everyone in the client's family. Often family members in large African American extended families are overwhelmed by the prospect of coming out to the whole family all at once.

It is important for the therapist to anticipate possible negative reactions to disclosure, especially in interracial lesbian relationships in which the other partner's race may become a more comfortable focus of the anger in the family. Therapists also should be aware that, despite their best efforts, the outcome may not be ideal for all parties. As this case illustrates, although the couple grew closer and Marion was out to all of her family members, her family still avoided open discussion of the lesbian relationship.

An educational strategy is important here. Both members of the couple need to be warned not to overreact to the initial response of family members, which may be negative. The person who is coming out is usually at a very different developmental stage of accepting lesbianism than is the person to whom she comes out. Her acceptance of her own lesbian orientation has taken time and did not take place overnight. An affirmative understanding or acceptance will not take place immediately for the family member either. Its absence at this juncture does not mean that it can never take place but that it may require time to develop. Furthermore, all of this may be compounded if the partner is White. The therapist must assist the couple in anticipating best and worst scenarios. At the end of each scenario they should be helped to problem-solve about different outcomes. Both members of the couple will require assistance in learning how to be supportive of each other during this difficult period.

AFRICAN AMERICAN LESBIAN COUPLES

Because of the extended nature of African American families, strong friendship ties between two African American adult women are very common. There is a culturally defined role within the African American community for the nonrelated adult girlfriend who has an often very intense nonsexual, spiritual, and emotionally connected relationship with an African American woman friend and her family. This is reflected in the greetings "girlfriend" or "sister," which acknowledge and confer kinshiplike status on a close adult female friend who is not blood-related but is experienced as intensely as "family." These women are often informally adopted by the family and are referred to by children and younger family members with terms such as *aunt, play aunt, play mama*, and *sister*. Sometimes there is a formal religious aspect to this relationship when this person is a godparent to a child in the family. Given the existence of this role in African American culture, the importance accorded to fictive kin, and because of the proclivity for African American families to deny the existence of lesbian relationships within their midst, it can be easy for African American families to avoid acknowledging the lesbian nature of a relationship between two adult women.

African American lesbian couples can sometimes collude in this denial by keeping their sexual orientation a secret. Others may not keep the information a secret but still never fully come out to their family members. Others couples may come out to their families without the families' dealing with the issue of the lesbian relationship and lifestyle but, rather, pretending that the lesbian relationship does not exist and accepting the lover in the culturally accepted role of "girlfriend" or "sister." Some African American families have evolved to the point that a lesbian couple is accepted and their relationship acknowledged by the extended family. It is important for clinicians to keep in mind the tremendous diversity of reactions. Different adaptations may exist among the various family members.

This diversity can also extend to the degree of involvement or participation that the lesbian couple has in the Black community and in the community's response as well. African American lesbian women often have children in their relationships. Because of the tradition of "multiple mothering" and grandmother involvement, it is likely that women in the extended family have been more involved in child rearing than their White counterparts (Boyd-Franklin, 1989; Greene, 1990b, 1994c).

Sometimes the question of who is raising the child or who is the ultimate authority in the child's life can be an issue or a problem in African American families. This is further complicated in the context of a lesbian family in which the generational boundaries are unclear. There are, for example, a number of dilemmas for the lesbian couple who are raising children within an extended family context (many of which are also common to heterosexual relationships). Therapists often view lesbian couples and families through the eyes of the couple. When children are involved, it is easy to feel as if one is treating only a "nuclear" lesbian family. In many African American couples, this assumption is often incorrect. The following case, involving two African American women who are raising a child with extended family involvement, illustrates the therapeutic importance of a multisystems, intergenerational view.

Case 2: African American Couple

Kadija, a twenty-nine-year-old African American lesbian women, and Aisha, her thirty-five-year-old African American lover of seven years, presented for couples and family therapy. They were raising Kadija's twelve-year-old son, Jamal, who was acting out at home and in school. They reported that they were intensely involved in each other's extended families. Within the last two years, they had been experiencing more conflict in their relationship. Both women dated the beginning of that conflict to their move from a separate apartment in Kadija's mother's house to a place of their own. Prior to the move, Kadija's mother had been Jamal's primary caretaker, as Kadija had been seventeen at the time of his birth.

Aisha, who had been a friend of the family before becoming Kadija's lover, was ambivalently accepted by both Kadija's mother and Jamal. While their lesbian relationship was never openly discussed, Kadija reported that she had come out to her mother and that her family knew about her involvement with Aisha. It was striking, however, that the couple reported that Jamal did not know the true nature of their relationship. As treatment progressed, it became apparent that prior to the move, Kadija's mother had served as a buffer between the couple and Jamal. Once the move occurred, they were unprepared for the full responsibility of raising a preadolescent child.

The therapist explored their denial of Jamal's knowledge of the true nature of their lesbian relationship. In a session alone with Jamal, the therapist discovered that Jamal was well aware of his mother's relationship with Aisha, and that he resented it—first, because he thought they were lying to him and second, because he was being teased by his friends. Finally, it became clear that Jamal had a very close relationship with his grandmother and had discussed his mother's lesbian relationship with her. Ironically, they both participated in the ruse of the denial. In addition, Jamal had been able to camouflage his mother's lesbian relationship from his peers as long as they all lived in his grandmother's house. The move had, in his words, "blown my cover."

The therapist facilitated a number of meetings in which she helped Jamal, Kadija, and Aisha talk more openly about the lesbian relationship. Both members of the couple were surprised at his anger and his embarrassment. As they began to talk about these issues, the tensions in the couple and the acting-out on Jamal's part began to ease. At the therapist's suggestion, Kadija's mother also was invited to participate in a few sessions in order to help all parties negotiate a new way of relating. It became apparent that Jamal and his grandmother often engaged in special alliances and that some of her directives to him were often different from those of Kadija and Aisha.

In the final phase of therapy, additional work was done with Kadija and Aisha to help them make separate time in their lives to nurture their relationship as a couple separate from other family members.

This case illustrates the complexity of extended family relationships within African American families. Therapists working with lesbian couples within this culture should be aware that although the couple may present for treatment, there are often many other family members involved. The collusion and denial evident in this family is not unusual in the African American community.

Therapy often serves the role of helping to open up discussion among family members on the taboo subject of the couple's lesbianism. Jamal's response as a preadolescent is also a common one. Boyd-Franklin (1989), in her book on Black families in therapy, discusses the impact of "toxic secrets." For Jamal, his mother's lesbianism is a toxic secret that is known on some level but denied and never fully discussed. Therapists working with African American lesbian couples with children must be sensitive to these issues and help the couple facilitate discussion with the young person involved. Timing is crucial, and therapists may have to work with family members individually at first in order to hear and understand their concerns before bringing the whole family together.

Finally, one of the most important aspects of this treatment is helping the couple to nurture each other and their relationship while these complex family dynamics are being explored in therapy. All of this work takes place in an environment that is antagonistic to African American lesbians and that contains little support for their relationships. Developing supportive social networks becomes another important aspect of this challenging work.

REFERENCES

Acosta, E. (1979, October 11). Affinity for Black heritage: Seeking lifestyle within a community. *Washington Blade*, pp. A-1, A-25.

Amaro, H. (1978). *Coming out: Hispanic lesbians, their families and communities.* Paper presented at the National Coalition of Hispanic Mental Health and Human Services Organization, Austin, TX.

Bass-Hass, R. (1968). The lesbian dyad: Basic issues and value systems. *Journals of Sex Research, 4,* 126.

Bell, A., & Weinberg, M. (1978). *Homosexualities: A study of human diversity among men and women.* New York: Simon & Schuster.

Boyd-Franklin, N. (1989). *Black families: A multisystems approach to family therapy.* New York: Guilford Press.

Brownworth, V. A. (1993, June). Linda Villarosa speaks out. *Deneuve, 3,* 16–19, 56.

Chan, C. S. (1989). Issues of identity development among Asian American lesbians and gay men. *Journal of Counseling and Development, 68,* 16–20.

Chan, C. S. (1992). Cultural considerations in counseling Asian American lesbians and gay men. In S. Dworkin & F. Gutierrez (Eds.), *Counseling gay men and lesbians: Journey to the end of the rainbow* (pp. 115–124). Alexandria, VA: American Association for Counseling and Development.

Christian, B. (1985). *Black feminist criticism: Perspectives on Black women writers.* New York: Pergamon.

Clarke, C. (1983). The failure to transform: Homophobia in the Black community. In B. Smith (Ed.), *Home girls: A Black feminist anthology* (pp. 197–208). New York: Kitchen Table-Women of Color Press.

Clarke, C. (1991). Saying the least said, telling the least told: The voices of Black lesbian writers. In M. Silvera (Ed.), *Piece of my heart: A lesbian of color anthology* (pp. 171–179). Toronto: Sister Vision Press.

Claybourne, J. (1978). Blacks and gay liberation. In K. Jay & A. Young (Eds.), *Lavender culture* (pp. 458–465). San Diego, CA: Harcourt Brace.

Clunis, M., & Green, G. D. (1988). *Lesbian couples.* Seattle, WA: Seal Press.

Collins, P. H. (1990). Homophobia and Black lesbians. In *Black feminist thought: Knowledge, consciousness, and the politics of empowerment* (pp. 192–196). Boston: Unwin Hyman.

Croom, G. (1993). *The effects of a consolidated versus nonconsolidated identity on expectations of African American lesbians selecting mates: A pilot study.* Unpublished doctoral dissertation, Illinois School of Professional Psychology, Chicago.

de Monteflores, C. (1986). Notes on the management of difference. In T. Stein & C. Cohen (Eds.), *Contemporary perspectives on psychotherapy with lesbians and gay men* (pp. 73–101). New York: Plenum.

Dew, M. A. (1985). The effects of attitudes on inferences of homosexuality and perceived physical attractiveness in women. *Sex Roles, 12,* 143–155.

Dyne, L. (1980, September). Is D.C. becoming the gay capital of America? *Washingtonian,* pp. 96–101, 133–141.

Espin, O. (1984). Cultural and historical influences on sexuality in Hispanic/Latina women: Implications for psychotherapy. In C. Vance (Ed.), *Pleasure and danger: Exploring female sexuality* (pp. 149–163). London: Routledge.

Falco, K. L. (1991). *Psychotherapy with lesbian clients.* New York: Brunner/

Mazel.

Garcia, N., Kennedy, C., Pearlman, S. F., & Perez, J. (1987). The impact of race and culture differences: Challenges to intimacy in lesbian relationships. In Boston Lesbian Psychologies Collective (Ed.), *Lesbian psychologies: Explorations and challenges* (pp. 142–160). Urbana: University of Illinois Press.

Garnets, L., & Kimmel, D. (1991). Lesbian and gay male dimensions in the psychological study of human diversity. In J. Goodchilds (Ed.), *Psychological perspectives on human diversity in America* (pp. 137–192). Washington, DC: American Psychological Association.

Glassgold, J. (1992). New directions in dynamic theories of lesbianism: From psychoanalysis to social constructionism. In J. Chrisler & D. Howard (Eds.), *New directions in feminist psychology: Practice, theory and research* (pp. 154–163). New York: Springer.

Gock, T. S. (1992). Asian-Pacific islander issues: Identity integration and pride. In B. Berzon (Ed.), *Positively gay* (pp. 247–252). Berkeley, CA: Celestial Arts.

Gomez, J. (1983). A cultural legacy denied and discovered: Black lesbians in fiction by women. In B. Smith (Ed.), *Home girls: A Black feminist anthology* (pp. 120–121). New York: Kitchen Table-Women of Color Press.

Gomez, J., & Smith, B. (1990). Taking the home out of homophobia: Black lesbian health. In E. C. White (Ed.), *The Black women's health book: Speaking for ourselves* pp. 198–213. Seattle, WA: Seal Press.

Greene, B. (1986). When the therapist is White and the patient Black: Considerations for psychotherapy in the feminist heterosexual and lesbian communities. *Women and Therapy, 5,* 41–66.

Greene, B. (1990a). African American lesbians: The role of family, culture and racism. *BG Magazine,* December, pp. 6, 26.

Greene, B. (1990b). Stereotypes of African American sexuality: A commentary. In S. Rathus, J. Nevid, & L. Fichner-Rathus (Eds.), *Human sexuality in a world of diversity* (p. 257). Boston: Allyn & Bacon.

Greene, B. (1990c). Sturdy bridges: The role of African American mothers in the socialization of African American children. *Women and Therapy, 10,* 205–225.

Greene, B. (1994a). Ethnic-minority lesbians and gay men: Mental health and treatment issues. *Journal of Consulting and Clinical Psychology, 62,* 243–251.

Greene, B. (1994b). Lesbian and gay sexual orientations: Implications for clinical training, practice and research. In B. Greene & G. Herek (Eds.), *Psychological perspectives on lesbian and gay issues: Vol. 1. Lesbian and gay psychology: Theory, research, and clinical applications* (pp. 1–24). Newbury Park, CA: Sage.

Greene, B. (1994c). Lesbian women of color: Triple jeopardy. In L. Comas-Diaz & B. Greene (Eds.), *Women of color: Integrating ethnic and gender identities in psychotherapy* (pp. 389–427). New York: Guilford Press.

Greene, B. (1995). Lesbian couples. In K. Jay (Ed.), *Dyke life: From growing up to growing old—a celebration of the lesbian experience* (pp. 97–106). New York: Basic Books.

Greene, B. (1996). African American lesbians: Triple jeopardy. In A. Brown-Collins (Ed.), *The psychology of African American women.* New York: Guilford Press.

Gutierrez, F., & Dworkin, S. (1992). Gay, lesbian, and African American: Managing the integration of identities. In S. Dworkin & F. Gutierrez (Eds.), *Counseling gay men and lesbians: Journey to the end of the rainbow* (pp. 141–156). Alexandria, VA: American Association for Counseling and Development.

hooks, b. (1981). *Ain't I a woman? Black women and feminism.* Boston: South

End Press.

Icard, L. (1986). Black gay men and conflicting social identities: Sexual orientation versus racial identity. *Journal of Social Work and Human Sexuality, 4*, 83–93.

Jeffries, I. (1992). Strange fruits at the purple manor: Looking back on "the life" in Harlem. *NYQ, 17*, 40–45.

Kanuha, V. (1990). Compounding the triple jeopardy: Battering in lesbian of color relationships. *Women and Therapy, 9,* 169–183.

Kite, M. (1994). When perceptions meet reality: Individual differences in reactions to lesbians and gay men. In B. Greene & G. Herek (Eds.), *Lesbian and gay psychology: Theory, research and clinical applications* (pp. 25–53). Newbury Park, CA: Sage.

Kite, M., & Deaux, K. (1987). Gender belief systems: Homosexuality and the implicit inversion theory. *Psychology of Women Quarterly, 11*, 83–96.

Loiacano, D. (1989). Gay identity issues among Black Americans: Racism, homophobia and the need for validation. *Journal of Counseling and Development, 68*, 21–25.

Mays, V., & Cochran, S. (1988). The Black women's relationship project: A national survey of Black lesbians. In M. Shernoff & W. Scott (Eds.), *The sourcebook on lesbian/gay health care* (2nd ed., pp. 54–62). Washington, DC: National Lesbian and Gay Health Foundation.

Mays, V., Cochran, S., & Rhue, S. (1993). The impact of perceived discrimination on the intimate relationships of Black lesbians. *Journal of Homosexuality, 25*, 1–14.

Morales, E. (1989). Ethnic minority families and minority gays and lesbians. *Marriage and Family Review, 14*, 217–239.

Moses, A. E., & Hawkins, R. (1982). *Counseling lesbian women and gay men: A life issues approach.* St. Louis, MO: Mosby–Year Book.

Newman, B. S. (1989). The relative importance of gender role attitudes toward lesbians. *Sex Roles, 21*, 451–465.

Omosupe, K. (1991). Black/lesbian/bulldagger. *Differences: A Journal of Feminist and Cultural Studies, 2*, 101–111.

Poussaint, A. (1990, September). An honest look at Black gays and lesbians. *Ebony*, pp. 124–131.

Roberts, J. R. (1981). *Black lesbians: An annotated bibliography.* Tallahassee, FL: Naiad Press.

Sears, V. L. (1987). *Cross-cultural ethnic relationships.* Unpublished manuscript.

Silvera, M. (1991). Man royals and sodomites: Some thoughts on the invisibility of Afro-Caribbean lesbians. In M. Silvera (Ed.), *Piece of my heart: A lesbian of color anthology* (pp. 14–26). Toronto: Sister Vision Press.

Smith, B. (1982). Toward a Black feminist criticism. In G. Hull, P. Scott, & B. Smith (Eds.), *All the women are White, all the Blacks are men, but some of us are brave* (pp. 157–175). Old Westbury, NY: Feminist Press.

Tafoya, T., & Rowell, R. (1988). Counseling Native American lesbians and gays. In M. Shernoff & W. A. Scott (Eds.), *The sourcebook on lesbian/gay health care* (pp. 63–67). Washington, DC: National Lesbian and Gay Health Foundation.

Taylor, A. T. (1983). Conceptions of masculinity and femininity as a basis for stereotypes of male and female homosexuals. *Journal of Homosexuality, 9*, 37–53.

Tremble, B., Schneider, M., & Appathurai, C. (1989). Growing up gay or lesbian in a multicultural context. *Journal of Homosexuality, 17*, 253–267.

Whitley, E. B., Jr. (1987). The relation of sex role orientation to heterosexual attitudes toward homosexuality. *Sex Roles, 17*, 103–113.

Wooden, W. S., Kawasaki, H., & Mayeda, R. (1983). Lifestyles and identity maintenance among gay Japanese-American males. *Alternative Lifestyles, 5,* 236–243.

Wyatt, G., Strayer, R., & Lobitz, W. C. (1976). Issues in the treatment of sexually dysfunctioning couples of African American descent. *Psychotherapy, 13,* 44–50.

23

SOCIAL CONSTRUCTION OF MARY BETH WHITEHEAD

Michelle Harrison

Although the testimony of mental health experts in custody cases is supposed to be scientific and objective, the experts' testimony in the Mary Beth Whitehead case was imbued with prevailing middle-class biases about good mothers and good parenting. Close review of the experts' reports fails to substantiate many of their assessments and recommendations and demonstrates instead a consistent bias in favor of the Sterns and against Mary Beth Whitehead.

Psychiatric expertise is often relied upon by the courts in evaluating the fitness or relative fitness of parents. Usually psychological reports and testimony are part of sealed court proceedings and thus only those directly involved learn their content and the basis for custody decisions. The case *In the Matter of Baby "M"* (1987), because of its public nature, has given us a unique opportunity to see the powerful role played by mental health professionals and how their perceptions created both the public and judicial characterizations of all the principals, but especially of Mary Beth Whitehead.

The premise underlying the use of mental health experts is that their testimony is both scientific and objective. However, mental health beliefs exist within the context of the culture at large. Prevalent beliefs about mental health reflect class (Gurslin et al. 1959, 1959–1960) and gender (Chesler 1972; Corea 1977) biases, as well as what constitutes pathological behavior (Broverman et al. 1970; Rosenhan 1973). The experts' testimony in the Mary Beth Whitehead case was imbued with prevailing middle-class beliefs about good mothers and good parenting.

The experts rendered their opinions regarding the future of Baby "M" (Sara Elizabeth Whitehead was the name on the birth certificate filed by her mother; the child's name was changed to Melissa Stern after Judge Sorkow's decision) based on reports of testing, interviews, and observations of the Whiteheads, Sterns, and Baby "M" (she will be referred to here as Sara Melissa, consistent with a coin-toss compromise by the experts). Close review of the content of those reports fails to substantiate many of the experts' assessments and recommendations and demonstrates instead that the Whiteheads' and Sterns' behavior was interpreted to fit an overall assessment of personality, character, and motivation that was biased in favor of the Sterns from the start.

Three experts, David Brodzinski, Ph.D., Marshall Schechter, M.D., and Judith Brown Greif, D.S.W., were chosen by Lorraine Abraham, Esq., the guardian *ad litem* appointed by the judge to represent the best interests of the child. On December 13, prior to any of the interviews, the three experts met with Ms. Abraham for "approximately 8 hours, that day as well as into the next day of December 14, 1986," and again at the conclusion of their observations (Schechter 1987, p. 2). Those three experts also conducted much of the interview and observation time together. Their meeting is relevant because of the similarity of their conclusions and recommendations and because of the consistent bias against Mary Beth Whitehead that pervaded their reports. One would hate to believe that the fate of Sara Melissa was sealed at the December 13 and 14 meeting of the experts with Ms. Abraham, but it is difficult not to do so. It was as if—once prejudged—Mary Beth Whitehead could do no right.

In addition to these three experts, Allwyn Levine, M.D., examined the Whiteheads and Sterns for the Sterns, and Harold Koplewicz, M.D., did so for the Whiteheads. Lee Salk, Ph.D., was asked by the Sterns' attorney to render an opinion, which he did solely on the basis of the reports of the other experts. Presumably the absence of any human contact with the people involved made it easier for him to describe Mary Beth Whitehead as a "surrogate uterus and not a surrogate mother" (Salk 1987, p. 2).

MOTIVATIONS FOR SURROGACY

Elizabeth Stern, M.D., Ph.D., and William Stern, Ph.D., were married in 1974 but decided to postpone having children because of Betsy Stern's studies and "financial considerations" (Levine 1987, p. E.S. 5). In 1979, without ever consulting a neurologist (her first consultation was in October 1986) to confirm or allay her fears, Betsy Stern sought counseling to deal with *having* multiple sclerosis. Hearing about a colleague's wife with multiple sclerosis who became temporarily paralyzed after a pregnancy, she became frightened of becoming pregnant. Betsy Stern's self-diagnosis of multiple sclerosis and her decision not to become pregnant went unquestioned by the experts. Without commenting on the degree of her fear or the appropriateness of her reaction, the experts praised her for having sought counseling.

The Sterns, having ruled out pregnancy as a means of having children, next considered adoption. They sought no agency help or advice but decided that their two different religions (he is Jewish, she Methodist) and their ages (late 30s) precluded that possibility. Bill Stern "stated that he was worried about the fear of AIDS in an adopted child and did not want a foreign child, such as a Korean, because the child would be different and therefore, he believed, would have more psychological difficulty" (Koplewicz 1987, p. 4). Regarding private adoption, Betsy Stern "had concerns about that process, sensing that they would in some way need to convince a woman to relinquish her baby" (Greif 1987, p. 11). At no time did the experts raise questions or reservations about two well-educated people with appropriate specialties (Betsy Stern is a pediatrician with a Ph.D. in human genetics; Bill Stern ran a genetics laboratory) who worried about AIDS in adopted children. No one seemed concerned that they rejected having a child who looked different.

Bill Stern is the last known surviving member of his family. Members of his extended family died in the Holocaust, and he has no siblings. Bill Stern "was the focus of his parents' lives" (Levine 1987, p. W.S. 3). His father died when he was twelve, his mother in December 1983. Bill Stern had an "ambivalent relationship with his mother through his formative years" (Brodzinski 1987, p. 12). Describing his going off to graduate school, Dr. Levine wrote: "Leaving his mother was extremely traumatic because of the sense that she had of being abandoned and he felt guilty" (Levine 1987, p. W.S. 7). It was in early 1984, within months of his mother's death, that Bill Stern saw an advertisement soliciting surrogate mothers, which suggested a way to have a genetic child. "For Mr. Stern the goal of maintaining the genetic family line was a chance to ward off existential loneliness" (Brodzinski 1987, p. 13). Another expert said, "Mr. Stern notes that there is a 'conventional streak' in him: had it been easier to adopt he would have chosen that route. He was drawn to the notion of surrogate parenting because it would enable him to have a biological link to another person, something he had been lacking since the death of his mother" (Greif 1987, p. 7).

Betsy Stern was drawn to mother surrogacy because it was "legal and voluntary" (Greif 1987, p. 11). Dr. Brodzinski interpreted her attitude as demonstrating "empathic capacity" (Greif 1987, p. 16). That the Sterns got themselves exactly what they both had stated they did not want, namely, for Bill Stern, a child who was "different," and for Betsy Stern, a child whose mother did not want to relinquish her, was unmentioned by the experts.

Regarding Mary Beth Whitehead's motivations for mother surrogacy, Dr. Schechter (1987, p. 30) wrote that she was interested in "being a surrogate parent to enhance a feeling of being novel and unique." He then used his interpretation of her motivation as the basis for concluding that she exhibited certain features of the Histrionic Personality Disorder portion of Mixed Personality Disorder. When Mary Beth Whitehead stated that she wanted to "give the gift of life," Dr. Brodzinski says her interest in being a surrogate mother "reflects a deep-seated narcissistic need" (1987, p. 21). Mary Beth Whitehead's naïveté as to what she was getting herself into by being a surrogate was interpreted as part of her impulsivity and self-damaging qualities, adding the Borderline Personality Disorder aspect to Dr. Schechter's final diagnosis of Mixed Personality Disorder (Schechter 1987, p. 27).

In contrast, the Stern's equally unresearched entry into surrogacy was accepted as normal behavior. With two Ph.D.s and an M.D. between them, they picked out the mother of their child from a picture book, an incomplete application, and a dinner with the Whiteheads at a restaurant. Like Dr. Salk, they may have seen the mother of their child as a "surrogate uterus," a carrier for Mr. Stern's genes, ignoring the fact that the child would carry Mary Beth Whitehead's genes as well.

One wonders what will happen if Sara Melissa is two or three or ten and acts or looks just like Mary Beth. Will the child forever have to deny behaviors that seem "like her mother's"? Will the Sterns forever be on the lookout for behaviors that are "like her mother's"? Will they see Mary Beth in Sara Melissa's strength, tenacity, passion? Alternatively, what will be the impact of Sara Melissa's being the last of her father's heritage? To what lengths will she have to go to perpetuate her father's genes and to deny her mother's? Who will she consider the grandmother to her own children, Betsy Stern or Mary Beth Whitehead? Dr. Brodzinski attempted to settle the heritage question by stating, "Mr. Stern will offer, by his presence alone, confirmation of her genealogical connections" (p. 30). He forgets that not by sperm alone are we created and, certainly, not by sperm alone do baby girls become women.

EVALUATIONS OF THE WHITEHEADS AND THE STERNS

All four adults (the Sterns, Mary Beth Whitehead and her husband, Richard) demonstrated impairment in tests of their intelligence as measured by Dr. Brodzinski. For Mr. Stern: "on the Picture Arrangement task, measuring sensitivity to part-whole relations, social judgment, and planning ability, he performed in the Borderline to Low Average range." Brodzinski added a comment that this test is highly sensitive to anxiety (1987, p. 11). Betsy Stern scored in the Low Average range (Brodzinski 1987, p. 15). Mary Beth Whitehead scored in the Average range (Brodzinski 1987, p. 20), as did Richard Whitehead (Brodzinski 1987, p. 24). If anxiety affects this test's results, it did so selectively. The experts did not consider that the Sterns might indeed have impairment of "part-whole relations, social judgment, or planning ability." When Mary Beth Whitehead did poorly on a test, it was considered a sign of psychopathology; when the Sterns did poorly it was considered either irrelevant or a sign of anxiety. All four adults were no doubt anxious, but the test results were not equivalent, showing impairment in social judgement and planning only for the Sterns.

Betsy Stern scored high on "a scale that measures a person's tendency to 'fake good'—that is, the tendency to respond to a question in a way that presents a picture of oneself as a socially desirable individual," which led Dr. Brodzinski to question the veracity of her self-reports. However, he concluded that she is "generally sincere and honest insofar as she understands and interprets the 'facts' of this case" (Brodzinski 1987, p. 15). Mary Beth Whitehead, however, impressed him as "*frequently* [his emphasis] covering up or selectively remembering past events" (Brodzinski 1987, p. 19). Mary Beth is "unwilling to expose herself" (Brodzinski 1987, p. 20), while "Mr. Stern states that he is very private about his religion and doesn't like to discuss it" (Koplewicz 1987, p. 4).

Bill Stern and Mary Beth Whitehead both showed a similar difficulty in distancing themselves from painful stimuli and from their current crisis (Brodzinski 1987, pp. 12, 20). Clearly, they were both in pain. Bill Stern was said to show a "dominance of reason over emotions. Indeed, there are strong tendencies in this gentleman toward a reserved or detached presentation of self—particularly in interpersonal situations. This pattern is defensive in nature and serves, in part, to bind his social anxiety." He was described as having difficulty handling emotions, protecting himself through defenses such as "denial, distancing, intellectualization, and rationalization" (Brodzinski 1987, p. 12). Dr. Brodzinski worried about whether Bill Stern would "smother" Sara Melissa—"that is, . . . foster an over-dependent and enmeshed relationship between Sara Melissa and himself. Although this is a possibility in a person whose (sic) has the character structure described above, my impression is that it is unlikely in the present case" (Brodzinski 1987, p. 13).

The experts were highly approving of the Sterns' utilization of and belief in mental health counseling. Using professionals was considered by the professionals in this case a universally successful answer to emotions, parenting questions, issues of identity, and so on. The experts minimized the Sterns' problems, because they used pastoral counseling and intended to seek such help for Sara Melissa. The Whiteheads had not utilized such services. Mary Beth did not make an assumption that her child would need professional help, although she expressed a willingness to seek it in the future if she or Sara Melissa needed it (Schechter 1987, pp. 11, 15). One expert said of her, "She classifies herself as a survivor and said that she reaches into herself and uses her own resources" (Levine 1987, p. 17). To these professionals, handling problems with the help of family and friends or alone, rather than utilizing mental health services, was evidence of mental illness.

Mary Beth Whitehead did reflect on her past actions, including her flight with her baby, and wondered aloud to the experts whether she had made the right decisions (Schechter 1987, p. 11). She expressed shame about her threats against Bill Stern (Levine 1987, p. M.B.W. 8). Yet the experts still condemned her for "an unwillingness on her part to see any character flaws in herself" and had "no expectation that she would avail herself of professional mental health counseling" (Levine 1987, p. M.B.W. 20). If she had accepted the authority of mental health professionals and had exhibited proper demeanor and respect to them, they might have been less biased against her in their recommendations.

Mary Beth Whitehead angered the experts, and their reactions were couched in diagnostic jargon. One said, "what initially struck me was her dogmatic and almost omnipotent sense of righteousness" (Levine 1987, p. M.B.W. 1). In an aside, another said, "Mrs. Whitehead often appears to be empathic, but usually is preoccupied with her own needs" (Brodzinski 1987, p. 21). Much of the experts' reactions seemed to come from Mary Beth Whitehead's sense of certainty as a mother, especially in regard to Sara Melissa: "From her perspective, the fact that she is the biological mother is sufficient in itself for determining the question of who gets custody of Sara Melissa" (Brodzinski 1987, p. 18). Many of her statements could be made by almost any mother of an infant, and their absence would ordinarily be seen as a deficiency of attachment, committment, and bonding.

The symbiosis that is a normal and necessary part of early mother-infant relationships may sound pathological out of context (Chodorow 1978). Like many new mothers, Mary Beth Whitehead said, "I know what every cry means; I know what she wants" (Levine 1987, p. M.B.W.2); "I need my baby and *my baby needs me*" (Brodzinski 1987, p. 22); "She wants me" (Brodzinski 1987, p. 23). About Mary Beth's reactions, Brodzinski reported, "She is experiencing the loss as a ripping apart of herself" (1987, p. 22). "She is now always thinking about her baby and wonders if she, Baby M, knows that her mother wants her and prays that she is not crying for her" (Schechter 1987, p. 10). The Sterns picked up three-day-old Sara Melissa at the Whitehead home on March 30, 1986. This is a description of what followed:

> The next day [Mary Beth Whitehead] asked to visit Sara Melissa and what she saw convinced her that the baby should be with her, namely that the cradle was in the baby's own room, not in the Stern's bedroom: 'She looked so lonely and helpless ... wrapped up in a blanket like a cocoon. I picked her up and never let her out of my arms; she was my child, it was what was right for her, she never cried.' (Greif 1987, p. 15)

The Sterns sought custody of Sara Melissa with termination of Mary Beth Whitehead's parental rights. They could see no value in the baby's having any contact with her mother. Their inflexibility in this matter was commented upon by the experts but did not seem to cause them concern: "Mr. Stern does not feel it would be in Sara Melissa's best interest to maintain ongoing contact with the non-custodial parent—whoever that might be" (Greif 1987, p. 9); "Dr. Stern does not favor the idea of access between Sara Melissa and her non-custodial parent, regardless of who is awarded custody" (Greif 1987, p. 12). Betsy Stern indicated to Dr. Koplewicz that "she will not entertain any participation in the child's life if Mary Beth Whitehead also participates" (Koplewicz 1987, p. 8). "Mr. Stern has indicated that should he not get custody, he believes that it is in Sara Melissa's best interests for her not to have contact with him ... instead of focusing on their own pain, he had projected it onto his daughter.... Mr. Stern's position neglects the sense of loss that children in Sara Melissa's situation often feel" (Brodzinski 1987, p. 14).

Sentences later, we learn that the Sterns would reconsider their position "should the professionals indicate that it is in Sara Melissa's best interests." It is easy to see how the professionals examining this couple found them so easy to recommend as custodial parents. They are true believers in the system in which the examiners believe. Since, by her manner, Mary Beth Whitehead did not demonstrate humility before them, even her willingness to listen was not heard. Nowhere in the reports was there a statement of her refusal to allow the Sterns visitation should she be granted custody. One expert said, "Mrs. Whitehead has stated that if she were given custody of the baby, she would encourage the Sterns to have visitation and participate in the major decisions of the baby's life" (Koplewicz 1987, p. 6). But her flexibility and agreement with the experts in this matter had no weight in their eyes.

EVALUATIONS OF PARENTING

The experts most clearly exposed their feelings about these two families when they wrote about the interaction of the Whiteheads (especially Mary Beth) with Sara Melissa and then of the Sterns with the baby. Sara was brought to the Whitehead home for four hours, after not having enjoyed a relationship with her older siblings, Tuesday or Ryan, or with Richard Whitehead since she was four months old. Her contact with her mother had consisted of two-hour visits twice weekly in a juvenile detention home. In this visit in front of the experts, Mary Beth Whitehead was said to have "failed pattycake" by saying "Hooray!" to the baby instead of "pattycake" (Schechter 1987, p. 13). Betsy Stern had responded with "pattycake" (p. 19). Richard Whitehead also gave the supposedly correct response. "Mr. Whitehead picked up the child, putting her into a flying position and when in this position she clapped her hands, he said, pattycake" (p. 13). Mr. Stern did not play pattycake at all.

In the courtroom, Dr. Schecter described, in now well-publicized reports, that the correct response was "pattycake," not "hooray," since "pattycake" reinforces the child's behavior. Laughter would be an appropriate response to these reports were it not for the seriousness of the proceedings and the weight given to the experts' testimony.

There were other biased assessments of the Whiteheads' and Sterns' parenting behaviors. When the baby crawled after Mr. Stern, it was indicative of her attachment to him (Brodzinski 1987, p. 18; Schechter 1987, p. 20). Not so for her mother. "When Mrs. Whitehead left the baby crawled toward where Mrs. Whitehead was in the kitchen. She smiled when she saw Mrs. Whitehead" (Schechter 1987, p. 12). The interpretation was that the baby showed "awareness" but "demonstrate[d] no anticipatory behaviors" toward Mrs. Whitehead (p. 12). Mrs. Whitehead was said to misinterpret the baby's signals: "Mrs. Whitehead also questioned if the baby were getting tired, as she was teething on a comb with no evidence of fatigue whatsoever" (p. 12). Next, "Mrs. Whitehead said that she always fell asleep in her arms" (p. 13). Then, without a comment that the baby had indeed been tired, it is noted that Mrs. Whitehead cautioned Ryan, her son, not to waken the baby by speaking too loudly. Dr. Schechter was critical of her because he did not think Ryan was being too loud (p. 14). Had the experts been biased toward Mrs. Whitehead, we might have read instead, "Here is a mother so perceptive that even though no one else in the room could tell the baby was tired, she knew. And she only sees her four hours a week. What a wonderful mother!"

Interpretation of Mary Beth Whitehead's Personality

The mental health experts in this case attempted to turn life experience and human coping mechanisms into pathology. Drs. Brodzinski and Schechter were especially upset at their perception that Mary Beth Whitehead is "the dominant one in her marriage" (Schechter 1987, p. 30) and the "controlling parent" (Brodzinski 1987, p. 26). For these assumed traits, the experts gave her a label of "Borderline Personality Trait." That the Sterns delayed having children because of Betsy Stern's medical training and her fears about multiple sclerosis received no comment. The Sterns attended holiday church services, although Mr. Stern "said that he never shared with his wife (who is Methodist) the fact that he was somewhat uncomfortable in being at non-Jewish religious services" (Levine 1987, p. W.S. 9), but Betsy Stern was not criticized for dominance.

The mental health experts saw Mrs. Whitehead as narcissistic because she "makes an assumption that because she is the mother that the child, Baby M, belongs to her" (Schechter 1987, p. 28). Further evidence of her narcissism was the cost of the suit that may lead to foreclosure of her house and long-term indebtedness for her family (Schechter 1987, p. 29).

Mary Beth Whitehead was said to engage in "magical thinking," which Dr. Schechter described as characteristic of "Schizotypal Personality Disorder." Magical thinking occurred, it was felt, in "the concept that if she became pregnant God would give her (infertile) sister a child" (Schechter 1987, p. 31). There is a thin but essential line that must be drawn between religious and magical thinking. Theologians are often called upon to separate the two and at times do so only with great difficulty. Judeo-Christian religion is replete with references to good works resulting in rewards won both on earth and in heaven. Mary Beth

Whitehead was raised within a religious tradition that sanctifies altruism and self-sacrifice.

Few human beings fail to look for meaning in the face of pain and loss. For Mary Beth Whitehead to do so was "omnipotence and omniscience" (Levine 1987, p. 15), especially given her statement that "she knows that she has been chosen by God to show people not to do surrogate mothering" (Levine 1987, p. 16). Mary Beth Whitehead is not the first or the only person to try to find meaning for others in her own personal tragedy.

CONCLUSION

There is a consistency to Mary Beth Whitehead's life. The experts may have described her as having an "emotional overinvestment" (Brodzinski 1987, p. 23) with her children, of having a "grandiose sense of giving" (Brodzinski 1987, p. 21) in becoming a surrogate, of believing that others may in some way gain from her suffering, but one has the sense that when she holds her child in her arms she is doing so not out of "best interests," not because "professionals" have told her to do so, but rather because "I need my baby and *my baby needs me*" (Brodzinski 1987, p. 22).

The experts did not help create clarity or provide guidance in this difficult case. They rendered conclusions based on impressions that were often not substantiated by their own reports. They allowed complex emotions and judgements to be fit into fixed, polarized, adversarial positions, and as a result, we do not know who Mary Beth Whitehead is, or who the others are.

The experts' omissions were glaring. They pretended that Sara Melissa will always be an infant, that she will not know the pain that surrounded her early life, that she will not learn of the pain brought to her mother and her siblings, or to her father and his wife. There are no pretty stories to tell this child, and all the professional counseling in the world will not undo what has been done and what will probably still be done. To pretend she is only half-rooted biologically will not help her into adulthood, much less through adolescence.

The experts have forgotten that Sara Melissa will grow and that she will eventually search for the answers to the questions they failed to ask. She will want to know why the system created to protect her best interests participated in an adversarial stance that could only allow her to have her mother or her father. She will ask why the court rewrote her birth certificate, making invisible half her heritage. She will want to know why her parents could not share their love, and why they could not allow her to share hers with both of them. She will eventually ask, why was this done to me? The answer will be steeped in class and gender bias and the inequities of power between fathers and mothers, and the social, professional, and legal systems that support that differential. She cannot help but see herself as ownable property subject to a contract dispute.

Beyond *In the Matter of Baby "M"*, the commodification of infants to be, the breeding of human beings for transfer of ownership, creates a new class of people whose lineage and ownership most clearly reflect our society's worst biases in regard to class, race, and gender.

REFERENCES

Brodzinski, D. 1987. *In the Matter of Baby "M"*, Doc. No. FM-25314-86E (Chan. Div./Fam. Pt., Bergen Co. Supr. Ct. NJ).

Broverman, I. K., D. M. Broverman, F. E. Clarkson, P. S. Rosenkrantz, and S. R. Vogel. 1970. "Sex-Role Stereotypes and Clinical Judgement of Mental Health." *Journal of Consulting and Clinical Psychology* 34:1–7.

Chesler, P. 1972. *Women and Madness*. New York: Doubleday.

Chodorow, N. 1978. *The Reproduction of Mothering*. Berkeley, CA: University of California Press.

Corea, G. 1977. *The Hidden Malpractice*. New York: Harper.

Grief, J. B. 1987. *In the Matter of Baby "M"*, Doc. No. FM-25314-86E (Chan. Div./Fam. Pt., Bergen Co. Supr. Ct. NJ).

Gurslin, O., R. Hunt, and J. Roach. 1959. "Social Class, Mental Hygiene and Psychiatric Practice." *Social Service Review* 33:237–244.

Gurslin, O., R. Hunt, and J. Roach. 1959–1960. "Social Class and the Mental Health Movement." *Social Problems* 7:210–218.

In the Matter of Baby "M". 1987. Doc. No. FM-25314-86E (Chan. Div./Fam. Pt., Bergen Co. Supr. Ct. NJ).

Koplewicz, H. S. 1987. *In the Matter of Baby "M"*, Doc. No. FM-25314-86E (Chan. Div./Fam. Pt., Bergen Co. Supr. Ct. NJ).

Levine, A. J. 1987. *In the Matter of Baby "M"*, Doc. No. FM-25314-86E (Chan. Div./Fam. Pt., Bergen Co. Supr. Ct. NJ).

Rosenhan, D. L. 1973. "On Being Sane in Insane Places." *Science* 179:250–257.

Salk, L. 1987. *In the Matter of Baby "M"*, Doc. No. FM-25314-86E (Chan. Div./Fam. Pt., Bergen Co. Supr. Ct. NJ).

Schechter, M. D. 1987. *In the Matter of Baby "M"*, Doc. No. FM-25314-86E (Chan. Div./Fam. Pt., Bergen Co. Supr. Ct. NJ).

24

COMMENT ON HARRISON: THE COMMODIFICATION OF MOTHERHOOD

Barbara Katz Rothman

The question is not whether or not Mary Beth Whitehead should be named "mother of the year." Mary Beth Whitehead is mother of the year. She has crystallized the issue of "surrogate mothering" for us, and "surrogacy" crystallized the issue of motherhood.

Like Michelle Harrison, I too am tempted to jump to the defense of Mary Beth Whitehead. I find myself doing it, over and over again, often by comparing myself to her. I'm good on pots and pans and pandas, but I don't even know the rules of pattycake. There's a Yiddish game we played—*sheyna sheyna fissella*, baby needs new *schichelah*, a *gezundt* in the baby's *bechelah.* Something about pretty feet, new shoes, and then I'm not too sure. So should my kids be taken away? I've defied authorities in child-rearing issues; I practically make a habit of it on medical issues. So should my children be taken away?

And so we find ourselves pleading the alternatives. Mary Beth Whitehead is not a bad mother. Or maybe we're all bad mothers. And the Sterns are no bargain either. Maybe there just aren't any good parents, no good mothers to be had. Nobody I know seems to be thrilled with the mothering they got. My mother once threw away a teddy bear of mine, though she denies it, swears I made that one up. Well, who're you going to believe? Certainly not a mother, not these days.

Which brings me to my real point. It's not just Mary Beth Whitehead who's in trouble, and it's not just surrogacy that's the issue. The problem is a deeper, more fundamental one. We are in the process of redefining motherhood, of changing the meaning of that basic, essential relationship. The "we" is the United States, probably the entire Western world, maybe the whole planet soon enough. As feminists, we are caught in a tricky spot facing these new definitions of motherhood. The old ones were so bad, we fought them so long, and now the new ones are worse— and we have not yet claimed a language of our own for motherhood, a woman-centered way of understanding motherhood.

The old definitions saw motherhood as a status. Women were mothers. Mothering was not something women *did*, it was something women *were.* Motherhood was in fact a master status, and everything women did was seen in terms of our motherhood, or our potential for motherhood. Motherhood and its demands, babies and children and their demands, defined women. We had to be what they needed.

That is the language Mary Beth Whitehead still speaks—my baby needs me, my baby is my life. We need to be together, we are one, mother and child.

The new language sees mothering as an activity, as a service, as work—and babies as a product produced by the labor of mothering. Babies, at least some babies, healthy white babies, are very precious products. Women, rather like South African diamond miners, are the cheap, expendable, not-too-trustworthy labor necessary to produce the precious product. That is the language of the contract Mary Beth Whitehead signed: a contract for services, payment on delivery. We are looking at the commodification of fetuses and of babies, and the proletarianization of motherhood.

Surrogacy is only the tip of the proverbial iceberg, only the most dramatic and obvious form of it. The real dangers lie deeper, threaten more women than just those signing surrogacy contracts.

In ordinary, home-grown pregnancies, we've seen the introduction of a variety of prenatal diagnostic tests, designed to find defective fetuses so that they can be aborted. Women are asked to go halfway through pregnancies, responsibly tending to the needs of the fetus, but always ready to terminate the pregnancy if the product is not acceptable. Rosalyn Weinman Schram has compared this kind of genetic counseling and prenatal testing to a form of quality control on the products of conception; the wrongful life suits, when a "defective" baby is born, are then a form of product liability litigation (Rothman 1986). The human costs, the woman's costs, the enormous maternal grief following the termination of such a pregnancy, are entirely discounted in the medical and social calculus. This tearing away of a part of a woman's body and soul, this abortion of a wanted and loved baby, is called "preventive" and "therapeutic" abortion.

There are other ways in which we see the increasing proletarianization of motherhood, and pregnant women as workers on a reproductive assembly line. It's there in the antismoking, antidrinking, "behave yourself" campaigns aimed at pregnant women. What are the causes of prematurity, fetal defects, damaged newborns? Bad mothers, of course. One New York City subway ad series shows two newborn footprints, one from a full-term and one from a premature infant. The ad reads, "Guess which baby's mother smoked while pregnant?" "Guess which baby's mother drank while pregnant?" "Guess which baby's mother didn't get prenatal care?" I look in vain for the ad that says, "Guess which baby's mother tried to get by on AFDC?" "Guess which baby's mother had to live in a welfare hotel?" "Guess which baby's mother was beaten by her husband?"

Women are laborers producing the precious products, but like most unskilled, poorly paid, disrespected workers, those who depend on their work do not trust them, want to monitor them, control them, keep them in line. A San Diego woman was arrested for the death of her baby. She misbehaved. Doctors and lawyers and ethicists think up "fetal abuse" statutes.

Once we focus on the precious fetus, once we create an image of fetuses as precious products, abandoned—not cradled, *abandoned*—in the womb, it is but a small step to hiring the workers and selling the fetuses. And so Baby M was created. A baby was ordered from a worker, but the worker got uppity and refused to turn over the product. A proletarian who won't stay alienated, who claims the product of her labor for herself, Mary Beth Whitehead says it's her baby. Stern claims it is his: his capital investment of sperm, his signed contract. And Baby M is a quality product, no doubt about that. So with the new perspective, the child as a product, as a commodity, we turn to those with competing claims and decide in court who has rights of ownership over the product—the worker or the employer?

The old and the new language of motherhood were used against Whitehead. When she claimed her intimate connection to the child, claimed that it is a part of her, it grew out of her flesh, in her body, claimed that this child is connected to her as deeply as one human being can ever be connected to another, then she was accused of biological determinism. Hasn't she seen *Kramer vs. Kramer*? Doesn't she know the revolution happened? Claiming the child needs her, the biological mother, made her a biological determinist, arguing against the new-found glories of father-love. (Never mind that it's Stern's wife who quits work to raise the baby—just remember all of those photos of him carrying the baby to the car from the courthouse.)

But if Whitehead had claimed, not that the child needs her, but that she needs the child, then she is a selfish mother. Real mothers, good old-fashioned mothers, loving devoted mothers, would never put their own needs above that of the child. If someone else can provide better for the child than she can, a truly unselfish mother would joyfully give up the child, wouldn't she?

Is there no language we can use to express the particular, unique relationship that is pregnancy? Has feminism nothing to offer Mary Beth Whitehead here? So often in contemporary American feminism we have found ourselves defending women's right to be like men, to enter into men's worlds, to work at men's jobs for men's pay. But what of our rights to be women? How have we addressed, or failed to address, that particular quandary? It's a different aspect of the distinction between "equal pay for equal work" and the much more troubling, much more revolutionary idea of "comparable worth." A woman being a lawyer is exactly the same as a man being a lawyer. A woman cop is just the same as a man cop. And a pregnant woman is just the same as.... Well, as, uh.... It's like disability, right? Or like serving in the army?

Pregnancy is just exactly like pregnancy.

There is nothing else quite like it. That statement is not glorification or mystification. It is a statement of fact. Having a baby grow in your belly is not like anything else that one can do. It is unique. If we're going to try to call it work, then we know it is women's work, and it's bound to be cheap labor.

Strangely enough, both patriarchal and a large segment of feminist thinking have come to essentially the same conclusion about what to do with the problem of the uniqueness of pregnancy: devalue it, discount it so deeply that its uniqueness doesn't matter. In strongly patriarchal frameworks the genetic tie for men is the only acknowledged parental tie—daddy plants a seed in mommy; women grow men's children; Mrs. John Smith bears John Smith, Jr. In a modified patriarchy, or in liberal feminism, we recognize the "paternity" rights of women; women too are acknowledged to have seeds. We also recognize the parenting rights of men; men, too, can mother. Children are "half hers, half his." Recognizing the paternity claims of women, their genetic tie, is like an "equal pay" argument. It is far less threatening to patriarchal values than is claiming the significance of the nurturing relationship that is pregnancy. It is less threatening to say children are equally the products of male and of female seed, and that equal bonding takes place at birth. Think how much more revolutionary it would be to claim "sweat equity": at birth, children belong to their mothers because mothers have put the work in; that they choose to share their children with others in their lives (including but not exclusively the father) is their gift to their loved ones.

In the "Baby M" case the judge recognized paternity claims, both Whitehead's and Stern's "paternity" claims. He said he would base his decision on the best interests of the child, but considered only two people as possible parents: the two genetic parents. He did not of course search the world for the best possible parents to the child. Two people had genetic, "paternity" claims on this child, and those were the only claims he recognized. The only question he would entertain in a custody decision was which of these two genetic parents would make the better parent socially. Any claim Mary Beth Whitehead tried to make about her superior rights to the child, her greater investment in the child, her willingness to share the child with the genetic father and his wife, were shot down as "irrelevant." As ultimately Mary Beth Whitehead was shot down as irrelevant. As ultimately motherhood itself is being shot down—just as the cheap labor unskilled women do.

REFERENCE

Rothman, Barbara Katz. 1986. *The Tentative Pregnancy: Prenatal Diagnosis and the Future of Motherhood.* New York: Viking-Penguin.

25

Resolving "Other" Status:
Identity Development of Biracial Individuals

Maria P. P. Root

Half-breed, mulatto, mixed, eurasian, mestizo, amerasian. These are the
"others," biracial individuals, who do not have a clear racial reference
group (Henriques, 1975; Moritsugu, Foerster, & Morishima, 1978) and
who have had little control over how they are viewed by society.
Because of their ambiguous ethnic identity and society's refusal to view
the races as equal, mixed race people begin life as *marginal people.*
Freire (1970) observes that *marginality is not a matter of choice, but
rather a result of oppression of dominant over subordinate groups.*

The challenge for a nonoppressive theory and therapy, as feminist perspectives attempt, is twofold. First, racism must be recognized and challenged within the therapist's and theorist's world. Without meeting this
challenge, it is unlikely that nonpathological models of mental health for
mixed race persons can be developed. Second, theoretical conceptualization and application to therapy must become multiracial and multicultural to accurately reflect the process of more than a single racial group. New
templates and models for identity development are needed which reflect
respect for difference. Necessarily, these theories will need to deviate from
traditional linear or systemic models which both have singular endpoints
to define mental health. These models are based upon male mental health,
or more recently, alternative models define white women's mental health.
Current models of mental health do not accommodate the process by
which individuals who have "other" identities, such as biracial and or
gay/lesbian, arrive at a positive sense of self-identity or maintain a positive
identity in the face of oppressive attitudes.

In this paper, the phenomenological experience of "otherness" in a biracial context is described and its sociopolitical origins explored. The integration of biracial heritage into a positive self-concept is complicated and
lengthy. An alternative model for resolution of ethnic identity is offered
which takes into account the forces of sociocultural, political, and familial
influences on shaping the individual's experience of their biracial identity. The uniqueness of this paper's approach is that several strategies of
biracial identity resolution are offered with no inherent judgment that one
resolution is better than another. Instead, the problems and advantages
inherent with each type of resolution are discussed. It is proposed that the
individual may shift their resolution strategies throughout their lifetime in
order to nurture a positive identity.

While early sociological theory might suggest that such a model as proposed here describes a "marginal personality" (Stonequist, 1937), or, in DSM-III-R nosology (American Psychiatric Association, 1987) "inadequate personality" or "borderline personality," recent research suggests that biracial young adults are generally well adjusted (Hall, 1980; Pouissant, 1987). Thus, the resolution of major conflicts inherent in the process of racial identity development may result in a flexibility to move between strategies which may reflect positive coping and adaptive abilities and be independent of the integrity of the individual's personality style.

ASSUMPTIONS ABOUT THE HIERARCHY OF COLOR IN THE UNITED STATES

Several general assumptions are made throughout this paper that are important for understanding the origins and dynamics of conflict surrounding the biracial individual. These dynamics further influence the developmental process of identity resolution.

First, in the United States, despite our polychromatic culture, we are divided into white and non-white. The positive imagery created by the "melting-pot" philosophy of the United States is relevant to white ethnic groups of immigrants such as the Irish, French, and Scandinavian people and not Americans of African, Asian, Hispanic, or, even on their home territory, American Indians. Cultural pluralism is neither appreciated nor encouraged by the larger culture.

Second, white is considered superior to non-white: the privileges and power assumed by whites are desired by non-whites. It is from this assumption that attempts are made to prevent racial mixing because free interaction assumes equality. A corollary of this assumption is that mixed race persons who are part white and can pass as such will be very likely to strive for this racial identity in order to have maximum social power and to escape the oppression directed towards people of color.

The third assumption is that there is a hierarchy of racial/cultural groups based upon their similarity to middle-class white social structure and values. Thus, in general, Asian Americans have a higher social status than Black Americans in White America.

The hierarchical social status system based upon color has oppressed biracial people in two major ways. Both stem from American society's fear of "racial pollution" (Henriques, 1975) (an attitude that was acutely reflected in Hitler's Germany). First, biracial persons have been given little choice in how they are identified. Any person with non-white ethnic features or traceable non-white blood is considered non-white (cf. Henriques, 1975). As a result, Poussaint (1984) notes than any individual with one black and one non-black parent is considered black. Because Asian ethnic groups can be equally oppressive in their fear of "racial pollution" (cf. Murphey-Shigematsu, 1986; Wagatsuma, 1973), a child that is half-Asian and half anything else, particularly black, is identified by the blood of the non-Asian parent. Mixed race persons from two minority groups are likely to experience oppression from the racial group of heritage which has higher social status. This method of "irrational," incomplete racial classification has made identity resolution for the biracial individual very difficult and oppressive.

The second source of oppression stems from society's silence on biracialism as though if it is ignored, the issue will go away. It was only as recently as 1967 that the Supreme Court ruled in the *Lovings* case of Virginia that anti-miscegenation laws were unconstitutional, a ruling based on an interpretation of the 14th amendment (1868) to the Constitution that could have been made any time in the previous 100 years (Sickels, 1972). Subsequently, the last twelve states with anti-miscegenation laws were forced to overturn them. However, this ruling does not change attitudes. Society still prohibits interracial unions (Petroni, 1973).

The assumption about the hierarchy of color is necessary for understanding the marginality of biracial persons who are part white. Because whites have been the oppressors in the United States, there is a mistrust by people of color of those accepted by or identified as white. Subsequently, those biracial individuals who are part white (and look white) will at times find it harder to gain acceptance by people of color by virtue of the attitudes and feelings that are projected onto them because of their white heritage and the oppression it symbolizes to people of color (Louise, 1988).

Being of mixed race, like being part of an interracial marriage, has meant different things at different times (e.g., whether it reflects sexual oppression of a minority group, or equity and similarity of racial groups). Nevertheless, mixed race persons have always had an ambiguous ethnic identity to resolve. *It is the marginal status imposed by society rather than the objective mixed race of biracial individuals which poses a severe stress on positive identity development*. There are few if any role models due to the lack of a clear racial reference group. Friends, parents, and other people of color usually do not comprehend the unique situation and intrapersonal conflict inherent in the resolution of an ambiguous ethnic identity for mixed race persons.

THE BEGINNINGS OF "OTHERNESS"

The themes described in the development of awareness of otherness in biracial persons have been highlighted in several recent research reports, e.g., Asian-White (Murphy-Shigematsu, 1986), Black-Asian (Hall, 1980), and Black-White mixes (Pouissant, 1984). The themes of the early years are around race, family acceptance, difference, and isolation. It is suggested that the intrapersonal and interpersonal conflicts which emerge out of these themes are circular and transitory. They reemerge at different points in development with a chance for a greater depth of resolution and understanding with each cycle.

The awareness of "otherness" or ambiguous ethnicity begins early, when a child starts to be aware of color around age three (Goodman, 1968), but before a sense of racial identity is formed. An ethnic name or non-ethnic name, which may not be congruent with how a child is perceived, can intensify this awareness. Initially this awareness develops from being identified as different from within any ethnic community. Questions and comments such as, "Where are you from?", "Mixed children are so attractive," and "You are so interesting looking," heighten the feeling of otherness. This acknowledgment of a child's ethnic mix or differentness is natural and not in and of itself harmful or particularly stressful. In fact, the special attention initially may feel good. It is the combination of inquisitive looks, longer than passing glances to comprehend unfamiliar racial-ethnic features (an "unusual or exotic look"), and comments of surprise on finding out that the child is one or the other parent's biological child *along with* disapproving comments and nonverbal communication that begin to convey to the child that this otherness is "undesirable or wrong." Suddenly, previously neutral acknowledgment or special attention is interpreted as negative attention. It is with these reactions that the child in her or his dichotomous way of knowing and sorting the world may label her or his otherness as bad. The child's egocentrism can result in assuming blame or responsibility for having done something wrong related to their color; subsequently, one may notice in young children peculiar behaviors to change racial characteristics such as attempts to wash off their dark color (Benson, 1981). Because the child is not equipped to resolve this conflict at such an early age, the conflict in its complexity is suppressed. It emerges only when negative experiences force the conflict to the surface.

During the early grade school years, children start comprehending racial differences consciously (Goodman, 1968). Self-concept is in part internalized by the reflection of self in others' reactions (Cooley, 1902). Subsequently, a significant part of identification of self in reference to either racial group is influenced by how siblings look, their racial identification, and people's reactions to them. Racial features can vary greatly among the children of the same parents; for example, in a Black-White family, one child may look white, one may look black, and one may look mixed.

They are teased by their schoolmates, called names, and are isolated—all the result of the prejudice that is transmitted by relatives, the media, and jokes. For those children who are products of interracial unions during foreign wars (i.e., WW II, Korean War, Vietnam War), fear of the "enemy," translated into national hatred towards the "enemy," may be projected onto interracial families and their children.

Once the child comprehends that there is a concept of superiority by color, she or he may attempt to achieve acceptance by embracing membership in the "hierarchically superior" racial group of their heritage, and rejecting the other half of their heritage. For example, Black-White children may want their hair straightened if it is kinky; Asian-White children may want blue eyes.

A teacher's oppressive assumptions and projections can also contribute to the marginality of the biracial child: This child may be singled out in ways that set her or him apart from peers. Unrealistic expectations of the child may be assumed, and misperceptions of the child's environment perpetuated. For example, in assuming that the child identifies with a culture unfamiliar to the teacher, she or he may be asked to "teach" the class about their racial/cultural group (while other children are not asked to do the same). By her or his action, the teacher is likely to project stereotypes onto the child with which they may not identify.

During the process of ethnic identity development, the biracial child from mid-grade school through high school may be embarrassed to be seen with one or both parents. This embarrassment reflects internalized oppression of societal attitudes towards miscegenation, possible internalized family oppression, as well as more typical American adolescent needs to appear independently functioning of their parents.

The Role of Family

The family environment is critical in helping the child and teenager to understand their heritage and value both races. A positive self-concept and view of people is promoted in interracial partnerships and extended families in which a person's value is independent of race though race is not ignored. This environment, whether it be as a single or two parent household, gives the individual a security that will help them weather the stress of adolescence. It is this unusual objectivity about people which determines the options the biracial person has for resolving their identity.

Unfortunately, the stress that has been experienced by interracial families, particularly those that have developed during wartime (e.g., Vietnam and the Korean War), has often resulted in a lack of discussion of race, discrimination, and coping strategies for dealing with discriminatory treatment. This silence has perhaps reflected these families' needs for a sanctuary from the painful issue of racial differences. Similar to issues of sexuality, the silence may also reflect the difficulty most people appear to have in discussing race issues.

Being identified with a minority group that is oppressed can generate feelings of inferiority within the biracial person, particularly if this parent is treated as such in the extended family. If the extended family is primarily composed of the socially dominant racial group, overt or covert prejudicial remarks against the parent with less racial social status will increase the child's insecurity about his or her acceptance. He or she may subsequently also devalue cultural and racial features associated with this parent in an attempt to be accepted.

Outright rejection of the parent with less racial social status, in the aspiration of being conditionally accepted by the dominant cultural group, reflects internalization and projection of discriminatory, oppressive attitudes towards one's own racial heritage (Sue, 1981) and creates tremendous intrapersonal conflict in resolving racial identity. Rejection at this age stems from the awareness that one is judged by those with whom one affiliates; color is a social issue that regulates acceptance and power.

In general, the intensity of the child's reaction is mediated by the racial diversity present in the community, the amount of contact the individual has with other biracial individuals, and the presence of equity among racial groups in their community (Allport, 1958). A child is much less likely to be embarrassed or to reject that part of their heritage that is judged negatively by society if there are ethnic communities which live side by side, if the parent with less racial social status has pride in themselves, and if parents have equal social status within the family. (It is important to be aware that persons of different races in relationships are not exempt from acting prejudicially or in an oppressive manner towards each other.) Based upon the pervasiveness of racism and the widespread oppression of women in American culture, it is hard to imagine equity in an interracial, heterosexual marriage.

Some families have a difficult start when an interracial relationship results in the severing of emotional and physical ties by the extended family such as in refusals to visit or accept a marriage or the children. It is a type of abandonment which contributes to mixed race children feeling more different and insecure than other children. Emotional cutoffs are more subtle than physical ones and can be equally damaging, e.g., biracial grandchildren are treated negatively compared to the rest of the grandchildren. This type of discrimination can be very subtle, such as loving treatment of biracial child combined with a simultaneous refusal to acknowledge biracial features. Cutoffs can also occur by non-white families and communities. For example, more traditional Japanese grandparents may refuse to accept grandchildren who are partly of any other race *or* ethnic background (e.g., Chinese). Rigid, impermeable physical, emotional, and psychological boundaries communicate hatred and judgment; they mirror to a greater or lesser extent community feelings.

The estrangement and isolation described above encourage denial and rejection of the part of self that has been unaccepted by the extended family; it is very difficult not to internalize this oppression and rejection. As in the case of people who are emotionally deprived of acceptance, some mixed-race persons will subsequently try to obtain the approval or acceptance of those persons who are least willing to give it. In the case of biracial children, they may place extra importance on the opinions of persons whose race is the same as the grandparents who initiated the cutoff. Alternately, they may displace anger towards the extended family onto strangers of the same race.

Summary

The process of identity development so far mirrors what Atkinson, Morten, and Sue (1979) describe as the first two stages of minority identity development. In the first stage (Conformity Stage), there is a preference for the dominant culture's values (which in the case of the biracial person may be part of their heritage). In the second stage (Dissonance Stage), information and experiences are likely to create confusion and challenge the individual's idealization of the dominant culture. It is at this point that the individual is usually reaching the end of elementary school and entering junior high school.

Due both to the adolescent's motivation to belong to a community or group and to the adolescent's reaction to a sense of injustice, the biracial individual may seek refuge and acceptance with the group that represents the other half of their heritage. The Minority Identity Development Model predicts that in the third stage (Resistance and Immersion) there will be a simultaneous rejection of the other part of their racial heritage, e.g., being angry and distrustful towards whites (Atkinson et al., 1979) or the racial-social group with greater status. However, this is where models for identity development are not adequate for the biracial individual's unique situation.

For the biracial individual to reject either part of their racial heritage continues an internalized oppression. In reality, it appears that some biracial persons attempt to do this, but the attempts are likely to be very shortlived due to powerful reminders of both sides of their racial heritage. To reject the dominant culture is to reject one parent and subsequently, an integral part of themselves that is unchangeable, particularly if it is the parent of the same sex. And because racial groups other than whites have their prejudices and fears, biracial individuals may feel neither fully accepted nor fully privileged by their other reference group. These individuals are harshly reminded of their ambiguous ethnic/racial status; they are an other. They are marginal until they achieve a unique resolution for themselves that accepts both parts of their racial heritage. In order to move out of marginal status they need to place less importance on seeking social approval and move beyond the dichotomy of thinking about the world and self as white versus non-white, good versus bad, and inferior versus superior. This strategy towards resolution requires children to do something for which in all likelihood they have few models to emulate.

FACING RACISM: THE END OF CHILDHOOD

In retrospective reports, biracial adults report differing degrees of awareness of the extent to which their biracial heritage increased the stress of adolescence (Hall, 1980; Murphy-Shigematsu, 1986). This awareness seems to be affected by the communities in which they have lived, parental support, acceptance by the extended family, racial features, and friends.

Junior high and high school are difficult developmental years as teenagers seek a balance between establishing a unique identity while pursuing conformity to peer values. For many biracial individuals, the teenage years appear to be encumbered by a process more painful than that of the monoracial person. Racial identity conflict is forced to the surface through increased peer dependence, cliques, dating, and movement away from the family.

Turmoil is generated when acceptance at home is not mirrored in the community. At an age in which one depends on peers' reactions as the "truth," teenagers may be angry at their parents for failing to prepare them, or for leading them to believe that they are wonderful, lovable, and likable. This inconsistency results in confusion, grief, and anger. Subsequently, conflicts of vague origin increase between children and parents; the adolescent sentiment, "You don't understand; no one understands!" takes on added meaning. Teenagers feel increasingly isolated when they do not know who to trust and as a result may become vulnerable to misinterpreting environmental cues. For those biracial individuals who feel a tremendous amount of alienation, they may dismiss the positive feedback about self and become extra sensitive to negative feedback. They may overcompensate academically and or in social relationships in order to prove their worth.

A dual existence may be reported by the biracial person; they may appear to be accepted and even popular, but may simultaneously continue to feel different and isolated. Morishima (1980) suggests that there may be more identity conflicts for Asian-White children because of their ambiguous appearance. Many White-Asians report feeling different regardless of growing up in predominantly white or Asian neighborhoods (Murphy-Shigematsu, 1986). In contrast, Black-White and Black-Asian persons' racial identities appear to be more influenced by their neighbors' color (Hall, 1980), though this difference may simply reflect the continuing, strong oppression of Blacks, leading to less freedom of choice for persons who are part Black. However, biracial adolescents may not relate their feelings of alienation to their biracial status, particularly in the case of those persons who have appeared to move well between and among racial groups. For therapists working with biracial persons, this source of alienation should always be kept in mind, especially with vague complaints of dissatisfaction, unhappiness, and feelings of isolation.

Dating brings many of the subtle forms of racism to the surface. For mixed race persons, all dating is interracial and can be fraught with all the tensions that have historically accompanied it (Petroni, 1973). The teenager who has seemingly been accepted by different racial groups and has friends of different races may be confronted with the old slur, "It's okay to have friends who are Black (Asian, White, etc.), but it's not okay to date one, and definitely not okay to marry one." A more subtle form of this racism occurs with parental encouragement of interracial friendships and even dating. However, more covert communication imparts the message, "you can date one, but don't marry one." For those biracial persons who can "pass" as white on the exterior, but do not identify as such, their attraction to non-whites may be met with statements such as, "You can do better than that." This statement is interpreted as a prejudicial comment towards their internal perception and identification of themselves. For some biracial persons this will be the first time that they experience barriers because of color or their socially perceived ambiguous race. For the child who has grown up in an extended white family and has been encouraged to act white and identify white, dating is painful. The teenager or young adult may avoid much dating and or continue in their activities in which these conflicts are absent.

A form of racism which surfaces during adolescence and may continue throughout life is "tokenism," which occurs both personally and vocationally. The biracial person's racial ambiguity and partial similarity by values or appearance may be used by a dominant group as a way of satisfying a quota for a person of color who is less threatening than a monoracial person of color (despite how the biracial person identifies). What makes this type of recruiting oppressive is that the group is using this person to avoid dealing with their racism; furthermore, they are assigning racial identity for the person and not informing her or him of their purpose. The group or organization subsequently uses their association with this person as evidence of their affirmative action or antiracist efforts. As a result, they have actually made this person marginal to the group.

Gender Issues

Like women, non-white persons have had to work harder to prove themselves equal by white, male standards. This observation is true for mixed race persons who may have to fight misperceptions that mixed race persons may be abnormal. The arenas in which biracial men and women have particular difficulties are different. Non-white men, because they have more social, economic, and political power than most women, are particularly threatening to White America. It is hypothesized that mixed race men will have a more difficult time overcoming social barriers than mixed race women; they will have to work harder to prove themselves and experience an oppression, which while shared by other minority group men, may exist also within their minority reference groups towards them.

On the other hand, because women in general are less threatening to the mainstream culture than men, mixed race women may not experience as much direct oppression as mixed race men. Biracial women may in fact be perceived as less threatening than monoracial women of color. They are likely to have difficulty comprehending, and then subsequently coping with pervasive myths that mixed race women are "exotic" and sexually freer than other women (Petroni, 1973; Wagatsuma, 1973). These myths appear to stem from myths that interracial relationships are based upon sex (cf. Petroni, 1973). Coupled with a lack of acceptance, some biracial women become sexually promiscuous in a search for acceptance (Gibbs, 1987). Mixed race women may also have more difficulty in relationships because of intersections of myths, lower status as women, and their search for an identity.

Summary

Racism challenges adolescent optimism. The young person's sensitivity to social approval and the human need for belonging make the resolution of biracial identity a long, uncharted journey. The path is determined by family, community, and peer values and environments. Racial features including skin color of self and family members also shape one's sense of racial identity.

To assume that the biracial person will racially identify with how they look is presumptive, but pervasive. Besides, the biracial person is perceived differently by different people. *Many persons make the mistake of thinking that the biracial person is fortunate to have a choice; however, the reality is that the biracial person has to fight very hard to exercise choices that are not congruent with how they may be visually and emotionally perceived.* She or he should have options to go beyond identifying with one or the other racial group of their heritage; the limitation of this dichotomy of options is oppressive and generates marginal status. To be able to have an expanded slate of options may shorten the journey and reduce the pain involved in resolution of biracial identity.

STRATEGIES FOR RESOLUTION OF "OTHER" STATUS

Several models for identity development exist both in the psychological and sociological bodies of literature. Minority models for identity development share in common the rejection of white values in order to appreciate minority values. However, as pointed out in the model of Atkinson et al. (1979), there is an inherent difficulty in rejecting "whiteness" if one is part white. In fact, the author proposes that for those individuals who are part white to manifest hatred towards whiteness probably reflects oppression within the nuclear and extended family system. For biracial persons who are a minority-minority racial mix, it is not clear how to apply this model.

A Beginning Schematic for Identity Development

I am proposing a schematic metamodel that might be used to understand the process of identity development for persons with different types of "other" status. This model is schematically a spiral where the linear force is internal conflict over a core sense of definition of self, the importance of which is largely determined by socialization (e.g., race, gender). Different sources of conflict may move the individual forward. It is proposed, however, that in each person's life there are at least one or two significant conflicts during critical developmental periods that move them forward. The circular or system forces encompass the political, social, and familial environments.

I suggest that in the identity development of the biracial person, the strongest recurring conflict at critical periods of development will be the tension between racial components within oneself. Social, familial, and political systems are the environments within which the biracial person appears to seek a sense of self in a circular process repeatedly throughout a lifetime. Themes of marginality, discrimination, and ambiguity are produced by these systems.

At all times, biracial persons contend with both parts of their racial heritage. Early in the process of identity development, after the child has become aware of race, she or he is likely to compartmentalize and separate the racial components of their heritage. The attention they give to aspects of their heritage may alternate (through not necessarily equally) over time. This alternating represents conflict and lack of experience and strategies for integrating components of self. Resolution reflects the lack of need for compartmentalizing the parts of their ethnic heritage.

The rest of this paper is dedicated to outlining four general resolutions of biracial identity. That there is more than one acceptable outcome confronts the limitations of traditional psychological theory which allows for only a single healthy endpoint. If there is another step in the contribution that feminist theory can make to personality development, it might be to provide flexibility and tolerance for more than a single definition of mental health.

The factors and criteria that determine each resolution are outlined. All resolutions are driven by the assumption that an individual recognizes both sides of their heritage. The resolutions that are proposed are an articulation of what appears on the surface: acceptance of the identity society assigns; identification with a single racial group; identification with both racial groups; and identification as a new racial group.

Acceptance of the Identity Society Assigns

Biracial people growing up in more racially oppressive parts of the country are less likely to have the freedom to choose their racial identity. They are likely to be identified and identify as a person of color which will be equated with subordinate status. This strategy reflects the case of a passive resolution that is positive but may stem from an oppressive process. However, it is possible for it to be a positive resolution if the individual feels they belong to the racial group to which they are assigned. Affiliation, support, and acceptance by the extended family is important to this resolution being positive.

Individuals who have largely been socialized within an extended family, depending on them for friendship as well as nurturance, are likely to racially identify with this group regardless of their visual similarity or dissimilarity to the extended family. One will tend to identify with the ethnic identify with which society views the family. The advantage of this identification is that the extended (well-functioning) family is a stable, secure reference group whose bonds go beyond visual, racial similarity.

This resolution is the most tenuous of the strategies outlined in that the individual may be perceived differently and assigned a different racial identity in a different part of the country. Because one's self-image in the mind's eye is stable across significant changes, the conflict and subsequent accumulated life experience would need to be tremendous to compel the individual to change their internally perceived racial identity. In the event of this challenge, the biracial person may work towards a more active resolution process. However, it is likely that she or he will still racially identify the same way but based on a different process such as identification with the extended family. Evidence of a positive resolution is that the individual would educate those persons with whom they interact of their chosen identity.

Identification with Both Racial Groups

Some biracial persons identify with both racial groups they have inherited. When asked about their ethnic background, they may respond, "I'm part Black and part Japanese," or "I'm mixed." This resolution is positive if the individual's personality remains similar across groups and they feel privileged in both groups. They may simultaneously be aware that they are both similar and different compared to those persons around them. However, they view their otherness as a unique characteristic of self that contributes to a sense of individuality.

This may be the most idealistic resolution of biracial status, but is available in only certain parts of the country where biracial children exist in larger numbers and mixed marriages are accepted with greater tolerance by the community such as on the West coast. This strategy does not change other people's behavior; thus, the biracial person must have constructive strategies for coping with social resistance to their comfort with both groups of their heritage and their claim to privileges of both groups.

Identification with a Single Racial Group

The result of this strategy sometimes looks identical to the strategy of assuming the racial identity that society assigns. It is different, however, in that the process is active rather than passive and is not the result of oppression. In this strategy, the individual chooses to identify with a particular racial/ethnic group regardless if this is the identity assumed by siblings, assigned by society, or matching their racial features. This is a positive strategy if the individual does not feel marginal to their proclaimed racial reference group and does not deny the other part of their racial heritage. This is a more difficult resolution to achieve in parts of the country which have the strongest prohibitions against crossing color lines (e.g., the South).

A major difficulty may be faced with this strategy when there is an incongruous match between how an individual is perceived by others and how they perceive themselves. With this strategy, the biracial person needs to be aware of and accept the incongruity and have coping strategies for dealing with questions and suspicion by the reference group. Some individuals will need to make a geographic move to be able to live this resolution more peacefully.

Identification as a New Racial Group

This person most likely feels a strong kinship to other biracial persons in a way that they may not feel to any racial group because of the struggle with marginal status. Identification as a new race is a positive resolution if the person is not trying to hide or reject any aspect of their racial heritage. This individual may move fluidly between racial groups but view themselves apart from these reference groups without feeling marginal because they have generated a new reference group. There are few examples of biracial groups being recognized in a positive way. Hawaii perhaps sees one of the best examples with the Hapa Haole (White-Asian) (Yamamoto, 1973).

A clear problem with this resolution is that society's classification system does not recognize persons of mixed race. Thus, this individual would continually experience being assigned to a racial identity and would need to inform people of the inaccuracy when it felt important to them.

Summary

I suggest that these strategies are not mutually exclusive and may coexist simultaneously, or an individual may move among them. Such movement is consistent with a stable, positive sense of identity if the individual does not engage in denial of any part of their heritage (internalized oppression). Two themes are common to the resolutions listed above. First, it is important that the biracial person accept both sides of her or his racial heritage. Second, the biracial person has the right to declare how they wish to identify themselves racially—even if this identity is discrepant with how they look or how society tends to perceive them. Third, the biracial person develops strategies for coping with social resistance or questions about their racial identity so that they no longer internalize questions as implying that there is something wrong with them. Rather, they attribute questions and insensitivities to ignorance and racism.

Resolution of biracial identity is often propelled forward by the internal conflict generated by exposure to new people, new ideas, and new environments. Subsequently, it is not uncommon that many individuals emerge out of college years with a different resolution to their racial identity than when they graduated high school. Furthermore, geography plays a large part in the options the individual has. Living in more liberal parts of the country may be necessary to exercise a wider range of options with less social resistance.

CONCLUSION

The multiple strategies for resolution of other status in this paper constitutes a proposal, challenge, and appeal to theorists of human personality development to be more flexible in considering the range of positive psychological functioning. Psychological theories have been oppressive in their narrow range of tolerance and allowance for positive mental health. As a result, many different types of people can relate to the search for a resolution of other status, though not necessarily based on racial/ethnic ambiguity. If theories of identity development allowed for a slate of equally valid resolutions of conflict around basic components of identity, fewer people may struggle with "identity crises." Because of the role that feminist theory has played in attempting to validate the experience of persons with "other" status by sexual orientation, religious/ethnic identity, etc., *it seems that feminist theorists and therapists may be the persons most able to develop flexible models of mental health that truly allow for diversity.* But first, more feminist theorists and therapists will have to reach out beyond their boundaries of cultural safety to understand issues of race.

Although it appears that the biracial person may have the best of both worlds, this is a naive assumption which presumes that she or he has unopposed freedom to choose how she or he wishes to be perceived. In reality all racial groups have their prejudices which when projected onto the biracial person are the creators of marginal status. The biracial person does not have a guaranteed ethnic reference group if they leave it to the group to determine if they can belong.

The key to resolving other status derived from ethnic ambiguity requires an individual to move beyond the dichotomous, irrational categorization of race by white versus non-white, which in turn has been equated with degrees of worth and privilege in our culture. Towards this goal, three significant assumptions can be made about the experience of the biracial person which subsequently affects their process of identity resolution.

First, the biracial person does not necessarily racially identify with the way she or he looks (Hall, 1980). Because self-image is an emotionally mediated picture of the self, one's perception of self is governed by more than racial features. One's image of self is shaped by the presence of absence of other people similar to them, the racial features of siblings, exposure to people of both races which they inherit, identification with one parent over another, peer reactions, and how the extended family has perceived them as children.

Second, unlike monoracial people of color, the biracial person does not have guaranteed acceptance by any racial reference group. Thus, minority models of identity development do not reflect the resolution of this situation which is the crux of the biracial person's marginal status. *Looking for acceptance from others keeps the biracial person trying to live by the "irrational" racial classification rules which may keep her or him marginal to any group.*

The third assumption is that there is more than one possible, positive resolution of racial identity for biracial persons. This assumption reflects a departure from traditional European, male-originated identity models which have a single, static, positive outcome. Furthermore, the *resolution strategies for biracial identity can change during a lifetime.* It is this ability to be flexible that may indeed determine both self-acceptance and constructive, flexible coping strategies.

Marginality is a state created by society and not inherent in one's racial heritage. *As long as the biracial person bases self-acceptance on complete social acceptance by any racial reference group, they will be marginal.* Freire (1970) clearly articulates the origin and subsequently difficult resolution of marginality,

> ... marginality is not by choice, [the] marginal [person] has been expelled from and kept outside of the social system.... *Therefore, the solution to their problem is not to become "beings inside of," but ... [people] ... freeing themselves; for, in reality, they are not marginal to the structure, but oppressed ... [persons] ... within it.* [pp. 10–11]

References

Allport, Gordon W. (1958). *The nature of prejudice.* Reading, MA: Addison-Wesley.

Atkinson, D., Morten, G., & Sue, Derald W. (1979). *Counseling American minorities: A cross cultural perspective.* Dubuque, IA: Brown Company.

Dien, D. S. & Vinacke, W. E. (1964). Self-concept and parental identification of young adults with mixed Caucasian-Japanese parentage. *Journal of Abnormal Psychology,* 69(4), 463–466.

Freire, Paolo (1970). *Cultural action for freedom.* Cambridge: Harvard Educational Review Press.

Gibbs, Jewelle Taylor (1987). Identity and marginality: Issues in the treatment of biracial adolescents. *American Journal of Orthopsychiatry,* 57(2), 265–278.

Goodman, M. E. (1968). *Race awareness in young children.* New York: Collier Press.

Hall, Christine C. Iijima (1980). *The ethnic identity of racially mixed people: A study of Black-Japanese.* Doctoral Dissertation, University of California, Los Angeles.

Henriques, Fernando (1975). *Children of conflict: A study of interracial sex and marriage.* New York: E. P. Dutton & Co., Inc.

Louise, Vivienne (1988). Of Color: What's in a Name? *Bay Area Women's News,* 1(6), 5,7.

Morishima, James K. (1980). *Asian American Racial Mixes: Attitudes, Self-Concept, and Academic Performance.* Paper presented at the Western Psychological Association convention, Honolulu.

Moritsugu, John, Foerster, Lynn, & Morishima, James K. (1978). *Eurasians: A Pilot Study.* Paper presented at the Western Psychological Association convention, San Francisco.

Murphy-Shigematsu, Stephen (1986). *The voices of amerasians: Ethnicity, identity, and empowerment in interracial Japanese Americans.* Doctoral Dissertation, Harvard University.

Petroni, Frank A. (1983). Interracial Dating—The Price Is High. In I. R. Stuart and L. Edwin (Eds.), *Interracial marriage: Expectations and Realities.* New York: Grossman.

Poussaint, Alvin F. (1984). Benefits of Being Interracial. *Children of interracial families* 15(6).

Sickels, Robert J. (1972). *Race, marriage, and the law.* Albuquerque, NM: University of New Mexico Press.

Stonequist, Everett (1935). The problem of the marginal man. *The American Journal of Sociology,* 41, 1–12.

Sue, Derald W. (1981). *Counseling the culturally different: Theory and practice.* New York: John Wiley & Sons.

Wagatsuma, Hiroshi (1973). Some Problems of Interracial Marriage for the Japanese. In I. R. Stuart and L. Edwin (Eds.), *Interracial Marriage: Expectations and Realities.* New York: Grossman.

Yamamoto, George (1973). Interracial Marriage in Hawaii. In I. R. Stuart and L. Edwin (Eds.), *Interracial Marriage: Expectations and Realities.* New York: Grossman.

26

USE OF AFRICAN-AMERICAN FAMILY STRUCTURES AND FUNCTIONING TO ADDRESS THE CHALLENGES OF EUROPEAN-AMERICAN POSTDIVORCE FAMILIES

Margaret Crosbie-Burnett
Edith A. Lewis

The experience of African-American families is used to inform European-American postdivorce families, including stepfamilies. Strategies and coping mechanisms that stem from a pedi-focal definition of family and are used in African-American families are suggested for postdivorce families to aid in their struggles with: welfare of dependent children, confusion about family roles and household boundaries, and the very definition of family. Implications for theory development, research, policy, and practice are included.

Information about healthy and adaptive family structures and functioning, beginning with theoretical models of *family* and extending to applications of these models that include family life education, therapeutic interventions, and public policy, has flowed in one direction traditionally—from the dominant European-American culture to populations of color (Lewis & Kissman, 1989). Naturally this information has reflected the ideals, values, and habits of the dominant culture. Consequently, the norm for family structure and functioning in the United States has been the traditional nuclear family. This process has resulted in incomplete portrayals of family life that have existed for generations for many families, particularly families of color.

Increasingly, European-American families are living in nontraditional family structures. Most of this change is a function of the dramatic increase in postdivorce families. These families are finding themselves struggling with many of the issues with which African-American families have been coping for centuries (Adams, 1978; Peters, 1981). These issues include: the welfare of children when one or both biological parents are not present in the home, the complexity and ambiguity of roles and relationships, the permeability of family and household boundaries, and the experience of having one's family structure defined by the dominant culture as outside the norm, and therefore deviant. The various structures of African-American families offer a rich source of information that addresses these issues. Much of the research done on these diverse families, however, has been ignored in reviews of family life written for the larger society (Taylor, Chatters, Tucker, & Lewis, 1990).

The purpose of this article is to focus on ways that the experience and strengths of African-American families (AA families) can inform European-American postdivorce families (EAPD families), whose ideology and frame of reference is based on the traditional nuclear family, leaving them ill-prepared to cope with the complex family structures and relationships in which they find themselves.

PEDI-FOCAL DEFINITION OF FAMILY

The continued welfare of dependent children as their parents change partners and households is probably the most important challenge to postdivorce families (Crosbie-Burnett, 1991; Emery, 1988; Hetherington, 1989; Hetherington & Arasteh, 1988; Hetherington & Clingempeel, 1992; Kurdek & Sinclair, 1988; Wallerstein, 1991; Weitzman, 1985). AA families have had to cope with the same challenge. Historically, in African societies strong communal interpersonal networks including extended families existed for the purpose of caring for children (Burgess, 1991; Rodgers-Rose, 1980). This tradition was amplified with the forced migration of Africans to the American colonies. During slavery, parents and children were sold away from each other at the whim of their owners (Rodgers-Rose, 1980; Staples, 1971). A slave child in this situation was cared for by the group of slaves with whom he or she lived. This meant that a child's very survival depended on other adults taking on parental roles for the child, with various adults contributing what they could.

In more recent history, a similar situation has existed for many African-American children. Many African-American mothers either lived in, or spent long days as maids for affluent families; sometimes fathers left the home for periods of time searching for work (Darity & Myers, 1984; Giddings, 1982). Regardless of the time in history, the challenge, however, is similar to that of EAPD families—the welfare of dependent children.

The very definition of *family* is at issue, and a change in definition suggests a response to this crucial challenge. Ahrons (1984) brought attention to the problem of the definition of family in the dominant culture by accurately noting that language about families does not reflect the reality of many postdivorce families. For example, there are no terms for some of the relationships found in remarried families, such as the relationship between mother and stepmother, even though the women in these roles may interact frequently in their efforts to rear the same child. Also, in postdivorce situations in which children spend time in each parent's home, the term binuclear family is more appropriate than calling either household a single-parent family (Ahrons & Rodgers, 1987).

Family Does Not Equal Household

Defining *immediate family* as the members of a household who are related by blood or marriage, exemplified by the way Census data are gathered, reflects the dominant culture's traditional definition of family. Similarly, within the patri-focal system of law that characterizes the United States, the legal definition of family is based on the legal status (e.g., legal marriage, separation, or divorce) between adults (Brandwein, Brown, & Fox, 1974; Kammerman, 1983; Weitzman, 1981). Defining the family based on the adults' legal relationship to each other discourages the continued interaction of parents and extended kin with children after parental divorce.

AA families, by contrast, traditionally are centered around the children, creating a pedi-focal family system. Thus, the family unit can be defined as including all those involved in the nurturance and support of an identified child, regardless of household membership (Brooks-Gunn & Furstenberg, 1986; Chatters, Taylor, & Neighbors, 1989; Stack, 1974). It means putting the needs of children above adult's conjugal needs. Children are prized, and being a part of their rearing is a privilege, not a burden (Wade-Lewis, 1989).

This way of thinking changes the bases of family relations from legal arrangements between biologically or legally related members to arrangements based on a child's needs. This conceptualization encourages extended family relationships for the benefit of children, and thereby increases the probability of assistance to children (Chatters, Taylor, & Neighbors, 1989; H. P. McAdoo, 1981; Wilson, 1989). This pedi-focal definition of family can promote continued responsibility for dependent children regardless of changes in relationships among adults. It has the potential to support cooperation and minimize hostility between adults and their kin in postdivorce families, because the goal of relating is not based on an ex-spousal relationship, but rather on a multiparental one (Ahrons & Rodgers, 1987).

Benefits of a Pedi-Focal Definition

One of the benefits of the pedi-focal definition of family is the inclusion of members of the community in the child's support system. The pedi-focal conceptualization of family assumes that children belong to the community and are the responsibility of any adults who are able to contribute to the child's well-being. Scholars have identified a language system in AA families that includes denotations for *fictive kin* (Adams, 1978; Aschenbrenner, 1978; Stack, 1974). This conceptualization enables families to include members who are not legally or biologically related, but have status and role responsibilities in the family.

Applications of Pedi-Focal Systems to Divorced Families

The applications to postdivorce families are many. For example, step-families that are trying to acknowledge membership for persons who are legally outsiders (e.g., a parent's new partner and the partner's extended family) might use these fictive kin terms to validate contributions to the nurturing of children. The extended family of a noncustodial parent can retain relationships with children. Also, within a pedi-focal system, the neighbor or child care–provider who oversees a single mother's child's homework daily is given the respect and authority needed to best make his contribution to the child's socialization. This validation process also facilitates and encourages nonparents to become involved, should a parent be unavailable for a period of time.

More specifically, two modifications of the traditional interactions between divorcing parents may increase the amount of attention paid to the children's needs at the time of the divorce and contribute to the development of a pedi-focal system. First, in divorce situations, relationships between parents (including each parent's extended family and friends) are often adversarial. Parents going through separation can offset this stance by identifying all the individuals from both sides who have been involved positively with the child and establishing mechanisms for their continued involvement. The goal is to act in the best interest of the child rather than in the interests of the parents. The separating parents thereby acknowledge and facilitate the continued significance of these individuals in the postdivorce life of the child, which minimizes the child's losses.

The second modification is to explicitly note in the final divorce stipulation that the divorcing parents will respect all individuals who may become involved in the support and nurturance of their children and will dedicate themselves to strengthening rather than undermining these relationships. This is meant to include future partners of the divorcing couple, and potentially step-grandparents and other extended family. Expectations that ex-spouses are supposed to cooperate with future parental figures may promote interactions that are beneficial to the children.

FLEXIBILITY OF ROLES AND RELATIONSHIPS

A corollary to the pedi-focal definition of family is the flexibility of roles and relationships. One of the critical problems facing EAPD families is determining how the child-related tasks of the expanded family unit will be distributed and executed by its members. Unlike the traditional nuclear family in which the division of labor is often based on traditional sex roles, divorced adults may have to perform tasks that are outside their usual parental roles. In addition, it is not clear what, if any, parental tasks should be fulfilled by stepparents. The potential for disagreements about the new division of labor abounds.

Androgynous Sex Roles

AA families can inform postdivorce family roles and relationships in several ways. The literature on AA families shows that sex roles are more androgynous in these families than in European-American families (Allen, 1981; J. McAdoo, 1981; Thornton, Chatters, Taylor, & Allen, 1990). Both males and females learn and perform what has been traditionally dichotomized as the instrumental and expressive functions. All children are taught to cook, clean, mend, build, and perform other necessary work for the benefit of the family unit. Thus, African-American women *and* men learn housekeeping and childrearing (Ahmeduzzaman & Roopnarine, 1992). With respect to African-American fathers in general, while the literature has documented that these men are less likely than fathers of other ethnic groups to live in the household with their children, this has not translated into a lack of involvement with their children (Danzinger & Radin, 1992; Stack, 1974). This challenge of staying involved with children with whom one does not live is shared by EAPD families' noncustodial and nonresidential parents.

Similarly, African-American women, including wives and mothers, have labored outside the home ever since slavery. Role flexibility occurs across generations as well; aging family members model flexibility in roles. For example, a grandfather may take on the childrearing function when parents are not available to do so (Beck & Beck, 1989; Burton & Bengtsen, 1985; Lewis, 1988a; Taylor, 1988). The welfare of children in EAPD families could be maximized if the distribution of the many child-related tasks could be based on the skills and resources of parents, stepparents, and other kin, rather than on prescribed family roles that are based on the traditional nuclear family.

Focus on Process Rather Than Outcome

Another dimension of this flexibility is a perspective on time that focuses on process rather than outcome (Spiegel, 1982). European-American culture is goal- and outcome-oriented (e.g., "Get the relationship with your ex-husband settled once and for all."). Control over outcome has been elusive for African Americans, an economically marginalized group. Education, housing, employment, and life expectancy parity with European Americans has not been reached by African Americans, even when one controls for economic status (Lewis, 1988b; Staples, 1981; Thurow, 1987). These basic aspects of living influence one's ability to perform family roles and have stable family relationships; when these aspects are not within one's control, or even predictable, family roles and relationships cannot be very stable.

A focus on process encourages learning communication and problem-solving skills that can be applied to the many difficult family situations that will inevitably present themselves, due to lack of predictability and control. This aspect of the African-American world view might help adults in EAPD families cope with the relative lack of control and influence that parental figures (e.g., former spouses and stepparents) may have over each other in the postdivorce, as compared to the predivorce, family.

Bicultural Socialization

This tolerance for ambiguity in roles and relationships, which differentiates AA families from families of European descent, stems from the bicultural experiences of AA families. These families must educate their members to live in at least two worlds—that of their ethnic community and that of the wider society (Peters & Massey, 1985; Ogbu, 1981; Lewis & Ford, 1990). Bicultural socialization requires that individuals learn at least two identities, including two sets of behaviors, exchange expectations, and roles. For those middle- and upper-income African Americans, learning a third set, based on class, is likely. Living in two cultures simultaneously means that situations arise in which role expectations and definitions of self and family are ambiguous, or even in conflict. Learning to anticipate and cope with this ambiguity about one's identity, specifically about who is in the family and who is not, and what role(s) one is supposed to perform in a variety of households, would be a useful skill for members of EAPD families.

African Americans have used a variety of strategies to cope with this phenomenon. First, with respect to the children, lessons learned from African-American children's socialization are helpful here. Directly presenting children with information about how their social status (e.g., as African American or stepchild) may be viewed in the wider society assists them in developing strategies for dealing with possible rejection or confusion in their encounters with social institutions' policies and practices, authority figures, neighbors, other children, and even friends.

Applications to Postdivorce Families

Bicultural socialization may benefit all postdivorce children and families. Children of divorce and remarriage live in a society that is still based on the ideology of the traditional, nuclear family. Understanding differences among people at an early age can lead to more favorable responses to other forms of difference in later life (Moraga & Anzaldua, 1983). Having books, magazines, and stories of postdivorce families available for children's use is one way to promote their understanding and embracing of the differences in families, rather than denying them, thus fostering their bicultural socialization. Self-help literature can help divorced-parents and stepparents to understand the ambiguity and contradictions in their roles and relationships, and, hopefully, to be more comfortable with their own bicultural status. Families could be encouraged to discuss television programs in which divorced or remarried families are portrayed, noting the similarities and differences in the family composition, life circumstances, and roles and relationships of family members.

PERMEABILITY OF FAMILIAL AND HOUSEHOLD BOUNDARIES

Differences Between Household and Family Boundaries Postdivorce

Closely related to the flexibility of roles and relationships is the permeability of familial and household boundaries. In traditional nuclear families, the household boundary and the family boundary are the same. Also, this boundary is not very permeable; a family member is either in or out of the family/household. This becomes problematic in EAPD families. Family membership does not equal household membership. For example, a child may go back and forth between households, being a part-time member of the father's household, while being considered a full-time member of the father's family. Similarly, a nonresidential biological father is not a member of his children's household, yet is likely to be considered a full-time member of his children's family. It is clear that the emotional and financial interdependence across two or more households in EAPD families does not fit the traditional nuclear family model of well-defined boundaries around the family/household.

Lessons From African-American Families

AA families have demonstrated the usefulness of permeable family and household boundaries (Aschenbrenner, 1978; Franklin & Franklin, 1985; H. P. McAdoo, 1981). Informed adoption of children by other family members is only one example of this permeability (Beck & Beck, 1989; Cherlin & Furstenberg, 1986). This permeability appears to exist even when education and income are controlled for among African Americans (McAdoo, 1980; Mutran, 1985). Persons may be members of families or households in some roles and not others, or for some periods of time, but not others. When the group's material and human resources are shared for the benefit of the community, particularly the children, then permeable boundaries are functional, and may even be necessary for survival under conditions of poverty. This flexibility has often been misconstrued in the literature as a nuclear unit's inability to separate from other units of family, be they units within other generations or across grown siblings (Lewis, 1989; Lewis & Kissman, 1989). A more accurate description of this phenomenon would highlight the functional linkage of households for the betterment of all members. It is a phenomenon that could serve well the multihousehold postdivorce family.

Use of Fictive Kin

The assumption of a parenting role is not restricted to blood kin. As a function of the pedi-focal definition of family, there is a tradition of fictive kin relationships that allows for those most able to take care of the children in the community to do so, as in the example of informal adoptions. The use of fictive kin for family support and exchange is well documented (Ahmeduzzaman & Roopnarine, 1992; Manns, 1981; Stack, 1974). In this practice, different parental roles may be filled by a variety of persons. For example, one person might contribute money to a child's support, while another focuses on nurturance and socialization, and still another gathers clothes from friends and relatives. A fourth may take responsibility for medical care or spiritual teaching. Non-blood– and non-legally–related persons may take on family roles and often have the same privileges with regard to children as the children's blood kin. This arrangement allows so-called single parents to share the parenting role and have coparenting relationships with those able to provide financial and human resources (Lewis, 1989; Lewis & Kissman, 1989; Taylor et al., 1990). Thus, the rearing of children is a coordinated effort between men and women in a loosely defined family system. EAPD families can benefit from an understanding of this flexibility in family-related roles and relationships, so that an emphasis can be placed on utilizing a variety of adults who are involved with the child to create a division of labor that is in the best interest of the child, rather than focusing solely on obligatory behaviors that are determined by legal or contractual arrangements, or by sex roles.

Applications to Postdivorce Families

An application of permeable household boundaries is exemplified by the use of the *genogram*. The culturally competent genogram can be easily adapted for use with postdivorce families. This genogram includes not only blood kin, but all individuals who have a stake in the family's presenting problem. Depending on how the problem is defined, different configurations of persons would be included in the genogram. For example, those who are part of a financial problem may be different from those who are important in an emotional crisis. Family includes different and overlapping subsets of persons when roles are flexible and boundaries are permeable (Lewis & Ford, 1990). In this application, parental and adult behaviors are driven by issue rather than structure.

POSTDIVORCE FAMILY STRUCTURES DEFINED AS DEVIANT

Facing the Deviant Label

In our dominant cultural ideology, the traditional nuclear family is the norm, and other family structures are, by definition *deviant*, and by implication, deficient (Bryant, Coleman, & Ganong, 1988; Ganong, Coleman, & Mapes, 1990). These "deviant" structures include postdivorce living arrangements such as single-parent households, step-families, and a variety of types of communal households, often created for economic reasons by postdivorce adults. This means that European-Americans, who are accustomed to having their institutions and behaviors defined as normal because they are part of the dominant culture, find their families defined as deviant and given second-class status (Cherlin, 1978; Crosbie-Burnett, 1989; Price-Bonham & Balswick, 1980). Coping with this prejudice is not easy. Psychologically internalizing the second-class status is demoralizing to the group and can affect an individual's sense of self-worth. It goes without saying that AA families have had much experience with being defined as deviant (Gilder, 1981; Hall, 1992; Sowell, 1975). Consequently, they have created coping mechanisms in response.

Relationships With Institutions

Insulating oneself from some traditional social institutions, for example, the legal institution, can be useful. Because the judicial system has no understanding of AA families and was negatively biased toward African Americans until the latter part of the 20th century, African Americans seldom used the courts as a remedy for familial matters (Lewis, 1988; Morrison, 1992; Stack, 1974). Family law and other family policies are designed to fit the idealized nuclear family, and thus are often problematic for both pedi-focal AA families and EAPD families. For example, stepparents still have virtually no legal rights vis-à-vis their stepchildren (Fine, 1989; Fine & Fine, 1992); family insurance coverage does not generally provide for cohabiting partners or for stepchildren who are not legally adopted. AA families have learned to cope with these limited perspectives on family in social institutions by creating and using informal systems to meet the needs of the family unit. For example, the informal adoption of children within the extended family is a way to keep the courts from choosing a child's legal guardian.

Identifying social institutions that respect diversity in families can counteract the "deviant" label. As compared to the legal system, spiritual institutions have been more adaptive to the needs of nontraditional families. For AA families, the church has served as a focal point with respect to social support as well as spirituality. For family members who are experiencing the transitions of divorce or remarriage, religious institutions and even educational institutions (Crosbie-Burnett, 1992, 1993; Crosbie-Burnett & Skyles, 1989) have the potential to serve a support function.

The diversity among alternative mutual support and aid institutions within African-American communities can provide some additional clues for European-American children and parents. At the time of divorce, sometimes the institutions with which families have previously been involved do not support family members' new status. For example, how does one address the inability of the noncustodial father to be present at the father-son activities designed by the Boy Scouts? A child cannot attain the Arrow of Light award without a male figure present. In

African-American communities, in order to ensure that these types of children's needs are met, African-American fraternal organizations have provided emotional and psychologial support for young men. The Black Male Responsibility Programs developed by the National Urban League address current issues facing young African-American males, such as employment, racism, parenthood, and AIDS. These groups are based on the premise that the children belong to the community.

EAPD families have used similar strategies for promoting social support. Groups like Parents Without Partners and the Stepfamily Association of America work to normalize the family structures and educate postdivorce families about how to cope with their struggles. Additional sources of support are needed for EAPD families.

Creating New Rituals

Creating alternative institutions and rituals can be useful. In AA families and communities, this has taken the form of frequent family reunions that include both blood and fictive kin. Dorothy Height and the National Association of Negro Women have sponsored large Black Family Reunions across the United States for several years, drawing hundreds of participants. Other organizations and families sponsor Kwanzaa celebrations (a seven-day celebration during December) across the country. Both the Black Family Reunions and Kwanzaa celebrations have the impact of teaching children and adults the history of African Americans through the African diaspora, supporting youth excellence in the present, and developing goals and objectives to guide future behavior. These types of rituals increase cohesiveness and problem solving within the expanded family unit.

The ritual of having large family celebrations may be useful for promoting cooperation and mutual support in the extended families of postdivorce and remarried families, especially if the rationale focuses on the benefit to the family's children. Within stepfamilies, creating new family rituals has been found to increase family cohesion (Whiteside, 1989).

References

Adams, B. (1978). Black families in the United States: An overview of current ideologies and research. In D. Shimkin, E. Shimkin, & D. Frote (Eds.), *The extended family in black societies* (pp. 173–180). Paris: Mouton Publishers.

Ahmeduzzaman, M., & Roopnarine, J. (1992). Sociodemographic factors, functioning style, and fathers' involvement with preschoolers in African-American families. *Journal of Marriage and the Family, 54,* 699–707.

Ahrons, C. R. (1984). The binuclear family: Parenting roles and relationships. In I. Koch-Nielsen (Ed.), *Parent-child relationship, postdivorce: A seminar report* (pp. 54–79). Copenhagen: The Danish National Institute for Social Research.

Ahrons, C. R., & Rodgers, R. H. (1987). *Divorced families: A multidisciplinary developmental view*. New York: Norton.

Allen, W. R. (1981). Moms, dads, and boys: Race and sex differences in the socialization of male children. In. L. Gary (Ed.), *Black men* (pp. 99–114). Beverly Hills, CA: Sage.

Aschenbrenner, J. (1978). Continuities and variations in black family structure. In D. Shimkin, E. Shimkin, & D. Frote (Eds.), *The extended family in black societies* (pp. 181–200). Paris: Mouton Publishers.

Beck, R., & Beck, S. (1989). The incidence of extended households among middle-aged black and white women: Estimates from a 5-year panel study. *Journal of Family Issues, 10*, 147–168.

Brandwein, R., Brown, C. A., & Fox, E. M. (1974). Women and children last: The social situation of divorced mothers and their families. *Journal of Marriage and the Family, 36*, 498–514.

Brooks-Gunn, J., & Furstenberg, F. F. (1986). The children of adolescent mothers: Physical, academic, and psychological outcomes. *Developmental Review, 6*, 224–251.

Bryant, Z. L., Coleman, M., & Ganong, L. H. (1988). Race and family structure stereotyping: Perceptions of black and white nuclear and stepfamilies. *Journal of Black Psychology, 15*, 1–16.

Burgess, N. (November, 1991). *Constructions of African women's sexuality*. Paper presented at the Preconference Workshop on Family Theory and Research Methods, National Council on Family Relations, Denver, Colorado.

Burton, L., & Bengtsen, V. (1985). Black grandmothers: Issues of timing and continuity of roles. In V. Bengtsen & J. Robertson (Eds.), *Grandparenthood* (pp. 61–77). Beverly Hills, CA: Sage.

Chatters, L. M., Taylor, R. J., & Neighbors, H. W. (1989). Size of the informal helper network mobilized in response to serious personal problems. *Journal of Marriage and the Family, 51*, 667–676.

Cherlin, A. (1978). Remarriage as an incomplete institution. *American Journal of Sociology, 84*, 634–650.

Cherlin, A. & Furstenberg, F. F. (1986). *The new American grandparent: A place in the family, a life apart*. New York: Basic Books.

Crosbie-Burnett, M. (1989). Application of family stress theory to remarriage: A model for assessing and helping stepfamilies. *Family Relations, 38*, 323–331.

Crosbie-Burnett, M. (1991). Impact of joint versus sole custody and quality of the coparental relationship on adjustment of adolescents in remarried families. *Behavioral Sciences and the Law, 9*, 439–449.

Crosbie-Burnett, M. (1992). The interface between non-traditional families and education: Empowering parents & families. *Family Science Review, 5*, 81–92.

Crosbie-Burnett, M. (in press). The interface between stepparent families and schools: Theory, research, policy, and practice. In K. Pasley & M. Ihinger-Tallman (Eds.), *Stepparenting: Issues in theory, research, and practice*. Westport, CT: Greenwood.

Crosbie-Burnett, M., & Skyles, A. (1989). Stepchildren in schools and colleges: Recommendations for educational policy changes. *Family Relations, 38*, 59–64.

Danzinger, S. & Radin, N. (1990). Absent does not equal uninvolved: Predictors of fathers' involvement in teen mother families. *Journal of Marriage and the Family, 52*, 636–642.

Darity, W. A., & Myers, S. L. (1984). Does welfare dependency cause female hardship? The case of the black family. *Journal of Marriage and the Family, 46*, 765–780.

Emery, R. E. (1988). *Marriage, divorce, and children's adjustment.* Newbury Park, CA: Sage.

Fine, M. A. (1989). A social science perspective on stepfamily law: Suggestions for legal reform. *Family Relations, 38,* 53–58.

Fine, M. A., & Fine, D. R. (1992). Recent changes in laws affecting stepfamilies: Suggestions for legal reform. *Family Relations, 41,* 334–340.

Franklin, A. J., & Franklin, N. B. (1985). A psychoeducational perspective on black parenting. In H. McAdoo & J. McAdoo (Eds.), *Black children* (pp. 194–210). Beverly Hills, CA: Sage.

Ganong, L., Coleman, M., & Mapes, D. (1990). A meta-analytic review of family structure stereotypes. *Journal of Marriage and the Family, 52,* 287–297.

Giddings, P. (1982). *When and where I enter: The impact of black women on race and sex in America.* New York: William Morrow.

Gilder, G. (1981). *Wealth and poverty.* New York: Basic Books.

Hall, R. (1992). African-American male stereotypes: Obstacles to social work in a multicultural society. *Journal of Multicultural Social Work, 1,* 77–89.

Hetherington, E. M. (1989). Coping with family transitions: Winners, losers, and survivors. Meetings of the Society for Research in Child Development. *Child Development, 60,* 1–14.

Hetherington, E. M., & Arasteh, J. D. (Eds.). (1988). *Impact of divorce, single parenting, and stepparenting on children.* Hillsdale, NJ: Erlbaum.

Hetherington, E. M., & Clingempeel, W. G. (1992). Coping with marital transitions: A family systems perspective. *Monographs of the Society for Research in Child Development, 57,* (2–3, Serial No. 227).

Kammerman, S. (1983). Fatherhood and social policy: Some insights from a comparative perspective. In M. E. Lamb & A. Sagi (Eds.), *Fatherhood and family policy* (pp. 23–37). Hillsdale, NJ: Erlbaum.

Kurdek, L. A., & Sinclair, R. J. (1988). Adjustment of young adolescents in two-parent nuclear, stepfather, and mother-custody families. *Journal of Consulting and Clinical Psychology, 56,* 91–96.

Lewis, E. (1988a). Role strengths and strains of African-American mothers. *Journal of Primary Prevention, 9,* 77–91.

Lewis, E. (1988b). *Social welfare and blacks in Michigan. State of black Michigan, 1988* (pp. 39–49). East Lansing, MI: Institute for Urban Policy, Michigan State University.

Lewis, E. (1989). Role strain in black women: The efficacy of support groups. *Journal of Black Studies, 20,* 155–169.

Lewis, E., & Ford, B. (1990). The Network Utilization Project: Incorporating traditional strengths of African-Americans into group work practice. *Social Work With Groups, 13,* 7–22.

Lewis, E., & Kissman, K. (1989). Factors in ethnic sensitive feminist social work practice. *ARETE, 14*(2): 23–31.

Manns, W. (1981). Support systems of significant others in black families. In H. McAdoo (Ed.), *Black families* (pp. 238–251). Beverly Hills, CA: Sage.

McAdoo, H. P. (1980). Black mothers and the extended family support network. In L. Rodgers-Rose (Ed.), *The black woman* (pp. 125–144). Beverly Hills, CA: Sage.

McAdoo, H. P. (Ed.). (1981). *Black families.* Beverly Hills, CA: Sage.

McAdoo, J. (1981). Black father and child interactions. In L. Gary (Ed.), *Black men* (pp. 115–130). Beverly Hills, CA: Sage.

Moraga, C., & Anzaldua, G. (Eds.). (1983). *This bridge called my back: Writings by radical women of color.* New York: Kitchen Table–Women of Color Press.

Morrison, T. (1992). *Race-ing, justice, en-gendering power*. New York: Pantheon Books.

Mutran, E. (1985). Intergenerational family support among blacks and whites: Response to cultural or to socioeconomic differences. *Journal of Gerontology, 40*, 382–389.

Ogbu, J. (1981). Black education: A cultural-ecological perspective. In H. McAdoo (Ed.), *Black families* (pp. 139–154). Beverly Hills, CA: Sage.

Peters, M. (1981). "Making it" black family style: Building on the strengths of black families. In N. Stinnett, J. deFrain, K. King, P. Knaub, & C. Rowe (Eds.), *Family strengths 3: Roots of well-being* (pp. 73–91). Lincoln: University of Nebraska Press.

Peters, M. (1985). Racial socialization of young black children. In H. McAdoo & J. McAdoo (Eds.), *Black children* (pp. 159–173). Beverly Hills, CA: Sage.

Peters, M., & Massey, G. (1985). Chronic vs. mundane stress in family stress theories: The case of black families in white America. *Marriage & Family Review, 6*, 193–218.

Price-Bonham, S., & Balswick, J. O. (1980). The noninstitutions: Divorce, desertion, and remarriage. *Journal of Marriage and the Family, 42*, 959–972.

Rodgers-Rose, L. (1980). *The black woman*. Beverly Hills, CA: Sage.

Sowell, T. (1975). *Race and economics*. New York: David McKay.

Spiegel, J. (1982). An ecological model of ethnic families. In M. McGoldrick, J. Pearce, & J. Giordano (Eds.), *Ethnicity & Family therapy* (pp. 31–51). New York: Guilford.

Stack, C. B. (1974). *All our kin*. New York: Harper & Row.

Staples, R. (Ed.). (1971). *The black family: Essays and studies*. Belmont, CA: Wadsworth.

Staples, R. (1981). The black American family. In C. Mendel & R. Haberstein (Eds.), *Ethnic families in America* (2nd ed.) (pp. 217–244). New York: Elsevier.

Taylor, R. (1988). Aging and supportive relationships among black Americans. In J. Jackson (Ed.), *The black American elderly: Research on physical health* (pp. 259–281). New York: Springer.

Taylor, R., Chatters, L., Tucker, B., & Lewis, E. (1990). Developments in research on black families: A decade review. *Journal of Marriage and the Family, 52*, 993–1014.

Thornton, M., Chatters, L., Taylor, R., & Allen, W. (1990). Sociodemographic and environmental influences on racial socialization by black parents. *Child Development, 61*, 401–409.

Thurow, L. (1987). Affirmative action in a zero-sum society. In R. Takaki (Ed.), *From different shores: Perspective on race and ethnicity in America* (pp. 225–230). New York: Oxford.

Wade-Lewis, M. (1989). The strengths of African-American stepfamilies. In N. Maglin & N. Schniedewind (Eds.), *Women and stepfamilies: Voices of anger and love* (pp. 225–233). Philadelphia: Temple University Press.

Wallerstein, J. S. (1991). The long-term effects of divorce on children: A review. *Journal of the American Academy of Child and Adolescent Psychiatry, 30*, 349–360.

Weitzman, L. J. (1981). The economics of divorce: Social and economic consequences of property, alimony and child support awards. *UCLA Law Review, 28*, 1183–1268.

Weitzman, L. J. (1985). *The divorce revolution: The unexpected social and economic consequences for women and children in America*. New York: Macmillan.

Whiteside, M. F. (1989). Family rituals as a key to kinship connections in remarried families. *Family Relations, 38,* 34–39.

Wilson, M. (1989). Child development in the context of the black extended family. *American Psychologist, 44,* 380–385.

Part VII

RECOGNIZING DIVERSITY, ENCOURAGING SOLIDARITY

27

POVERTY, SOCIAL RIGHTS, AND THE QUALITY OF CITIZENSHIP

Roger Lawson
William Julius Wilson

Although poverty and inequality have increased in Europe and in Canada, the most severe consequences of the social and economic dislocations of the past two decades have occurred in the United States. This was already readily apparent in the late 1970s but became more pronounced during the 1980s, when the Reagan administration pursued policies aimed at improving the living standards of the broad middle class and relied on economic growth to trickle down and take care of the problems of the poor.

By the second half of the 1980s, the American poverty rate among the nonelderly population rose to more than double that of most European countries and to almost three times the level in West Germany. Even when the elderly are included, the United States had the highest national poverty rate of all thirteen countries represented in the LIS data base (Rainwater 1991). Even more significant were the changing depth or severity of poverty in the United States and the sharply divergent patterns of poverty concentration between racial minorities and whites.

In recent years, the United States Census Bureau established what might be called "the poorest of the poor" category, that is, those individuals whose annual income falls at least 50 percent below the officially designated poverty line. In 1975, 30 percent of all the poor had incomes below 50 percent of the poverty level; in 1988, 40 percent did so. Among blacks, the increase was much sharper, from 32 percent in 1975 to nearly half (48 percent) in 1988 (U.S. Bureau of the Census 1988).

As the comparisons with Europe suggest, these trends can be seen as the outcome of a distinctive response to poverty that has long prevailed in the United States. As Rainwater (1991) has noted, "America's various wars on poverty, unlike those of some continental European countries, have been particularly preoccupied with the situation of the very worst off in society, with the situation of the lower class rather than that of the working class more broadly." This difference has been reflected in the way antipoverty and social policy agendas have been structured. In most European welfare states, the prevailing view for much of the postwar period has been similar to that described by a French official. "A policy for the poor," he suggested, "is a poor policy ... the general principle underlying steps to help the most disadvantaged is to ensure that they get the maximum benefit from programs which apply to the population as a whole. Rather than specific measures, the idea is to pay specific attention to groups in difficulty within the context of general measures" (Lion 1984).

By contrast, most American "welfare" and antipoverty programs, including the Great Society's War on Poverty programs in the 1960s, have emphasized targeting and means testing rather than universalistic social policy. As such, they have been relatively autonomous arrangements for the "poor" that have developed largely in isolation from broader national concerns with employment or indeed from macroeconomic interventions more generally. Politically and institutionally they have been sharply differentiated from mainstream social policies, especially social security, health, and housing, for the "stable" working class and middle class. Moreover, the American response to poverty has been typically characterized by a predilection for "programs" rather than "policy" and especially for decentralized and fragmented programs and experiments.

A number of excellent historical studies have shown that the American approach to poverty is part of the peculiar policy legacy of the New Deal (see, e.g., Weir, Orloff, and Skocpol 1988; Katz 1986, 1989; Patterson 1981). These studies demonstrate how the development of nationwide social security programs under the New Deal marked an important extension of social citizenship to the "deserving" working class (i.e., workers with good job prospects and the ability to pay regular contributions). These programs were not only backed by a strong federal bureaucracy, they also had a broad base of public support, including support from the middle classes who gained from the improvements in social security entitlements.

However, the New Deal did much less to address the problems facing people with low skills and status, including many blacks migrating out of the rural South, who were prone to bouts of joblessness, low and fluctuating incomes, and poor health. Policy initiatives that would have rebounded to their benefit, such as attempts to establish a firm national commitment to full employment or to a nationwide health care program, were notably unsuccessful in the 1930s and 1940s. The United States also lacked the combination of laws, union power, and customs used in Europe after 1945 to raise the bottom of the labor market. Instead, under the New Deal system, efforts to combat the real threat of poverty among the weakest sections of society were confined to a number of disjointed, second-tier programs grouped under the rubric of "welfare." With much weaker administrative capacities than social security, the fate of these programs was largely dependent on the altruism of the nonpoor.

The historical analysis shows how the development of second-tier "welfare" programs from the New Deal not only restricted the scope of antipoverty initiatives but also reinforced traditional concerns with the "underserving poor" and, more importantly, images of the poor and of many black Americans as a class apart in American society. In many important respects, the Great Society programs of the 1960s helped sustain these images.

Although the War on Poverty appeared to herald a new and less divisive era in social policy, its impact on social rights contrasted sharply with the extension of political and civil rights to blacks in the 1960s. The poor gained some notable improvements in welfare benefits, but from policies that did little in practice to integrate the recipients into the economic and social life of mainstream society. On the contrary, issues like unemployment and the growth of female-headed households among the newly urbanized black poor were still treated as distinctive welfare issues to be addressed through "special interest" programs. As one study puts it, "despite a greater willingness to expend resources on the poor ... the labor economists and sociologists who became architects of the poverty programs in the 1960s saw efforts to change the behavior of the poor as the most promising route to ending poverty—for poverty was, by definition, not a national economic problem" (Weir, Orloff, and Skocpol 1988: 206). Even the more radical measures of the War on Poverty, such as the efforts in the Community Action Programs to secure poor and minority group control of social policy institutions, effectively maintained the separation of poverty policy from broader issues of social solidarity and wider economic and workplace concerns (Klass 1983).

The events of the past two decades have exposed the real weaknesses of the targeted welfare programs. As Skocpol (1988: 309) has argued, "When the political going gets rough for public social policies, as it has in the United States since the 1970s, policies that lack clear political and cultural legitimation as expressions of social compassion and collective solidarity are difficult to either defend or extend against individualist, market-oriented, and anti-statist attacks." Put another way, the most significant welfare state backlash in this period has occurred, not where social spending is highest, but in countries like the United States, where there has been a more marked "us/them" divide in social policy between programs for the broad middle mass in society and programs for the poor. As Korpi (1980) explains, this dualism "in effect splits the working class and tends to generate coalitions between the better off workers and the middle class thus creating a larger constituency for welfare-backlash. In fact, the 'welfare backlash' becomes rational political activity for the majority of citizens."

But the welfare backlash is also activity that has been fueled by the way America's antipoverty efforts have in the long run fostered group misunderstanding and isolation and distrust of the poor. A weakening of community support for the poor—or what Alan Ryan (1992) has called "the retreat from caring"—is another of the broader themes associated with the new configurations of poverty. Ryan used the phrase in a commentary on the new "tough love" policies advocated by both Democrats and Republicans in the 1992 U.S. presidential campaign and particularly on the way even Democrats appeared to despair of the poor.

The 1992 Democratic party platform took a line that ten years earlier would have been denounced as "blaming the victim." Why this exasperated mood seemed so widespread was, to Ryan, a puzzle, given the low costs of the social programs that evoked so much hostility. However, he attributed it partly to despair at the apparent intractability of black poverty and, more specifically, to the decline of basic formal and informal institutions in ghetto neighborhoods. This placed severe constraints on welfare services in locating their clients but, more importantly, made it "harder to recruit community organizers who provide grassroots support to go with government assistance."

The problem of who now speaks for the poor is raised in Guy Standing's discussion in *Poverty, Inequality, and the Future of Social Policy* of the dramatic erosion of trade union rights and influence on both sides of the Atlantic. As he argues, unions have sometimes been castigated for representing mainly relatively secure male employees. But, in reality, union membership has often in the past made a substantial difference for the most vulnerable groups in the labor market. His figures for the United States in the late 1980s are worth repeating: "whereas white men gained a wage premium of about 50 cents an hour from union membership, black men gained about $1.61, Hispanic men about $2.18, white women about $0.83, black women $1.23 and Hispanic women $1.53."

The retreat from caring in the United States reflects a more widespread sense of pessimism about the intractability of poverty and the failure of welfare programs than has been evident in Europe. The European comparisons indicate that much of the problem in the United States stems from the limited range of tools available for combating poverty. Without the support of more universal social services or labor market interventions, welfare programs have attempted to do too much, not too little. However, the prevalent mood in America by the 1970s and 1980s offered a very different interpretation. To many middle Americans, the nation's poorest citizens had come to be virtually synonymous with a "welfare class" posing a growing threat to the public peace and to dominant American norms. To be more specific, as a study of social standing in America in the 1970s showed, lower America was seen to be separated into two status subdivisions. At the bottom of the ladder was the welfare class, people who were described in terms of their behavioral and cultural deficiencies by the great majority of those interviewed in the study, and who were seen as being caught up in a "welfare way of life" that undermined initiative and encouraged apathy, alienation, and normlessless. Above them were people who were "lower class but not the lowest": Significantly, they were "accorded their superior standing 'because they are never on welfare' or 'only occasionally' (and 'if on, they're trying to get off')" (Coleman and Rainwater 1979).

The heavy emphasis on the individual traits of the welfare poor and on the duties or social obligations of welfare recipients is not unique to the general public. This "common wisdom" has been uncritically incorporated into the work of many poverty researchers. Throughout the 1960s and 1970s, the expanding network of poverty researchers in the United States paid considerable attention to the question of individuals' work attitudes and the association between income maintenance programs and the work ethic of the poor. They consistently ignored the effects of basic economic transformations and cyclical processes on the work experiences and prospects of the poor.

However, despite this narrow focus, these very American researchers have consistently uncovered empirical findings that undermine, rather than support, assumptions about the negative effects of welfare receipt on individual initiative and motivation. Yet these assumptions persist among policymakers, and "the paradox of continuing high poverty during a period of general prosperity has contributed to the recently emerging consensus that welfare must be reformed" (Melville and Doble 1988). Although it is reasonable to argue that policymakers are not aware of a good deal of the empirical research on the effects of welfare, the General Accounting Office (GAO), an investigative arm of Congress, released a study in early 1987 that reported that there was no conclusive evidence for the prevailing beliefs that welfare discourages individuals from working, breaks up two-parent families, or affects the child-bearing rates of unmarried women, even young unmarried women.

The GAO report reached these conclusions after reviewing the results of more than 100 empirical studies on the effects of welfare completed since 1975, analyzing the case files of more than 1,200 families receiving public assistance in four states, and interviewing officials from federal, state, and local government agencies. Nonetheless, despite the report's findings, the growth of social dislocations among the inner-city poor and the continued high rates of poverty have led an increasing number of policymakers to conclude that something should be done about the current welfare system to halt what they perceive to be the breakdown of the norms of citizenship. Indeed, a liberal-conservative consensus on welfare reform has recently emerged that features two themes: (1) The receipt of welfare should be predicated on reciprocal responsibilities whereby society is obligated to provide assistance to welfare applicants who, in turn, are obligated to behave in socially approved ways; and (2) able-bodied adult welfare recipients should be required to prepare themselves for work, to search for employment, and to accept jobs when they are offered. These points of agreement were reflected in the discussions of the welfare reform legislation passed in the United States Congress in 1988.

These two themes are based on the implicit assumption that a sort of mysterious "welfare ethos" exists that encourages public assistance recipients to avoid their obligations as citizens to be educated, to work, to support their families, and to obey the law. In other words, and in keeping with the dominant American belief system, *it is the moral fabric of individuals, not the social and economic structure of society, that is taken to be the root of the problem* (Wacquant and Wilson 1989).

The poverty tradition in the United States, including the lack of comprehensive programs to promote the social rights of American citizens, is especially problematic for poor inner-city blacks who are also handicapped by problems that originated in the denial of civil, political, and social rights to previous generations. And their degree of current economic deprivation and social isolation is in part due to the limited nature of institutionalized social rights in the United States (Schmitter-Heisler 1991). Indeed, the effects of joblessness on all the poor in the United States are far more severe than those experienced by disadvantaged groups in other advanced industrial Western societies. While economic restructuring and its adverse effects on lower-income groups has been common to all these societies in recent years, the most severe consequences of social and economic dislocations have been in the United States because of the underdeveloped welfare state and the weak institutional structure of social citizenship rights. Although all economically marginal groups have been affected, the inner-city black poor have been particularly devastated because their plight has been compounded by their spatial concentration in deteriorating ghetto neighborhoods, neighborhoods that reinforce weak labor force attachment.

In short, the socioeconomic position of the inner-city black poor in American society is extremely precarious. The cumulative effects of historic racial exclusion have made them vulnerable to the economic restructuring of the advanced industrial economy. Moreover, the problems of joblessness, deepening poverty, and other woes that have accompanied these economic changes cannot be relieved by the meager welfare programs targeted to the poor. Furthermore, these problems tend to be viewed by members of the larger society as a reflection of personal deficiencies, not structural inequities.

Accordingly, if any group has a stake in the enhancement of social rights in the United States, it is the inner-city black poor. Unfortunately, given the strength of the American belief system on poverty and welfare, any program that would improve the life chances of this group would have to be based on concerns beyond those that focus on life and experiences in inner-city ghettos. The poor and the working classes struggle to make ends meet, and even the middle class has experienced a decline in its living standard. Indeed, Americans across racial and class boundaries continue to worry about unemployment and job security, declining real wages, escalating medical and housing costs, childcare programs, the sharp decline in the quality of public education, and crime and drug trafficking in their neighborhoods.

These concerns are reflected in public opinion surveys. For the last several years national opinion polls consistently reveal strong public backing for government labor market strategies, including training efforts, to enhance employment. A 1988 Harris poll indicated that almost three-quarters of the respondents would support a tax increase to pay for childcare. A 1989 Harris poll reports that almost nine out of ten Americans would like to see fundamental change in the United States' health care system. And recent surveys conducted by the National Opinion Research Center at the University of Chicago reveal that a substantial majority of Americans want more money spent on improving the nation's educational system and on halting rising crime and drug addiction.

These poll results suggest the possibility of new alignments in support of the enhancement of social rights. If a serious attempt is made to forge such an alignment, perhaps it ought to begin with a new public rhetoric that does two things: focuses on problems that afflict not only the poor, but the working and middle classes as well; and emphasizes integrative programs that promote the social and economic improvement of all groups in society, not just the truly disadvantaged segments of the population.

REFERENCES

Ashton, D., and Maguire, M. 1991. "Patterns and Experiences of Unemployment." In *Poor Work: Disadvantage and the Division of Labour*, edited by P. Brown and R. Scase, 40–55. Milton Keynes & Philadelphia: Open University Press.

Balsen, W., et. al. 1984. *Die neue Armut*. Cologne: Bund Verlag.

Caraley, D. 1992. "Washington Abandons the Cities." *Political Science Quarterly* 107: 1–27.

Coleman, R., and Rainwater, L. 1979. *Social Standing in America*. London: Routledge & Kegan Paul.

Dean, H., and Taylor-Gooby, P. 1993. *Dependency Culture: The Explosion of a Myth*. New York and London: Harvester Wheatsheaf.

Economist. 1992. "All Quiet on the Racial Front?" 325 (7788), December 5th–11th, London.

Freeman, R. 1983. "Public Policy and Employment Discrimination in the United States." In *Ethnic Pluralism and Public Policy*, edited by N. Glazer and K. Young, 124–144. Lexington, Mass.: D.C. Health.

Katz, M. 1986. *In the Shadow of the Poorhouse: A Social History of Welfare in the United States*. New York: Basic Books.

———. 1989. *The Undeserving Poor: From the War on Poverty to the War on Welfare*. New York: Pantheon.

Klass, G. 1983. "Explaining America and the Welfare State: An Alternative Theory." *British Journal of Political Science* 15: 427–450.

Korpi, W. 1980. "Social Policy and Distributional Conflict in the Capitalist Democracies." *West European Politics* 3(1).

Lawson, R. 1987. "Social Security and the Division of Welfare." In *Inside British Society: Continuity, Challenge and Change*, edited by G. Causer, 77–97. New York: St. Martin's Press.

Leibfried, S., and Tennstedt, F., eds. 1985. *Politik der Armut und die Spaltung des Sozialstaats*. Frankfurt am Main: Suhrkamp.

Lion, A. 1984. "An Anti-poverty Policy or a Social Development Policy? A French Point of View." In *Anti-Poverty Policy in the European Community*, edited by J. Brown, 100–112. London: Policy Studies Institute.

Marklund, S. 1986. "The Swedish Model—Work and Welfare." *ASW Impact* December.

Melville, K., and J. Doble. 1988. *The Public's Perspective on Social Welfare Reform*. The Public Agenda Foundation, January.

OECD, 1988. *The Future of Social Protection: The General Debate*. Paris: Organization for Economic Co-operation and Development.

Patterson, J. 1981. *America's Struggle Against Poverty*. Cambridge, Mass.: Harvard University Press.

Rainwater, L. 1991. *Poverty in American Eyes*. Luxembourg Income Study, CEPS/INSTEAD. Mimeo.

Ryan, A. 1992. "The Retreat from Caring." *The Times*, London, August 12.

Sampson, R., and W. J. Wilson. 1994. "Toward a Theory of Race, Crime, and Urban Inequality." In *Crime and Inequality*, edited by J. Hagan and R. Peterson. Stanford: Stanford University Press.

Schmitter-Heisler, B. 1991. "A Comparative Perspective on the Underclass." *Theory and Society* 20:455–483.

Schneider, U. 1993. *Solidarpakt gegen die Schwachen: Der Rückzug des Staates aus der Sozial-politik*. München: Knaur.

Skocpol, T. 1988. "The Limits of the New Deal System and the Roots of Contemporary Welfare Dilemmas." In *The Politics of Social Policy in the United States*, edited by M. Weir, S. Orloff, and T. Skocpol, 293–312. Princeton, N.J.: Princeton University Press.

Smith, S. 1989. *The Politics of "Race" and Residence*. London: Polity Press.

Standing, G. 1986. *Unemployment and Labour Market Flexibility: The United Kingdom*. Geneva: International Labour Office.

Statistisches Bundeamt. 1993. *Sozialhilfe*. Wiesbaden: Statistisches Bundeamt.

Townsend, P., et al. 1987. *Poverty and Labour in London*. London: Low Pay Unit.

U.S. Bureau of the Census. 1988. "Money Income and Poverty Status in the U.S." In *Current Population Reports*, Series P-60. Washington, D.C.: Government Printing Office.

Vincent, D. 1991. *Poor Citizens*. London and New York: Longman.

Wacquant, L., and W. J. Wilson. 1989. "Poverty, Joblessness and the Social Transformation of the Inner City." In *Reforming Welfare Policy*, edited by D. Ellwood and P. Cottingham, 70–102. Cambridge, Mass.: Harvard University Press.

Weir, M. 1993. "Race and Urban Poverty: Comparing Europe and America." Center for American Political Studies, Harvard University, Occasional Paper 93–9, March.

Weir, M., Orloff, A., and Skocpol, T. 1988. "The Future of Social Policy in the United States: Political Constraints and Possibilities." In *The Politics of Social Policy in the United States*, edited by M. Weir, S. Orloff & T. Skocpol, 421–446. Princeton, N.J.: Princeton University Press.

Wilson, W. J. 1987. *The Truly Disadvantaged: The Inner City, The Underclass, and Public Policy*. Chicago: University of Chicago Press.

———. 1991. "Studying Inner-City Social Dislocations: The Challenge of Public Agenda Research." *American Sociological Review* 56:1–14.

———. 1995. *Jobless Ghettoes: The Disappearance of Work and its Effect on Urban Life*. New York: Knopf.

28

THE CASE FOR A RACE-SPECIFIC POLICY

Stephen Steinberg

Needless to say, all poverty is contemptible, and it is easy and tempting to call for a color-blind assault on poverty. The problem with the color-blind left, like the color-blind right, is that it is willing to pay lip service to the unique oppression of blacks, but is unwilling to address it outside of a larger social agenda. In my view, by virtue of their unique oppression, blacks have historical and moral claim to having their grievances redressed before those of other groups. Blacks should not have to queue up with the other displaced workers in the nation's rust belt. For their underclass status is not merely the result of plant shutdowns. It is the end product of three centuries of racial oppression.

From a national standpoint, too, the black underclass warrants special priority, again because of its special history. For the black underclass represents not just economic dislocation, income maldistribution, and social injustice; it represents all that, *and* racism. The black underclass is the present-day manifestation of America's greatest crime, and is a blot on American democracy. At stake is not just social and economic justice, but the very soul of the nation.

Just as William Julius Wilson's analysis led him to "a universal program" for change, the foregoing analysis suggests the need for a race-specific public policy. Several elements of such a policy are outlined below:

1. We need a national commitment to eliminate ghettos. It is remarkable how we, as a nation, have become inured to the odious moral connotations of this term. We talk about "ghettos" with the same neutrality that we talk about "suburbs." Ghettos are nothing less than the shameful residue of slavery. It took one century after this nation declared its own freedom from colonial domination to abolish slavery. It took another century, and a protracted and bloody civil rights struggle, to end official segregation. It is time for a third stage that will eliminate racial ghettos, and destroy the less visible barriers that manifest themselves in a host of inequities ranging from lower incomes to higher mortality.

2. The elimination of ghettos would entail large-scale programs of urban reconstruction, like those proposed by Wilson and others. These programs, however, should have the specific purpose of eliminating ghettos, lest they become a pork barrel for a myriad of "urban" and "minority" constituencies. Furthermore, in my view, these economic policies must not ignore the racial and cultural dimensions of the underclass. For economic policy to

work, it is imperative that local groups and individuals be empowered so that the process of reconstruction can occur from within, rather than being imposed from outside. Only community-based groups can bridge the chasm that separates the underclass from mainstream society, and marshal the cultural and spiritual resources to effect meaningful change.

This is the correct application of the culture-of-poverty thesis. When Oscar Lewis wrote that "the elimination of physical poverty *per se* may not be enough to eliminate the culture of poverty," he pointed to the need to combat apathy and despair "by organizing the poor and giving them a sense of belonging, of power and of leadership."[1] In his book *The Black Underclass*, Douglas Glasgow also showed how street-corner men and former convicts and addicts were mobilized, in the wake of the Watts Riot and the infusion of federal funds, to work as constructive agents for change.[2] My point is that not only the ends, but the means as well, must be race-specific.

3. We should not be diverted by the adamant opposition to affirmative action, and the split in the liberal coalition over this issue. Affirmative action has been hotly contested because it is the most radical development in race policy since Reconstruction. It is radical because it legitimated the principle of compensation for past wrongs, and provided a fool-proof mechanism for achieving racial parity—one which has achieved significant results in major employment sectors.

For example, in 1973 the American Telephone and Telegraph Company, one of the largest employers in corporate America, entered into a six-year agreement with the Equal Employment Opportunities Commission to correct prior discriminatory employment practices. By 1982 the percentage of minority craft workers had increased from 8.4 percent to 14 percent. The proportion of minorities in management increased even more—from 4.6 percent to 13.1 percent.

Raw numbers point up the impact of affirmative action even more vividly. The number of black employees at IBM increased from 750 in 1962, to 7,251 in 1968, to 16,546 in 1980. Under threat of litigation, governmental agencies have pursued affirmative action programs even more aggressively. To take one key example, since the late 1960s the number of black police officers nationally increased by 20,000. These diverse examples testify to the profound impact that affirmative action has had on black representation in both the private and public sectors.[3]

These examples also rebut the claim, made by Wilson and others, that affirmative action primarily benefits those who are "already advantaged." As William Taylor has pointed out: "The focus of much of the effort has been not just on white collar jobs, but also on law enforcement, construction work, and craft and production jobs in large companies—all areas in which the extension of new opportunities has provided upward mobility for less advantaged minority workers."[4]

Having laid the groundwork and survived the harrowing legal battles, we should not turn away from affirmative action as a strategy for rectifying past wrongs.[5] On the contrary, affirmative action should be extended into all areas of our economy and society. Wilson is right to worry that its benefits will not filter down to the underclass, but this is not an insurmountable problem. Our statisticians have demonstrated their skill at classifying who belongs to the underclass. The challenge is to make this designation a ticket to a good job, instead of what Richard McGahey has called "poverty's voguish stigma."[6]

4. We need manpower policies that will assess immigration policy with respect to its impact on native workers, and minority workers in particular. Again, this raises issues that trouble the liberal conscience, and demands hard moral choices. However, as Otis Graham, Jr., wrote in *Dissent* in 1980, immigration restriction should be considered, "not simply in the interest of national economic efficiency, but as the only way to extend economic opportunity to our own disadvantaged."[7]

In the past quarter-century, when some three million industrial jobs disappeared, the nation absorbed over eleven million legal immigrants, not to speak of millions of undocumented workers. Thus, at the same time that we have been exporting jobs we have been importing workers—in even greater numbers. It may be true, as some have argued, that many of these immigrants are not in direct competition with the underclass.[8] Others are, however, and while this simple truth seems to elude the experts, it is acutely realized by average blacks who are in direct competition with immigrants. This was evident during the recent "riots" in southern Florida, where protesters voiced their resentment about the influx of Hispanic and Haitian refugees.[9] Whatever salubrious effects immigration may have for the economy as a whole, it can hardly be denied that the absorption of well over eleven million immigrants in the last quarter-century has compounded the job crisis for the nation's thirteen million black workers. Once again, the nation is pursuing a short-sighted policy of importing foreign labor instead of upgrading the skills of our marginal domestic workers.

I hasten to add that this is not an argument for blanket restriction. There are other compelling moral and political considerations that must be taken into account when shaping immigration policy. For one thing, different nationalities have different historical and moral claims. This is particularly true of nations previously conquered or colonized by the United States, including Mexico. Secondly, although immigration policy generally has been governed by self-interest, the United States *has* functioned as an asylum for the dispossessed, and we cannot in good conscience slam the door on desperate political and economic refugees. These legitimate concerns, however, must be balanced against the interests of unemployed and marginal native workers who pay the price of current immigration practices.

Nursing is a case in point. To meet a critical shortage of nurses, the United States has been importing tens of thousands of foreign nurses, largely from the Philippines and the West Indies. At the same time, we have been closing down nursing schools throughout the United States, instead of expanding subsidies and creating channels of opportunity for blacks and other marginal groups. No doubt, it is cheaper and more expedient to import nurses trained at some other nation's expense. However, such a shortsighted policy would be inconceivable if our nation's unresolved racial problems were high on the national agenda.

The agenda outlined above is clearly not politically realistic, now or in the forseeable future.[10] Indeed, critics of an earlier version of this essay contended that it is self-contradictory to argue, as I do, that racism is pervasive and endemic, and at the same time, to propose race-specific solutions that would arouse the adamant opposition of most whites. According to these critics, blacks are too weak politically to "do it on their own." Only by entering into broader coalitions, and supporting a larger agenda, can they hope for political deliverance. Thus, like Wilson, they opt for a "universal program of reform" that would attack the institutionalized inequalities which include but are not limited to racial inequality. In this view, blacks stand to gain more by participating in this larger movement than they are likely to achieve by pursuing a specifically black agenda.

My critics were particularly affronted by my suggestion that blacks have historical and moral claim to have their problems redressed before others. Is one hungry child any less deserving of our compassion than another? Don't other groups—Indians, chicanos, women, Appalachian whites, displaced steel workers—also have compelling historical and moral claims? Is it moral or helpful to quibble about which groups suffered more? To engage in "comparative suffering" can only be divisive, and detract from a common struggle against oppression and inequality. The only moral path, and the only politically viable one, is the pursuit of political goals that would eliminate the institutionalized inequalities that are at the root of all these inequities.

Granted, these are powerful arguments, not to be dismissed lightly. Furthermore, I am willing to concede the moral high ground to my critics. After all, they are guided by a comprehensive vision of a more egalitarian society, rather than what they construe as a divisive concern with the interests and welfare of specific groups. The issue, though, is whether a millennial political and moral agenda, despite its worthy intentions, ends up as a pious evasion of difficult, and often unpleasant, moral and political choices.

A number of considerations must be weighed in assessing the merits and practicality of a race-specific policy as opposed to the universal program advocated by Wilson and others:

1. Whether or not a race-specific policy is politically realistic, it is incumbent on us as social scientists to put forward an analysis and agenda that is faithful to history and responsive to the racial crisis that afflicts this society, with terrible repercussions for whites and blacks alike. It is important to go on record with a clear, unequivocal statement that is *not* calibrated to political reality. This is not just a matter of intellectual and moral rectitude. Even from a political standpoint, it is important to establish a principled position before compromising with "political reality." If

we allow praxis to govern analysis, we run the risk of losing sight of the theoretical and moral underpinnings of our own position.

What, then, is to be said about Wilson's "hidden agenda?" On the premise that programs targeted for blacks are anathema to most whites, he argues that "the hidden agenda for liberal policymakers is to improve the life chances of the truly disadvantaged groups such as the ghetto underclass by emphasizing programs to which the more advantaged groups of all races and class backgrounds can positively relate."[11] However, it is not altogether clear what assumptions lurk behind Wilson's policy facade. Is it that he actually favors a race-specific policy, but believes he has to "hide" programs intended for blacks by extending benefits to whites? Or is his point that the contemporary sources of black disadvantage have little to do with race, and therefore class-based politics become necessary? Or does he, like some of the color-blind left, champion the cause of all disadvantaged groups—"regardless of race," as it were—and therefore see racial inequality only as a manifestation, albeit a special one, of larger and more pervasive inequalities? It would be far better had Wilson laid all his racial and class cards on the table before bowing to the exigencies of practical politics.

2. "You are right historically and you are right morally," my critics tell me, "but you are disastrously wrong politically. Not only is there no political constituency for race-specific programs, but worse than that, such an approach is self-defeating since it triggers a reactionary backlash."

In the first place, there would have been no civil rights revolution, and there would be no significant black middle class today, if blacks had been deterred by the inevitable white backlash. Ever since the Montgomery boycott, there have been solemn voices of "moderation" admonishing blacks to curtail their militancy lest they provoke reaction and alienate even their white supporters. Yet if there is any wisdom in hindsight, it is that militancy brought results despite—and perhaps because of—the racial polarization that ensued.

In a recent op-ed piece in the *New York Times*, Wilson again makes his case for "coalition politics and race-blind programs.[12] He worries aloud that a race-specific approach only translates into Republican electoral victories. The politics of backlash are not so simple and predictable, however. One could argue that the Democratic Party would lose more white support if blacks worked inconspicuously within the Party than it would if blacks were an obtrusive and militant force *outside* the Party. This latter strategy, paradoxically, might actually enhance the political viability of the Democratic agenda, without asking blacks to become politically invisible.

In any event, Wilson's case against race-specific politics would be more compelling if his "universal approach" were in fact politically viable, and if "full employment" were more than a mirage on the political horizon. This is hardly the case, however. His proposals, especially his advocacy of full employment, would entail a vast expansion in the welfare state and major restructuring of political and economic institutions. This may be the ultimate goal of any radical politics, but it can hardly be claimed to be politically realistic at the present time.

On the other hand, a race-specific approach does not entail major changes in basic institutions. Its major aim is the integration of blacks into the economy and labor force, whether this is achieved through manpower policy, enforcement of anti-discriminatory legislation, affirmative action, or development projects aimed at ghettos and the ghetto underclass. By itself this is not a radical agenda, and perhaps this is why it is not appealing to some of my activist critics. If this is so, however, it points up a major disjunction between a black agenda and a radical agenda, a point that warrants more analysis and soul-searching than it has received thus far.

Thus, what renders a race-specific agenda politically unrealistic is not that it is too "radical," but only that, as Wilson suggests, whites will not support programs targeted for blacks. But is this necessarily the case? Many of the Great Society programs were directly or indirectly targeted for the inner-city (the politically acceptable euphemism for the ghetto). Furthermore, affirmative action, which is explicitly a race-specific policy, has at various times received the approval of all and concerted opposition, but has achieved significant results. Similar policies have been implemented in other nations, including Israel, and despite furious and sometimes violent opposition, governments have not capitulated to reaction. It is strange and unbecoming to see activists on the left succumbing to the white backlash because it is "divisive" among their own constituency. What, then, does this vaunted coalition have to offer blacks if they must subordinate their legitimate and urgent demands to the interests and prejudices of their white allies?

Furthermore, it is not a given that the opposition to race-specific policies cannot be overcome. Enlightened leadership, perhaps under the aegis of an independent black political party, might make some headway in convincing the American public that impoverished and crime-ridden ghettos and a volatile underclass are not in the national interest. Unfortunately, as Harold Cruse has been arguing for decades, there has been a failure among black leaders to adequately define and advance a black agenda.[13] The notion that the black protest movement, once it achieved its legislative agenda, was impotent in dealing with the massive problems of poverty and unemployment has been a debilitating and self-fulfilling myth. The nearly thirty million blacks in the United States generally share a racial and political consciousness and potentially constitute the basis of a formidable political movement. If such a movement defined a clear political agenda, mobilized the ghetto population, aroused the conscience of sympathetic whites, made effective use of its base in the political establishment, and developed a strategy for exerting pressure both within and outside the electoral system, it could make a significant political difference.

At least it is not obvious that such a movement would be destined to failure. It has the advantage of a number of political assets that were absent when the civil rights movement emerged: the franchise; a sizable black middle class that could potentially provide leadership and resources; a political base in local, state, and national government; a far more favorable climate of tolerance in the nation as a whole; and finally, a political legacy in the form of consciousness, organization, and tactics developed during the ten-year civil rights struggle. As during the sixties, it may be spontaneous eruptions of rage among ghetto youth that finally galvanize protest and frighten the white power structure to pay attention to the immense human tragedy in the nation's ghettos. Those who dismiss a race-specific strategy as "unrealistic" could never have predicted the civil rights revolution, since it originated from even greater political inertia and weakness, and faced even more insuperable obstacles.

3. There is historical irony in the claim that blacks cannot "do it on their own," but must join in coalitions with larger agendas. The black liberation movement has been the major catalyst of progressive change for the past thirty years. Directly and indirectly, it helped to ignite protest movements among other marginal and stigmatized groups, including Third World minorities, women, homosexuals, and the handicapped, and it was a major factor—if not *the* major factor—in galvanizing support for a war on poverty. By heightening political consciousness and by challenging the legitimacy of the established order, the black liberation movement also paved the way for the student movement and the antiwar movement, culminating in the emergence of the New Left.

This is not to deny the need for coalition. At issue, however, is the axis of this coalition. Should blacks be urged to enter into a coalition with other progressive groups, and subordinate their demands to a larger agenda? Or, paradoxically, would the progressive agenda be better served if progressive groups channeled their energies and resources into a revitalized black protest movement? As in the past, a national commitment to eliminate the vestiges of slavery in the United States would inevitably unleash other forces of change, and compel the nation to attend to its unfinished social agenda.

4. Finally, a comment about "comparative suffering." In my view, it is vitally important to acknowledge that two groups—Indians and blacks—have suffered a unique oppression in America. To be sure, other groups have suffered prejudice and discrimination, and countless injustices. But what is there to compare with wars of extermination, the appropriation of Indian land, and the banishing of the surviving population to reservation wastelands? What claims are the moral equivalent to two centuries of slavery, and another century of second-class citizenship, codified in the nation's laws and pervading every social institution? More is involved here than historical and moral truth. The whole justification—indeed, the only justification—for race-specific public policy is that certain groups have been victims of crimes of such magnitude and with such enduring consequence that "equal opportunity" is not enough, and special remedial policies become necessary.

In the final analysis, this is what is most disturbing about Wilson's thesis regarding "the declining significance of race" and his advocacy of universal, as opposed to race-specific, public policy. It absolves the nation of responsibility for coming to terms with its racist legacy, and takes race off of the national agenda.

NOTES

Acknowledgement: In writing this paper, I benefited from an extended dialogue with Neil McLaughlin. We generally disagreed, but he was a redoubtable and unyielding sparring partner, and this forced me to think through and clarify my position. Gertrude Ezorsky provided me with valuable source material and criticism. I presented an earlier version of this essay to the irascible "Monday lunch" group at Queens College, and the spirited debate that ensued provided the basis for the concluding section to this piece.

1. Oscar Lewis, *La Vida* (New York: Vintage, 1968), p. 1ii.
2. Douglas G. Glasgow, *The Black Underclass* (New York: Vintage Books, 1981), chapter 8.
3. These figures come from chapter 4 of "A Report of the Citizen's Commission on Civil Rights," 620 Michigan Ave. N.E., Washington, D.C. 20064. For a lucid statement concerning the history, rationale, and objectives of affirmative action, see "Affirmative Action in the 1980s: Dismantling the Process of Discrimination," United States Commission on Civil Rights, Clearinghouse Publication 70 (November 1981).
4. William L. Taylor, "*Brown*, Equal Protection, and the Isolation of the Poor," *Yale Law Journal* 95 (1986), p. 1714. Wilson, in fact, quotes this very passage, but goes on to portray affirmative action as a "creaming" process that primarily helps "those with the greatest economic, education, and social resources among the less advantaged individuals" (p. 115). To be precise, affirmative action clearly does not reach those who are worst off. However, those who are reached can hardly be described as the "cream" of black society: they are socially and economically marginal, and have few, if any, alternative channels of mobility. The key point, as Taylor shows even with respect to professional schools, is that gains associated with affirmative action involve real mobility, "not simply changing occupational preferences among middle class minority families" (p. 1714). For other defenses of affirmative action, see Herman Schwartz, "Affirmative Action," in Leslie W. Dunbar, ed., *Minority Report* (New York: Pantheon Books, 1984), pp. 58–74; and Herbert Hill, "The Opposition to Affirmative Action," *New Politics*, V. I, No. 2 (Winter 1987), pp. 31–82.
5. Of course, as we are finding out, "surviving the harrowing legal battles" is not irreversible. The Supreme Court recently rendered a decision that jeopardizes affirmative action programs in 36 states and 200 local governments. The test case was a Richmond, Virginia, law that channeled 30 percent of public works funds to minority-owned construction companies. When the law was passed less than 1 percent of the city's construction contracts had been awarded to

minority-owned businesses in the previous five years. At the time half the city's population was black. The majority on the Court insisted on a stringent standard of proof that such underrepresentation was the result of deliberate discrimination. Their claim, of course, is that they are upholding the principle of a color-blind society. In his dissenting opinion, on the other hand, Justice Blackmun wrote: "I never thought I would live to see the day when the city of Richmond, Virginia, the cradle of the Old Confederacy," having voluntarily tried to "lessen the stark impact of persistent discrimination," would then see its effort struck down by "this Court, the supposed bastion of equality." *New York Times*, January 24, 1989, p. 1.

6. Richard McGahey, "Poverty's Voguish Stigma," *New York Times,* March 12, 1982, p. A29.

7. Otis L. Graham, Jr., "Illegal Immigration and the Left," *Dissent* 27:3 (Summer 1980), p. 344. In New York City, for example, there were about 650,000 immigrant workers in 1979, comprising one-fifth of the total work force. The areas of largest immigrant concentration were as follows: manufacturing, 178,000; restaurants, 42,000; hospitals, 35,000; construction, 31,000. There were also large concentrations in various service industries, such as hotels, laundries, beauty shops, and shoe repair and tailor shops. Marcia Freedman, "The Labor Market for Immigrants in New York City," *New York Affairs* 7:4 (1983), p. 9.

8. For example, see Michael Piore, "Another View on Migrant Workers," *Dissent* 27:3 (Summer 1980), pp. 347–51, and Roger Waldinger, "Changing Ladders and Musical Chairs: Ethnicity and Opportunity in Post-Industrial New York," *Politics and Society* 15:4 (1986–87), pp. 373, 380.

9. "Dreams and Despair Collide as Miami Searches For Itself," *New York Times*, January 23, 1989, p. 1; "A Brightly Colored Tinderbox," *Time,* January 30, 1989, pp. 28–9.

10. For an incisive analysis of the decline of race-specific public policy, see Gary Orfield, "Race and the Liberal Agenda: The Loss of the Intergrationist Dream, 1965–1974," in Margaret Weir, Ann Shola Orloff, and Theda Skocpol, eds., *The Politics of Social Policy in the United States* (Princeton: Princeton University Press, 1988), pp. 313–356.

11. William Julius Wilson, *The Truly Disadvantaged* (Chicago: University of Chicago Press).

12. William Julius Wilson, "How the Democrats Can Harness Whites and Blacks in '92," *New York Times*, March 24, 1989, p. A31.

13. Harold W. Cruse, *The Crisis of the Negro Intellectual* (New York: William Morrow, 1967) and *Plural But Equal* (New York: William Morrow & Co., 1987).

29

The Family Values Fable

Judith Stacey

A Bedtime Story for the American Century

Once upon a fabulized time, half a century ago, there was a lucky land where families with names such as Truman and Eisenhower presided over a world of Nelsons, Cleavers, and Rileys. Men and women married, made love, and produced gurgling Gerber babies (in that proper order). It was a land where, as God and Nature had ordained, men were men and women were ladies. Fathers worked outside the home for pay to support their wives and children, and mothers worked inside the home without pay to support their husbands and to cultivate healthy, industrious, above-average children. Streets and neighborhoods were safe and tidy. This land was the strongest, wealthiest, freest, and fairest in the world. Its virtuous leaders, heroic soldiers, and dazzling technology defended all the freedom-loving people on the planet from an evil empire that had no respect for freedom or families. A source of envy, inspiration, and protection to people everywhere, the leaders and citizens of this blessed land had good reason to feel confident and proud.

And then, as so often happens in fairy tales, evil came to this magical land. Sometime during the mid-1960s, a toxic serpent wriggled its way close to the pretty picket fences guarding those Edenic gardens. One prescient Jeremiah, named Daniel Patrick Moynihan, detected the canny snake and tried to alert his placid countrymen to the dangers of family decline. Making a pilgrimage from Harvard to the White House, he chanted about the ominous signs and consequences of "a tangle of pathology" festering in cities that suburban commuters and their ladies-in-waiting had abandoned for the crabgrass frontier. Promiscuity, unwed motherhood, and fatherless families, he warned, would undermine domestic tranquility and wreak social havoc. Keening only to the tune of black keys, however, this Pied Piper's song fell flat, inciting displeasure and rebuke.

It seemed that overnight those spoiled Gerber babies had turned into rebellious, disrespectful youth who spurned authority, tradition, and conformity, and scorned the national wealth, power, and imperial status in which their elders exulted. Rejecting their parents' gray flannel suits and Miss America ideals, as well as their monogamous, nuclear families, they generated a counter-culture and a sexual revolution, and they built unruly social movements demanding student rights, free speech, racial justice, peace, and liberation for women and homosexuals. Long-haired, unisex-clad youth smoked dope and marched in demonstrations shouting slogans like "Question Authority," "Girls Say Yes to Boys Who Say No," "Smash Monogamy," "Black is Beautiful," "Power to the People," "Make Love, Not War," "Sisterhood is Powerful," and "Liberation Now." Far from heeding Moynihan's warning, or joining in his condemnation of "black matriarchs," many young women drew inspiration from such mothers and condemned Moynihan instead for "blaming the victims."

Disrupting families and campuses, the young people confused and divided their parents and teachers, even seducing some foolish elders into emulating their sexual and social experiments. But the thankless arrogance of these privileged youth, their unkempt appearance, provocative antics, and amorality also enraged many, inciting a right-wing, wishful, "moral majority" to form its own backlash social movement to restore family and moral order.

And so it happened that harmony, prosperity, security, and confidence disappeared from this once most fortunate land. After decimating African American communities, the serpent of family decline slithered under the picket fences, where it spewed its venom on white, middle-class victims as well. Men no longer knew what it meant to be men, and women had neither the time nor the inclination to be ladies. Ozzie had trouble finding secure work. He was accused of neglecting, abusing, and oppressing his wife and children. Harriet no longer stayed home with the children. She too worked outside the home for pay, albeit less pay. Ozzie and Harriet sued for divorce. Harriet decided she could choose to have children with or without a marriage certificate, with or without an Ozzie, or perhaps even with a Rozzie. After all, as front-page stories in her morning newspaper informed her, almost daily, "Traditional Family Nearly the Exception, Census Finds."

As the last decade of the century dawned, only half the children in the land were living with two married parents who had jointly conceived or adopted them. Twice as many children were living in single-parent families as in male-breadwinner, female-homemaker families. Little wonder few citizens could agree over what would count as a proper family. Little wonder court chroniclers charted the devolution of the modern family system in books with anxious titles such as: *The War Over the Family*, *Embattled Paradise*, *Disturbing the Nest*, *Brave New Families*, *The Way We Never Were*, *Fatherless America*, and *Families on the Faultline*.

The clairvoyant Daniel Patrick Moynihan found himself vindicated at last, as political candidates from both ruling parties joined his hymns of praise to Ozzie and Harriet and rebuked the selfish family practices of that rebellious stepchild of the Nelsons, Murphy Brown.

END OF THE MODERN FAMILY SYSTEM

The era of the modern family system had come to an end, and few could feel sanguine about the postmodern family condition that had succeeded it. Unaccustomed to a state of normative instability and definitional crisis, the populace split its behavior from its beliefs. Many who contributed actively to such postmodern family statistics as divorce, remarriage, blended families, single parenthood, joint custody, abortion, domestic partnership, two-career households, and the like still yearned nostalgically for the *Father Knows Best* world they had lost.

"Today," in the United States, as Rutger's historian John Gillis so aptly puts it, "the anticipation and memory of family means more to people than its immediate reality. It is through the families we live *by* that we achieve the transcendence that compensates for the tensions and frustrations of the families we live *with*." Not only have the fabled families of midcentury we live *by* become more compelling than the messy, improvisational, patchwork bonds of postmodern family life, but as my bedtime story hints, because they function as pivotal elements in our distinctive national imagination, these symbolic families are also far more stable than any in which past generations ever dwelled.

In the context of our contemporary social, economic, and political malaise, it is not difficult to understand the public's palpable longing for the world of innocence, safety, confidence, and affluence that Ozzie and Harriet have come to signify. Unfortunately, this nostalgia does little to improve conditions for the beleaguered families we live *with*, and a great deal to make them even worse. The family-values campaign helped to fuel the passage of budget-cutting and anti-welfare "reform" measures that will plunge the growing ranks of our least fortunate families, and especially the children whose interests the campaign claims to serve, into ever-greater misery and decay. For apart from exhorting or coercing adults to enter or remain in possibly hostile, even destructive marriages, family-decline critics offer few social proposals to address children's pressing needs. Further stigmatizing the increasing numbers who live in "nontraditional" families will only add to their duress.

We can watch *Ozzie and Harriet* reruns as long as we like, but we cannot return to the world it evokes, even if we wish to. What we can do, and what I sorely believe we must do instead, is to direct public attention and resources to measures that could mitigate the unnecessarily injurious effects of divorce and single parenthood on the fourth of our nation's children who now suffer these effects. Having surmised that one must fight fables with fables, I offer my personal utopian wish list of such genuinely "pro-family" measures:
- restructure work hours and benefits to suit working parents;
- redistribute work to reduce under- and overemployment;
- enact comparable-worth standards of pay equity so that women as well as men can earn a family wage;

- provide universal health, prenatal and child care, sex education, and reproductive rights to make it possible to choose to parent responsibly;
- legalize gay marriage;
- revitalize public education;
- pass and enforce strict gun control laws;
- end the economic inequities of property and income dispositions in divorce;
- house the homeless;
- institute a universal national-service obligation;
- fund libraries, parks, public broadcasting, and the arts;
- read a fable of democratic family values to the children of the next millennium.

SELECTED BIBLIOGRAPHY OF RECENT SOURCES

Compiled by Maya Parson

Amott, Teresa L., and Julie Mattaei. *Race, Gender, and Work: A Multicultural Economic History of Women in the United States*. Boston, MA: South End Press, 1991.

Anderson, Karen. *Chain Her by One Foot: The Subjugation of Women in Seventeenth-Century New France*. London: Routledge, 1991.

Anderson, Margaret L., and Patricia Hill Collins, eds. *Race, Class, and Gender: An Anthology*. Second edition. Belmont, CA: Wadsworth, 1995.

Aponte, Harry J. *Bread and Spirit: Therapy with the New Poor: Diversity of Race, Culture, and Values*. New York: Norton, 1994.

Aswad, Barbara C., and Barbara Bilge, eds. *Family and Gender among American Muslims: Issues Facing Middle-Eastern Immigrants and Their Descendents*. Philadelphia: Temple University Press, 1996.

Auhagen, Ann E., and Maria von Salisch. *The Diversity of Human Relationships*. Cambridge, MA: Cambridge University Press, 1996.

Baca Zinn, Maxine, and D. Stanley Eitzen. *Diversity in Families*. Fourth Edition. New York: HarperCollins Publishers, 1996.

Baca Zinn, Maxine. "Family, Feminism, and Race in America." *Gender and Society*. 4:1 (1990): 68–82.

———. "Feminist Rethinking from Racial-Ethnic Families." *Women of Color in U.S. Society*. Eds. Maxine Baca Zinn and Bonnie Thorton Dill. Philadelphia: Temple University Press, 1994. 303–314.

Bankston, Minzhou, and Carl L. Bankston III. *Growing Up American: How Vietnamese Children Adapt to Life in the United States*. New York: Russell Sage Foundation, 1998.

Barrett, James R., and David Roediger. "Inbetween Peoples: Race, Nationality and the 'New Immigrant' Working Class." *Journal of American Ethnic History*. 16:3 (1997): 3–44.

Benería, Lourdes and Catharine R. Stimpson, eds. *Women, Households, and the Economy*. The Douglass Series on Women's Lives and the Meaning of Gender. New Brunswick, NJ: Rutgers University Press, 1987.

Benkov, Laura. *Reinventing the Family: The Emerging Story of Gay and Lesbian Parents*. New York: Crown Publishers, 1994.

Benson, J. E. "Households, Migration, or Community Context." *Urban Anthropology*. 19 (1990): 9–29.

Berry, Mary Frances. *The Politics of Parenthood: Child Care, Women's Rights, and the Myth of the Good Mother*. New York: Viking, 1993.

Billingsley, Andrew. *Climbing Jacob's Ladder: The Enduring Legacy of African-American Families*. New York: Simon and Schuster, 1992.

Blumberg, Rae Lesser, ed. *Gender, Family, and Economy: The Triple Overlap*. Newbury Park, CA: Sage Publications, 1991.

Boris, Eileen, and Elisabeth Prügl, eds. *Homeworkers in Global Perspective: Invisible No More*. New York: Routledge, 1996.

Boris, Eileen. "Unwed and Unwanted? New Perspectives on Social Welfare." *Journal of Policy History*. 7:3 (1995): 365.

Bowman, Phillip J. "Coping with Provider Role Strain: Adaptive Cultural

Resources among Black Husband-Fathers." *The Journal of Black Psychology.* 16 (Spring 1990): 1–21.

Boydston, Jeanne. *Home and Work: Housework, Wages, and the Ideology of Work in the Early Republic.* New York: Oxford University Press, 1990.

Brenner, Johanna, and Barbara Laslett. "Gender, Social Reproduction, and Women's Self-Organization: Considering the U.S. Welfare State." *Gender and Society.* 5 (September 1991): 311–333.

Brewer, Rose. "Race, Class, Gender and U.S. State Welfare Policy: The Nexus of Inequality for African-American Families." *Color, Class, and Country: Experiences of Gender.* Eds. Gay Young and Bette J. Dickerson. London: Zed Books, 1994. 115–127.

Brewer, Rose. "Theorizing Race, Class, and Gender: The New Scholarship of Black Feminist Intellectuals and Black Women's Labor." *Theorizing Black Feminisms: The Visionary Pragmatism of Black Women.* Eds. Stanlie M. James and Abena P. A. Busia. London: Routledge, 1993. 13–30.

Cabaj, Robert P. and David W. Purcell, eds. *On the Road to Same-Sex Marriage: A Supportive Guide to Psychological, Political, and Legal Issues.* San Francisco: Jossey-Bass Publishers, 1997.

Chan, Sucheng. *Asian Americans: An Interpretive History.* Twayne's Immigrant Heritage of America Series. Boston: Twayne Publishers, 1991.

Chang, Grace. "Undocumented Latinas: The New 'Employable Mothers.'" *Mothering: Ideology, Experience, and Agency.* Eds. Evelyn Nakano Glenn, Grace Chang, and Linda Rennie Forcey. New York: Routledge, 1994. 259–285.

Chang, Hedy Nai-Lin, Amy Muckelroy, and Dora Pulido-Tobiassen. *Looking In, Looking Out: Redefining Child Care and Early Education in a Diverse Society.* San Francisco: California Tomorrow, 1996.

Chase-Lansdale, P. Lindsay, and Jeanne Brooks-Gunn, eds. *Escape from Poverty: What Makes a Difference for Children?* Cambridge, MA: Cambridge University Press, 1995.

Chauncey, George. *Gay New York: Gender, Urban Culture, and the Making of the Gay Male World, 1890–1940.* New York: BasicBooks, 1995.

Chow, Esther Ngan-Ling, and Catherine White Berheide. *Women, the Family, and Policy: A Global Perspective.* Albany: State University of New York Press, 1994.

Chow, Esther Ngan-Ling, Doris Wilkinson, and Maxine Baca Zinn, eds. *Race, Class, and Gender: Common Bonds, Different Voices.* Gender in Society Reader. Published in Cooperation with Sociologists for Women in Society. Thousand Oaks, CA: Sage Publications, 1996.

Collier, Jane Fishburne, and Sylvia J. Yanagisako, eds. *Gender and Kinship: Essays Toward a Unified Analysis.* Stanford, CA: Stanford University Press, 1987.

Collins, Patricia Hill. *Black Feminist Thought: Knowledge, Consciousness, and the Politics of Empowerment.* Perspectives on Gender, Volume 2. Boston: Unwin Hyman, 1990.

Comas-Diaz, Lillian, and Beverly Greene, eds. *Women of Color: Integrating Ethnic and Gender Identities in Psychotherapy.* New York: Guilford Press, 1994.

Comer, James P., and Alvin F. Poussant. *Raising Black Children: Two Leading Psychiatrists Confront the Educational, Social, and Emotional Problems Facing Black Children.* New York: Plume, 1992.

Coontz, Stephanie. *The Way We Never Were: American Families and the*

Nostalgia Trap. New York: BasicBooks, 1992.

Coontz, Stephanie. *The Way We Really Are: Coming to Terms with America's Changing Families.* New York: BasicBooks, 1997.

Davis, Larry E., and Enola K. Proctor. *Race, Gender, and Class: Guidelines for Practice with Individuals, Families, and Groups.* Englewood Cliffs, NJ: Prentice Hall, 1989.

Del Carmen, Rebecca, and Gabrielle N. Virgo. "Marital Disruption and Nonresidential Parenting: A Multicultural Perspective." *Nonresidential Parenting: New Vistas in Family Living.* Eds. Charlene E. Depner and James H. Bray. Newbury Park: Sage Publications, 1993. 13–36.

Dickerson, Bette J., ed. *African-American Single Mothers: Understanding Their Lives and Families.* Sage Series on Race and Ethnic Relations, Volume 10. Thousand Oaks, CA: Sage Publications, 1995.

Dill, Bonnie Thorton, Maxine Baca Zinn, and Sandra Patton. "Feminism, Race, and the Politics of Family Values." *Report from the Institute for Philosophy & Public Policy.* 13 (Summer 1993): 13–18.

Dill, Bonnie Thorton. *Across the Boundaries of Race and Class: An Exploration of Work and Family among Black Female Domestic Servants.* New York: Garland, 1994.

Dilworth-Anderson, P., L. M. Burton, and L. B. Johnson. "Reframing Theories for Understanding Race, Ethnicity, and Families." *Sourcebook of Family Theories and Methods.* Eds. Pauline G. Boss et al. New York: Plenum Press, 1993. 627–645.

Duncan, Greg J. and Jeanne Brooks-Gunn, eds. *Consequences of Growing Up Poor.* New York: Russell Sage Foundation, 1997.

Dunn, Dana, ed. *Workplace/Women's Place: An Anthology.* Los Angeles: Roxbury Publishing Company, 1997.

Dykeman, Cass, J. Ron Nelson, and Valerie Appleton. "Building Strong Working Alliances with American Indian Families." *Social Work in Education.* 17:3 (July 1995): 148–158.

Edelman, Peter B., and Joyce A. Ladner, eds. *Adolescence and Poverty: Challenge for the 1990s.* Washington, DC: Center for National Policy Press, 1991.

Edin, Kathryn and Laura Lein. *Making Ends Meet: How Single Mothers Survive Welfare and Low Wage Work.* Russell Sage Foundation, 1997.

Edwards, Laura F. "Sexual Violence, Gender, Reconstruction, and the Extension of Patriarchy in Granville County, North Carolina." *North Carolina Historical Review.* 68:3 (1991): 237–260.

Espiritu, Yen Le. *Asian American Women and Men: Labor, Laws, and Love.* The Gender Lens Series. Thousand Oaks, CA: Sage Publications, 1996.

Farley, Reynolds, ed. *State of the Union: America in the 1990s.* New York: Russell Sage Foundation, 1995.

Ferguson, Ann. "The Intersection of Race, Gender, and Class in the United States Today." *Rethinking Marxism.* 3 (Fall–Winter 1990): 45–64.

Folbre, Nancy. *Who Pays for the Kids? Gender and the Structures of Constraint.* London: Routledge, 1994.

Franklin, Donna. *Ensuring Inequality: The Structural Transformation of the African-American Family.* New York: Oxford University Press, 1997.

Gibbs, Jewelle Taylor, Larke Nahme Huang, and Associates. *Children of Color: Psychological Interventions with Minority Youth.* San Francisco: Jossey-Bass Publishers, 1989.

Gillis, John R. *A World of Their Own Making: Myth, Ritual, and the Quest for Family Values.* New York: BasicBooks, 1996.

Glenn, Evelyn Nakano, Grace Chang, and Linda Rennie Forcey, eds. *Mothering: Ideology, Experience, and Agency.* Perspectives on Gender. New York: Routledge, 1994.

Glenn, Evelyn Nakano. "From Servitude to Service Work: Historical Continuities in the Racial Division of Paid Reproductive Labor." *Unequal Sisters: A Multicultural Reader in U.S. Women's History.* Second Edition. Eds. Vicki L. Ruíz and Ellen Carol DuBois. New York: Routledge, 1994. 405–435. [Article originally published in *Signs.* 18:1 (1992)]

Glenn, Evelyn Nakano. "Gender and the Family." *Analyzing Gender: A Handbook of Social Science Research.* Eds. Beth B. Hess and Myra Marx Ferree. Newbury Park, CA: Sage Publications, 1987. 348–380.

Gonzalez-Mena, Janet. *Multicultural Issues in Child Care.* Second edition. Mountain View, CA: Mayfield Publishing Company, 1997.

Gordon, Linda, ed. *Women, Welfare, and the State.* Madison: University of Wisconsin Press, 1990.

Greene, Beverly A. "What Has Gone Before: The Legacy of Racism and Sexism in the Lives of Black Mothers and Daughters." *Women and Therapy.* 9:1/2 (1990): 207–230.

Greene, Beverly A. *Ethnic and Cultural Diversity Among Lesbians and Gay Men.* Psychological Perspectives on Lesbian and Gay Issues, Volume 3. Thousand Oaks, CA: Sage Publications, 1997.

Gresham, Jewell Handy. "White Patriarchal Supremacy: The Politics of Family in America." *The Nation.* July 24/34, 1989: 116–122.

Grossberg, Michael. "Children's Legal Rights? A Historical Look at a Legal Paradox." *Children at Risk in America: History, Concepts, and Public Policy.* Youth Social Services, School and Public Policy Series. Ed. Roberta Wollons. Albany: State University of New York Press, 1992. 111–140.

Gutiérrez, Ramón A. *When Jesus Came, the Corn Mothers Went Away: Marriage, Sexuality, and Power in New Mexico, 1500–1846.* Stanford, CA: Stanford University Press, 1991.

Hardy, Kenneth. "The Theoretical Myth of Sameness: A Critical Issue in Family Therapy Training and Treatment." *Journal of Psychotherapy and the Family.* 6 (1989): 17–33.

Harrison, Algea, et al. "Family Ecologies of Ethnic Minority Children." *Child Development.* 61 (1990): 347–362.

Hertz, Rosanna, and Faith I. T. Ferguson. "Childcare Choice and Constraint in the United States: Social Class, Race, and the Influence of Family Views." *Journal of Comparative Family Studies.* 27:2 (1996): 249–280.

Higginbotham, Elizabeth and Mary Romero, eds. *Women and Work: Exploring Race, Ethnicity, and Class.* Women and Work, Volume 6. Thousand Oaks: Sage Publications, 1997.

Hill, Robert B. *The Strengths of African-American Families: Twenty-five Years Later.* Washington, DC: R & B Publishers, 1997.

Hill, Robert B., with Andrew Billingsley et al. *Research on the African-American Family: A Holistic Perspective.* Westport, CT: Auburn House, 1993.

Hing, Bill Ong. *Making and Remaking Asian Americans through Immigration Policy, 1850–1990.* Stanford, CA: Stanford University Press, 1993.

Hoff, Joan. "The Limits of Liberal Legalism: Marriage, Divorce, Pregnancy, and Abortion." *Law, Gender, and Injustice: A Legal History of U.S. Women.* Feminist Crosscurrents. New York: New York University Press, 1991. 276–315.

Hondagneu-Sotelo, Pierrette. "Overcoming Patriarchal Constraints: The Reconstruction of Gender Relations among Mexican Immigrant Women and

Men." *Gender and Society.* 6 (September 1992): 393–415.

Hsyashi, Brian Masuru. *For the Sake of Our Japanese Brethren: Assimilation, Nationalism, and Protestantism Among the Japanese of Los Angeles, 1895–1942.* Stanford, CA: Stanford University Press, 1995.

Ingoldsby, Bron B., and Suzanna Smith, eds. *Families in Multicultural Perspective.* New York: Guilford Press, 1995.

Ishwaran, K. *Family and Marriage: Cross-cultural Perspectives.* Revised edition. Toronto: Thompson Educational Publishing, 1992.

Jacobs, Janet L. "Gender, Race, Class, and the Trend Toward Early Motherhood: A Feminist Analysis of Teen Mothers in Contemporary Society." *Journal of Contemporary Ethnography.* 22:4 (January 1994): 442 et seq.

Jencks, Christopher, and Paul E. Peterson, eds. *The Urban Underclass.* Washington, DC: Brooking Institute, 1991.

Kamerman, Sheila B. "Gender Role and Family Structure Changes in the Advanced Industrialized West: Implications for Social Policy." *Poverty, Inequality, and the Future of Social Policy: Western States in the New World Order.* Eds. Katherine McFate, Roger Lawson, and William Julius Wilson. New York: Russell Sage Foundation, 1995. 231–256.

Kaplan, Lisa, and Judith Girard. *Strengthening High-Risk Families: A Handbook for Practitioners.* New York: Lexington Books; Toronto: Maxwell Macmillan, 1994.

Katz, Jane, ed. *Messengers of the Wind: Native American Women Tell Their Life Stories.* New York: Ballantine, 1995.

Katz, Michael B., ed. *The "Underclass" Debate: Views from History.* Princeton, NJ: Princeton University Press, 1993.

Knaefler, Tomi Kaizawa. *Our House Divided: Seven Japanese American Families in World War II.* Honolulu: University of Hawaii Press, 1991.

Knight, G. P., L. M. Virdin, and M. Roosa. "Socialization and Family Correlates of Mental Health Outcomes among Hispanic and Anglo-American Children." *Child Development.* 65 (1994): 212–224.

Kozol, Jonathan. *Amazing Grace: The Lives of Children and the Conscience of a Nation.* New York: Crown Publishers, 1995.

Laird, Joan, and Robert-Jay Green. *Lesbians and Gays in Couples and Families: A Handbook for Therapists.* San Francisco: Jossey-Bass Publishers, 1996.

Lamphere, Louise, Patricia Zavella, Felipe Gonzalez, with Peter B. Evans. *Sunbelt Working Mothers: Reconciling Family and Factory.* Ithaca, NY: Cornell University Press, 1993.

Lamphere, Louise. *From Working Mothers to Working Daughters: Immigrant Women in a New England Industrial Community.* Ithaca, NY: Cornell University Press, 1987.

Laosa, Luis M. "Ethnicity and Single Parenting in the United States." *Impact of Divorce, Single Parenting, and Stepparenting on Children.* Eds. E. Mavis Hetherington and Josephine D. Arasteh. Hillsdale, NJ: Lawrence Erlbaum Associates, Publishers, 1988. 23–49.

Leonard, Karen Isaksen. *Making Ethnic Choices: California's Punjabi Mexican Americans.* Asian American History and Culture Series. Philadelphia: Temple University Press, 1992.

Leong, Russell, ed. *Asian American Sexualities: Dimensions of the Gay and Lesbian Experience.* New York: Routledge, 1996.

Levine, James A., and Edward W. Pitt. *New Expectations: Community Strategies for Responsible Fatherhood.* New York, NY: Families and Work Institute, 1995.

Lewin, Ellen. "Negotiating Lesbian Motherhood: The Dialectics of Resistance and

Accomodation." *Mothering: Ideology, Experience, and Agency*. Eds. Evelyn Nakano Glenn, Grace Chang, and Linda Rennie Forcey. New York: Routledge, 1994. 333–353.

Logan, Sadye L., ed. *The Black Family: Strengths, Self-Help, and Positive Change*. Boulder, CO: Westview Press, 1996.

Luker, Kristin. *Dubious Conceptions: The Politics of Teenage Pregnancy*. Cambridge, MA: Harvard University Press, 1996.

Lynn, Laurence E., and Michael G. H. McGeary, eds. *Inner-City Poverty in the United States*. Washington, DC: National Academy Press, 1990.

Maffi, Mario. *Gateway to the Promised Lands: Ethnic Cultures on New York's Lower East Side*. New York: New York University Press, 1995.

Marsiglio, William, ed. *Fatherhood: Contemporary Theory, Research, and Social Policy*. Research on Men and Masculinities, Volume 7. Thousand Oaks, CA: Sage Publications, 1995.

May, Elaine Tyler. *Homeward Bound: American Families and the Cold War Era*. New York: BasicBooks, 1988.

McAdoo, Harriette Pipes, ed. *Black Families*. Third edition. Thousand Oaks, CA: Sage Publications, 1996.

McAdoo, Harriette Pipes. *Family Ethnicity: Strength in Diversity*. Newbury Park, CA: Sage Publications, 1993.

McGoldrick, Monica, Joe Giordano, and John K. Pearce. *Ethnicity and Family Therapy*. Second edition. New York: Guilford Press, 1996.

Mindel, Charles H., Robert W. Habenstein, and Roosevelt Wright Jr., eds. *Ethnic Families in America: Patterns and Variations*. Third edition. New York: Elsevier Press, 1988.

Mink, Gwendolyn. *The Wages of Motherhood: Inequality in the Welfare State, 1917–1942*. Ithaca, NY: Cornell University Press, 1995.

Mintz, Steven, and Susan Kellogg. *Domestic Revolutions: A Social History of American Family Life*. New York: The Free Press, 1988.

Mishel, Lawrence R., et al. *The State of Working America, 1996–97*. Armonk, NY: Economic Policy Institute, 1997.

Morales, E. S. "Ethnic Minority Families and Minority Gays and Lesbians." *Homosexuality and Family Relations*. Eds. F. W. Bozett and M. B. Sussmen. New York: Harrington Park Press, 1990.

Nelson, Margaret K. "Family Day Care Providers: Dilemmas of Daily Practice." *Mothering: Ideology, Experience, and Agency*. Eds. Evelyn Nakano Glenn, Grace Chang, and Linda Rennie Forcey. New York: Routledge, 1994. 181–209.

Newman, Katherine. *Falling From Grace: The Experience of Downward Mobility in the American Middle Class*. New York: The Free Press, 1988.

Okun, Barbara F. *Understanding Diverse Families: What Practioners Need to Know*. New York: The Guilford Press, 1996.

Oliver, Melvin L., and Thomas M. Shapiro. *Black Wealth/White Wealth: A New Perspective on Racial Inequality*. New York: Routledge, 1995.

Ong, Paul, Edna Bonacich, and Lucie Cheng, eds. *The New Asian Immigration in Los Angeles and Global Restructuring*. Philadelphia: Temple University Press, 1994.

Palmer, John L., Timothy Smeeding, and Barbara Boyle Torrey, eds. *The Vulnerable*. Washington, DC: The Urban Institute Press, 1988. [Distributed in the United States and Canada by The University Press of America, Lanham, MD]

Patterson, Charlotte J. "Lesbian Mothers, Gay Fathers, and Their Children."

Lesbian, Gay, and Bisexual Identities Over the Lifespan: Psychological Perspectives. Eds. Anthony D'Augelli and Charlotte Patterson. New York: Oxford University Press, 1995.

Pesquera, Beatríz M. "In the Beginning He Wouldn't Even Lift a Spoon: The Division of Household Labor." *Building With Our Hands: New Directions in Chicana Studies.* Eds. Adela de la Torre and Beatriz M. Pesquera. Berkeley: University of California Press, 1993.

Peters, Virginia Bergman. *Women of the Earth Lodges: Tribal Life on the Plains.* North Haven, CT: Archon, 1995.

Phillips, Kimberley L. "'But It Is a Fine Place to Make Money': Migration and African-American Families in Cleveland, 1915–1929." *Journal of Social History.* (Winter 1996): 393–413.

Phinney, Jean S., and Mary Jane Rotheram, eds. *Children's Ethnic Socialization: Pluralism and Development.* Newbury Park, CA: Sage Publications, 1987.

Polakow, Valerie. *Lives on the Edge: Single Mothers and Their Children in the Other America.* Chicago: University of Chicago Press, 1993.

Quadagno, Jill S. *The Color of Welfare: How Racism Undermined the War on Poverty.* New York: Oxford University Press, 1994.

Rank, Mark R. *Living on the Edge: The Realities of Welfare in America.* New York: Columbia University Press, 1994.

Renzetti, Claire M. "Violence in Lesbian Relationships: A Preliminary Analysis of Causal Factors." *Journal of Interpersonal Violence.* 3 (December 1988): 381–399.

Robertson, Claire. "Africa into the Americas? Slavery and Women, the Family and the Gender Division of Labor." *More than Chattel: Black Women and Slavery in the Americas.* Eds. David Barry Gaspar and Darlene Clark Hine. Bloomington: Indiana University Press, 1996.

Robinson, Paulette J., and Billy T. Tidwell, eds. *The State of Black America 1996.* New York: National Urban League, 1996.

Robson, Ruthann. "Resisting the Family—Repositioning Lesbians in Legal Theory." *Signs.* 19 (Summer 1994): 975–996.

Romero, Mary. "'I'm Not Your Maid. I Am the Housekeeper': The Restructuring of Housework and Work Relationships in Domestic Service." *Color, Class, and Country: Experiences of Gender.* Eds. Gay Young and Bette J. Dickerson. London: Zed Books, 1994. 71–83.

Root, Maria, ed. *Filipino Americans: Transformation and Identity.* Thousand Oaks, CA: Sage Publications, 1997.

Root, Maria, ed. *The Multiracial Experience: Racial Borders as the New Frontier.* Thousand Oaks, CA: Sage Publications, 1996.

Roschelle, Ann R. *No More Kin: Exploring Race, Class, and Gender in Family Networks.* Understanding Families Series. Thousand Oaks, CA: Sage Publications, 1997.

Rosenblatt, Paul C., Terri A. Karis, and Richard D. Powell. *Multiracial Couples: Black and White Voices.* Understanding Families, Volume 1. Thousand Oaks, CA: Sage Publications, 1995.

Rosenthal, Marguerite G. "Single Mothers in Sweden—Work and Welfare in the Welfare-State." *Social Work.* 39 (May 1994): 270–278.

Rothman, Barbara Katz. "Beyond Mothers and Fathers: Ideology in a Patriarchal Society." *Mothering: Ideology, Experience, and Agency.* Eds. Evelyn Nakano Glenn, Grace Chang, and Linda Rennie Forcey. New York: Routledge, 1994. 139–157.

Rothman, Barbara Katz. "Women as Fathers: Motherhood and Child Care under a Modified Patriarchy." *Gender and Society.* 3 (March 1989): 89–104.

Ruíz, Vicki. *Cannery Women, Cannery Lives: Mexican Women, Unionization, and the California Food Processing Industry, 1930–1950.* Albuquerque: University of New Mexico Press, 1987.

Saba, George W., Betty M. Karrer, and Kenneth V. Hardy, eds. *Minorities and Family Therapy.* New York: Hawthorn Press, 1990.

Schnarch, Brian. "Neither Man nor Woman: Berdache—A Case for Non-Dichotomous Gender Construction." *Anthropologica.* 34: 1 (1992): 105–121.

Schorr, Lisbeth B. *Common Purpose: Strengthening Families and Neighborhoods to Rebuild America.* New York: Doubleday, 1997.

Scott-Jones, Diane. "Adolescent Childbearing: Whose Problem? What Can We Do?" *Kappan Special Report.* (November 1993): K5.

Seccombe, Wally. *Weathering the Storm: Working-Class Families from the Industrial Revolution to the Fertility Decline.* London: Verso, 1993.

Segura, Denise A. "Working at Motherhood: Chicana and Mexican Immigrant Mothers and Employment." *Mothering: Ideology, Experience, and Agency.* Eds. Evelyn Nakano Glenn, Grace Chang, and Linda Rennie Forcey. New York: Routledge, 1994. 211–233.

Shaw, Stephanie J. "Mothering Under Slavery in the Antebellum South." *Mothering: Ideology, Experience, and Agency.* Eds. Evelyn Nakano Glenn, Grace Chang, and Linda Rennie Forcey. New York: Routledge, 1994. 237–258.

Shelton, Beth Anne, and Daphne John. "Ethnicity, Race, and Difference: A Comparison of White, Black, and Hispanic Men's Household Labor Time." *Men, Work, and Family.* Research on Men and Masculinities Series, Volume 4. Ed. Jane Hood. Thousand Oaks, CA: Sage Publications, 1993: 131–150.

Sherman, Arloc. *Wasting America's Future: The Children's Defense Fund Report on the Costs of Child Poverty.* Boston: Beacon Press, 1994.

Sidel, Ruth. *Keeping Women and Children Last: America's War on the Poor.* New York: Penguin Books, 1996.

Sjoberg, Gideon, et al. "Family Life and Racial and Ethnic Diversity—An Assessment of Communitarianism, Liberalism, and Conservatism." *Journal of Family Issues.* 16 (May 1995): 246–274.

Skolnick, Arlene S., and Jerome H. Skolnick, eds. *Family in Transition: Rethinking Marriage, Sexuality, Child Rearing, and Family Organization.* Seventh edition. New York: HarperCollins Publishers, 1992.

Skolnick, Arlene, and Stacey Rosencrantz. "The New Crusade for the Old Family." *The American Prospect.* 18 (Summer 1994): 59.

Snipp, C. Matthew. *American Indians: The First of This Land.* New York: Russell Sage Foundation, 1989. [For the National Committee for Research on the 1980 Census]

Solinger, Rickie. *Wake Up Little Susie: Single Pregnancy and Race Before Roe V. Wade.* New York: Routledge, 1992.

Spain, Daphne, and Suzanne M. Bianchi, eds. *Balancing Act: Motherhood, Marriage, and Employment among American Women.* New York: Russell Sage Foundation, 1996.

Spickard, Paul R. *Mixed Blood: Intermarriage and Ethnic Identity in Twentieth-Century America.* Madison: University of Wisconsin Press, 1989.

Stacey, Judith. *Brave New Families: Stories of Domestic Upheaval in Late Twentieth-Century America.* New York: BasicBooks, 1990.

Stack, Carol B. *Call to Home: African Americans Reclaim the Rural South.* New York: BasicBooks, 1996.

Stavig, Ward. "'Living in Offense of Our Lord': Indigenous Sexual Values and Marital Life in the Colonial Crucible." *Hispanic American Historical Review.*

75 (1995).

Stevenson, Brenda E. *Life in Black and White: Family and Community in the Slave South.* New York: Oxford University Press, 1996.

Tamura, Eileen. *Americanization, Acculturation, and Ethnic Identity: The Nisei Generation in Hawaii.* Urbana: University of Illinois Press, 1994.

Taylor, Robert J., James M. Jackson, and Linda M. Chatters, eds. *Family Life in Black America.* Thousand Oaks, CA: Sage Publications, 1997.

Taylor, Ronald L., ed. *African-American Youth: Their Social and Economic Status in the United States.* Westport, CT: Praeger Publications, 1995.

Taylor, Ronald L., ed. *Minority Families in the United States: A Multicultural Perspective.* Englewood Cliffs, NJ: Prentice Hall, 1994.

Thompson, Linda, and Alexis J. Walker. "Gender in Families: Women and Men in Marriage, Work, and Parenthood." *Journal of Marriage and the Family.* 51 (November 1989): 845–871.

Thorne, Barrie, and Marilyn Yalom. *Rethinking the Family: Some Feminist Questions.* Revised edition. Boston: Northeastern University Press, 1992.

Toliver, Susan D. *Black Families in Corporate America.* Understanding Families Series. Thousand Oaks, CA: Sage Publications, 1998.

Toro-Morn, Maura I. "Gender, Class, Family, and Migration: Puerto Rican Women in Chicago." *Gender and Society.* 9:6 (1995): 712–726.

Um, Shin Ja. *Korean Immigrant Women in the Dallas-Area Apparel Industry: Looking for Feminist Threads in Patriarchal Cloth.* University Press of America, 1996.

Voydanoff, Patricia, and Linda C. Majka, eds. *Families and Economic Distress: Coping Strategies and Social Policy.* Newbury Park, CA: Sage Publications, 1988.

Wilkerson, Margaret B., and Jewell Handy Gresham. "Sexual Politics of Welfare: The Racialization of Poverty." *The Nation.* (July 24/31, 1989): 126–132.

Williams, Lucy A. "The Right's Attack on Aid to Families with Dependent Children." *The Public Eye: A Publication of Political Research Associates.* 10: 3/4 (1996): 1–18.

Williams, Walter L. *The Spirit and the Flesh: Sexual Diversity in American Indian Culture.* Boston: Beacon Press, 1992.

Wilson, William Julius. *When Work Disappears: The World of the New Urban Poor.* New York: Knopf, 1996.

Wrigley, Julia. *Other People's Children: An Intimate Account of the Dilemmas Facing Middle-Class Parents and the Women They Hire to Raise Their Children.* New York: BasicBooks, 1995.

Zambrana, Ruth, ed. *Understanding Latino Families: Scholarship, Policy, and Practice.* Thousand Oaks, CA: Sage Publications, 1995.

Zavella, Patricia. *Women's Work in Chicano Families: Cannery Workers of the Santa Clara Valley.* Anthropology of Contemporary Issues. Ithaca, NY: Cornell University Press, 1987.

Many thanks to Stephanie Coontz, Peta Henderson, Lee Lyttle, and Gabrielle Raley for their help with this bibliography.

PERMISSIONS ACKNOWLEDGMENTS

The following essays were previously published. Permission to reprint is grate-fully acknowledged here.

BONNIE THORNTON DILL, "Fictive Kin, Paper Sons, and *Compadrazgo*: Women of Color and the Struggle for Family Survival." Reprinted from *The Journal of Family History*, Vol. 13, No. 4, (1988), pp. 415–431. Reprinted by per-mission of Sage Publications, Inc. DAVID WALLACE ADAMS, excerpts from *Education for Extinction: American Indians and the Boarding School Experience, 1875–1928* by David Wallace Adams, 1988. Reprinted by permis-sion of the University Press of Kansas. NIARA SUDARKASA, "Interpreting the African Heritage in Afro-American Family Organization." Reprinted from *Black Families*, edited by Harriette Pipes McAdoo (1988), pp. 27–43. Reprinted by permission of Sage Publications, Inc. EVELYN NAKANO GLENN, "Split Household, Small Producer, and Dual Wage Earner: An Analysis of Chinese-American Family Strategies." Reprinted from *Journal of Marriage and the Family*, Vol. 45, No. 1 (1983), pp. 35–46. Copyright © 1983 by the National Council on Family Relations, 3989 Central Avenue, N.E., Suite 550, Minneapolis, MN 55421. Reprinted by permission. STEPHANIE COONTZ, "Working-Class Families, 1870–1890." Reprinted from *The Social Origins of Private Life* by Stephanie Coontz, 1988, pp. 287–325. Reprinted by permission of Verso. GEORGE J. SÁNCHEZ, excerpts from *Becoming Mexican American: Ethnicity, Culture, and Identity in Chicano Los Angeles, 1900–1945*, by George J. Sánchez, 1993. Reprinted by permission of Oxford University Press. JACQUELINE JONES, "Southern Diaspora: Origins of the Northern 'Underclass.'" Reprinted from *The "Underclass" Debate: Views From History*, edited by Michael B. Katz (1993), pp. 27–54. Copyright © 1993 by Princeton University Press. Reprinted by permis-sion of Princeton University Press. RAYNA RAPP, "Family and Class in Contemporary America: Notes Toward an Understanding of Ideology." Reprinted from *Science and Society*, Vol. 42, (1978), pp. 278–300. Reprinted by permission of the Guilford Press. PATRICIA HILL COLLINS, "Shifting the Center: Race, Class, and Feminist Theorizing About Motherhood." Reprinted from *Mothering: Ideology, Experience, and Agency*, edited by Evelyn Nakano Glenn, Grace Chang, and Linda Rennie Forcey (1994), pp. 45–65. Reprinted by permission of Routledge and the author. KAREN BRODKIN SACKS, "Toward a Unified Theory of Class, Race, and Gender." Reprinted from *American Ethnologist*, Vol. 16, No. 3 (August 1989), pp. 534–550. Reprinted by permission of the American Anthropological Association. Not for further reproduction. MAXINE BACA ZINN, "Social Science Theorizing for Latino Families in the Age of Diversity." Reprinted from *Understanding Latino Families: Scholarship, Policy, and Practice*, edited by Ruth E. Zambrana (1995), pp. 177–189. Reprinted by permission of Sage Publications, Inc. LILLIAN B. RUBIN, excerpts from *Families on the Fault Line: America's Working Class Speaks About the Family, the Economy, Race, and Ethnicity* by Lillian B. Rubin, 1994. Copyright © 1994 by Lillian B. Rubin.

Reprinted by permission of HarperCollins Publishers, Inc. PIERRETTE HONDAGNEU-SOTELO, "Women and Children First: New Directions in Anti-immigrant Politics." Reprinted from *Socialist Review*, Vol. 25, No. 1, (1995), pp. 169–190. Copyright © Center for Social Research and Education. Reprinted by permission of Duke University Press. NAZLI KIBRIA, "Migration and Vietnamese American Women: Remaking Ethnicity." Reprinted from *Women of Color in U.S. Society*, edited by Maxine Baca Zinn and Bonnie Thornton Dill (1994), pp. 247–261. Copyright © 1994 by Temple University Press. Reprinted by permission of Temple University Press. PIERRETTE HONDAGNEU-SOTELO and MICHAEL A. MESSNER, "Gender Displays and Men's Power: 'The New Man' and the Mexican Immigrant Man." Reprinted from *Theorizing Masculinities*, edited by Harry Brod and Michael Kaufman, pp. 200–218. Reprinted by permission of Sage Publications, Inc. JUDITH STACEY, "Gay and Lesbian Families Are Here; All Our Families Are Queer; Let's Get Used to It!" Originally appeared as "Queer Like Us: Gay and Lesbian Families" in *All Our Families*, edited by Steve Sugarman, Mary Ann Mason, and Arlene Skolnick. Reprinted by permission of Oxford University Press. BEVERLY GREENE and NANCY-BOYD FRANKLIN, "African-American Lesbians: Issues is Couples Therapy." Reprinted from *Lesbians and Gays in Couples and Families*, edited by John Laird and Robert-Jay Green (1996), pp. 251–271. Reprinted by permission of Jossey Bass Publications. MICHELLE HARRISON, "Social Construction of Mary Beth Whitehead." Reprinted from *Gender and Society*, Vol. 1, No. 3 (1987), pp. 300–311. Reprinted by permission of Sage Publications, Inc. BARBARA KATZ ROTHMAN, "Comment on Harrison: The Commodification of Motherhood." Reprinted from *Gender and Society*, Vol. 1, No. 3 (1987), pp. 311–316. Reprinted by permission of Sage Publications, Inc. MARIA P.P. ROOT, "Resolving 'Other' Status: Identity Development of Biracial Individuals." Reprinted from *Women and Therapy*, Vol. 9 (1990), pp. 185–205. Reprinted by permission of the Haworth Press. MARGARET CROSBIE-BURNETT and EDITH A. LEWIS, "Use of African-American Family Structures and Functioning to Address the Challenges of European-American Postdivorce Families." Reprinted from *Family Relations*, Vol. 42, No. 3 (1993), pp. 243–248. Copyright © 1993 by the National Council on Family Relations, 3989 Central Avenue, N.E., Suite 550, Minneapolis, MN 55421. Reprinted by permission. ROGER LAWSON and WILLIAM JULIUS WILSON, "Poverty, Social Rights, and the Quality of Citizenship." Reprinted from *Poverty, Inequality, and the Future of Social Policy*, edited by Katherine McFate, Roger Lawson, and William Julius Wilson (1995), pp. 693–714. Copyright © 1995 by the Russell Sage Foundation. Reprinted by permission of the Russell Sage Foundation, New York. STEPHEN STEINBERG, "The Case for a Race Specific Policy." Reprinted from an article by Stephen Steinberg entitled, "The Underclass: A Case for Color Blindness" which appeared in *New Politics*, Vol. 2 (1995), pp. 51–58. Reprinted by permission of *New Politics*. JUDITH STACEY, "The Family Values Fable,: Reprinted from *National Forum: The Phi Kappa Phi Journal*, Vol. 75, No. 3 (Summer 1995). Copyright © 1995 by Judith Stacey. Reprinted by permission of the publishers.